PRAISE

FOR

THE NEW AMERICAN DEMOCRACY

BY FIORINA AND PETERSON

"This book is in a class by itself. The value of the electoral approach which Fiorina and Peterson have taken is that it is simultaneously powerful and simple. It is capable of explaining a great deal about the American political system and, at the same time, requires little in the way of course restructuring."

—Jon Hurwitz, University of Pittsburgh

"I think this text is a truly new and giant step forward. I believe the theme [of a new democratic era] is 'right on.'. . . I will adopt this text the next time I teach the class and will show it to colleagues. I found it truly enjoyable to read and think students will find it quite enjoyable as well."

—John H. Parham, Minnesota State University

"In my American Government course, I use the idea of 'a new politics' or the 'new American politics,' and I am convinced, with a textbook like this one, that the task of conveying this theme would be much more effective. Given its clear theme, excellent writing, and organization, I will adopt Fiorina and Peterson's textbook."

—Michael E. Meagher, University of Missouri

"A fresh approach to studying one our oldest institutions. It captures the attention of the reader and stimulates deep intellect. It builds citizenship and a comprehensive understanding of what our system of government has evolved into."

—Charles E. Menifield, Murray State University

ABOUT
THE AUTHORS

MORRIS P. FIORINA

Morris P. Fiorina is Professor of Political Science and Senior Fellow of the Hoover Institution at Stanford University. He received a B.A. from Allegheny College in Meadville, Pennsylvania, and a Ph.D. from the University of Rochester. Before moving to Stanford, he taught at the California Institute of Technology and Harvard University.

Fiorina has written widely on American government and politics, with special emphasis on representation and elections. He has published numerous articles, and five books: *Representatives, Roll Calls, and Constituencies; Congress—Keystone of the Washington Establishment; Retrospective Voting in American National Elections; The Personal Vote: Constituency Service and Electoral Independence* (coauthored with Bruce Cain and John Ferejohn); and *Divided Government*. He has served on the editorial boards of a dozen journals in the fields of political science, economics, law, and public policy, and from 1986 to 1990 he served as chairman of the Board of Overseers of the American National Election Studies. He is a member of the National Academy of Sciences.

In his leisure time, Fiorina favors physical activities, including hiking, fishing, and sports. Although his own athletic career never amounted to much, he has been a successful youth baseball coach for fifteen years. Among his most cherished honors is a plaque given by happy parents on the occasion of an undefeated Babe Ruth season.

PAUL E. PETERSON

Paul E. Peterson is the Henry Lee Shattuck Professor of Government and Director of the Center for American Political Studies at Harvard University. He received his B.A. from Concordia College in Moorhead, Minnesota, and his Ph.D. from the University of Chicago.

Peterson is the author of numerous books and articles on federalism, urban politics, race relations, and public policy, including studies of education, welfare, and fiscal and foreign policy. He received the Woodrow Wilson Award from the American Political Science Association for his book *City Limits* (Chicago, 1981). In 1996 his book *The Price of Federalism* (Brookings, 1995) was given the Aaron Wildavsky Award for the best book on public policy. He is a member of the American Academy of Arts and Sciences.

It is not only when writing a textbook that Peterson makes every effort to be as accurate as possible. On the tennis courts, he always makes correct line calls and has seldom been heard to hit a wrong note when tickling the ivories.

D. STEPHEN VOSS

D. Stephen Voss is Assistant Professor of Political Science at the University of Kentucky. He received his Ph.D. from Harvard University, studying with Gary King, and specializes in voting and elections with a particular focus on racial politics in the U.S. South. A New Orleans native, Voss also has two bachelor's degrees from Louisiana State University—one in history and one in print journalism.

Voss has authored or coauthored articles in various political science journals, including the *American Journal of Political Science, Journal of Politics, Public Opinion Quarterly, State Politics and Policy Quarterly,* and *American Politics Research*. He also coauthored *CliffsQuickReview American Government* and is working on the Federal Elections Project with David Lublin of American University. Prior to entering academia, Voss was a political reporter for Gannett News Service and edited a top-selling travel guide, *Let's Go: USA*.

Voss spends his leisure time listening to hard-edged rock, jazz, and blues; enjoying first-person-shooter video games; watching *The X-Files* and David Lynch videos; and dabbling in fantasy role-playing. This exposure to hyperviolent media entertainment has not resulted in any acts of criminal aggression, so far as he knows.

Penguin Academics

AMERICA'S NEW DEMOCRACY

Penguin Academics

AMERICA'S NEW DEMOCRACY

MORRIS P. FIORINA
Stanford University

PAUL E. PETERSON
Harvard University

D. STEPHEN VOSS
University of Kentucky

Longman

New York   San Francisco   Boston
London   Toronto   Sydney   Tokyo   Singapore   Madrid
Mexico City   Munich   Paris   Cape Town   Hong Kong   Montreal

Vice President and Publisher:	Priscilla McGeehon
Senior Acquisitions Editor:	Eric Stano
Development Manager:	Lisa Pinto
Development Editor:	Barbara Muller
Senior Marketing Manager:	Megan Galvin-Fak
Supplements Editor:	Kelly Villella
Media Supplements Editor:	Patrick McCarthy
Production Manager:	Joseph Vella
Project Coordination, Text Design, and Electronic Page Makeup:	Thompson Steele, Inc.
Photo Research:	Photosearch, Inc.
Senior Cover Manager/Designer:	Nancy Danahy
Cover Photo:	© Eyewire, Inc.
Manufacturing Buyer:	Al Dorsey
Printer and Binder:	Quebecor World—Taunton
Cover Printer:	Phoenix Color Corp.

For permission to use copyrighted material, grateful acknowledgment is made to the copyright holders on pp. C-1–C-2, which are hereby made part of this copyright page.

Library of Congress Cataloging-in-Publication Data

Fiorina, Morris P.

    America's new democracy / Morris P. Fiorina, Paul E. Peterson, D. Stephen Voss.--1st ed.

      p.cm.

    Includes bibliographical references and index.

    ISBN 0-321-09248-1 (alk. paper)

     1. Democracy--United States. 2. United States--Politics and government. I. Peterson,

Paul E. II. Voss, D. Stephen (Dennis Stephen). III. Title.

JK1726.F55 2002

320.473--dc21   2001038579

Please visit our Web site at http://www.ablongman.com

For more information about the Penguin Academic Series, please contact us by mail at Longman Publishers, attn. Marketing Department, 1185 Avenue of the Americas, 25th Floor, New York, NY 10036, or by email at http://www.ablongman/feedback

ISBN 0-321-09248-1

1 2 3 4 5 6 7 8 9 10—QWT—03 02 01

To Michael and Joseph,
citizens of the new
American democracy
—M. P. F.

To David, Sarah, and John
—P. E. P.

To Sir Gareth and Princess Corrine,
who yearn for a time before
America's new democracy
—D. S. V.

CONTENTS

PART TWO
INGREDIENTS OF
AMERICA'S NEW DEMOCRACY
91

PART THREE
THE AMERICAN
POLITICAL SYSTEM
231

PART FOUR
OUTPUTS FROM THE
POLITICAL SYSTEM
421

CHAPTER 13 | *CIVIL LIBERTIES* 422

PREFACE

College-age people are prepped for skepticism when they approach the study of American government. Students do not struggle with the concept that institutions or practices may malfunction. Hidden motives, corrupt bargains, social injustice, rampant incompetence—these are precisely what many (if not most) undergraduates today expect to encounter. Of course, not all students react to bad news in the same way. Some smirk knowingly. Some thump their chests and demand radical reform. Most shrug or yawn. Precious few, however, gasp in surprise.

Many popular political science works reinforce the pessimism of the age, especially with regard to democratic politics. They downplay the importance of mass political behavior—and teach that elites actually run the U.S. government, with limited regard for the voting public.[1] This book, by contrast, offers a guardedly optimistic perspective. We encourage readers to approach sky-is-falling-down political rhetoric with the same skepticism that they instinctively turn on patriotic cheerleading. Our purpose is to cultivate a mirror image of analytical techniques already in place—to get readers in the habit of looking beyond the surface when appearances are *negative,* not only when they are positive.

Admittedly, institutions or practices that seem to function effectively in fact sometimes do not. Yet sometimes institutions or practices that appear unseemly— those that draw on base motives, express questionable values, or seem to lack an underlying logic—actually perform surprisingly well. This is an optimistic, yet even-handed, orientation—one that seeks the virtues as well as the vices of American government. Our form of optimism may sound alien to modern readers, especially those who have learned about politics primarily from journalistic sources. But it dates back to the Enlightenment "political science" of the nation's founders (in particular, James Madison) and is a dominant mode of thinking among several contemporary schools in the political science discipline.

The intellectual perspective described here motivates the book's central theme: Elections (or at least the anticipation of them) matter more in America's political system now than they have in the past, than they do in other industrialized democracies, or than other political writers usually recognize. Votes are the main currency in the political market, so influencing them drives political behavior even when the connection is not obvious. Fiorina and Peterson first articulated this claim while writing a textbook in 1993, and at the time they expected the argument to meet with substantial resistance. Most of the developments they described were fairly recent. But eight years under Bill Clinton's "horse-race presidency" have lessened the novelty of the argument—and, if anything, turned it into conventional wisdom.[2] This new book lies squarely in the mainstream of scholarly thinking about American politics.

A UNIFIED APPROACH TO AMERICAN GOVERNMENT

Regardless of whether one accepts this book's central argument, it serves as a valuable organizing framework for learning to think critically about American government (or, for that matter, simply for learning about the government). It compels readers to consider which institutions might promote public influence despite themselves and then to probe why. It also encourages readers to resist the temptation to blame democratic failure when institutions or practices do not function well, instead prompting them to recognize the voting public's own role in creating political dilemmas. We regularly ask whether voters "got what they asked for." This message of empowerment tempered by responsibility is an important one for young Americans to encounter, wherever they fall on the range from moral outrage to apathy.

The book's theme and its intellectual perspective link every chapter. An introductory chapter announces the emphasis on popular influence, especially as transmitted through democratic elections. The remaining 14 chapters then each deal with a subject conventionally covered by American government texts. Rather than consign culture, opinion, and electioneering to single chapters, however, we continue to trace their effects through American political institutions all the way to the shape of public policies. Every chapter begins with a vignette that either illustrates the voting public's power or seems to contradict it. We then use the stories to draw larger lessons about popular influence on each component of the American political system. We emphasize the electoral incentives that political actors face, how those incentives shape institutions, and how the institutions translate competing pressures into public policy. Thus, the result is more a unified book than a textbook, albeit one written for newcomers to the topic.

CHALLENGING TODAY'S STUDENT

Instructors often operate on the implicit view that their students are not adequately motivated to undertake college work. They presume that undergraduates will not endeavor to learn new words or to think through complex ideas. This viewpoint has led some instructors to oversimplify their courses and some textbook authors to avoid sophisticated arguments. Having each taught American government for many years, we are not unsympathetic with the pressures these educators face.

Nevertheless, we suspect that the main problem for typical students is neither stupidity nor laziness but simple boredom. Our experiences as educators at both private and public universities suggest that most students who are engaged by a subject are perfectly willing to do the work necessary to learn, even if it means checking a dictionary occasionally or reading a paragraph a second time. Rather than blame students for their boredom, therefore, we hypothesize that political science textbooks need to do a better job of conveying why the subject is both interesting and relevant to students who lack an inherent love of the subject.

Given our premise, this book intentionally challenges college undergraduates. We treat readers as mature and thoughtful people, curious about their world but impatient with authors who waste their time. To meet the requirements of this demanding audience, we have done everything possible to make learning more pleasant without undercutting the vitality of politics. Each chapter is an extended essay told in a uniform authorial voice, not a series of disembodied topics. We tell stories. We emphasize meaning and significance, the "bottom line." We use the active voice, straightforward sentences, and nontechnical language whenever possible. We do not just define or describe; we interpret and sometimes provoke. Our hope is that readers will find this approach as satisfying an antidote for their boredom as our own undergraduate students have.

FEATURES OF THE BOOK

This book grew out of a textbook by Fiorina and Peterson called *The New American Democracy*.[3] It is not just an "essentials edition" of the parent text, however. As part of the *Penguin Academics* series from Longman Publishers, *America's New Democracy* is an alternative for instructors and readers who want to move away from standard textbooks—those who prefer a learning tool unified by a strong framework upon which to attach facts picked up along the way. Voss has adapted the book so that it differs substantially from the source. The key changes are as follows:

- Greater focus on the book's underlying theme, including transition sections (a) linking each introduction to the book's central argument and (b) explaining how the body of the chapter illustrates popular influence in the political system. Chapters are organized to work readers through the logic connecting each topic to electoral influences.

- Large sections of new or substantially revised material, including new introductions for Chapter 1 (the 2000 presidential election), Chapter 3 (the federal drinking age), and Chapter 13 (the McVeigh execution) and updated or revised introductions for many others.

- A reorganized table of contents, with the material broken up to facilitate use in a 15-week course. This is accomplished by offering larger, merged chapters on the executive branch (including coverage of the presidency and bureaucracy), on elections (including presidential and congressional elections), on political factions (including parties and interest groups), and on public policy (including domestic, economic, and foreign policy).

- Up-to-date information on such topics as racial redistricting, civil-liberties law, U.S. trade policy, relations with the Middle East, the federal budget, and civil rights for American minorities.

This new book does retain the essential elements that have attracted so many college instructors to the Fiorina and Peterson product.

- **Election Connection** boxes describe the relationship between popular will and particular institutions or policies (including new ones treating Senator James Jeffords' 2001 defection from the Republican party and the rally-'round-the-flag public response to terrorism).

- **Critical-thinking questions** follow most graphics (including many new photos and cartoons), encouraging readers to consider the significance of numerous political issues.

- The book offers an extensive **Glossary** defining terms bold-faced in the text that is intended to help with vocabulary commonly used in the discussion of American politics.

- At the end of each chapter an **On the Web** feature directs readers to Web sites where they can find more information on the topics discussed.

SUPPLEMENTS

INSTRUCTOR'S MANUAL/TEST BANK

Prepared by Danny Adkison of Oklahoma State University, each chapter of this resource manual contains an overview, learning objectives, key terms, an outline of the chapter, ideas for lectures or discussion, and numerous multiple-choice, short-answer, true-false, and essay questions.

TESTGEN EQ COMPUTERIZED TESTING SYSTEM

This easy-to-master electronic supplement on CD-ROM includes all the test items in the printed test bank. The software allows you to edit existing questions and add your own items. Tests can be printed in several different fonts and formats.

ACKNOWLEDGMENTS

We want to thank the many people who helped out during the preparation of this book. Candice Y. Wallace, Gareth J. Voss, and Kathleen J. Elliott performed superbly as research assistants. University of Kentucky Professors Brad Canon, Don Gross, Stuart Kaufman, and Mark Peffley all provided advice on chapters relating to their areas of expertise (judicial politics, congressional elections, ethnic conflict, and media politics, respectively). Chris White helped motivate the Federalism introduction. Lori Allen and Beverly Clayborne offered helpful staff support whenever it was sought. Also, Voss is grateful for the encouragement he has received as a faculty member in the University of Kentucky's College of Arts and Sciences, not only from the college's administration but also from the many University of Kentucky undergraduates who have toiled to make his experience teaching American Government so stimulating. He dedicates the book to his two children, Gareth James Voss and Corrine Faye Elliott, whose knight-and-princess fantasies suggest rather royalist leanings but who nevertheless tolerate their father's interest in mass political behavior.

We also wish to express the deepest gratitude to those who have assisted with editions of the text from which this book draws. Bruce Nichols first argued the need for a new-century approach in introductory texts on American government. The Center for Advanced Study in the Behavioral and Social Sciences provided generous support for Peterson's work on the first edition during his academic year there. Harding Noblitt of Concordia College read the entire first-edition manuscript in search of errors of fact and interpretation, which saved the authors much embarrassment. In addition, portions were read by Danny Adkison, Sue

Davis, Richard Fenno, Gary Jacobson, Barry Rabe, and Chris Stamm, whose comments helped with fact checking. Larry Carlton supplied important factual material. Research assistants included Ted Brader, Jay Girotto, William Howell, Donald Lee, Jerome Maddox, Kenneth Scheve, Sean Theriault, and Robert Van Houweling. We extend our special thanks to Bert Johnson and Martin West of Carleton College and Harvard University, respectively, and to Sam Abrams of Stanford University for the multitude of tasks they undertook to see the second edition of *The New American Democracy,* on which this book draws most heavily, into publication. Rebecca Contreras, Alison Kommer, Shelley Weiner, and Sarah Peterson provided staff assistance.

M. P. F.
P. E. P.
D. S. V.

FOUNDATIONS
OF
AMERICA'S NEW DEMOCRACY

DEMOCRACY IN THE UNITED STATES

Election night 2000 was not a proud moment in the annals of American journalism. The problems began at 8:00 P.M. eastern standard time, just after polls had closed in the first handful of states. Americans were still casting votes across the heartland and up and down the West Coast when the television networks announced a major development in the presidential election. One after another the networks declared, based on their election-night polls, that Democratic Vice President Al Gore had taken Florida—even though some of the state's voting booths had not yet even closed.[1]

Losing Florida would have dealt a crushing blow to the presidential ambitions of Texas Governor George W. Bush, the Republican nominee. His brother Jeb governed the state, so trouble there—where his campaign held a home-field advantage—probably would have signified even more trouble in other swing states that he and Gore had contested closely. Anyway, few informed observers thought that Bush could win the presidency without near-solid support from the South, and especially from such a large southern state as Florida.[2]

When Bush appeared before the television cameras soon afterward, though, seated in his shirtsleeves with tie askew, he did not appear particularly worried. He joked with companions on screen, then announced to the cameras that no one should write him off yet. "The networks called this thing awfully early, but the people who are actually counting the votes are coming up with a little different perspective," he warned. "And so ... I'm pretty darn upbeat about things."[3]

Bush staffers were much less jocular. They jumped quickly to chastise the networks for making their declarations so early in the night, when they could still influence many voters across the country. "This is an unfortunate rush to judgment by the media," Mark McKinnon, Bush's senior media consultant, told ABC. "I think there's going to be some real serious discussion about this." No doubt reporters initially assumed that Bush's smiles were false bravado, hiding his campaign advisers' knowledge that the election was lost.

The election, though, was not lost. As the numbers poured in from Florida, it became clear that Gore was not receiving the expected level of support. The networks finally threw out their predictions after half of Florida's precincts had reported results. "We realized we were in trouble, and we pulled it back," explained ABC spokesperson Carolyn Smith, describing the situation faced by all the networks. They declared Florida once again "too close to call" and stuck to that judgment throughout the night—even as the Florida tally mounted—no doubt wishing to avoid a second embarrassment.

Finally, in the wee hours of the morning, the networks could no longer resist and set themselves up for humiliation again. They declared Florida for Bush this time and announced his election as the nation's forty-third president. The few TV screens still shining across the United States showed smiling pictures of Governor Bush, with the American flag rippling behind him. Only later did watchers learn that Florida would end the night as it began, still much too close to call.

If election night 2000 marked the low point in political news coverage, many observers considered the days that followed the low point of twentieth century American politics. The whole presidential election hinged on one state, the state governed by a candidate's brother, and it quickly became clear that the nation's election laws and voting technologies were not precise enough to resolve such a close contest in a manner satisfactory to everyone.

Thousands of ballots had gone uncounted. Many thousands more had been miscast by voters who did not understand what they were supposed to do with the ballot. In one Florida county, Palm Beach, a poorly designed ballot resulted in perhaps 3,000 votes being miscast for Reform Party candidate Pat Buchanan. It is hard to say who deserved those votes, since Buchanan's spot on the ballot placed him between the two major-party candidates, but the quantity involved was more

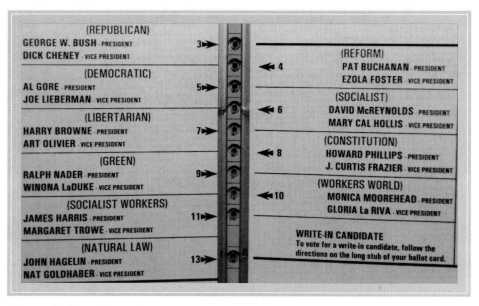

A butterfly doomed to extinction

Palm Beach County, Florida, used a "butterfly ballot" in the 2000 presidential election that caused many voters to choose Reform Party candidate Pat Buchanan accidentally. Buchanan's ballot slot fell between that of the two major-party candidates, but many specialists argue that Gore lost the bulk of these miscast votes. Florida followed the debacle with a major overhaul of its election law. Why might Gore supporters be more likely to punch the wrong hole on this ballot?

than enough to make up any difference between votes for Bush and those for Gore.[4] Media reports turned up examples of dead people and felons voting, of people being turned away at the polls because precincts could not handle the traffic, of absentee military ballots being disqualified because of technicalities.[5]

Florida began the slow process of recounting votes to make sure that Bush had won. But with so much of the process in doubt, it seemed inevitable that ultimate resolution of the contest would have to come from the courts. Legal teams for both candidates began filing suits and countersuits, throwing around provisions in Florida law and constitutional doctrine to swing the state over to their cause.

The legal battle did little to increase national confidence in the election. Florida's Republican secretary of state made a series of judgments about the timing of recounts that would benefit the Republicans. The Democratic state attorney general responded with contrary legal interpretations that would benefit the Democrats. The Florida Supreme Court, dominated by Democratic judges, favored an interpretation of state law that would assist Gore. But the U.S. Supreme Court, dominated by Republican appointees, overruled their judgment as unconstitutional—only then guaranteeing a Bush victory. The debate operated under a veneer of legal reasoning, but if anything only added to the sense that Americans might never know who really won the 2000 election.

One election result did appear certain: This "debacle" could only fuel feelings of impotence and political cynicism already rampant in the country. For that matter, even foreign observers felt compelled to declare their loss of faith in American elections.[6] If campaigns in the United States could be resolved by such a haphazard (and seemingly partisan) procedure, many asked, then why should anyone bother to vote? Who would accept that the attitudes, opinions, and values of regular citizens can influence elected leaders? Who would believe that elections really matter anymore?

NEVERTHELESS, THE CENTRAL THEME OF THIS BOOK IS THAT ELECTIONS ARE the key to understanding contemporary American democracy. Not only are elections more important in the United States than in other democracies, but they are also more important today than they were in most earlier periods of U.S. history. Americans have developed *a unique conception of democracy* that requires frequent citizen participation, with the result that *elections are plentiful* and *politicians are permanently campaigning.* The need to please a fickle and demanding electorate therefore drives political behavior across the nation's institutions, both the formal ones set up by law and the informal ones—such as political parties, interest groups, and the mass media—that also help shape the American political system.

THE ELECTION CONNECTION: KEEPING GOVERNMENT IN LINE

Americans do not trust government as much as they did a generation ago, as indicated by Figure 1.1. Citizens believe that government costs too much and delivers too little. They think politics is needlessly contentious and often corrupt. Many are unenthusiastic about major-party presidential candidates and yearn for new leaders, such as former wrestler Jesse Ventura, elected governor of Minnesota in 1998. Many are suspicious about the established TV networks and newspapers, preferring such alternative information providers as talk show hosts and cable programs. Many believe they have little influence over government, despite frequent opportunities to give leaders feedback. They are frustrated enough with existing political processes that they support radical reforms, such as constitutional amendments to limit the number of terms elected officials may serve.[7]

We think that this growing cynicism is misguided, given the importance of elections in contemporary politics, but not necessarily dangerous. To some extent, suspicion of government is healthy. By their very nature, governments threaten human liberty. The great German sociologist Max Weber wrote that **government** is the only institution in society with a "monopoly of the legitimate use of physical force."[8] Government is the only institution that *legally* can take people's property (by taxing them), restrict their movements (by imprisoning them), and even kill them (by executing them). As George Washington put it, a century before Weber, "Government is not reason, it is not eloquence—it is force."[9]

Why have governments at all, then? Different thinkers have provided different answers to that question. Thomas Hobbes, a great English political theorist, made the most basic case. A world without government would be nothing less than "a war of all against all," he claimed. Life would be "nasty, brutish and short."[10] Because he saw the consequences as so dire, Hobbes determined that government must possess absolute power to protect itself. Few Americans today accept this undemocratic conclusion. At the same time, almost everyone accepts that some form of government is necessary, and for much the same reason Hobbes offered: to protect people from each other's abuses, if nothing else. As former president James Madison once put it, "If men were angels, no government would be necessary."[11]

Those who participate in politics generally do so because they want to use government's great power to realize their visions of a better society. Obviously there are other ways to improve a community, a nation, or the world—such as charities or volunteer efforts. But government is a convenient means to force

FIGURE 1.1

Americans have grown increasingly skeptical of the national government

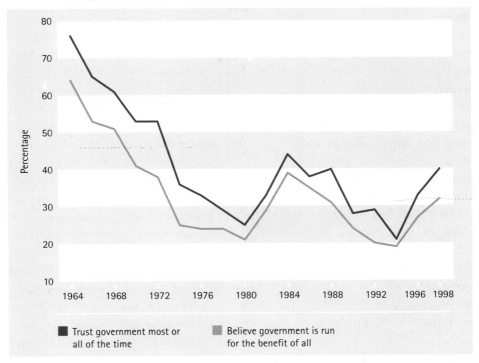

NOTE: Data on the 1986 responses to the second question do not exist.

SOURCE: The American National Election Studies.

everyone else to work toward the same vision, and to do so speedily. In other words, government is designed for the times when people disagree rather than when they agree. It offers a legitimate means to resolve those disagreements, and to back up society's decisions with force if necessary. For that reason, citizens *should* be wary of its power. In particular, the size, scope, and shape of government are among the most critical decisions that a society must make.

TYPES OF GOVERNMENT

British author Samuel Johnson once commented, "I would not give half a guinea to live under one form of government than another. It is of no moment to the happiness of an individual."[12] Johnson's comment is silly, at best. Lives can be terribly damaged or greatly improved, depending on the type of government under which people live. The system of government matters. Aristotle recognized this fact 23 centuries ago when he classified governments into three general types: government by one person, by the few, and by the many.

Few Americans today support government dominated by a small number of people. When a single ruler, such as an emperor or a tsar, controls government, that person may put the welfare of the people first, last, or anywhere in between. An absolute ruler answers to no one. Giving one person so much power is risky, and few are so deserving of that trust. Government by the few may appear slightly better, since members of a ruling class can compete with each other. They may try to improve social conditions as a means of attracting public support. But without periodic elections, a small ruling group usually can remain unified enough to exploit its position and acquire wealth at the expense of the rest of society.

Government by one person
Pol Pot murdered millions of his fellow Cambodians—all in the name of progress.

That most Americans support rule by the many does not, however, settle every question about the form of government. Not every system of popular rule is the same. Government in which all citizens share power is called **democracy,** after the Greek word *demos,* meaning "people." In its purest form, **direct democracy,** all citizens participate directly in making government decisions. Direct democracy still exists in a few New England villages, where policies are made at town meetings, but for most levels of government direct democracy is only practical with a few political issues at a time.

Government by the many usually takes the form of a **representative democracy,** or **republic,** an *indirect* form in which citizens select the officials who govern them. In a representative system voters do not select policies, but free elections are still the key to liberty—as Soviet dictator Joseph Stalin recognized when he said, "The disadvantage of free elections is that you can never be sure who is going to win them."[13]

THE AMERICAN MODEL OF DEMOCRACY

Political theorists disagree over how much popular control is desirable. Some prefer that citizens take an active role in government. Democracy is more than just a decision-making procedure for them; it is also an educational forum. A citizenry improves itself while deciding the community's future. By being inclusive, by transforming "conflict into cooperation," the process combines everyone's perspective to produce better policies.[14] Elections play a critical role in this *popular model of democracy* because they are the mechanism for instructing officials about public wishes. Obviously, this idea requires informed citizens who are capable of voting prospectively—that is, by looking to the future.

Critics question whether average citizens should take more than a passive role in government. Too much participation produces lots of talk but little action, and also makes compromises more difficult. Citizens may be capable of judging a candidate retrospectively—that is, by looking at past performance when they vote, keeping good leaders and removing bad ones. But they are neither equipped for, nor interested in, selecting among competing policy proposals.[15] These critics favor instead a *responsible model of democracy,* in which elected officials choose policies but must answer to the people afterward for their decisions.

In the real world, of course, pure types do not exist; all democracies combine popular and responsible features. Yet the United States has always been a more popular democracy than its European counterparts. Indeed, from the earliest days of the republic, the principles of popular democracy have been an important part of American thought. "Where annual elections end, there slavery begins," said the second president, John Adams, arguing that citizens must have frequent opportunities to instruct and judge their representatives.[16] When the French scholar Alexis de Tocqueville visited the United States during the 1830s, he was astounded by the extent of popular participation. "It must be seen to be believed," he exclaimed to his fellow French citizens. "No sooner do you set foot on American ground than you are stunned by a kind of tumult. . . . Almost the only pleasure an American knows is to take part in the government and discuss its measures."[17]

Yet the best way the founders could envision to preserve popular control was a system of responsible representation. James Madison in particular believed that protections on paper—which he called "parchment barriers"—were no guarantee of good government. Rules alone would not prevent abuses of power. Rights listed in the Constitution would survive only under a system of **checks and balances.** Divide power among different representatives chosen in different elections at different times, Madison explained, and give them the authority to resist each other. Elected officials would naturally keep an eye on their rivals.

"Ambition must be made to counteract ambition. The interest of the man must be connected with the constitutional rights of [his office]."[18] In this way, the framers constructed a responsible democracy, yet one in which popular elections play a central role. Two hundred years without tyranny validate their choice.

THE ROLE OF ELECTIONS IN AMERICA

American politics has evolved over the course of two centuries to allow greater popular participation. More and more of the population have gained full rights of citizenship. The connection between representatives and the public has become increasingly direct. National institutions have become less insulated from popular influence. And the number and frequency of elections, coupled with the more extensive campaigning that accompanies them, have increased. These trends have accelerated dramatically in recent decades—to the extent that calling the system America's "new democracy" is no exaggeration.

The political system that we describe in this book may be summarized as follows: Ambitious politicians offer proposals that are crafted to help get them elected. Their proposals are shaped by polls indicating the state of public opinion. Public opinion may shift, however, because—although it is rooted in stable, underlying values—opinion responds to social change, political debate, and the way the media portray social problems. When elected officials deliver on popular promises to the public, they take issues away from potential challengers. When they fail to deliver on such promises, they give their opponents ammunition. Ambitious politicians, public opinion, the media, constant electoral pressures—all are key elements of modern American politics.

HALF A MILLION ELECTED OFFICIALS, AND THEN SOME

The United States has more elections, selecting more officials for public office, than any other country on Earth. This simple fact is one important key to understanding why elections are so influential. Unbelievable as it may seem, more than half a million people in the United States are elected officials, about one official for every 500 Americans. If all elected officials lived in one place, the population would exceed that of Cleveland.[19]

National elections, in which voters choose the officials of the federal government, occur every two years. These important elections determine the president, the vice president, 100 senators, and 435 members of the House of Representatives. But these elections, which receive the bulk of news coverage, are just the tip of the iceberg.

State elections allow the citizens of each of the 50 states to choose their public officials. In every state, voters elect the governor and the state legislature, and in nearly all states they also elect the lieutenant governor, the treasurer, the state's attorney, the auditor, and perhaps state public utility commissioners.

The number of elections explodes at the local level. In *local elections,* voters in cities elect mayors and city councils. Voters in the more than 3,000 counties elect sheriffs, county treasurers, and county boards, among other officials. Voters elect the members of 90 percent of the nation's 16,000 school boards, as well as numerous officials responsible for the governance of towns, villages, and special districts.

Even the judicial system—often viewed as insulated from political pressure—is permeated by elections. In 37 states, voters elect at least some judges. Altogether, Americans select more than 1,000 state judges and about 15,000 county, municipal, and other local officers of the court.[20] Moreover, in recent years judges have been increasingly subject to **recall elections,** in which dissatisfied citizens try to remove sitting officials during their terms.

The result? Americans must vote constantly to stay involved. Just to take one example, professors at the University of Houston estimate that a resident of Houston is represented by 126 elected officials, judges included.[21] We challenge our readers to find other jurisdictions in which citizens vote for even more officials!

Although half a million elected officials sound like a lot, there are far more elections than there are elected officials. First, many officials must win two or more elections before they can take office. In the **primary election,** each party chooses a nominee, who then squares off against the other parties' nominees in the **general election**—which selects the officeholder. *Nonpartisan elections,* where candidates do not run with party labels, also sometimes use primaries to narrow the field of candidates.

Some elections do not choose officials at all, but instead allow the people to decide on public issues directly. In 27 states and the District of Columbia, citizens may change state law at the ballot box.[22] Some states allow **initiatives,** proposed laws or constitutional amendments placed on the ballot by citizen petition. Some states decide policy through **referenda,** laws or state constitutional amendments proposed by a legislative body that require voter approval before going into effect. A few states, such as California, frequently have more initiatives and referenda on the ballot than elected offices to be filled.

Other countries do not have nearly so many elections. Consider Great Britain, which elected John Major prime minister in 1992 and replaced him with Tony Blair five years later. In each of these elections, Britons voted for only one person—a candidate for parliament. Between these two elections, Britons voted on only two other occasions, for only two offices—local councillor and representative to the European Community.

In the time between Bill Clinton's two election victories, the French voted four times: for Parliament in 1993, for president in April and May of 1994 (France has a two-round system), and for local mayors in 1995. Similarly, between 1992 and 1996 the Japanese voted five times, twice each for the upper and lower houses of the Diet (their parliament) and once for local officials.

U.S. citizens even vote a lot more often than other North Americans. At most a Mexican citizen votes four times in a four-year period: in presidential, congressional, state, and municipal elections. A Canadian votes at most three times (national, provincial, and municipal) in a four-year period, except for an occasional referendum, such as Quebec's 1995 vote on sovereignty.[23]

Observers from other countries are struck by the seemingly constant presence of Americans at the polling booths. British analyst Anthony King observes:

> Americans take the existence of their elections industry for granted. Some like it; some dislike it; most are simply bored by it. But they are all conscious of it, in the same way that they are conscious of Mobil, McDonald's, Larry King Live, Oprah Winfrey, the Dallas Cowboys, the Ford Motor Company, and all the other symbols and institutions that go to make up the rich tapestry of American life. In a meaningful sense, America is about the holding of elections.[24]

THE LIMITS OF VOTING

Stressing the importance of elections may create a rather rosy picture. To avoid any misunderstanding, therefore, we must emphasize three qualifications, and they are (1) that elections involve more than what takes place in the voting booth, (2) that elections do not always express the popular will, and (3) that elections are not the only important force in American politics.

First, our notion of electoral influence is very broad. We are referring not just to what happens on election day, nor even just to what goes on during campaigns. Rather, when we write about the importance of elections, we include the anticipation of, and the preparation for, future elections. Looking ahead affects what presidents propose, what they sign, and what they veto; what Congress passes and what it kills; whom groups support and whom they oppose; and whom and what the media cover or ignore.

A second important clarification is that when we stress the importance of elections, we are *not* making a naïve claim that "the people" rule. Just as the winner of an Olympic event may have been determined on the training fields years earlier, so the outcomes of elections may be determined by the actions of candidates, groups, contributors, the media, and other political actors far in advance of the actual campaigns. Most fund-raising is done by groups who wish to promote special political interests. Liberal and conservative groups, economic and environmental groups, women's groups, minority groups, or whatever—all have a perfectly legitimate right to participate in politics. But all have a point of view, usually one that is narrower than that of the typical voter.

Moreover, even in today's technologically advanced world, campaigns require workers as well as money. This is particularly true of lower-level campaigns. Volunteers circulate petitions, stuff envelopes, knock on doors, make phone calls, stage rallies, create photo opportunities, and drive voters to the polls. To get volunteers, candidates may appeal to **single-issue voters,** people who care so deeply about some particular issue that a like-minded candidate can draw them into the political process. Candidates naturally give greater weight to the activists from whom they recruit their campaign workers.

Turnout

In 2000, despite massive get-out-the-vote efforts, barely more than half of the electorate showed up at the polls. Political parties are always trying to activate more of their supporters to turn out and shift the balance of power in the election. Why don't people vote?

Once elections are underway, many potential voters choose not to participate. Even in the 2000 presidential election, only 51 percent of the adult population voted. Turnout rates in other elections are much lower—in the single digits(!) in some local races. Groups of people who vote at higher rates, such as the elderly, enjoy disproportionate political influence.[25]

Primary elections have especially low turnout. The primary electorate is much more educated, and much more interested in politics, than the average American citizen. Republican primary voters tend to be more conservative than the typical American, and Democratic primary voters tend to be more liberal. To win primary elections, candidates may appeal to the more extreme elements of their parties. By the time typical voters get involved in the general election, their choice may be between two unappetizing candidates.

Sometimes elections allow powerful special interests to block actions desired by the majority. Sometimes leaders elected by different majorities at different times or in different regions fight each other to a standstill. It is possible that inattentive voters can be manipulated by biased information or confused by complex political issues. Elections are thus not always free, accurate, and effective expressions of national sentiment.

Finally, to say that elections are a key ingredient in American democracy—even *the* key ingredient—is not to deny that other elements are important as well. Elections are part of a complex political system. Comprehending how they operate in America's new democracy sometimes requires understanding the historical evolution of American government, the political behavior of individual Americans, the workings of the country's basic institutions, and the policies that the government produces. All of these topics, which are closely bound up with elections, thus receive thorough treatment in the chapters that follow. First, though, we consider a different drawback to a system driven by elections: the cost of the stressful contests themselves.

THE PERMANENT CAMPAIGN

The new American democracy is marked by a **permanent campaign**.[26] The term literally means that campaigning never ends; the next election campaign begins as soon as the last one has finished, if not before. The dust from the 2000 elections had barely settled before speculation turned to which candidate would challenge President Bush four years later. Commentators began discussing a presidential bid by First Lady Hillary Clinton before she was even sworn in as New York's junior U.S. senator.

The deeper meaning of the term *permanent campaign* is that the line between campaigning and governing has disappeared. How an elected official governs is, in effect, just another strategic campaign decision. Injecting campaign tactics into government may result in short-term thinking, a more combative governing style, and more emphasis on image than on substance.[27] Not everyone takes such a critical view of the rise of the permanent campaign, but most observers recognize its significance.

CAUSES OF THE PERMANENT CAMPAIGN

At least seven developments have moved American democracy in a popular direction by contributing to the permanent campaign.

SEPARATION OF ELECTIONS   In principle, all public officials could be elected on the same day and serve, say, the same four-year term of office. Everyone would stand for reelection simultaneously. Such an arrangement—one gigantic election day every four years—would greatly reduce the time taken up by campaigning and voting.

A century ago, most officials *were* elected on the same day. In 1885 a graduate student named Woodrow Wilson wrote that "This is preeminently a country of frequent elections, and few states care to increase the frequency by separating elections of state from elections of national functionaries."[28] In Wilson's time citizens of most states cast votes simultaneously for president, senator, representative, governor, mayor, state representative, state senator, city councillor, and so forth.

Today few states still follow this pattern.[29] Most Americans now turn out to vote for president at one general election, for governor at another, and for mayor at yet another. Primary elections, as well as those for local offices, are held earlier in the election year. Initiatives and referenda may be held on still other occasions. As a result, Americans are repeatedly called to the polls. For example, a conscientious Californian generally has to vote on eight separate occasions every two years. There is very little "quiet time."

DECAY OF PARTY ORGANIZATIONS   Since just before the Civil War, the two major parties in the United States have been the Republicans and the Democrats. These parties give voters a choice by advocating different political philosophies. Conservatives are called the "right" or the "right wing," and liberals, the "left" or the "left wing."*The Republican party leans in a conservative direction,

---

*The origins of this terminology lie in the French Assembly that sat after the French Revolution (1789–1795). In the Assembly, conservatives sat on the right side of the chamber and liberals on the left (as you face the podium). The U.S. Congress and some other world legislatures follow a similar practice today

generally favoring smaller government, lower taxes, less regulation of business activity, and traditional family values. The Democratic party leans in a liberal direction, usually favoring a strong federal government, more extensive social programs, more regulation, and toleration of alternative lifestyles. Issue positions shift only gradually, providing continuity and familiarity to political life. For this reason, parties simplify the choices voters must make.

A century ago many of the state and local party organizations were called machines, because they were strong, disciplined organizations that could mobilize large numbers of voters on election day. Candidates relied on their parties when elections rolled around. But various reforms and social changes killed the machines. As a consequence, today's politicians cannot depend on party workers to deliver the vote. They must build their own organizations almost from scratch.[30] Such personalized support is less reliable than the organized support once shared by a party's candidates, and requires extensive time and resources to maintain.[31]

SPREAD OF PRIMARIES   In most countries, party leaders select candidates for office. A century ago this was the standard procedure in the United States as well. According to reformers, candidates were picked in "smoke-filled rooms" by party "bosses." To eliminate the corruption that often accompanied such deal making, reformers passed laws giving voters the right to select party nominees in primary elections.

Although they came into use about a century ago, primaries did not become the dominant mechanism for nominating presidential candidates until after World War II, as shown in Figure 1.2. The first presidential candidate who owed his nomination in any significant degree to winning primaries was Dwight D. Eisenhower, elected in 1952. As late as 1968, the Democratic nominee, Hubert Humphrey, did not enter a single primary.

Today primaries contribute substantially to the permanent campaign. They greatly increase the number of elections. Moreover, because primaries often are held months in advance of the general election, they shorten the time between one election and the next. Behind-the-scenes planning for the presidential election of 2000 began in early 1997. The campaign was under way by mid-1999, more than six months before the primaries began in the spring of the year 2000 and only two and a half years into Clinton's second term. Nor is the permanent campaign limited to the White House. Some members of the House of Representatives face primaries more than six months before their two-year terms end. On April 9, 1996, for example, a Texas Republican was defeated in a primary scarcely 15 months after he had taken the oath of office.

FIGURE 1.2
The number of presidential primaries has increased greatly in the past three decades

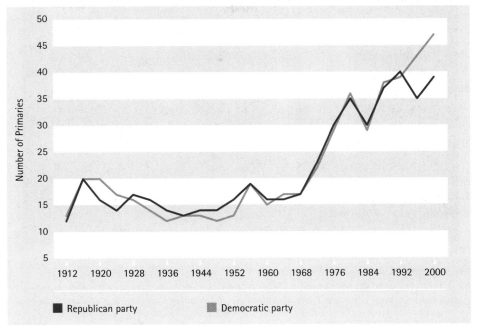

SOURCE: Harold Stanley and Richard Niemi, *Vital Statistics on American Politics.* (Washington, DC: CQ Press, 2000), p. 62 and data compiled by Sam Abrams.

MASS COMMUNICATIONS Technological progress also has helped make campaigns continuous. Fifty years ago, party workers simply passed out flyers and posted signs when the formal campaign began. Today's candidates make every effort to get their names in the papers and their pictures on television. Moreover, interactive mass communications provide citizens with more opportunities to talk back to politicians. Long-distance telephone rates are so low that many people are willing to call anywhere in the United States. Dozens of cable television channels enable candidates to communicate with small, well-defined audiences. C-SPAN provides continuous coverage of congressional debates, giving people outside Washington a chance to observe public officials directly. Radio talk shows have increased in popularity. Candidate and interest-group Web sites on the Internet have proliferated, and conversation on the Internet (although often erroneous and conspiratorial) is perhaps the fastest-growing mode of political communication.

The effects of technological change have been intensified by changes in the culture of the mass media. The demand for content has been greatly increased by

The permanent campaign
Candidates begin campaigning far in advance of the actual presidential election and often find the whole experience terribly draining. Texas Governor George W. Bush's exhaustion shows in this election-night photo, in which he tries to nap on wife Laura's shoulder. Is it feasible, or even a good idea, to limit the time candidates may campaign?

24-hour news services. Any move a politician makes might end up on television, and virtually every move a prominent politician makes is now evaluated for its political motives and implications. Partly as a consequence of the media's insatiable appetite for news, the distinction between public and private life has eroded. The financial and medical histories of elected officials are treated as public business, and reporters ask candidates almost any question imaginable, no matter how tasteless or unrelated to politics and government. Campaigning never ends because the public never stops watching.

PROFUSION OF INTEREST GROUPS The personal organizations that today's candidates put together are built in large part from the numerous interest groups that have formed during the past generation. When political scientists wrote about interest groups at mid-century, they referred mostly to a few large business, labor, and agricultural organizations. Now, there are thousands of generally smaller, more narrowly focused organizations. Many are outgrowths of the social movements of the 1960s (such as the antiwar, civil rights, women's, and environmental movements).

Technology has played a role as well. In the precomputer, "snail mail" era, it was far more difficult for small economic interests even to locate each other, let alone organize. Today, interest groups can monitor the actions of elected officials electronically and then post information about political developments on their Web sites or send blanket e-mail to their members. Technology provides the means to put the actions of public officials under a microscope, and interest-group leaders have more than enough incentive to do so.

PROLIFERATION OF POLLS The permanent campaign owes much to the profusion of polling. Leaders always have been concerned about public opinion, of course. The framers of the U.S. Constitution were particularly concerned with how others would perceive their handiwork, since they wanted the document ratified and respected. Abraham Lincoln waited for a military victory before issuing the Emancipation Proclamation, abolishing slavery in the Confederate states, so that a happy northern public would be more inclined to support it. Politicians traditionally are portrayed as having their "ears to the ground" and their "fingers to the wind." But until the introduction of modern polling, beliefs about the state of public opinion were only guesses.

Modern polling techniques are much more precise and provide everyone the same information. Polling has become a major industry, in part because elected officials hunger for information about the state of the public mind. Of course, it is not just the politicians who want to know about the state of public opinion. The media have become increasingly focused on it as well, as Figure 1.3 shows. Some critics charge that the media find it easier to "manufacture" news by taking a poll and writing about it than to write about real news.

Polling contributes to the permanent campaign by making opinions immediately available. When a new issue arises, politicians no longer wonder about the savvy position to take; they find out within days or sometimes hours. Even if elected officials wanted to make decisions without thinking about their political implications, it would be difficult to do so. They are bombarded with such information at every turn.

MONEY Campaigning is expensive. Polls, political consultants, and TV ads cost a great deal of money. And because candidates now have personal organizations, they do not share many resources with each other. The total cost of election campaigns thus has increased dramatically in the past three decades. Campaigns for the House of Representatives, for example, were more than five times more expensive in 1996 than in 1976.[32]

FIGURE 1.3

Poll coverage exploded between the mid-1960s and mid-1970s

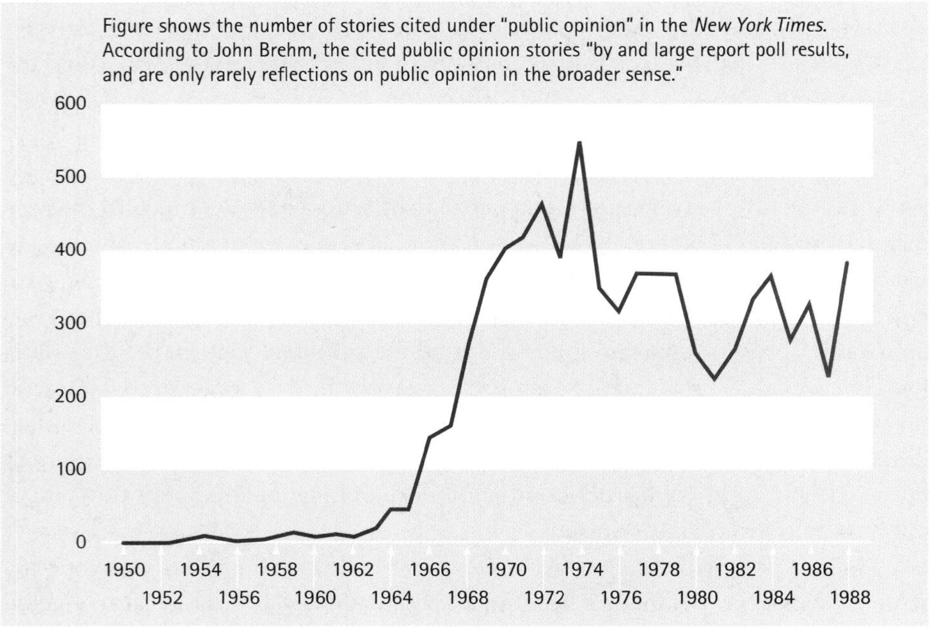
Figure shows the number of stories cited under "public opinion" in the New York Times. According to John Brehm, the cited public opinion stories "by and large report poll results, and are only rarely reflections on public opinion in the broader sense."
600
500
400
300
200
100
0
1950
1952
1954
1956
1958
1960
1962
1964
1966
1968
1970
1972
1974
1976
1978
1980
1982
1984
1986
1988

SOURCE: John Brehm, *The Phantom Respondents* (Ann Arbor, MI: University of Michigan Press, 1993), p. 4.

Elections may occur every few years, but the quest for money is continuous. Nearly all governors serve four-year terms, but current estimates are that incumbents in large states must raise an average of $50,000 *every week of their terms* to fund reelection campaigns.[33] Similarly, U.S. senators serve six-year terms. The framers thought that such long terms would help insulate senators from popular pressures and allow them to act more deliberately than members of the House. But most contemporary observers believe that the Senate today is just as electorally sensitive.[34] One reason is that senators must raise more than $15,000 every week of their six-year terms to run for reelection.

In recent years the scramble for money has led to a series of fund-raising scandals, some involving public officials with long-standing reputations for honesty and integrity. In consequence, public interest groups have placed the issue of campaign finance on the public agenda. Another, more basic cost of this need for cash is that public officials must be concerned with the next election even when it is years away.

REFORM?

The United States pays a price for the pervasiveness of its elections. Continuous electioneering creates a governmental system that is unattractive in many respects. Scandals—real and trumped-up—are common; inefficiency and stalemate are widespread; important policy problems fester; and effective actions are delayed or compromised into ineffectiveness.[35]

Even though American government understandably frustrates many citizens, we should view proposals for radical reform skeptically. Reforms often call for further movement toward popular democracy—more elections, more opportunities to exert popular pressure, or less power for appointed officials. Americans apparently believe, with John Dewey, that "The cure for the ailments of democracy is more democracy."[36] Such reforms overlook the tremendous popular pressure that political leaders already face. Indeed, popular influence on government may be one cause of the very problems reformers wish to address.[37]

America is a diverse country, and those who elect public officials—their **constituencies**—reflect that diversity. People have conflicting interests and values. If elected officials wish to follow their **electoral incentives,** and remain in office, they must attend to the demands generated by these diverse constituencies. Reconciling so many demands requires compromise. Unlike chief executives in the business world, presidents cannot fire members of Congress, governors cannot remove members of their state legislatures, and mayors cannot dismiss members of their city councils. Political leaders either must persuade their opponents or bargain for their support, a process that becomes harder when the public is more attentive and involved. This being the case, reforms that shift American politics in a still more popular direction may worsen problems of stalemate and delay rather than eliminate them.

THE BENEFITS OF THE SYSTEM: A PRETTY GOOD GOVERNMENT

Although single-issue voters and other kinds of special interests at times wield unequal influence, such groups lose much of their clout when a clear majority of the voters takes a strong interest in a highly visible subject. The same is true whether voters demand a policy change or prefer to stop one. Elected officials cannot routinely take positions contrary to those of their constituents and expect to escape the wrath of the electorate indefinitely.

Moreover, majorities remain potentially powerful even when the public is uninformed about or unaware of an issue. Elected officials realize that the media spotlight may suddenly shine into what seemed to be a dark corner. Challengers looking for campaign issues contribute to this danger, poring over the incumbent's record, searching for unpopular votes cast, positions taken, or statements made. Most of the time, incumbents think twice before taking actions in back rooms if those actions cannot be defended once the doors are opened.[38]

Because leaders are never sure which issue will explode, they tend to be cautious in handling all of them. Hence, the power of minorities is limited by the potential threat that the majority will become aroused. Ordinarily, a majority rules not so much by actively articulating its views as through the calculations of public officials who anticipate majority opinion long before it asserts itself. For example, Bill Clinton signed an historic welfare reform bill about which he had serious doubts because he knew a veto would have made welfare reform a major campaign issue.

We began this chapter by noting an irony of America's new democracy: Americans have been growing increasingly unhappy with a government over which they have more influence than ever. Now that we have explained how thoroughly American majorities exercise their influence, it should be clear that the sour national mood is difficult to justify. Serious problems and unresolved conflicts certainly exist, but most are the natural result of an active and diverse voting public, not the result of an arrogant and inattentive government. The political system is much more successful than commentary often suggests.

Too often, critics apply unrealistic standards of evaluation. An old maxim— frequently quoted by former President Clinton—states that "the *best* is the enemy of the *good*." Any policy or institution will fall short when judged against some abstract standard of perfection. Perfection does not exist in the real world, but the wish for it makes people unhappy with their government and their leaders. The search for perfection can cause harm because people often abandon the "pretty good" for something worse. Democracy's defenders cite Winston Churchill's remark that "democracy is the worst form of government except all those other forms that have been tried."[39] The great American judge Learned Hand similarly commented, "Even though counting heads is not an ideal way to govern, it is at least better than breaking them."[40] These observations apply with special force to America's new democracy.

Across the entire sweep of human history, most governments have been controlled by one or a few. Many were tyrannical; a government that did not murder and rob its subjects was about as good a government as people could expect. Tragically, tyrannical governments are not just a matter of ancient history. Only a bare majority of the world's population today lives under governments that can reasonably be considered democratic, and in the twentieth century, governments caused the deaths of 170 million people, a number that *does not include those who died in wars*.[41] In recent years Americans have watched in horror as civil war or genocide has erupted in Northern Ireland, Cambodia, Iraq, Azerbaijan, Bosnia, Rwanda, Burundi, Chechnya, Albania, Zaire, Kosovo, East Timor, and Sierra Leone. Official tyranny—and worse—remains a contemporary reality.

To be sure, Americans should not set too low a standard for their political life. No one would seriously argue that Americans should be satisfied just because their country has avoided dissolving into chaos. But Americans must apply realistic standards when evaluating their political system. Critics selectively cite statistics showing that the United States is worse than Canada in one respect, worse than Japan in another respect, worse than Sweden in some other respect, and so on. But can one conclude with confidence that any comparable national government works better on the whole? We think the answer is no.

Only when comparing the United States with other countries do we see that American democracy, for all its faults, has an unmatched record of maintaining order, encouraging prosperity, protecting freedom, and redressing injustices. Citizens in the United States enjoy rights and privileges that citizens in other lands die to achieve. Not only can American citizens vote more often, but Americans also can speak their minds more freely, find out more easily what their government is doing, and deal with a government less likely to discriminate against them.

Citizens of the United States have a government with a better record than most at protecting them against foreign aggression while avoiding unwise involvement in foreign conflicts. On average, citizens of the United States are wealthier than citizens of any other comparably large country. They are better housed, better fed, and better clothed. Their physical environment is better protected against degradation. Even the large fiscal deficits that were such a political concern in the 1980s and 1990s compared favorably to the deficits of most other industrial countries.

Of course, the United States is not the best at everything. Poverty rates are higher in the United States than in countries with comparable living standards. More homeless people are visible on city streets than in other industrialized countries—a sign that either the safety net has gaping holes or poor people in the United States move about more freely than those in other nations.[42] More people lack access to adequate medical care than in other developed democracies. The distribution of income is less equal than in other developed democracies. More people are murdered and more are imprisoned than in almost any other industrialized country. Just why the United States does poorly at some things and well at others is considered in the pages that follow. But not much would be gained by substituting the institutions of any other country for the ones that the United States now has. The United States, for all its problems, has as good a government as exists anywhere, and a better one than most.

CHAPTER SUMMARY

The 2000 presidential contest initially appears to validate public disillusionment with American institutions, and to challenge our focus on elections. Yet the conclusion of that race was ambiguous only because the majority was so tiny. The legal maneuvering that decided the contest only became necessary because voters were evenly divided between the two candidates. The vote itself, therefore, was a testament to how important elections really are. Anticipation of the contest drove the behavior of both Bush and Gore for years. They worked hard to frame successful political messages, planned their presidential bids far in advance, and campaigned aggressively to win over swing voters. It was their electioneering that produced such a close vote. The experience hardly serves to uphold a criticism that elections do not matter.

More than ever before, and more than in other democracies, electoral influences drive politics in the United States. Elections have always served a central role in American political thought because the framers relied on a system of checks and balances to protect freedom. But the role played by elections has grown because there are so many elective offices in the United States, because terms of office generally are short, and because Americans select candidates in primaries and vote directly on propositions. Public officials must permanently campaign as a result of numerous technological, institutional, and social changes; electoral considerations can never be far from their minds. The result is a responsive political system that, although imperfect, is still the envy of much of the world.

KEY TERMS

checks and balances, p. 9
constituency, p. 21
democracy, p. 8
direct democracy, p. 8
electoral incentive, p. 21
general election, p. 11

government, p. 6
initiatives, p. 11
permanent campaign, p. 14
primary election, p. 11
recall elections, p. 11
referenda, p. 11

representative democracy
(republic),
p. 8
single-issue voter, p. 13

ON THE WEB

DemocracyNet
www.dnet.org
This online voter guide with state-specific information is a project of the Center for Governmental Studies and the League of Women Voters.

The Federal Election Commission (FEC)
www.fec.gov
This online portal of the FEC provides easy-to-use information regarding all aspects of elections—from electoral histories to campaign finance contributions.

Project Vote Smart
www.vote-smart.org
This richly informative site is supported by a nonpartisan group. It contains biographical histories, voting records, campaign finances and promises, and performance evaluations of elected officials and candidates.

SUGGESTED READINGS

Cronin, Thomas. *Direct Democracy: The Politics of Initiative, Referendum, and Recall.* Cambridge, MA: Harvard University Press, 1989. A comprehensive study of direct democracy in the United States that takes a balanced view of the costs and benefits of citizen policy making.

Downs, Anthony. *An Economic Theory of Democracy.* New York: Harper, 1957. Seminal theoretical discussion of how elections shape the activities of voters, candidates, parties, and interest groups.

King, Anthony. *Running Scared: Why Politicians Spend More Time Campaigning Than Governing.* New York: Free Press, 1996. Provocative study by a British political scientist who shows how elections shape contemporary American politics.

Morone, James A. *The Democratic Wish.* New York: Basic Books, 1990. Brilliant historical analysis that shows how Americans have long tried to cure the ills of democracy by extending citizen participation.

Schattschneider, E. E. *The Semi-Sovereign People.* New York: Holt, 1960. Classic analysis that explains why elections do not ensure equal political influence.

Tocqueville, Alexis de. *Democracy in America,* Vols. I and II, Philips Bradley, ed. New York: Knopf, 1945. Nineteenth-century French observer's insightful interpretation of the democratic experiment in the United States.

ESTABLISHING A
CONSTITUTIONAL
DEMOCRACY

CHAPTER OUTLINE

The story of the U.S. Constitution's framing does not, at first glance, appear to support our claim that elections dominate American politics. The 55 men who gathered in Philadelphia in 1787, to write the charter that has become the world's longest living constitution, arrived there under false pretenses. They had been selected by their state legislatures to amend the current charter, the Articles of Confederation, not to start from scratch and write a new constitution. Yet they tossed out the Articles on the fourth day, and instead started working on a new document drafted in advance by Virginia delegate James Madison.

The Articles of Confederation were quite explicit about the proper legal procedure for changing them. Every state legislature had to approve alterations. Article 13 specified that the Articles had to be "inviolably observed. . . . Nor shall any alteration at any time hereafter be made in any of them; unless such alteration be . . . confirmed by the legislatures of every state." The framers knew, however, that the new constitution they envisioned would never get past Rhode Island. The state legislature there was so hostile to a stronger centralized government that it had not even bothered to send delegates to the convention.

The framers did not see any justice in letting one or two small states prevent the rest of the nation from adopting a different sort of system. So they ignored the law and wrote in the Constitution that the proposed government would take effect if it had the approval of only nine states. They also did not trust the state legislatures who had appointed them, and so they ignored the law a second time. The Constitution specified that the states would decide whether to ratify it, making no mention of the currently elected legislatures.

If word of their actions were to leak out, the Constitutional Convention might have faced disruption from angry mobs. The membership consisted of wealthy, young "demi-gods," as Thomas Jefferson called them, not typical citizens. They were leaders willing to spend a hot summer in a poorly ventilated hall without pay, debating the fine points of governance, only because they had ambitious plans for changing the political system. But most of their fellow Americans were poor farmers, jealous of the rights of their own states and fearful of what a strengthened national government might do to individual liberties.

So to keep their discussions secret, the framers imposed a gag rule and swore members to secrecy. Today, such a promise may sound silly, since it is hard to keep news bottled up among such a large number of people. But at the time a gentleman's word of honor was one of his most prized possessions.[1] The deliberations were able to proceed with very few leaks about what was taking place inside. Indeed, most of our knowledge of the convention comes from Madison's notes, which he kept from the public until after his death.[2]

Once the framers had completed their handiwork, the Confederation Congress moved swiftly to install the "legal revolution." Congress submitted the Constitution to the states for approval 11 days after the convention ended. Some of the most supportive states moved swiftly to build up momentum behind the document, and to do so before opponents could prepare themselves for a fight. The states held elections to select delegates for their individual constitutional conventions, elections in which many Americans (including women, racial minorities, and much of the poor) could not vote. The process moved so swiftly, and news spread so slowly, that participation was quite low, even among those who could vote.

Those supporting the Constitution were much better prepared than the opponents were. Their leaders knew the document intimately and possessed the resources to promote it. Some well-known figures did fight hard to stop ratification. Patrick Henry, the great American patriot, was one of these. "Before the meeting of the late Federal Convention at Philadelphia a general peace, and a universal tranquility prevailed in this country," Henry warned. But now, "I conceive the republic to be in extreme danger. Here is a revolution as radical as that which separated us from Great Britain. . . . All pretensions to human rights and privileges are rendered insecure, if not lost."[3] New York's powerful governor, George Clinton, also resisted. But neither talent nor time was on their side, and the Constitution eventually won ratification.

THE WHOLE PROCESS WAS RATHER UNSEEMLY. A group of young discontents appointed to do a job instead ignored both their instructions and the law, worked in secrecy to redesign the political system, and then exploited numerous strategic advantages to win official approval for their plans. It was not what most Americans envision when they think of "free and fair elections," and it seems to challenge the central theme of this book. If American politics is driven by elections more than is true in other democracies, then how do we explain the minor role voting played in creating the political system in the first place? Was the country from its beginning nothing more than a sham democracy?

That topic is the subject of this chapter. Its purpose is to show you that elections played a minor role only because the framers were good politicians. They worked hard to anticipate problems their Constitution might face with the voters, and they made compromises—including the adoption of ten amendments protecting individual liberty that many thought unnecessary—to minimize those difficulties. They designed a framework for government that was sensitive to inherited political traditions, revolutionary experiences, and lessons learned during the early years of independence. It was precisely the Constitution's success at meeting these requirements that allowed its rapid adoption and its continuing legitimacy.

THE COLONIAL EXPERIENCE WITH DEMOCRACY

A small group of religious dissenters, now remembered as the Pilgrims, set sail for Britain's Virginia colony in 1620. To help cover costs for the voyage, they had loaded the ship *Mayflower* with many other Europeans who did not share their religious beliefs, who simply wanted to seek their fortunes. However, the ship never reached Virginia (either because it was blown off course, as claimed, or because the Pilgrims never really intended to live in a colony led by Anglican tobacco planters in the first place). Instead, the *Mayflower* arrived in what is now Provincetown, Massachusetts. Imagine the dismay of the ship's ambitious immigrants when they looked out and, instead of seeing Virginia's rich tobacco fields, encountered New England's bare and rocky shoreline!

The Pilgrim leaders knew that they would have to pacify the disappointed passengers if they were going to found a new colony.[4] They also realized that they lacked a clear governmental framework, one that mirrored their belief that individuals should decide both religious and political matters for themselves. Before leaving the ship, therefore, the settlers signed the **Mayflower Compact,** the first document in colonial America in which the people gave their express consent to be governed. Thus, democratic principles were established from the very beginning of New England's colonial settlement.[5]

GOVERNANCE OF THE COLONIES

European settlement spread across the eastern shores of the North American continent. Several of the most successful colonies, like the Maryland colony Lord Baltimore established for fellow Catholics, also began as a means to accommodate minority religious beliefs. Others initially formed as **proprietary colonies,** governed either by a prominent English noble or by a company. Companies founded settlements, such as the Jamestown colony, almost exclusively for economic gain, including the search for gold. When their colonies ran into financial difficulty, they often became **royal colonies,** governed by the king's representative with the advice of an elected assembly. Nine of the 12 colonies had reverted to royal control by the Revolutionary War.

Radical social and religious beliefs did not enjoy much influence in proprietary and royal colonies. Yet local institutions still helped prepare colonists for democratic principles. Power was divided between the governor and an elected assembly—usually a two-chamber legislature. Governors were appointed by either proprietors or the king and were the most serious threat to self-government. They could veto any legislation passed by the assemblies, and they controlled the distribution of enough jobs and benefits to sway legislators. Many took advantage of this **patronage** power. In Massachusetts, for example, 71 percent of the members of the 1763 assembly had been appointed justices of the peace, giving "the Governors vast Influence."[6]

The assemblies had the power to levy taxes, and they eventually used this authority to achieve broader influence. Many obtained financial control of the salaries of governors and their appointed officials.[7] In most cases, members elected to assemblies were substantial community members, which added to their influence. For example, Thomas Jefferson won election to the Virginia assembly after organizing his community to clear the Rivanna River for navigation by trading boats.[8]

VOTING QUALIFICATIONS

Although assemblies were gaining control over colonial affairs, this did not mean the colonies were democratic in the modern sense of the word. From the very beginning, women, slaves, and indentured servants were excluded from the voting rolls, as Table 2.1 illustrates. Even white male voters usually had to meet certain property qualifications: In Virginia they had to own 25 acres and a house. In Maryland and Pennsylvania, voters needed to be worth 50 acres or 40 pounds. By 1750 these qualifications disenfranchised as much as one-quarter to one-half of the male population.[9]

THE SPREAD
OF REVOLUTIONARY IDEALS

The colonial era established solid foundations for the American democratic experiment. Despite limits on voting, elections made a difference because elected assemblies held the power to tax and spend. The democratic practices that began during the colonial period were reinforced by the struggle for independence.[10] Liberties that the colonists took for granted suddenly had to be defended from the king's power.

AMERICAN POLITICAL THOUGHT

By the time of the revolution, political thinkers who influenced the patriots had long discarded the notion that kings had a God-given right to rule, which was called **divine right.** In its place stood the following three revolutionary principles:

1. Government arises from the consent of the governed.
2. Power should be divided among separate institutions.
3. Citizens should govern themselves to the extent feasible.

Each of these principles shaped the writing of the Constitution.

CONSENT OF THE GOVERNED   As early as 1651, the great English political theorist Thomas Hobbes said that kings rule by the consent of the governed. He still defended giving kings absolute power, but only because such a government was necessary to prevent anarchy.[11] Later thinkers retained the idea of consent but looked to elections as a means for government to seek popular approval more frequently. Foremost among these thinkers was John Locke, an English writer whose *Second Treatise on Government* (published in 1690) probably influenced the Declaration of Independence more than any other work.

TABLE 2.1

VOTING QUALIFICATIONS BY COLONY AT THE TIME OF THE REVOLUTION

Despite the restrictions on who was eligible to vote, can elections held in the colonies be said to have been democratic in any way? In your opinion, who must be eligible to vote if a country is to qualify as a democracy?

COLONY	QUALIFICATIONS
Massachusetts	Male, 21 years old, property owner
New Hampshire	Male, 21, except paupers
Rhode Island	Male, 21, debt-free
Connecticut	Male, 21, property owner, civil in conversation
New York	Male, 21, property owner or renter, six months residence
New Jersey	Male, 21, one year residence
Pennsylvania	Male, 21, taxpayer, two years residence
Virginia	Male, 21, property owner
Maryland	Male, 21, property owner, one year residence
North Carolina	Male, 21, property owner, one year residence
South Carolina	Male, 21, white, taxpayer, property owner, two years residence
Georgia	Male, 21, taxpayer, six months residence

SOURCES: Robert J. Dinkin, *Voting in Revolutionary America: A Study of Elections in the Original Thirteen States, 1776–1789* (Westport, CT: Greenwood Press, 1982); Robert J. Dinkin, *Voting in Provincial America: A Study of Elections in the Thirteen Colonies, 1689–1776* (Westport, CT: Greenwood Press, 1977).

SEPARATED POWER   Hobbes was ruthlessly coherent. Accept his premise that individuals are selfish and shortsighted, and his conclusion that power must remain undivided seems almost inevitable. But the English people, more pragmatic than consistent, rejected Hobbes's defense of kingly strength. Instead, Locke argued that governmental power took both legislative and executive forms, each requiring a different institution.[12] A country's founders should create a **separation of powers,** so that these two institutions would not encroach upon each other. Nearly 60 years after Locke's writings, the French philosopher Montesquieu added a third institution. These three separate powers are as follows:

1. *Legislative power,* the making of law, exercised by an elected assembly if possible

2. *Executive power,* the enforcement of law, exercised by a single person

3. *Judicial power,* the application of law to particular situations, exercised by independent judges

Great political theorists often come to conclusions that differ little from existing practice. So it was with Locke, whose theory closely resembled English government. England had a legislature, or parliament, consisting of two chambers: the House

Thomas Hobbes
Thomas Hobbes (1588–1679) thought that humans are by nature warlike and selfish. His treatise Leviathan *held that the only way to maintain human society was for individuals to consent to rule by a single, all-powerful leader or government.* How did Locke modify Hobbes's theory?

of Lords (representing the aristocracy) and the House of Commons (representing the people). The king exercised executive powers. The House of Lords appointed judges. Locke's genius consisted of making theoretical sense of English practice, offering a way of thinking about a government that had evolved haphazardly over many centuries.

PARTICIPATORY DEMOCRACY Not long after Locke wrote, British practice changed. Power began concentrating in a small group of ministers drawn from Parliament but appointed by the king. Patronage and corruption, not a balance of power among separated institutions, held the system together.[13]

This patronage-based system provoked intense opposition from a group known as **Whigs,** who developed a theory of citizen rights and representation. The most important political thinker among the Whigs was James Harrington. In place of kingly rule, exercised through parliamentary control over a large nation, Harrington favored self-governing cities. Each would be a republic, protecting the freedoms of its residents. Ordinary citizens would select from their own number virtuous leaders who would serve for short periods of time.[14] The Whig theory of representation was explicated forcefully in *Common Sense,* written by Thomas Paine.[15] The book, which American colonials read widely in the months before independence, calls for frequent elections so that representatives establish a "common interest with every part of the community."

TAXATION WITHOUT REPRESENTATION

Whig criticism of the British government made sense to many American colonists. The rough equality of colonial America stood in sharp contrast to the court intrigues in London. And the more Parliament imposed taxes and interfered in colonial affairs, the more corrupt England's system appeared.

The revolutionary movement began as a tax revolt. British military costs were rising, so Lord of the Treasury George Grenville decided colonists should pay for the troops defending them. The British government started in 1765 with enactment of the **Stamp Act,** which imposed a tax on pamphlets, playing cards, dice, newspapers, marriage licenses, and other legal documents. Colonial taxes were lower than those the British themselves paid, so the new policy seemed reasonable. But to the colonists, who had never before paid a direct tax and were accustomed to managing their own affairs, it was an outrageous imposition.

Colonial leaders opposed what they viewed as taxation without representation. King George III did not raise taxes on England without consulting the elected Parliament. Why should he be able to tax colonists without consulting their elected assemblies? To organize their protest, nine colonies sent delegates to a Stamp Act Congress, the first political organization uniting leaders from throughout the colonies. It gave clear expression to the American demand for representative government.[16]

In Boston a group of citizens calling themselves the "Sons of Liberty" decided to enforce resolutions passed by the Stamp Act Congress. They hanged the city's proposed tax collector in effigy and then looted his home—and that of the lieutenant governor for good measure. As violence spread throughout the colonies, tax collectors resigned their positions, others refused to take their places, and colonial assemblies banned the importation of English goods, making home-spun clothes fashionable. Patrick Henry, who was one of the more outspoken members of the Virginia assembly, warned, "Caesar had his Brutus; Charles the First his Cromwell; and George the Third *may profit by their example.*" When someone shouted "Treason!" Henry replied, "If *this* be treason, make the most of it." In the face of rhetoric that compared King George with rulers who were overthrown and killed, the Stamp Act became unenforceable, and within a year Parliament repealed the legislation.[17]

Revenue stamp

One of the infamous revenue stamps that fired colonists' opposition to the tax imposed on the American people by the Stamp Act of 1765. This particular two-pence stamp appeared on an almanac. Why were many patriots so opposed to this tax? Were they correct in saying it was unfair?

The British ignored American demands for representation. They also unwisely replaced the stamp tax with a tax on tea, arousing passions even further. Antitax groups led by such prominent men as Samuel Adams and John Hancock stirred up rebellious colonists. They characterized themselves as patriots dedicated to defending American liberties. In 1773 many patriots organized the Boston Tea Party, a nighttime foray in which protesters disguised as American Indians dumped chests of tea into the city's harbor. Outraged at such law-breaking, Parliament punished the Bostonians by shutting down democratic institutions in the Massachusetts colony. It withdrew the colony's charter, closed its colonial assembly, banned town meetings, blockaded the Boston harbor, and strengthened the armed garrison stationed in the city.

THE CONTINENTAL CONGRESSES

The colonists responded by calling the **First Continental Congress** in 1774. Attended by delegates from 12 of the colonies, the Continental Congress issued a statement of rights and called for a boycott of British goods. Patriots assembled guns and trained volunteers for military exercises in Massachusetts.

To put down the rising insurrection, British soldiers marched out from Boston's harbor on April 19, 1775, in search of weapons hidden in the nearby countryside. Paul Revere helped spread a warning that British redcoats were coming, though, so 600 patriots were able to arm themselves. Ralph Waldo Emerson later claimed that the first shots they fired were "heard round the world." Certainly, word of the shots spread throughout the colonies, even to the Virginia assembly, where Patrick Henry cried, "Give me liberty, or give me death!"

Delegates from all 13 colonies soon journeyed to Philadelphia to participate in the **Second Continental Congress,** the political authority that directed America's struggle against Britain. The Continental Congress proclaimed a **Declaration of Independence** on July 4, 1776, withdrawing the United States of America from Great Britain. No single document better expresses the democratic spirit that animates American politics. Written mainly by Thomas Jefferson, the Declaration of Independence both denounces King George III and declares the country's commitment to the rights of "life, liberty, and the pursuit of happiness." This radical revolutionary statement "epitomizes and summarizes" a train of political thought that originated in England, but which the colonists had made their own.[18]

For seven long years the patriots valiantly fought British soldiers. The **Tories,** colonists who opposed independence, lost their property and were imprisoned or chased off; some 80,000 fled to London, Nova Scotia, or the West Indies. In 1783 the British recognized American independence in the Treaty of Paris.

GOVERNMENT AFTER INDEPENDENCE

The Revolutionary War generated intense discussion of many philosophical ideas by the colonists. They rejected taxation without representation and instead embraced consent of the governed, separation of powers, and the rights of the people. The state governments they constructed implemented these ideals. Of course, the 13 new states at first mostly kept their colonial institutions as they were, "with Parliament and the King left out."[19] But the pace of democratization began to accelerate. Eight of the 13 states eased property qualifications for voting, and five lowered them for candidates to the lower houses of state legislatures.[20] Fewer state legislators possessed great wealth, especially in the North, giving new political opportunities to those from more modest backgrounds. Ten states required that governors be elected annually, and six limited the number of terms they could serve.[21]

Some believed that the Whig theory of the rights of man should apply to women. Abigail Adams proposed giving women their rights and liberties as well. She warned that if "attention is not paid to the ladies we are determined to foment a rebellion, and will not hold ourselves bound by any laws in which we have no voice, or representation." But even her husband, John, who later became the nation's second president, argued against making such changes. "There will be no end of it," he said. "Women will demand a vote; lads from twelve to twenty-one will think their rights not enough attended to; and every man, who has not a farthing, will demand an equal voice."[22]

THE ARTICLES OF CONFEDERATION (1781–1789)

The new country needed, above all, a sense of unity. In one of its more inspired decisions, the Second Continental Congress helped bring the nation together by appointing George Washington, a Virginia plantation owner, as commander of a continental army—even though initially most soldiers came from northern colonies. But although the Continental Congress was prompt to take necessary military steps, reaching constitutional decisions took much longer. The idea of creating a national government was so foreign to the colonial experience that it took the Continental Congress nearly five years to install the country's first constitution, the Articles of Confederation.

Ratified in 1781, the Articles of Confederation, in its own words, amounted to little more than a "firm league of friendship" in which "each state retains its sovereignty, freedom and independence." The Articles granted the Continental Congress limited power. It could declare war but could raise an army only by requesting states to muster their forces. Congress could not tax citizens; it had to rely on voluntary state contributions, and as a result, the national government could not pay its debts. Congress could negotiate tariffs with other nations, but so could each state.

Most significantly, the Continental Congress could not protect interstate commerce. Instead, states imposed trade barriers on one another. New York, for example, taxed New Jersey cabbage and Connecticut firewood.[23] The states also could coin their own money, flooding the country with many different currencies. Constant quarrels over the relative worth of different state coins impeded trade among the states.

Members of the Continental Congress were elected annually by state legislatures. Each state, no matter how large or small, was equally represented. On all important issues, a supermajority of 9 states (out of 13) had to agree before action could be taken, and changing the Articles required every state to agree.

The Articles of Confederation did not create a system of divided powers along the lines Locke had envisioned. Instead, the Continental Congress wielded all national powers, such as they were. There was no independent executive. Congress often lacked a **quorum,** the minimum number who must be present, so without adequate attendance to do business, much of the legislature's work fell upon an unwieldy Committee of the States. Nine of the 13 delegates had to agree before the committee could take action. Judicial functions were left to the states, except that disputes between states were settled by ad hoc committees of judges selected by the Continental Congress. Discontent with the Articles grew as the national government proved too weak to grapple with peacetime problems.

A GROWING SENSE OF DREAD

Many influential voices in government worried about more than just operating procedures, however. They also grew troubled about the rise of a "levelling spirit" among the common people. Commoners took to putting on airs, wearing fancy clothing once restricted to the higher orders. They showed disrespect toward their social betters. Most of all, they applied the same disruptive tactics and radical ideas to their new governments—gathering in informal conventions to void unpopular laws and electing leaders from among their own number—that the revolutionaries had once applied to the British.[24]

The biggest problem came from former revolutionary soldiers, who were not being treated very well after the war.* Unlike their officers, who had organized into a politically influential secret society called the **Order of the Cincinnati,** rank-and-file soldiers did not receive much government aid. Many ended the war in debt and took on even more debt to resume their delayed farming careers. But then a combination of high state taxes and economic downturns caused them to default on loans. Soon these war heroes had to watch as bank representatives arrived to seize their properties, or they had to sell the land to wealthy merchants (including some of their former officers!) for a pittance.

Not every former patriot was willing to endure such bad fortune. A group of ex-soldiers from the continental army descended on Congress in 1783 and demanded their rightful back pay. Members fled to Princeton College to avoid

---

*Indeed, they had not been treated very well *during* the war. At one point the Continental Congress had to pass a law limiting soldier beatings to restrain George Washington's whip! See Merrill Jensen, *The New Nation: A History of the United States during the Confederation, 1781–1789* (New York: Vintage, 1965), p. 33.

the mob. **Shays's Rebellion,** a 1786 uprising in western Massachusetts led by Revolutionary War captain Daniel Shays, was especially frightening. The rebels, unable to pay their taxes or mortgages, tried to intimidate local courts into forgiving their debts. It took months to suppress the rebellion because too many political figures sympathized with the debtors.

Domestic unrest raised serious questions about political stability, but threats from foreign countries were even more disturbing. The British disputed the boundary between its Canadian colonies and the United States. Also, the British navy routinely intercepted American ships and dragooned U.S. sailors into service, claiming that anyone who spoke English must be British unless they could prove otherwise. Spain, in possession of Florida and the lands west of the Mississippi, claimed large segments of what is today Mississippi and Alabama (see Figure 2.1). Even France, a revolutionary ally, blocked U.S. trade with its islands in the West Indies and demanded repayment of war loans. The Continental Congress found it difficult to resolve these disputes because it could not prevent states from engaging in their own negotiations with foreign countries.

THE CONSTITUTIONAL CONVENTION

None felt the deficiencies in the Articles more keenly than the men who became America's founders. George Washington, an avid speculator in land west of the Appalachian mountains, was frustrated by government's sluggishness at building up the country's interior and at running Native Americans off the land. James Madison despaired at Congress's inability to raise money. Alexander Hamilton mourned the lack of a strong executive.

A group of reformers met to discuss constitutional changes in 1786 at what became known as the **Annapolis Convention,** but only five state delegations attended. Hamilton persuaded the Annapolis Convention to propose another meeting of delegations in Philadelphia for the next year, a plan that Madison had little trouble selling to the Congress in the aftermath of Shays's Rebellion. Every state legislature except Rhode Island's sent delegates to the Constitutional Convention with instructions to formulate amendments for the Articles.

The delegates to the Constitutional Convention did not constitute a cross section of the population. The people who met in Philadelphia were bankers, merchants, plantation owners, and speculators in land west of the Appalachians.[25] They believed the country needed a centralized government that could provide political stability, mediate conflicts among the states, and defend the nation.[26]

Most of those content with the Articles stayed away. Patrick Henry, when asked to be a delegate, refused, saying he "smelt a rat." Others simply were not

FIGURE 2.1

Map of competing claims

This map shows only some of the competing claims being made in North America in 1787. Because the British had a superior navy, the United States was, in a sense, surrounded by foreign powers. How did this threat influence the debates over the Constitution?

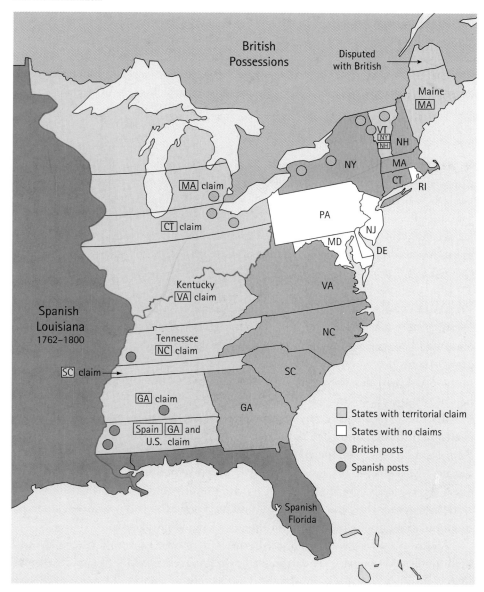

SOURCE: Edgar B. Wesley, *Our United States: Its History in Maps* (Chicago: Denoyer-Geppert Co., 1965), p. 37.

interested. Of the few skeptics who did attend, ten abandoned the convention before the Constitution was completed. When the work was done, the Constitution passed out of the convention with almost unanimous support; only three of the remaining delegates refused to sign.

Yet the delegates did not agree on all issues. They had strong political connections within their home states and therefore represented different regions with conflicting interests. Two divisions were paramount. Delegates from big states often disagreed with delegates from small states. And delegates from the southern slave states opposed those from northern states, whose economies did not depend on slavery. Delegates also disagreed over which sorts of changes voters would accept.

SCHEMES OF REPRESENTATION

The delegates' differences were submerged during the opening weeks of the convention, when a spirit of unity and reform filled the Philadelphia hall. But as the four-month convention progressed, delegates pulled back from some of the more far-reaching reforms and searched for compromises that would produce a document that could be ratified.[27] The first of these revolved around how to constitute the legislative branch.

THE VIRGINIA PLAN Madison had prepared a constitutional draft, with Washington's active involvement, prior to the gathering in Philadelphia. His Virginia Plan proposed massive changes in the design and powers of the national government. It created a separation of powers along the lines that Locke had recommended, with a president to hold the executive power and a supreme court to handle disputes between individuals from different states.

Instead of a single congress like the one established under the Articles, Madison proposed two chambers. The lower chamber—like the future House of Representatives—was elected by the voters. The upper chamber—like the future Senate—was elected by state legislatures. Representation in these chambers differed dramatically from the pattern existing under the Articles. Instead of each state having one vote, the number of both representatives and senators depended on population, giving much more influence to the largest states.

Madison's plan gave the national government vast powers far beyond those held by the old congress. The proposed new congress could legislate on all matters that affect "the harmony of the United States" and could negate "all laws passed by the several states."[28] It also could use force to ensure that states fulfilled their duties. To win popular support, the Virginia Plan called for ratification by state convention delegates "expressly chosen by the people."[29]

THE NEW JERSEY PLAN   The Virginia Plan received strong support from two of the most populous states—Virginia and Pennsylvania—as well as from states that expected to grow rapidly in population in the next few years—North Carolina, South Carolina, and Georgia. Delegates from smaller states, especially New Jersey and Delaware, were not very pleased. Two weeks or so into the convention, these states offered an alternative design, prepared by William Patterson, that became known as the New Jersey Plan, the small-state proposal for constitutional reform.

The New Jersey Plan also separated powers into three branches, but instead of creating a house and senate, it kept a one-chamber congress in which each state had a single vote. It also envisioned a more limited national government, in which the congress possessed only specific powers, such as levying taxes on imported goods, compelling states to pay their share of taxes, and regulating "trade & commerce with foreign nations" and among the states. The judicial branch could hear only specific types of cases, such as those involving treaties or foreigners.[30]

Despite these limitations, the New Jersey Plan strengthened the national government well beyond what existed under the Articles. The supporters of the New Jersey Plan were not so much opposed to a stronger government as afraid that the big states would control it. As one delegate observed at the time, "Give New Jersey an equal vote, and she will dismiss her scruples, and concur in a National system."[31]

THE CONNECTICUT COMPROMISE   The convention nearly collapsed when a majority of the delegates rejected the New Jersey Plan. Delegates from the small states considered leaving Philadelphia, which would have killed all hope of ratification. The large states flirted with the idea of forming their own union and then using economic pressure to force small states to join.

The most divisive issues were turned over to a committee controlled by moderates. The committee reported back a compromise offered by delegates from the middle-sized state of Connecticut. The Connecticut Compromise created a house where representation was proportionate to population and a senate in which all states were represented equally. Small states liked the proposed senate, large states, the house (see Figure 2.2).

Once the delegates accepted what became known as the "Great Compromise," they found it relatively easy to broker other differences. Following the Virginia Plan, they created a government with three branches, dividing powers among

FIGURE 2.2

The Connecticut Compromise

Vital to the success of the Constitutional Convention, the Connecticut Compromise allowed both large and small states to have a voice in Congress. These pie charts illustrate the proportion of seats in each congressional chamber controlled by the original 13 colonies.

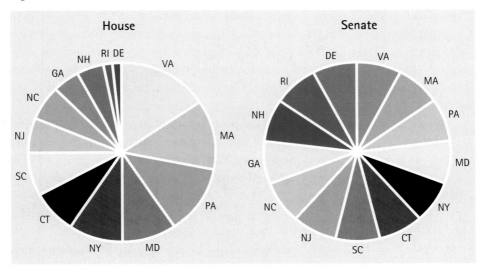

them. But in a provision consistent with the New Jersey Plan, they limited the powers of all three. The result was a Constitution quite different from the Articles (see Table 2.2).

CONGRESS

Congress received only specific powers. But the delegates created a loophole by saying that Congress has the power to "make all laws which shall be necessary and proper for carrying into Execution" its duties. What exactly does this mean? Some thought the **necessary and proper clause** allows only what is absolutely essential. Other delegates thought it meant just about anything convenient and useful. The phrasing was ambiguous enough that delegates could interpret the language to their own liking.

The question of property qualifications for voting was a delicate one because northern merchants preferred limitations based on wealth and southern planters preferred limitations based on land ownership. Rather than settle the dispute, the Constitution let states establish their own, aside from requiring that anyone eligible

TABLE 2.2

THE CONSTITUTION AND THE ARTICLES
OF CONFEDERATION COMPARED

Many provisions of the Constitution directly address the failures of the Articles of Confederation.

WEAKNESSES OF THE ARTICLES OF CONFEDERATION	HOW ADDRESSED IN CONSTITUTION
Congress could not levy taxes.	Congress has power to levy taxes (Article I, Section 8).
States could restrict commerce among states.	States cannot regulate commerce without the consent of Congress (Article I, Section 10).
States could issue their own currency.	States are prohibited from coining money (Article I, Section 10).
Executive was not independent of Congress.	An independently elected president holds the executive power (Article II).
There was no national judicial system.	The Supreme Court was created, and Congress was granted the power to establish lower federal courts (Article III, Section 1).
Amendments to Articles had to have unanimous approval of states.	Large majorities are necessary to amend the Constitution, but there are several different ways to do so (Article V).

SOURCE: Articles of Confederation; U.S. Constitution, articles listed. See Appendix.

to vote for the lower chamber of a state legislature could vote in elections for the House of Representatives. The wording therefore allowed states to exclude poor citizens from voting however they liked, yet guaranteed the vote to everyone already eligible (that is, those who would decide whether to ratify the Constitution). This open-ended language later permitted the gradual, state-by-state extension of the right to vote to many excluded from the electorate in 1787.

THE EXECUTIVE

Some analysts have claimed that many convention delegates secretly harbored a desire to create an executive who had powers comparable to those of a British king.[32] But except for Alexander Hamilton, who actually made a proposal along these lines, the delegates were too practical to treat such an idea seriously. They knew that voters would reject out of hand a constitution that threatened the return of another King George.

Instead, the Constitution keeps presidential power under tight congressional control. The president is commander-in-chief of the armed forces, but only

Congress can declare war. The president can call Congress into session and speak before the membership but cannot dismiss Congress or prevent it from meeting. The president may veto congressional legislation, but Congress can override the veto with a two-thirds vote.

Other presidential powers require senatorial **advice and consent,** support for a presidential action by a designated number of senators. For example, the president can sign treaties with foreign countries, but treaties take effect only if two-thirds of the senators agree. Also, the president can appoint both judges and executive branch officers, but a majority of the Senate must confirm them.

The impeachment clause makes clear the president's ultimate dependence on political support from Congress. The House of Representatives can impeach the president for "Treason, Bribery, or other high Crimes and Misdemeanors." If impeached, the president is tried in the Senate. If convicted by a two-thirds vote, the president is removed from office. Although no president has ever been removed in this way, Bill Clinton was tried but not convicted, Andrew Johnson avoided conviction by only one vote, and Richard Nixon chose to resign in the face of almost certain impeachment and conviction.

THE ELECTORAL COLLEGE

Although the Constitution sharply checks presidential power, delegates to the Constitutional Convention still expected the president to be a powerful political figure. As a consequence, they debated at great length the method for presidential selection. Once again, the dispute divided big states and small ones. A president chosen by popular vote or by the House of Representatives would owe political allegiance to big states, where most people lived. A president selected by the Senate would give the small states extra clout.

The delegates finally agreed on a compromise: the creation of a complicated two-stage procedure that remains in effect today. The first stage involves selection of an Electoral College. Each state chooses electors in proportion to its number of senators and representatives. For example, Texas now has 32 electoral votes, because it elects two senators and 30 representatives. (In addition, as a result of the passage of the Twenty-Third Amendment, the District of Columbia casts three votes.) If a candidate receives a majority of the electoral vote (50 percent plus 1 vote), that person is elected president. In the 2000 election George W. Bush won 271 electoral votes, one more than needed to become president.

But if no candidate receives a majority in the Electoral College, the action moves to the House of Representatives. If, for example, the vote of the Electoral College in 1996 had split three ways among Bill Clinton, Robert Dole, and Ross

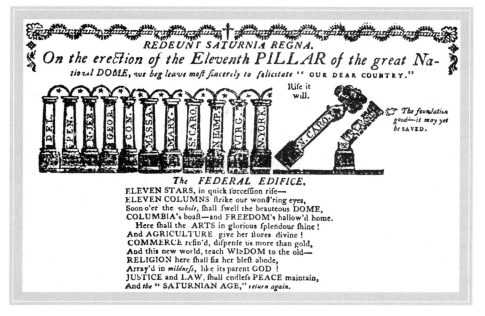

Ratification

At the time of this cartoon's publication, only 11 states had ratified the Constitution. The cartoonist eagerly awaited North Carolina ("Rise it will") and Rhode Island ("The foundation good—it may yet be saved") joining the new Union. Why was Rhode Island the last state to ratify the Constitution?

Perot and if none had received more than 50 percent, then the election would have been decided in the House. The last time this happened was in 1824.

The Constitution does not require that voters choose the members of the Electoral College. Instead, the manner of selecting electors was left up to the states. Constitutional silence on this key matter was not accidental. Some delegates thought the president should be elected by the people; others believed this could lead to mob rule. The Constitutional Convention compromised on the question, as it did on so many, by leaving the issue up to the states. Not until 1864 did the last state, South Carolina, give voters the power to select electors directly (though by the 1820s, electors were chosen by the voters in the great majority of states).[33]

Some think the Electoral College compromise has proved to be less successful than the Connecticut Compromise. In the 2000 election, for example, the candidate who won the most popular votes was not selected president (as was also true in 1824, 1876, and 1888). Some scholars favor eliminating the Electoral College altogether, on the theory that the candidate receiving the most popular votes should win the election. Others think that the Electoral College, for all its

Should the Electoral College Be Reformed?

Delegates to the Constitutional Convention found it difficult to agree on the best way of selecting the president of the United States. The compromise they reached was a two-stage procedure that was sufficiently complicated that both sides could claim victory:

FIRST STAGE. The first stage gives the advantage to big states. Each state chooses as many electors as it has representatives and senators; the electors vote for presidential candidates; if no candidate has a majority, the three top vote getters go to the second stage.

SECOND STAGE. The second stage gives the advantage to small states. Members of the House of Representatives vote by state delegation; each delegation has one vote and must choose from the top three candidates. The winner must receive a majority.

The presidential election of 2000 set off intense new criticisms of the Electoral College. Albert Gore won the national popular vote, but the winner of the presidency depended on a few votes in Florida. Yale's Jonathan G. S. Koppell pointed out that the Electoral College was a byproduct of an outdated controversy. "It is time to rethink a system that is designed to satisfy the political exigencies of the late 18th century," he argued. Political scientist Benjamin Barber of Rutgers University went further, criticizing the Electoral College as a "dormant sore on the body politic which has now gone cancerous." Richard Nathan of the State University of New York at Albany agreed that there was cause for concern. "This is a delicate time for our political system. It is broke, and we need to do something," he claimed.

Some even speculated that in future close elections, candidates would seek out "rogue electors" who would switch their votes in the December balloting. Such efforts, said Electoral College expert Walter Burns, could set off "a constitutional crisis that will put this country in a third-world category where elections are decided in the streets."

But others argued that the Electoral College had served its purpose for hundreds of years. What was more, the Electoral College may have prevented the 2000 election from becoming a larger crisis. "If anything, this has really established the utility of the electoral vote system," Kenneth Janda argued. "If we were deciding by popular vote, there would be calls for a nationwide recount, and we would find disputed ballots in every nook and cranny of the country. Now, at least the issue is confined to one state." Political scientist Nelson Polsby warned that moving to a popular vote system "would encourage splinter parties, spoilers, and nuisance candidacies—hence more, not less, of Ralph Nader and Pat Buchanan."

What do you think?

- Is the Electoral College outdated and possibly dangerous?
- To eliminate the potential for future crises, should presidents be chosen directly by a plurality of voters, no matter where they live?
- Would this reform make it easier for third-party candidates to win elections? Would the reform undermine the two-party system? Would it endanger the role of states in the federal system?

SOURCES: Jonathan G. S. Koppell, "Some States Are More Equal Than Others," *Los Angeles Times* (November 9, 2000): B11; David Broder, "Bizarre Twists Raise Fairness Issue," *Washington Post* (November 9, 2000): A01; Mary Leonard, "How Popular Mandate Can Mean Defeat," *Boston Globe* (November 9, 2000, Third Edition): D1; Nelson Polsby, "Election 2000: What Does it All Mean? No Reason to Fix a System That Works," *Boston Globe* (November 9, 2000, Third Edition): A19.

faults, helps assure that presidential candidates enjoy support across the country (see the Election Connection, "Should the Electoral College Be Reformed?").

THE JUDICIAL COMPROMISE

Most convention delegates thought the country needed a supreme court to adjudicate conflicts between the states. They also found it fairly easy to agree that justices should be nominated for lifetime positions by the president and confirmed by a majority of the Senate.

The delegates differed over whether the Supreme Court needed lower federal courts to assist it. Advocates of the Virginia Plan thought lower federal courts were needed because state courts "cannot be trusted with the administration of the National Laws."[34] Advocates of the New Jersey Plan said the state courts were sufficient. They also thought "the people will not bear such innovations."[35] The delegates compromised on the issue by leaving it to Congress to decide whether lower federal courts were needed. The first Congress created a system of lower federal courts, whose essentials remain intact today.

The delegates also apparently disagreed on whether the Supreme Court should be given the power of **judicial review,** authority to declare laws null and void on the grounds that they violate the Constitution. There is no record of anyone rising to its defense when two delegates spoke against the idea, yet the lack of debate is probably best explained by political expediency. Judicial review had provoked controversy in North Carolina and Rhode Island, and convention delegates avoided the issue because it might have endangered ratification.

Instead of calling for judicial review, convention delegates inserted into the Constitution an ambiguous phrase that has become known as the **supremacy clause,** which binds judges to treat the Constitution as the "supreme Law of the Land." To some, this phrase simply told state judges to be mindful of the Constitution when interpreting state laws. To others, it gave the Supreme Court the power to declare both state and federal laws unconstitutional, an interpretation that the Court would lock into place 20 years later.

THE SLAVERY ISSUE

The delegates never seriously contemplated using the Constitution to eliminate slavery (although one delegate said it was their moral duty to do so). Indeed, the Constitution avoided mentioning slavery altogether. Southern states never would have ratified a constitution that threatened their economic system.

The debate over slavery took other forms. The North and the South split over tariffs, or taxes on imported goods. Southerners feared this provision would protect northern manufacturing at the expense of southern slave plantations.

Meanwhile, Northerners wanted to end the international slave trade. Most southerners argued that the slave trade, however despicable, was necessary to fuel economic growth in the unsettled parts of the South. The two sides compromised, with southern delegates accepting tariffs in exchange for delays in ending the slave trade. The Constitution required that Congress wait until 1808, roughly 20 years later, before interfering with the "importation of such persons as any of the states now existing shall think proper to admit."

Northern delegates did not want to count slaves when figuring state representation in the House. Southerners thought they should be counted. On the other hand, Southerners did not want slaves counted for purposes of taxation, which Northerners endorsed. The two sides came up with the **three-fifths compromise,** which counted each slave as "three-fifths" of a person for purposes of both taxation and representation.

AMENDMENTS TO THE CONSTITUTION

The delegates to the Constitutional Convention, realizing that the document they were writing was imperfect, discussed methods for amending the Constitution. Small states wanted unanimous consent of state legislatures, which would sharply limit amendments. Southern states also feared an easy amendment process that might endanger slavery. Big states believed that a unanimity rule would lead to stagnation and protracted conflict.

The resulting compromise allowed proposal and then ratification of amendments by any one of four different procedures, as shown in Figure 2.3. The simplest, and the most frequently used, way to amend the Constitution requires a two-thirds vote in both houses of Congress and then ratification by three-quarters of the state legislatures. Of the 27 amendments to the Constitution, 26 followed this procedure. On one occasion, the amendment repealing Prohibition, state legislatures were bypassed in favor of state ratifying conventions attended by elected delegates (the same procedure used to ratify the Constitution itself).

Amending the Constitution requires such overwhelming majorities that only 17 amendments have been enacted since the initial 10, which are known as the Bill of Rights. Thousands of amendments proposed over the decades have failed to win approval. A possible amendment must jump hurdles so high that even popular proposals fall short. For example, in the 1970s many people thought that the Equal Rights Amendment, which said that men and women have "equality of rights under the law," would win approval. The amendment received overwhelming support from both houses of Congress in 1971–1972 and was quickly ratified by 34 states. But when the proposed amendment became intertwined with abor-

FIGURE 2.3

Amending the Constitution: a two-stage process

Why did the founders make the amendment process so complicated?

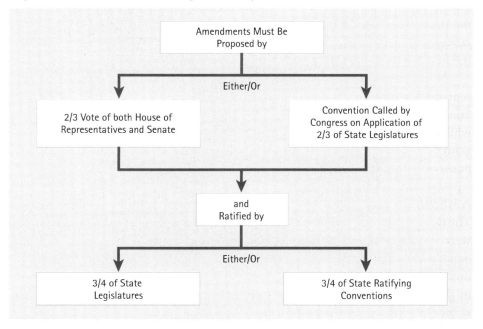

SOURCE: U.S. Constitution, Article V. See Appendix.

tion and other disputed issues, it failed to win ratification by the necessary final three state legislatures.[36]

The one kind of amendment that seems capable of jumping the high hurdles needed to achieve adoption is one that extends democratic electoral practices. Despite the complicated procedures that are in place, 13 amendments ratified since the Bill of Rights have tightened the electoral connection well beyond what was originally envisioned by the Constitution—by broadening the electorate, by extending civil liberties, or by making more direct the connections between leaders and voters. Five amendments specifically extended suffrage to citizens previously excluded from voting: African Americans, women, young people (aged 18 to 21), residents of the District of Columbia, and those unwilling or unable to pay a poll tax. Eight other amendments also have corrected procedural deficiencies thought to be inconsistent with democratic practice (see the Election Connection, "Amendments to the Constitution").

ELECTION CONNECTION

Amendments to the Constitution

Amendments to the Constitution have extended liberties and tightened the election connection.

AMENDMENT	YEAR RATIFIED	PROVISION
XII	1804	Distinguishes electoral vote for president and vice-president.
XIII	1865	Abolishes slavery.
XIV	1868	Guarantees citizens the right of due process and equal protection before state law. Removes the three-fifths compromise from the Constitution.
XV	1870	Extends suffrage to African Americans.
XVII	1913	Permits direct election of senators.
XIX	1920	Extends suffrage to women.
XX	1933	Shortens the time between election and the day members of Congress and the president assume office.
XXII	1951	Imposes a two-term limit on presidents.
XXIII	1961	Extends presidential suffrage to residents of the District of Columbia.
XXIV	1964	Abolishes taxes on voting.
XXV	1967	Determines the procedure for filling the office of the vice-president if it becomes vacant.
XXVI	1971	Extends suffrage to 18-year-olds.
XXVII	1992	Postpones congressional pay raises until after next election.

SOURCE: U.S. Constitution, amendments listed. See Appendix.

THE FIRST NATIONAL ELECTION

Delegates to the Constitutional Convention generally agreed that a stronger central government was needed. They made numerous compromises to hammer out the details of the new system. Voters in 1787 were receptive to constitutional reform because the country's mood had lost much of the idealism that had unified it during the Revolutionary War. Persistent economic and political difficulties had also eroded the new nation's confidence. Many blamed the situation on the Articles of Confederation.

But even though the Articles were unpopular, ratification of the Constitution was hardly inevitable. Victory was achieved only because the **Federalists,** those who campaigned for ratification of the Constitution, provided strong leadership. They mobilized voters, sidestepped obstacles, and crafted powerful arguments in favor of ratification.

The Federalists offered an anxious public not only a new constitution but also the return of its revolutionary leader, General George Washington. Washington presided over the Constitutional Convention and was expected to become the first president. Other prominent Revolutionary War figures also helped write the Constitution and then campaigned on its behalf. Benjamin Franklin, the diplomat who had secured France as an ally, took part as a quiet-spoken elder statesman. James Madison, a key member of the Continental Congress, provided intellectual leadership. Alexander Hamilton, a hero at the decisive battle of Yorktown, emerged as a rising star during the New York ratification campaign.

The **Anti-Federalists,** those who opposed ratification of the Constitution, lacked a national leader. The one man who could have galvanized the opposition, Declaration of Independence author Thomas Jefferson, was serving in Paris as minister to France. He shared many Anti-Federalist beliefs and worried that the Constitution did not protect civil liberties adequately, but he admitted to his friend Madison that the document still deserved ratification.

With energy and organization on their side, the Federalists easily won the first rounds in the ratification struggle. Conventions in four of the smaller states—Delaware, New Jersey, Georgia, and Connecticut—ratified the document by an overwhelming vote within four months of its signing in September 1787.[37] Pennsylvania also quickly approved, thanks to Ben Franklin's prestige and some strong-arm tactics (although a vocal minority at its state convention distributed a stinging critique of the document). By the end of 1788, Federalists had persuaded 11 of the 13 states to ratify the Constitution, and George Washington was elected president in February 1789. North Carolina ratified later that year. Rhode Island, which had refused even to send delegates to the Constitutional Convention, finally gave its grudging approval on May 29, 1790 (see Table 2.3).

THE BILL OF RIGHTS

The delegates to the Constitutional Convention made one mistake so serious that it nearly ruined their chances of securing ratification: They failed to include within the Constitution clauses that clearly protected individual liberty. It is surprising that the delegates to the Philadelphia Constitutional Convention, who in other respects showed excellent political judgment, made such a serious miscalculation. Their lapse is instructive, however, because it reveals clearly how much

TABLE 2.3

VOTING OF DELEGATES AT CONSTITUTIONAL RATIFYING CONVENTIONS

Article VII of the Constitution provided that "The Ratification of the Conventions of nine States, shall be sufficient for the Establishment of this Constitution."

STATE	DATE	YES VOTES	NO VOTES	PERCENTAGE
Delaware	Dec. 7, 1787	30	0	100.0
Pennsylvania	Dec. 11, 1787	46	23	66.7
New Jersey	Dec. 18, 1787	38	0	100.0
Georgia	Jan. 2, 1788	26	0	100.0
Connecticut	Jan. 9, 1788	128	40	76.2
Massachusetts	Feb. 6, 1788	187	168	52.7
Maryland	Apr. 26, 1788	63	11	85.1
South Carolina	May 23, 1788	149	73	67.1
New Hampshire	June 21, 1788	57	47	54.8
Virginia	June 25, 1788	89	79	53.0
New York	July 26, 1788	30	27	52.6
North Carolina	Nov. 21, 1789	194	77	71.6
Rhode Island	May 29, 1790	34	32	51.5

SOURCE: Lauren Bahr and Bernard Johnson, ed., *Collier's Encyclopedia*, Vol. 7 (New York: P. F. Collier, 1992), p. 239.

their success relied on compromise with popular sentiments. The Constitution could not win widespread support until Federalist politicians promised to add a Bill of Rights.

The Virginia assembly, in 1776, had passed a Bill of Rights protecting free speech, the right of the propertied to vote, the right to a trial by jury, the right not to be compelled to testify against oneself, and other civil liberties.[38] Most of the other states had also incorporated statements of rights into their constitutions, or at least had approved them by statute. Yet when South Carolina's Charles Pinckney proposed guaranteeing freedom of the press at the Constitutional Convention, a majority voted his motion down—on the grounds that regulation of speech and press was a state responsibility.[39] The convention majority simply failed to appreciate how powerfully the demand for protections against governmental tyranny would resonate.

The Federalists recognized their mistake during the fight over ratification in Massachusetts. They narrowly secured the state's support, and this only after promising to amend the Constitution so that it would protect freedoms directly. Victories in Virginia and New York required similar guarantees. Two states, North Carolina and Rhode Island, remained unsatisfied. They withheld ratification until the Federalists made good on their promise. The first ten amendments to the U.S. Constitution resulted from this struggle for popular support. Their protections include the following:

- Freedom of speech, press, and assembly (Amendment I)
- Free exercise of religion (Amendment I)
- Right to bear arms (Amendment II)
- Security against unreasonable searches and seizures (Amendment IV)
- Protection from being be forced to testify against oneself (Amendment V)
- Guarantee of trial by jury (Amendments VI and VII)
- Protection against cruel or unusual punishment (Amendment VIII)

THE ANTI-FEDERALIST LEGACY

The Anti-Federalists at least partly won their fight for a Bill of Rights; some of the amendments they desired won approval. Yet their criticism of the Constitution was broader than the lack of a Bill of Rights. Drawing on the Whig theory of rights and representation, the Anti-Federalists attacked the Constitution as a blueprint for national tyranny. They said undercutting the states would take power from the people. The number of representatives in Congress would be too small to include a wide variety of citizens from all parts of the United States. Presidents could become virtual kings, because they could be reelected again and again for the rest of their lives. The reelection of senators and representatives would create a political aristocracy.[40]

The Anti-Federalists failed to defeat the Constitution and could not change most of the constitutional provisions that worried them. However, their electoral efforts were not wasted. They forced the framers to defend their handiwork and explain what different constitutional provisions meant. Publication of the ***Federalist Papers***, for example, emerged as part of the ratification fight in New York. This series of newspaper essays defending the Constitution—written by Alexander Hamilton, James Madison, and John Jay, under the pen name "Publius"—are generally regarded as the finest essays on American political theory ever written.[41] These explanations, constructed to attract popular approval, later shaped how judges and elected officials interpreted the document.

Nor did the Anti-Federalist critique of centralized power fall entirely on deaf ears. Later, politicians such as Thomas Jefferson and Andrew Jackson articulated a message similar to theirs. These leaders governed with a narrow view of what the national government should do. The Constitution that operated for much of the nineteenth century was thus a mixture of Federalist words and Anti-Federalist ideals.

THE CONSTITUTION:
AN ASSESSMENT

The debate over the Constitution did not end with its ratification. The influential historian Charles Beard wrote in 1913 that the Constitution represented a victory for the propertied classes against the masses of the people.[42] Beard pointed out that wealthy people wrote the document and that only people with property were allowed to vote on ratification. But modern-day historians Bernard Bailyn and Gordon Wood see it as having moved the country toward the ideals of citizen rights and representation that motivated the revolutionary patriots.[43] In their view, the Whig ideals that spurred the war of independence are given practical expression in the Constitution.

Both sides of this debate probably overstate their cases. The adoption of the Constitution consolidated changes in citizen participation and representation that had already taken place in many states. The adoption of the Constitution did not extend the right to vote, but neither did it further restrict it. The Constitution divided powers that had been lodged in a single representative body under the Articles of Confederation, but each of the new entities—House, Senate, president, the courts—was ultimately grounded in the people. This electoral connection grew after 1789, as a more popular democracy evolved within the framework of the Constitution.

FLAWS

The Constitution certainly contained much to criticize. Written by 55 prosperous gentlemen, the document fell far short of expressing contemporary democratic ideals. But we cannot judge eighteenth-century decisions by twenty-first-century principles. Most flaws written into the Constitution were necessary to achieve ratification. The one big mistake the convention could most certainly have avoided, neglecting to include a Bill of Rights, was corrected by the first Congress. That the Constitution could win support from a uniformly white, male, property-owning population—and still leave open the possibility for greater democratization in the centuries to come—is to the honor, not the discredit, of those who met in Philadelphia.

ACHIEVEMENTS

The delegates wrote a document that contributed to solutions for four of the most immediate and pressing problems facing the United States. First, it created a unified nation capable of defending American sovereignty from foreign threats. True, the United States would fight an unsuccessful war against Britain in 1812. But the Constitution kept the country from splintering at a time when Britain, France, and Spain were all looking for a piece of the action in the New World. Instead of falling prey to European ambitions, the United States profited from European divisions by seizing the opportunity to make the Louisiana Purchase, in 1803, which doubled the size of the country. The new lands were eventually incorporated into the Union as new member states.

Second, the new Constitution facilitated the country's economic development by outlawing state currencies and eliminating state tariffs. As a result, trade among states flourished, and the United States grew into an economic powerhouse faster than any had expected.

The Constitution also created a presidency that was first filled by George Washington, the country's most beloved political leader. His great prestige gave the national government the additional strength needed to overcome many difficulties the new nation encountered (see the Election Connection, "George Washington Is Elected").

Finally, the Constitution was a compromise document, one written to maintain loyalty across a young country. The interests of big states and small states, northerners and southerners, commercial entrepreneurs, farmers, property owners, and debtors all were woven into the constitutional fabric.

In the two centuries that have followed, the main lines of conflict changed. People no longer worry much about divisions between big and small states or differences between commerce and agriculture. But the Constitution still gives many different groups and interests clear opportunities to voice their concerns. In addition to solving immediate problems, the Constitution created a framework that facilitated an ever more popular democratic experiment.

CONSTITUTIONAL AMBIGUITY: A VIRTUE   Even the ambiguities embedded in the Constitution have provided benefits. Written as compromises among conflicting interests, such vague phrases as "necessary and proper" and "supreme Law of the Land" have had the elasticity necessary to accommodate powerful

ELECTION CONNECTION

George Washington Is Elected

The first presidential election was extremely dull. No issues arose and no campaign allegations were made; the vote was unanimous. Yet the votes cast by the Electoral College on February 4, 1789, may have been as important as any ever cast. The election of George Washington as the nation's first president got the country off to a good start.

Unanimity was certainly an advantage, because the election process itself created many questions. In only five states did the voters choose the electors. Electors in two states—Rhode Island and North Carolina—did not vote because their states had yet to ratify the Constitution. The New York legislature, still opposed to the Constitution, refused to pick any electors. In New Jersey the electors were designated by the governor and his council. In four other states the electors were chosen by the legislatures.

Yet virtually everyone was pleased with the new president. Though a great war hero, he had always deferred to the Continental Congress. As a former member of the Virginia colonial legislature, he did not disdain politics. Because he was both a speculator in western lands and a slave owner (known for his generous treatment of those who worked for him), he was acceptable to both northern and southern states.

What do you think?
- Are war heroes as politically popular today?
- Should the powers of a public office be influenced by who is likely to hold it?

SOURCE: Stanley Elkins and Eric McKitrick, *The Age of Federalism* (New York: Oxford University Press, 1993); Thomas A. Lewis, *For King and Country: The Maturing of George Washington, 1748–1760* (New York: HarperCollins, 1993.)

social and political forces the founders could not have anticipated. Subsequent chapters discuss ways in which the compromises of 1787 have been redefined and given new meaning in response to changing political circumstances.

The Constitution's extraordinary adaptability over a prolonged period of time constitutes no small accomplishment. Although the United States is often thought of as a relatively new country, its governing arrangements have remained intact for much longer than those in most other countries. Of all the great industrial democracies, only the British system comes close to enjoying basic governing arrangements that date back as far as those of the United States. And even the democratic features of British government are newer than those of the United States. Not until 1867 did most British men get the right to vote.

Most other countries have much newer constitutions. The latest Russian constitution was adopted in 1993. The current Spanish constitution was promulgated in 1978. The French constitution dates back only to 1958, the Danish to 1953, and the German, Italian, and Japanese constitutions to the late 1940s.

THE STAIN OF SLAVERY   Despite everything positive that can be said for the Constitution, the stain of slavery remains indelible. The Constitution validated the slave trade and indicated that each slave only counted as three-fifths of a person. The Constitution also required free states to return escaped slaves to the places from which they had fled.

Dividing and checking concentrations of power prevented the tyranny of the majority. But they also prevented a majority from undoing the tyranny of slavery. By denying the national government the capacity to end slavery peacefully, separation of powers helped perpetuate the slave system at a time when the practice was disappearing throughout the rest of the world.

Perhaps it would have been too much to ask of any constitution that it provide the tools for resolving what had become an intractable problem. Perhaps it was, as Abraham Lincoln once said, inevitable that "every drop of blood drawn with the lash shall be paid by another drawn with the sword."[44] It is not easy to think how the delegates to the Constitutional Convention could have designed a constitution that would have both freed slaves and won ratification by the voters of 1788.

CHAPTER SUMMARY

The colonists who settled the eastern coast of North America established incomplete but meaningful rules of democracy through such institutions as the Mayflower Compact and elected colonial assemblies. These democratic institutions were reinforced by the spread of philosophical ideals during the Revolutionary War, ideals that formed the basis for the U.S. Constitution.

The Constitution was written to rectify difficulties the country experienced under the Articles of Confederation. The national government could not raise its own army, levy its own taxes, or regulate commerce among the states. Many leaders believed the country was too weak to fend off potential threats from Britain, Spain, and France.

When drafting the new Constitution designed to address needs unmet by the Articles of Confederation, the delegates to the Constitutional Convention designed a new basic law that would be acceptable to the voters who were asked to ratify it and yet sufficient to win the loyalty of voters who would follow. Many compromises were necessary. Congress was given not a general power but a set of specific powers, along with the capacity to do anything "necessary and proper" to carry them out. Differences of opinion between delegates from big and small states were resolved by creating two legislative chambers with different schemes of representation. The Constitution provided that the president is selected via a complicated two-stage system. The Supreme Court is neither given nor denied the power of judicial review. Differences between the North and South were settled via compromises. The convention delegates erred by excluding a Bill of Rights but ultimately agreed during the ratification debate to add one.

The Constitution curbed the powers of state governments, gave Congress additional authority, created a presidency of limited powers, and established the Supreme Court as the head of the judicial system. By dividing power between the states and the national government and by further dividing the power of the national government among the legislative, executive, and judicial branches, the Constitution provided an enduring system of limited government well designed to protect the liberties of the citizens. Subsequent changes to the document have only increased popular control of the national government.

KEY TERMS

advice and consent, p. 44

Annapolis Convention, p. 38

Anti-Federalists, p. 51

Declaration of Independence, p. 35

divine right, p. 30

Federalist Papers, p. 53

Federalists, p. 50

First Continental Congress, p. 35

judicial review, p. 47

Mayflower Compact, p. 29

necessary and proper clause, p. 42

patronage, p. 30

proprietary colony, p. 29

Order of the Cincinnati, p. 37

quorum, p. 37

royal colony, p. 29

Second Continental Congress, p. 35

separation of powers, p. 32

Shays's Rebellion, p. 38

Stamp Act, p. 33

supremacy clause, p. 47

three-fifths compromise, p. 48

Tories, p. 35

Whigs, p. 33

SUGGESTED READINGS

Adams, Willi Paul. *The First American Constitutions: Republican Ideology and the Making of the State Constitutions in the Revolutionary Era.* Chapel Hill: University of North Carolina Press, 1980. Reveals that much of what seems original in the Constitution was already in place in many states.

Bailyn, Bernard. *The Origins of American Politics.* New York: Knopf, 1968. Identifies the sources of the American Revolution in colonial thought and practice.

Beard, Charles A. *An Economic Interpretation of the Constitution of the United States.* New York: Free Press, 1913. Interprets the writing of the Constitution as an effort by the wealthy to protect their property rights.

Elkins, Stanley, and Eric McKitrick. *The Age of Federalism.* New York: Oxford University Press, 1993. Authoritative account of political life during the first decade after the adoption of the Constitution.

ON THE WEB

National Archives and Records Administration
www.nara.gov/exhall/charters/constitution/conmain.html
The National Archives and Records Administration provides the full text of the Constitution, biographies of each of its signers, and high-resolution images of the document itself.

Internet Encyclopedia of Philosophy
www.utm.edu/research/iep/l/locke.htm
The Internet Encyclopedia of Philosophy provides a biography of John Locke, as well as a review of his important works.

PBS
www.pbs.org/ktca/liberty/
This site, the companion to a PBS series on the American Revolution, provides a comprehensive account of the Revolutionary War, including timelines, accounts of battles, and biographies of key figures.

Avalon Project at Yale Law School
www.yale.edu/lawweb/avalon/federal/fed.htm
The Avalon Project at Yale Law School presents online all 85 *Federalist Papers,* which can be searched by keyword.

Morgan, Edmund S., and Helen M. Morgan. *The Stamp Act Crisis: Prologue to Revolution.* Chapel Hill: University of North Carolina Press, 1953. Readable account of key events leading to the revolution.

Roche, John P. "The Founding Fathers: A Reform Caucus in Action." *American Political Science Review* 55 (December 1961): 799–816. Identifies the election connection at the Constitutional Convention.

Wood, Gordon S. *The Radicalism of the American Revolution.* New York: Knopf, 1992. Portrays the unleashing of a democratic ideology during the struggle for independence.

FEDERALISM

I t only took 47-year-old Clarence William Busch two days out on bail from his hit-and-run drunken-driving charge before he killed a little girl. Thirteen-year-old Cari Lightner was in the middle of a Saturday afternoon stroll when Busch swallowed her young life. His car careened straight across a bicycle path, struck the slim teen from behind, and left in its wake a mangled body that died within the hour.[1]

That Busch's personal struggles finally resulted in a death was not particularly surprising. When he sat behind the wheel that fateful day, Busch already had two drunken-driving convictions under his belt, not counting the most recent charge. What is more surprising is that the repercussions from this all-too-common tragedy did not stop with its impact on the lives of the killer and his victim's family. Cari's mother, a Sacramento real estate agent, quickly transformed her grief into a political crusade—one, incidentally, that would impact the lives of college students across the nation.

Candy Lightner formed the organization Mothers Against Drunk Driving (MADD) within a week of her daughter's death and first set about challenging statutes that allowed repeat offenders back into their cars. Her efforts started small: a campaign of "knocking on doors" in the California capital. But Candy, despite her lack of administrative experience, within four years built MADD into a national organization of 258 chapters and 300,000 members.

Candy's thirst for "revenge" did not stop with those caught driving intoxicated. Instead, her agenda spread to encompass young adult drinkers of all sorts. Teenagers account for a disproportionate share of drunk-driving accidents, so MADD demanded laws to take away the whole age group's right to drink.[2] The effort gained credibility in 1983 when the President's Commission on Drunk Driving proposed raising the drinking age to 21. The National Highway Traffic Safety Administration also weighed in, projecting that a higher minimum would reduce highway deaths by 13 percent.[3]

At first, President Ronald Reagan and other Republicans resisted turning these recommendations into federal law. Modern conservatives generally endorse allowing states to determine their own social regulations, and Reagan preferred to adhere to that principle. But the political situation grew stickier as many states resisted changing their own laws. By the middle of 1984, only 23 states forbade drinking for those under 21, and 19 states had declined to do so.[4] The final blow came when New York's legislature failed to raise the state's drinking age, despite a strong push by the governor. New York was a mecca for young drinkers from New Jersey and Pennsylvania, who created a "blood zone" on the state borders as they journeyed back home.

Congressional delegations from New York's two neighboring states placed MADD's agenda on the front burner. One New Jersey Democrat authored a measure to impose a national drinking age. As his legislative assistant explained, "The day of more rights for kids has passed." But this suggestion seemed to run afoul of rights for states as well, since the Twenty-first Amendment gives states the authority for liquor laws. Instead, Representative James Howard of New Jersey suggested following the same strategy that, in 1973, he had used to force states to lower their speed limits to 55 miles per hour. He proposed legislation formally allowing states to set their own drinking ages but yanking away millions of dollars in federal highway funds from any state whose limit remained below 21.*

The House passed this indirect national drinking age by voice vote, with very little opposition, and polls supported raising the minimum—prompting the White House to switch positions. Transportation Secretary Elizabeth Dole announced during a MADD rally on the Capitol steps that President Reagan now supported the legislation. It then passed the Senate, 81 to 16, opposed primarily by conservatives unhappy with the strong-arm treatment that states would face.[5] Reagan eventually signed the National Minimum Drinking Age Act into law.

But the battle did not end there. Eight states still refused to cave in until the 1986 deadline arrived, and four actually passed on the "blackmail portion" of federal highway funds for a year by holding out until June 1987.[6] Others changed their laws only in protest. Florida, for example, specified that the age would drop again the minute any federal court struck down the Act.[7]

South Dakota, supported by the other holdout states, took a challenge all the way to the U.S. Supreme Court. Its attorneys argued that Congress was trying to do an end run around the state's constitutional rights. South Dakota endorsed lower drinking ages, they explained, because otherwise teenagers would engage in "surreptitious drinking."[8] They argued it was the state's prerogative to make such a judgment. But the Court wouldn't swallow it. Chief Justice Rehnquist wrote for a seven-justice majority in *South Dakota v. Dole* (1987) that Congress can use federal budgetary power to pressure states—regardless of whether the law Congress wants changed falls under its jurisdiction. He called the potential million-dollar losses "relatively mild encouragement," prompting a spokesperson for the National Conference of State Legislatures to scoff, "I don't think many of them will hold out. They simply need the money."[9]

---

*States that did not raise their drinking ages would lose 5 percent of their highway construction funds in 1986 and 10 percent starting in 1987.

Let the good times roll

States have varying cultures, and this diversity can lead to wide differences in their social regulations. The state of Louisiana's southern half, for example, still bears heavy influence from its days as a colony of France and then Spain. This spicy Latin mix, augmented by carnival celebrations and musical festivals, leads to a more-tolerant attitude toward alcohol than found in states with an Anglo-Saxon heritage. Here we see the city's French Quarter inundated with revelers, many of them under age. If a region's attitudes seem "unenlightened," when should the nation impose its cultural preferences? When should it defer to local tastes and let states do their own thing?

No state held out against the *letter* of the law; the coercion worked. But Louisiana's state legislature did resist the *spirit* of the law. It's no accident that Louisiana was the last to surrender to federal pressure. The state began as a French colony, later was a Spanish colony, and in her southern region still contains many cultural attitudes redolent of Latin Catholicism rather than Anglo Puritanism. Alcoholic beverages are more likely to be part of normal family life there.[10] Louisiana also attracts a substantial (and young) tourism trade, hosting numerous music festivals as well as Mardi Gras (a carnival celebration called the "greatest free show on Earth"). Raising the drinking age simply did not conform to Louisiana's interests or her political culture.

So the Louisiana legislature left a major loophole in its 1986 alcoholic beverage regulation. Legislators made it illegal to drink under age 21, but imposed penalties only on those selling alcohol to teenagers under 18. This loophole made enforcement impossible for a decade. And when the loophole finally collapsed in 1995, worn down by continued federal pressure, the Louisiana Supreme Court responded by trying to roll the entire age limit back to 18, ruling that a higher limit represented unconstitutional age discrimination! But one New Orleans columnist, at least, predicted that raw federal power would force a reversal of the decision: "So long as they got the bomb, and we [only] got the Tenth Amendment, the feds are going to win every time."[11] Louisiana's court reheard the case in the face of severe threats from the Clinton administration and then backpedaled—with one judge switching his vote and a new judge joining the majority—in a decision the state's top liquor lobbyist derided as "totally political."[12] The drinking age went up again, loopholes gone.

At long last Louisiana conformed to national norms, and young adults were saved from demon liquor in every state, right? Wrong. Not even Louisiana's 1996 surrender was final. One poll showed that fewer than half of Louisiana men endorsed the higher drinking age and that respondents aged 18 to 20 over-whelmingly opposed it.[13] A strong majority of the legislators in the state house, unimpressed by the federal mandate, voted in favor of a 1999 constitutional amendment to restore the old limit—although they fell 18 votes short of the supermajority needed.[14]

And Louisiana still has loopholes. Young adults may drink with parents or in private residences. Both chambers of the legislature explicitly rejected an attempt to keep young adults out of bars. Despite complaints from law-enforcement offi-cials, they are still free to enter entertainment establishments that serve liquor in order to "hear good music."[15] And there's always the question of how aggressively police enforce a law that lacks local sympathy. Two teenage brothers interviewed in 1996 said they had little trouble finding booze in the New Orleans French Quarter. "Once in a while we'll get hassled trying to buy liquor in a supermar-ket," 17-year-old Patrick Grimmace explained. "But never on Bourbon Street."[16]

THE WINDING PATH FOLLOWED BY AMERICA'S NATIONAL DRINKING AGE illustrates why the structure of intergovernmental relations—seemingly so tech-nical—has been an intense source of conflict from the nation's founding. It shows the important value preserved by letting states do their own thing: social regula-tions that better fit the culture and interests of people in each state and less dan-ger of a national majority bullying regional minorities. It shows how hard states will fight to retain their distinctiveness. At the same time, it shows how a deter-mined national majority can force deviant states to conform to its demands, espe-cially when a few states seem bound to a policy that the rest of the nation consid-ers backward or unwise.

The story also illustrates why the American political system has tilted over time toward the national government. It shows that federal courts ultimately bear the burden of deciding between competing claims of authority—a responsibility that, more often than not, they exercise to expand the power of the national government of which they are part. It shows another reason the balance has tipped as well: the muscle provided by congressional grants. But the story also shows that, even in their weakened condition, state and local governments still have influence. As long as the nation relies on them to implement programs, then local officials will enjoy some discretion.

THE FEDERALISM DEBATE

Most nations have **unitary governments,** in which all authority is held by national governments. Such a system may divide the country into local jurisdictions, but these are simply administrative outposts in that they lack independent authority (or **sovereignty**). By contrast, the United States has a federal system consisting of two formal units: the *national government* and the *state governments*.* **Federalism** divides power, so that each fundamental unit has the authority to act independently (called **dual sovereignty**).

As a principle of government, federalism attracts a fair bit of skepticism. The great fighter for Venezuelan independence, Simón Bolívar, once observed, "Among the popular and representative systems of government, I do not approve of the federal system: It is too perfect; and it requires virtues and political talents much superior to our own."[17] Splitting up authority may prevent a nation from responding quickly during a crisis, and may exacerbate problems during times of conflict.

Yet federalism seems ideally suited to a nation characterized by so much geographical, ethnic, and cultural diversity. It provides a useful way to resolve conflicts that can tear other countries apart, by allowing subdivisions to "do their own thing." Federalism also helps promote the nation's economic development, since it leaves states with the authority and interest to focus on internal needs. As early as the 1830s, the keen French observer Alexis de Tocqueville noted, "One can hardly imagine how much division of sovereignty contributes to the well-being of each of the states that compose the Union. In these small communities ... all public authority [is] turned toward internal improvements."[18]

Both Supreme Court decisions and the outcome of key elections have defined and redefined the nature of American federalism (see Figure 3.1). Supreme

---

*Local governments—such as cities, counties, towns, and school districts—are also important parts of government in the United States, but they are not fundamental units in the U.S. federal system in the same way that the national and state governments are. According to a long-standing legal doctrine known as *Dillon's rule* (after the Iowa state judge John Dillon), local governments are in legal terms mere "creatures of the state" that a state legislature may alter or abolish at any time.

FIGURE 3.1

Development of American federalism

Nationally elected leaders, state legislators, and courts have all been instrumental.

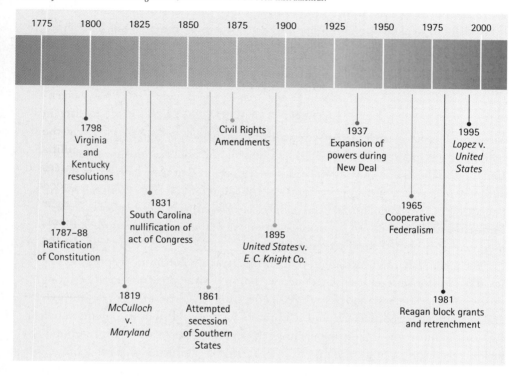

Court decisions have had a fundamental impact because the Supreme Court has the power of judicial review—that is, the authority to declare laws null and void on the grounds that they violate the Constitution (see Chapter 11). When the Supreme Court declares a national law unconstitutional, it also expands the arena in which states are sovereign. When it declares state laws unconstitutional, which it does more often, the result is a stronger national government.

Elections have been no less important for defining American federalism. Quite apart from the indirect influence they have on the Supreme Court's makeup, elections can have direct and immediate effects on the federal system. Indeed, for much of early American history, the national government remained weak precisely because elected officials intentionally limited the power they tried to exercise in many areas of national life. Centralization increased when Americans elected new leaders who wanted to exercise more authority.

FEDERALISM IN THE CONSTITUTION

Balancing national and state power has been a challenge since the country's founding. The Federalists (some say they should have been called "Nationalists") favored a strong national government. They believed that national strength was needed to overcome rivalries among the states. The Anti-Federalists (some say they were the real "Federalists") wanted the states to retain as much power as possible, fearing that a powerful national government could trample the liberties of the people.

The Constitution itself represents a compromise between these competing views (see Table 3.1). To appease those who wanted a weak national government, the document does not give Congress general legislative authority; in theory Congress can exercise only those powers specifically enumerated in the Constitution. States hold independent power too—for example, over the militia (today known as the National Guard). In addition, the Constitution guarantees existing state boundaries; no state can be stripped of its territory or divided into parts without its consent. The Anti-Federalists also won (as part of their fight for enactment of the Bill of Rights) passage of the Tenth Amendment, which emphasizes that states retain all power not delegated specifically to the federal government.

TABLE 3.1

CONSTITUTIONAL DIVISION OF POWER
BETWEEN NATIONAL AND STATE GOVERNMENTS

POWERS GRANTED TO THE NATIONAL GOVERNMENT	POWERS GRANTED TO THE STATE GOVERNMENTS
Conduct foreign affairs	
Raise armies and declare war	Maintain state militias (the National Guard)
Regulate imports and exports	
Regulate interstate commerce	Regulate commerce within the state
Regulate immigration and naturalization	
Establish and operate federal court system	Establish and operate state court systems
Levy taxes	Levy taxes
Borrow money	Borrow money
Coin money	
Provide for the general welfare	
Make laws "necessary and proper" to accomplish the above tasks	Exercise powers not granted to national government

At first, supporters of states' rights suggested that a state government could nullify national laws that infringed on its authority (see the Election Connection, "The Nullification Doctrine"). The doctrine of **nullification** was seldom invoked, however, and it died with the Civil War. Once nullification had been laid to rest, it was up to the federal courts to interpret what the Constitution had to say about federalism.

The Constitution contained numerous phrases that federal judges would be able to use, eventually, to expand federal power. It contained the **supremacy clause** declaring national law superior to state law, the **commerce clause** giving Congress control over interstate trade, and the **spending clause** giving Congress access to a very deep purse. Finally, Congress received great flexibility in carrying out its enumerated powers from the **necessary and proper clause.** Combined, these ambiguous phrases laid the groundwork for a significant centralization of power in the national government, to which the Fourteenth Amendment added after the Civil War (see Chapters 13 and 14).

THE SUPREMACY CLAUSE   The Constitution states that national laws "shall be the supreme Law of the Land . . . any Thing in the . . . Laws of any State to the Contrary notwithstanding." This statement comes close to saying (yet does not quite say) that only the national government is truly sovereign. It was used early in the nation's history as a basis for rejecting the nullification doctrine in *McCulloch* v. *Maryland,* a sweeping Supreme Court decision, handed down in 1819, that is among the most important the Court has ever made.[19]

The case revolved around the Bank of the United States, an entity that commercial interests thought vital to economic prosperity but that many farmers and debtors resented. Responding to popular opinion, the state of Maryland levied a tax on the bank. James W. McCulloch, an officer of the bank's Maryland branch, refused to pay and took his case to the Supreme Court. The Court ruled in favor of McCulloch. Maryland could not tax a federal bank, Chief Justice John Marshall, an ardent Federalist, explained. The "power to tax involves the power to destroy."[20] If a state government could tax a federal agency, then states could undermine national sovereignty—which the supremacy clause would not allow.

THE NECESSARY AND PROPER CLAUSE   The Constitution gives Congress authority "to make all laws which shall be necessary and proper for carrying into Execution the . . . Powers vested by this Constitution in the government of the United States." The words *necessary and proper* were first analyzed by Justice

The Nullification Doctrine

Many Americans considered the Constitution a limit on national government, an understandable impression given the strong wording of the Tenth Amendment and the ambiguity of other clauses. Indeed, some thought state sovereignty so complete that they propounded the doctrine of nullification, which says that state legislatures can invalidate unconstitutional acts of Congress.

States first used this doctrine in 1798. In that year, the Federalist Congress was upset by criticisms of their party, and especially of President John Adams during a foreign-policy crisis with France. They feared the growing power of Vice President Thomas Jefferson and the Democratic-Republican party he led. Congress passed the Sedition Act, a ban on criticism of most national leaders (except Jefferson). Opposition newspaper editors were soon imprisoned, and even Congressman Matthew Lyon was sentenced to four months in jail for insulting Adams. Federalists no doubt hoped censorship could suppress Jefferson's presidential campaign against Adams.

Outraged Jeffersonians in Virginia and Kentucky initially invoked the nullification doctrine, passing state resolutions to void the laws. Jefferson and his protégé, James Madison, wrote the resolutions, arguing that the Sedition Act of 1798 was unconstitutional. The doctrine's legal status remained unresolved, however, because their attempt to shut off debate backfired on the Federalists.

Closing newspapers and arresting people for political speeches undermined any claim that Jefferson's "French party" threatened liberties the Federalists would protect. The Democratic-Republicans took firm control of the national government after 1800, and a new Congress discontinued Sedition Acts.

The main application of the doctrine took place when regional conflict between the North and South started heating up. During the Jackson administration the conflict focused on tariffs, or taxes on imports, which Southern planters generally opposed but Northern merchants generally supported. Former Vice President John Calhoun's supporters in South Carolina called a state convention, which declared the tariff null and void in the state. President Jackson prepared to use armed force to crush the dissidents, but cooler heads prevailed. Congress passed a new tariff, and South Carolina agreed to pay it.

Southern leaders continued to espouse the doctrine of nullification—and to maintain their right to secede peacefully from the Union—because they were afraid that the national government would take away their slaves. Abraham Lincoln's election brought the issue to a head in 1860, since Lincoln represented the antislavery Republican party. The South seceded from the Union in response to his election. Only after half a million soldiers had died and the countryside had been laid to waste was the doctrine of nullification finally repudiated.

What do you think?
- If the national government passed unconstitutional legislation today, should state governments resist?
- If so, what prevents abuse of the power?
- If not, how can federalism help guarantee rights and liberties?

SOURCE: Stanley Elkins and Eric McKitrick, *The Age of Federalism* (New York: Oxford University Press, 1993).

Marshall in the same decision that challenged the doctrine of nullification, *McCulloch* v. *Maryland*.

Maryland argued that Congress had no authority to establish a national bank, because a bank was not *necessary* for Congress to carry out its delegated power to coin money. But Justice Marshall rejected such an interpretation. The language, he explained, does not mean *absolutely* necessary; it only means convenient. "Let the end be legitimate," he said. "Let it be within the scope of the Constitution, and all means which are appropriate, which are plainly adapted to that end, which are not prohibited, but consistent with the letter and spirit of the Constitution, are constitutional."[21]

Since the *McCulloch* v. *Maryland* decision, the courts have generally found that almost any means selected by Congress is "necessary and proper." As a result, the necessary and proper clause has come to be known as the "elastic clause" because over the centuries it has stretched to fit almost any circumstance.

THE COMMERCE CLAUSE   The Constitution gives Congress power "to regulate commerce . . . among the several states." The meaning of these words has been the subject of heated dispute. In the nineteenth century, the courts understood *interstate* (between-state) commerce to exclude exchanges that did not overtly cross state lines. Thus, for example, the Supreme Court's 1895 ruling in *United States* v. *E. C. Knight Co.* said that Congress could not break up a monopoly that had a nationwide impact on the price of sugar because the monopoly refined all its sugar within the state of Pennsylvania.[22]

The Great Depression eventually led to a change in how courts understood the commerce clause, because it ushered in a long period of Democratic dominance (see Chapter 8). In particular, voters sent Franklin Delano Roosevelt (FDR) to the White House because he promised to fight the Depression aggressively. FDR initiated what he called the **New Deal**—a wide array of proposals expanding the federal government's power to stimulate economic recovery.

The Supreme Court resisted empowering the national government at first, but after Roosevelt's landslide reelection in 1936, the Court began reinterpreting the commerce clause to suit his proposals. At first, doctrine changed slowly. For example, the Supreme Court permitted a New Deal law protecting union organizers, the Wagner Act, only because "industries organize themselves on a national scale."[23] But FDR's appointees increasingly expanded the legal definition of interstate commerce.

For example, in 1941 a farmer sowed 23 acres of winter wheat on his own land to feed his own family and his own livestock. This act violated crop quotas imposed under New Deal legislation, but the farmer challenged the limits as unconstitutional. What took place entirely on his farm, he argued, bore no relation to commerce "among the several states." Yet the Supreme Court ruled against the farmer in *Wickard* v. *Filburn* (1942), reasoning that he was depressing worldwide wheat prices by taking care of his own needs.[24] In other words, Congress could obligate the farmer to "resort to the market" for grain rather than grow it himself! With such an expansive definition, almost nothing falls outside the reach of Congress.

This broad interpretation of the commerce clause remained unquestioned until 1992, when Alphonso Lopez, a teenager with neither a criminal record nor a history of troublemaking, foolishly carried a .38-caliber handgun to his San Antonio high school. Needless to say, this was a violation of Texas state law. Rather than leave the matter to the local justice system, though, a U.S. district attorney decided to prosecute Lopez using 1990's Gun-Free School Zone Act.

Waves of grain?
Before the New Deal, the Supreme Court ruled that the power of Congress to regulate commerce generally only applied to goods produced or processed in multiple states. But the New Deal court decided that Congress can prevent farmers from growing food even if their produce will never leave the farm. Do you think the framers envisioned a national government that could regulate agriculture so closely?

This law made bringing a dangerous weapon near school grounds a federal offense. Lopez received a sentence of six months in the penitentiary, but he appealed the case, arguing that Congress had exceeded its enumerated powers by trying to control Texas's public schools. *U.S.* v. *Lopez* (1995) resulted in a victory for Lopez, who avoided jail and instead joined the Marines.

The *Lopez* case also represented a victory for states trying to slow expansion of the federal government. Chief Justice Rehnquist dismissed arguments that Congress could regulate the "business" of public schools because they influence interstate commerce. Since then the Supreme Court has continued to place limits on Congress's ability to intervene in state and local affairs. In 1997, the Court expanded the thrust of the *Lopez* decision by declaring unconstitutional a federal law that required state and local law enforcement officials to check the backgrounds of those seeking to buy handguns. The commerce clause does not allow the federal government to issue orders to state officials.

THE SPENDING CLAUSE   The Constitution gives Congress authority to collect revenues for the "general welfare." The New Deal Supreme Court considered the meaning of this clause when it ruled on the constitutionality of the social security program for senior citizens enacted in 1935. A taxpayer had challenged the program as oriented toward the specific welfare of the elderly and not the general welfare. But the Supreme Court, in tune with FDR's enlarged conception of federal power, said it was up to Congress to decide whether any particular program was for the general welfare "unless the choice is clearly wrong."[25] So far, the Court has never found Congress "clearly wrong."

Not only has the Supreme Court refused to restrict the purposes for which Congress can spend money, it has also granted Congress the right to attach almost any regulation to the money it spends. *South Dakota* v. *Dole* (1987), discussed in the introduction to this chapter, is a recent example. The Supreme Court rejected South Dakota's contention that teenage drunkenness bore little relation to road repair; both involve "highway safety."[26] States could always refuse the money. Only one justice expressed general concern with the power of Congress to "buy compliance with the few things that otherwise exceed its grasp."[27]

The congressional power to tax and spend has remained one of the broadest congressional powers because the federal government's scope expands every time it raises taxes. The more revenue extracted from state economies by federal taxation, the more cash-strapped state governments need to get the funds back through grants—and therefore the more willing they must become to meet congressional stipulations. Some scholars consider the national government's spending authority "the greatest threat to state autonomy."[28] For this reason, it is important to understand how the national government distributes funds to state and local government.

COOPERATIVE FEDERALISM

Political scientist Morton Grodzins first propounded the theory of **marble-cake federalism,** or cooperative federalism. Grodzins criticized those who viewed government as a layer cake, each level independent of and separate from the other.[29] He pointed out that, in practice, agencies from different levels of government work together, combining and intertwining their functions to such an extent that the intergovernmental system more appropriately resembles a marble cake.

For example, law enforcement requires cooperation among agencies, such as the Federal Bureau of Investigation, state highway traffic control, the county sheriff's office, and local police departments. According to Grodzins, all levels of government should work together because it assures that the policy process (1) represents many different interests in society, (2) grows out of compromise, and (3) draws on the shared expertise of professional administrators with similar values.

The 1964 election of Lyndon Johnson, together with an overwhelming Democratic majority in Congress, provided an opportunity to test more fully Grodzins's theory of cooperative federalism. Over the next few years, Congress passed a broad range of legislation that greatly enlarged the number, size, and complexity of intergovernmental grants—programs funded in part by the federal government but administered more locally. In 1930 only $85.8 million was spent on intergovernmental grants to local governments.[30] Grants to state and local governments grew to $43.6 billion by 1962, and by 1982 they had more than tripled to $147.5 billion (see Figure 3.2).*

Growth in the number and size of intergovernmental grants was facilitated by their popularity with most members of Congress. Many found they could profit politically from new projects begun in their home districts. As Senator Barry Goldwater said, "I don't care what the piece of equipment is—or how bad it is—if it's done in his state, the senator has to stand up and scream for it."[31] Though grants have often been criticized as mere pork-barrel projects, most grants are well received by the cities or towns lucky enough to get the money.

Representative Joe McDade of Pennsylvania, for example, proved to be one of the grand masters of grant making. From his position as ranking Republican on the House Appropriations Committee, McDade secured federal monies to help build a center for the performing arts, fund a microbiology institute for cancer research at the University of Scranton, restore an antique aqueduct, construct McDade

*Unless otherwise indicated, all amounts in this chapter are calculated in 1998 dollars.

FIGURE 3.2

Growth and decline in federal grants to states and localities

Expenditures for categorical grants continue to rise, whereas expenditures for block grants have declined in recent years.

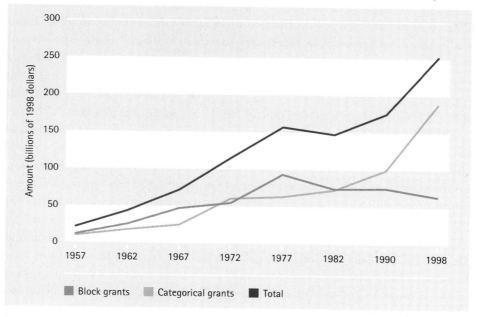

SOURCES: Paul E. Peterson, *The Price of Federalism* (Washington, DC: Brookings, 1995), Ch. 5; U.S. Bureau of the Census, *Federal Aid to the States for Fiscal Year 1998*. (*Note:* Totals exclude defense expenditures. Deriving precise estimates of block and categorical grants is a difficult undertaking. Here we have employed grants used mainly for developmental purposes as a proxy for block grants and grants used mainly for redistributive purposes as a proxy for categorical grants.)

Park (including a tourist-friendly museum on the history of coal mining) in Lackawanna County, turn the home of minor novelist Zane Grey in Lackawaxen into a national historic site, finance a flood-control project, and convert a railroad station into a fancy hotel and restaurant. Needless to say, McDade was extraordinarily popular with his constituents. Although he was under indictment on charges of "racketeering, conspiracy and accepting about $100,000 in illegal gratuities," McDade won reelection to Congress in 1994.[32]

CATEGORICAL GRANTS   Although Republicans like Representative McDade sometimes benefit from federal grants, the theory of cooperative federalism is particularly well suited to Democratic party philosophy. Many Democrats see federal grants as a way to encourage state and local governments to address needs they have previously ignored, and thus they favor **categorical grants.** These grants include regulations that specify how the money must be spent. Most have had social welfare purposes, such as job training, elimination of hunger through food stamps, and educational programs for the disabled.

The **War on Poverty,** a wide-ranging set of programs designed to enhance economic opportunities for low-income citizens, became the most famous and controversial of all categorical grant programs. Enacted in 1964 at the height of the civil rights movement, this series of poverty initiatives required involvement of the poor in program implementation to the maximum extent feasible. Examples include the popular Head Start program for preschoolers and the Job Corps, a residential education and training program. Nevertheless, the War on Poverty faced severe criticism. Not only did local officials often feud with the poverty warriors, some blame the program for the wave of civil violence that swept through American cities in the two years following its adoption.

PROBLEMS OF IMPLEMENTATION   The War on Poverty was only one of many categorical grant programs that came under tough scrutiny from those who studied their **implementation**—the way in which grant programs are actually administered at the local level. Critics note three reasons why intergovernmental grants are not as effective as expected:[33]

1. National and local officials often block one another, making it impossible to get much done. For example, when Lyndon Johnson tried to build "new towns" for the poor on vacant federal land, he encountered the opposition of local officials who objected to the program's adverse effects on local property values.[34] Virtually no new towns were built.

2. When many participants are involved, delays and confusion are almost inevitable. It took over four years to get a job creation program in Oakland under way. Political scientists Jeffrey Pressman and Aaron Wildavsky pointed out that the long delay was caused at least in part by the sheer number of agencies involved in the decision. The program required 70 separate clearances. Even if each took an average of only three weeks (not an unreasonable length of time), the total delay would be over four years.[35]

3. Federal policy makers often raise unrealistic expectations by using exaggerated rhetoric, thereby guaranteeing disappointment. It was a mistake to equate moderately funded programs with a war.

BLOCK GRANTS   Some problems with intergovernmental cooperation smooth out as categorical grant programs mature. Nevertheless, the criticism has proved quite influential. To simplify federal policy, Congress replaced many categorical grants with **block grants,** intergovernmental grants with a broad set of objectives, a minimum of restrictions, and maximum discretion for local officials.

The move toward block grants occurred in three distinct waves, each influenced by the political circumstances prevailing at the time. The first wave of block grants began under President Nixon. The most comprehensive, **general revenue sharing,** gave state and local governments a share of federal tax revenues to be used for any purpose whatsoever. During this first wave, block grants did not replace categorical grants so much as supplement them—a necessary compromise for Nixon to get block grants past Democrats in Congress. As a consequence, the total size of the intergovernmental grant program continued to grow throughout the 1970s, eventually costing more than $155 billion (see Figure 3.2).

The second wave of block grants came at the beginning of Ronald Reagan's administration, which enjoyed a Republican majority in the Senate. Reagan succeeded in converting a broad range of categorical grants in education, social services, health services, and community development to block grants. During this second wave, the new block grants not only had fewer restrictions than those they replaced, but their funding levels were also reduced.[36] The amount spent on block grants fell from $93.5 billion in 1977 to $64.1 billion in 1998, and most of this reduction occurred in the early 1980s. General revenue sharing was eliminated in 1985, and the community development block grant, a major grant program for cities across the country, was cut from $7.7 billion in 1980 to $4.6 billion in 1998.[37]

The third wave of block grants took place after the congressional election of 1994, when Republicans captured control of Congress. Earlier initiatives had not touched large social programs, such as Medicaid and Aid to Families with Dependent Children (AFDC). But in 1996 Congress transformed the AFDC program into a block grant that gave states almost complete discretion over the way monies could be used (see Chapter 15). Congress also tried to transform the Medicaid program into a block grant, but this effort was forestalled by a presidential veto. Despite continued Republican pressure to return responsibilities to the states, expenditures on categorical grants have continued to rise (see Figure 3.2).

WHAT'S WRONG WITH FEDERAL GRANTS?

Perhaps the best argument against both categorical and block grants is that even though they are often defended as a way of equalizing resources across the country,[38] federal grants in fact do not have this effect. Instead, wealthier states usually receive more federal money than poorer states. On average, the ten richest states in the country have gotten much more money per resident from block grants than other states (see Figure 3.3). Election pressures make it difficult for Congress to direct federal dollars to needy parts of the country. Members fight to get as much money as possible for their home districts. If they do not, their election opponents can make it a campaign issue.

The experience of Massachusetts Senator Edward Kennedy, a Democrat, provides an illuminating example. In 1988 Kennedy ran on the campaign slogan "He can do more for Massachusetts," a reference to his many Washington connections

FIGURE 3.3

Block grants for traditional governmental services

Richer states usually get more money than poorer states. Is this unfair, or do rich states deserve more because they pay more to the federal government in taxes?

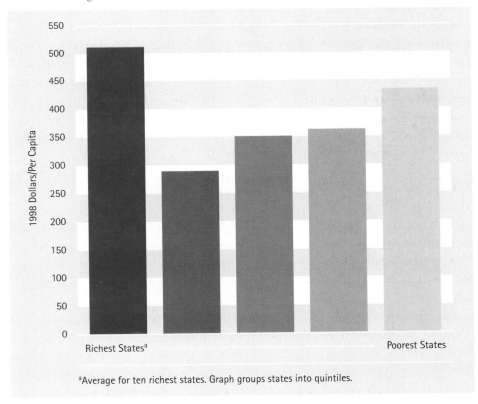

ᵃAverage for ten richest states. Graph groups states into quintiles.

SOURCE: U.S. Bureau of the Census, *Federal Aid to the States for Fiscal Year 1998,* April 1999, Table 1.

dating back to when his brother was president. When Kennedy ran for reelection in 1994, a study showed that Massachusetts was receiving only 97 cents back for every dollar paid in taxes (instead of the $1.01 it had received in 1988). The finding fetched the following headline in a local newspaper: "State's Share of Federal Dollars Drops: Kennedy's Record in Last Decade, a Campaign Issue."[39] Although Kennedy still won reelection, the vote was surprisingly close.

Perhaps the best argument in favor of federal grants is that they are necessary to maintain properly funded social programs. When states are not subject to federal regulation, they try to shift the burden of serving the needy to other states. In Minnesota, a state with generous poverty programs, the proportion of new welfare recipients from out of state increased from 19 to 28 percent between 1994 and 1995, a time when other states were placing limits on benefits. "We're really concerned," a county official said.[40] Fear of migration from other places creates a vicious cycle of cuts that President Clinton has called a "race to the bottom."

Although the debate over grants has polarized between those in favor of a wide variety of intergovernmental grants and those opposed to all of them, the most sensible solution may lie in a mixed approach. In areas where state and local governments have traditionally concentrated their efforts, including transportation, sanitation, and education, it may be appropriate to keep the federal role to a minimum. States and localities provide these services whether they receive federal aid or not, and are likely to know their own needs best. But in other areas, such as Medicaid and food stamps, it may be important to establish federal standards so that states do not "race to the bottom."

THE CONTEMPORARY FEDERALISM DEBATE

The debate over federalism continues today. It divides the two major political parties. Republicans tend to prefer a decentralized government because state and local officials are closer to the people, more in touch with their needs, and less likely to waste taxpayer dollars. Conversely, Democrats tend to think that many serious social problems require a national solution; they do not trust local majorities to be fair.

In the early 1990s, debate focused on the issue of **unfunded mandates**—which occur when the national government imposes regulations on state and local governments without covering the costs. This strategy is tempting to members of Congress because it allows them to "solve" social problems without raising taxes. By 1993, countless mandates had reached the statute books, including prison reforms, environmental laws, and social-welfare benefits.[41] A number of state and local officials held "National Unfunded Mandates Day" on October 27, 1993, to protest such policies—complaining that cities were suffering "spending without representation."[42]

Despite the long-standing popularity of unfunded mandates on Capitol Hill, the 1994 election at least temporarily slowed their growth. Republicans campaigned in favor of **devolution,** the return of governmental responsibilities to state and local governments. After taking over Congress, they passed a statute banning any new law that is not adequately funded. However, if Congress wishes, it can—and sometimes does—ignore the law and pass new mandates anyway.

The Supreme Court has also worked to limit the elasticity of the necessary and proper clause through rulings that have attracted some criticism. For example, in *New York* v. *U.S.* (1992), the Supreme Court declared that Congress cannot give direct orders to states. This case dealt with the disposal of radioactive waste,

Congress dumped a problem on the states, but the Supreme Court said no
Citizens organized protests and demonstrations whenever a town was named as a potential site for a waste dump. Why did the Supreme Court reject Congress's response to this "Not in My Back Yard" (NIMBY) problem?

which has become a particularly annoying political problem. Millions of cubic feet of such waste must be buried someplace where it cannot be disturbed for thousands of years.[43] The dilemma has become an elected official's nightmare: Something needs to be done, and there is no way of doing it without making some people angry—really angry.

Easily alarmed at the very word *radioactive,* citizens organize protests and demonstrations whenever a town is mentioned as a potential radioactive dump. Everyone knows the stuff has to go somewhere, but everyone also says, "Not In My Back Yard." This response is generally known as the **NIMBY problem.** After stewing fitfully over the NIMBY problem for several years, Congress discovered a politically painless solution: It required each state either to find an adequate burial site for its waste or to become legally responsible for any damages the waste might cause. Rather than make tough decisions itself, Congress decided to place an unfunded mandate on governors and state legislatures.

As a result, the debate over domestic radioactive waste shifted to the states. In no state was the issue more hotly debated than in New York. Often, when state officials identified a potential dump, they were run off the site and burned in effigy.[44] Under the pressure of the federal law, New York officials decided to ignore the opposition and dump the waste in Cortland and Allegany counties. But the elected boards for the two counties, to keep faith with county voters, filed suit claiming that the federal law was unconstitutional. Supreme Court Justice Sandra Day O'Connor, writing for the majority, said Congress could not force states or local governments to bury their nuclear waste; such direct orders violate state sovereignty.[45] Old ideas of sovereignty clearly have been revived.

STATE AND LOCAL GOVERNMENT

American government may have become more centralized, but that does not mean the states and localities are withering away. Quite the contrary. The national government has increased its authority, but lower levels of government usually bear responsibility for implementing policy. These lower levels are the ones often actually spending the funds collected through taxation and distributed according to competitive grants or according to specific formulas. State and local governments are the ones actually hiring new bureaucrats to implement federal mandates (see Chapter 10). For this reason, someone wishing to understand America's new democracy needs to consider how these independent administrative units actually operate.

LOCAL GOVERNMENT

Local governments now play a more prominent role in the federal system than they have for decades. Even before the most recent devolution, nearly half of all domestic government expenditure was paid for by taxes raised by state and local governments. This pattern is in keeping with long-standing American traditions (see Figure 3.4).

Nearly a century ago, the British scholar James Bryce identified the key role played by local governments in the American federal system:

> *It is the business of a local authority to mend the roads, to clean out the village well or to provide a new pump, to see that there is a place where straying beasts may be kept till the owner reclaims them, to fix the number of cattle each villager may turn out on the common pasture, [and] to give each his share of timber cut in the common woodland.*[46]

FIGURE 3.4

Domestic expenditure of governments

State and local governments spend almost as much as the national government.

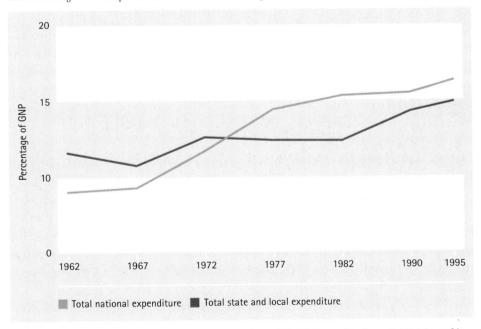

SOURCES: Paul E. Peterson, *The Price of Federalism* (Washington, DC: Brookings, 1995); U.S. Bureau of the Census, *Statistical Abstract of the United States,* 1998.

The nature of the work has modernized since Bryce's observation, but the basic functions remain much the same. Local governments maintain roads; take care of the parks; provide police, fire, and sanitation services; run the schools; and perform many other functions that affect the everyday lives of citizens.

THE NUMBER AND TYPES   Local governments constitute a growing presence, at least in sheer numbers. There were over 73,000 in 1997, up from about 46,000 in 1942. The basic unit in most states is the county, although not all counties are alike. In some states they manage school systems, welfare programs, local roads, sanitation systems, sheriff's offices, and an array of other governmental activities. In other states they hardly have any duties. Many counties are divided into townships—there are nearly 17,000 of them nationwide—which take care of local road maintenance and other small-scale activities. As the population has become concentrated in urban areas, the total number of municipalities—cities, suburbs, and towns—has increased to nearly 20,000. In most states, these municipal governments have assumed many of the responsibilities once performed by counties.

States, counties, and municipalities have also created an extraordinary array of special districts—nearly 30,000 in all. Each special district has responsibility for only one or a few specific governmental functions. Such governments are unique in that they overlap the boundaries of other local governments, sometimes spanning many different municipal jurisdictions. Special districts account for most of the increase in the number of local governments over the last 50 years. Some special districts run schools, others manage parks, and still others administer transportation systems or garbage collection. Even as specific a task as mosquito abatement can be the responsibility of a special district.

LOCAL ELECTIONS   Elected officials run most local governments, although heads of special districts are sometimes appointed. In the United States as a whole, the total number of elected local officials approaches half a million people. But despite the large number of local elections, actual rates of citizen participation in them are surprisingly low. If a particularly colorful candidate runs for mayor, or if ethnic or racial issues rise up, large numbers of voters can show up at the polls. But usually the local electorate is about half the size of the presidential electorate.[47]

The sheer number of elected officeholders often makes local elections confusing. The near invisibility of local elections also helps reduce local participation rates.[48] Newspaper coverage is haphazard. Local governments often hold their elections at times that coincide with neither state nor national elections, which further reduces turnout.[49] Few understand that local governments also oversee the administration of national elections and may organize voting in a way that discourages participation. This local responsibility became a key issue in the close 2000 presidential election, when some voters in Palm Beach County, Florida, claimed that the county's confusing ballot design had led them to vote for the wrong candidate.

POPULARITY OF LOCAL GOVERNMENT This diverse, half-democratic system might seem irrational and doomed to fail. Yet local governments remain popular. According to survey results, 37 percent of the population trust their local governments more than other levels of government, compared to only 19 percent who trust the federal government the most (see Figure 3.5). Only 8 percent feel their local governments are most wasteful of their tax dollars, compared to 66 percent who feel this way about the federal government.

One explanation for the apparent popularity of local government, despite the low profile of its elections, is the ability of people to "vote with their feet"—that

FIGURE 3.5

Evaluations of federal, state, and local governments

Why do you think more people trust local government than other governments?

In which of the following governments do you have the most trust?

What government do you feel wastes the most of your tax money?

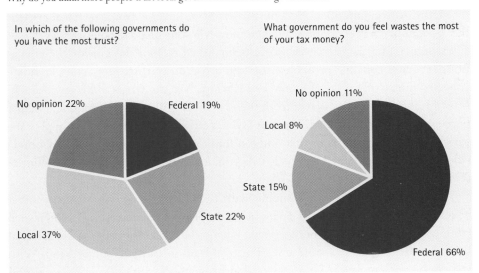

No opinion 22%
Federal 19%
State 22%
Local 37%

No opinion 11%
Local 8%
State 15%
Federal 66%

SOURCE: Thomas R. Dye, "Federalism: A Return to the Future," *Madison Review* 1 (Fall 1995): 3.

is, to move from one community to another—if they are unhappy. Americans are a mobile people: Over 17 percent move each year.[50] Every local government official knows that if the government is inefficient or unresponsive, population and property values will drop. As a result, most local governments have good reason to be mindful of their constituents' needs and desires.

The ability to move is important, because it allows people to "shop" for the type of locality in which they wish to live. Some people favor sex education programs and condom distribution in schools; others do not. Some people think refuse collection should be publicly provided; others prefer to recycle their own garbage. Some people think police protection should be intensive; others think an intrusive police presence violates civil liberties. By giving people a choice, the diversity of local governments reduces conflict and enhances citizen satisfaction.

LIMITS ON LOCAL GOVERNMENT　　Local governments often do not have the resources to meet the needs of the poor, the sick, and the disabled. If a local government tries to provide substantial services, it runs the risk of attracting more needy people and driving away those expected to pick up the tab. For example, in the early 1990s, Framingham, Massachusetts, provided a broad range of social services to disadvantaged residents, including group homes for recovering drug and alcohol abusers, halfway houses for juvenile offenders, counseling centers, and other programs for the poor. Although the programs were well administered, the growing number of clients provoked complaints from town leaders that the community was becoming "a magnet for everyone else's problems."

Complaining that taxpayers were being asked to foot the bill for the education, security, and fire protection of low-income nontaxpayers, one candidate appealed effectively to local voters by insisting, "We can't afford this anymore."[51] Most local governments agree; from their own tax dollars, they spend less than 1 percent of the gross national product (GNP) on social programs. But such is the variety of local government that one can find exceptions to this (as to any other) rule; San Francisco and New York City, for example, provide a broad range of social services.

Local governments also compete with each other to attract businesses that generate the economic activity necessary to improve communities. Although such competition has positive benefits, in that it keeps localities sensitive to the needs of their wealth producers, sometimes the competition can get out of hand. With state help, one county in Kentucky outbid its neighbors for a Canadian steel mill employing 400 people. It ended up costing the state $350,000 for every job created. Such bidding wars have spread across the country. As one Michigan official put it, "Right now, all we are doing is eating each other's lunch. At some stage we have to start thinking about dinner."[52]

In other cases, cities compete to secure or retain professional sports teams. In 1995 Cleveland Browns owner Art Modell abruptly decided to move his football franchise to Baltimore, which had promised a new stadium and other financial incentives. Baltimore's mayor and Maryland's governor participated in the negotiations for the team and helped announce the move. Meanwhile, Cleveland officials were incensed. Mayor Michael White likened the move to "a kick in the teeth."[53] Undaunted, the city of Cleveland worked with major financial backers to bring a professional football team back to the city, this time as an expansion team. In 1999 the expansion Cleveland Browns played their first season in a brand-new $283 million stadium.

STATE GOVERNMENT

The federal government's design was adapted from constitutions in many states. Thus it is not surprising that the basic organization of most state governments bears a strong resemblance to that found in the U.S. Constitution. Just as Congress has the Senate and the House, legislatures have an upper and a lower chamber in all states except Nebraska (which has only one chamber). All states have multitiered court systems roughly comparable to that of the federal system. And every state has an independently elected governor, the chief executive of the state, whose responsibilities roughly parallel those of the president.

State governments differ in many important ways, however. State legislatures vary greatly in size. Most lower houses have around 100 representatives; but Alaska, Delaware, and Nevada each have about 41 members, while in New Hampshire the lower house comprises 398 legislators. Some state governments hold their elections in even-numbered years, in conjunction with federal races; others do not. In some states, administrative officers such as the secretary of state and the attorney general are elected, whereas in other states the governors appoint these officials.

State policies vary as well. For example, there is significant variation in the legality of assisted suicide, the rules governing a woman's access to an abortion, and social welfare policies across states. In South Dakota most consumer fireworks are permitted, but in Georgia even sparklers are against the law. In Nevada gambling is legal, yet in Idaho it is a misdemeanor. Until the federal government clamped down on it, states varied widely in their minimum drinking ages as well.

FIGURE 3.6

States with divided government

Increasingly, the governor of a state belongs to a party different from the party that controls one or both houses of the state legislature. Is this pattern an accident or the result of conscious decisions by voters?

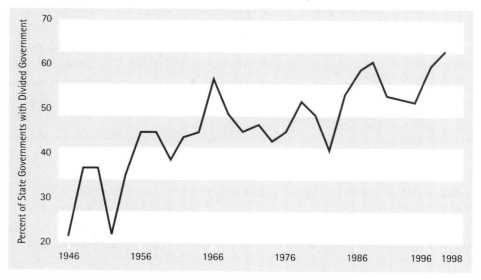

SOURCES: Morris Fiorina, *Divided Government* (Needham Heights, MA: Allyn and Bacon, 1996); *The Book of the States,* Vol. 32: 1998–1999 (Lexington, KY: The Council of State Governments, 1998).

STATE ELECTIONS   Despite differences among states, state elections bear a strong resemblance to national elections. The same two political parties—the Republicans and Democrats—are the dominant competitors in nearly all state elections. A new trend toward competitive politics and divided government has developed in most states (see Figure 3.6). Democrats have had the advantage in state legislative races; Republicans have elected governors more often. The voters may like this split in power: Each party can act as a check on the other, and government does not drift to either political extreme.[54]

VARIATION IN RESPONSIBILITIES   The size and range of state responsibilities have grown dramatically in recent decades. As a percentage of GNP, state expenditures increased by over 60 percent between 1962 and 1995. States bear heavy responsibilities for financing education at all levels. They maintain parks, highways, and prisons. They manage welfare and Medicaid programs that serve low-income populations. They give grants to local governments to help pay for police, fire, and other basic governmental services.

The amount spent on government services varies from state to state. For one thing, wealthier states spend much more on public services. In 1995 the state and local governments in the ten richest states spent an average of $6,600 per person on public services, whereas in the ten poorest states they spent, on average, less than $4,500 (although of course the purchasing power of a dollar may be greater in a poor state).[55] Federal grants have done little, if anything, to reduce fiscal inequalities.

Expenditures are also affected by elections. Each party has its favorite type of public service. Democrats in the legislature tend to prefer high expenditures for social services. The more Republicans who win, the higher the expenditure for traditional government services.[56]

As state government has become more complicated, state legislatures have also become more professional. That is, they have lower turnover rates, higher salaries, more staff, and longer sessions. In 1995 California's legislature was among the most modern. Its members remained in session throughout the year, receiving $72,000 in salary, retirement benefits, and handsome daily expense payments as well as the services of a full-time staff. Turnover rates were only about 18 percent. By contrast, Wyoming paid its legislators $125 dollars a day and limited its legislative sessions to a maximum of 40 working days in odd-numbered years and 20 days in even years. It had a turnover rate twice that of California.[57] During the 1990s, voters reacted against the professionalization of state government, as many states limited the terms of legislators, cut their staffs, and reduced their salaries and benefits.

THE RESURGENT GOVERNORS   Being governor of a medium- to large-sized state has historically been one of the best ways to position oneself for a presidential run. Three of the last four U.S. presidents have been governors, and former governors have been major candidates in every presidential election campaign since 1976. George W. Bush's popularity as governor of Texas, coupled with the advantages of a well-known family name, quickly catapulted him into the presidential limelight.

Since 1950 many states have strengthened the office of governor by lengthening terms of office, reducing term limitations, and enhancing the governor's veto power over legislation. Most governors now have a **line item veto,** a power that allows them to reject specific parts of a bill. Ten governors have a particularly strong form of the line item veto that allows them to eliminate or cut particular spending items.[58] In part because of their newfound strength, governors became influential players in several national policy debates in the 1980s and 1990s.

STATE ECONOMIC ACTION   In the nineteenth century, state governments played an active role in their economies, granting charters to private corporations and investing their resources to assist in the development of key industries. After the New Deal, the states faded in importance, but many became active again in the 1980s and 1990s—seeking to reinvigorate their business climate through tax incentives and actively recruiting firms from out of state.

States with large economies and significant international exports, such as California and Texas, arranged trade missions to countries such as Mexico, Japan, and Canada. Some of these missions met with greater success than most thought possible. In 1987, California governor George Deukmejian traveled to Japan to promote the sale of California rice. Most experts scoffed at his efforts, arguing that native Japanese rice was central to the country's national pride, culture, and self-sufficiency. "Negotiating for rice is like negotiating for Mt. Fuji," said one trade consultant. Nevertheless, the governor's efforts did not go unrewarded: By the late 1990s, Japan imported $100 million worth of rice from California, accounting for 20 percent of the state's rice crop. The skeptics had to admit they were wrong.[59]

CHAPTER SUMMARY

Federalism divides sovereignty between the states and the national government. Its existence in the United States is the result of a compromise between Constitutional Convention delegates who believed that a strong national government was necessary to preserve stability and those who feared that centralized power would lead to tyranny. The compromise that resulted does not define governmental powers clearly. As a result, the nature of American federalism has changed in response to numerous events, including key elections.

The election of strong Democratic majorities in the 1960s allowed the national government to put in practice a theory known as cooperative or marble-cake federalism, which holds that all levels of government can and should work together. In accordance with this theory, the federal government increased tax revenues but then distributed the new funding back to state and local governments through new federal grants. Many of these grants were categorical in nature; they contained restrictions that specified how the money should be spent. Republicans have tried to limit the restrictions placed on states and otherwise to increase state power. But even after numerous judicial appointments made by Republican presidents and a Congress controlled by the Republican party, the changes have been modest.

Despite the expansion of federal power, state and local governments remain vital components of the federal system. Nearly half of domestic spending by government comes out of state and local budgets, so these governments can play key roles in economic development. Governors are well-known political figures, often positioned to seek the presidency. Though few citizens participate in local elections, local governments are the most popular of all governmental levels, in part because people can "vote with their feet"—that is, they can choose local communities suited to their tastes.

The growing power of the national government in some ways represents a frustration of popular desires, since Americans generally trust their local officials more. They are annoyed by a federal bureaucracy that hands down orders, ignoring local needs. Yet the principled desire for a weaker national government is not strong; it usually falls by the wayside when states block one's policy goals. So frustration with centralized government should not conceal an important fact: the new balance in favor of national power has made it easier for popular majorities to change American social life rapidly. Centralization is an important part of the background in which America's new democracy operates.

KEY TERMS

block grant, p. 76

categorical grant, p. 74

commerce clause, p. 68

devolution, p. 79

dual sovereignty, p. 65

federalism, p. 65

general revenue sharing,
   p. 76

implementation, p. 75

line item veto, p. 87

marble-cake federalism,
   p. 73

McCulloch v. *Maryland,* p. 68

necessary and proper clause,
   p. 68

New Deal, p. 70

NIMBY problem, p. 80

nullification, p. 68

sovereignty, p. 65

spending clause, p. 68

supremacy clause, p. 68

unfunded mandates, p. 78

unitary government, p. 65

War on Poverty, p. 75

SUGGESTED READINGS

Conlan, Timothy. *From New Federalism to Devolution: Twenty-Five Years of Intergovernmental Reform.* Washington, DC: Brookings, 1998. Excellent analysis of changing federal policy.

Elazar, Daniel. *American Federalism: A View From the States.* New York: Harper & Row, 1984. Discussion of various regional political cultures in the U.S.

Elkins, Stanley, and Eric McKitrick. *The Age of Federalism.* New York: Oxford University Press, 1993. Account of the first decades of the federal system under the Constitution.

Fiorina, Morris, *Divided Government.* New York: Macmillan, 1992. Explains why control of many state governments is divided between the Democratic and Republican parties.

Peterson, Paul E. *The Price of Federalism.* Washington, DC: Brookings, 1995. Contrasts the responsibilities of national, state, and local governments.

Riker, William H. *Federalism: Origin, Operation, Significance.* Boston: Little, Brown, 1964. Theoretical treatise on federalism.

ON THE WEB

National League of Cities
**National Conference of State
  Legislatures**
National Governor's Association
www.nlc.org
www.ncsl.org
www.nga.org
Several interstate governmental organizations provide information and policy priorities for state and local governments.

Urban Institute
www.urban.org/
On this Web site, the Urban Institute presents information about its ongoing

assessment of new programs whereby responsibility devolves to the states.

Federalism
www.min.net/~kala/fed/
Created by a doctoral student at George Washington University, this Web site covers nearly every aspect of federalism, from philosophy to economics to history.

Part Two

$\rightarrow$ —◆— $\leftarrow$

INGREDIENTS OF AMERICA'S NEW DEMOCRACY

AMERICAN POLITICAL CULTURE

More than six years of war filled the interval between the Minutemen's stand at Concord and the British surrender at Yorktown ending the Revolutionary War. At times the military position of the colonies was desperate, but in the end the newly formed Continental Army and the colonial militias defeated the finest standing army in the world.

Well, not exactly. The Americans had a little help from their friends. The French Marquis de Lafayette and the German Baron Johann de Kalb were among Washington's top generals (although de Kalb died after suffering 11 wounds in hand-to-hand combat).[1] When Washington's army was shivering at Valley Forge and the American cause appeared to be lost, another German, Baron Friedrich Wilhelm von Steuben, arrived on the scene. An expert in military drill, von Steuben transformed the untrained Americans into a disciplined force that could stand against British regulars.

A Polish general, Casimir Pulaski, known as the father of the American cavalry,[2] was mortally wounded leading an international unit (Americans, Poles, Irish, French, and Germans) against British fortifications at Savannah. Another Pole, Thaddeus Kosciuszko, designed the defenses at Saratoga, where Americans stopped the British from separating New England from the other colonies. He also designed the fortifications at West Point that Benedict Arnold tried to betray to the enemy. A Spanish commander in New Orleans, Don Bernardo de Galvez, organized a force of 1,200 men, including 80 free blacks and 160 Indians, and sailed up the Mississippi, taking British forts as far north as Natchez. Then he captured Mobile and Pensacola. In all, de Galvez's racially diverse unit took about 3,000 British soldiers out of the fight.[3] Without all of this "foreign aid," Americans might be singing "God Save the Queen" at the start of baseball and football games.

At the time, it was not unusual for soldiers to fight under a foreign flag. Generally, they were mercenaries—professional soldiers who fought for pay. For example, the Hessians whom Washington defeated on his midnight raid across the Delaware River were British employees. On the American side, however, soldiers often were volunteers. High-ranking officers worked without pay until after the war. Kosciuszko donated his military compensation to the emancipation of slaves. These foreigners joined the American side, at least in part, because of their attraction to the kind of country being created.

This international contribution to the "American" Revolution is underappreciated, but then so is the international contribution to "America" as a whole. Millions of people have followed in the footsteps of those eighteenth-century foreign soldiers, opting to become part of the democratic experiment. Americans are more ethnically and religiously diverse than the citizens of other democracies.

Most of the world's multiethnic governments have been either short-lived (like Yugoslavia) or authoritarian (like the Austro-Hungarian and Soviet empires). The United States is the exception, an unusual example of diverse people coexisting peacefully under the same democratic government.[4]

Carl Friedrich, a professor who immigrated to the United States from Germany, explained in 1935 why so many immigrants find it possible to adopt America as a new homeland: "To be an American is an ideal, while to be a Frenchman is a fact."[5] The meaning of American citizenship differs from that found in most of the world. Other countries define citizenship by race or ethnicity. Members of a dominant racial or ethnic group *automatically* enjoy a citizen's rights and privileges, whereas others may not be eligible at all. By contrast, there is no American ethnicity; an American may belong to any ethnic group. To be a "good American" refers not to a nationality but to a set of beliefs and values that people of any heritage may choose to embrace.

Yet Friedrich's comment hints at a strange contradiction. Americans share "an ideal"—a set of basic assumptions about the nature of a good society—more so than citizens in other democracies. Certainly the United States has its share of controversy and disagreement, but nothing comparable to the wide range of conflicting elements often found in Europe. European nations have had strong parties favoring various extreme ideologies, from the far left to the far right. By contrast, efforts to establish an official church or a workers' paradise are outside the mainstream of legitimate political discourse in the United States.

HOW DOES SUCH A DIVERSE SOCIETY DEVELOP SUCH A UNIFIED WORLD view? Understanding that paradox—political consensus coexisting with cultural diversity—forms the core focus of this chapter. We describe the diversity, outline the unifying philosophy, and then explain how they can coexist. As you read, however, keep in mind why these fundamental ideals even matter.

The values of a country's citizenry grow out of the people's historical experiences and economic conditions. These values determine how laws operate and whether they survive the passage of time. They mold how politicians behave and how institutions work. If American laws conflicted sharply with social realities, they would be replaced or ignored. Conversely, carting the U.S. Constitution to a troubled country, such as Yugoslavia or Burundi, would not magically transform their government into a carbon copy of this one.

For these reasons, it is important to take a close look at the American people—who they are, and what they value. These traits, which some scholars call the **political culture,** form the context for America's new democracy. Both cultural diversity and political consensus operate in the background whenever the

United States holds an election, requiring public officials to respect America's unity amidst diversity.

SOCIAL DIVERSITY

John Jay wrote in the second *Federalist Papers* essay that Americans were "one united people; a people descended from the same ancestors, speaking the same language, professing the same religion." Such statements remind us that the *Federalist Papers* were primarily campaign documents, for Americans were not nearly so similar as Jay alleged. His exaggeration of American unity was a political tactic, an appeal to rise above serious divisions that threatened ratification of the Constitution.

Contrary to Jay's claim, America in the New World was not settled by "one united people." Although the British were most numerous, other nationalities were well represented. The Dutch settled New York, and the Swedes established settlements in what are now Delaware and eastern Pennsylvania. The French were present on the northern and western borders, and the Spanish in the South (although the latter never were very numerous). As for the British, they were not all of a kind. New England was settled by Puritans, whereas Virginia settlers were loyal to the Church of England. Maryland was a grant to Lord Baltimore, who welcomed his fellow Catholics, and Pennsylvania welcomed Quakers. Moreover, after 1700, British immigration came increasingly from Scotland, Wales, and Ireland, and the indentured servants (who made up half the populations of Pennsylvania, New York, and New Jersey) included thousands of Germans, Scandinavians, Belgians, French, and Swiss. And these were only the voluntary immigrants; the involuntary immigrants—slaves—were from Africa.[*] All in all, historians estimate that in 1763, only 50 percent of the colonial population was English and nearly 20 percent was African American.[6]

You may react skeptically to this description of colonial variety. After all, a mixed group of Europeans and their slaves does not correspond to our modern-day view of diversity. But keep in mind that those northern European Christians (Catholics, Calvinists, and Lutherans) pillaged, raped, and murdered each other on a monumental scale during the Thirty Years' War (1618–1648); one-third of the population of what is now Germany died during the conflict. Near the end of that period, Puritan dissenters from the Church of England fought Royalist defenders of Church and Crown in the English Civil War (1642–1653). Ultimately, the king and the archbishop both lost their heads. (This conflict had a faint echo in Maryland, incidentally, as Catholics, Puritans, and Anglicans for a time engaged in a "minor civil war.")[7] For perhaps the most appalling contradiction of the notion

---

[*]Native Americans, whose numbers had been decimated by wars and disease, were viewed as separate nations altogether.

A religious martyr
An Illinois mob murders Mormon prophet Joseph Smith in 1844. The diversity represented by his religion's polygamist practices was intolerable to Illinois Protestants—who feared a growing population of Mormons voting as a bloc in county elections. Are there examples (presumably less extreme) of conflict over diversity in your community today? Are there limits to diversity? Is there something society simply ought not tolerate?

that northern European Christians were all alike, consider the St. Bartholomew's Day Massacre that began on August 24, 1572. In a forerunner of Hitler's Final Solution, French Catholics wielding swords, axes, and crude firearms moved from door-to-door and farm-to-farm to kill 30,000 French Calvinists.

In the contemporary United States, **diversity** refers to when people of color live among the white majority, when people who follow European traditions coexist with those holding other religious beliefs, and when people with unconventional lifestyles enjoy the same rights and privileges as those who are more traditionally oriented. But diversity is relative to time and place. In 1640 Catholics looked upon Protestants with no more understanding (and possibly with less) than that with which a Muslim looks upon a Jew today. In 1844 Illinois Protestants murdered Mormon leader Joseph Smith, because, among other things, the Mormons practiced polygamy, an intolerable violation of "family values" as understood in that era. And to white Americans in 1900, Greeks and Italians were people of color who threatened the nation's racial purity.

Relative to other countries, and to the times, America has always been diverse. The national motto, imprinted on the United States seal and on several coins, *E Pluribus Unum*—"out of many, one"—explicitly recognizes this diversity. So does the myth that the United States is a melting pot, in which many peoples are melted down to form a new metal tougher than any of the ingredients.[8] The Statue of Liberty, looking over Ellis Island where so many immigrants enter the country, symbolizes this commitment to diversity.

Multiculturalism offers a rival notion of American diversity—a notion not of a "casserole" in which ingredients are baked together but of a "salad bowl" of vibrant colors and tastes. Distinctive ethnic cultures should be preserved and respected by everyone in the larger society, producing a spicier and more flavorful mix. This view is a matter of considerable political controversy today. Critics describe a unique threat, posed by today's social diversity, to the dominant American political culture. Defenders, meanwhile, stoke their fears by attacking the dominant culture as inherently hostile to outsiders. They exaggerate both the cultural uniformity of the American past and the distinctiveness of the present. Both sides betray a troubling lack of historical awareness.

The simple truth is that earlier generations found the immigrants of their eras just as "different" as do contemporary generations. Current debate ignores the difficulty with which earlier waves of immigrants assimilated into American society. In fact, the desire of distinct ethnic and religious groups to preserve some part of their distinctiveness underlies much of the country's history of conflict and has directly shaped the political culture itself.

A NATION OF IMMIGRANTS THEN

The United States did not restrict immigration at the time of its founding, but not everyone was happy about it. One of the most cosmopolitan Americans of the time, Benjamin Franklin, expressed his resentment of Germans in various letters:

> *Why should* Pennsylvania, *founded by the* English, *become a colony of Aliens, who will shortly be so numerous as to Germanize us instead of our Anglifying them, and will never adopt our Language or Customs any more than they can acquire our Complexion? [emphasis in original].*[9]

Despite such misgivings, land was plentiful and labor scarce. The more rapidly the territory could be populated, the more rapidly economic development would follow. Immigration gradually increased, until by mid-century immigrants from England, Ireland, and Germany were arriving in numbers as high as 400,000 per year. Irish immigration became a major political controversy. Some Protestants feared that Catholics would put their allegiance to the Pope above their loyalty to the United States and might even plot to overthrow the government. Cartoonists of the period depicted the Irish as hairy, apelike people. In the 1854 elections, the anti-Catholic Know-Nothing party won 43 seats in the House of Representatives—a number comparable to 80 seats in today's House. (The party's name came from its secret password, "I know nothing about it.")

Immigration increased considerably in the 1860s and continued at a high rate until World War I. In the 1860s and 1870s, the first of an eventual half-million French Canadians crossed the northeastern border of the United States, and several million Scandinavians joined a continuing stream of English, Irish, and Germans (see Figure 4.1). Again, by today's standards such groups may seem alike, but many historians argue that a principal cause of conflict in the late nineteenth century was "ethno-cultural."[10]

FIGURE 4.1

Timeline: Immigration to the United States

The quantity and national origin of immigration to the United States has changed sharply over time.

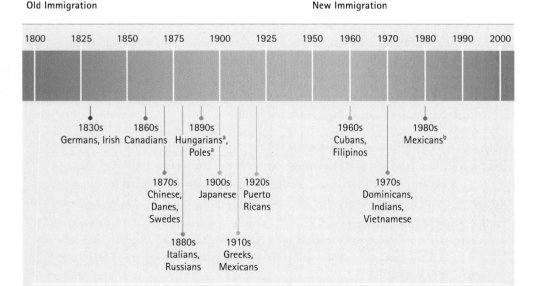

Old Immigration

New Immigration

[a]Estimated because immigrants from the Austro-Hungarian Empire were not separately classified before World War I.

[b]Mexican immigration first reached 100,000 in the 1910s. However, in terms of new immigration, Mexican immigration peaked in the 1980s with over 1.65 million immigrants to the United States.

NOTE: During these decades, immigration by the indicated nationality group first reached 100,000.

SOURCES: Stephanie Bernado, *The Ethnic Almanac* (Garden City, NY: Doubleday, 1981), pp. 22–140; U.S. Immigration and Naturalization Service (www.ins.gov)

Indeed, cultural issues tended to define the major political parties of the era. Native Protestants usually flocked to the Republican party in the Midwest and East, whereas the Democrats sank roots in the immigrant Catholic communities. Politics revolved around such issues as the prohibition of alcohol, public funding of parochial schools, bilingual schools (mostly German, but French in New England), and Sunday blue laws—laws that restricted commercial and recreational activities on Sundays. The German Lutherans were an important swing group in some Midwestern states; they generally voted Republican but swung to the Democrats when conservative Protestants within the Republican party attempted to legislate on cultural issues. In Wisconsin, for example, the Republicans lost only two statewide elections between 1858 and 1890. One came after the party raised liquor license fees, and the second, after they passed a measure requiring English-language instruction in the schools. According to Richard Wayman, "Throughout much of Eastern Wisconsin, German immigrants jealously guarded what they regarded as their right to preserve many of the customs they brought with them from Europe."[11]

Meanwhile, the adoption of the Fourteenth Amendment gave citizenship to African Americans, who constituted about the same proportion of the population in 1865 (one-eighth) as they do today. Because they did not choose to emigrate, but were forcibly abducted from their homelands, the African American experience differs from that of other immigrants. Nevertheless, it is important to point out that between Emancipation and the 1890s, when repression deprived them of fundamental political rights (see Chapter 14), African Americans played an active role in electoral politics.[12]

African Americans were not the only non-Europeans to assume a place in the United States. The Chinese were the first Asians to immigrate on a significant scale. More than 20,000 Chinese participated in the California Gold Rush, which began in 1849.* More than 100,000 Chinese laborers helped build the western links of the transcontinental railroads. At first Americans viewed these newcomers as peaceful, hard-working (and cheap) labor. Soon, however, a backlash set in. The charge against Chinese immigrants was much like the one heard today against other groups: Cheap foreign labor undercuts the American standard of living.[13]

The character of immigration changed beginning in the 1880s, as the country attracted millions of migrants from southern and eastern Europe. The new immigrants again seemed threatening to many "real Americans," a term that had grown to embrace all of northern and western European origin.[14] A best-selling

---

*Only two-thirds of the forty-niners were Americans, and only two-thirds of the Americans were white; large numbers of Cherokee Indians and African Americans panned for gold. On the multicultural character of California after it was annexed to the United States, see Ronald Takaki, *A Different Mirror* (Boston, MA: Little, Brown, 1993), Ch. 8.

book by Madison Grant of the American Museum of Natural History, published in 1916, warned that the United States was receiving "a large and increasing number of the weak, the broken, and the mentally crippled of all races drawn from the lowest stratum of the Mediterranean basin and the Balkans, together with hordes of the wretched, submerged populations of the Polish ghettoes."[15]

Again, the charges have a contemporary ring: Americans of northern European Protestant stock soon would be a minority in their "own" country, overwhelmed by waves of people embracing Catholicism, Judaism, and Eastern Orthodoxy. Such sentiments were by no means limited to a small fringe of the population. Indeed, ethnic stereotypes even appeared within official government documents.[16] No one should ever think that the American melting pot resembled *Mister Rogers' Neighborhood,* a community of harmony and love.

Not all opposition to immigration reflected bigotry. Some opposed further immigration for concrete reasons. Union leaders believed that continued immigration would undercut the bargaining power of workers. And, indeed, American business encouraged immigration as a source of cheap labor. The Progressives, a reformist political movement, wanted to close the borders because immigrants strongly supported what they viewed as corrupt urban political machines.

For many reasons, then, anti-immigration sentiment grew. Congress passed the Chinese Exclusion Act in 1882 to combat the "Yellow Peril." An immigration law adopted in 1917 required a literacy test that favored English speakers.[17] A series of laws passed in the 1920s restricted immigration and gave explicit preference to those from northern and western Europe.[18] The Japanese and other Asians joined the Chinese on the list of groups excluded altogether. By 1930 the era of the open door had ended.* But before the United States closed its doors, more than 35 million people had left hearth and home to "look for America." These immigrants and their children were a large component of the growth of the United States from a country of about 10 million inhabitants in 1820 to one of more than 100 million in 1920.

Restrictions on immigration were part of a general reactionary movement that broke out after World War I. In the "Red Scare," immigrants were persecuted as carriers of Bolshevik, anarchist, and other subversive foreign ideologies. And religious bigotry surged: Anti-Catholic and Anti-Jewish sentiments spawned a second Ku Klux Klan in the 1920s that counted 25 to 30 percent of the adult male Protestant population in its membership.[19] Not surprisingly, the 1928 Democratic presidential nomination of Catholic Al Smith caused a virulent reaction.[20] Several

---

*Mexicans continued to enter the southwestern states to work in American agriculture (joining those who had been incorporated when the United States took the territory from Mexico), and after World War II, Puerto Ricans in significant numbers emigrated to New York City.

bigoted media demagogues were popular during the Great Depression, and discrimination against Catholics and Jews was widespread into the 1930s.

Gradually tensions died down. The cumulative effects of economic troubles, World War II, revulsion against the Holocaust, the Cold War, and generational change led to a reduction in hostility. Ivy League universities dropped informal admissions quotas against Jewish students around 1950, for example. However, the period spanning the early 1930s to the mid-1960s was only a brief interlude between the cultural conflict of yesterday and that of today.

A NATION OF IMMIGRANTS NOW

The Immigration Act of 1965 opened the door to the largest surge of foreigners since the 1890s. This has given rise to the contemporary debates about such issues as bilingual education and the provision of social services to immigrants.

The 1965 legislation abandoned the national-quotas system, which had favored northern Europeans. As a result, immigration from Latin America and the West Indies increased rapidly. In addition, hundreds of thousands of new immigrants from Vietnam, Korea, Cambodia, India, Iran, the Philippines, and other countries became the first numerically significant Asian groups since the Japanese in the early years of the twentieth century (see Figure 4.1). In the 1980s the absolute number of immigrants—about 9 million—was higher than in any previous decade, although lower as a proportion of the population than it had been at the turn of the century. Three million came from Mexico, Central America, and the Caribbean, and nearly as many from Asia. Nearly half a million came from South America and almost 200,000 from Africa. These figures include only legal immigrants; an estimated 5 million people now live in the United States illegally.[21]

As a result of this newest wave of immigration, by 1995 the proportion of the population of European origin had dropped to about three-quarters, and it is projected to fall to less than two-thirds in the next two decades. Whites of European origin are already a minority in California and in many large cities.

THE NEW IMMIGRATION

Immigration is once again a political issue. In 1994 California voters overwhelmingly passed Proposition 187, an initiative that denied state services to illegal immigrants and their children (see the Election Connection, "California's Proposition 187"). Support for the measure was high even in counties where very few immigrants lived.[22] And from 1995 to 1996, the question of eligibility for governmental services such as welfare was a matter of intense controversy at the national level. Much of this contemporary debate over immigration would sound very familiar to Americans of the early 1900s. Does providing services to immigrants impose a burden on native citizens? Do immigrants take jobs from native workers and drive native shopkeepers out of business?

Such fears are not new, but that does not mean they are totally groundless. There are four problems associated with immigration today that are somewhat different from those of the past. First, in contrast to earlier periods in American history, immigrants are not entering an economy hungry for unskilled labor. There is no exploding railroad industry to absorb today's immigrants as it absorbed the Irish and the Chinese. There is no expanding steel industry sending representatives to southern and eastern Europe to recruit laborers. The American economy is moving away from manufacturing to a globally integrated service and information economy. Many Americans, especially those lacking skills, face severe difficulties in the transition. Research indicates that competition from immigrants undercuts the wages of low-skilled Americans who are already struggling to make ends meet.[23]

Second, levels of government do not share the burdens and benefits of immigration equally.[24] Studies show that immigrants strengthen the national economy. They pay nearly as much in taxes as they consume in government services. But most of the taxes paid by immigrants are federal income and social security taxes. This revenue does not go directly to the states and cities responsible for providing social services to new migrants. Yet during the 1980s, more than 75 percent of new immigrants went to six states: California, New York, Texas, Florida, New Jersey, and Illinois. This disparity focuses the costs of immigration much more narrowly than the benefits. Heavy immigration forces local and state governments to cut services, raise taxes, and beg for money from higher levels of government, options that elected officials naturally view as unpleasant.

Third, both the United States and the world face a looming environmental crisis, one tied to an expanding population. The fertilizers and pesticides that help grow food contaminate water used for drinking or for recreation. Chemicals needed to produce consumer goods, and fuels used to transport both people and products, all cause health problems. Trees are cut down and unpopulated areas devastated to make room for housing developments and roads. Isolated locales once treasured for vacations, for outdoor sports, or just for their natural beauty may not be so isolated any more. Providing utilities like energy or water sometimes strains communities, as does disposing of garbage and other wastes.

All of these concerns worsen as the population increases, and immigrants account for half of the country's population growth. Obviously, many sorts of policies can address the declining quality of life associated with overcrowding, and shifts in population from one country to another may not worsen global problems. But concern with the environment does prompt many to question the virtue of admitting even more people from other countries.[25]

ELECTION CONNECTION

California's Proposition 187

California is on the cutting edge of American social and economic trends. Perhaps for that reason political controversies often surface there first. Such was the case with the immigration issue in 1994. Almost half of the nation's 4 to 5 million illegal immigrants live in California. Taxpayer resentment of the burden of providing services (education, Medicaid, welfare, and police) interacted with ethnic antagonisms and an economic slowdown to create a backlash in the form of Proposition 187. This initiative would have denied state and local services to illegal immigrants and their children and would have instructed all government employees, including teachers, to report suspected illegal immigrants to immigration authorities. Although opponents of the measure charged that it was unconstitutional, and many proponents agreed, both sides believed it would send an important signal.

During the summer, incumbent Republican Governor Pete Wilson was trailing Democratic challenger Kathleen Brown by 20 points in the polls, but Wilson was an experienced politician with a good instinct for important issues. He embraced Proposition 187 and led the campaign for its adoption. Brown opposed it. Immigration was not the only issue in the campaign, and Brown was widely viewed as a poor campaigner; but by mid-October Wilson transformed his double-digit deficit in the polls into a double-digit lead. In the Republican sweep a few weeks later, he thrashed Brown 55 percent to 40 percent.

Wilson's attempt to parlay his big victory into the Republican presidential nomination failed, and as expected, the courts eventually overturned Proposition 187's provisions. But the campaign demonstrated the political importance of the immigration issue. In 1995 the new Republican Congress proposed legislation to discourage illegal immigration and restrict the benefits that legal immigrants could receive (although the version ultimately signed in 1996 did not include most of the provisions dealing with legal immigrants).[a]

What do you think?

- Should government actively check the citizenship status of people, which raises privacy concerns?

- Should people not legally in the country automatically be deported?

- Why might a nation provide social services to a population that is not supposed to be within its borders?

- How do we treat the children of illegal immigrants, who are citizens if they are born here?

[a]Dan Carney, "As White House Calls Shots, Illegal Alien Bill Clears," *Congressional Quarterly Weekly Report* (October 5, 1996): 2864–2866.

Finally, whereas late-nineteenth-century law barred a person "likely to become a public charge," the immigration law adopted in 1965 gives preference to those with relatives already in the country. Two-thirds of all immigrants today are relatives of those already present. In consequence, a higher proportion of dependent persons—especially older people—have been admitted in recent years than in previous eras.[26] Current U.S. immigration policy admits fewer taxpayers and more people in need of services than the law that gave first preference to productive workers. Even if immigrants as a group pay as much in taxes as they consume in services, many American taxpayers ask why they should admit *anyone* likely to be a drain on resources.

These are all material explanations for opposition to immigration. Over and above economic costs, however, many opponents of immigration regard it as a threat to the American political culture. They believe that people who speak different languages, believe in different religions, and practice different customs could threaten American unity. They fear a divided society, in which groups retain their own narrow identities and fight each other for power and influence. They urge the United States to close the door before too much *pluribus* destroys the *unum*.[27] To understand these fears, however, we need to know precisely what these Americans seek to defend.

PHILOSOPHICAL UNITY

From the French visitor Alexis de Tocqueville in the 1830s to the Swede Gunnar Myrdal in the 1940s, visitors have claimed that Americans agree on a common core of values defining what it is to be American. These beliefs usually are described as "individualist," and the political culture they produce is generally referred to as a "liberal" one.[28]

Classical **liberalism** emerged in Europe after medieval thought disintegrated in the religious wars of the seventeenth century. Whereas earlier philosophies viewed human nature as sinful, requiring authority to keep it in check, liberalism empowered the individual. Authority does not come from God, according to liberal thinkers like Locke and Rousseau, but is derived from a "social contract" conferring privileges and duties on everyone, both rulers and ruled.

The social contract preserves individual rights that are more fundamental than the hereditary privilege of the nobility or the religious privilege of the clergy. Having certain inviolable rights is necessary because liberal thinkers view altruistic sentiments—that is, the desire to "do good"—as too weak to provide a reliable basis for government. Human beings are willing to oppress (or at least mistreat) others if allowed, so rights are a necessary protection.[29]

Instead of viewing individuals as the product of political society, a view that goes back to the Greeks, liberalism makes society the product of individuals. You might wonder what difference this makes. Consider Democratic President John F. Kennedy's famous exhortation: "Ask not what your country can do for you; ask what you can do for your country." Classical liberals shudder at these words. If society is nothing more than a collection of individuals, then any sacrifice for the "greater good" is simply something taken away from one person and given to another.[30]

What kind of political system follows from such a philosophy? A small government, one that treats everyone equally under the law, limited by individual rights—rights to religious exercise, to free expression, and to their own property. Governments in such a system are merely instrumental, not ends or values in themselves. The political system exists to serve individuals, and may be retained or jettisoned depending upon how well it meets these obligations.

The preceding paragraph should have a familiar ring, for the ideas are the basis of America's political system. Indeed, the second paragraph of the Declaration of Independence is little more than a summary of these ideals: political equality, rights, and limited and instrumental government. The Constitution and its Bill of Rights form an elaborate statement of the limits under which government should operate. For this reason, the American constitutional tradition often is called a liberal tradition.

Do not confuse liberal *philosophy* with liberal *politics,* however. The classical meaning of the term *liberal* is more akin to the contemporary term *libertarian,* which signifies skepticism of government interference in all spheres of life. By contrast, these days a "liberal" politician is one who supports higher taxes and more generous governmental programs. These different meanings naturally create confusion; for example, a classical liberal like Nobel Prize–winning economist Milton Friedman is often called a "conservative." What unites both sorts of liberals is a concern for freedom in the broader sense; they agree liberty is a good thing but differ on whether the welfare state promotes or hinders it.

Writers may exaggerate America's philosophical consensus. Many refer to the "American creed" or the "American ethos." Terms like these suggest a more unified and well-defined set of beliefs than actually exists. Some scholars argue that writers in the liberal tradition have downplayed the importance of a competing tradition, called **civic republicanism,** that existed at the time of the Revolution.[31] Civic republicanism placed more emphasis on virtue and on the welfare of the community than on individual rights. Over time it lost ground to liberalism, but the tradition certainly has not disappeared—as indicated by the positive response given to President Kennedy's message of self-denial.[32] Modern advocates use the label "communitarian."[33]

Other critics point out that the ideals exalted in the liberal tradition often did not extend very far in practice.[34] American settlers destroyed Native American tribes, and African Americans did not enjoy equal rights until a century after the Civil War. Full rights and privileges did not extend to women until even later, and the rights of other minority groups, such as homosexuals, remain matters of political controversy today.

We agree that there has been a tendency to exaggerate the scope, unity, and inclusiveness of the "American consensus." But even granting these reservations, there is plenty of evidence that Americans agree to certain basic liberal principles that set them apart from the citizens of other democracies.

AMERICAN INDIVIDUALISM

Perhaps the most striking difference between Americans and people elsewhere lies in the emphasis Americans place on individual responsibility. Figure 4.2 reports the results of a survey conducted in 14 democracies that asked respondents whether they "completely agree" that "It is the responsibility of the state

FIGURE 4.2

Americans emphasize individual responsibility much more than people elsewhere

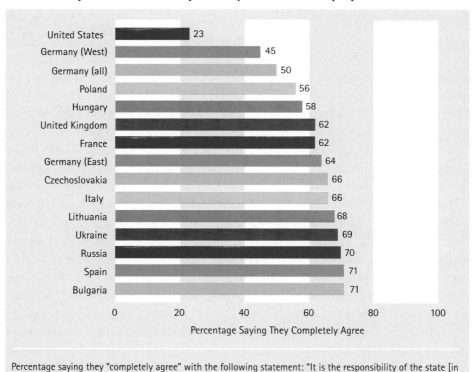

Percentage saying they "completely agree" with the following statement: "It is the responsibility of the state [in the United States, "the government"] to take care of very poor people who can't take care of themselves."

SOURCE: Everett Carll Ladd, *The American Ideology* (Storrs, CT: The Roper Center, 1994), p. 79.

FIGURE 4.3

Americans are far less supportive of government actions to reduce economic inequality than people elsewhere

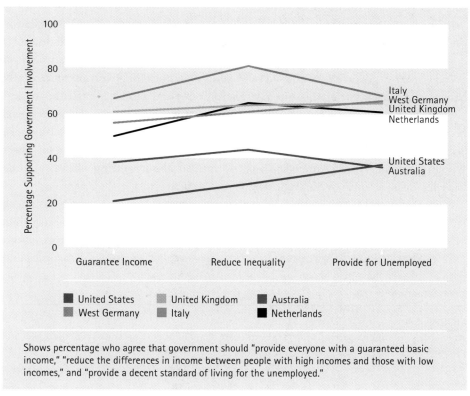

Shows percentage who agree that government should "provide everyone with a guaranteed basic income," "reduce the differences in income between people with high incomes and those with low incomes," and "provide a decent standard of living for the unemployed."

SOURCE: Ladd, *The American Ideology*, p. 75.

('government' in the United States) to take care of very poor people who can't take care of themselves." Note that less than a quarter of the American respondents opted for governmental responsibility, a proportion that is only half as large as that in the next closest country (Germany).

Another survey of six long-established Western democracies found Americans to be similarly uniform in their belief that individuals are responsible for their own welfare. As shown in Figure 4.3, less than a quarter of Americans supported a government-guaranteed income, disagreeing with majorities of Germans, British, Italians, and Dutch. Fewer than one in three Americans rejected the notion that government should reduce income inequality. And little more than one-third of Americans believed that the government should guarantee a decent standard of living for the unemployed, compared to an average of two-thirds in the four European democracies. Interestingly, Australia seems to occupy a middle position between the individual responsibility favored by Americans and the governmental responsibility favored by Europeans. Australia, too, is a society of immigrants.

The American preference for individual responsibility is not simply stinginess. Rather, Americans are suspicious of government. They fear its power and doubt its competence. In Samuel Huntington's view, "the distinctive aspect of the American creed is its anti-government character."[35] People skeptical of government naturally have qualms about letting the state take their money and hand it out to others.

Anyway, Americans believe that individual responsibility works. Americans consider hard work the key to success; perseverance pays off. People elsewhere are less likely to put much faith in personal effort. As a consequence, an overwhelming majority of Americans are optimistic about getting ahead—unlike those elsewhere, even in Australia (see Figure 4.4).

One would think that those at the bottom of the economic ladder would be far less optimistic than those at the top. In fact, the American belief in individual achievement bears little relation to one's personal success. As shown in Figure 4.5, even the poorest Americans reject a government-guaranteed income, and

FIGURE 4.4

Americans are much more optimistic about their chances of getting ahead than people elsewhere

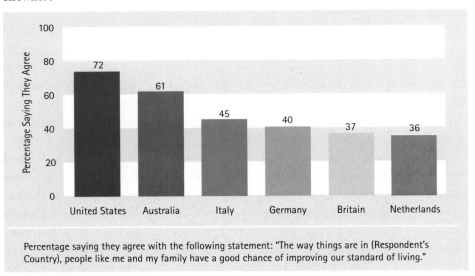

Percentage saying they agree with the following statement: "The way things are in (Respondent's Country), people like me and my family have a good chance of improving our standard of living."

SOURCE: Ladd, *The American Ideology*, p. 76.

FIGURE 4.5

Even less-affluent Americans share the individualistic values of the larger society

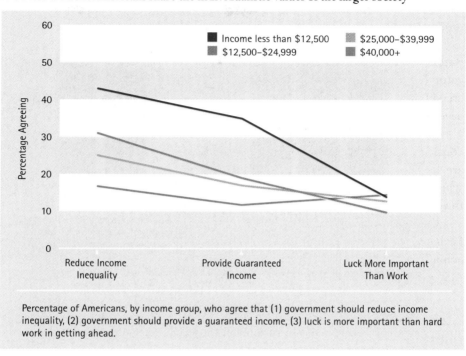

Percentage of Americans, by income group, who agree that (1) government should reduce income inequality, (2) government should provide a guaranteed income, (3) luck is more important than hard work in getting ahead.

SOURCE: Ladd, *The American Ideology*, p. 68.

only the very poorest feel that the government should reduce income differences. There is no relationship between income and belief in hard work: Four-fifths of the poorest Americans downplay the importance of luck, just as do four-fifths of the most affluent.

Other studies offer similar results. They reveal that poor Americans are as likely as others to embrace the "work ethic" and as likely to take personal responsibility for their condition.[36] The poor dislike the progressive income tax almost as much as the rich.[37] And perhaps the most powerful illustration of American individualism lies in the attitudes of minorities. African Americans and Latinos clearly share in the American Dream less often than whites do. On average they earn less, work in less prestigious occupations, and suffer discrimination in many forms. It comes as no surprise, then, that they are a bit less likely than whites to embrace the American Dream. But it does come as a surprise that they embrace it as often as they do. Black and Latino Americans are quite similar to white

FIGURE 4.6

Even racial and ethnic minorities share the individualistic values of the larger society

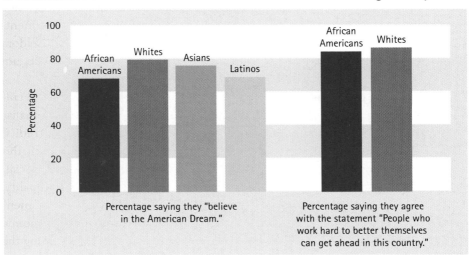

SOURCE: Adapted from data reported in "People, Opinions and Polls: An American Dilemma (Part II)," *The Public Perspective* (February/March 1996): 19–35.

Americans (see Figure 4.6). In sum, even those who face an extra burden in the American social order still support its basic premises.[38]

THE TENSION BETWEEN INDIVIDUALISM AND EQUALITY

Liberal philosophy attaches great importance to equality, and writers in the liberal tradition typically mention it just after liberty. Indeed, they thought liberty and equality reinforce each other. A free people would be a hard-working people and achieve economic success. An independent, economically secure middle class would safeguard society from threats to liberty.

Early in American history liberty and equality probably did go together. Alexis de Tocqueville and other early nineteenth-century visitors were struck by the extent of social and economic equality in the United States. But economic development weakened the association between liberty and equality. The Industrial Revolution produced great concentrations of private wealth. Under such conditions, liberty and equality became detached. The only way to stop free people from working to collect profit is to inhibit their ability to compete, limit their production, or take away their earnings.

Great inequalities now exist in the United States. The income distribution changed little during the past six decades; earlier improvements have disappeared since the early 1970s.[39] Naturally, some Americans have become disillusioned with a political system that can tolerate such inequalities. But reform movements typically focus on curbing the worst abuses of corporate power; they seldom attack the foundations of the economic system. Americans generally do not demand that government eliminate or even sharply reduce inequalities.

The explanation of this apparent inconsistency is that American political culture only supports a certain kind of equality. Liberalism emphasizes equality before the law; one person has the same rights as another, regardless of heredity, religious faith, or connections with public officials. As is consistent with this philosophical heritage, Americans display a strong commitment to legal, social, and political equality. But Americans are not committed to economic equality. Rather, they agree with Madison, who thought "diversity in the faculties of men" would inevitably produce inequalities.[40] Many Americans regard economic inequality as fair, and celebrate entrepreneurs who become rich by providing the nation with products or services it wants to buy.

Today it is customary to talk about this distinction in terms of the difference between **equality of opportunity** and **equality of results.** Americans strongly support equality of opportunity. Everyone should have a fair chance. Attempts to bring about equality of results, by contrast, may involve rewarding people who are undeserving. Intelligence and hard work should bring special rewards.

Affirmative action for minorities and women is controversial precisely because it falls between these two sorts of equality. Americans favor affirmative action when survey questions are clear that equal opportunity is the goal: Ninety-four percent agree that "Our society should do what is necessary to make sure that everyone has an equal opportunity to succeed." Seventy-nine percent agree that "After years of discrimination, it is only fair to set up special programs to make sure that women and minorities are given every chance to have equal opportunities in employment and education."

But Americans just as strongly oppose affirmative action when the survey questions indicate that equality of outcome is the goal: Eighty-six percent do not think "blacks and other minorities should receive preference in college admissions to make up for past inequalities." Eighty percent do not think "blacks and other minorities should receive preference in hiring to make up for past inequalities."[41]

As far as most Americans are concerned, equality of opportunity should be sufficient. The rest is up to the individual. This belief also shows up in government policy. As critics have pointed out, the United States spends a smaller proportion of its national income on social welfare than most other democracies do. But the United States historically has spent a larger proportion of its national income on education than other democracies have. Education is a means by which individuals improve their skills and make themselves useful. That idea resonates with Americans.[42] Direct government assistance, in contrast, looks like a handout. Americans are uncomfortable with that idea.

RELIGION AND INDIVIDUALISM: CONTRADICTION OR COMPLEMENT?

Some democracies have an established church, an official religion that may be subsidized by the government. The Anglican Church is the established church in Great Britain, the Catholic Church in Italy, the Lutheran Church in Norway, and the Eastern Orthodox Church in Greece. Yet as Figure 4.7 shows, even in countries with established churches, citizens are not so involved with religion as

FIGURE 4.7
Americans are far more involved with religion than people elsewhere

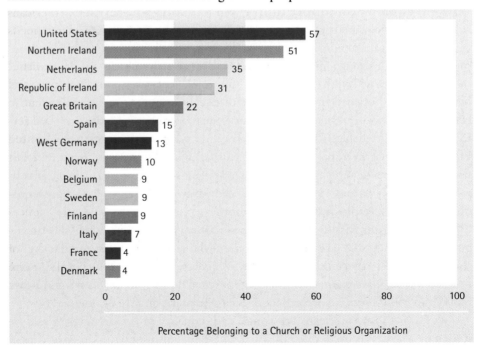

Percentage Belonging to a Church or Religious Organization

SOURCE: Ladd, *The American Ideology*, p. 71.

Americans are. Americans are more likely to believe in God, to attend religious services, and to report that religion plays an important role in their lives. Some observers find American religiosity difficult to square with the notion of a liberal creed. How can so many individualists join organizations oriented toward identifying a collective moral code?

People seeking religious freedom carried out much of the original settlement of the United States. These deeply religious people were trying to escape oppression by the established churches of Europe. Of course, they had no problem with established religion in principle, as long as it was *theirs.* The Congregational Church, for example, was the established church of Connecticut until 1818 and of Massachusetts until 1833.* The agreement to maintain a "wall between church and state" only emerged as a strategy to help so many different religions get along in one nation.[43]

Throughout history, religiously motivated Americans have attempted to use government to change society. They have tried to use laws to encourage (and perhaps coerce) people into "moral behavior." Thus, at various times and places, laws have restricted recreational activities on Sundays, prohibited people from drinking, and censored what people could read or watch. And Americans tend to evaluate their politicians in relatively moralistic terms.[44] A majority of Americans report that they will not vote for an otherwise-qualified candidate who happens to be an atheist.[45]

The religious roots of the United States thus may explain the "moralistic" nature of American politics. But is the influence of the Puritans, Quakers, and others who landed on American shores more than 300 years ago still present in the habits of contemporary Americans? Are the religious roots of the original settlers sufficient to explain the persistence of religious sentiment in the United States? The moral impulse seems too strong to be nothing more than habits left over from centuries before. After all, the nation organized in reaction against religious privilege, emphasizes individual autonomy, and celebrates personal achievement. Presumably it would have developed a more worldly personality unless religion served some modern function.

One explanation emphasizes diversity—America's incredible number of religions, from mainstream denominations to tiny sects. If a person rejects one religion, there are numerous alternatives, and exceptionally hard-to-please

---

*The constitutional prohibition of the establishment of religion originally applied only to the federal government, and even today archaic provisions in some state constitutions require public officials to believe in a deity. See "In (Blank) We Trust," *Economist* (October 12, 1996): 32.

worshipers can always start their own. This range of options makes it easy to find a comfortable match, whereas citizens typically have a much smaller range of choices in other countries.

A religious institution supported by government subsidy need not cater to its membership; the state forces them to pay for the church either way. By contrast, a church that must compete to retain members and attract their contributions must keep followers happy. American clergy are motivated to adapt their "product" to the changing interests and values of their members and to provide services and auxiliary activities (youth clubs, sports clubs, and even singles clubs) that members value. Americans may be more involved with religion than people in other countries because, stimulated by the sort of competition that liberalism demands, American churches offer them more reasons to be.

Another intriguing explanation of the persistence of religiosity in the United States has been proposed by Robert Booth Fowler, a scholar who argues that the liberal tradition and religiosity do not conflict. He maintains, in fact, that just the opposite is true—the liberal tradition creates a deep need for religion. People steeped in the liberal tradition jealously guard their rights and hold themselves personally responsible for their successes and failures. They create a society characterized by social mobility and rapid change. Fowler suggests that many people find life in such a society precarious, or at least somewhat lonely:

> *Religion has aided liberalism by being a* refuge *from liberalism. . . . [I]t provides an escape from liberal culture, a place of comfort where individualism, competition, this-worldly pragmatism, and relentless rationalism do not hold sway. In a liberal country with liberal citizens, religion is a place where one can come home . . . and then emerge refreshed for the battles of life in the liberal world.*[46]

Thus, Fowler sees religion as filling a gap in American lives. In contrast, citizens of more collectivist democracies are already part of something larger than themselves. They already have a higher authority, the state, to help order their lives. They may have less need for a religious dimension.

Fowler's theory would help explain the great religious "awakenings" that periodically wash over the United States. According to historians, the first such awakening occurred in the colonies in the 1730s and 1740s. The second started around 1800 and continued into Jackson's presidency (1828–1836). The third began in the 1890s and lasted about two decades. Some believe that the United States is now in a fourth awakening. These religious awakenings typically precede periods of reform, and so may reflect a growing gap between the ideals Americans hold dear and the conditions that individualism creates.[47]

Such arguments are plausible enough: Competition creates material prosperity, but some people eventually begin to wonder whether there is something more to life than money. Others are appalled by the self-serving behavior necessary to succeed. Thus people may turn to religion for different reasons: as an avenue to personal satisfaction or as a means of restraining the behavior of others. The resurgence of evangelical Protestantism in the 1980s may have been in part a reaction to the excesses of the 1960s, a reaction that occurred when the baby boomers— the "me generation"—came of age.

WHY A LIBERAL POLITICAL CULTURE?

We now return to the question posed at the start of the chapter. How can we explain the apparent contradiction: a population that is strikingly diverse in its ethnic, racial, and religious makeup but surprisingly uniform in the beliefs and values that constitute its political culture? How has American political culture survived waves of immigrants bred in different social environments? Both traditional and newer explanations of the American commitment to individualism help answer that question.

TRADITIONAL EXPLANATIONS OF AMERICAN INDIVIDUALISM

Traditional explanations assume that ideas interact with social conditions. As suggested by writers like Alexis de Tocqueville and Louis Hartz, the early settlers brought with them liberal ideas, and in contrast to the established social structure of Europe, they found nothing in the United States to dispute such ideas. Hartz, especially, emphasizes the lack of a feudal tradition in the United States. There was no hereditary aristocracy or established church to provide the basis for the kind of conservative and clerical viewpoints that persist even today in Europe. Nor was there an oppressed peasant class that might form the basis for radical agrarian parties.

Perhaps as important as what the United States lacked, however, is what it had. In particular, it had a great deal of land. North America was a sparsely populated continent over which the United States steadily expanded.[48] Some historians suggest that the frontier operated like a social safety valve: Rather than revolt against intolerable conditions (the only option in the settled countries of Europe), struggling citizens found it easier to pack up their belongings, move west, and start again.

A plentiful supply of land and a scarcity of labor meant that ambitious individuals could and did succeed. The individualistic values the early settlers brought with them were reinforced by conditions in the new country. And with few competing values reinforced by the nation's history, a liberal political order and a market economy thrived. As Hartz comments,

> *where the aristocracies, peasantries, and proletariats of Europe are missing, where virtually everyone . . . has the mentality of an independent entrepreneur, two national impulses are bound to make themselves felt: the impulse toward democracy and the impulse toward capitalism.*[49]

Generations of radical scholars have plaintively asked, "Why no socialism in America?"[50] The simplest answer is that Americans never saw much need for it. Why risk trying to change the political system, as a strategy for personal improvement, when more direct methods are readily available? Under the conditions that prevailed, individual effort usually was enough to provide an acceptable life for most people.

Still, questions remain. The frontier closed more than a century ago, and labor shortages have not been of much concern for more than half a century. So even if social conditions in the nineteenth century reinforced the beliefs and values of the early settlers, of what relevance is that today? Moreover, the millions of immigrants who arrived after the Civil War were not from liberal societies. Most of them came from authoritarian states with established churches, and most had lived their lives in communal peasant societies that *did* have feudal traditions. What is the basis for *their* adherence to the individualist values of the liberal tradition?

One simple explanation might be that the culture perpetuates itself through **political socialization.** That is, children may receive liberal values in the family and then find them reinforced in schools, churches, and other organizations. Socialization may perpetuate a consensus established in the eighteenth century, a consensus so dominant that it was able to assimilate tens of millions of immigrants who arrived a century and more later.

Many find such an explanation insufficient, however. One of the principal means by which immigrants were integrated into American society was through the efforts of political parties, particularly the urban machines that we discuss in Chapter 8. The urban machines were not the embodiment of liberal, individualist values. On the contrary, the machines were something of an anomaly in the larger American political culture. They were clannish, with an emphasis on obedience and loyalty rather than on independence. It is unlikely that such a political social-ization taught immigrants to value liberal ideals.

Newer explanations

More recent explanations for survival of the liberal tradition focus on American institutions. Political scientist Sven Steinmo argues that scholars have misunder-stood the liberal tradition. Rather than liberal ideas shaping American govern-ment and politics, Steinmo argues the opposite—that the government of the United States creates and reinforces the ideas.[51] Specifically, he argues that American government is so fragmented and decentralized that it can rarely act in a positive way to improve society. Often it is "gridlocked," or unable to act—and when it does act, it often does so via the exchange of political favors among spe-cial interests. In consequence, successive generations of Americans learn the same basic lesson: Look to yourself because you cannot look to government, and best keep government limited because it will usually act against the public interest.

Given their institutions, Americans would have learned this lesson whether they were originally individualists or not, and new waves of immigrants learn what the natives already know. Steinmo's argument reminds us that, once estab-lished, institutions that originally *reflected* particular beliefs and values may come to *reinforce* those beliefs and values. Material conditions in the United States today may be far different from those of the nineteenth century, but political institu-tions are similar and work to preserve the ideas that gave rise to them.

It is even possible that immigrants are healthy for the liberal tradition. Rather than posing a threat to American traditions, as many feared, the flow of diverse peoples to America may have reinforced and strengthened American tra-ditions. How could that be the case? The answer lies in what statisticians refer to as *self-selection*. With the tragic exception of African Americans, immigrants came to the United States voluntarily. It is possible that the sort of person most likely to leave family, friends, and village behind is exactly the sort of person most likely to reinforce the liberal tradition.

Remember that through most of history immigration was not a matter of tak-ing a train to Dublin, Frankfurt, or Rome and catching a flight to New York. Before the Civil War the journey usually took months, as immigrants walked to a port and then suffered through a long journey below deck on a sailing ship. Even after the Civil War, when the steamship shortened the ocean voyage and the rail-road shortened the land journey, the trip still took weeks. Many (if not most) of the people who booked passage knew that they would never see their relatives or their homes again.[52] What kind of people made such a decision?

In all probability the people who migrated already were—relative to their own societies—unusually individualistic. They were more willing to leave the communal order of Europe, more ambitious, more willing to run risks in the hope of bettering themselves. In Hartz's words, they were more likely to possess "the spirit which repudiated peasantry and tenantry."[53] Bigoted as it was, even the Immigration Commission in 1911 recognized that "emigrating to a strange and distant country, although less of an undertaking than formerly, is still a serious and relatively difficult matter, requiring a degree of courage and resourcefulness not possessed by weaklings of any class."[54] In short, although they had never heard of the liberal tradition, immigrants already possessed much of its spirit.

If so, immigration and the resulting diversity never were a threat to American values. On the contrary, successive waves of immigrants rejuvenated those values. People who were willing to endure hardships, eager to work hard, and convinced that they could have a better life were scarcely the kind who would support an oppressive government or religion. Rather, whatever their skills or education, the immigrants included many of the kind of ambitious individuals who already resided in the United States.

True, many came to the United States when they were pushed off their land, when crops failed, or when work was nowhere to be found. Emigration under such circumstances may not seem to have occurred by choice. Nevertheless, not everyone in poor or troubled countries chose to try life in the United States. Many chose to remain in their homelands, enduring the miserable conditions in which they found themselves. The few who did emigrate, therefore, still exercised a politically meaningful choice. And those who felt least at home in the United States probably were disproportionately represented among the third of all immigrants who eventually returned to their home countries.

We believe that this earlier pattern continues to hold. Today's immigrants have left their homes and families in Asia, Africa, and South America. They have endured hardships to come to a new land with a different culture and language. In some extreme cases they have risked life and limb to emigrate, as with the boat people of southeast Asia who braved pirates, sharks, and storms, and with the Cubans who swam from rafts to the Florida coast. Such people display a kind of individual initiative that can fairly be considered "American," regardless of their nationality!

During the 1994 battle over California's Proposition 187, which would have denied government services to illegal immigrants and their children, two prominent Republicans, William Bennett and Jack Kemp, raised eyebrows by opposing the initiative publicly.[55] Similarly, in 1996 Rudolph Giuliani, the Republican mayor of New York, made news by denouncing congressional attempts to limit immigrant eligibility for welfare and other governmental services.[56] In the 2000 presidential campaign, George W. Bush appealed directly for support in immigrant communities. The positions of these politicians conflicted with the popular image that Republicans are unsympathetic to the disadvantaged. Their statements and behavior also seemed to run counter to their partisan self-interest, since minority group members typically support Democrats.

These Republicans appeared to be betting that the earlier pattern of American history will continue in the future. They were betting that the Mexican laborers, Korean grocers, and Middle Eastern service station operators are today's successors to the Irish laborers, Italian grocers, and Jewish shopkeepers of generations past. They were betting that although ethnic activists often ally with the Democratic party, most members of those ethnic groups are focused more on economics than on politics. Over time, such people become middle-class Americans concerned about their tax rates, their schools, and their property values—and willing to consider Republican appeals.

There is some evidence that they made a good gamble. On the basis of extensive surveys—intended to gauge patriotism, trust in government, tolerance, and economic individualism—political scientist Rodolfo de la Garza reports that Puerto Ricans who express lower support for these values tend to be those who are foreign born and Spanish dominant. As they and their mainland-born children learn English, their support for these values becomes indistinguishable from that of Anglos who find themselves in similar socioeconomic conditions.[57]

De la Garza's studies of Mexican immigrants reach very similar conclusions.[58] So does research on other ethnic groups. As shown in Figure 4.8, a 1995 Gallup survey found that immigrants—even those who have been in the country ten years or less—are virtually indistinguishable from native-born Americans, both in their beliefs about economic opportunity and in their general attitudes toward assimilation.[59] Demographic data suggest similar conclusions. One widely noted study reports that, judging on the basis of standard measures of assimilation (citizenship, home ownership, English acquisition, and intermarriage), today's immigrants "overwhelmingly do what immigrants have always done: slowly, often painfully, but quite assuredly, embrace the language, cultural norms and loyalties of America."[60] Other studies suggest that the use of English as a principal language is occurring *more* rapidly among the children of today's immigrants than among children of past immigrants.[61]

In sum, the evidence is mounting that American society is evolving along a path that does not support either the fears of diversity's opponents or the claims of novelty and uniqueness made by its proponents. Ethnic, racial, and religious diversity can coexist with agreement on basic values. On balance, today's diversity is more likely to reinforce than to undermine the American political culture.

FIGURE 4.8

Impressions, immigrants' beliefs about American culture, are strikingly similar to those of the native-born

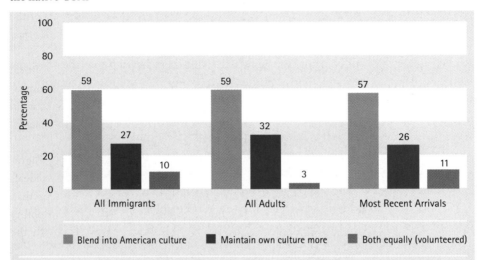

Question: Which do you think is better for the United States: To encourage immigrants to blend into American culture by giving up some important aspects of their own culture, or to encourage immigrants to maintain their own culture more strongly, even if that means they do not blend in as well?

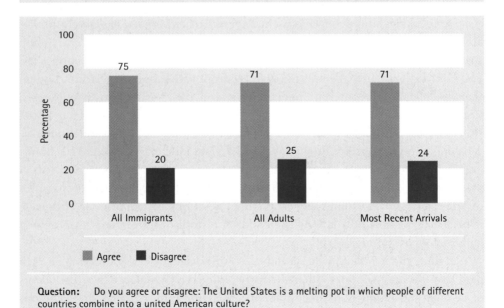

Question: Do you agree or disagree: The United States is a melting pot in which people of different countries combine into a united American culture?

SOURCE: Gallup survey reported in *The Public Perspective* (August/September 1995): 15.

CHAPTER SUMMARY

For more than two centuries the United States has been a study in contrasts. On the one hand, this country always has been diverse socially, containing a wider array of ethnic and religious groups than most other lands. On the other hand, the diverse citizenry of the United States has long shown a higher level of agreement on fundamental principles than is found in other democracies.

America's fundamental political principles grew out of a classical liberal political philosophy stressing the rights and liberties of individuals, while giving much less emphasis to their duties and obligations to the community. Today, that philosophy is reflected in a greater emphasis on individual responsibility and hard work, as well as greater suspicion of government, than is found in other countries.

Throughout American history, many native-born citizens have feared that immigration threatened the distinctly American political culture. Yet American political ideals have proved surprisingly resilient. In all likelihood, immigrants reinforce rather than weaken the spirit of individualism in the United States. The very fact of their mobility suggests that they possess an ambitious, individualistic outlook compatible with the American political culture.

KEY TERMS

civic republicanism, p. 105

diversity, p. 96

equality of opportunity, p. 111

equality of results, p. 111

liberalism, p. 104

multiculturalism, p. 97

political culture, p. 94

political socialization, p. 116

SUGGESTED READINGS

Borjas, George. *Heaven's Door: Immigration Policy and the American Economy.* Princeton, NJ: Princeton University Press, 1999. Argues that immigration has hurt the poorest native-born workers, especially African Americans. Calls for restricting immigration and limiting it to better educated and more highly skilled people.

Erie, Steven. *Rainbow's End: Irish-Americans and the Dilemma of Urban Machine Politics, 1849–1985.* Berkeley, CA: University of California Press, 1988. Interesting account of the Irish urban machines that played an important role in American political history.

Hartz, Louis. *The Liberal Tradition in America.* New York: Harcourt, 1955. A classic, if impenetrable, discussion of the liberal tradition that argues the absence of feudalism allowed liberal ideas to spread without resistance in the United States.

Kleppner, Paul. *The Cross of Culture.* New York: Free Press, 1970. This example of the "ethno-cultural" school of political history provides a detailed account of political conflict in the Midwest from the rise of the Republican party to the end of the nineteenth century.

ON THE WEB

Immigration and Naturalization Service
www.ins.usdoj.gov
This comprehensive site, maintained by the U.S. Department of Justice, covers all facets of immigration in the United States. It provides statistical reports on the history of immigration to the United States, as well as information on the current guidelines for becoming an American citizen.

Academic Information: Religion Gateway
www.academicinfo.net/ religindex.html
An annotated directory of Internet resources for the academic study of religion, this site is supported and maintained by a graduate of the University of Washington's Comparative Religion program.

Lipset, Seymour Martin. *American Exceptionalism.* New York: Norton, 1996. The latest work on the American political culture by an eminent senior scholar who has spent much of his career studying it.

Menendez, Albert. *Religion at the Polls.* Philadelphia: Westminster Press, 1977. Survey of the association between religion and voting since the founding of the country.

Mills, Nicolaus, ed. *Arguing Immigration: Are New Immigrants a Wealth of Diversity … Or a Crushing Burden?* New York: Simon & Schuster, 1994. This collection of essays provides a good overview of the contemporary debate.

Schlesinger, Arthur, Jr. *The Disuniting of America.* Knoxville, TN: Whittle, 1991. An eminent senior historian complains about the contemporary influence of multiculturalism.

5

PUBLIC OPINION

After months of wrangling over oil, territorial boundaries, and war debts, the nations of Iraq and Kuwait descended into armed conflict on August 2, 1990. Iraqi troops surged across the Kuwaiti border, and subjugated that small state in a single day.[1]

Such open aggression in the Middle East posed a difficult challenge for Republican President George H. W. Bush, who had a reputation for foreign-policy expertise to uphold. Bush reacted without hesitation. He condemned the invasion in the strongest possible terms and on November 29 secured a United Nations (UN) resolution authorizing member states to expel Iraqi forces from Kuwait. It was an impressive diplomatic victory for Bush because the UN had not condoned member states going to war since the Korean conflict four decades earlier.

Bush's administration faced a tougher challenge convincing the Democratic Congress. Members began deliberating shortly after New Year's Day but waited until January 12, after an impressive televised debate in the Senate, to approve using military force. Democrats accounted for virtually all of the opposition. They raised the specter of Vietnam, charged that a war in the Middle East would be more about oil than aggression, and asked for additional time for economic sanctions to work. Nevertheless, in the end 86 Democrats in the House and 10 in the Senate joined Bush's effort, enough to assure victory. The vote in the House was 250 to 183, and in the Senate, a closer 52 to 47. Bush's presidential leadership seemed to win out over partisan squabbling, an impressive political victory.

By early 1991, a million UN troops lined the Kuwait border to face the invaders. The air war began a day after the January 15 deadline for Iraq's withdrawal. Broadcasting from downtown Baghdad during the bombardment, CNN showed Americans stunning military footage of technologically advanced weaponry. The ground offensive followed on February 24, and again the contest was almost completely one-sided. Allied forces outflanked the entrenched Iraqi troops and in four days drove them from Kuwait—with only 89 Americans dead and 38 missing in action.[*] By contrast, at least 50,000 Iraqis perished in the conflict. On March 6, more than a week after the shooting had stopped, President Bush was able to declare before Congress, "The war is over." The United States had achieved an impressive military victory under his leadership as commander-in-chief.

The evening news telecasts showed throngs of jubilant Kuwaitis parading through the streets chanting "Bush! Bush! Bush!" The reaction at home was more muted, but no less favorable. In the aftermath of the war, President Bush's

---

[*]Not until a decade later was it clear that physical illnesses called the Gulf War syndrome resulted from exposure to burning nerve gases and toxins.

FIGURE 5.1

The rise and decline of President Bush's approval ratings

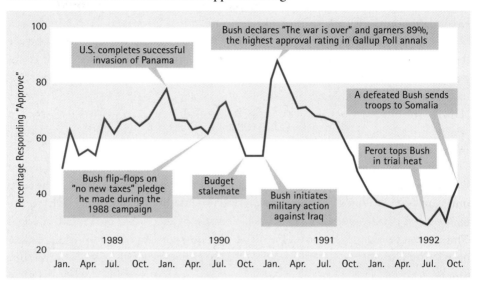

SOURCE: Gallup poll (www.gallup.com).

approval ratings soared, reaching unprecedented heights—as much as 90 percent in some polls (see Figure 5.1). Most people conceded his reelection, only a year and a half away. Prominent Democrats who had been mentioned as likely opponents—House Majority leader Richard Gephardt, Senators Sam Nunn and Bill Bradley, and New York Governor Mario Cuomo—all thought better of taking on the seemingly unbeatable Bush. With the Democratic "first team" on the bench, the field of play was left to "minor leaguers" like Arkansas Governor Bill Clinton.

Yet even as his strongest opponents were conceding him the election, Bush's fortunes were slipping. The American public forgot about the war and turned its attention to the struggling economy.[2] As Figure 5.1 shows, within a year of his great success in the Persian Gulf, Bush's approval rating dropped by 50 percent. He went into the election as one of the least popular presidents of the past 50 years and lost to Clinton in a three-way race.

BUSH'S TURBULENT OPINION RATINGS REFLECT A LARGER TRUTH ABOUT America's new democracy. Voters have very high expectations for their leaders, and often use election time to express their displeasure. Leaders always must fear public whims, and cater to them when possible, or they will not lead for long. This is why public officials spend lots of money and effort to anticipate public demands. At the same time, public opinion can be terribly capricious, flitting from one issue to the next. The public, operating collectively, has limited knowledge, a short attention span, and rather sloppy methods for decision making. Public opinion is difficult to measure accurately. It is also open to manipulation, and sometimes indulges its worst impulses. For these reasons, elections capture the people's demands imperfectly. Elections drive American politics, but it is not always clear what drives voters.

WHAT IS PUBLIC OPINION AND HOW IS IT FORMED?

The reason for public opinion's importance is captured aptly by political scientist V.O. Key's definition: "those opinions held by private persons which governments find it prudent to heed."[3] Democratic governments find it "prudent" to heed the opinions of private persons, of course, because of elections. Note that in Key's conception, public opinion can, but need not, be expressed actively. Even if public opinion is silent, or "latent," public officials may act or fail to act because they fear arousing it. This is the so-called law of anticipated reactions, whereby elections influence government even though they do so indirectly and passively.[4] The common phrase, "Public opinion wouldn't stand for that," acknowledges that public opinion can exercise power subtly.

The opinions that people hold reflect numerous influences. Most of these sources are stable: values, self-interests, education. But applying them to particular issues may not be straightforward. And some influences—such as the media—can shift rapidly. Thus, even a politician who tries to "give the people what they want" may be surprised come election day.

Children begin to form political attitudes at an early age. Research carried out in the 1950s and 1960s generally concluded that the single most important **socializing agent** was the family, and that within the family the mother was most important—she spent far more time with the children in that era. Studies found that many children identify themselves as Democrats or Republicans well before they have any idea what the parties stand for. And older children are very likely to share the party affiliation of their parents. A few scholars concluded, however, that schools were more important than family.[5]

In recent decades the increases in single parenthood and in the divorce rate have left many children in one-parent families. Moreover, the proportion of mothers who work outside the home has doubled since the 1960s. It is plausible, then, to suppose that the relative importance of the family as a socializing agent has declined, but there is little recent research to test such a supposition.

Socialization often works indirectly, by forming the beliefs and values on which individuals act later in life. For example, a very young child may learn fear of, or comfort with, nudity—and this psychological orientation may shape adult attitudes about such political issues as strip club restrictions or pornography bans. But sometimes socializing agents consciously try to activate political attitudes. The Catholic Church officially opposes abortion, and rank-and-file Catholics are indeed less accepting of abortion than are mainline Protestants and Jews.[6] Most fundamentalist Protestant churches officially condemn homosexuality, and rank-and-file members are indeed less tolerant of homosexuality.[7] From the 1930s to the 1980s, labor unions typically supported the Democratic party, and union members were indeed typically more Democratic in their voting than other blue-collar workers.[8] Whether the influences lie in the distant past or in the present, differences among people with different socialization experiences emerge regularly on all kinds of issues.

Although people form many of their attitudes in childhood, their political views continue to develop over the course of their lifetimes. Childhood socialization can be reversed by adult experiences, and especially by one's *personal interests*.[9] For example, blue-collar workers are more sensitive to a rise in unemployment that throws them out of work, while professionals and managers are more sensitive to a rise in inflation that drives up interest rates and depresses the overall business climate.[10] In 1978 California homeowners were significantly more likely than renters and public employees to support Proposition 13, the famous initiative that rolled back property taxes.[11] People often evaluate public policy by asking, "What's in it for me?"

Education contributes to both socialization and self-interest, but it belongs in a separate category because of the unique role it plays. More highly educated people are more tolerant of minority groups and deviant practices, as shown in Figure 5.2.[12] It may be that values emphasized in higher education—logical argument, open-mindedness, unemotional analysis—predispose the educated to accept diversity. Or it may be that college professors consciously try to make students critical of their own backgrounds. Either way, higher education is generally associated with a more tolerant outlook. Higher education also is associated with a greater sense of **political efficacy**—the belief that the citizen can make a difference by acting politically.

In recent years many people have expressed the fear that *mass media* increasingly shape public opinion. Overall, little evidence to date supports the worst fears of media critics. For example, an extensive study of opinion change during the 1980 presidential campaign found that in the aggregate, TV and newspaper exposure had only marginal effects on preexisting views.[13] And more recently,

FIGURE 5.2

Higher education is associated with greater tolerance of diversity

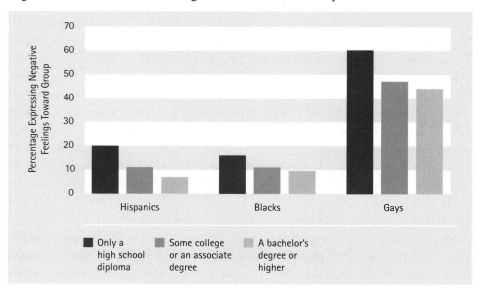

SOURCE: American National Election Study, 1994.

despite the overwhelmingly negative coverage President Clinton received during the Lewinsky scandal, his job performance ratings scarcely budged. Nevertheless, under some circumstances, the media can move public opinion—if not directly, then by determining how values, interests, and education come together to shape a person's political beliefs. This instability makes public opinion hard to predict. It is also hard to measure.

MEASURING PUBLIC OPINION

In the nineteenth century, measuring public opinion was an art form. Politicians looked at informal straw polls, consulted community leaders, or scanned the newspapers' editorial pages to understand the public mood. But the process was less like science and more like "reading tea leaves."[14] The advent of modern survey research in the 1930s (pioneered by George Gallup) clarified public opinion, making it a much more powerful political force. The key to this change was the scientific design and administration of randomized surveys, which has become a standard tool of the modern campaign.

Most often researchers measure public opinion via telephone polls. Various firms and academic organizations contact individuals, ask them questions, and report the responses. Of these, Gallup is the most widely recognized name. Newspapers, magazines, and TV networks also sponsor regular polls—NBC News/Wall Street Journal, CBS News/New York Times, ABC News/Washington Post, USA Today/CNN—and base major stories on them.[15]

The general public is sometimes suspicious of survey research, refusing to believe that fewer than 2,000 people can speak for an entire nation. They may be right to distrust polls, but the reason for skepticism is misplaced. Statisticians have demonstrated that a few thousand people usually will mirror the opinion of 200 million adults quite well—as long as everyone has a roughly equal chance of being polled. That is, the small group needs to be a **random sample** of the population. For this reason, telephone surveys often use random-digit dialing; to equalize the odds of selection, a computer randomly selects which numbers to call within a given telephone exchange. People with unlisted numbers may be irritated when they answer their phones and hear pollsters, but no one has given out their numbers—the computer has found them by accident!

Random samples are not perfect, and the polls that use them do not get the answer exactly right, but the existence of such **sampling error** does not make them unreliable. Consider a simple example to illustrate. Suppose that every reader of this book flipped a coin 1,500 times. The most likely result, the "right" answer in this instance, would be 750 heads—because a coin flip turns up heads half the time. But of course some of you would get a few more heads by chance, and some, a few more tails—that's the sampling error. Statistical theory tells us precisely how much each experiment would bounce around the typical result. It is a statistical fact that 95 percent of the time we would find between 705 and 795 heads, between 47 and 53 percent. This range is what pollsters mean when they report that surveys have a "margin of error" of plus or minus 3 percent: 95 percent of the time their survey method would turn up an estimate within 3 points of the right answer.

Even with a representative sample, however, the calculated sampling error may exaggerate the accuracy of the survey. Typically, more than half the original sample either never answer the phone or refuse to be interviewed.[16] Research shows that surveys tend to underrepresent men, young people, whites, and the wealthy.[17] In 1996, for example, pre-election polls overestimated Bill Clinton's margin over Robert Dole. Some commentators claimed that this was because pro-Democratic groups were more likely to respond to the polls than pro-Republican groups.[18]

The key to getting an unbiased sample is to make sure that individuals cannot affect whether they are in or out of the sample. For example, if we were to poll attendees at a hockey game, an opera, or even a political science lecture, our sample would be suspect, because the members of each of these groups share a common interest—in hockey, opera, or political science—that brought them together. This common interest differentiates them from the American population at large.

The same is true for call-in surveys conducted by radio and TV stations. These may be good ways to generate listener or viewer interest, but they have no more scientific value than letters to the editor or the feedback heard by elected officials at town hall meetings do. People who take the time and trouble to participate are those who care most. They are not representative of the much larger population.

The latest rage is Internet polls. The problem with Internet polling was highlighted by a mildly embarrassing experience suffered by the Democratic National Committee (DNC) in January 2000. The DNC Web site includes a weekly opinion poll. The poll in question noted that the United States was enjoying a large budget surplus and asked people to vote for one of two ways to use the surplus: "saving Social Security, strengthening Medicare, and paying down the debt," or "implementing George W. Bush's $1.7 trillion risky tax scheme that overwhelmingly benefits the wealthy." Surprisingly, when the results were tabulated, 72.2 percent of the respondents favored "risky" tax cuts for the rich. Mischievous Republicans monitoring the opposition had voted in the Democrats' poll![19] This amusing episode illustrates the problem with allowing the sample to determine itself. Thus, survey researchers must be continually on guard against **selection bias,** the error that occurs when their sample systematically includes or excludes people with certain types of attitudes. In a scientific poll, the investigator must control who is included in the sample and who is not.

MISMEASURING PUBLIC OPINION

Poll stories routinely report sampling error, but despite the attention it gets, sampling is a relatively unimportant source of error in most professional surveys. Various kinds of **measurement error** are much more troublesome. The reason is that someone's opinion is not an objective fact like the length of a stick. We can all measure a stick, and if we are careful, our measurements will be quite similar. But opinions are not physical facts. Beliefs and judgments may be hard to quantify and often are expressed as casual answers to questions the respondent has never really thought about. For that reason, how people answer a poll depends very much on the wording of the questions. Here is a striking example that embarrassed a reputable polling firm.

THE HOLOCAUST POLL FIASCO   The Holocaust Memorial Museum opened in Washington, D.C., in the spring of 1993. Coincident with the dedication of the museum, the American Jewish Committee released startling data from a survey conducted a few months earlier by Roper Starch Worldwide, a respected commercial polling organization. The poll indicated that 22 percent of the American public believed it "possible . . . the Nazi extermination of the Jews never happened" and that another 12 percent were unsure. In total, one-third of all Americans apparently had doubts about whether the Nazis murdered 6 million Jews in World War II.

The news media jumped on the story, which fit the preconceptions of editorialists and columnists eager to find shortcomings in their fellow citizens. What was wrong with the American people? Had the educational system failed so miserably that in the short span of 50 years the worst genocide in history had become a matter of mere opinion? Was anti-Semitism so widespread and deeply ingrained in the population that Holocaust denials by the lunatic fringe were making headway? What did the Holocaust poll say about the American people?

Very little, it turned out. The Gallup organization—a Roper business competitor—soon demonstrated that the Roper poll was gravely mistaken, because Roper had asked a confusing question. The exact wording of Roper's question was

Does it seem possible, or does it seem impossible to you that the Nazi extermination of the Jews never happened?

One of the first rules of survey research is to keep questions clear and simple. The Roper question fails that test because it contains a double negative (impossible . . . never happened)—a grammatical construction long known to confuse people.

Gallup conducted a new poll in which half of the sample was asked the Roper question with the double negative and the other half were asked an alternative question,

Does it seem possible to you that the Nazi extermination of the Jews never happened, or do you feel certain that it happened?

The differences in question wording may seem minor, but it made a great deal of difference. In the half of the sample that was asked the Roper question, one-third of the respondents again replied that it was possible the Holocaust never happened or that they were unsure, but in the half that were asked the alternative question, less than 10 percent of the sample were Holocaust doubters. Roper eventually retracted its initial poll results after doing its own follow-up studies. The whole episode had been the product of a simple mistake.[20]

Embarrassed by a poll

The 1993 opening of the Holocaust Memorial Museum was accompanied by a polling embarrassment that underscored the necessity of keeping public opinion poll questions clear and simple. Why might a person have answered yes to the following: "Does it seem possible, or does it seem impossible to you that the Nazi extermination of the Jews never happened?"

THE IMPORTANCE OF WORDING   The point of the Holocaust poll example is that no one accused the Roper organization of choosing a bad sample. Roper asked a poorly constructed question, and the results gave a reliable indication of how Americans would respond to that bad measurement (something Gallup's follow-up survey confirmed).

What looks like minor variations in question wording can produce significant differences in measured opinion. This is especially likely when the variations involve the substitution of emotionally or politically "loaded" terms for more neutral terms. A classic example comes from the controversy over social spending. Consider the following survey question:

> *We are faced with many problems in this country, none of which can be solved easily or inexpensively. I'm going to name some of these problems and for each one I'd like you to tell me whether you think we're spending too much money, too little money, or about the right amount.*[21]

When the public was asked about "welfare" in the spring of 1994, the responses showed that a large majority of Americans believed that too much was being spent:

Too little	13%
About right	25%
Too much	62%

Conservatives might take heart from such a poll and use it to argue that public assistance to the poor should be slashed. But when the same people in the same poll were asked about "assistance to the poor," a similarly large majority responded that too little was being spent:

Too little	59%
About right	25%
Too much	16%

Liberals might take heart from such a poll and use it to argue that welfare spending should increase.

Looking at these two questions together, though, it's hard to tease out any real preference. Both invoke the same policy, but different stereotypes. "Welfare" carries negative connotations; it seems to prompt people to think of lazy and undeserving recipients, so-called welfare cheats. But "assistance to the poor" does not seem to invoke these negative images. Here is clearly a case where the careless (or clever) choice of question wording can produce contradictory findings on a major public issue.

Loaded questions are far from the only problem. Responses to opinion polls also vary with question format.[22] People tend to give more consistent answers to questions that allow graduated responses (agree strongly, agree somewhat, neither agree nor disagree, disagree, disagree somewhat, and disagree strongly) than to either/or questions (agree/disagree). More people will choose a "don't know" or "not sure" answer if it is offered to them than if they have to volunteer it. People respond differently, when asked to choose between two sides of a question, if they hear the supporting arguments for each position first. People respond differently if earlier questions in the survey prompt them to think along certain lines. And people respond differently when surveyed after significant social, economic, or political developments than when surveyed before such events.[23]

CHARACTERISTICS
OF PUBLIC OPINION

Why should the measurement of public opinion be so sensitive to how it is measured? As we have said, public opinion is not an objective quantity like length or weight. On the contrary, public opinion often makes it very hard to obtain reliable measurements.

Public opinion often is uninformed

Americans are an accommodating people. If a pollster asks a question, many will cooperate by giving their best answer, even if they have not thought about the question or have no basis for deciding. A 1989 survey provides an extreme example. People were asked to rate 58 ethnic and nationality groups. Although one group included in the list ("Wisnians") was fictitious, 29 percent of the sample ranked them anyway.[24]

Most people have little or no information about public affairs. The extent of popular ignorance is most obvious when surveys pose "factual" questions. As shown in Figure 5.3, in 1995 only one quarter of the voting-age population knew how long U.S. senators serve. Barely half could name the Speaker of the House (Newt Gingrich, who had been on the cover of *Time* magazine), and only 60 percent could recall the name of the vice president (Al Gore). Almost half had no idea which branch of government interprets the Constitution.

Elections are not standardized tests, of course; voting intelligently does not require knowing the answers to all sorts of factual questions. But widespread ignorance extends beyond such factual questions to important matters of government and public policy. During the 1995 federal government shutdown, 40 percent of Americans were unaware that the Republicans controlled both houses of Congress (and 10 percent did not know that the president was a Democrat). And by more than a 2-to-1 margin, Americans believed—absolutely wrongly—that the federal government spent more on foreign aid than on Medicare. In fact, the United States spends four times as much on Medicare as on foreign aid, and the ratio is growing.[25]

Why do people have so little knowledge of basic facts and issues? The answer is that most people seldom pay attention to politics. News magazines sell far fewer copies than entertainment and lifestyle magazines do. Far more Americans watch sitcoms like *Ally McBeal* and *ER* than watch PBS's *NewsHour with Jim Lehrer*. Figure 5.4 presents various contrasts in the entertainment habits of the American public.

Upon learning the full extent of popular ignorance, some politically involved students react critically, jumping to the conclusion that apathetic Americans are irresponsible people who fall far short of the democratic ideal. Such reactions overlook the reasons why people pay so little attention to public affairs.

The simple fact is that most people have little time for politics; it is something of a luxury interest. They work hard to take care of the "necessities"—paying the bills, caring for families, and nurturing personal relationships. They may not have time or energy for the *New York Times* and *Nightline* after dropping off and picking up children, commuting, working, and housekeeping. The effort required to stay informed competes with human necessities like recreation and relaxation.

FIGURE 5.3

Americans are not very knowledgeable about the specifics of American government

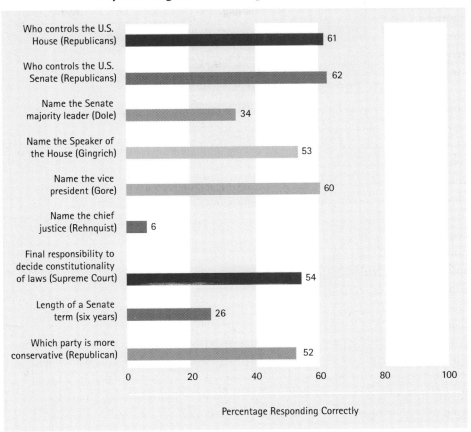

NOTE: This survey was conducted by Princeton Survey Research Associates in late November 1995 and early December 1995, after the Republicans took control of Congress for the first time in 40 years and during the federal budget impasse of 1995. Correct answers appear in parentheses.

SOURCE: "Why Don't Americans Trust the Government?" (Menlo Park, CA: The Kaiser Foundation, 1996).

Those who criticize ordinary citizens for their lack of attention to public affairs often have jobs that enable them to stay informed with little effort. For example, in a university environment, political conversation is a common diversion, and for many professors and students being informed is relevant to academic pursuits. Likewise, many journalists have jobs that involve following politics: If they are not informed, they are not doing their jobs. But most Americans do not face these incentives, a fact that critics in academia and the media tend to forget. Nor is it clear what such people would do with their knowledge of public affairs if they were able to obtain it.

FIGURE 5.4

Interest in politics is much lower than interest in popular culture and entertainment

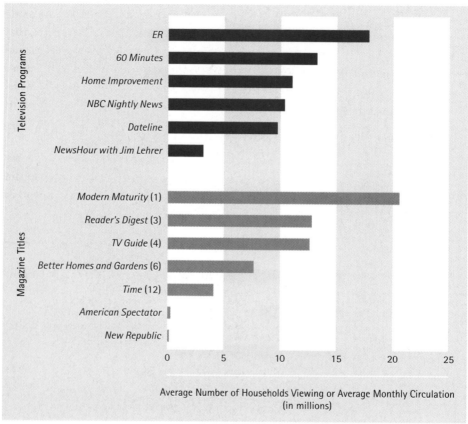

NOTE: The television ratings for prime time shows are for the period between September 1, 1998, and May 26, 1999. The magazine circulation figures are for the period between July 1, 1998, and December 31, 1998.

SOURCES: *The World Almanac and Book of Facts, 2000;* Nielsen Media Research; and the Web sites of the magazines and programs.

The general point is that gathering, processing, and storing information is neither effortless nor free. For most Americans, bearing such **information costs** brings them little tangible return.[26] Few citizens believe that they have enough power to influence how conflicts in Kosovo, Afghanistan, or the next crisis spot will resolve. And when faced with a costly activity that has no obvious benefit, many of them quite rationally decide to minimize their costs. Thus, from a logical standpoint, the puzzle is not why so many Americans are ill-informed; the puzzle is why so many are as informed as they are.[27]

Of course, information costs do not fall equally heavily on all people. Education makes it easier to absorb and organize information; thus it comes as no surprise that more-educated Americans are better informed than less-educated ones (see Figure 5.5). In addition, the benefits of information are not the same for all people on all issues. Most people will be better informed on issues that directly affect their lives. Parents and teachers are more knowledgeable than other citizens about school operations and budgets. Human services providers are more knowledgeable about welfare and other public assistance policies. Steel workers have strong views on foreign imports. Such **issue publics** are different from the large mass of citizens in that their members' occupations make information cheaper to obtain, as well as more relevant, interesting, and valuable.[28]

In addition to varying across people and issues, the costs and benefits of being well informed may vary over time as well. When a tax revolt erupts or a debate over condom distribution in the schools flares up, information levels surge as

FIGURE 5.5

Higher education is strongly associated with greater knowledge of politics and government

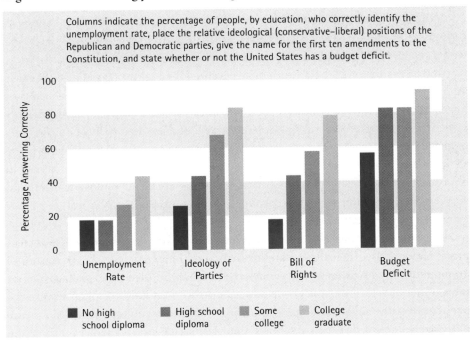

Columns indicate the percentage of people, by education, who correctly identify the unemployment rate, place the relative ideological (conservative–liberal) positions of the Republican and Democratic parties, give the name for the first ten amendments to the Constitution, and state whether or not the United States has a budget deficit.

SOURCE: Data are taken from Michael Delli Carpini and Scott Keeter, *What Americans Know About Politics and Why It Matters,* p. 189.

people get caught up in the controversy. But after the burning issues are resolved and the controversy subsides, information levels also return to normal.[29]

Of course, some people consider it their duty as citizens to be informed, so they stay attuned to public affairs simply because they believe it is the "right thing" to do. Other people follow public affairs because they find it intrinsically interesting, in the same way that some follow sports or the arts. For such people, staying informed is a matter of taste or values, not the result of any tangible benefit from being informed. What others view as costs, they see as a source of satisfaction.[30]

Finally, we note that Americans are not unique in paying little attention to public affairs. Citizens in other countries are similarly inattentive and similarly lacking in knowledge. A 1998 British Gallup poll, for example, found that only 40 percent of Britons knew that the United States once was part of the British Empire![31]

PUBLIC OPINION IS NOT IDEOLOGICAL

Another characteristic of public opinion that makes it easy to misinterpret is that even when people have reasonably firm views on issues, those views often are surprisingly unconnected to each other. That is, the American people are not very ideological.

People who are deeply interested and involved in politics, whether as activists or as office holders—traditionally called **political elites**—tend to have well-structured **ideologies** that unite their positions on policy issues. To know that such a person is a "liberal" or a "conservative" is to know a good deal, because underlying principles mold their system of beliefs. Ordinary citizens are another matter. Philip Converse showed long ago that ordinary citizens—traditionally called the **mass public**—are nonideological.[32] Rather than believe consistently in either activist or minimal government, an important trait distinguishing liberals and conservatives, citizens generally favor federal spending in some areas but oppose it in others. They favor regulation in some areas but oppose it in others. They favor toleration for some groups in some situations, but not for other groups in other situations.

In fact, Converse and his assistants found that only 3 percent of the 1950s electorate thought ideologically, a number that could be expanded to a maximum of 16 percent only by using a very generous definition of "ideology." The most common frame of reference was group allegiances: To what kinds of people were the parties sympathetic? The second most common frame of reference was "the nature of the times": How had the parties and their candidates performed recently? Even when generously classified, though, ideologues were no more numerous than citizens who could articulate virtually nothing of political relevance. In the 1960s there was some increase in ideological thinking, as educational levels rose and the parties became more polarized, but the thought patterns of ordinary Americans remain far less ideologically coherent than elites often presume.[33]

Even when the standard for ideological thinking is weak, the evidence for widespread ideology is absent. For example, *when given the option*, one-quarter to one-third of the population will not even classify themselves on a liberal–conservative scale, and another one-quarter put themselves exactly in the middle: "moderate, middle of the road."[34]

There is a common tendency to interpret the nonideological thinking of ordinary Americans in a negative light and to presume that preferences with little obvious interconnection are somehow less valid than those with a predictable structure. Here again, we disagree with such pessimistic judgments. In our view, ideologies are as much *social* as logical constructions. Personal views aside, can anyone explain the logical connection among supporting low capital gains tax rates, being pro-life, opposing gun control, and favoring high defense spending? Positions on such issues may go together for liberal and conservative elites, but why? Maybe it is political elites who should be viewed critically.

That ideologies are matters of social construction and convention is shown by the way they change over time.[35] From the 1930s through the 1950s, *liberal* implied a belief in government intervention in the economy to control powerful corporations, to provide a safety net for ordinary citizens, and to supply collective goods (such as electricity to rural areas) that the private sector could not supply profitably. In the 1960s the terms of political debate shifted. Although present earlier, racial attitudes and opinions about civil rights became much more important components of liberalism than they were previously. By the time *liberal* became a dirty word in the campaigns of the 1980s, the term was synonymous with tolerance of personal irresponsibility and contempt for traditional values.

The American people have a strong pragmatic strain, often noted by international observers accustomed to a more ideological style of political discourse. Perhaps nonideological views should be taken as evidence of American common sense. Whether you regard ideological thinking as good or bad, however, bear in mind one point. Because they presume that ideological thinking is the norm, party and issue activists, media commentators, and many public officials will conclude too much on the basis of opinion polls and voting returns. Support for one variety of government action may indicate nothing about support for another seemingly similar government action. Support for a candidate's position on one issue may suggest little or nothing about that candidate's "mandate" to act on seemingly related issues. The nonideological nature of public opinion means that elites often hear more than the voters are saying.

PUBLIC OPINION OFTEN IS INCONSISTENT

Given that people often have not thought about issues or the connections among them, it should come as no surprise that public opinion often is also inconsistent. Opinions with little basis are not likely to abide when survey questions change emphasis or as time passes. For example, in 1980, when Ronald Reagan defeated Jimmy Carter and the Republicans made striking gains in Congress, many in the media interpreted the election results as a "resurgence of conservatism" or a "turn to the right" in American politics. The evidence, however, was confusing.[36]

A poll taken in 1978 reported that an overwhelming 84 percent of the citizenry thought the federal government was spending too much money. A smaller majority thought that the federal government had gone too far in regulating business. Popular sentiments like these appear to foretell the Reagan victory that followed. But then again, the same poll asked the *same people* which domestic programs they favored cutting and which areas of business activity they favored deregulating. Surprisingly, majorities often indicated that most domestic activities deserved *higher* funding or *more* regulation. Similarly, after the Republican congressional victories in 1994, polls reported that large majorities wanted to balance the budget but not to cut specific programs, especially not the large entitlement programs causing the budget deficits.[37] Such contradictory views recall the old maxim that "everybody wants to go to heaven but nobody wants to die."

Obviously, such contradictory views confuse political debate, distorting whatever message voters try to send during an election. President Reagan claimed—with some justification—that he had been elected to cut government spending and deregulate the economy. Democratic leaders in Congress claimed—with some justification—that their party had been returned to power so that they could protect existing spending and regulatory programs. Both claims were plausible given the public opinion data. In 1994 Republican congressional leaders believed they had a mandate to balance the budget (see the Election Connection, "Public Opinion and the 1994 Republican Contract with America"). But when they attempted to slow the growth of Medicare spending, they discovered that the mandate did not extend that far.

Why is public opinion so inconsistent? Obviously, ignorance is part of the explanation. People are unaware how little is being spent on programs such as welfare and foreign aid. Thus, they believe, erroneously, that cutting such unpopular programs will free up sufficient funds to maintain popular ones. Some voters also believe that waste and inefficiency are so pervasive that simply streamlining government operations would allow painless spending increases.

Not all examples of inconsistency reflect insufficient and inaccurate information, however. Citizens are so consistently inconsistent when applying general principles to specific cases that other explanations must be at work. We have seen that people favor cutting spending in general but not specific programs. They also oppose amending the Constitution but favor amendments to require a balanced budget, limit congressional terms, and ban flag burning. And, perhaps most interesting of all, they support fundamental rights but regularly make numerous exceptions.[38] As Figure 5.6 shows, most citizens favor "free speech for all"—but

FIGURE 5.6

Americans tend to endorse general principles but make numerous exceptions to them

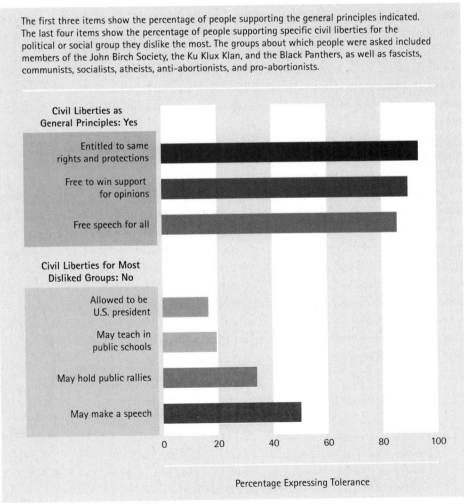

The first three items show the percentage of people supporting the general principles indicated. The last four items show the percentage of people supporting specific civil liberties for the political or social group they dislike the most. The groups about which people were asked included members of the John Birch Society, the Ku Klux Klan, and the Black Panthers, as well as fascists, communists, socialists, atheists, anti-abortionists, and pro-abortionists.

Civil Liberties as General Principles: Yes

- Entitled to same rights and protections
- Free to win support for opinions
- Free speech for all

Civil Liberties for Most Disliked Groups: No

- Allowed to be U.S. president
- May teach in public schools
- May hold public rallies
- May make a speech

Percentage Expressing Tolerance

SOURCE: Data are taken from John Sullivan, James Piereson, and George Marcus, *Political Tolerance and American Democracy* (Chicago: University of Chicago Press, 1982).

then half refuse to agree that a member of their most disliked group should be allowed to give a speech. Similarly, they believe in the separation of church and state but favor prayer in schools!

It is easy to label such inconsistencies hypocrisy, and some do. Or such inconsistencies may indicate that ordinary people do not have a clear understanding of rights, and perhaps they do not. But there are other, more positive interpretations as well. To the law professor, the newspaper editor, or the political activist, rights may be viewed as absolutes. Letting government infringe on guaranteed protections leaves open the possibility that government will water them down until they are meaningless. But Americans tend to be pragmatists. Few distrust their elected government so much that they are unwilling to bend the rules once in a while. The absolutist language of rights is foreign to the problem-solving American way of thinking. Rights are good things, but they must be balanced against other values.[39] To adults familiar with life's conflicts and tradeoffs, the legalistic language of rights belongs in the realm of theoretical argument, not the realm of real-world politics. They may feel no contradiction in advocating a right while simultaneously endorsing significant exceptions.[40]

THE PERILS OF POLLING: PUBLIC OPINION ON ABORTION

The Supreme Court handed down the *Roe* v. *Wade* decision in 1973, striking down restrictions on a woman's right to terminate a pregnancy in the first three months (and limiting restrictions on that right in the second trimester). Since then, the issue has never left the national agenda, so most Americans probably decided long ago where they stand on the issue. Nevertheless, the abortion issue provides striking illustrations of the features of public opinion discussed in the preceding pages, especially its apparent inconsistency and its nonideological nature.

When the same survey question is repeated over time, public opinion is strikingly constant. For example, a National Opinion Research Center (NORC) question reads as follows:

Please tell me whether or not you think it should be possible for a pregnant woman to obtain a legal abortion if

1. *the woman's health is seriously endangered?*
2. *she became pregnant as a result of rape?*
3. *there is a strong chance of serious defect in the baby?*
4. *the family has low income and cannot afford any more children?*
5. *she is not married and does not want to marry the man?*
6. *she is married and does not want any more children?*

ELECTION CONNECTION

Public Opinion and the
1994 Republican Contract with America

The 1994 congressional elections have been described as an "electoral meteorite that slammed into the American political landscape."[a] Although many observers thought that the Republicans had a chance to win the Senate, few gave them a serious chance to capture the House. When the dust thrown up by the "electoral meteorite" cleared, however, the Republicans had captured both chambers for the first time in 40 years, and the pundits were speculating that a new electoral era had dawned.

The architect of the Republican victory was soon-to-be Speaker of the House Newt Gingrich, and his vehicle was called the Contract with America. In late September, Gingrich had organized a Washington rally where more than 350 Republican candidates signed a contract promising voters that within 100 days of taking control of Congress, the new House majority would adopt a package of congressional reforms and vote on ten planks dealing with the following issues: balanced budget, crime, welfare, families, a middle-class tax cut, national security, senior citizens' benefits, capital gains taxes, legal reforms, and congressional term limits.[b] Democrats, as well as many nonpartisan commentators, had scoffed at this Republican media event. Not only did they think that many of the Republican proposals were electoral losers, but also conventional wisdom holds that the out-party should simply attack the in-party, not promise anything specific.

Gingrich and the Republicans stood firm. Criticism of the Contract with America did not make them back away from it. Indeed, they reemphasized it, even publishing it in *TV Guide,* a popular magazine with a huge circulation. The Republicans were confident in their strategy for a simple reason: The Contract with America had been carefully put together with the aid of modern public opinion research methods. On average, the proposals in the Contract with America were supported by comfortable majorities in national surveys, and the language that was used—the "frames"—had been carefully tested in focus groups (small groups of citizens brought together to talk about the proposals).[c] The Republicans believed that the more widely publicized the Contract with America, the better for them it would be. Of course, the Contract with America was not the only factor in the election, but the Republicans' beliefs proved to be more accurate than the Democrats'. In mocking the Contract with America, Democrats were swimming against the current of public opinion. In many cases they were swept away.

If imitation is the sincerest form of flattery, then the 1996 Democrats flattered the 1994 Republicans. In the summer of 1996, Minority Leader Richard Gephardt unveiled a new "Families First" agenda for the Democrats. It provided for tax breaks for child care and health costs and promised to get tough on crime and balance the budget. This time, the Republicans did the mocking, dismissing Families First as "nothing more than a product designed by their pollsters and their elite leadership in Washington."[d]

Some critics argue that the use of public opinion research methods to craft campaign appeals is troubling. Others argue that candidates have always tried to advocate what voters want and that modern methods simply give them a more accurate way to do so.

(continued)

(continued from previous page)

What do you think?

- Do polls give good, needed information to elected officials, or do they allow politicians to avoid the hard work of considering public policy?
- Is the use of public opinion research methods to craft campaign appeals a negative development or a positive development? Why?

- How could this development be reversed?

[a]Robert W. Merry, "Voters' Demand for Change Puts Clinton on the Defensive," *Congressional Quarterly Weekly Report* (November 12, 1994): 3207.

[b]Clyde Wilcox, *The Latest American Revolution* (New York: St. Martin's Press, 1995), pp. 48–56, Appendix A.

[c]On public support for the Contract with America proposals, see "The Direction Specified in Most of the 'Contract's' Planks Finds High Public Backing," *Public Perspective* (February/March 1995): 29.

[d]John Yang, "'Contract with America,' Meet 'Families First,'" *The Washington Post* (National Weekly Edition, July 1–7, 1996): 13.

After moving in a liberal direction in the late 1960s, opinion stabilized at the time of the Roe decision, stayed remarkably constant for two decades, and then moved slightly in a conservative direction in the late 1990s (see Figure 5.7). On average, Americans favor legal abortion in half of the circumstances, with large majorities supporting abortion in the first three ("traumatic") circumstances, but more people regularly opposing abortion in two of the second three ("elective") circumstances.[41] Opinion changed little after the 1989 *Webster* v. *Reproductive Health Services* decision, which opened the way for some state regulation of abortion, or after the 1992 *Planned Parenthood* v. *Casey* decision, which upheld some of the specific restrictions imposed by Pennsylvania. Thus, the complicated picture that follows is not the result of uninformed, unconcerned citizens giving haphazard responses to polls. The difficulties run deeper.

Consider the effects of question wording shown in two surveys that bracketed the 1989 *Webster* decision.[42] A *Los Angeles Times* poll asked,

> *Do you think a pregnant woman should or should not be able to get a legal abortion, no matter what the reason?*

By close to a 2-to-1 margin (57 percent to 34 percent), Americans thought she should not. As pro-life spokespersons claimed, Americans were pro-life. Should Democratic campaign consultants have advised their clients to flip-flop to the pro-life side in anticipation of the next election? Well, probably not. A few months later, a CBS News/*New York Times* survey asked,

> *If a woman wants to have an abortion, and her doctor agrees to it, should she be allowed to have an abortion or not?*

By more than a 2-to-1 margin (58 percent to 26 percent), Americans said yes. As the pro-choice spokespersons claimed, America had a pro-choice majority.

FIGURE 5.7

Popular attitudes toward abortion have been remarkably stable since *Roe* v. *Wade* (1973)

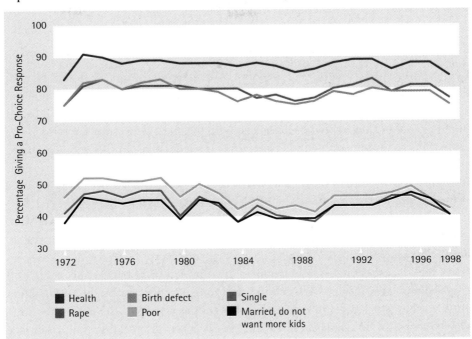

NOTE: Respondents who answered "don't know" are included in the calculation.

SOURCE: Calculated by the authors from the General Social Survey 1972–1998 Cumulative Data File.

Should Republican campaign consultants have advised their clients to flip-flop to the pro-choice side?

Which poll was right? Probably neither. Upon close examination, both survey questions are suspect. Each contains words and phrases that predispose people to answer in one direction. The first question uses the phrase "no matter what the reason." Most Americans are not *unconditionally* pro-choice, any more than their other political ideals are unconditional. If forced to choose yes or no, some genuinely pro-choice people will say no, believing that there must reasons for an abortion that even they would consider invalid. The CBS News/*New York Times* question leans in the opposite direction. A doctor's approval suggests a reasoned decision based on medically justifiable grounds. Some generally pro-life people might agree to permit abortion in such a case. Thus, even on an issue where many people have stable, considered opinions, variations in question wording can make a big difference in the answers they give.

A survey also can skew answers by how it **frames** an issue, encouraging the respondent to answer questions from one point of view rather than another. For example, a CBS News/*New York Times* poll asked the following question:

> *Even in cases where I might think abortion is the wrong thing to do, I don't think the government has any business preventing a woman from having an abortion.*[43]

By close to a 3-to-1 margin (69 percent to 24 percent), Americans agreed with that sentiment. Apparently, the country stands firmly in support of abortion rights. On the other hand, when another CBS News/*New York Times* poll asked people whether they agreed or disagreed with the stark claim that "abortion is the same thing as murdering a child," Americans were deeply split (46 percent agreed and 41 percent disagreed). Similarly, a plurality or majority of Americans regularly agrees that "abortion is morally wrong" (51 percent agreed, and 34 percent disagreed in the aforementioned CBS News/*New York Times* poll).[44]

The first question uses a *choice* frame. Individualistic Americans favor freedom of choice, especially when it involves freedom from governmental interference. The second and third questions use an *act* frame. Many Americans who favor choice nevertheless are troubled by the act of abortion. So even poll respondents with stable, well-defined positions on abortion might react differently to these variations in questions—depending upon which values the interviewer seems to be asking them to endorse. It is no surprise that the pro-choice side of the debate consistently employs one frame, the pro-life side the other. Nor is it any surprise that an accomplished politician like then-President Clinton, recognizing the conflict felt by many Americans, announced that he was pro-choice and against abortion.

Consistently inconsistent, Americans are pragmatic, not ideological, on the abortion issue. They favor the right to choose, but not an unconditional right to choose in every conceivable circumstance. Surveys show that rape, birth defects, and threats to the mother's health and life are overwhelmingly viewed as justifiable circumstances, but personal convenience and gender selection are not. The mother's age, financial condition, and marital status divide the population deeply. For this reason Americans oppose overturning *Roe*, but as Figure 5.8 shows, they approve of state laws that make abortion more difficult, and they oppose public funding. About 60 percent of the public approved of the Supreme Court's *Casey* decision, and Democrats were just as likely to approve as Republicans were. Political folklore claims that the Supreme Court follows the election returns, but in the recent abortion decisions, it might well be said that the Supreme Court followed the opinion polls.

FIGURE 5.8
Americans tend to favor abortion rights, but with restrictions

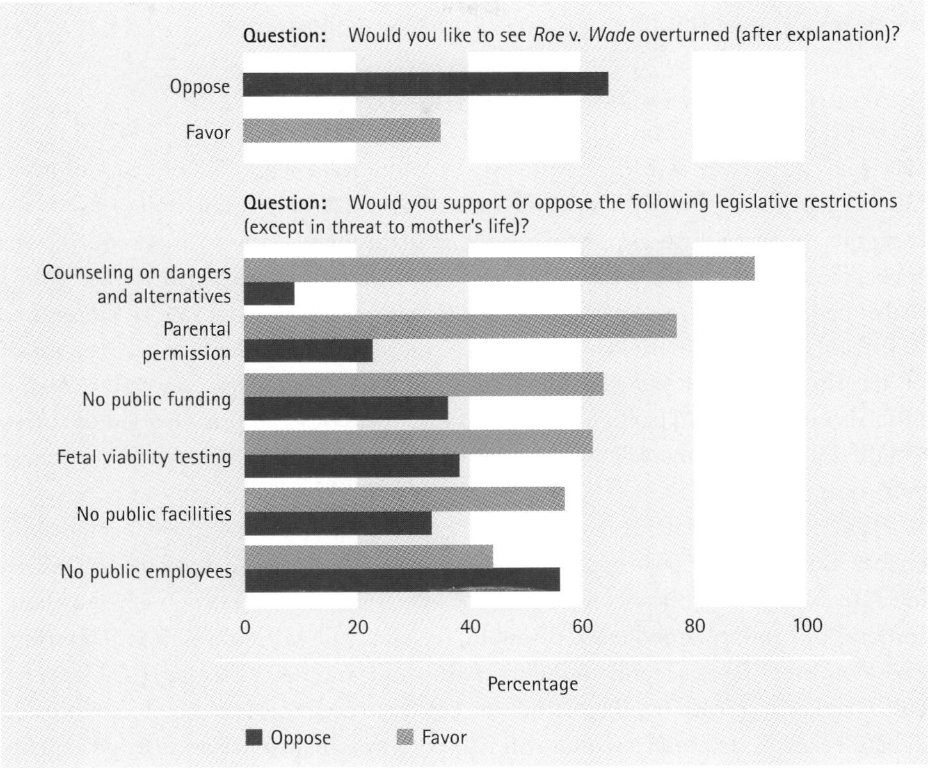

Question: Would you like to see *Roe* v. *Wade* overturned (after explanation)?

Oppose
Favor

Question: Would you support or oppose the following legislative restrictions (except in threat to mother's life)?

Counseling on dangers and alternatives
Parental permission
No public funding
Fetal viability testing
No public facilities
No public employees

0 20 40 60 80 100

Percentage

■ Oppose ▨ Favor

SOURCE: Gallup, July 6–7, 1989.

GOVERNING BY PUBLIC OPINION?

Never before have politicians been so well equipped to measure and interpret public opinion. Clinton's White House in particular developed a reputation for "the way policy and politics were routinely interwoven in his decision-making process." Critics regularly complain that policy is too "poll driven." During the 2000 presidential campaign, George W. Bush promised that he would end the permanent campaign. "A responsible leader . . . makes decisions based upon principle, not based upon polls or focus groups," he told an audience in Michigan. Six months into his presidency, though, observers noted that the Bush White House was polling about twice a month.[45] The permanent campaign seems inescapable.

The presidency aside, however, there is no guarantee that public policy will follow opinion even when preferences are fairly clear. The reason is that although individual politicians may be highly responsive to public opinion, the system as a whole may not be. Recent tragic events provide an illustration.

A DISCONNECT BETWEEN PUBLIC OPINION AND PUBLIC POLICY: GUN CONTROL

On April 20, 1999, two male students at Columbine High School in Colorado killed 12 of their peers and wounded more than 20 others. The killers used two shotguns, a semiautomatic pistol, and a semiautomatic rifle in their murderous spree. This was the fourth school shooting in little more than a year. Other young males had shot teachers or students in West Paducah, Kentucky; in Jonesboro, Arkansas; and in Springfield, Oregon. Whether because of the cumulative impact or the sheer scale of the rampage, the Columbine shootings energized elected officials into action. In particular, antigun members of Congress decided to revive a stalled juvenile crime bill so that they could use it as a vehicle for passing new gun control laws.

One controversial measure was a Senate proposal to require background checks on potential customers at gun shows. The measure initially had failed because many Republican lawmakers saw it as an undue burden on gun consumers, but the inflamed state of public opinion following the school shootings gave some of them second thoughts. After still another shooting (in Conyers, Georgia), the Senate reconsidered its earlier decision. The highly publicized debate reached its climax with a roll call vote in which senators divided equally for and against the proposal, allowing Vice President Al Gore to use his constitutional tie-breaking power to give the idea Senate approval. By much wider margins the Senate adopted other provisions mandating trigger locks on or lock boxes with every handgun sold, outlawing imports of high-capacity ammunition clips, and raising the age at which juveniles could buy handguns and assault weapons. The amended bill passed the Senate by a comfortable margin and then went to the House of Representatives.

House Republican leaders also thought that the aroused state of public opinion required some response. Speaker Denny Hastert (R-IL) commented that "This is one of those rare times when the national consensus demands that we act" and promised that the House would pass a gun control measure.[46] But the issue was now thoroughly entangled in partisan politics. Vice President Gore obviously believed that his highly visible gun control stance would aid his presidential bid, and congressional Democrats hoped to use the issue to help regain control of the Congress in 2000. The key target group was suburban voters—especially women, whom polls showed favored gun control more than men did.[47] To appeal to them, Democrats framed the issue as one of protecting children by restricting access to guns.

The Democrats were not united, however. A senior Democrat, John Dingell of Michigan, was an avid hunter and a former National Rifle Association board member. Dingell worked with Republican leaders to develop an amendment that would weaken the Senate's gun show restrictions. Forty-five Democrats followed Dingell and joined Republicans to pass the weaker provision. However, angry liberal Democrats who believed the legislation did not go far enough then joined with angry conservative Republicans who felt it still went too far and rejected the bill! The House adjourned, so no gun control provisions resulted from the furor over Columbine.

At first glance this story seems to be one of irresponsible or even corrupt behavior by the Congress. Certainly, that is the way the media portrayed it. The story line offered by the media was simple: Public opinion counted less than the campaign contributions and arm twisting of the NRA. But this account is too simplistic. Members of Congress do not get reelected by opposing an aroused majority of their constituents in exchange for an interest-group endorsement or a $5,000 PAC contribution. Rather, the failure of the House to pass gun control measures shows the imperfect connection between aggregate public opinion and national public policy.

Members of Congress represent congressional districts of 630,000 or so people, whose opinions may be very different from those of the country as a whole. The national distribution of opinion is of little importance to members of Congress, unless they happen to be considering a run for the presidency; the distribution of opinion in their districts is what counts. And what counts even more is the distribution of opinion among the voters who elected them. So it is no surprise that the minority of Democrats who followed Dingell's lead came mainly from rural and mixed districts, where guns tend to be a more important part of daily life. A large majority of representatives who voted against gun control may well have voted in accordance with the sentiments of majorities *in their districts.*

Still, given the high level of support for the gun control provisions, it is likely that some representatives did vote against district majorities. Was this the NRA at work? To some extent, probably yes, but remember that interest-group endorsements and campaign contributions don't vote. There have to be voters in the district who will act on the group's support. The problem for gun control activists is that their supporters are much less likely to act on their convictions than are their opponents, who see government attempts to monitor guns or limit their availability as an attack on personal freedom. As Democratic Minority Leader Richard Gephardt (D-MO) conceded, "The 80 percent that are for gun safety just aren't for it very much. They're not intense."[48] Indeed, although most polls registered a high level of support for gun control, the same polls indicated that the public did not regard it as one of the more important issues facing the country. One national poll indicated that gun control ranked twelfth in importance as a voting issue in the next election.[49] Not many supporters of gun control are intense, **single-issue voters** (if they vote at all), but the opponents of gun control certainly are. Indeed, Dingell and the Democrats who followed him pointed out that popular support for gun control was at least as high earlier in the decade as it was after Columbine, but despite that fact, Democrats lost their congressional majority in 1994 in part because of the party's support for the ban on assault weapons.

In sum, even when a clear majority opinion exists, it may not translate directly into public policy. Opinions filter through political institutions such as the electoral system. Such filtering takes account of the fact that some people feel much more passionately about an issue than others.

DOES PUBLIC OPINION MATTER?

We note that individual members of the public are nonideological. But as political scientist James Stimson has observed, the public at large certainly understands that the Democrats are to the left of the Republicans on most issues.[50] Moreover, the public knew that Ronald Reagan was farther to the right than Richard Nixon was and that George McGovern was farther to the left than Jimmy Carter was. It may not be possible to separate the nuances of public opinion from the noise, but the general direction or "mood" of the public may be easier to gauge. Stimson shows, for example, that if hundreds of survey questions are analyzed together, they indeed yield a portrait of an electorate that was turning to the right in the years leading up to Reagan's election.[51]

In the same vein, Benjamin Page and Robert Shapiro have argued that, viewed *collectively,* the public is reasonably "rational." Analysis of thousands of poll questions asked between 1935 and 1980 shows that, in the aggregate, public opinion is more stable than the opinions of individual members of the public are and that public opinion reacts to new developments in logical ways. Moreover, taking such a broad, long-term view, Page and Shapiro find that American public policy follows public opinion. When trends in opinion are clearly moving in one direction, public policy follows. The more pronounced the trend, the more likely policy is to follow it, especially when the public wants policy to move in a liberal direction.[52] Similarly, recent research shows that when federal spending goes up, public preferences for continued increases go down, an effect that indicates some broad public recognition of the direction in which government policy has moved.[53]

The newer findings of Stimson, Page and Shapiro, and others provide an important corrective to much of the earlier work on public opinion. Although the opinions of the individuals who make up the public are often poorly informed, unconnected, inconsistent, and changeable, the process of aggregation may cancel out individual error and enable the central tendency to emerge. Think of a grade school orchestra. Individually, the young musicians are so unsteady that it is difficult to identify the tune each is playing; but put them all together, and the audience can make out "Twinkle, Twinkle Little Star." So it is with public opinion. On some issues and at some times, public opinion and public policy may not be closely aligned, but if one looks at the general direction of policy as shaped by the electoral system, public opinion usually gets its way.

Many framers of the U.S. Constitution feared and distrusted public opinion. They deliberately chose institutions that would constrain it. The Constitution, which provides for federalism, the separation of powers, a bicameral legislature, a Bill of Rights, six-year Senate terms, and the Electoral College, certainly was not designed to translate public opinion directly into public policy. On the contrary, the Constitution sought to insulate senators and presidents from public opinion, allowing them to exercise leadership. But in America's new democracy, elected officials always watch for shifts in public opinion that could cost them their jobs come election time.

CHAPTER SUMMARY

Public opinion is a basic element of democratic politics, but measuring public opinion is an inexact science at best. The question wording, the sample, and the complexity of the issues make designing good public opinion polls very tricky. On many issues, including abortion, the public truly does not have answers that are easily quantified in a bar graph for an American government textbook. Public opinion exerts its influence largely through the calculations of public officials who understand that they can be challenged in free elections and must consider the distribution and intensity of views on any issue. Elected officials clearly will hesitate to defy the will of an aroused public, but even unexpressed public opinion may influence the actions of politicians who fear arousing it.

Despite the importance of public opinion, governing by opinion poll is difficult and perhaps undesirable. Citizens tend not to be well informed; their views are not firmly held, can change quickly, and often are not connected to other, seemingly related views. For these reasons, poll results often are misleading and often are misinterpreted by politicians and journalists. In the long run, American democracy follows public opinion, but public policy does not always respond to shifts in public opinion over the short term.

KEY TERMS

frames, p. 146

ideologies, p. 138

information cost, p. 136

issue publics, p. 137

mass public, p. 138

measurement error, p. 130

political efficacy, p. 127

political elites, p. 138

random sample, p. 129

sampling error, p. 129

selection bias, p. 130

single-issue voter, p. 150

socializing agent, p. 126

SUGGESTED READINGS

Cook, Elizabeth, Ted Jelen, and Clyde Wilcox. *Between Two Absolutes: Public Opinion and the Politics of Abortion.* Boulder, CO: Westview, 1992. Careful, disinterested description and explanation of American attitudes toward abortion.

Herbst, Susan. *Numbered Voices: How Opinion Polling Has Shaped American Politics.* Chicago: University of Chicago Press, 1993. An informative historical survey of the growth of opinion polling, with a critical examination of its impact on contemporary politics.

Jacobs, Lawrence, and Robert Shapiro. *Politicians Don't Pander: Political Manipulation and the Loss of Democratic Responsiveness.* Chicago: University of Chicago Press, 2000. Provocative argument that today's politicians follow their own strongly held preferences and that polls are only a tool used to determine how best to frame the positions that the politicians personally favor.

Page, Benjamin, and Robert Shapiro. *The Rational Public.* Chicago: University of Chicago Press, 1992. Monumental study of public opinion from the 1930s to the 1990s. The authors argue that, viewed as a collec-

tivity, the public is rational, however imperfect the individual opinions that members of the public hold.

Schuman, Howard, and Stanley Presser. *Questions and Answers in Attitude Surveys.* New York: Harcourt, Academic Press, 1981. A comprehensive study of the effects of question wording, form, and context on survey results.

Stimson, James. *Public Opinion in America: Moods, Cycles, and Swings.* Boulder, CO: Westview Press, 1991. Statistically sophisticated examination of American public opinion from the 1960s to the 1990s, in which the author finds that public opinion was moving in a conservative direction in the 1970s but reversed direction around the time of Reagan's election.

Zaller, John. *The Nature and Origins of Mass Opinion.* New York: Cambridge University Press, 1992. An influential reinterpretation of public opinion findings that argues that people do not have fixed opinions on many subjects. Rather, their responses reflect variable considerations stimulated by the question and the context.

ON THE WEB

American Association for Public Opinion Research
www.aapor.org
An academic association interested in the methods, applications, and analysis of public opinion and survey research. This site includes access to the *Public Opinion Quarterly* index and its contents.

The Roper Center for Public Opinion Research
www.ropercenter.uconn.edu
An academic, nonprofit center for the study of public opinion maintaining the world's largest archive of public opinion data.

The National Opinion Research Center
www.norc.uchicago.edu
Based at the University of Chicago, the social science data site provides access to survey history, a library of publications, links, and information on general social survey methodology.

INDIVIDUAL PARTICIPATION

On the morning after the 1992 national elections, large headlines summed up the presidential outcome: Clinton Beats Bush! But farther down their front pages, many papers carried another story: Turnout Rises! Around 55 percent of the voting-age population had cast presidential votes, a 5 percent increase over 1988. Even more important than the amount by which voter **turnout** increased was the simple fact that it *did* increase, for between 1960 and 1992 voting rates had dropped almost continuously from one presidential election to the next. Many observers hoped that these headlines pointed the way to a revitalized electoral system.

Alas, 1992 proved to be little more than a blip. Less than half of Americans voted for president in 1996, the lowest figure since 1924. Indeed, if we set aside the 1920 and 1924 elections (for which women had just received the right to vote), the 1996 turnout figure was the lowest for a presidential year since the United States became a mass democracy in 1828. The news was not much better in 2000, as barely more than half the eligible electorate voted despite the closeness of the contest. And turnout is ordinarily highest in presidential contests; it drops even lower in other elections.

International observers of American politics probably were surprised by the attention given to the 1992 turnout. After all, more than three-quarters of the British voted when they defeated Prime Minister John Major in 1997. Turnout was an almost unimaginable (to Americans) 96 percent in the 1996 Australian parliamentary elections. In 1999 the turnout rate was 91 percent in the Belgian parliamentary elections, 89 percent in the South African parliamentary elections, and 93 percent in the Indonesian parliamentary elections. By the standards of other democracies, turnout in American national elections is exceptionally low.

Not everyone is concerned about low voter turnout though. Unlike a century ago, some point out, there are no poll taxes, literacy tests, gender barriers, or property requirements to block access to the voting booth. Voters *choose* to stay away. Some are apathetic; some are ignorant; some are simply self-centered. Why badger such people? What would they bring to an election?[1]

Others are more troubled. Voting is widely regarded as the fundamental form of democratic participation. If a bare majority votes, how representative are the public officials they elect, and how legitimate are the actions these officials take? Not very, they argue. Political theorist Benjamin Barber charges that "In a country where voting is the primary expression of citizenship, the refusal to vote signals the bankruptcy of democracy."[2]

Whether or not one is concerned about low participation, it presents a puzzle. The United States is a rich country, with citizens who have high levels of education. Usually democracy thrives in such a setting, and voting is the *only* form of democratic participation for the great bulk of the population. It is intriguing so few do even that.

LOW VOTER TURNOUT IS INTERESTING FOR ONE OTHER REASON. It threatens our claim that elections drive American politics. Why would voter participation be significantly *lower* if elections had a *greater* impact on politicians in America than in other countries? Americans presumably have enough common sense to decide whether an activity is worth their effort. Surely most would vote if they learned from observation that elections were important. Therefore, maybe Americans do not vote because their experience contradicts our interpretation.

Certainly this thinking contains an element of truth. Some Americans do stay out of politics because they doubt their ability to make a difference. But most explanations for why Americans do not vote have very little to do with the importance of elections or who wins them. Americans vote at a higher rate than the statistics usually imply, and—leaving aside voting—they participate in politics at a *higher* rate than citizens in other countries. To the extent voter participation is lower, it results from the shape of American institutions and does not undermine the relevance of elections.

Before explaining these claims, however, it is important to review the history of the **franchise,** or right to vote, in the United States. Equipped with this background, you will be ready to understand why many people do not participate actively in America's new democracy.

A BRIEF HISTORY OF THE FRANCHISE IN THE UNITED STATES

A single political party, the Democratic–Republicans, dominated the United States in the early nineteenth century. The party's members in Congress met in a caucus before each presidential election to nominate their candidate, who invariably won. But in 1824 the caucus could not unite behind a single nominee. As a result, four candidates vied for the office; they included Secretary of State John Quincy Adams (son of the second president), War of 1812 hero General Andrew Jackson, and Speaker of the House Henry Clay of Kentucky.

Although Jackson received the largest share of the popular vote, 50 percent more than his closest competitor, no one managed a majority in the Electoral College. The election went to the House of Representatives, as specified in the

Constitution. There, Speaker Henry Clay delivered the victory to Adams, who in turn appointed Clay secretary of state, a position once considered the stepping-stone to the presidency. The losers condemned this sequence of events as evidence of a "corrupt bargain" between Adams and Clay.

THE BIRTH OF MASS DEMOCRACY

Ironically, this instance of popular frustration produced one of the nation's most dramatic moves toward full democracy. Jackson's supporters were so outraged that they redoubled their efforts for the next presidential election. They linked local political organizations together across the country, and they spread their campaign outward to the newly settled West. They pressured for change in election laws, sometimes successfully. For example, four states transferred the right to choose presidential electors from their legislatures to the voters. Turnout increased in all the other states. In total, more than three times as many men voted for electors in 1828 as had voted in 1824, and Jackson easily defeated Adams.[3]

Despite the tripling of voter turnout between 1824 and 1828, only about 56 percent of the adult male population voted in 1828. The problem was not necessarily lack of interest. Many men had no choice. Property qualifications for voting varied from state to state and were very unevenly enforced, but in various forms they continued into the 1830s. Most states restricted the franchise to taxpayers until the 1850s. Not until the eve of the Civil War could it be said that the United States had universal white male **suffrage** (another term for franchise).

Not all voter qualifications were economic. Until the 1830s, a few states limited voting to those who professed belief in a Christian god. Jews were not permitted to vote in Rhode Island as late as 1830. Blacks generally could not vote until after the Civil War, and they lost their rights again a generation later by means of poll taxes, literacy tests, white primaries, and other discriminatory procedures (see Chapter 14). Only modern electoral reforms, such as the Voting Rights Act of 1965, effectively expanded the franchise to African Americans.

Women briefly enjoyed the right to vote in New Jersey after the Declaration of Independence. They lost it in 1807, and more than sixty years passed before another state granted women voting rights. Wyoming became the first state to extend the franchise to women in national elections in 1890. Eleven other states, mostly in the West, had followed by 1916. Finally, in 1920 the Suffrage Movement won its crowning victory when the Nineteenth Amendment was ratified (see Figure 6.1).

The last extension of the franchise came with the adoption of the Twenty-sixth Amendment. Prior to 1971, most states did not grant the vote to those under age

FIGURE 6.1

The right to vote in the United States has been steadily expanded

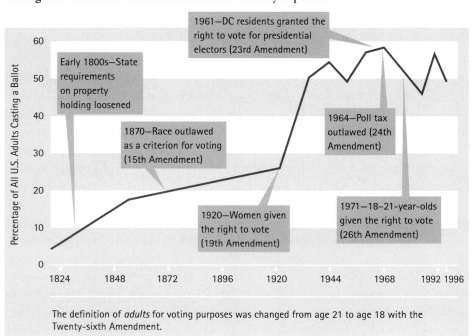

The definition of *adults* for voting purposes was changed from age 21 to age 18 with the Twenty-sixth Amendment.

NOTE: Extending the franchise to new groups does not always result in better turnout.

SOURCE: Adapted from Harold W. Stanley and Richard G. Niemi, *Vital Statistics on American Politics 1999–2000* (Washington, DC: CQ Press, 2000), p. 12.

21. This restriction became an embarrassment during the Vietnam War, however, since it implied that soldiers mature enough to die in Asian jungles were not mature enough to choose political leaders. Even Republican President Richard Nixon supported extending the suffrage to include those 18 and older, despite the certainty that young voters of the era would oppose both him and his party.[4]

WOMEN'S SUFFRAGE AND THE IMPORTANCE OF ELECTIONS

The uneven expansion of the franchise illustrates the overwhelming power of free elections to make a society even more democratic over time. Elected leaders naturally want to expand the influence of social groups that support them. And once a few members of a social group achieve political power, no politician wants to explain why others like them should remain powerless. Promising to give a group more influence in future elections is a fairly cheap way to attract its support, or at least forestall its opposition. This dynamic operated to expand voting rights for blacks and the young, but it was most apparent in the case of women's suffrage.

Fewer than a dozen states allowed women to vote in 1916. Many influential Democratic politicians opposed giving them the franchise. They believed that women were more likely to support Republican reformers. Women would vote against labor unions, against liquor interests, and against machine politicians—all key Democratic constituencies. Moreover, southern Democrats worried that granting voting rights to women would raise African American aspirations for similar rights.

Democratic President Woodrow Wilson, who was running for reelection that year, did not have a clear position on women's suffrage. Indeed, he once dodged the issue by saying that the question had never come to his attention. But Wilson was in a difficult spot. He had won the 1912 election in a three-way race, receiving only 42 percent of the popular vote. His 1916 opponent, Republican Charles Evans

Demonstrating for women's suffrage

The suffragists put considerable pressure on President Woodrow Wilson to support the Nineteenth Amendment. Women initially received the franchise in only a few western states. How did that increase the pressure on politicians to support a constitutional amendment?

Hughes, supported women's suffrage, and one-sixth of the country's electoral votes belonged to states where women could vote. If Wilson came out against a constitutional amendment to expand the franchise, he risked moving Hughes one-third of the way toward an Electoral College majority.

So Wilson decided to ignore the wishes of many Democrats, and signaled his moderate support for the cause. He promised to vote in favor of a 1916 women's suffrage referendum in New Jersey, his home state. Partly on the strength of this moderate position, Wilson was able to carry 10 of the 12 women's suffrage states and narrowly win reelection. Politicians quickly jumped on the bandwagon, passing a constitutional amendment through Congress and the states in time for women to vote in the 1920 presidential election nationwide. Interestingly, the United States was far ahead of most of the world in granting full rights of citizenship to women. France did not allow women to vote until 1945, and the last Swiss canton did not enfranchise women until 1990![5]

INTERNATIONAL COMPARISONS OF VOTER TURNOUT

The United States expanded the franchise more quickly than other advanced democracies. Today every mentally competent, law-abiding citizen who has reached the age of 18 may vote. Elections are a central institution of American politics. It is therefore puzzling (and perhaps a bit embarrassing) that Americans participate at low levels (see Table 6.1). The truth is not quite as dire, however, as the statistical comparisons published in newspapers often imply. Procedures for calculating turnout differ from country to country, and the differences systematically lower American turnout figures relative to those in other democracies.

COMPUTING TURNOUT

Turnout would seem to be simple enough to measure. The U.S. Bureau of the Census calculates official turnout in presidential elections as the number of people voting for president divided by the number of people in the voting-age population. This definition seems straightforward, but it lowers American turnout as much as 5 percent relative to other countries. Consider the numerator, the number of people voting for president. If you believe that all the candidates are bums and you either don't vote for president or don't pick a recognizable candidate, you are not counted as having voted. Other countries are more flexible. In France, for example, unhappy voters have long scribbled an offensive suggestion across their ballots (the English translation has initials "F. Y."). French election offi-

TABLE 6.1

AMERICANS ARE LESS LIKELY TO VOTE
THAN ARE THE CITIZENS OF OTHER DEMOCRACIES

The figures represent the average turnout (in percentages) in elections to the lower house of the legislature or parliament in 37 countries, 1960–1995.

COUNTRY	AVERAGE TURNOUT (%)	COUNTRY	AVERAGE TURNOUT (%)
Australia (14)[a]	95	Costa Rica (8)	81
Malta (6)	94	Norway (9)	81
Austria (9)	92	Israel (9)	80
Belgium (12)	91	Portugal (9)	79
Italy (9)	90	Finland (10)	78
Luxembourg (7)	90	Canada (11)	76
Iceland (10)	89	France (9)	76
New Zealand (12)	88	United Kingdom (9)	75
Denmark (14)	87	Ireland (11)	74
Venezuela (7)	85	Spain (6)	73
Bulgaria (2)	80	Japan (12)	71
Germany (9)	86	Estonia (2)	69
Sweden (14)	86	Hungary (2)	66
Greece (10)	86	Russia (2)	61
Lithuania (1)	86	India (6)	58
Latvia (1)	85	United States (9)	54
Czech Republic (2)	85	Switzerland (8)	54
Brazil (3)	83	Poland (2)	51
Netherlands (7)	83		

[a]Number of elections.

SOURCE: Adapted from Mark Franklin, "Electoral Participation," in Lawrence Le Duc, Richard Niemi, and Pippa Norris, eds., *Comparing Democracies* (Thousand Oaks, CA: Sage, 1996), p. 218.

cials count such ballots, whereas most American officials would not.[6] Or if you cast a "frivolous" write-in vote (actual examples from U.S. elections are Rambo, ZZ Top, and Batman), election officials in many jurisdictions ignore your vote rather than tabulating it as "other." The decision to exclude some ballots lowers U.S. turnout figures by 1 to 2 percent per election.[7]

More important are factors that affect the denominator, the number of people in the voting-age population. The **voting-age population** refers to the number of people over the age of 18, a number that includes some groups legally ineligible to vote: felons, people confined to mental or correctional institutions, and (most important) noncitizens. Counting the entire voting-age population rather than only the eligible voting-age population lowers U.S. turnout figures by another 3 percent.[8]

Other countries use a different denominator in their turnout calculations: the registered population. More than 30 percent of the American voting-age population is unregistered. When turnout is measured as the number voting among **registered voters**—those who have signed up according to the requirements prevailing in their states and localities—U.S. figures jump to the mid-range of turnout in industrial democracies.

Since registered American voters turn out at levels typical of other democracies, it is tempting to conclude that registration requirements are part of the problem. Voter registration is automatic in most of the world, a function performed by the central government. American practice differs in making registration entirely the responsibility of the individual, and one-third of the eligible population does not bother to register. It is not clear whether simplifying registration would make a significant difference, though. A few states have no registration, or let voters register at their polling stations on election day, yet turnout still falls well below the levels in many European countries.[9] Activists tried to increase voting by pushing 1993's "motor voter" law, which required motor vehicle offices to double as voter registration offices—but preliminary evidence suggests this reform changed little.[10] Statistical simulations suggest that liberalizing registration procedures would increase national turnout only about 9 percent.[11]

HOW AMERICAN INSTITUTIONS HOLD DOWN TURNOUT

Registration requirements may not explain low voter turnout, but other legal differences between Europe and the United States may. Voting is compulsory in some countries.[12] Greek electoral law provides for imprisonment of nonvoters for up to 12 months. That penalty is never applied, but other democracies do penalize nonvoters, at least sometimes. Australian law allows for fines of up to $50 for not voting (without a valid excuse), and 4 percent of nonvoters apparently must pay. Belgium also imposes fines. In addition to having their identification papers stamped "Did Not Vote," Italian nonvoters have their names posted on community bulletin boards. Nonvoters risk the possibility of unsympathetic treatment at the hands of public officials and criticism from their friends.

Turnout in democracies with compulsory voting is almost 15 percent higher than it is in other democracies.[13] No doubt American turnout in American elections would increase if the government punished those who abstain! But it is not clear that, to Americans, the ideas of democracy and forced voting go together.

Several additional institutional variations raise the costs of voting for Americans. Elections in America traditionally are held on Tuesdays, an ordinary workday. In most of the rest of the world, either elections are held on Sundays or election days are proclaimed official holidays. In Italy, workers receive free train fare back to their places of registration, usually their hometowns, so in effect the government pays for family reunions.

Also, keep in mind that the United States conducts more elections than other countries do.[14] In most European countries, citizens vote only two or three times in five years—once for members of Parliament, once for representatives to the European Union, and perhaps once for small numbers of local officials. The burden is much less than American voters face, so turnout statistics for a single American election are not comparable with those for a single European election. Some have suggested, not completely tongue in cheek, that turnout in the United States should be calculated as the percentage who vote at least once during a four-year period. This number would be closer to turnout figures for other countries.[*]

Finally, some states use lists of registered voters to select people for jury duty, a task that many Americans wish to avoid. Fear of losing many days' work if a trial is extended (think about the O. J. Simpson criminal trial!) probably is sufficient to motivate some citizens to forfeit their right to vote. One study concluded that in such jurisdictions, turnout is 5 to 10 percent lower than it otherwise would be.[15] And this consideration leaves out the many Americans who do not register because they think, wrongly, that they live in such jurisdictions!

All in all, both intentionally and accidentally, American practices raise the costs of voting relative to those in other countries. When some citizens understandably react to those costs by failing to vote, editorialists criticize them for their lack of public spirit. Scholars, meanwhile, are puzzled that turnout is so low in such a wealthy, educated country, where civic attitudes encourage popular participation. But the nation's laws are not equally encouraging. Political scientist Bingham Powell estimates that differences in electoral institutions, chiefly registration systems, depress American turnout between 10 and 15 percent relative to that in Europe.[16] In sum, it costs Americans more to vote, and they receive less support for voting than citizens in most other countries.

---

[*]Interestingly, Switzerland also asks voters to turn out frequently, and the turnout rate there is comparable to the American rate.

WHY AMERICANS
VOTE LESS OFTEN THAN
IN THE PAST

For many people the problem is not only that turnout levels in the United States are lower than in other advanced democracies, but also that turnout has fallen over time (see the Election Connection, "The Decline of Voting after 1896"). The declines have been steepest during the past generation, falling steadily in presidential elections between 1960 and 1988 before hitting a half-century low in 1996 (see Figure 6.2). In off-year elections, turnout declined more erratically, but it is significantly lower now than it was a generation ago. Steven Rosenstone and Mark Hansen report that the minorities of people who work in campaigns or attend political or governmental meetings also declined in number, although other studies reach slightly different conclusions. Even those who participate in such minimal ways as signing petitions are slightly fewer in number now than a generation ago.[17]

To many observers these declines in popular participation suggest that something is terribly wrong with American politics. This concern was reinforced in the

FIGURE 6.2
Turnout in the United States has declined since 1960

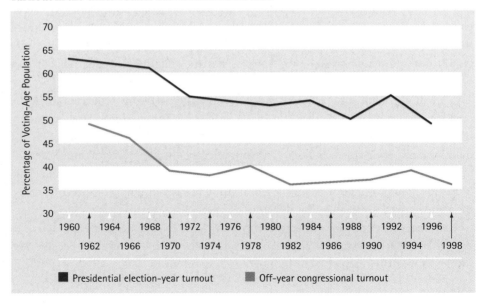

SOURCE: Norman Ornstein, Thomas Mann, and Michael Malbin, *Vital Statistics on Congress, 1999–2000* (Washington, DC: American Enterprise Institute, 2000), p. 48.

The Decline of Voting after 1896

In the late nineteenth century, American turn-out levels reached all-time highs; in the five elections leading up to 1896, turnout averaged 80 percent of the male voting-age population. In the five elections following 1896, however, turnout averaged just 65 percent, and it has never since reached the late-nineteenth-century highs.[a]

What happened in 1896? As we explain in Chapter 8, many political historians consider 1896 to be the central election in a critical era, a period in which voting alignments changed in significant and lasting ways. The decades from the end of the Civil War to the mid-1890s were the most electorally competitive in American history. The parties of this period were stronger than before or since; historians liken them to military organizations.[b] Supported by the patronage system, the parties had ample *resources* to mobilize the electorate. And given the intense electoral competition, the parties had the *incentive* to mobilize the electorate—defeat would throw tens of thousands of party workers out of their jobs.

But political developments were undercutting both the resources and the incentives that buoyed up the parties.[c] Civil service and other reforms were beginning to eat away at the patronage system. And between 1888 and 1896, 90 percent of the states instituted some kind of personal registration system, raising the citizens' costs of voting and restricting the parties' ability to vote the dead, vote people twice (or more!), vote the ineligible, and engage in other corrupt practices that raised turnout.[d]

Meanwhile, the Populists, a radical third party representing the agricultural West, merged with the Democrats and nominated William Jennings Bryan, who thundered that the Republicans would not be allowed to "crucify mankind on a cross of gold." After taking a look at Bryan, an ample majority of voters decided to chance the Republican candidate, William McKinley. It was more than a temporary victory. In large areas of the North and Midwest, the Democrats stopped being competitive. Their national majority now secure, the Republicans abandoned the South to the Democrats, who completed their disfranchisement of black Americans as well as many poor whites.

With party competition greatly reduced in much of the country, the parties no longer had the incentive to mobilize supporters, and Americans no longer believed it was important to vote. Meanwhile, reforms continued to sap the material resources the parties had relied on, and party organizations went into long-term decline. Although political historians continue to argue about the relative importance of the institutional and political factors that led turnout to decline, 1896 clearly was a watershed between a high-turnout, highly competitive electoral era and a low-turnout era of Republican dominance.[e]

What do you think?

- If many Americans of earlier generations voted because they were paid to do so, in effect, should we be as concerned about low turnout levels today as many are? Why or why not?
- If compulsory voting (the "stick") is unacceptable, why not pay people (the "carrot") to vote? For example, your ballot stub could be a ticket in a lottery with large cash

(continued)

(*continued from previous page*)

prizes. (This would have the additional effect of helping close the gap between turnout of the poor and that of the wealthy.)

[a]Walter Dean Burnham, "The Turnout Problem," in A. James Reichley, ed., *Elections American Style* (Washington DC: Brookings, 1987), Table 5.3.

[b]Richard Jensen, "American Election Campaigns: A Theoretical and Historical Typology," presented at the 1968 Meetings of the Midwest Political Science Association.

[c]Walter Dean Burnham, *Critical Elections and the Mainsprings of American Politics* (New York: Norton, 1970), Ch. 4.

[d]Philip Converse, "Change in the American Electorate," in *The Human Meaning of Social Change*, Angus Campbell and Philip Converse, eds. (New York: Russell Sage, 1972), pp. 263–337.

[e]See the articles, comments, and rejoinders by Walter Dean Burnham, Philip Converse, and Jerrold Rusk in *American Political Science Review* (September 1974).

late 1970s when analysts noted that participation was declining at the same time that trust in government was declining—recall Figure 1.1. Many feared that declining trust threatened the entire political system, and that declining turnout was but an early symptom. Research soon showed, however, that the two trends were largely unrelated. That is, turnout declined among the trusting and the cynical alike, and the former were no more likely to vote than the latter.[18]

What makes the decline in turnout all the more puzzling is that two other developments in the past three decades led to an expectation of *rising* turnout. First, court decisions, federal legislation such as the Voting Rights Act and its amendments, and the Twenty-fourth Amendment to the Constitution have removed numerous impediments to voting. For example, poll taxes and literacy tests were abolished, state and local residency requirements were shortened, registration was made simpler and more convenient, bilingual ballots were permitted, and absentee voting was made easier. Such reforms were especially effective in the South, where they helped overcome the legacy of racial discrimination.

Second, socioeconomic change should have raised turnout in the post-1964 period. Education is the single strongest predictor of turnout. Higher educational levels produce a keener sense of civic duty and help people deal with the complexities of registering and voting. Researcher Ruy Teixeira estimates that, other things being equal, the net effect of socioeconomic changes, chiefly education, should have been to raise national turnout by about 4 percent.[19]

What, then, explains the decline in turnout? There is less agreement here than there is on the explanations for turnout differences between the United States and other democracies. Journalists often take voters to task for being lazy and uninvolved, while criticizing the candidates for being uninspiring and unworthy. But the question of why some people vote while others abstain is certainly more complicated than newspaper editorials usually imply.

For one thing, although citizens of other democracies generally vote at much higher levels than do Americans, turnout is on the decline elsewhere as well. In 17 of 19 advanced democracies around the world, turnout in the 1990s was lower than in the 1950s.[20] So the sources of declining turnout clearly cannot be unique to the United States. Rosenstone and Hansen divide the reasons for voting into two general categories: individual motivations and outside mobilization.[21]

THE DECLINE OF INDIVIDUAL MOTIVATIONS TO VOTE

Individual motivations reflect the personal costs and benefits associated with voting. If you are paid by the hour and you take time off in order to vote, you lose a portion of your wages. If you are a parent who cares for small children, you must pay a sitter or drag the kids along in order to vote. Even if you are a professional with flexible hours, you do less work on election day if you take the time to vote.

Moreover, not all costs are tangible. When you spend time on political activity, you have less time to spend on other, perhaps more attractive or fulfilling, activities. For some people with little education or information, the entire voting situation is confusing and uncomfortable. Staying home enables them to avoid such discomfort. If you are surprised that such minor considerations could lower turnout, consider that turnout generally falls when the weather is unpleasant.[22]

There also are benefits to voting, of course. One reason, though not the only one, why historical turnout levels were so high (sometimes more than 75 percent outside the South) is that many people were paid to vote. For example, scholars estimate that the going price of a vote in New York City elections in the 1880s was $2 to $5 (expressed in 1990 dollars) and that prices soared as high as $25 in particularly competitive circumstances.[23] Material rewards are a much rarer benefit of voting today, but direct payments for voting (sometimes called "walking around money") still exist here and there.

And for some citizens, elections still directly affect their material interests. For example, local government employees vote in low-turnout local elections at higher rates than people employed in the private sector, and government employees in general vote at higher rates, other things being equal.[24] For such individuals, elections give them influence at picking their own bosses.

Today, however, most of the material benefits of voting have faded. The incentives are primarily psychological. Some people take civic norms to heart and feel a duty to vote; they avoid guilt by voting. Others take satisfaction in expressing their preferences for candidates or positions on issues, much as they might enjoy cheering for athletic teams. Such psychological sources of satisfaction are called **psychic benefits of voting.**

Dilbert's philosophy of representation

Some Americans, like Dilbert in the accompanying cartoon, consider voting a duty rather than merely a right. Voting is the central act of participation, one these Americans find personally gratifying. Other Americans neglect voting and seek representation through protests or other focused activities.

Psychic benefits are important, because a single vote seldom affects the outcome. It is very rare for elections to approach a tie.[25] With a small committee, every member has the potential to tip the scale, but in an election any single voter is relatively insignificant. Almost 100 million Americans voted in the 1996 presidential election, despite the lowest turnout rate in 70 years. In the 1998 elections for the U.S. House of Representatives, an average of 141,000 citizens voted in each congressional race. A voter would have been unreasonable to think the outcome depended upon whether he or she voted.[26] The personal benefits of voting generally do not exceed the costs, which has dismal implications for turnout.

Thus, psychic benefits are critical. They do not depend on whether a voter affects the outcome. A voter with a strong sense of duty, who takes considerable satisfaction from expressing a preference, gets those benefits just by casting a vote. These incentives have declined over time, however. Americans once expressed their political preferences by marching around in uniforms or attending festivals. Now they do so in the privacy of a voting booth, simply pulling a lever or coloring in an arrow or punching out a chad. Such an anonymous manner of expressing preferences gives many potential voters little satisfaction. And, as we discuss in Chapter 4, Americans are individualistic; they are unlikely to respond to civic duty alone.

The result is that Americans today are disengaged from the electoral process. They are not so interested in politics and don't care much about who wins each election.[27] Thus, they do not see as much riding on their decisions as in years past, and they probably get less intrinsic satisfaction from supporting admired candidates or parties.

Another political factor that has lowered the benefits of voting is that elections have become less competitive. As we discuss in Chapter 7, the advantage of incumbency in congressional elections increased greatly between the mid-1960s and the mid-1990s, and a similar process occurred more slowly in state legislative elections. Many presidential elections in the 1970s and 1980s were landslides, and gubernatorial elections had become less competitive as well. Rosenstone and Hansen find that in states with competitive gubernatorial campaigns in presidential election years, turnout is 5 percent higher, other things being equal.[28] In a result consistent with such arguments, turnout dropped 5 percent in 1996 when Bill Clinton led Bob Dole by a comfortable margin from start to finish.

Furthermore, with election polls so common, voters are more likely than ever to know when contests are foregone conclusions. The notion that one's vote actually makes a difference must seem more outlandish than ever. The puzzle is not that turnout is so low in the United States but, rather, that turnout is as high as it is.

THE DECLINE OF OUTSIDE ENCOURAGEMENT TO VOTE

Parties, groups, and activists are often concerned about the **mobilization** of their potential supporters (although they are less so in uncompetitive elections). Campaign workers provide baby-sitters and rides to the polls, thus reducing the individual costs of voting. They apply social pressure by contacting citizens who haven't voted and reminding them to do so. Various groups and social networks to which individuals belong also exert social pressures, encouraging the feeling that one has a responsibility to vote.

Political parties were especially important at mobilizing voters in the past. Rosenstone and Hansen observe that

> . . . *party mobilization underwrites the costs of political participation. Party workers inform people about upcoming elections, tell them where and when they can register and vote, supply them with applications for absentee ballots, show them the locations of campaign headquarters, and remind them of imminent rallies and meetings. Campaigns drop by to pick up donations, telephone reminders on the day of the election, and drive the lazy, the harried, the immobile, and the infirm to the polls.*[29]

These mobilization efforts have declined over time. Parties still are active, of course, and candidate organizations are more active than ever. But the nature of their efforts has changed. Polling and media advertising are probably not good substitutes for the kind of pound-the-pavement, doorbell-ringing workers who used to dominate campaigns. Voters may be motivated by the coaxing of a campaign worker standing at the front door or telephoning late in the afternoon of election day, but those same voters may not be motivated by an impersonal TV spot or a taped telephone message urging them to vote.[30] Thus, a change in style from labor-intensive to high-tech campaigning may have indirectly contributed to declining turnout. Nor are social movements, such as the civil rights, antiwar, and other movements, active enough to take up the slack, as they were during the turbulent 1960s.

THE DECLINE OF SOCIAL CONNECTEDNESS

A final explanation for declining turnout falls somewhere between personal and outside motivations. Stephen Knack raises the possibility that common thinking about voting is misconceived. Rather than voting being the fundamental political act, voting may instead be a social act—a way to be part of the community. Voters may take pleasure from having an excuse, once in a while, to gather in a local building and make contact with their neighbors. Voting is related to giving blood, donating to charities, doing volunteer work, and other forms of community involvement.[31]

Voters would respond to these incentives only if they felt connected socially to those around them. **Social connectedness** is the extent to which people are in fact integrated into society—their families, neighborhoods, communities, churches, and other social units. Social connectedness may well have declined over time. Older Americans grew up in a simpler age, when Americans were less mobile and more trusting of their fellow citizens. They may be more connected than are younger Americans, who have grown up in a highly mobile society where cynicism about their fellow citizens is widespread.

Certainly young people seldom vote, and not simply because of their stage in life. Rather, political scientist Warren Miller has shown that declining voter turnout is a result of what social scientists call a **compositional effect:** a change in the people who compose America's potential electorate rather than a change in behavior.[32] Turnout is declining because of the simple fact that older Americans, who have always been accustomed to voting at high rates, are dying and being replaced by younger Americans who have never voted much. Another political scientist, Robert Putnam, argues that the younger generation is less likely to participate in other ways as well.[33]

It is less clear whether social connectedness explains turnout directly. Investigators have examined the possibility, but they are stuck using relatively crude indicators of social connectedness, such as marriage rates, home ownership, church attendance, and length of residence in a community. Nevertheless, such studies find that decreased social connectedness accounts for as much as one-quarter of the decline in presidential election turnout.[34] (Interestingly, although being married is associated with higher turnout, being *newly* married apparently lowers the odds of voting. Voting is probably not high on the priority list of newlyweds![35])

IS LOW TURNOUT A PROBLEM?

Low voting rates probably would not stimulate as much discussion as they do if all social and economic groups in America exhibited the same voting rates. But people differ in their ability to bear the costs of voting, in the strength of their feeling that voting is a duty, and in how often they are the targets of mobilization. Consequently, as Figure 6.3 indicates, turnout rates differ considerably across social and economic groups.[36]

Highly educated people are far more likely to vote than people with little formal education. Education instills a stronger sense of duty and gives people the knowledge, analytic skills, and self-confidence to meet the costs of registering

FIGURE 6.3
Group differences in turnout, 1996

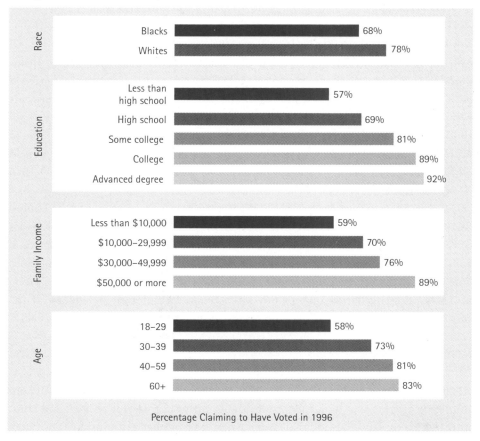

SOURCE: American National Election Studies.

and voting. Over and above education, income also has a significant effect. The wealthy are far more likely to vote than the poor. Affluence, too, reflects a set of skills and personal characteristics that help people overcome barriers to voting.

Studies of turnout in the 1970s concluded that, once differences in education, age, and income were factored out, blacks were at least as likely to vote as whites.[37] But more recent research finds that blacks are somewhat less likely to vote than whites, even taking into account differences in income and educational levels.[38] One suggestion is that African Americans were disillusioned by the failure of the Jesse Jackson's campaigns in 1984 and 1988.[39] Other minorities, such as Latinos and Asians, still face language barriers, though the situation is gradually improving.[40]

Turnout increases with age until one becomes very old, when the trend reverses. People presumably gain experience as they age, experience that makes it easier for them to overcome any barriers to voting. They also become more socially connected, as well as more settled in a life situation that clarifies their political preferences.

Interestingly, the relationships between socioeconomic characteristics and turnout are consistently stronger in the United States than they are in other democracies. Indeed, in some countries there is almost no relationship between education and income on the one hand and voting on the other.[41] The reason is not that in other democracies education and income have effects different from those in the United States; it is that elsewhere parties are much more effective at mobilizing their supporters. In particular, European Social Democratic parties do a far better job of getting their less-advantaged potential voters to the polls than the Democratic party does in the United States.

Given who votes and why, should the relatively low turnout rate in the United States be a cause for concern? Quite a few answers have been offered on both sides of this question. Democrats generally decry low turnout while Republicans tend to be more complacent, because many people assume that the electorate is more conservative than the voting-age population at large is. On the other hand, among scholars, differing views on turnout often hinge on different beliefs about the motives for voting. We briefly sketch three arguments on each side of the debate.

LOW TURNOUT IS NOT A PROBLEM: THREE ARGUMENTS

AN OPTIMISTIC ARGUMENT   Many of those concerned about low turnout implicitly assume that high turnout indicates enthusiasm about politics and commitment to making the political order work. Maybe that assumption is not correct. Some skeptics suggest that high turnout may indicate tension or conflict. People may vote because they believe losing would be unacceptable. Consider the experience of Austria and Germany as their democratic governments crumbled and the Fascist parties took power in the 1930s.[42] Turnout in those elections reached very high levels, but this probably reflected disillusionment and desperation more than commitment and enthusiasm. The 1992 presidential election is a less extreme case in point. Turnout rose, but did this indicate a healthier political system? On the contrary, by many indications people were "mad as hell"—frustrated and upset with their government. Low turnout therefore may be a sign of the health of a political system, a sign of stability. As political scientist Samuel Huntington summarizes the view, "The effective operation of a democratic political system usually requires some measure of apathy and noninvolvement on the part of some individuals and groups."[43]

AN ELITIST ARGUMENT   On average, nonvoters are less educated than voters. Studies also show them to be less informed, less interested in politics, and less concerned about it. Such voters may be more susceptible to getting caught up in political fads. They may be vulnerable to deceptive political advertising, or even outright manipulation. Some therefore argue that the quality of electoral decisions is higher if no special effort is made to increase turnout. For example, social theorist David Reisman once remarked, "Bringing sleepwalkers to the polls simply to increase turnout is no service to democracy."[44] Columnist George Will is even more succinct. "Smaller is smarter," he says.[45] Of course, the process of encouraging people to vote might inform them at the same time. But the elitist argument has gained credence since the 2000 election, in which many voters apparently were incapable of following the instructions on their ballots, for example either voting for the wrong person or voting for multiple candidates.

A CYNICAL OR RADICAL ARGUMENT   Some radicals contend that it is not the nonvoters but the voters who are a cause for concern. According to this viewpoint, elections don't matter—they are charades. Real decisions are made by power elites far from the popular arena. If so, voting is merely a symbolic act that makes the masses feel they have a say in how they are governed. Turnout doesn't matter because elections don't matter. Of course, we disagree strongly with this latter argument. As we stress throughout this book, elections matter a great deal—in some cases, too much.

LOW TURNOUT IS A PROBLEM:
THREE ARGUMENTS

LOW TURNOUT REFLECTS A "PHONY" POLITICS   Low turnout may reflect disgust with an American politics that does not address "real" issues of concern to minorities and the poor. What are real issues? Basically, they involve economics: jobs, health care, housing, income distribution, and education. Instead, the parties debate "phony" **social issues** relevant to the upper-middle-class: rights of free expression, gun control, feminism, animal rights, capital punishment, and gay rights. This argument often is made by Democrats and other progressive thinkers nostalgic for the New Deal coalition (see Chapter 8). On the other hand, the decline of economic issues may simply result from a stronger national economy. Times are relatively good, so voters worry less about their pocketbooks and more about the direction of society.

LOW TURNOUT DISCOURAGES INDIVIDUAL DEVELOPMENT   Classical political theorists from Aristotle to John Stuart Mill emphasized that democracy has an important educational component. Participation in democratic politics stimulates individual development. Participants become better citizens and better human beings, which in turn enables them to take society to a higher level. From the standpoint of this argument, low turnout signifies a lost opportunity. The argument is rather persuasive when applied to participation in intensive, face-to-face processes like local board or council meetings. It seems less relevant to impersonal processes like voting in a national election.[46] Nevertheless, it reminds us that voting may shape more than just an election. It may shape the voters themselves and help determine what manner of people they are.

THE VOTERS ARE UNREPRESENTATIVE   The most obvious concern arising from low turnout is that it produces an unrepresentative electorate. The active electorate is wealthier, whiter, older, and better educated than the potential electorate. However, numerous studies suggest that voting patterns do not bias election results. The policy views and the candidate preferences of nonvoters differ little from those of voters. Some studies have even found that at times the conservative candidate was more popular among nonvoters—Ronald Reagan in 1984, for example.[47]

How can this be? In the first place, although minorities and the poor vote less often than whites and the affluent do, the difference is only a matter of degree. Thus blacks are less likely to vote than whites, but only about one-eighth of all the nonvoters are black. Similarly, the more highly educated are more likely to vote, but 25 percent of the nonvoters have some college education. Nonvoters are not all poor, uneducated, or members of minority groups. Plenty of nonvoters are affluent, well educated, and white—particularly those who have relocated. According to the U.S. Bureau of the Census, nearly one in five Americans moves during the two-year interval between national elections.[48]

In the second place, few groups are as one-sided in their political inclinations as African Americans, who voted roughly 9 to 1 Democratic in the 2000 presidential election. If turnout among most other groups were to increase, the Democrats might get more than half the additional votes, but the Republicans would get a fair proportion as well. Teixeira calculates that, if all the Hispanics and African Americans in the country had voted in 1988 at levels 10 percent higher than that of whites and if all the white poor had voted at a level 10 percent higher than that of the white rich, the Democratic candidate, Michael Dukakis, would still have lost by two and a half million votes.[49] Not all elections are so one-sided, of course, but given the improbability that minorities and the disadvantaged could ever be mobilized at such high levels, it is even more doubtful that realistic changes in turnout would produce a sea change in American politics.

Still, as a Marxist might point out, there could be an element of "false consciousness" here: Because present nonvoters are uninformed and uncommitted, they fail to understand or act on their true interests. The political or social changes necessary to increase their voting would also greatly increase their knowledge and produce a different political outlook. This line of argument could be settled only by greatly increasing turnout and seeing whether the preferences of nonvoters change.

DOES TURNOUT MATTER?

Our view is that nonvoters and voters have diverse motives. Some nonvoters are content while others are alienated, and the same goes for voters. High turnout can indicate either high approval of the political order or serious dissatisfaction with it. Nonvoters don't have much information, but as we see in Chapter 5, neither do many voters. Low turnout does make the actual electorate somewhat less representative than the potential electorate, but not as much as critics often assume. Some potential voters undoubtedly are discouraged by a politics that discusses issues of little relevance for them, but other citizens turn out to vote precisely because of their concern with such issues. And although participation fosters citizenship, we are doubtful that the simple impersonal act of casting a vote fosters it very much. In short, we find some validity in each of the arguments presented; we reject in its entirety only the argument that elections don't matter. Low turnout is a cause for concern, yes, a cause for despair, no.

OUTSIDE THE VOTING BOOTH

Americans turn out at lower levels than citizens in other democracies. Moreover, they are significantly less likely to participate in other ways than they are to vote. Only one-third of Americans report having signed a petition, and a similar number claim to have contacted a government official at one time or another. Substantially fewer have made financial contributions to a party or candidate, attended a political meeting or rally, or worked in a campaign. Two-thirds of Americans participate in no way beyond voting.[50]

It is a bit surprising, then, to learn that Americans are *more* likely to engage in these less-common forms of participation than are the citizens of some countries where turnout is much higher. Figure 6.4 shows that even though only a relatively small number of Americans work in campaigns or contact public officials, more of them do so than citizens in other democracies do. Explanations vary.

- Because there are far more offices and government bodies in the United States, there are far more opportunities to contact officials, attend board meetings, and so forth. Even if Americans were less likely to take advantage of any particular opportunity, the sheer number of chances would result in a higher level of political participation than in other countries where opportunities are more limited.

- America's individualistic political culture, with its emphasis on rights and liberties, encourages Americans to contact public officials and to protest government actions. In contrast, the political cultures of most other democracies are more deferential to authority and discourage ordinary citizens from taking as active a role in politics as that taken in the United States. Citizens elsewhere are less likely to protest government decisions, and when they do, their governments are more likely to ignore them.

- Because American political parties are weaker today than in earlier eras, candidates construct numerous personal organizations, many of whose members are temporary. In other countries a small cadre of committed party workers shoulders most of the burden of campaigning year in and year out, but in the United States campaigns are fought by much larger

FIGURE 6.4

Americans are more likely than citizens in other democracies to participate in ways more demanding than voting

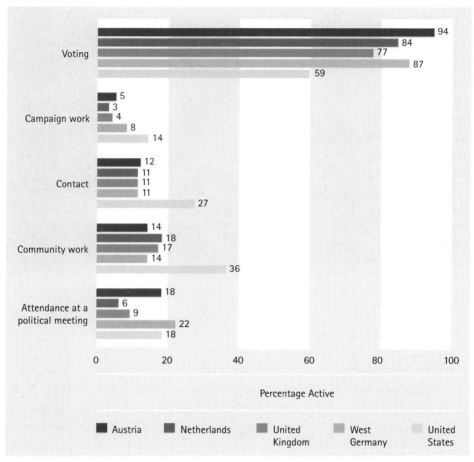

Percentage Active

■ Austria ■ Netherlands ■ United Kingdom ■ West Germany □ United States

SOURCE: Adapted from Sidney Verba, Kay Lehman Schlozman, and Henry Brady, *Voice and Equality* (Cambridge, MA: Harvard University Press, 1995), p. 70.

groups of "occasional activists." These are enthusiastic amateurs who drift in and out between protest and politics, depending on whether particular candidates or issues arouse their enthusiasm.[51]

- Finally, many Americans participate in politics indirectly by joining or supporting interest groups. These groups take a more direct role by soliciting

Political protest

Americans may not turn out to vote quite as much as other nations, but protests are very common in Washington, DC. Here, Kosovar Albanians march in front of the White House in support of the NATO bombings. Protest is an often controversial form of participation. When should it be? Why or why not?

their members for signatures or contributions, encouraging them to go to meetings, and so forth. There are far more groups and associations active in politics in the United States than in other countries, and hence there are far more opportunities for participation through groups. Groups are particularly likely to be the source of "unconventional" participation: protests, demonstrations, and civil disobedience.

CHAPTER SUMMARY

A majority of the American electorate stays away from the polls in most elections. To some extent this pattern results from barriers to participation. Registration is left to the individual, voting is less convenient than elsewhere, and citizens are called on to vote often. In addition, mobilizing agents, such as parties and unions, are weaker in the United States than in other modern democracies; Americans get less encouragement from larger organizations than do citizens of other democracies. Nevertheless, turnout statistics exaggerate the difference between the United States and other democracies—and Americans are more likely to engage in other forms of participation than citizens of democracies elsewhere.

The declining rates of participation in the United States are more difficult to understand, especially since other democracies have experienced a similar trend. Reforms have lowered the costs of voting, and educational levels have gone up; but Americans seem less interested in politics than ever. The explanations for such disenchantment are a matter of much debate. But for our purposes, low turnout appears to be irrelevant. Evidence is thin that low turnout alters the election results. Nonvoters are not all the same, and they do not differ from voters as much as is usually presumed. Elections do not matter any less simply because some voters choose to stay home.

KEY TERMS

compositional effect, p. 170

franchise, p. 156

mobilization, p. 169

psychic benefits of voting,
 p. 167

registered voters, p. 162

social connectedness,
 p. 170

social issues, p. 174

suffrage, p. 157

turnout, p. 155

voting-age population,
 p. 162

SUGGESTED READINGS

Piven, Francis, and Richard Cloward. *Why Americans Don't Vote.* New York: Pantheon, 1988. This critical commentary on nonvoting in the United States contends that "have-nots" are systematically discouraged from voting.

Rosenstone, Steven, and John Mark Hansen. *Mobilization, Participation, and Democracy in America.* New York: Macmillan, 1993. Comprehensive statistical study of electoral and governmental participation from the 1950s to the 1980s, with particular emphasis on the decline in turnout.

Teixeira, Ruy. *The Disappearing American Voter.* Washington, DC: Brookings, 1992. Comprehensive statistical study of turnout from the 1960s to the 1980s, with particular emphasis on the turnout decline and the difference between turnout in the United States and in other democracies.

Verba, Sidney, Kay Schlozman, and Henry Brady. *Voice and Equality: Civic Volunteerism in American Politics.* Cambridge, MA: Harvard University Press, 1995. Fascinating discussion of the development of political skills in nonpolitical contexts, such as churches. Strong on attention to differences involving race, ethnicity, and gender.

Wolfinger, Raymond, and Steven Rosenstone. *Who Votes?* New Haven, CT: Yale University Press, 1980. A statistical study that relies on huge Census Bureau samples and thus provides the best estimates of the relationships between demographic characteristics and voting, though in a limited number of elections (1972 and 1974).

ON THE WEB

The League of Women Voters
www.lwv.org
A nonpartisan political organization, the League of Women Voters encourages the informed and active participation of citizens in government.

Project Vote Smart
www.vote-smart.org
This wide-ranging site is supported by a nonpartisan group that gathers and distributes biographical histories, voting records, campaign finances and promises, and performance evaluations of elected officials and candidates.

A History of the Suffrage Movement
www.rochester.edu/SBA/
history.html
An online history project with links dealing with the Nineteenth Amendment and the history of voting rights in the United States. This site is maintained by the University of Rochester.

NATIONAL
ELECTIONS

elevision networks announced Bill Clinton's election as the nation's forty-second president at 10:30 P.M. on November 3, 1992. No doubt Clinton was thrilled and relieved. He had survived a grueling contest—one in which he had been savaged by accusations of extramarital sex, draft dodging, and pot smoking—to attain the highest office in the land. Yet if this announcement marked the end of one campaign, it is only a slight exaggeration to say that it also marked the beginning of the next. His White House honeymoon was short-lived.

Clinton was a "minority president," having received only 43 percent of the popular vote. Republican candidates had won the presidency in five of the last six elections, three times by landslides—so Clinton's victory appeared a minor setback. Republicans presumed that the Arkansas governor would have a short stay in the White House. Six days after the election, one Republican senator already was campaigning in New Hampshire, and another had filed a statement of candidacy.

Republicans in Congress quickly served notice that they would oppose the minority president's agenda. Senate Republicans killed his economic stimulus program by refusing to allow it to come to a vote. Then, both Senate and House Republicans voted unanimously against Clinton's budget, which passed by one vote in the House and only by virtue of Vice President Gore's tie-breaking vote in the Senate.[1] Other defeats followed, including the national health insurance plan Clinton delivered to Congress.

Resistance seemed to be working. The public apparently did not blame those who obstructed Clinton's proposals. Indeed, voters began to perceive that Clinton was more liberal than originally thought. As opponents characterized his early record, Clinton favored gays and opposed guns; he had raised taxes and proposed a massive government takeover of health care; and he had broken his campaign promise by doing absolutely nothing about welfare. These accusations resonated with the public. Polls indicated that many Americans resented taxes and had grown skeptical of ambitious government programs. They believed the Democratic party did not share their values, and Republicans charged that Clinton was nothing more than a liberal sheep in the clothing of a moderate wolf.

Two years later, in the 1994 elections, the Democrats lost control of both the House and Senate, giving their opposition control of the legislative branch for the first time in 40 years. Some congressional Democrats blamed the president for their electoral misfortunes, and many thought he would follow them into defeat in 1996. But Clinton did not gain his reputation as "the comeback kid" for nothing. He hired a moderate, Richard "Dick" Morris, as his campaign adviser, and he began recasting himself as a centrist. He signed a welfare reform law opposed by liberals in his party and concentrated on balancing the budget without threatening popular middle-class programs for the elderly. By the time the 1996 campaign season rolled around, Clinton enjoyed a comfortable lead in the polls and stayed ahead of opponent Senator Robert Dole throughout the campaign. He coasted to an easy Electoral College victory, taking even Republican mainstays such as Florida.

The 2000 election followed the opposite pattern. As it approached, Clinton had held the White House for eight years and would leave it a popular president. He had fashioned an appealing, middle-of-the-road program. He had worked with Republicans to reduce the national deficit and had allowed respected Republican appointee Alan Greenspan to remain in charge of the Federal Reserve Board. Apparently as a result, the Clinton administration had presided over an unprecedented period of economic growth. His presidency was marred by scandal, most notably deceptions growing out of Clinton's extramarital affair with a young White House intern, but few in the administration shared blame for these personal peccadillos.

Vice President Al Gore thus seemed guaranteed to retain the White House for the Democratic party. He also was a southerner with a moderate policy stance, except on the environment, and was implicated in few of the White House scandals. The economy remained strong, and his campaign, well funded. He left his party's national convention with a solid showing in the polls. Standard statistical models used to predict presidential elections generally indicated that Gore would win handily.[2] And his opponent was a relatively inexperienced politician, Texas Governor George W. Bush, whose main advantages seemed to be his family's influence and a boyish charm.

Once again the election held a surprise. Despite an aggressive primary battle with Arizona Senator John McCain, Bush was able to unite with his rival. He also attracted the endorsement of billionaire Ross Perot, whose independent campaign in 1992 helped dethrone Bush's father. Bush was comforting to both business Republicans and cultural Republicans, since he spoke like an evangelist but offered economic proposals pleasing to corporate interests.[3] The fringes of his party did not demand that he take many unpopular policy stands to satisfy them.[4]

Gore, by contrast, faced repeated threats to his liberal base. Vanquishing respected New Jersey Senator Bill Bradley in the Democratic primaries required him to form ties with national labor unions early on. Then, in the general election he faced a serious challenge from the Green party candidate, activist Ralph Nader—a credible national figure who appealed directly to leftists upset with White House moderation when dealing with international corporations. Unlike

The gloves were off
Some critics charged that Gore ran a poor campaign in 2000, since he rarely mentioned the economic successes of the Clinton administration. His demeanor in presidential debates appeared aggressive and unappealing. Why do you think that Gore's theme was "I'm going to fight for you" instead of "You've never had it so good"?

Bush, therefore, Gore could not soften his message to appeal to wavering voters. He worked closely with liberal advisers and portrayed himself in a belligerent fashion—someone who would "fight for you."[5]

Gore may have hammered the final nail into his own coffin during the presidential debates. His impolite demeanor—sighing audibly during Governor Bush's answers and frequently demanding the last word—did not fit with his campaign image as a representative of the common people.[6] And he squandered his reputation for command of policy details with numerous faulty statements, which critics interpreted as lies.[7] The result? For the second presidential election in a row, the winner was someone thought to have little chance two years before.

THESE TWO UPSET VICTORIES UNDERSCORE THE DIFFERENCE BETWEEN how journalists approach elections and how political scientists understand them. Media coverage emphasizes personalities and short-term campaign strategies, rather than long-term regularities guiding voter behavior. Journalists focus on how much money the candidates raise, or how clever their ads are. They trace small shifts in the polls to recent campaign events. Once one contest appears settled, they wipe the slate clean and turn to speculation about the next.

By contrast, political scientists view much of voting behavior as predictable in advance. The public enters an election period with attitudes and loyalties mostly in place, although it may take some time to sort out their priorities and apply them to the options at hand.[8] The most important question for voters is how close their values are to those of the candidates. Nor can candidates simply pick the message Americans want to hear. They enter an election constrained by their own political histories, by the alliances they have formed, and by the opponents they face—not just by their personalities. So once the cast of characters stabilizes, for most voters their choice is obvious. *This predictability makes elections look less important than they are.*

Some voters may be shaken from their initial impulses, but they require a credible reason to abandon one candidate and even better reasons to embrace another one. And *the power of money is limited:* it is simply a resource to publicize those reasons. A few genuinely undecided voters exist, but their relative lack of political interest or information makes them both hard to reach and unlikely to behave all the same way. They rarely exercise the muscle to swing elections for national office.

Finally, institutions may help one candidate or hinder another—for example when they shape how votes are counted. But election law is complicated and highly decentralized, so rules are difficult to manipulate, especially once a contest is underway. Unless two candidates are equally pleasing to the typical citizen, *methods of counting votes will not influence the election result.*

The difference between how journalists and political scientists view national elections is not just a quibble between two sets of professionals. The journalistic approach helps explain why Americans would be cynical about the system, blaming bad candidates or unfair media coverage or campaign-finance abuses for results they dislike. But *strategies, media, and money mostly matter only during the nomination process*—and, even then, less than people commonly think. These factors rarely influence the final showdown. Once one realizes that the main force guiding elections is the abiding dispositions of American voters, a different culprit for cynicism emerges. The problem is not that Americans lack influence, but that the electoral system is oriented toward giving even a divided public what it wants.

VOTING BEHAVIOR:
THE IMPORTANCE OF ELECTIONS

Citizens exhibit considerable continuity in voting behavior. This "electoral inertia" explains why presidential candidates know ahead of time that they will probably lose some states and win others. It is also why some congressional districts feature hard-fought campaigns, while in others no one challenges the sitting representatives. Elections sometimes are uneventful not because voters are powerless, but because they exercise their power in ways that political actors can anticipate.

Many people decide how they will vote before a campaign begins. Either they always vote the party line, or they have strong opinions about the candidates. In presidential elections, typically one-third to one-half of the electorate decides how to vote *before the primaries.* According to American National Election Studies surveys, one-half to two-thirds of the electorate decides how to vote before the fall campaign gets under way. The figure was 51 percent in 1988, when no incumbent ran, and 63 percent in 1996, when Clinton sought reelection. Hence strategy typically cannot influence most voters.

How can people make up their minds before candidates debate their policies and programs? The answer is simply that Americans have a longer time horizon than the considerations that dominate news coverage. Voter preferences accumulate for years, long before a single contest gets under way. They emphasize party loyalties and government performance, not policy proposals and candidate personalities.

PARTY LOYALTIES AND GROUP IDENTITIES

About two-thirds of the American electorate view themselves as Democrats or Republicans. Political scientists call this allegiance **party identification,** or party ID.[9] Party ID was once thought to be much like a religious affiliation: learned in childhood, resistant to change, and unrelated to the group's actual doctrines.[10] In fact, partisanship does respond to events and ideas, but only gradually.[11] Party ID thus provides continuity from election to election.

For example, the Civil War and Reconstruction created many yellow-dog Democrats in the South—people who wouldn't vote for a Republican if the Democratic nominee were a yellow dog. Eventually white southerners began to vote Republican in national elections, but they took much longer to switch party labels. Similarly, the Great Depression left many northerners intensely committed to the New Deal Democratic party of Franklin Roosevelt. Even the growing number of self-professed independents usually find themselves closer to one party than another.[12]

Party ID makes most elections quite predictable, even before candidates decide whether to run or how to manage their campaigns. Certain groups consistently vote Democratic, and others, steadily Republican (see Table 7.1). African Americans, urbanites, and Catholics have traditionally been Democratic groups. The wealthy, rural residents, southerners, and white Protestants—especially Evangelicals—tend to vote Republican. The increase in political independents has not undermined this predictability.

A "gender gap" has also sprung up, dividing the political preferences of men and women—and in the last two presidential elections it has been stronger than ever before (see Figure 7.1). Robert Dole would have won the 1996 election if only men had voted! Gender differences in voting do not result from so-called

TABLE 7.1

GROUPS DIFFER IN THEIR SUPPORT FOR THE PARTIES

	PERCENTAGE VOTING REPUBLICAN				
POPULATION CATEGORY	BUSH 2000	DOLE 1996	BUSH 1992	BUSH 1988	REAGAN 1984
White	54	46	40	59	64
Hispanic	31	21	25	30	37
African American	8	12	10	12	9
Poor (< $15,000/year)	37	28	23	37	45
Affluent (> $50,000/year)	52	48	44	62	69
Union	37	30	25	42	46
White Protestant	63	52	47	66	72
Catholic	47	37	35	52	54
Jewish	19	16	11	35	31
Big-city resident (population > 500,000)	26	25	28	37	n/a
Suburban resident	49	42	39	57	61
Rural resident	59	46	40	55	67
Lives in the East	39	34	35	50	53
Lives in the Midwest	49	41	37	52	58
Lives in the South	55	46	43	58	64
Lives in the West	46	40	34	52	61

SOURCE: "Portrait of the 2000 Electorate," *New York Times* (December 20, 2000). Available at time of publication at http://www.nytimes.com/images/2000/12/20/politics/elections/nwr_portrait_education.html.

women's issues, which men and women view similarly.[13] Rather, the gap appears to stem more from long-standing gender differences over the use of force and over the responsibility of government to address social ills (see Table 7.2).[14] It is not clear whether such differences grow out of childhood socialization, biology, self-interest, or some combination of factors.[15] The political preferences of women are not all the same, though; married women tend to have preferences much closer to those of men.[16] The electoral gap flows naturally from each gender's political preferences.[17]

FIGURE 7.1

Since 1980 women have consistently voted more Democratic than men

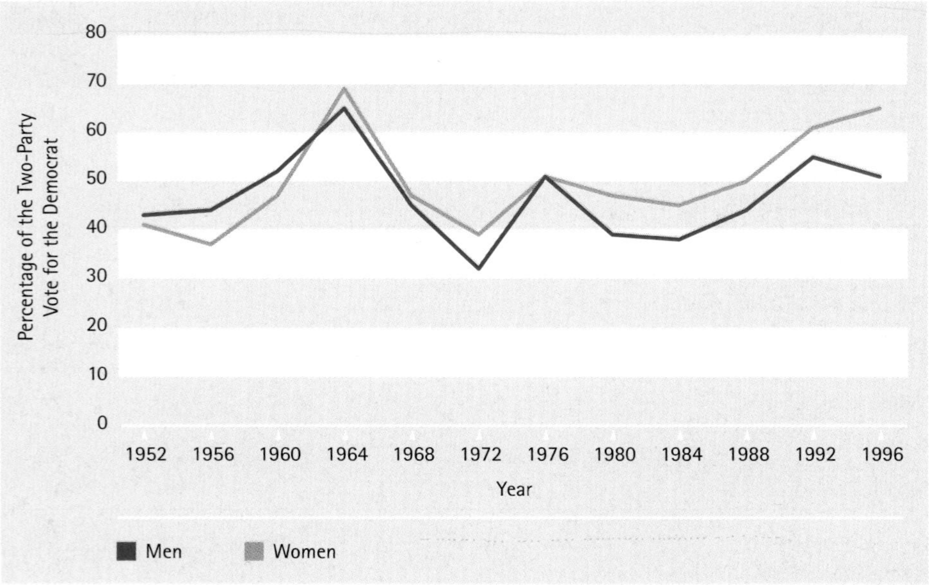

Year

■ Men   ▨ Women

SOURCE: The Gallup Organization.

Politicians are aware of how various groups differ politically. For the strongest partisans, the campaign is irrelevant; come hell or high water, they will vote their party IDs. Since potential candidates know how many members of each group appear in a given state or congressional district, they can strategize around such data. They usually need not wait for the formal election to respond to known voter preferences.

GOVERNMENT PERFORMANCE

Not every voter consistently supports the same political party. Typically, these voters react to the performance of current elected officials, though, and not so much to personalities or campaign promises.[18] Assessing performance does not require hours watching C-SPAN or reading the *New York Times*. Rather, voters can judge economic conditions from their own experiences and from word-of-mouth stories. They can judge other social conditions by observing their communities, schools, and workplaces.

Sometimes voters are upset about a problem and eager for government to do *something* about it. Thus, candidates talk about "getting tough on crime," "fix-

TABLE 7.2

Women's and men's attitudes

	WOMEN	MEN
Role of Government		
Consider self conservative	29%	43%
Say government should provide fewer services	30	45
Rank poverty and homelessness are among the country's most important problems	63	44
Believe government should guarantee medical care for all	69	58
Favor affirmative action programs for blacks and other minority groups	53	41
Force/Violence		
Thought American bombers should attack all military targets in Iraq, including those in heavily populated areas	37	61
Say handguns should be illegal except for use by police and other authorized persons	48	28
Favor the death penalty	76	82
Approved of caning a teenager in Singapore who committed acts of vandalism	39	61
Approve of the way the Justice Department took Elian Gonzalez from his Miami relatives	35	52

SOURCES: *The Public Perspective* (August/September 1996): 10–27; *The Public Perspective* (July/August 1994): 96; Gallup Tuesday Briefing, May 2, 2000.

ing the health-care system," or "getting guns out of the hands of children." These are important political issues, to be sure, but they do not evoke specific policy solutions. Such appeals merely tap into a general judgment of government performance.

The 1984 presidential election provides a classic illustration of how voters look toward past performance (often called **retrospective voting**). Surveys showed that, on many issues, voters were closer to the Democratic nominee, Walter Mondale, than to President Reagan. A majority considered tax increases inevitable (Mondale's position), doubted "Star Wars" (the missile defense system dear to Reagan's heart), rejected Reagan's call for increased defense spending, and disliked Reagan's policies toward Central America.[19] Nevertheless, Reagan carried 49 states. A few policy differences aside, most voters approved of Reagan's overall performance as president.

Voters hardly can be blamed for adopting shortcuts like retrospective voting. They are not equipped to judge among policy proposals, and candidates may not keep their promises anyway. Good performance by government suggests competent leadership, so voters reasonably choose not to "fix something that ain't broke."[20] Bad times, on the other hand, add credibility to any claim that someone else ought to get a shot at running the government. A campaign can "spin" an administration's record creatively, but it is difficult to make virtues out of a bad economy or an unpopular war—no matter how clever the media experts or how expensive their advertisements.

PUBLIC POLICIES

Policies and programs are the essence of elections for the most politically active citizens. These voters view campaigns as long-running debates, opportunities for candidates to educate the electorate about alternative paths the country may choose and to persuade voters to follow one of them. However, voters seldom use policy proposals to determine their choice among candidates.[21] One reason is that policy debates often are complex and people have limited information. To cite one extreme example, President Clinton's 1993 health care proposal required 1,342 printed pages, and that was just one of the options! How could voters possibly be expected to evaluate such complex issues?

Moreover, voters often are unsure where the candidates stand. Research on the 1968 election, for example, found that views on U.S. policy in Vietnam were mostly unrelated to the presidential vote. How could that be true, when disagreement about the war was tearing the country apart? The answer is that the positions of the candidates gave voters no basis on which to choose. The Democratic nominee, Hubert Humphrey, kept wavering. The Republican, Richard Nixon, refused to reveal his position, since to do so would undermine his "secret plan" to end the war. In the end, befuddled voters assessed both candidates as though they supported the same policy.[22]

One occasional exception is a social or cultural policy, such as prayer in schools or abortion. Such issues are "easy" in the sense that voters generally know where they stand. Moreover, the desired outcome and the policy that achieves it are one and the same: allow school prayer or ban it, or stop abortions or permit them.[23] Yet even these "hot-button" issues allow candidates to equivocate. In 2000 Gore tried to distance himself from gun control, emphasizing gun licenses rather than weapons bans and espousing the rights of hunters. Bush gave mixed messages on abortion: he was unhappy with the Food and Drug Administration's decision to allow sale of the abortion pill, RU-486, but claimed uncertainty about whether the next president could reverse the ruling.

THE QUALITIES OF THE CANDIDATES

Not surprisingly, the individual candidates are a major source of *change* in how people vote from election to election.[24] In a country that exhorts voters to "support the person not the party," the nature of the candidates is a major influence on how people vote. But it is important to keep in mind several cautions.

First, personality is seldom the most important candidate quality. In fact, detailed analysis of what people like and dislike indicates that most of the traits they mention are relevant to governing: intelligence, integrity, experience.[25] Voters may admire a president open enough to smooch with his wife on national television. They may not relish the thought of four years listening to a stumbling speaker or hearing lectures from an arrogant one. But there is little evidence that these considerations sway votes.

Public display of affection
Al Gore's aggressive kiss reportedly surprised wife Tipper at the Democratic National Convention. Whatever her reaction, "The Kiss" electrified some pundits, who credited it for Gore's bounce in the polls. But humorist Dave Barry thought Gore resembled an alien depositing an egg sac. Is it important to have an affectionate national leader, or is that relevant only to a personality contest?

Second, after the election there is a tendency to downgrade the loser's personal qualities and upgrade the winner's. Journalists reinforce this tendency by habitually explaining politics in personal terms. Many Republicans dismissed Senator Robert Dole as a terrible choice after his defeat in 1996. Yet two years earlier, during the Republican takeover of Congress, Dole was viewed as the rare "grown-up" in Washington, an admirable man possessing warmth and a quick wit. He was a mature, experienced public official who could fill the leadership vacuum. Did the election expose Dole as anything else? No, but his charisma was insufficient to unseat a moderate incumbent backed by peace and prosperity. Clinton's enemies preferred to blame Dole rather than credit the president. Similarly, Michael Dukakis received praise before the 1988 election and criticism afterward. Dukakis hadn't changed, but many in the Democratic party found it easier to blame their messenger than to admit that the electorate had rejected their message.

There are some striking contrasts between what voters actually think of candidates during a given campaign and how popular history later views the combatants. John F. Kennedy is the best example, since he is now legendary as the charismatic king of a new Camelot, an inspiring leader who died under a lone gunman's bullet. JFK was not loved half as much in life as he is in death. During the 1960 election, the public considered Kennedy's opponent, Richard Nixon, more experienced and better qualified than the young senator.[26] JFK owed his narrow victory primarily to the fact that he was the standard bearer of the majority party, although the Democratic party has since declined in support (see Figure 7.2).[27] What lives on in political folklore may have little connection to why people voted the way they did.

Finally, we should remember that what people think about a candidate is partly based on political compatibility—whether they belong to the same party, whether the politician has performed well, and whether the politician espouses similar values. Thus, candidates are important, but there is a tendency to misunderstand how. Personality looks much more influential than it really is.

THE POWER OF CONGRESSIONAL INCUMBENTS

It is not hard to see how presidential elections might ensure public influence. The contests are almost always energetic ones, covered heavily in the media. Voters pay attention and participate at relatively high rates. The importance of congressional elections may seem less obvious, though, since they are seldom competitive. Sitting members of Congress, called incumbents, often do not face serious opposition. When they do encounter real opponents, incumbents rarely lose because they possess many electoral advantages.

FIGURE 7.2

The Democratic advantage in party identification has eroded

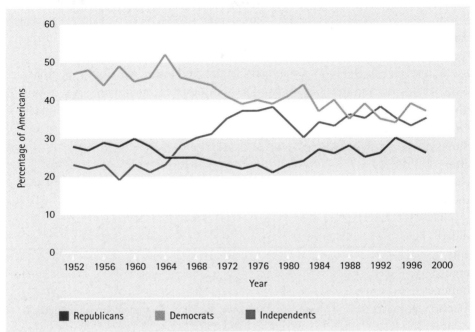

SOURCE: American National Election Studies.

The true measure of voter strength is not how often they replace elected officials, however. Low congressional turnover is itself a symptom of how much elections matter. Journalists, and even the politicians themselves, seem to consider
incumbency the single most important factor in winning House elections—but
that claim is inaccurate. Rather, party long has been and continues to be the dominant influence, just as it is in presidential elections.

Partisan control of the House seldom changes, and House incumbents seldom lose, because many House districts are **safe seats.** Preferences are so one-
sided that these districts are almost certain never to elect representatives of a
different party. The importance of partisanship explains why the Democrats
could maintain unbroken control of the House of Representatives between 1954
and 1994, despite the departure of all but three of their 1954 incumbents during
the period.[28]

One reason why party remains the most important factor in House elections
may be that many voters know little, if anything, about specific candidates. Only a

third of the citizenry can recall the names of their incumbents, and even fewer can remember anything they have done for their districts. Only 10 percent or so can remember how incumbents voted on a particular bill. Challengers are even less known. Lacking information, many people simply pick the party with which they generally sympathize. In House elections, 70 percent or more of all party identifiers typically stick with their party's candidate.[29]

If not the single most important factor in House elections, incumbency clearly is the second most important factor. Moreover, incumbency has grown in importance while party has declined. Statistical studies of House elections have found that the **incumbency advantage**—the electoral benefit of being an incumbent after taking into account other relevant traits—has grown from about 2 percent before 1964 to as high as 12 percent in some recent elections.[30] The increase has not been smooth; rather, the incumbency advantage surged in the late 1960s, bounced around that high level until 1986, then declined in the 1990s (see Figure 7.3).

FIGURE 7.3

The advantage of incumbency surged in the mid-1960s

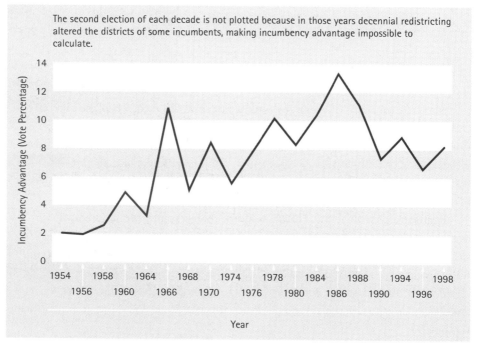

The second election of each decade is not plotted because in those years decennial redistricting altered the districts of some incumbents, making incumbency advantage impossible to calculate.

SOURCE: Calculated by the authors using the Gelman–King method. See Andrew Gelman and Gary King, "Estimating Incumbency Advantage Without Bias," *American Journal of Political Science* 34 (November 1990): 1, 142–164.

This development does not betray a decline in voter influence, however. Just the opposite. It indicates the growing electoral connection between voters and representatives. Legislators are extremely sensitive to their constituents' wishes, more so than members of Congress from earlier eras. The reasons are straightforward: (1) Elected officials are more likely to think of politics as a job and wish to retain office, (2) technological changes make elected officials less able to hide their actions and better able to determine what voters want, (3) electoral fortunes are less likely to rise or fall based upon ties to national political parties, and (4) elected officials remain in office longer if they cater to the tastes of local voters and provide the services that constituents demand.

THE GROWING ELECTORAL INCENTIVE Until the late nineteenth century, many more congressional representatives quit than were defeated. Job conditions were not very attractive. The national government was weak, and the District of Columbia little more than a swamp.[31] Ambitious politicians, especially outside the South, often found state government a better outlet for their energies.[32] Even those members willing to serve multiple terms sometimes were prevented from doing so by rotation practices, whereby political factions in a congressional district "took turns" holding the congressional seat. Abraham Lincoln, for example, stepped down from the House of Representatives in 1848 after serving only one term.[33] Average service in the House did not reach three years until after 1900.

The early Senate was also far from being a stable body. In the first ten years of the republic, more than one-third of the Senators failed to serve out their terms. More Senators resigned during their terms, before 1820, than were denied reelection by their state legislatures! Although they had the opportunity to stay longer than members of the House, many chose to leave.[34]

Today, things are quite different. The Congress is the world's foremost example of what political scientists call a professional legislature. Its members are full-time legislators who stay for long periods. Relatively few members quit voluntarily, and many intend to remain in Congress indefinitely. This professional interest in retaining their jobs prompts representatives to be electorally sensitive, if not hypersensitive. Contemporary incumbents fare so well precisely *because* they are so electorally aware; they anticipate threats to their reelection and act to avoid them.

CHANNELS OF COMMUNICATION More congressional decisions are public now than they were a generation ago. Until 1971, many House votes were cast by standing, speaking (aye–nay), or depositing colored cards (called tellers) into boxes—procedures that camouflaged each member's position. But rule changes that year made it easy to demand a **roll-call vote**—in which each member declares a vote for the record—and the number of roll calls in an average session more than doubled. Recorded votes are risky because they are available to interest groups or opposition researchers seeking campaign issues. Damaging votes need not be highly visible ones. Even an obscure vote can come back to haunt a member years later.[35]

Compensating for the increased scrutiny is the improved information members of Congress have about their constituents. Not only do their offices have fax machines, e-mail, and World Wide Web pages—technologies undreamt of a few decades ago—but also travel subsidies and other perks have expanded greatly.[36] Members were reimbursed for only three trips to their districts per year in 1960. By 1976 the number had increased to 26, and today there is no limit except the overall budget allocated to each member. Members travel to their districts 30 to 50 times a year! Important business is thus rarely scheduled for Mondays or Fridays because so many members travel on those days. Moreover, members can afford to conduct surveys if they want a scientific way to learn the views of constituents. Today's representatives therefore probably make fewer mistakes based on bad information than their predecessors did, and are better prepared than ever before to serve as "delegates" to the national government.[37]

Members of Congress also can compensate for increased scrutiny by communicating with constituents directly. Congressional use of the **frank**—free postage for official business—has grown, and computerized mailing lists make the tool more useful. Not surprisingly, congressional mailings to constituents are more frequent in even-numbered (election) years than in odd-numbered years. However, newsletters cannot be mailed within 90 days of an election, and members cannot include more than two personal photos per page.

THE DECLINE OF PARTY   At one time parties were powerful enough to bully members of Congress into sticking with the leadership, even if it meant casting votes that would damage them in their districts. In modern times, fewer constraints prevent legislators from acting on the electoral incentives they face and the information they have. Legislators can support the interests of their district—liberal or conservative, with the president or against, and so forth— except under unusual circumstances (see the Election Connection, "The Political Death of MMM"). This flexibility tends to make voters in a district happier with their representative (although it may make leadership in Congress more difficult). Thus, one reason why fewer incumbents are defeated is that fewer give their constituents reasons to defeat them.

The Political Death of MMM

The year 1992 was the so-called year of the woman. Four new female senators were elected, and the number of women representatives rose from 28 to 47. One of the newcomers to the House of Representatives was Democrat Marjorie Margolies-Mezvinsky, commonly known as MMM, a popular local newscaster, who was the first Democrat in 76 years to be elected from Pennsylvania's thirteenth district. She had defeated her Republican opponent in November by less than 1 percent of the vote.

Normally, a member's first election is the hardest. Once in office, she can utilize the advantages of incumbency to expand her support among constituents. So long as she behaves prudently and does not give potential challengers a damaging issue, she can anticipate reelection with very high probability. MMM gave her constituents such an issue—eight months after the election, when the House considered the final version of Bill Clinton's deficit reduction plan.

It was a sweeping package of spending cuts and tax increases that would chart the course of governmental economic policy for the next five years. Not a single Republican would support the plan; the income tax increases were unacceptable to them. And even though these tax increases fell entirely on affluent Americans, some Democrats were opposed to the plan because it included small increases in gasoline taxes and other elements that they disliked. Democratic leaders worked feverishly to muster a majority. President Clinton himself worked the phones, calling undecided Democrats and telling them that he had to have their vote—his presidency was at stake.

For MMM the situation was a political nightmare. She already had voted against each

of Clinton's three key economic proposals, including the deficit reduction package that was once again on the floor. On that earlier occasion she had announced, "I promised the voters of Montgomery County that I would not vote for an across-the-board tax increase—and tonight I kept that promise."[a] Since then, she had reassured her constituents that she would continue to oppose the plan. Now she was under intense pressure from the president and Democratic leaders to reverse her stand.

At the conclusion of electronic voting, the tally stood at 216 to 216. A majority of the full house (218 of 435) is required to pass the budget. Pat Williams, a Democrat from Montana, had agreed to support the president, if necessary, so MMM's vote would decide the fate of the plan and, by implication, Clinton's presidency. Surrounded by supportive Democrats and "with the demeanor of someone being marched to her own hanging," she approached the well of the House to cast a written vote. Gleeful Republicans chanted "Goodbye, Marjorie!"[b] MMM may have saved the Clinton legacy, but the cost was her political life.

In 1994 President Clinton himself appeared in her district, and the Democratic leadership helped raise more than $1,600,000 in campaign funds; but it wasn't enough to save MMM. The Republican she defeated in 1992 returned for a second try, and although he raised less than two-thirds as much money, MMM still could not overcome her damaging vote. She was swept under the national Republican tide, receiving only 45 percent of the vote. MMM is the exception that proves the rule: Incumbents win regularly only because they do what constituents want.

(continued)

(continued from previous page)

What do you think?

- Does a representative who knowingly bucks the preferences of her home district provide an inspiring example of political leadership, or does she betray the voters who placed her in office?
- Are public officials who shift their policy preferences according to the polls pandering to an ill-informed electorate or properly carrying out their jobs as popular representatives?
- To what extent do your answers to the last two questions vary depending upon whether you agree with the elected official or the public?

[a]Martha Angle, "Tallying Up the Thank-Yous," *Congressional Quarterly Weekly Report* (May 29, 1993): 1344.

[b]Quoted in George Hager and David Cloud, "Democrats Tie Their Fate to Clinton's Budget Bill," *Congressional Quarterly Weekly Report*, (August 7, 1993): 2127, 2125.

Parties are also weaker in the electorate. Although these days 70 percent of voters select their parties' candidates, that figure is low by historical standards.[38] Voters are more open to diverse appeals, which encourages candidates to court voters of all parties.[39] Constituents often find good reasons to ignore partisanship. Since the late 1960s, the rate at which voters support incumbents of a different party has often been close to 50 percent.[40]

Meanwhile, representatives know that their own partisan constituencies are less secure. They cannot take votes for granted. It is seldom sufficient to vote for party proposals or stick with their leadership. They usually must seek additional, more personal, reasons for district voters to support them. Constituency service often fills this need.

CONSTITUENCY SERVICE   You may think of members of Congress primarily as *lawmakers*. Making laws is their principal business and main constitutional responsibility. But members of Congress do much more than legislate. The official title of House members is "representative," and most people's view of representation involves a wide range of activities.[41]

One chore that occupies a great deal of the time and effort is district service—making sure that congressional districts get a fair share (or more) of federal programs, projects, and expenditures.[42] Some members of Congress are famous for their efforts to bring such economic benefits to their districts. Even Americans who disapprove of pork barrel legislation usually applaud when their representatives and senators bring home the bacon, and they reward them at the ballot box for it.

Another activity to which modern representatives devote a great deal of attention is constituent assistance, or "casework." Citizens, groups, and businesses frequently encounter difficulties in qualifying for government benefits or in complying with federal regulations. When their problems are not solved through normal channels, they appeal to members of Congress for assistance. About one in six voters reports having contacted a representative for information or assistance. In overwhelming numbers, they were satisfied with the resolution of their problems and, again, showed their gratitude at the polls.[43]

In many other countries, an administrative official called an ombudsman assists citizens when they must deal with the government bureaucracy. In the United States, members of Congress serve this role, hiring large staffs to help with the chore.* Some observers compare members of Congress to CEOs (chief executive officers) of small businesses.[44] Each House member heads an office system—one part in Washington and one or more parts in the district—and directly employs an average of 18 personal staff assistants, more than 40 percent of whom are assigned to district offices.[45] Indeed, it has been said that Capitol Hill is the headquarters of 535 political machines.

Such was not always the case. In 1950 the average representative had three staff employees. And as late as 1960, nearly a third of the representatives did not have permanent district offices. The 1960s and 1970s were a period of unparalleled growth in congressional staffs. The ombudsman role has grown in importance because of the federal government's expansion.[46] More subsidies and more regulations resulted in more opportunities for members of Congress to engage in constituent assistance. The number of citizens who reported contacting their representatives for this purpose tripled between 1958 and 1978.[47] Thus, at the same time that strength of party affiliation was declining, an expanding federal government conveniently stimulated constituent demands that members of Congress were able and willing to meet.

District service and constituent assistance often are included together under the general term **constituency service.** These two activities share an important characteristic that sheds some light on why the incumbency advantage does not undermine elections. When members of Congress take positions on issues, they please some groups and antagonize others. On controversial issues, their positions may lose them as many votes as they gain. But when incumbents provide valued services to constituents, nearly everyone approves. Small wonder that, by a 5 to 1 margin (judging from one survey), House administrative assistants

---

*Senators have larger staffs than House members do. The size depends on a state's population.

consider constituency service the most important factor helping their employers stay in office.[48] Incumbents seldom lose because they have become much better at making constituents happy.

NATIONAL FORCES IN CONGRESSIONAL ELECTIONS

Former Speaker of the House Thomas P. "Tip" O'Neill (D-MA) once commented that "all politics is local." O'Neill's remark partly reflected the parochial politics of Massachusetts, but it also is a reminder that members of Congress ultimately must answer to people in thousands of separate localities. Modern congressional elections have become less susceptible to national political forces generated by presidents, parties, and economic conditions.[49]

Presidential **coattails**—the tendency of presidents to carry their own party's candidates for Congress into office—have declined in strength.[50] More voters today split their tickets, voting for presidential and congressional candidates of different parties.[51] Moreover, fewer voters seem to treat voting in an election year without a presidential contest as a way to send the president a message. From the time of the Civil War until 1998, the president's party lost House seats in every off-year election except one (1934). But **midterm loss** has been declining (see Figure 7.4). The limited connection between presidential and congressional elections indicates the independent importance of each contest.

The 1994 elections challenged the prevailing view of incumbent insulation. Democrats lost 52 seats in the House, the largest rupture since 1946, and 8 in the Senate. A strong national tide apparently swept away the Democratic Congress.[52] However, even the 1994 surprise owes less to national forces than many supposed. Democrats did experience severe incumbent losses in 1994; yet 85 percent of the party's House incumbents who ran still won reelection, and a handful of Democratic losses in the early 1990s resulted from district changes intended to help elect minorities to office.[53]

Furthermore, the role of national forces was short-lived. Many of the new Republicans retained their seats in 1996 by the same time-honored techniques once used by their Democratic predecessors: putting distance between themselves and an unpopular leader (House Speaker Newt Gingrich) and highlighting activities on behalf of their districts.[54] In the 1996 elections, 91 Republican House candidates managed to win districts carried by President Clinton. The Monica Lewinsky scandal did little to hurt Democratic congressional candidates in 1998; most successfully distanced themselves from the President, for example, by canceling fund-raisers at which he was to appear.[55]

Two years later, the 2000 congressional elections had no national theme at all. Control of both chambers was at stake, so party leaders urged candidates to

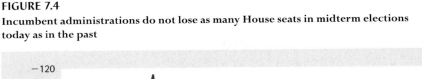

FIGURE 7.4

Incumbent administrations do not lose as many House seats in midterm elections today as in the past

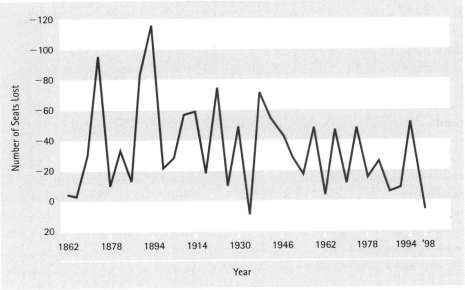

SOURCE: Norman J. Ornstein et al., eds., *Vital Statistics on Congress, 1995–1996* (Washington, DC: Congressional Quarterly, 1996), p. 55.

seek the most effective messages, even if it meant highlighting their differences with the leadership. The results were reminiscent of the incumbency-dominated elections of the 1970s and 1980s. Only 8 House incumbents lost, out of 412 who ran (although, as usual, senators had a rougher time).

To the extent national forces are regaining strength, it may be because political parties have become more active. Parties control more campaign resources that candidates wish to attract.[56] The congressional parties are more unified than they were a generation ago, and the differences between Republicans and Democrats are greater.[57] Congress contains few moderates. Thus voters today usually are presented with a clear choice between two candidates who hold distinct positions on national issues. Such clear differences can overwhelm local factors or the candidate's personal traits.

Interest groups help link congressional elections through issue advocacy. In 1998, for example, the National Rifle Association spent $2.3 million on ads, and it is by no means the biggest spender. Indeed, in 1998 groups began running ads without the knowledge of (and sometimes in defiance of the wishes of) their candidates. In a spring special election in California, for example, pro-life groups attacked the Democratic candidate even though the Republican opponent did not want abortion to be an issue in the race. As the campaign progressed, groups supporting business, environmentalism, and the "Religious Right" jumped in.[58] Even the parties got into the act. Forcing candidates to address national issues does not necessarily reduce popular influence.

THE SENATE PARADOX

The founders intended the House of Representatives to be highly sensitive to popular wishes. However, they viewed the Senate differently. The Constitution originally provided for senators to be chosen by state legislatures, not elected by the people. According to Madison, the insulated Senate would proceed "with more coolness, with more system, and with more wisdom, than the popular branch."[59]

Neither institution has evolved in the manner Madison and the founders expected. The House as a whole is not very responsive to changes in the national mood, since most members succeed at constructing political identities satisfying to their local constituencies. On the other hand, the Seventeenth Amendment (adopted in 1913) exposed senators to popular election.* Senators must stay sensitive to public opinion.

Of course, elections are never far from the mind of any member of Congress. Members of the House put their fates on the line every other November, not counting the primary campaigns that are under way scarcely more than a year after they take the oath of office. But if anything, the situation is worse for senators (see Figure 7.5). Not only are one-third elected every two years, but Senate campaigns are so expensive that typically incumbents must raise an average of just over $15,000 every week of their terms. This time-consuming, psychologically draining activity keeps all of them aware of their need to maintain political support. Plus senators represent more diverse constituencies, who are therefore harder to please. And because their offices are more powerful and have a higher visibility, senators are more likely to face strong opponents.

RECONSIDERING THE IMPORTANCE OF CAMPAIGNS

The importance of the campaign is exaggerated. Contrary to what the media imply, many presidential elections are decided before the campaign begins. Conditions in the preceding four years and the government's response to those conditions generally determine the outcome. Political scientist James Campbell has calculated that between 1948 and 1996, the campaigns probably were decisive in 1948 and 1960, two exceedingly close elections. Campbell adds that the 1976

---

*Many states adopted various popular-voting procedures for their senators as early as the mid-nineteenth century.

FIGURE 7.5

Representatives get reelected more often than Senators

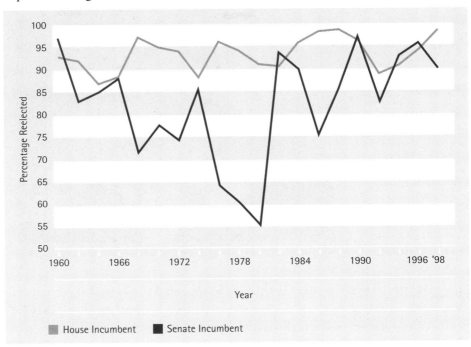

SOURCE: Norman J. Ornstein et al., eds., *Vital Statistics on Congress, 1995–1996* (Washington, DC: Congressional Quarterly, 1996), pp. 60–61.

and 1980 campaigns "may have possibly been decisive." In the other nine elections, the outcome was largely predetermined.[60] Certainly campaigns do matter, but only when the electorate is otherwise closely divided.[61]

Campaigns are shaped by what takes place long before the election. A card game provides a good analogy. Who wins often depends on the deal of the cards. No matter how skillfully one plays, it may not overcome a bad hand. In politics, some cards are dealt years, even decades, before the election. The Democrats drew the "Herbert Hoover Depression" card in 1932 and played it successfully for an entire generation. The Republicans drew the "Decline of Law and Order" card in 1968 and were still playing it two decades later. Other cards are drawn in the four years since the last election. Good economic conditions are aces dealt to the incumbent party; poor conditions are aces dealt to the opposition. International embarrassments and costly wars also may serve as trump cards.

Media coverage seldom mentions the luck of the draw, since most of this is "old news." Journalists generally neglect the main explanations for who wins, the topic

The Ragin' Cajun
*Bill Clinton's political con-
sultant in 1992, a
Louisiana native named
James Carville, is known for
his irreverence and wacky
sense of humor. But he
understood the science of
politics enough to realize
that an economic recession
would bother voters more
than the Arkansas gover-
nor's personal scandals.*

on which they expend so many words and so much ink. They praise and criticize campaigns, as though strategic decisions operate on a level playing field; they forget that social and economic realities often dictate how the game is played.

Did the fact that Massachusetts Governor Dukakis lost to Vice President Bush in 1988, while Arkansas Governor Clinton beat the same man four years later, indicate that Dukakis ran a poor campaign and Clinton a brilliant one? Dukakis surely could have done some things better, and Clinton certainly found his way out of a few tight spots.[62] But a recession made the Bush administration a much fatter target in 1992 than the Reagan–Bush administration was in 1988. As Clinton's adviser, James Carville, put it, "It's the economy, stupid!" The 1996 Dole effort is another example; his campaign was lackluster because he had no chance to win.[63] The economy and the conservative image that the Republican party projected in 1995 and 1996 had Dole against the ropes before the fight even began.

The importance of the campaign emerges in close contests. If a race is about even when the election begins, then any minor event or clever ploy can tip the balance among the few swing voters. Biased media coverage or a few extra advertisements may make a difference. But then so can any number of happenstances—trying to pinpoint the "cause" of victory or defeat becomes futile. Nor does the rarity of such close contests justify the emphasis campaign strategy receives in the news.

CAN REFORMS IMPROVE THE SYSTEM?

Thus far, we have been very optimistic about the importance of elections in American politics. Despite the media attention to campaigns and character, these are mostly short-term, frivolous factors that operate only at the margins. Voters generally choose how to vote in a sensible manner, following their long-term party loyalties and medium-term evaluations of government performance. Attention to a candidate's policy positions is mostly limited to what they say about a candidate's values, and the criteria used to judge candidate quality are mostly connected to evaluations of competence rather than personality.

Congressional incumbents seldom fail to win reelection, but their success only underscores the importance of elections. They expend extensive effort trying to please constituents and scare off potential challengers. To the extent parties are once again growing influential in Congress, the explanation appears to be that American voters have become more divided politically and interest groups do not allow congressional candidates to hide from divisive national issues. Senators are even less insulated from electoral pressures than members of the House. All told, elections matter more than ever, whether or not they happen to produce dramatic political changes.

Despite this optimism, three topics worry many would-be reformers: (1) the role of money in national politics, (2) the apparent unfairness of some electoral institutions, and (3) the haphazard nature of the nomination process. In each case, critics exaggerate distortions in the nation's democratic process. Further, the practices and laws that most bother reformers sometimes provide underappreciated benefits. What would result after fixing specific flaws in the electoral system might not be better—and could be much worse—than what the United States has now.

CAMPAIGN FINANCE: THE ROLE OF MONEY

National officeholders generally must win two stages of election: a nominating campaign in which they become the standard bearer of a particular political party, and a general election in which they defeat other parties' nominees to win the office. The process usually requires large sums of money, some of which the federal government collects. The money comes from the voluntary checkoffs on Americans' income tax returns and is distributed by the Federal Elections Commission (FEC).

FINANCING NOMINATION CAMPAIGNS   Qualifying presidential candidates may have their fund-raising matched, dollar for dollar, as long as they agree not to exceed a prespecified spending limit. In 2000, the FEC spending limit for the nomination campaign was $40.5 million. This limit was low enough that two candidates, Steve Forbes and George W. Bush, chose to forego **matching funds.** Bush had already raised $70 million without federal aid before the primary season began.[64] By the time he defeated John McCain and clinched the nomination, Bush had already spent $63 million, half again as much as he would have been permitted to spend had he accepted matching funds.[65] Most candidates prefer to accept the money, however.

Eligibility for campaign subsidies is not automatic. To be eligible, a candidate must raise at least $5,000 in each of 20 states, with no contribution larger than $250. Most serious candidates do not find it very difficult to raise $100,000 in a single year, as required by the law. Even minor candidates have qualified, although they generally do not raise much money after they do.

Staying eligible is harder than becoming eligible. Candidates must comply with spending limits in each state. To continue receiving matching funds throughout the primary season, they also must attract substantial voting support. A candidate who fails to receive at least 10 percent of the vote in two consecutive primaries loses eligibility and can regain it only by getting 20 percent or more of the vote in a later primary. Thus a struggling campaign may find itself deprived of funds just when it most needs them. And once candidates become strong, government money helps ensure that they stay that way.

FINANCING PRESIDENTIAL CAMPAIGNS   Presidential campaign funding was a very simple proposition from the mid-1970s to the mid-1990s. Under the terms of the 1974 Federal Elections Campaign Act (FECA), the general-election campaign is publicly funded. The FEC gives major-party candidates subsidies (Bush and Gore received approximately $67.5 million each in 2000), and in return the candidates agree not to raise and spend any more. Thus, from 1974 to 1992, most observers believed that the nominees of the major parties were adequately and equally funded.

Beginning in the 1990s, however, campaigns increasingly relied on funding that is not subject to federal regulation. Unlike the hard cash provided to an individual candidate, this unregulated **soft money** never reaches the nominee's hands. Nor may the nominee coordinate how it is spent. Instead, interest groups, labor unions, and individual donors turn over large campaign contributions to party committees who are not subject to FECA restrictions.

Parties legally may take contributions of any size and spend the money to promote their candidates for office indirectly. Soft money contributions to the parties exploded in the 1990s. In 1992 the parties raised about half as much in soft money as their candidates received in public funds. In 1996 soft money raised by the parties far exceeded public funds, and preliminary estimates for 2000 suggest that the pattern has continued.

SPENDING IN THE GENERAL-ELECTION CAMPAIGN   Labor Day traditionally is the official start date for the fall campaign, although today's nominees take shorter breaks after the summer conventions than in the past. From the start of the campaign until election day (the first Tuesday after the first Monday in November), the candidates maintain an exhausting pace, and the campaign dominates the news.[66]

Campaign consultants oversee the expenditure of the large sums of money raised. These specialists in modern, candidate-based campaigns have replaced party leaders, who supervised strategy in earlier eras. Modern campaigns retain pollsters expert in measuring surges and slumps in public opinion. Media consultants schedule the candidate's time, design campaign ads (or spots), and stage media events that attract the interest of reporters. Derided by critics as "handlers" or "hired guns," some campaign consultants have become celebrities.

The most important category of general-election spending is for what the FEC calls electronic media—TV and radio advertising—and the lion's share goes to television. In 1996 over 60 percent of both Clinton's and Dole's general-election spending was for electronic media.[67] Although campaign advertising is widely criticized, studies have consistently found that it is informative; those exposed to ads know more about the candidates and where they stand than those not exposed.[68] The issue content of ads actually has increased in recent years.[69] The emphasis on issues has come with a cost, however; ads are increasingly negative in tone.[70] Rather than make positive cases for themselves, candidates offer memorable criticisms of their opponents.[71]

FINANCING CONGRESSIONAL CAMPAIGNS   House elections have become increasingly expensive: Average total spending in each House race was more than half a million dollars in 1998, with 87 candidates spending over a million.[72] Moreover, the gap between incumbents' spending and that of their challengers is wide and has grown wider since 1980 (see Figure 7.6). For many of today's reformers, the explanation for the advantage of incumbency is simple and self-evident: money.

Money certainly affects candidate visibility, and congressional challengers are seriously underfunded. Furthermore, attracting so much campaign cash requires

FIGURE 7.6

The spending gap between incumbents and their challengers

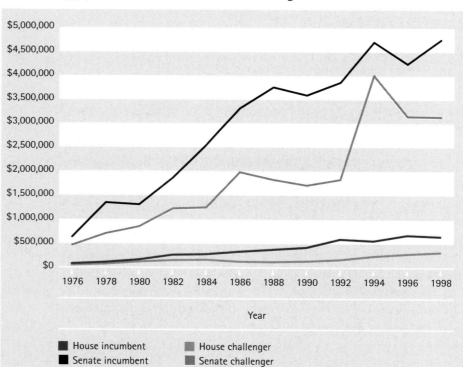

SOURCE: Norman J. Ornstein et al., eds., *Vital Statistics on Congress, 1999–2000* (Washington, DC: American Enterprise Institute, 2000), p. 81.

extensive effort from elected officials, a chore they often dislike (see the Election Connection, "Tongue-in-Cheek Fund-Raising"). Nevertheless, research on congressional election financing paints a surprisingly complicated picture. Although money contributes to the electoral advantage that incumbents enjoy, its contribution is less than often supposed.

Researchers have found that campaign spending gives what economists call *diminishing returns:* The more a candidate spends, the less impact an additional dollar can have. In particular, for an incumbent who already has perquisites of office worth as much as a million dollars a year, an extra $100,000 has less impact than it would if spent by a challenger who lacked taxpayer-provided resources. For this reason, sophisticated advocates for increasing electoral competition oppose low

Tongue-in-Cheek Fund-Raising

All members of Congress who plan to run for reelection spend a significant amount of time raising money, but many find it an unpleasant, if not demeaning, task. Some find ways to inject a bit of humor into the process, as this fund-raising letter from Massachusetts Democratic Representative Barney Frank illustrates.

February 1998

Dear Liz and Gary:

Fortunately, having been in electoral politics for 25 years, serving as a State Representative and then as a Member of the U.S. House of Representatives, I've had a good deal of experience in choosing the lesser evil. And that is what I am doing right now as I dictate this letter. Indeed, this letter is in fact the lesser evil in question—I am about as eager to write it as you are to read it. But writing it wins out over the greater evil which is to try to get reelected in 1998 without any campaign funds.

I believe I am mellowing as I get older and am somewhat nicer than I used to be, but I concede that I am not yet at the point where I can win reelection on charm alone—which brings me to this letter, which in turn I hope brings you to send me some money.

I realize that fundraising is in lower repute this year than it has ever been, but since the various recipients of this letter and I have been engaged in campaign fundraising—that is I have been engaged in fundraising and the recipients have, fortunately for me, been willing to engage in fund giving (semantically I suppose the opposite of fundraising should be fundlowering but that does not seem fully opposite)—and I will now confess that while dictating I have entirely lost track of where this sentence was going so I will simply end it.

To return to the point I was trying to make, it's an election year, I am running for reelection, and while I do not anticipate having to spend millions of dollars, I will have to spend more than I now have so if you think it is a good idea for me to be reelected, I hope you will send me some money.

Barney

Paid for by the Barney Frank for Congress Committee
Box 260, Newtonville, MA 02160

What do you think?

- Does an electoral system that requires elected officials to hustle for money undermine democracy by giving more influence to those with deep pockets, or does it increase democracy by making representatives defend their records directly to their close supporters?

- Would public funding of elections make representatives more arrogant and unresponsive to individual supporters, since they could count on campaign funding from government, or would it make them even more humble than Frank was in his witty contribution request?

spending limits because they would hurt challengers, who need to compensate for the incumbents' name recognition and perks.[73]

Incumbents may receive so much money in part because they are so likely to win, rather than the reverse. The mid-1960's surge in the incumbency advantage preceded the explosion of congressional campaign spending. Moreover, the growth of Political Action Committees (PACs) took place after the adoption of campaign finance reform laws in 1974, when incumbents had already developed a significant advantage. Heavy spending by an incumbent generally signals that the incumbent is in trouble.[74] Of the ten highest-spending representatives in 1998, four lost. The great majority of incumbents probably would still be reelected if campaign spending were slashed.

Perhaps the most discouraging impact of campaign spending today is one that is difficult to observe, let alone measure. Because it takes so much money for a challenger to mount a serious campaign—$600,000 in the estimation of political scientist Gary Jacobson—many potential challengers probably never enter the race.[75] Why invest so much money for what is at best a long shot? Thus, substantial campaign funds may be most important as a deterrent: Money can't buy the candidate love, but perhaps it can scare off rival suitors.[76]

In recent years the topic of campaign finance reform has received enormous attention. Many citizens view the system as little more than bribery. Columnist Dave Barry writes, "Basically, our campaign finance system works this way: Donors give money to politicians, who then use the government to do favors for the donors."[77] Although this may exaggerate the current system's negative effects, there is no question that citizens are disgusted with it. They are cynical about government, suspecting that politicians care only about what wealthy interests have to say. With unhappiness so widespread, reform may be politically necessary. One presidential hopeful, John McCain, made it the centerpiece of his campaign in 2000.

Even if the campaign-finance system is fundamentally flawed, however, it is not certain what sort of electoral reform would improve matters. Spending is heavily regulated in other democracies. In Britain neither parties nor individual candidates for office are permitted to buy broadcast time to communicate directly with potential voters! They are limited to a small number of publicly financed addresses by national party leaders. In Germany the law restricts parties to the free air time provided by TV networks; they may not buy additional ads.[78] Such restrictions on campaign messages do not appear consistent with the First Amendment, or with American values in favor of free expression.

Many other democracies provide at least some degree of public financing.[79] But using government money to subsidize campaigns requires some method of deciding eligibility and also how much money to give. The country could not turn over millions of dollars to any person or party choosing to throw a hat into the ring. The typical response is to look back at the previous election. For example, in many countries the parties receive public subsidies in proportion to the number of votes they received in the previous election or the number of seats they hold in parliament.* It is hard to see how a system geared toward rewarding past successes would make either incumbents or dominant parties any less secure than they are now.

THE ROLE OF ELECTORAL INSTITUTIONS

The United States operates on the principle that everyone should have equal influence over government. This commitment fuels widespread distaste for the role of money in national elections, for example, and undergirds the one-person–one-vote legal doctrine. Systems of representation never give everyone equal influence in practice, however. Full equality is impossible to implement, if for no other reason than the electoral system must accommodate other social goals—including efficiency, individual autonomy, protection of minorities, and fidelity to tradition.

Inequality may open election laws to criticism, but embracing dramatic changes without giving due consideration to their social costs is unwise. Two institutions in the U.S. system cause voter influence to vary—the Electoral College in presidential elections and legislative districts in congressional elections. Each distorts the straightforward "will of the people." Yet tampering with the current system could carry considerable costs.

THE ELECTORAL COLLEGE   The presidential candidate who garners the most votes—the so-called **popular vote**—does not necessarily win. Four times in American history, the candidate who came in second became president, including George W. Bush in 2000.† The reason for this discrepancy is the Electoral College. Each state possesses a certain number of **electoral votes** and selects the rules that determine which candidate(s) will receive them. If a candidate wins more of the battles for electoral votes, then the total quantity of individual votes received nationwide is irrelevant.

The Electoral College distorts popular preferences by distributing unequally the electors who cast electoral votes. Each state picks one elector for each House and Senate seat in Congress (with an additional three electors assigned to the

---

*Examples include Austria, Belgium, Denmark, Finland, Germany, Mexico, Sweden, and Turkey.
†The other three were John Quincy Adams in 1824, Rutherford Hayes in 1876, Benjamin Harrison in 1888.

District of Columbia under the terms of the Twenty-third Amendment). Because every state has two senators, influence is not proportional to population; small states get a numerical advantage. The smallest states receive yet another advantage because of the guarantee that they will each get at least one House member no matter how small their populations.

For example, with two senators but only one seat in the House, Wyoming has three electoral votes—approximately 1 electoral vote per 151,000 residents. With two senators but 52 seats in the House, California has 54 electoral votes, approximately 1 vote per 550,000 residents, a ratio only one-third as large as Wyoming's. Using 2000 figures, a candidate theoretically could become president with the electoral votes of states containing only 46 percent of the U.S. population.

Large states have tried to compensate for their disadvantage by assigning all of their electors to the candidate receiving the most votes. This system is sometimes called **winner-take-all voting** and is present in all states except Maine and Nebraska. Because large states have so many electoral votes to distribute, they are often the most attractive targets for campaign activity. And because large states tend to be diverse, they are usually competitive, another trait that draws candidate attention.

Experts disagree whether, on balance, the Electoral College favors large states, small ones, or balances power. Their disagreements usually hinge on rather technical differences in how they evaluate influence.[80] But the small-state advantage helped President Bush tease out a victory over former Vice President Gore, since many Bush states were small ones. And the winner-take-all system explains why candidates often win big Electoral College majorities despite modest advantages in the popular vote. In 1996 Clinton won 49 percent of the popular vote but 70 percent of the electoral vote.

For more than a century the popular and electoral vote winners were the same, so the Electoral College received little attention. The 2000 election changed that. At first many observers thought Al Gore might win the presidency with a minority of popular votes. Bush seemed quite strong in the Republican "L" (depicted in Figure 7.7), a cluster of heartland states that consistently vote for the GOP.* Yet Gore seemed capable of tipping the balance in enough swing states to win without a popular majority. Concentrating his support in rural states would have cost Bush the election. As it turned out, Gore's policy proposals played well in coastal areas, and urban voters mobilized heavily behind him, so that he trounced Bush in a handful of densely populated states. But he lost the electoral vote.

*Between 1968 and 1988, 21 states with 191 electoral votes voted six consecutive times for the Republican candidate. Only the District of Columbia, with 3 electoral votes, was so loyal to the Democrats.

FIGURE 7.7

The Republican "L"

The base on which GOP majorities were built in presidential elections in the 1970s and the 1980s was a wide swath of states called the Republican "L." It takes in the Rocky Mountain region, the Plains states, and the entire South. With Alaska thrown in, these states have a total of 233 electoral votes (270 are needed to win). Bill Clinton cracked the "L" but it reemerged in 2000.

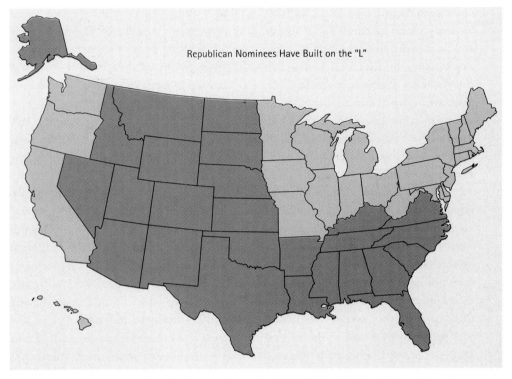

Republican Nominees Have Built on the "L"

SOURCE: "Republican Nominees Have Built on the "L," *Congressional Quarterly Guide to the 1996 Republican National Convention* (August 3, 1996): 9.

Anger that the system cost Democrats the White House no doubt will lead to reform proposals in the coming years.[81] Norms of equal influence have become very strong. It seems unjust to many Americans that the majority might find its desires frustrated. It is therefore worth considering what useful role the Electoral College might play.

Breaking up votes by state requires that a candidate have broad appeal. Winning a state overwhelmingly is not as important as winning lots of different states. The 2000 election illustrates this dynamic. Gore crushed Bush in California and New York, so he won the popular vote. (Remove either state and Gore lost handily.) But Bush squeaked through in the Electoral College because he won a larger variety of states. The system therefore discourages politicians from adopting a strategy that unites a minority of the country (whether Southerners or city dwellers or anyone else) while dividing the majority. Divisiveness does not pay off.

The Electoral College also may reduce the importance of money. It allows candidates to focus their resources on undecided states. Candidates still may choose to spend vast sums, blanketing battleground states with ads, but these excessive expenditures bring diminishing returns more quickly. The two-party candidate with fewer resources may not suffer as much under the current system.

Finally, the Electoral College may reduce corruption. Presumably electoral misbehavior is easiest in states where partisanship is most one-sided. Public officials are more likely to share interests, and citizens are most uniform on who should win the presidency. The potential for statewide corruption peaks in states where it is least likely to make a difference. In other words, the Electoral College assures that vote totals matter only as a state becomes less lopsided, when the competing sides are better able to demand fair and honest procedures.

Replacing the Electoral College with a popular vote system certainly would equalize political influence (although probably less than people think). Yet doing so would change very few elections, judging from the past, and it could make a difference only in elections when the public does not clearly favor one candidate or the other. A popular-vote system meanwhile might bring costs: encouraging discriminatory campaign appeals, forcing candidates to find resources adequate to compete for votes nationwide, and rewarding states that can find ways (fair or foul) to pile up overwhelming majorities for their candidate of choice.

Whatever happens to the Electoral College, it is clear that the current system shapes campaign strategy. If you are a citizen of Kansas or Utah, or of Mississippi or Massachusetts, you might scarcely have known the 2000 election was taking place. Your states were written off by one party and taken for granted by the other. But if you were a citizen of Florida, Pennsylvania, Missouri, West Virginia, or another "battleground" state, you were bombarded with campaign ads, and the candidates visited your state numerous times. The candidates also recast their issue positions to appeal to the swing states, with Gore edging away from his strong antigun stance and Bush distancing himself from social conservatives.

APPORTIONMENT OF CONGRESSIONAL DISTRICTS   Using electoral districts to determine the nation's legislators also frustrates the will of the majority. This is obvious for the Senate. The Constitution gives every state two senators, regardless of population.* The House presents a more complicated picture, since

---

*This provision can be amended only with the consent of every state (Article 5).

Fair weather for Republicans

Population growth in the heavily Republican Sun Belt has outpaced that in the North, causing congressional districts to migrate southward. The Detroit area of Michigan, where this cartoon was first published, has been especially hard hit. Do you think it is harder for a region to recover if it loses political power when the area goes into decline?

representatives run in election districts that shift periodically. The Constitution requires a census every decade. After each census, the 435 seats in the House are apportioned among the states according to their populations; hence, the term **reapportionment.**

Currently, six states have populations so small that they each get only one representative, a minimum guaranteed by Article I. After the smallest states receive their representatives, the remaining congressional districts must be of almost precisely equal population. This provision applies both within states and, to the extent possible, across them. Nationally, the shift in congressional districts from state to state has favored the GOP. Northeastern and Midwestern states have lost House seats to the South and Southwest, as population has shifted to the predominantly Republican Sun Belt.

Once states learn their allotments, they set to work **redistricting**—drawing the boundaries of the new districts to equalize population. In most states the legislature does the work, but in five states bipartisan commissions do the job, and several others have a more complicated process. Redistricting is often highly contentious, because political careers depend on which voters get placed in which districts. Politicians often accuse each other of **gerrymandering**—that is, of drawing the lines to benefit a certain group. Often the courts are pulled into the process. (See Chapter 14, on Civil Rights, for a discussion of gerrymandering intended to elect representatives of a certain race or ethnicity.) But every district still ends up with the same population.

Aside from those in a few small states, therefore, everyone receives the same amount of House representation. The inequality comes with the system of electing one member per district and granting the seat to the person who wins the most votes in a general election—called the single-member, simple plurality (SMSP) system. The system disadvantages minorities, racial and otherwise. A candidate who receives fewer votes than the leading candidate does, even if that person gets 49 percent, wins nothing. Any minority spread out over many districts will remain unrepresented unless it becomes dominant in at least one place.

Recognizing these realities, some critics question the electoral system itself. Some suggest that the United States should shift to **proportional representation,** in which a party receives congressional seats according to its share of the vote. Certainly, such a system would equalize influence, compared to the current system. Yet it could undermine the ombudsman role served by legislators. The current system assigns each locality a particular member of Congress, responsible for defending that area's interests before the national government. An alternate system, which pooled votes over a large geographical area or even the nation as a whole, would sever this direct link between legislator and voter.

Proportional representation systems also carry a risk. They might assist fringe parties dedicated to undermining the political system.[82] Even parties with few supporters could garner enough votes to win at least one seat, so the incentive to choose mainstream politicians would diminish. The party system might splinter enough that social conflicts would all have to be settled within the halls of government, among combative representatives, rather than through the coalition building that candidates often require to win elections in a district-based system.

THE NOMINATION PROCESS

The role that incumbent war chests play in chasing off qualified challengers is not the only problem with the manner in which candidates for office are recruited and nominated. If any segment of the electoral system dampens popular influence, and in a fashion that is difficult to justify, it is a nomination process that limits the range of choices voters can express.

PRESIDENTIAL NOMINATIONS   The United States is unusual among world democracies for its lengthy, participatory process of nominating candidates for chief executive. One British correspondent calls it "a bizarre ritual."[83] In most democracies, party activists and leaders choose nominees. But in the United States every citizen, whatever the depth of his or her commitment, may participate in selecting among possible candidates for the two major parties. Barriers are minimal for participation in a **caucus**—a meeting of candidate supporters—or a **primary election**—a preliminary election. At the presidential level, nearly three-quarters of the states choose their delegates in primary elections, and the remainder choose them in caucuses. Because caucus states tend to be smaller, most of the delegates are chosen in primaries.

The caucus is a rather time-consuming process. Supporters of the respective candidates meet in each voter precinct to start the process of delegate selection. Generally, they gather in public places, such as town halls or public schools, but sometimes they meet on quasi-private property, such as restaurants. These precinct gatherings are only the beginning, however, because the process has a number of stages. For example, the Iowa caucuses are the first major test for candidates, because they occur very early in the election year. But these caucuses only choose delegates to the county conventions held in March, which then choose delegates to the May congressional district conventions, who move on to state conventions held in June!

Democratic caucuses are constrained by national party rules that require proportional representation for the supporters of different candidates, as well as equal numbers of male and female delegates where possible. Any registered Democrat is eligible to participate. Republican caucuses are less open. Some limit participation to party officials and workers. Some use variants of proportional representation, and some continue to use winner-take-all voting procedures.[84]

Caucus turnout is extremely low—typically in single digits. About 6 percent of the voting-age population participated in the 2000 Iowa caucuses. This figure was not unusually low; the 12 percent turnout in the 1988 Iowa caucuses, when both parties had competitive contests, is believed to be the highest caucus turnout ever recorded. Caucus participants of both parties are unrepresentative of the general population in terms of income and education, and ideologically they tend to be more extreme than their party's broader base of party identifiers.

Primaries take many forms across the states. In **closed primaries** only party members can vote—and only in the primary of the party in which they are registered. Some primaries are only "semiclosed" because they allow independents to select party primaries and vote as well. **Open primaries** allow any registered voter to select one party's primary and vote in it, even if that person is a member of another party. Most of the southern and upper midwestern states have open primaries. A few Pacific Coast states experimented with "blanket primaries," in which a voter selects a party primary for each office, but in 2000 the U.S. Supreme Court struck down the California law (see the Election Connection, "The Blanket Primary").

Variation in primary laws was significant in the 2000 election season because of the candidacy of John McCain. McCain won in New Hampshire, a semiclosed-primary state, because he received heavy support among independents. Then he scared George W. Bush in South Carolina and won in Michigan—both open-primary states. He was less successful in states where only registered Republicans could participate.

The parties generally would prefer to control participation in their primaries. Even third parties often prefer closed primaries, because they fear how easily an active group can take over a small party—as Pat Buchanan's supporters illustrated in the 2000 election, when they won control of the Reform party from Ross Perot's old allies.

EVOLUTION OF THE NOMINATION PROCESS   The direct primary is an American invention, a Progressive reform that swept across the states in the early twentieth century. Despite their adoption at the state and local levels, however, primaries did not determine presidential nominations for another half-century.[85] As late as 1968, Vice President Hubert Humphrey won the Democratic nomination without entering a single primary. Primaries simply served as beauty contests used by particular candidates to show party leaders their popular appeal. These leaders—mayors, governors, and other public and party officials—actually controlled the delegates to national conventions.

The Republicans were the first to begin moving toward greater popular participation in their nominating process. In 1964 Senator Barry Goldwater, an insurgent from Arizona, won the nomination by edging out the party's establishment candidate in the California primary.[86] But the real push to openness came after Humphrey's presidential nomination. Many liberal activists had supported "peace" candidates Eugene McCarthy and Robert Kennedy, who opposed the war in Vietnam.[87] These candidates won most of the year's primaries, driving President Lyndon Johnson from the race in the process. Their supporters thus were outraged that the nomination went to Johnson's vice president. The party adopted its current process to mollify the antiwar movement.[88]

ELECTION CONNECTION

The Blanket Primary

In the 2000 elections, the states of Alaska, California, and Washington chose candidates for office using what are called blanket primaries.[a] Any registered voter can participate in such primaries, and all receive the same ballot. All the candidates for a given office—Democratic, Republican, and minor party—are listed together, and a voter can vote for any party's candidate for each office to be filled. Thus, a voter could vote for a Republican Senate candidate, a Democratic House candidate, a Libertarian gubernatorial candidate, a Peace and Freedom secretary of state candidate, and so on. Because such primaries ignore considerations of party membership and party loyalty, they have been called "free love" primaries; voters can switch from party to party and don't have to make any commitments!

The California parties sued to overturn the state's blanket primary, which had passed by a popular initiative over their bipartisan opposition in 1998, on the grounds that it violated their constitutional right of free association. Lower court decisions were appealed to the Supreme Court. In June of 2000 in *California Democratic Party* v. *Jones,* the Supreme Court overturned the California blanket primary, sending its supporters back to the drawing board to attempt to devise some constitutionally permissible alternative.

Supporters of the blanket primary make two main arguments. First, they claim that it increases turnout because members of a party with no exciting contests might be drawn to the polls by an exciting race in the other party. Second, they claim that blanket primaries moderate politics because conservative Republicans usually win in Republican primaries, and liberal Democrats, in Democratic primaries. Allowing everyone into a party's primary increases the likelihood that moderates can win.

Opponents of the blanket primary argue that it allows parties to be "hijacked by drive-by voters with no durable interest in the parties, acting on transitory whims, or even to make mischief by burdening a party with a weak candidate."[b]

What do you think?
- Do the goals of boosting turnout and encouraging moderation outweigh restricting the parties' rights of free association?
- Given that two major parties together control the electoral process, is it right to exclude people who are not party members (one-third of the voting age population) from choosing candidates?

[a]In California, however, although voters could vote for any presidential candidate, delegates were allocated in proportion to the votes cast by party members only.

[b]George Will, "'Blanket' Primary Can Hijack a Party," *San Francisco Chronicle* (May 1, 2000): A23.

The past two decades have seen much tinkering with the rules, but the broad outlines of the system have not changed. In 2000 all of the Republican delegates and about 80 percent of the Democratic delegates were chosen in primaries and caucuses.[*] The general pattern today is for candidates to build extensive

[*]The Democrats generally reserve about 20 percent of their slots for elected officials and party leaders called *superdelegates.*

organizations in the states where the first caucuses and primaries are held. Here the emphasis is on "retail politics," face-to-face contact with voters.[89] An early victory can lead to greater support and more news coverage in the caucuses and primaries that follow.

STRENGTHS AND WEAKNESSES OF THE NOMINATION PROCESS
Despite its participatory nature, many observers are critical of the presidential nomination process.[90] Their concerns fall into two broad categories, one procedural, the other political.

The nomination process is sequential: Candidates organize and campaign in one state, then pack up and move on to the next one. The problem, critics complain, is that the process starts before citizens are interested in the election and

Information overload

The American public apparently lacks the endurance for a long election season. They do not pay attention while the early candidate selection process takes place, and they bore of the campaign before the election ends. States have worsened the problem by "front-loading" their primaries. Do you think the United States should change election laws to shorten the presidential campaign? Or will that give too much of an advantage to candidates with early money and name recognition?

outlasts citizen endurance.[91] For example, the January 2000 candidate debate carried by NBC in prime time drew an audience of 4.7 million. That was only a bit larger than the audience for reruns of *Buffy the Vampire Slayer* and only 60 percent as large as the audience for *WWF Smackdown!*[92] Many candidacies therefore die before voters are tuned in to the campaign.

The long process may bore ordinary voters and leave the nominees "damaged goods" after they exit the grueling process. Yet it shines a bright light on candidates, revealing a great deal of information about them that Americans choose to consider when they vote. Is it better for voters to be ignorant of personal shortcomings or the questionable activities of a public servant, flaws that often went unknown before the modern nomination process? Opinions differ. The scrutiny may expose bad leaders, but the lack of personal privacy also may drive away some good leaders. Indeed, some have suggested (jokingly?) that anyone willing to expose every aspect of his or her life to media scrutiny is not the kind of person who should be in power.

And so the procedural argument goes, back and forth. The structure of the nomination process has positive and negative qualities, and any change is soon criticized. For example, in 1996 and 2000 the primaries were "front-loaded"; many states moved their primaries to early dates in hopes that the nomination contests would be decided more quickly and the winners would have more time to unify their parties and plan for the fall election campaign.[93] As Figure 7.8 shows, these hopes were fulfilled. But then critics charged that this front-loading gave an advantage to well-known, establishment candidates who could raise large sums of money to pay for national campaigns.

A second set of criticisms focuses on the *politics* of the nomination process. Reformers who instituted primaries claimed they were giving "power to the people"—the new procedure would empower ordinary citizens at the expense of the party bosses. In fact, other elites rose up to be the new bosses: political activists and the media.

Political activists have always exercised more influence than ordinary citizens, because they participate. Caucus turnout is extremely low, and although primary turnout is higher, it is still much lower than that in general elections. Of the 18 states that voted while the nominations were still undecided in 2000, 12 set turnout records, but the average turnout was only 13.6 percent![94] Even more important, activists work in campaigns and give money to candidates; they help mobilize others.

None of this would be a cause for concern if the activists were like everyone else. But activists differ in politically relevant ways. Not only are their views more intense, but party activists' positions are more extreme as well (see Table 7.3).

FIGURE 7.8

In 1996 and 2000 the presidential nominations were decided earlier than ever

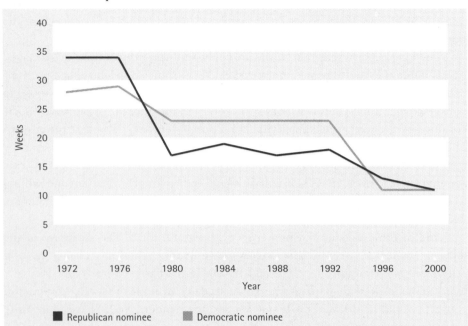

SOURCE: Data compiled by Sam Abrams through various news reports.

Candidates often must conform to these policy positions if they wish to win nominations. Consequently, the primary process may force candidates to take positions far from the center of the political spectrum where the mass of Americans is located.

Democratic candidates generally are more liberal, and Republican candidates generally more conservative, than the average voter. That being said, primary electorates do not appear to be very far from the party mainstream, even if convention delegates and campaign workers may be.[95] To the extent the system is unrepresentative, the problem seems to center on caucuses and in the fund-raising arena.[96]

Another consequence of the enhanced influence of activists in the nominating process is that they skew the political debate. To someone following the process, it may seem that the most important issues facing the United States are so-called hot-button issues, such as abortion and gun control. Although issues like these are important, ordinary voters do not view them as crucial. They may prefer that the spotlight turn to bread-and-butter issues, such as education, medical care, and prosperity.

TABLE 7.3

PARTY ACTIVISTS ARE NOT MODERATES

Surveys find that on most issues, Democratic activists tend to be more liberal than Democratic identifiers and Republican activists more conservative than Republican identifiers. Here is how national convention delegates compared to their parties' supporters in 1996. Democratic delegates were more extreme than identifiers on eight of ten issues, and Republican delegates, more extreme on nine of ten issues.

ISSUE	DEMOCRATIC		REPUBLICAN	
	DELEGATES	IDENTIFIERS	IDENTIFIERS	DELEGATES
Government should do more to solve the nation's problems	76%	53%	20%	4%
Government should regulate the environment and safety practices of business	60	66	37	4
Government should promote traditional values	27	41	44	56
Abortion should be permitted in all cases	61	30	22	11
Assault weapons should be banned	91	80	62	34
It is necessary to have laws to protect racial minorities	88	62	39	30
Affirmative action programs should be continued	81	59	28	9
Organized prayer should be permitted in public schools	20	66	69	57
Trade restrictions are necessary to protect domestic industries	54	65	56	31
Children of illegal immigrants should be allowed to attend public school	79	63	46	26

SOURCE: From CBSNews/*New York Times* Poll results distributed by Michael Kagay at the Annual Meeting of the American Political Science Association, San Francisco, August 31, 1996.

The media are the second group that gained influence from the nomination process, since journalists are the ones responsible for interpreting confusing primary and caucus developments for the American people. Some critics claim that the press trivializes elections by emphasizing matters other than policy and performance. The press reports the horse race—who is ahead and by how far, who is coming up "on the rail," and who is fading from contention. This emphasis has increased over time such that, for the last couple of decades, four-fifths of election coverage focuses on the race aspect.[97]

Journalists also tend to swarm around what many observers regard as trivia—scandals, gaffes, and campaign feuds. Accounts of modern presidential campaigns are littered with stories like Jimmy Carter's revelation to *Playboy* magazine that he had felt "lust in his heart" and Bill Clinton's less-speculative forays into amorous activity. The media like sleaze. Defenders of the media like to point out, though, that sleaze attracts viewers and sells papers. The public gets what it pays for.

The media warp public perception of elections in other ways. For example, Iowa, the first caucus state, and New Hampshire, the first primary state, receive a disproportionate share of news coverage. Some critics ask whether two sparsely populated, rural states should play such an important role in determining candidate viability or, indeed, in determining who is the front runner.[98]

Finally, some observers complain that the media no longer merely report the nomination process but have become important players in it. News stories have become overwhelmingly interpretive, rather than simply factual.[99] For example, in every campaign there is a widely publicized "expectations" game. The question is not so much whether candidates win or lose but how they perform relative to "expectations." And who sets these expectations? The media!

The classic example occurred in 1972, when Senator Edmund Muskie's campaign never recovered from his showing in the New Hampshire primary. Muskie won the primary over George McGovern 46 percent to 37 percent. But New Hampshire was next to Muskie's home state—Maine—so the media expected him to do well, whereas they thought that South Dakotan McGovern's showing was unexpectedly strong. The momentum that McGovern took out of New Hampshire carried him to the Democratic nomination.

The media are more influential in the primaries than in the general-election campaign. Voters cannot use party cues to decide among candidates in primaries, because they all belong to the same party. Nor is presidential performance of any use. Normally, all the candidates in the incumbent party's primaries defend the president's record, whereas all the candidates in the other party's primaries criticize that record. Consequently, citizens use other information to choose among the candidates, and in most cases the media provide it. In particular, the electorate usually wishes to know which candidates are serious, and campaign coverage gives that signal. None of these sources of media influence appears in the general election.

Whatever your view of the pros and cons of the American nomination process, it is now well established and, so, unlikely to change except in marginal ways for the foreseeable future. Many of the problems that bother critics do not trace back to national law, but to the combined decisions of political parties, individual states, and media organizations. Even if reformers did succeed at changing the process, the alternatives may be worse than the current system.

Holding all primaries on the same day could increase the role of money and national stature. Trying to increase the amount of candidate information available or the number of candidates might result in overload and drive citizens out of the process even more than they already are. Opening up the nomination process might hinder the ability of party leaders to recruit and promote strong candidates able to create a national constituency. The only obvious possible enhancement would be if citizens became more attentive to their political decisions and more savvy about evaluating potential candidates—and that is the one thing that reformers probably cannot legislate.

WHO NOMINATES THE VICE PRESIDENT? Before the establishment of the contemporary nomination process, the conventions chose the vice presidential candidates as well as the presidential candidates. Today, the choice is completely in

The moral high ground
Al Gore's ticket surged in the polls after Connecticut Senator Joseph Lieberman joined it as Gore's running mate. Lieberman seemed an inspired choice. Not only did his Jewish faith attract lots of media attention, his devoutness also set up a nice contrast with the sex scandals of the Clinton administration. Some observers have mentioned Lieberman as a potential presidential candidate in 2004. Judging from your own community, do you think many voters would be prejudiced against a Jewish candidate? Would Lieberman face an extra burden, or would he get a fair shake?

the hands of the presidential nominees. The presidential nominees simply announce their choices, and the conventions accept them. Usually they attempt to select a nominee who will help the ticket (or at least not hurt it).[100]

Bush's choice of Dick Cheney offset his inexperience with national politics; Cheney was a widely respected former Cabinet secretary and congressman. Gore chose Connecticut Senator Joseph Lieberman, whose religiosity and early criticism of the Monica Lewinsky affair innoculated his ticket against contamination by the outgoing Clinton administration's scandals. Recent choices for vice president, as often as not, have been better respected nationally than the men who chose them.

THE CONGRESSIONAL NOMINATION PROCESS   The congressional nomination process is much simpler than the presidential one: A nominee for the House or Senate must win at most one primary election, not a sequence across many states. In a few states party conventions can nominate candidates, but in most states primary voters do the job.

The dates of **filing deadlines** and primary elections vary widely across states.[101] The filing deadline is the latest date on which a politician who wishes to be on the ballot must file official documents with and/or pay fees to state election officials. In 2000 the dates ranged from January 3 in Texas to August 18 in Louisiana. The earliest primaries started on March 7, and the last, on September 23. Thus, some candidates know whether they will have opponents and who they are as much as nine months earlier than others.

The hardest-fought primaries occur when a seat becomes "open" because an incumbent dies, retires, resigns, or opts to run for another office. If both parties have strength in the area, the primaries in both parties are hotly contested. If only one party is strong, its primary will be a donnybrook, because the winner is viewed as the next member of Congress. **Open seats** are critical to political change within a party because few incumbents lose primaries. In the ten elections held since 1980, a total of 50 House incumbents and 6 Senate incumbents were defeated in primaries, and not many more faced tough races. This record does not prove that primaries are unimportant. Incumbent primary successes probably indicate the same thing as general-election successes do: Incumbents behave in such a way as to keep their constituencies satisfied and preempt a strong challenge.

CHAPTER SUMMARY

Many traits that reformers dislike about the American electoral system result from the quantity of popular input, rather than the limits on it. For example, incumbency advantages in congressional elections largely result from the effort incumbents put into satisfying voters back home. They work hard to anticipate how constituents wish them to vote and work even harder providing constituency service for their districts. Even senators must campaign continually to retain their power, contrary to what the founders originally expected. They cannot simply ride national political forces to victory.

The American nomination process is far more open than the nomination processes of other democracies. It gives rank-and-file voters more influence in the United States than the processes in other countries, and it gives "outsider" candidates a chance by enabling them to pull off upsets in early primaries and caucuses. If the system has any serious flaw, it is probably the way campaign finance, party activists, and the media can run off or shut out candidates that ordinary voters have not had adequate time to consider. But even this influence may be exaggerated, and at any rate no obvious reform is available to fix it.

Campaigning is often misunderstood. It is not an independent force that determines election outcomes. Rather, the campaign itself is shaped by events and conditions in the years leading up to the election. The reason campaigns are limited in their impact is that most voters do not make up their minds on the basis of campaigns. People vote for the parties they favor, vote against leaders when they dislike the government's performance, consider policy differences when they are easy to compare, and weigh candidate traits relevant to governance. Only a minority decide how to vote late in the campaign, by using knowledge of particular candidates or the particular things they say.

Finally, . . . a puzzle. If this description of voting behavior is accurate, why did Al Gore lose? Even statistical models popularized by political scientists—which take into account some (but certainly not all) of the insights introduced in this chapter—suggested that he should have won easily. Does Gore's loss prove that campaign tactics actually matter, in the rare instance when a party messes up? Certainly Gore's personality turned off some voters, even some who agreed with him on the issues. Yet Bush's demeanor grated on many voters as well. It is more likely that Gore's loss indicates the complex way in which party, performance, and policy preferences operate.

Incumbents receive credit for good times because voters assume they will continue to do what they have done before. Gore was not the incumbent, however, but his second in command. He distanced himself from the Clinton administration and its scandals. He had to counteract Bill Bradley's primary challenge, as well as Ralph Nader's Green party presidential bid, by emphasizing liberal policy reforms rather than maintenance of the status quo. As one critic sarcastically observed, Gore's theme was "You've never had it so good, and I'm mad as hell about it."[102] If anything, Bush ran as the incumbent, drawing from Clinton's moderate playbook more often than Gore did. Swing voters may have considered Bush likely to continue the pattern of compromise they associated with the outgoing administration and favored him as a result.

KEY TERMS

caucus, p. 217

closed primaries, p. 217

coattails, p. 200

constituency service, p. 199

electoral vote, p. 211

filing deadlines, p. 226

frank, p. 196

gerrymandering, p. 216

incumbency advantage, p. 194

matching funds, p. 206

midterm loss, p. 200

open primaries, p. 218

open seats, p. 226

party identification, p. 186

popular vote, p. 211

primary election, p. 217

proportional representation,
p. 216

reapportionment, p. 215

redistricting, p. 215

retrospective voting, p. 189

roll-call vote, p. 196

safe seat, p. 193

soft money, p. 206

winner-take-all voting,
p. 212

SUGGESTED READINGS

Brady, David. *Critical Elections and Congressional Policy Making*. Stanford, CA: Stanford University Press, 1988. Prize-winning account that ties together congressional elections, processes, and policy making.

Brown, Clifford, Lynda Powell, and Clyde Wilcox. *Serious Money.* Cambridge, England: Cambridge University Press, 1995. A detailed empirical study of who contributes to presidential campaigns and why.

Butler, David, and Bruce Cain. *Congressional Redistricting.* New York: Macmillan, 1992. Readable account of the redistricting process, with comparisons to practices in other democracies.

Campbell, James. *The Presidential Pulse of Congressional Elections.* Lexington, KY: University of Kentucky Press, 1993. Detailed analysis of national forces operating in midterm elections.

Canon, David. *Actors, Athletes, and Astronauts.* Chicago: University of Chicago Press, 1990. Interesting study of how political amateurs run for and occasionally win seats in Congress.

Fenno, Richard. *Home Style.* Boston: Little, Brown, 1978. Influential study of how House members interact with constituents, earning their trust.

Fiorina, Morris. *Congress—Keystone of the Washington Establishment,* Second Edition.

New Haven, CT: Yale University Press, 1989. A critical look at the implications of constituency service for national policy making.

Hibbing, John. *Congressional Careers.* Chapel Hill: University of North Carolina Press, 1991. Detailed study of career development of modern U.S. representatives after their initial election.

Holbrook, Thomas. *Do Campaigns Matter?* Thousand Oaks, CA: Sage, 1996. A scientifically rigorous study of the impact of presidential campaigns.

Kahn, Kim, and Patrick Kenney. *The Spectacle of U.S. Senate Campaigns.* Princeton, NJ: Princeton University Press, 1999. Detailed study of how candidate strategies, media practices, and voter decisions interact in contemporary Senate campaigns.

Mayer, William, ed. *In Pursuit of the White House 2000: How We Choose Our Presidential Nominees.* Chatham, NJ: Chatham House, 2000. An informative collection of essays covering all facets of the contemporary nominating process.

Mayhew, David. *Congress—The Electoral Connection.* New Haven, CT: Yale University Press, 1974. Influential work that shows how much of congressional structure and behavior can be explained by the assumption that reelection is the most important goal of members.

ON THE WEB

The United States Electoral College
www.nara.gov/fedreg/elctcoll
A detailed explanation of the electoral college as well as an historical database of presidential election data. The site is maintained by the National Archives and Records Administration and has links to other government data sets pertaining to elections on all levels of government.

Common Cause
www.commoncause.org/index.html
Common Cause is a nonprofit, nonpartisan citizen's lobbying organization promoting open, honest, and accountable government. This site contains a searchable database of special-interest soft-money contributions to the Democratic and Republican national party committees, as well as a database of materials that focus on the impact of big money in politics.

Presidential Election Statistics
www.multied.com/elections/
A graphical presentation on each of the U.S. presidential elections, providing both electoral and popular votes. This site is run by MultiEducator Incorporated, an online education company that offers free access to many of its files over the Internet.

Federal Election Project
www.american.edu/academic.depts/spa/ccps/elections
A repository for 2000 election statistics at the precinct level, compiled by David Lublin at American University and Steve Voss at the University of Kentucky.

American National Election Studies
www.umich.edu/~nes/
Probably the single most important source of data for students of American elections. This impressive collection of election surveys conducted from the 1950s to the present is the source of many of the figures and tables that appear in this book.

Voter Information Services
www.vis.org/
A site that includes scorecards, voting records, and various public interest groups' ratings for members of the U.S. Congress.

Part Three

THE AMERICAN POLITICAL SYSTEM

POLITICAL PARTIES
AND INTEREST GROUPS

embers of the House Education Committee were hard at work on a major bill in February 1994, when California Democrat George Miller offered what appeared to be an acceptable amendment.[1] Miller's proposal would have withheld federal grant money from school districts using teachers who were not certified officially in their subjects. Approving the amendment must have been an easy decision. Committee members could claim that they had taken affirmative steps to improve teacher qualifications, without spending any additional money.

Miller's amendment promised other political advantages to the Democrats dominating the committee. The mandate was sure to please two interest groups whose members frequently support their party: unions and universities.* Teachers' unions favor certification requirements, because they reduce competition from skilled, but uncertified, teachers. Education schools favor certification requirements because professionals, no matter how skilled, would have to go through one of their programs before being allowed to teach. But these eyes were not the only ones watching.

A home school advocate who had been following the proceedings contacted Richard Armey (R-TX) to inquire whether the amendment would affect home school teachers. Unbeknown to many people, including most members of Congress at the time, between 500,000 and 1 million American children are educated at home—many by conservative Christian parents opposed to the secular values of the educational profession. Uncertain about the impact of the proposal, Armey sought the advice of the Home School Legal Defense Association. The association's lawyers suggested that, given the tendency of the courts to interpret legislative mandates broadly, the proposal did threaten uncertified parents educating their children at home.

The reaction was fierce and immediate. In a letter to Congress that illustrates the fevered pitch of political rhetoric today, the Home School Legal Defense Association charged that the House proposal was "the equivalent of a nuclear attack upon the home schooling community." Employing modern communications technologies, the interest group set out to mobilize the potential constituency of home schoolers and their ideological sympathizers.

Electronic communications carried the warning to every corner of the United States, and in a matter of days the echoes came back loud and clear. The home school constituency generated more than half a million communications, tying up Capitol Hill switchboards and overwhelming fax machines. A few days

*The term "interest group" may not suggest a college or university. But American universities, especially private institutions, are quite active in lobbying government.

later a second wave of electronic thunder rolled across Capitol Hill after the home school coalition convinced groups representing private schools that they, too, were endangered by the proposed mandate.

Many members of Congress—blithely unaware of what was going on in one of 275 committees and subcommittees—went home for the Presidents' Day recess and were caught in the blast of a constituency explosion. Some of them were verbally ambushed at town meetings by constituents incensed that Congress might be planning to destroy home schools. And when members tried to reach their offices to figure out what was going on, they found the lines jammed! Armey could not get through from Texas, and other members had to call staff at their homes to learn the nature of the problem.

In the face of such an outcry, the House sounded a full retreat. Before galleries packed with home school advocates, the committee offered a floor amendment to kill the Miller provision and add statutory language specifically exempting home schools from the legislation's scope. It passed 424 to 1; Representative Miller stood alone. Not completely satisfied, Armey introduced a further amendment declaring that the legislation did not "permit, allow, encourage or authorize any federal control over any aspect of any private, religious or home school." To be on the safe side, the House passed this amendment too, 374 to 53.

THIS EPISODE GRAPHICALLY ILLUSTRATES ALL THE PERCEIVED ILLS OF interest-group democracy. It shows large organizations trying to use federal power to reduce competition and steer people into paying for training they may not need. It shows a small, but intense, minority able to send the nation's entire legislative branch scrambling for cover. It shows the extent to which public policies emerge from fear and political calculation rather than from careful deliberation.

James Madison warned against the "mischiefs of faction"—against the danger of allowing self-interested pressure groups to take over the reins of government. Yet to many Americans, Madison's worst nightmares appear to have been realized. How did the United States reach such a pass, where special interests war in the halls of Congress and the "public interest" plays so little obvious role? Were the mechanisms of democracy so easy for factions to seize? What happened to the golden era of American politics, in which citizens influenced their government through political parties with mass appeal?

This chapter explains how the United States moved from a system ruled by political parties to the contemporary system of interest-group democracy. However, we do not accept the value-laden tone of much of the criticism that special interests face. As the chapter shows, the era of party control was not so golden, and interest groups did not seize anything. Rather, *the United States made a series of policy decisions intended to weaken political parties.* Some of these changes responded directly to problems with a party-dominated process. But citizens still needed some medium through which to communicate demands on their government. *Interest groups rose up to fill the void that weakening political parties had left behind.*

POLITICAL PARTIES: A NECESSARY EVIL?

When George Washington left office in 1796, he warned his fellow citizens about "the spirit of party": "It agitates the community with ill-founded jealousies and false alarms, kindles the animosity of one part against another, foments occasional riot and insurrection." Washington's warning came too late—the spirit of party already was loose, never to be confined again. Both Treasury Secretary Alexander Hamilton's ambitious policies and numerous problems in foreign affairs had caused deep divisions within the young republic.

Support for Hamilton's program was strongest in New England. It was generally endorsed by commercial interests and by those in favor of strong government under a strong executive. Opposition to Hamilton was strongest in the South and West, especially among agrarian interests (many of whom were particularly outraged by Hamilton's tax on whiskey). Those averse to a strong executive also gravitated to the opposition, which was centered in the Virginia congressional delegation led by James Madison. Both Hamilton's and Madison's embryonic parties had their own newspapers, which they used to revile each other.[2] Critics of Hamilton vilified him and his followers as monarchists and British sympathizers. The Madison supporters were maligned as radicals and French sympathizers.

In 1796 John Adams, Washington's vice president, won the presidency. Thomas Jefferson, Washington's secretary of state, came in second in the Electoral College voting and thus became the new vice president. Over the course of the next few years, Jefferson and Madison laid the foundations of a new electoral alliance. Jefferson, who regularly glorified the small farmer, began to reach out to urban interests. By the next presidential election he and Madison had concluded an alliance with the New York Republicans under Governor George Clinton and New York City political operative Aaron Burr. By all accounts a superb organizer, Burr delivered the New York legislature, which chose the presidential electors. New York's 12 electors were the key to the 1800 election—Jefferson and Burr finished eight votes ahead of President Adams.

Thus, within eight years of the adoption of the Constitution, a two-party presidential race had been fought. The Constitution contains not a word about political parties, but they have been active in U.S. national politics almost since the founding. Indeed, some historians claim that the individual colonies had parties even earlier.[3] It is hard to imagine a government without them.

All modern democracies have **political parties.** Traditionally defined as groups of like-minded people who band together in an attempt to take control of government, political parties serve as the main connection between ordinary citizens and the public officials they elect. Parties nominate candidates for office, shape the electoral process, and mobilize voters. And after elections have determined the winners, parties also coordinate the actions of elected officials in the government.

Despite the presence of parties almost since the founding, however, Americans have not always accepted the roles they play in the American political system. Periodically, voters have grown unhappy with the major parties available to them and expressed their displeasure by supporting new organizations (see Table 8.1). Often these periods of instability caused significant changes in the political system, or evoked demands for reform that stripped parties of their organizational strength.

THE TWO-PARTY SYSTEM

Two major parties have dominated elections for national office throughout two centuries of American history. Americans therefore understandably regard a two-party system as a natural state of affairs. Third parties regularly arise, including the fledgling Reform Party (see the Election Connection, "The Reform Party and the Elections of 1992, 1996, and 2000"). But they nearly all disappear soon afterward, either because they are a reaction to a particular problem or because one of the major parties coopts their main issues.[4] Only once has a third party replaced a major party—the Republicans displaced the Whigs in the 1850s.

The number of political parties may result from how a country's laws translate popular votes into control of public offices.[5] The United States relies almost exclusively on the **single-member, simple plurality (SMSP) system.** Elections for office take place within geographic units (states, congressional districts, city wards, and so on), and the candidates who win the most votes win the elections. This electoral system is characteristic of the "Anglo-American democracies" (England and its former colonies). It is often called the first-past-the-post system; just as in a horse race, the winner is the one who finishes first, no matter how many others are in the race or how close the finish.

In the SMSP electoral system, winning is everything—finishing in any position except first gets nothing. Thus, if small parties have more in common with

TABLE 8.1

THIRD PARTIES IN U.S. HISTORY

CANDIDATE (PARTY, YEAR)	SHOWING	SUBSEQUENT EVENTS
Martin Van Buren (Free Soil party, 1848)	10.1 percent 0 electoral votes	Party drew 5 percent in 1852; supporters then merged into Republican Party
James B. Weaver (Populist party, 1892)	8.5 percent 22 electoral votes	Party supported Democrat William Jennings Bryan in 1896
Theodore Roosevelt (Progressive party, 1912)	27.4 percent 88 electoral votes	Party supported GOP nominee in 1916
Robert M. La Follette (Progressive party, 1924)	16.6 percent 13 electoral votes	La Follette died in June 1925
Strom Thurmond (States' Rights Democratic party, 1948)	2.4 percent 38 electoral votes	Democrats picked slate acceptable to South in 1952
Henry A. Wallace (Progressive party, 1948)	2.4 percent 0 electoral votes	Party disappeared
George C. Wallace (American Independent party, 1968)	13.5 percent 46 electoral votes	Wallace ran in Democratic primaries in 1972 until he was injured in assassination attempt
John B. Anderson (National Unity Campaign, 1980)	6.6 percent 0 electoral votes	Anderson withdrew from elective politics
H. Ross Perot (Independent, 1992)	18.7 percent 0 electoral votes	Perot formed new party (Reform) to take part in 1996 and 2000 presidential elections
H. Ross Perot (Reform party, 1996)	8.5 percent 0 electoral votes	Perot adopted a lower profile
Patrick Buchanan (Reform party, 2000)	< 1 percent 0 electoral votes	Buchanan appeared to be finished in national politics
Ralph Nader (Green party, 2000)	3 percent 0 electoral votes	Nader failed to qualify for federal funding in 2004

NOTE: The list excludes many third-party candidates who received less than 2 percent of the popular vote. Other third parties that won at least 2 percent of the vote include the Liberty party (1844); the Greenback party (1880); the Prohibition party (1888, 1892); and the Socialist party (1904, 1908, 1912, 1916, 1920, 1932).

SOURCE: Adapted from Kenneth Jost, "Third-Party Prospects," *The CQ Researcher* (December 22, 1995): 1148. Updated with 1996 and 2000 election returns.

The Reform Party and the Elections of 1992, 1996, and 2000

In the 1992 presidential election, H. Ross Perot, a colorful Texas multimillionaire, received 19 percent of the vote in a three-way race with Bill Clinton and George Bush. This was the best showing by a third candidate since Theodore Roosevelt's Bull Moose insurgency in 1912.

After preliminary preparations, Perot announced on CNN's *Larry King Live!* in early 1992 that he would run for president—if his supporters could get his name on the ballot in all 50 states. His candidacy caught on, and his poll numbers rose rapidly; by May several polls showed a statistical dead heat among the three candidates. With visibility came critical examination, however, and doubts rose about his personality and temperament; the campaign started slipping in the polls. Perot temporarily withdrew from the race in July, but once his supporters qualified his name for the ballot in all 50 states, he reentered the race. In total, Perot spent $65 million of his personal fortune.

Surveys showed that Perot supporters tended to be people who had not previously been involved in politics. They were "between" the two parties in terms of their policy stands: neither as socially conservative as Republicans nor as socially liberal as Democrats. They did not want to spend more money on new programs like traditional Democrats, nor did they want to cut taxes like many Republicans. Instead, they wanted to attack budget deficits, Perot's signature issue.[a]

After the election Perot transformed his campaign organization, "United We Stand, America," into a citizen watchdog group and continued to speak out on national politics. In 1994 he urged his supporters to "send a message," helping the Republicans capture control of Congress. In late 1995 Perot announced on CNN that he would encourage the formation of a third party. The new Reform Party would not compete in the 1996 primaries but would compete in the general election. The Federal Election Commission announced that, on the basis of its 1992 showing, the party would be eligible for $30 million in federal matching funds.

Perot did much worse in 1996, winning only 9 percent of the vote. But the party did not fade away as many expected. In 1998 the Reform Party ran more than 180 candidates for a variety of offices and even managed to elect a governor, former professional wrestler Jesse Ventura, in Minnesota. With $12.6 million in federal matching funds available for 2000 and a network of supporters in place, the Reform Party nomination was still worth something.

The party split badly in late 1999. Ventura resisted appeals that he run for president. Multimillionaire real estate developer Donald Trump also considered running and then decided against it. Finally former Republican Pat Buchanan moved in, and his socially conservative supporters swamped the Reform Party—winning access to government subsidies that had been earned by a very different sort of candidate. The money was not enough; Buchanan received less than 1 percent of the popular vote in 2000.

What do you think?

• Will the Reform Party go the way of most third parties and die out? Why will it, or won't it, survive?

• Has its impact been large or small, particularly in budget matters?

[a]"The Perot Phenomenon," *The Public Perspective* (September/October 1992): 91–95.

each other than with the largest party, they have an incentive to join together. Dividing the opposition simply plays into the hands of the largest party. Citizens, in turn, realize that voting for a small party is tantamount to "wasting" their votes—unless party sympathizers are so concentrated that they can win in a particular geographical unit.[6] Thus, voters tend to support one of the two larger parties. These calculations work against third parties.

In most of the world's other democracies, however, the electoral system is some version of **proportional representation (PR).** In such systems, elections may (as in Germany) or may not (as in Israel) take place within geographic units, but even if they do, each unit elects a number of officials, with each party winning seats in proportion to the vote it receives. Multiple political parties are much more likely under a PR system because votes for a third party seldom go to waste. One study found that the average number of parties in proportional representation systems was 3.7, while the average number in SMSP systems was 2.2.[7]

POLITICAL PARTIES IN U.S. HISTORY

The United States has always had two parties, but the system has not remained static throughout the country's history. When Washington issued his warning, parties were not unlike "court factions" in a monarchical government: groups of nobles who engaged in "palace intrigues." The electoral system has gone through numerous changes since then: the development of parties appealing to the masses, the collapse of a major party and birth of a new one, and wild fluctuations in the balance of power between Republicans and Democrats.

Realignment theorists view American political history as a succession of electoral eras, often referred to as party systems (see Table 8.2).[8] Within each era, elections are similar, in that each social and economic group consistently supports one party. The minority party rarely wins the presidency, unless it can find a military hero to nominate or identifies some other temporary opportunity. But at some point a crisis disrupts the tidy arrangement of voters. Factions within the major parties may start fighting each other, or strong third parties may arise. Voter turnout surges in response to the excitement. Finally, a **critical election** (or realigning election) alters the existing electoral alignment altogether. New groups enter the electorate, or influential groups switch parties for good, solidifying the terms of political conflict for a generation or more.

THE FIRST PARTY SYSTEM (JEFFERSONIAN)   Some historians date the first party system from the early 1790s to about 1824. The overriding issue during this period was the proper balance of power between national and state

TABLE 8.2

THE PARTY-SYSTEMS INTERPRETATION OF U.S. ELECTORAL HISTORY

First (Jeffersonian) Party System: 1796–1824[a]
  7 Democratic–Republican presidential victories
  1 Federalist victory

Second (Jacksonian) Party System: 1828–1856
  6 Democratic victories
  2 Whig victories

Third (Civil War and Reconstruction) Party System: 1860–1892
  7 Republican victories
  2 Democratic victories

Fourth (National Republican) Party System: 1896–1928
  7 Republican victories
  2 Democratic victories

Fifth (New Deal) Party System: 1932–1964
  7 Democratic victories
  2 Republican victories

Sixth (Divided Government) Party System: 1968–??
  6 Republican victories
  3 Democratic victories

[a]Years are approximate.

governments. Commercial interests in the young republic supported the Federalists, especially in New England. Agricultural interests supported the Jeffersonians, especially in the South and West. The Jeffersonians (or Democratic–Republicans) were the dominant party, winning the presidency seven consecutive times from 1800 to 1824, but the system splintered when a "corrupt bargain" denied General Andrew Jackson the presidency in 1824—after he had won both the popular *and* the electoral vote.

THE SECOND PARTY SYSTEM (JACKSONIAN DEMOCRACY) After Jackson's defeat in 1824, he and his allies laid the groundwork for another presidential campaign. They sought to mobilize more potential voters—spreading the Democratic party outward from Washington and downward into the grassroots. They succeeded with a vengeance: Between 1824 and 1828, turnout in the presidential election tripled, sweeping Jackson into office. The Jacksonian Democrats were the world's first mass party; one of their efforts' principal architects, Martin Van Buren, is sometimes called the father of parties.[9]

Jackson and Van Buren believed in the old adage "To the victors belong the spoils." They freely and openly passed out government jobs and contracts to consolidate their hold on power. Until it splintered in the sectional conflicts of the 1850s, the Jacksonian Democracy lost only two presidential elections to the Whigs—in 1840 to William Henry Harrison and in 1848 to Zachary Taylor, both of whom were war heroes. The Democrats also controlled Congress through much of this period.

The second party system continued many conflicts from the previous alignment, especially those over the proper power of the federal government. Jackson vigorously opposed having a national bank. The opposition Whig party, led by Kentuckian Henry Clay, endorsed programs of internal improvement led by the national government. Forces also clashed over rates of taxation on imported goods.

As the system matured, however, sectional differences over slavery intensified. By the late 1840s, both parties were crumbling from internal dissension. Dissatisfied citizens began challenging the system under third-party banners. The Free Soilers opposed the expansion of slavery into the territories.* Then, from 1854 to 1856, a new Republican party rose to replace the Whigs. The badly split Democrats nominated both northern and southern candidates for president in 1860. Together with the Constitutional Union candidate, they received nearly 60 percent of the popular vote. But the Electoral College and winner-take-all election system translated Abraham Lincoln's 40 percent of the vote into a victory— which ultimately sparked a Civil War.

THE THIRD PARTY SYSTEM (CIVIL WAR AND RECONSTRUCTION) War seldom enhances democracy, but the Civil War realignment produced the most competitive electoral era in American history.[10] The Democrats maintained a base in the House of Representatives during the Civil War and then took control in 1874 following the South's readmission to the Union. The Republicans maintained control of the Senate, though, since the wartime government had admitted several sparsely populated western states that dependably elected Republican senators.[11]

At the presidential level, the third party system became known as "the period of no decision." From 1876 to 1892, no presidential candidate received as much as 51 percent of the popular vote. In two elections (that of Rutherford Hayes in

---

*Another third party, the Know Nothings, opposed immigration, especially of Catholics.

1876 and that of Benjamin Harrison in 1888), the Electoral College chose a president who had come in second in the popular vote. The dominant issue at the beginning of the period was Reconstruction, but after 1876 economic issues took center stage. The rise of large business organizations, industrialization and its associated dislocations, and a long agricultural depression generated the political issues of this party system.

During this era, party organizations reached their high point. Bitter memories of the Civil War left many people committed to the party of the Union (Republicans) or of the rebels (Democrats), and these citizens voted a straight party line. Indeed, independents often were viewed as traitors. With feelings so strong and politics so competitive, the parties exerted tremendous effort in campaigns.[12] Moreover, there were thousands of immigrants and former slaves to be fed and housed, employed, and marched to the polls. Parties reached such a high level of organization in many cities that they were referred to as **machines.**[13]

The depression of the 1890s plunged much of the country into misery. Agricultural protest, common throughout the period, gave rise to the Populist movement—which seriously challenged the major parties in the South and West. Eventually Populists fused with the Democrats to form a worker–farmer alliance, which nominated William Jennings Bryan for president in 1896.[14] Bryan was a master of fiery rhetoric, but many of his allies were extremists, so his nomination sent many urban voters scurrying to the Grand Old Party (GOP), as the Republicans are sometimes called. The "period of no decision" was over; Americans had decided.

THE FOURTH PARTY SYSTEM (INDUSTRIAL REPUBLICAN)   The critical election of 1896 inaugurated a period of Republican dominance.[15] The Democrats contracted to their base in the old Confederacy. The Republicans lost the presidency only twice during the fourth party system: in 1912, when Democrat Woodrow Wilson won a three-way race, and again in 1916, when Wilson narrowly held his post on a platform of keeping the United States out of World War I (which he did not do).

Wilson's unique success owed much to a factional split within the GOP. The Republican party included two wings, the old guard of pro-business conservatives and a progressive wing (see the Electoral Connection, "The Progressives"). President William McKinley, elected in 1896 and reelected in 1900, was a solid member of the Republican old guard. But the Progressives had found a sympathizer in his vice president. When McKinley fell to an assassin's bullet in 1901, young Teddy Roosevelt brought their ideas into the White House. An energetic

The Progressives

The Progressive reform movement arose, in the 1890s, in the wake of rapid industrialization and urbanization. Its attempt to bring order to a nearly chaotic society culminated in major innovation to almost every facet of public and private life in the United States. Progressives sought to improve fairness in the political system, the economy, and the standards of everyday living. In the words of progressive Senator Robert M. La Follette, "The supreme issue, involving all the others, is the encroachment of the powerful few upon the rights of the many."

Because of the somewhat contradictory nature of the various branches within progressivism, controversy continues today over the membership and goals of this extremely diverse movement. It is viewed by some as primarily designed to protect the middle class from being squeezed out of power by an ever-growing working class on the one hand and by the increasing power of big business on the other. Others claim the source of the movement to have been the workers themselves, and still others credit business leadership. Progressives have alternately been called self-sacrificing reformers bent on improving the quality of American life and condescending meddlers better at social control than social reform.

Whatever their motivations, Progressives tackled any number of the nation's ills, with varying degrees of success. Although Progressives accepted popular democracy in theory, they were outraged by some democratic practices. Progressives thus became active in government reform, notably the destruction of political machines in favor of a more intellectualized democracy. They combined elitist reforms, such as literacy tests, with measures of direct democracy, such as primaries and citizen initiatives. As with most progressive reforms, this transformation originated on the local level and only gradually spread.

The great trusts—large companies so powerful as to be immune from decisions made by individual workers or consumers—were attacked and broken down via regulation and tariff reform. A variety of tax reforms were introduced in an effort to distribute the nation's wealth more evenly. A constitutional amendment allowed income taxes for the first time. Additional legislative achievements changed child labor laws, industrial working conditions, and workers' compensation provisions.

Following an era of relatively passive chief executives who served as administrators rather than as policy shapers and leaders, progressivism marked the return of strong, active presidents, such as Theodore Roosevelt and Woodrow Wilson. It was also characterized by great faith in the ability and skills of professionals to remedy society's ills.

What do you think?

- When is legislation just a proposal, and when is it a "reform"? Or is the term nothing more than a label people attach to their preferences?

- How active should society be at reforming its institutions? Should a society move slowly and defer to traditional practices unless it is faced with serious problems, or should it experiment with changes frequently to find the best system possible?

SOURCE: Excerpted from Nancy Unger, "Progressivism (circa 1890s to 1917)," in L. Sandy Maisel, ed., *Political Parties and Elections in the United States: An Encyclopedia* (New York: Garland, 1991), Vol. 1, pp. 888–889.

and colorful president, Roosevelt was easily elected in his own right in 1904 and served another four-year term.

His successor met with less success. William Howard Taft was not as astute a politician, and as the Republican party's split widened, President Taft increasingly allied himself with the old guard. Roosevelt returned home from safari in 1910 and took up the progressive banner again. He hammered Taft in the 1912 primaries, but an alliance of professional party operatives and southern delegations gave Taft the nomination anyway. So Roosevelt's supporters formed a new Progressive (or Bull Moose) party, and he ran for president as the new party's nominee. Not only did this split give Democrat Woodrow Wilson the White House, it marked the first and only time a third-party candidate has attracted more votes than a major-party nominee.

This temporary rift within Republican ranks did not end the fourth party system, however. Republicans again controlled the presidency during the 1920s. Two other forces began to threaten their dominance. One worked slowly: Urban populations in the North opposed Republican conservatism, and they were growing. Many urbanites were Catholic or Jewish, and they found the Democratic party a more comfortable home. Al Smith of New York won the Democratic presidential nomination in 1928, the first time a major party ran a Catholic for president.[16]

The great stock market crash of 1929 was more sudden, and more damaging to the incumbent party. The Great Depression of the 1930s resulted in unemployment levels over 20 percent. A third of the nation's banks failed; a quarter of families lost their savings.[17] The Republicans lost the House in the midterm elections of 1930, and then the critical elections from 1932 to 1936 established a new party system.

THE FIFTH PARTY SYSTEM (NEW DEAL)   The fifth party system was a class-based alignment like those found in modern European democracies. In 1936, after Franklin D. Roosevelt's first term, the Democrats became the party of the "common people" (blue-collar workers, farmers, and minorities), while the Republicans became, more than ever, the party of established interests. The former accounted for a lot more voters than the latter, leading to a period of Democratic dominance. Only Republican war hero Dwight Eisenhower was able to crack the Democratic monopoly on the White House, and only from 1952 to 1954 did the Republicans control Congress as well as the presidency.

The South formed a major component of FDR's coalition early on, but Democratic politicians struggled to reconcile the region's expectations with those of liberals and African Americans in northern cities. Gradually party leaders began weaning themselves off of the southern white vote. FDR won repeal of the 104-year-old **two-thirds rule,** which required that the Democratic nominee receive a two-thirds majority of national-convention delegates. With its elimination in 1936, the South no longer could veto unacceptable presidential candidates.

Southerners could not resist the growing national pressure for racial change once they lost influence over their party. The white South began abandoning Democratic presidential candidates a decade later. The Deep South bolted the party rather than vote for President Truman in 1948, since he had begun taking small steps toward racial equality. Then southerners—along with other voters upset with the pace of social change—left in droves when President Johnson pushed an aggressive civil rights agenda through Congress in the mid-1960s. By 1968 the Democratic party was at war with itself, and Republican Richard Nixon was elected president.

Preaching to the converted
Vice President Al Gore made a strong push to turn out African American voters late in the 2000 presidential campaign, including this appearance at a black church in Tennessee. His attempt continued a long party tradition of courting minority voters. Democrats locked up the black vote starting in the 1960s through aggressive appeals, including an ambitious social welfare agenda as well as support for race-conscious policies, such as affirmative action. But their strong civil rights stand may have ended the New Deal party system by driving away white southerners and the urban working class.

THE SIXTH PARTY SYSTEM (DIVIDED GOVERNMENT) For much of the past generation, scholars have debated whether the United States developed a sixth party system. What puzzles them is that, although the Democrats lost all but one presidential election in two decades, they never lost control of the House during that time and held the Senate through most of it. And then, just when the White House changed hands, Republicans seized control of Congress. Voters display a high rate of **ticket splitting,** supporting the presidential and congressional candidates of different parties in the same election. This evidence leads some scholars to argue that perhaps American parties have grown too weak to realign into a new party system.[18]

In retrospect, though, most scholars agree that the mid-1960s were another critical transition period. The third-party presidential campaigns of Alabama Governor George Wallace revealed just how much resentment racial activism had caused—even in the North. The Vietnam conflict also led to a popular reaction against the Democratic leadership. And as the first wave of baby boomers entered college, young people challenged conventional norms about drug use and sexual behavior. These social issues alarmed their more traditional elders, a struggle that took on political dimensions as both New Left and Religious Right groups gained influence. Once again, the Democrats were split between their old and new wings, while Republicans allied themselves with more conservative Middle America.

WHAT PARTIES DO

American parties may have changed their issue alignments and even their names over time, but the two-party system has existed almost from the country's inception. This durability has done little to endear political parties to the American public. Americans do not regard parties as a fundamental institution of democratic governance. Mostly they are indifferent, but many Americans think that government would be better off if no parties existed at all.[19]

Political scientists typically challenge the conventional wisdom against parties. E. E. Schattschneider, for example, devoted much of his life to making the case for the vital role played by political parties. In introducing his classic work, *Party Government*, he wrote that "modern democracy is unthinkable save in terms of the parties."[20] Professional organizations in political science at times have called openly for stronger parties.[21] What critical functions do strong parties carry out?

THE PLUS SIDE OF STRONG PARTIES Without political parties to *organize political life*, it is likely that democracy would be too disorganized to operate except at the local level.[22] Parties coordinate the actions of hundreds, indeed thousands, of public officials. At each level of government, executives count on the support of their fellow partisans in the legislature, and legislators trust the information they get from their fellow partisans in the executive branch. Parties also coordinate across levels of government—as when, in 1995, Democratic governors convinced some Democratic members of Congress that they should support far-reaching welfare reform proposals. Parties need to maintain unity, or their "brand names" will not mean anything.

Party members correctly believe that they will be judged according to their collective performance.[23] This belief gives them an incentive to *fashion a party record worth defending* at the polls. Parties identify problems, publicize them, and advance possible solutions. The competitive struggle for power motivates them to educate the public and fashion a policy agenda. They also recruit strong candidates who will help the parties win new offices, and (like predators) seek to identify vulnerable members of the other side.[24] Where parties are weak, as they were in the American South during the first half of the twentieth century, politics degenerates, taking on a more personal quality as factions contend for private benefits.[25]

Not all problems can be solved by clever policy proposals. Occasionally interests conflict, and some sort of compromise becomes necessary. And even if satisfying every specific interest were possible, the end result might detract from the general interest. For example, granting every individual's spending demand can lead to deficits, inflation, high interest rates, and other national costs. Parties help *synthesize societal demands into public policy.* Because parties compete nationwide, they offer a mix of benefits and burdens to everyone. Yet they must do so in a way that appears beneficial to the general interest, or they suffer at the polls—as the Democrats did in 1984 or the Republicans in 1996.

Imagine that no parties helped *winnow the field of candidates.* Rather than choosing between two candidates for most offices, voters would be faced with many more. The candidates would lack party labels, so voters would have to learn about each set of candidates to determine their preferences. And if elections had more than two serious candidates, officials would frequently enter office with a minority of the vote. Politics thus would become much more complicated than it is now.

THE MINUS SIDE OF STRONG PARTIES Americans hold political parties in relatively low esteem, despite the valuable functions they can perform, for two reasons. First, the fact that parties *can* play a valuable role in politics is no guarantee that they *will.* Politicians do not organize parties to promote the public good. They want to win elections and gain power; organizing politics happens to be a good way to do that.[26] Public officials devote real effort to maintaining their parties, but only because parties help them govern. A second and more important reason why Americans are suspicious of political parties is that party influence is a double-edged sword. Parties strong enough to organize politics are also strong enough to abuse their power. Each of the positive functions that parties can perform may be corrupted.

A strong party that controls its members can become the equivalent of an elected dictatorship, a charge the Progressives leveled at urban machines. They can force voters to choose between two stark choices, even on issues for which more than two options (should) exist. They may recruit celebrities, or party hacks good at winning elections, rather than qualified people good at administering government.

Parties may choose to suppress issues rather than address them. For example, the parties avoided the slavery issue during the first half of the nineteenth century, and the Democrats suppressed issues of racial equality in the first half of the twentieth. Third-party candidate Ross Perot's support in the 1992 presidential election came disproportionately from voters concerned about the deficit who believed that neither the Republicans nor the Democrats would do much about it.[27]

THE MILLENNIUM. THE TIGER AND THE LAMB LIE TOGETHER

The Tammany Tiger

A cartoonist's negative view of the Tammany Hall Machine, which ruled New York City, preying on the innocent. Political machines were very effective at organizing (and holding) power. But does this sort of organization further democracy?

The parties may attempt to confuse responsibility, so that they can escape any blame for bad times and win undeserved credit for good ones. Worse, rather than helping to solve a public problem, opposition parties may concentrate on blocking the governing party's attempts. The temptation to torpedo the other party's initiatives is especially strong when **divided government** exists—when one party holds the presidency but does not control Congress—because then voters will be unsure who is responsible for lingering social problems.[28]

At its extreme, party divisiveness can create or exacerbate cleavages and conflicts among citizens—just as Washington warned two centuries ago. During the 1980s Democrats charged that Republican campaigns inflamed racial resentments. We agree with that charge. For their part, Republicans charged that Democrats divided the country by pandering to disparate groups—African Americans, Hispanics, gays, feminists, labor, and the elderly—rather than constructing a vision of a larger society. We agree with that charge too.

THE BALANCE SHEET   So, on balance, are parties good or bad? Scholars value parties because they *can* make very useful contributions to democratic politics and government. When evaluating party performance, scholars generally do not examine parties in isolation; rather, they usually use the comparative standard, "relative to having no parties." Reformers, on the other hand, see that parties often *do not* make useful contributions and, indeed, often abuse their power. Moreover, reformers generally apply absolute standards, failing to ask whether there is an alternative institution that could replace parties and do a superior job. Whichever view you hold, one thing is clear: American political parties are weak, and reforms have only made them weaker. We turn to that subject now.

WHY ARE AMERICAN PARTIES SO WEAK?

Parties have never been as strong in the United States as they are in other industrialized countries. In most of the world, parties are fairly unified organizations, more like third parties in the United States. People join parties in the same way they join clubs: They pay dues, receive official membership cards, and have a right to participate in various party-sponsored activities (such as nominating candidates). Americans who travel abroad often are surprised to find that parties elsewhere have buildings, full-time staffs, and even newspapers and television stations. Party members in government are much more united than they are in the United States, and party candidates run much more coordinated campaigns than those seen in the candidate-centered politics of the United States.

Historically, the United States did not have true national party organizations. Rather, what passed for national organizations were temporary associations of state parties that briefly joined together every four years to elect a president. Similarly, party members in government have generally not been terribly cohesive. Both parties (but especially the Democrats) have suffered from regional splits, and both parties have incorporated conflicting interests—agricultural versus commercial, and so forth.[29] Because parties lack unified memberships, modern American commentators often discuss parties primarily in terms of adherents to the parties in the electorate, ordinary citizens who identify themselves as Democrats or Republicans.

For most of the twentieth century it appeared that political parties in the United States—whatever the concept of party one used—were in decline. Progressive era reforms wounded state and local organizations, and changes after World War II undercut the national associations. Party cohesion and presidential support in Congress declined.[30] The number of adherents to the two parties began dropping in the mid-1960s as well, to be replaced by self-professed "independents." But by the mid-1980s, the first two of these trends reversed: Party organizations became more active again, and parties were becoming more important in government.

PARTY ORGANIZATIONS UNDER FIRE   Party organizations were at their strongest when the Progressive movement began. They went into decline because of deliberate public policies promoted by reformers. The two principal resources that parties depend on are control of patronage—or the dispensation of government jobs and contracts—and control of nominations for office. Progressive reforms limited both of these.

Patronage was gradually eliminated by regular expansions of civil service protection (see Chapter 10). After World War II, unionization of the public sector also gave government workers a layer of protection from partisan politics.* Today, the president controls fewer than 4000 appointments.[31] At the height of the spoils system—and with a much smaller federal government—presidents controlled well over 100,000.[32] Similarly, governors and big-city mayors who once controlled tens of thousands of jobs today control only a few thousand. Meanwhile, party control over nominations was greatly weakened by the spread of the direct primary, an important Progressive reform (see Chapter 7).

Deprived of their principal resources, modern American parties had few sticks and carrots with which to work. Electoral defeat did not mean that people would lose their jobs; hence, they were less inclined to support parties unquestioningly. Similarly, outsiders could challenge parties for their nominations—and if they won, the parties had no choice but to live with the result. Controlling neither the livelihoods of ordinary voters nor the electoral fates of public officials, party organizations atrophied.

However, deliberate political reforms are not entirely to blame for the weakening of American parties. Other factors also contributed to their decline. For one thing, the communications revolution lessened the need for traditional parties. Candidates could raise funds through direct-mail appeals and then reach voters directly with ads. Elections have become less labor-intensive; party workers are no longer critical to reelection.[33] And in the United States political parties do not control communications outlets the way they do in some European countries.

A second development that undercut U.S. parties was the post–World War II increase in mobility—social, economic, and residential. Better-educated voters have less need of parties to make sense of politics. And as the suburbs grew,

---

*The largest union in the AFL-CIO today is the American Federation of State, County and Municipal Employees.

the traditional, urban-based parties came to represent an ever-smaller proportion of the population—while the new, decentralized suburbs went largely unorganized.

Still a third development that may have weakened parties was the so-called reapportionment revolution set off by the Supreme Court's one-person–one-vote decisions in the 1960s.[34] Prior to these decisions, political jurisdictions tended to coincide with natural communities. In the lower houses of many state legislatures, for example, every county had a seat. Thus, a natural association existed between legislators and their local parties. In the aftermath of the reapportionment revolution, however, legislative districts often cut across cities, counties, and other jurisdictions in the pursuit of numerical equality, racial balance, and other considerations. Today, a legislator's district may stretch across numerous counties, and a city or town may be divided into several districts. Such fragmentation broke apart the relationship between legislators and local parties.

THE REVIVAL OF PARTY ORGANIZATIONS?　In the view of long-time observers, party reforms often were misconceived.[35] One important reason for inappropriate policy solutions is that reformers overlook the reasons why aspiring politicians form and maintain parties. Reformers fail to appreciate that parties inevitably act to promote their own political interests. Attempting to force parties to behave contrary to their interests often leads to reforms that don't work or even to consequences worse than the original problem the reforms were intended to address.

The reforms did not even kill parties. Rather, it was clear by the 1980s that creative politicians had found new uses for the old organizations. Leading this effort were Republicans such as William Brock, chairman of the Republican National Committee (RNC) from 1976 to 1982. Brock and the Republicans first saw the possibilities of adapting parties to the modern age. They used direct mail technology to raise large sums of money. They hired full-time political operatives who were campaign experts. They retained lawyers who knew how to exploit loopholes in the campaign finance laws as well as specialists skilled in computers and other technologies. They made these consultants and services available at low cost to Republican candidates nationwide. Congressional campaign committees began actively recruiting candidates for office, a level of national intervention that would have been unthinkable half a century earlier.

For their part, the Democrats imitated the Republicans, although they did so later and less successfully until the Clinton presidency. National organizations are no longer the weakest level of party organization, as they were through most of their 150-year history. Today, the national committees are active and well financed, and they have been joined by senatorial and congressional campaign committees. Together these national committees have helped rejuvenate lower-level party organizations, which had started rebuilding as early as the 1960s.[36]

In contrast to a generation ago, most state parties have permanent headquarters and employ full-time staff. Many conduct statewide polls. They provide campaign aid and recruit candidates more actively than they did a few decades ago. The state and local party organizations clearly have a more tangible existence today than they did at mid-century.[37]

Still, the debate is not over. Some knowledgeable observers remain skeptical about whether these new national parties are really stronger. John Coleman asks whether the parties are resurgent or "just busy."[38] Others grant that the parties are more active now but argue that the newer activities do not make them stronger "parties" in any traditional sense. According to these critics, the party organizations essentially have become large campaign consulting firms.

Moreover, despite the impressive efforts of the newly constituted parties, they contribute only a fraction of the resources spent on electioneering. They still do not have control over candidates the way parties did a century ago or the way they do in most other democracies today. Indeed, in 1995, when House Speaker Newt Gingrich suggested in a memo that rebellious freshmen members of the House Agriculture Committee would have their committee assignments changed, it was the Speaker who was forced to back down![39]

PARTIES VERSUS INTEREST GROUPS

Some political theorists believe that the power of interest groups is negatively correlated with the power of parties—when parties are strong, groups are weak, and vice versa.[40] Strong parties can provide electoral resources and deliver the vote. Their efforts free candidates from dependence on interest-group resources on the one hand and insulate them from interest-group reprisals on the other. Furthermore, both sorts of groups serve similar functions. They bring together like-minded citizens into institutions that can work for their interests and their policy preferences. When parties are too weak to represent voters before government, it may be natural that citizens create private associations to carry out the task for them.

Regardless of whether Americans *must* choose between strong parties and strong interest groups, it is certainly true that interest groups proliferated in the

Progressive era when reformers were systematically attacking the parties. They surged again in the 1960s and 1970s, when American parties reached a nadir, before their recent recovery. Just as nature is said to abhor a physical vacuum, so it may be that political vacuums cannot persist. If parties do not fill them, interest groups will.

If this argument is valid, then the real alternative to party domination of the electoral process is not some ideal form of popular control, but some other system of skewed influence. As the next section shows, the contemporary political system that replaced party-dominated government is not clearly better than the one it replaced, but not clearly worse.

INTEREST GROUPS: A BIASED CHORUS?

Many Americans participate in politics indirectly by joining or supporting private associations—organizations that are made up of people with common interests and that participate in politics on behalf of their members. Although only half the adult population votes in presidential elections, more than three-quarters of Americans belong to at least one group. On average they belong to two, and they make financial contributions to four.[41] In comparison to citizens of other nations, Americans are joiners.

Of course, not all the groups with which people are associated are political groups. Many are social clubs, charities, service organizations, church groups, and so forth. But there are literally thousands of groups that do engage in politics, and even seemingly nonpolitical groups often engage in political activity. For example, parent–teacher organizations often are active in school politics; neighborhood associations lobby about traffic, crime, and zoning policies; and even hobby or recreation groups mobilize when they perceive threats to their interests—witness the National Rifle Association!

GROWTH AND DEVELOPMENT OF GROUPS

Americans have a long-standing reputation for forming groups. In his classic book *Democracy in America*, Alexis de Tocqueville, the nineteenth-century French visitor to the United States, noted this tendency. "Americans," he wrote, "are forever forming associations. . . . At the head of any new undertaking, where in France you would find the government or in England some territorial magnate, in the United States you are sure to find an association."[42]

However natural and long-standing the American propensity to form interest groups, there is no doubt that there are more political groups today than ever before. Nor has group formation in the United States been a steady process. Rather, it has occurred in several waves, with the greatest wave of group formation in American history occurring in the 1960s and 1970s. In fact, one study found that 40 percent of the associations with Washington offices were formed after 1960.[43]

Before the Civil War, few national organizations existed. Life revolved around "island communities" unconnected to each other by social or economic links.[44] Regions produced much of what they consumed themselves. As the railroads connected the country after the Civil War, though, a national economy developed— and national associations, such as labor unions, were not far behind.

Another major wave of group organization occurred during the Progressive era, roughly 1890 to 1917. Many of today's most broad-based associations date from that era; the Chamber of Commerce, the National Association of Manufacturers, and the American Farm Bureau Federation are examples. These associations often unite economic interests, but other associations founded during the Progressive era had other goals. For example, the National Association for the Advancement of Colored People (NAACP) was formed as part of an effort to improve the fortunes of black Americans.

The wave of group formation from 1960 to 1980 is by far the largest and the most diverse. Thousands of additional economic groups formed, but they tended to be narrower than earlier ones; the American Soybean Association and the Rocky Mountain Llama and Alpaca Association are two examples. Similarly, in commerce and manufacturing, numerous specialized groups joined the older, more broad-based ones. "Government interest groups" formed to represent public-sector workers. All kinds of specialized occupational associations formed as well. These included a few that influence the lives of young Americans, such as the National Association of Student Financial Aid Administrators. One researcher estimated that almost 80 percent of the interest groups active in the 1980s represented professional or occupational constituencies.[45]

The other 20 percent consisted of shared interest groups, many of which have formed in recent decades. Some are actively political, working for particular points of view. Liberal groups, such as the National Organization for Women (a feminist group) and People for the American Way (a civil liberties group), are deeply involved in politics, as are such conservative groups as the Christian Coalition (which promotes traditional morality) and Operation Rescue (an antiabortion group). Many "citizens" groups, such as Common Cause (a political reform group), Greenpeace (an environmental group), and the National Taxpayers' Union (an antitax group) are less than a generation old. Many of these have such a narrow focus that they are called "single-issue groups."

A "single-issue group"—the National Rifle Association

The National Rifle Association (NRA) was founded shortly after the Civil War to promote marksmanship, and it grew into an organization of hunters, target shooters, and gun collectors. By the mid-twentieth century, the NRA operated firearms and hunter safety programs and trained law enforcement officers. With a presence in every state, it takes the lead in opposing gun control legislation. Its PAC is usually one of the top ten contributors to congressional elections, and it employs some 80 lobbyists. The NRA is one of the best examples of a single-issue group, *a group focused on one issue to the exclusion of virtually everything else.*

Other groups are not primarily political but have a political side. For example, the American Association of Retired Persons (AARP), established in 1958, is the largest voluntary association ever, with more than 33 million members—and still growing! AARP is a major player whenever Social Security or Medicare is on the political agenda. Under the right circumstances almost any group may become involved in politics. A sports association for snowmobilers and mountain bikers may seem as apolitical as a group can get, but when government threatens to restrict their use of public lands, then such organizations gear up for a political battle.

Not all active interest groups have elaborate formal organizations with membership dues, journals, meetings, conventions, and so forth. Some are little more than addresses for teams of lawyers to whom sympathizers send contributions. One study found that of 83 public interest groups examined, 30 had no membership at all![46] Some large corporations maintain their own Washington offices, as do hundreds of state and local governments and even universities.

The explosion of groups is partly reactive; the expansion of government activity has given people more reasons to form groups. Business groups, for instance, may form in reaction to governmental regulations or because they see opportunities to procure government subsidies. Group formation also responds to opportunities; groups expand whenever a change in communications or transportation technology allows them to do so. Computer databases, for example, permit the generation of all kinds of specialized mailing lists. People with common interests can communicate easily and cheaply via the Internet. And once a group forms on one side of an issue, its opponents usually need to get organized or lose the fight.

FORMING AND MAINTAINING INTEREST GROUPS

That so many Americans belong to so many associations often leads people to overlook the difficulties that groups face.[47] Women's groups contain only a small fraction of the female population. Few blacks join the NAACP. Most gun owners do not belong to the NRA. As these examples suggest, millions of people do *not* join or support associations whose interests they share.

Supporting a group requires the investment of personal *resources*. Contributing money or paying dues is the most obvious cost, but the time required for group activities can be significant too. One commits resources when the *incentive* to do so—the expected benefit—justifies the investment.

Incentives take many forms, and different groups rely on different incentives. Political scientist James Q. Wilson divides incentives into three categories.[48] The first he calls *solidary*. Some people join a group for social reasons; they simply wish to associate with particular kinds of people. Membership in the group is an end in itself. Most such groups are nonpolitical, though—such as Greek organizations on a college campus. Political groups rarely use solidary incentives. It is unlikely that people join the National Taxpayers' Union to enjoy the company of other taxpayers!

A second category of incentives is *material*. Some people join a group because membership confers tangible benefits. IBM does not belong to various trade associations because its executives like to socialize with other computer executives. They have plenty of other opportunities to do that. IBM belongs because the trade associations are seen as a way to protect and advance corporate interests. Material incentives also play a role in some political groups. Workers may join a politically active union because it gives exclusive access to some jobs.

Finally, some people join groups for *purposive* reasons. They are committed to the group's goals and wish to advance them. They want to save the whales, bring about a liberal or conservative Congress, end abortion, or preserve freedom of choice. Obviously, many political groups concentrate on purposive incentives and attract members by promising to work for public-policy changes. Many interest groups oriented toward material benefits, by contrast, have declined in influence relative to purposive groups, as has happened with unions (see Figure 8.1). At the same time, however, interest groups that work only to improve government

FIGURE 8.1

Union membership has declined significantly since mid-century

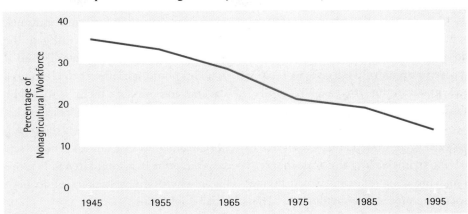

SOURCES: George Kurian, *Datapedia of the United States: 1790–2000* (Lantham, MD: Bernham Press, 1994), p. 80; *Almanac of the 50 States,* 1997 ed. (Palo Alto, CA: Information Publications, 1997).

policy often experience the greatest difficulty attracting active members. The **free-rider problem** hinders their efforts.

THE FREE-RIDER PROBLEM When a group works to change policies, people can enjoy the benefits even if they have not joined—and therefore did not share the costs. Nor is it easy to punish, in other ways, those who refuse to help. At the same time, individual contributions usually will not make any measurable difference in whether, or to what extent, the benefits are produced. Thus, the incentive is to free ride on the efforts of others.[49]

If you donate $20 to Greenpeace, does your contribution guarantee the survival of some particular baby seal? If you donate several hours of your time to march for the end of hunger, does your contribution measurably reduce the amount of malnutrition in the world? Although most well-meaning people are reluctant to admit it, in each case the truthful answer is no. If you don't contribute, just as many baby seals will live or die, and world hunger will be no different. So if your sacrifice makes no difference, why contribute?

Furthermore, most policy changes and social improvements are **public goods** rather than private ones. You cannot walk into a store, buy them, and consume them yourself—like pizzas or stereos. Individuals receive the benefit whether they contribute or not. If world hunger declines or more seals swim in the oceans, everyone lives in a better world, not just those who worked to make it happen. So if you get the same benefit regardless of your actions, why contribute?

Most political goals are public goods unaffected by individual contributions, which poses a major obstacle to group survival. Two considerations mitigate the severity of the free-rider problem, though. First, small groups generally find it easier to organize their efforts. If a few neighbors pool their efforts to clean up a nearby vacant lot, it is easy to identify the slackers and pressure them. It would be unthinkable, however, for a large city to rely on volunteers to maintain city parks. Second, other things equal, the free-rider problem is less severe when the group works for an immediate and tangible benefit. Cleaning up a vacant lot is more satisfying than cleaning the atmosphere. Feeding the poor in a soup kitchen is more satisfying than reducing world hunger. This is why bumper stickers often urge socially concerned individuals to "Think globally, act locally."

Material incentives can be public goods as well. If General Motors lobbies successfully for a tariff or quota on Japanese cars, Ford still will enjoy the benefits (lower competition, and higher prices). If members of the Corn Growers' Association pool their efforts to get a higher corn subsidy, even growers who are not members reap the benefit of the higher subsidy. The free-rider problem therefore even affects groups seeking material improvements. Only those groups based on social incentives escape it; because membership itself is the benefit, most people outside the group receive nothing.

The most important implication of the free-rider problem for democratic politics is that "special" interests will be able to overcome it more easily than "public" interests will. Other things being equal, small groups organized for narrow purposes have an organizational advantage over large groups organized for broad purposes. For example, a small number of corporations seeking millions of dollars in government subsidies will find it easier to organize an association than the millions of consumers who might each pay an extra nickel as a result.

OVERCOMING THE FREE-RIDER PROBLEM   On first learning about the free-rider problem, some skeptics protest, "What if everyone felt that way?" Well, a great many people do, which is why interest groups struggle to stay powerful. The tactics they use are not always pretty.

Labor unions may rely on coercion—and sometimes even outright violence—to enforce a decision among workers to strike, for example. Milder forms of coercion are widespread. For example, professional and occupational associations lobby governmental jurisdictions to hire, approve, or certify only their members, thus making membership a condition of working or practicing in that jurisdiction. Such requirements are ways of coercing potential free riders into joining the associations that represent their trades and professions.

Many groups develop **selective benefits** available only to their members. They may publish journals containing useful information. They may provide consulting services, giving members a place to call when they need help. The American Association of Retired Persons (AARP) offers the most notable example of this strategy for overcoming the free-rider problem. For a mere $8 per year, members gain access to the world's largest mail-order pharmacy (where volume buying keeps prices low); low-cost auto, health, and life insurance; discounts on hotels, air fares, and car rentals; and numerous other benefits. Even a senior citizen who disagrees with the AARP's political positions finds it hard to forgo membership! The political activity in which the group engages may be secondary to the selective benefits it provides.

Many groups owe their existence to **political entrepreneurs,** members who take the lead in setting up and operating the groups.[50] For example, some individuals, institutions, or corporations may have such a large stake in the group goal that they are willing to bear more than their share of the effort. They let others free ride on them to give the appearance of broad-based support. For such large actors, political activity is simply a good business decision.

Similarly, a rich individual with a deep commitment to the group goal may be able to make a difference. Your $20 contribution to Greenpeace may have no measurable impact, but if you could fork over a million dollars, you may actually save some seals. Someone so committed to a purpose also may set up and maintain his or her own group. For example, Ralph Nader, the ascetic lawyer who ran for president in 2000, did more than anyone else to organize the consumer movement and has devoted his life to it. Motives vary for this sort of dedication (or fanaticism, from the point of view of opponents). Sometimes people hold ambitions for political office, sometimes they enjoy feeling powerful, and sometimes they simply are swept along by political tides. But they occasionally make a big difference in politics.

One often overlooked organizer is the government itself. As the role of government expanded in the 1960s and 1970s, activists needed new ways to implement programs through a decentralized federal system. One strategy was to stimulate and subsidize organizations. Once formed, local groups could help develop standards and regulations, publicize them, and carry them out. To those trying to build a stronger welfare state, these groups were politically useful as well because, once established, they would be able to fight against shrinking government. Not surprisingly, associations that receive federal funds are more than twice as likely to support expanded government activity—and, by implication, elected officials who expand it—as groups that do not.[51] The government subsidized political groups who would then help it grow bigger.

Despite the prevalence of free-rider problems, people do not always evaluate their political activities from a self-interested viewpoint. Sometimes individuals simply get caught up in a **social movement** and join the bandwagon. These broad-based demands for social change have a long history in American politics. The abolitionist movement is one of the best known. Dedicated to ending slavery, this movement forced the issue onto the national agenda. It played a role in the political upheaval of the 1850s and, ultimately, in the outbreak of the Civil War. The civil rights movement is another, more modern, example of a social movement. Few abolitionists or civil rights marchers ever received benefits equivalent to the costs they paid.

Social movements build on emotional or moral fervor. Many activists dedicate themselves to what they see as a higher cause and receive inherent pleasure from being part of that effort. When individuals adopt a moral perspective, they may ignore the considerations that normally would lead them to free ride. Still, social movements typically mobilize only small proportions of their prospective constituencies. Moreover, emotional and moral fervor are temporary social conditions, so movements have a tendency to lose momentum. For a social movement to exert continued influence, it must find a way to "institutionalize" itself—to spin off formal associations that face the same free-rider pressures as other interest groups.

HOW INTEREST GROUPS INFLUENCE GOVERNMENT
The variety of groups, associations, and institutions that make up the interest-group universe engage in a wide array of political activities.

LOBBYING   Many attempt to influence government the old-fashioned way: by lobbying public officials. **Lobbying** consists of attempts by group representatives personally to influence the decisions of public officials. **Lobbyists** draft bills for friendly legislators to introduce, testify before congressional committees and in agency proceedings, meet with elected officials and present their cases (sometimes at posh resorts where the officials are the guests), and provide public officials with information.

Corporations account for the lion's share of traditional lobbying, spending upwards of $1.5 billion per year.[52] There are federal and state laws that require lobbyists to register, but because of disagreement about what lobbying is and who is a lobbyist, as well as lack of enforcement, those who register are only a fraction of those engaged in lobbying.[53] For example, the *American Lobbyists Directory* lists

Lobbyists at work
Three gentlemen collectively representing the Public Health Association, the Campaign for Tobacco Free Kids, and the American Heart Association. What strategies are most effective for these interest groups, focused on protecting the public health?

65,000 legally registered federal and state lobbyists, but estimates are that in Washington alone, there are upwards of 90,000.[54]

The term "lobbyist" has negative connotations (we doubt that many parents plan for their children to grow up to be lobbyists). Movies, novels, and even the newspapers often portray lobbyists as unsavory characters who operate on the borders of what is ethical or legal—and often step across them. Research suggests this characterization is an exaggeration. Although there are examples of shady behavior by lobbyists, such transgressions are hardly the norm. Certainly, most analysts believe that corrupt behavior by interest-group lobbyists is less widespread today than in previous eras of American history. Numerous conflict-of-interest laws and regulations, along with an investigative media ever on the lookout for a hint of scandal, make outright corruption in today's politics relatively rare.

For the most part, lobbyists provide public officials with information and arguments to support their political goals. They tend to deal with officials already sympathetic to their positions, providing them ideas and support. Lobbyists have little incentive to distort information or lie. To do so would mislead their allies and undermine their credibility. Many political scientists think that lobbyists serve a useful purpose, injecting valuable information into the legislative process.

GRASSROOTS LOBBYING   Today, Washington lobbying is often combined with so-called **grassroots lobbying.** Outside-the-beltway pressure supplements inside-the-beltway persuasion. Whereas lobbying consists of attempts to influence government officials *directly*, grassroots lobbying consists of attempts to influence officials *indirectly* through their constituents. The home schooling example that opened this chapter illustrates the process. A Washington association communicates with its grassroots supporters, who in turn put pressure on their elected representatives. As one health care lobbyist put it recently,

> *One of the perceptions about lobbying is that you go out drinking, and the guy's your buddy so he does you favors. . . . Those days are long gone. That sort of thing may work on tiny things like a technical amendment to a bill, but on big, important issues personal friendships don't mean a thing. I'll bet we could have done just as good a job as we did [on influencing health care reform] without ever going to the Hill or ever talking to a member of Congress. It is knowing when and how to ask the troops in the field to do it.* [55]

This sort of lobbying is not new. The Anti-Saloon League, a prohibition group, included more than 500,000 names on its mailing list nearly a century ago—long before dependable long-distance telephone service, let alone computers, the fax, and e-mail! [56] But grassroots lobbying is especially effective now that Congress is decentralized (see Chapter 9). Inside-the-beltway strategies worked when only a few leaders required persuasion, but government is generally more open than in the past. It is not so easy for Washington insiders to make private deals; it is more important than ever to show popular support for their groups' positions. Moreover, the availability of cheap communications technologies makes grassroots lobbying much easier.

ELECTIONEERING AND PACs   Personal and grassroots lobbying attempts to influence public officials on specific matters. Another way to promote a group's goals is to influence who gets elected in the first place. Groups have always been involved in the electoral process, supporting some candidates and opposing others. But as the role of party organizations in campaigns has eroded and as campaigns have become more expensive, groups have become more active than ever before. Electioneering is probably the fastest-growing group tactic, and a principal vehicle of this tactic is the political action committee.

Political action committees (PACs) are specialized organizations for raising and spending campaign funds. Many are connected to interest groups or associations. They come in as many varieties as the interests they represent. [57] Some, such as the realtors' RPAC and the doctors' AMPAC, represent big economic interests. Others are smaller. Beer wholesalers, for example, have

SixPAC. Not all PACs serve economic interests, and politicians sometimes form their own.[58]

There is widespread public dissatisfaction with the role of PACs in campaign finance. It is therefore ironic that the proliferation of PACs is partly an unintended consequence of previous attempts in the early 1970s to reform the campaign finance laws (see the Election Connection, "Interest Groups, Free Speech, and Campaign Finance").[59] They began in the early 1970s as a direct response to reforms, and have enjoyed explosive growth in the past few decades. From a mere handful in 1970, they proliferated rapidly in the 1980s (see Figure 8.2).

PACs have played an increasingly prominent role in congressional campaign finance. Reflecting their business associations, most PACs tend to give instrumentally, which means that they donate to the members of key committees regardless of party. When the Democrats were in the majority in Congress, some of their

FIGURE 8.2
PACs formed rapidly after the 1974 Federal Election Campaign Act (FECA) reforms

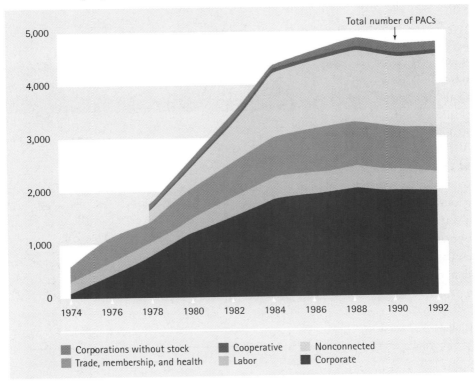

Corporations without stock Cooperative Nonconnected
Trade, membership, and health Labor Corporate

SOURCE: Paul Herrnson, *Congressional Elections* (Washington, DC: CQ Press, 1995), p. 106.

members became highly dependent on business contributions, and critics charged that this dependence affected their legislative judgment.[60] When Democrats became a minority after the 1994 elections and contributions began to favor their rivals (see Table 8.3), they became much more favorable to campaign finance regulation that restricted PACs.

As with interest-group corruption in general, the PAC problem in particular may be somewhat exaggerated by the popular media. Most PAC contributions are small and are intended as a way to gain access to public officials. Most research has failed to establish any significant relationship between contributions and votes.[61] Evidence even suggests that politicians extort PACs, pressuring them to buy tickets to fund-raisers and otherwise make contributions as a condition of continued access. For example, a former congressional staffer told one of us the following story:

> In our office we loved the FEC [Federal Election Commission] reports. We'd comb through them and list all the business groups who had contributed to our opponent.

TABLE 8.3

BUSINESS PAC CONTRIBUTIONS TEND TO FOLLOW POLITICAL POWER

	CONTRIBUTIONS TO REPUBLICANS JAN.—FEB. 1993 (DEMOCRATIC MAJORITY)	CONTRIBUTIONS TO REPUBLICANS JAN.—FEB. 1995 (REPUBLICAN MAJORITY)
American Dental Association	27%	90%
American Bankers Association	52	87
American Hospital Association	53	81
Ameritech	35	79
AT&T	36	79
American Institute of CPAs	45	87
Home Builders	45	71
Realtors	75	91
RJRNabisco	69	81
United Parcel Service	55	78

SOURCE: Jonathan Salant and David Cloud, "To the 1994 Election Victors Go the Fundraising Spoils," *Congressional Quarterly Weekly Report* (April 15, 1995): 1057.

ELECTION CONNECTION

Interest Groups, Free Speech, and Campaign Finance

Of all the things that contemporary Americans find unsatisfactory about their politics, campaign finance ranks near the top. Many people believe that free-spending special interests exercise too much influence over government actions and that free-spending candidates are able to buy elections. John McCain was able to capitalize on such sentiments to give Republican presidential nominee George W. Bush a scare in the early 2000 primaries.

Despite widespread dissatisfaction, however, and the efforts of public interest groups, little by way of reform has occurred. For one thing, any reforms have to be approved by elected officials whose electoral self-interest is at stake. Their positions give them a view of reform very different from that held by disinterested citizens. But another important part of the problem is that proposed reforms seem to be at least partly in conflict with constitutional freedoms. For example, in 1996 a proposal to ban PACs achieved considerable support in the House of Representatives, but opponents claimed that such a ban was patently unconstitutional.

In an important 1976 decision, *Buckley* v. *Valeo,* the U.S. Supreme Court held that Congress could not limit spending by either candidates or interest groups: Because it costs money to publicize one's views, limiting spending was equivalent to limiting expression.[a] Others disagree. Presidential candidate Bill

Bradley argued that "I do not believe that a rich man's wallet is in free-speech terms the equivalent of a poor man's soapbox."[b] And an expert campaign finance lawyer discounts constitutional arguments and characterizes the contemporary system of campaign finance as "felonious bribery."[c]

What do you think?

- Would Americans still have free speech if government limited how much they could spend on buying advertisements to promote their views?
- To ensure the integrity of the electoral process, should some rights of speech and expression be sacrificed, either in the courts or by amending the Constitution?
- Would limits on spending help incumbents, who attract lots of contributions, or challengers, who need more cash to make a name for themselves?
- Given the importance of money in conducting a modern campaign, where is the line between constitutionally protected campaign contributions and illegitimate bribes?

[a]For background on the constitutional issues that arise in campaign finance reform debates, see Beth Donovan, "Constitutional Issues Frame Congressional Options," *Congressional Quarterly Weekly Report* (February 27, 1993): 431–437.

[b]Adam Clymer, "Senate Kills Measure to Limit Spending in Congress Races," *New York Times* (June 26, 1996): A16.

[c]Daniel Lowenstein, "Political Bribery and the Intermediate Theory of Politics," *UCLA Law Review* 32 (1985): 784–851.

Then we'd call them up and say, "Hey, we noticed that you contributed to our opponent's campaign. The Congressman just wants you to know that there are no hard feelings. In fact, we're holding a fund-raiser in a few weeks; we hope you'll come and tell us your concerns."

PERSUADING THE PUBLIC   In recent years a phenomenon called issue advocacy has grown in prominence. Groups conduct advertising campaigns designed to move public opinion in regard to some policy proposal. Estimates suggest that $150 million was spent on issue advocacy in the 1996 presidential campaign and $260 million during the 1998 congressional campaigns. Preliminary figures suggest that these amounts were greatly exceeded during the 2000 campaigns.[62]

Many groups communicate with citizens even when no specific legislation or regulation is at issue. Their goal is to build general support for the group and its interests. Thus, in the 1970s, the Mobil Oil Corporation began paying to have columns printed on the editorial page of the *New York Times.* Sometimes these were "advocacy ads" directed at a specific government activities or proposed laws, but more often they were simply attempts to convey ideas favorable to the industry.

One communications technique that is a product of modern electronic communications is **direct mail.**[63] Groups compile computerized mailing lists of people who may be favorable toward their leaders or causes and then send out printed or computer-generated materials soliciting financial contributions. Often, in an attempt to scare or provoke the recipients into contributing, the mailing exaggerates the threat the group faces. Some groups depend almost completely on direct-mail fund-raising for their budgets. The citizens group Common Cause, for example, prides itself on its dependence on small contributions.[64] Once again, the rise of the Internet makes the direct-mail strategy both easier and cheaper.

Finally, any group likes to have favorable media coverage for its activities and points of view. Thus, groups are always on the lookout for opportunities to get such coverage—opportunities to plant stories, to associate themselves with popular issues and candidates, and to position themselves as opponents of unpopular issues and candidates. In sum, whether they call it public relations or education, communication with a wider audience is a significant concern for many interest groups.

LITIGATION   Many groups impatient for social change either do not wish to wait for the public to get behind them or doubt that they will ever persuade enough people. Instead, they file lawsuits and concentrate on persuading the legal community of the rightness of their causes.[65] Liberal groups tend to be more active in the courts, but conservative groups use litigation strategies as well. Not all legal tactics involve direct lawsuits. Some groups stage demonstrations in front of courthouses to influence judicial decision making. Others file *amicus curiae* (a Latin term meaning "friend of the court") briefs in cases in which they are not otherwise directly involved.

Naturally, legal action is not a strategy oriented toward democratic majorities. The growth of lawsuits may be the most significant limit on popular influence in America's new democracy. On the other hand, lawsuits are a way for individual citizens to challenge entrenched government officials and force them to be responsive. So the growth of litigation limits the popular will in some ways but enhances it in others.

DIRECT ACTION   The United States has a long history of citizens engaging in **direct action** to influence government policy. From the Revolutionary War itself, to abolitionist raids before the Civil War, to urban riots and violent strikes, protests are as American as apple pie.[66] Forms of direct action are often used by social movements, whose members previously have not been organized, who lack access to power, and who lack the resources to use other strategies. The media—TV in particular—find direct action newsworthy and thus communicate the protests to locales far beyond where they occur.

HOW INFLUENTIAL ARE INTEREST GROUPS?

The answer to this question is a matter of enormous disagreement. On the one hand, some critics believe that interest groups dominate American politics. One critic charges that the United States suffers from "demosclerosis," a condition in

Ghosts of the sixties
Not since the 1960s have Americans seen these kinds of militant protestors, who disrupted the city of Seattle during a meeting of the World Trade Organization. How extensive must protests be before they are no longer simply free speech, but instead lawless action?

which interest groups clog the veins and arteries of the body politic.[67] Another claims that Americans have the best Congress "money can buy."[68] Certainly the volume of interest-group activity and their massive expenditures of resources amount to strong circumstantial evidence that groups are influential.

On the other hand, academic research yields less clear conclusions. Indeed, some of the most expert students of interest-group politics contend that most groups cancel each other out.[69] There are so many groups, and so many *opposing* groups, that the efforts of one association offset the efforts of another. Also, it is likely that particular interests were more influential in the past than most individual interests are today. Changes in American politics have undermined the classic "iron triangles" that once governed areas of policy.

IRON TRIANGLES   Observers of American politics in the 1940s and 1950s noted that a collusion of congressional committees, executive agencies, and interest groups dominated many policy areas.[70] These three actors worked hand in hand to form a subgovernment that was almost entirely responsible for the particular policy in question. A congressional committee provided an agency with budgetary support. The agency produced outcomes favored by the interest group. The interest groups provided campaign support to the members of the congressional committee. Some of these three-way alliances were so tight, and therefore so hard to penetrate, they received the name **iron triangles.**

The preconditions once necessary to sustain iron triangles are almost gone. Congress has changed, making the committees weaker. Interest groups have proliferated, so most associations have rivals who will not leave their influence unchallenged. In particular, citizens groups representing consumers, environmentalists, and taxpayers can oppose the excesses of special-interest politics. And the media are less likely to ignore examples of special-interest profiteering. In the spring of 1996, for example, an effort to help milk producers raise prices collapsed after CBS anchor Dan Rather called it an "attempted rip-off of the consumer" on his evening news program.[71] Iron triangles melt in the glare of publicity.

ISSUE NETWORKS   Many scholars believe that a new form of policy environment has arisen. The new **issue networks** are bigger, broader, and much looser connections of interest groups, politicians, bureaucrats, and policy experts.[72] Given the enormous variety of interest groups today, the proliferation of policy experts, and the overlap among many policies, issue networks are much more open than subgovernments and much less stable in their composition. However, scholars disagree how organized these "networks" really are. Some claim that the term exaggerates the degree of organization that characterizes interest-group activity in Washington today.[73] Others suggest that the term overlooks the influence of organized interests in new policy areas.[74]

In short, judgments about the general importance of interest groups remain as divided as ever. Probably the safest conclusion about interest groups is that their influence is conditional: It ranges from weak to strong, depending on the conditions under which groups try to mold policy. Groups are most influential when they act on low-profile issues, when they attempt to block action rather than originate it, when they are unopposed, and when they have plentiful resources.[75] Once again, the real world of American democracy is more complicated than many popular commentators suggest.

INTEREST GROUPS AND DEMOCRATIC POLITICS

Participation is easier for people who have more resources. Thus, it is no surprise that the affluent contribute more than the poor and that two-worker families with small children participate less than those whose family situations give them more free time.[76] More generally, a large institution or corporation has more resources to contribute than a solitary citizen. No doubt this is one the reason that Americans hold interest groups in such low regard.[77] They seem to violate the American principle that everyone enjoy equal influence on government.

On the other hand, equal influence can never be more than an ideal. Party-dominated government did not give Americans equal influence either. Political scientists thus have not held interest groups in as low regard as ordinary citizens have. In fact, one mid-century school of thought assigned groups a central place in American politics.[78] Pluralists held that American politics should consist of an interplay of numerous interests, organized into associations. Under such a system, groups would exercise countervailing power, and public policies would emerge from compromise. Policies would be moderate and change incrementally.

Pluralism is out of fashion today, because it overemphasizes how representative groups are. As critic E. E. Schattschneider once observed, "The flaw in the pluralist heaven is that the heavenly chorus sings with a strong upper-class accent."[79] The free-rider problem gives an advantage to small special interests. In particular, economic groups and funding recipients benefit, at the expense of the broader population of consumers and taxpayers. Furthermore, rather than check and balance each other, interest groups often cooperate—demanding a mixture of higher prices and tax breaks at the expense of the national economy.[80]

Perhaps most importantly, when groups clash, the result is a more negative politics than that which occurs when individuals deal with the political system directly. Ordinary citizens have multiple attachments and affiliations. A retired couple, for example, naturally favors higher Social Security and Medicare expenditures. But they might demand less for themselves, knowing that the result would be higher taxes on their children or lower government expenditures on their grandchildren's schools. Leaders of interest groups for the elderly, by contrast, typically see their job as the maximization of group benefits. They have no incentive to be reasonable or to balance competing social goals. As a result, AARP has been attacked as an organization composed of "tax-loving former teachers and government employees" who favor an "age-based welfare state."[81]

This crowding out of moderate demands by more extreme ones is reinforced by the tendency of group activists and leaders to be more zealous in their views and more committed to group goals than nonmembers or even rank-and-file members (see Table 8.4). It is doubtful that most regular men and women who supported the Equal Rights Amendment (ERA) for women wanted to send

TABLE 8.4

THE EXTREMISM OF GROUP ACTIVISTS AND LEADERS

One study compared the views of 100 top leaders in environmental groups with the views of scientific experts—in this case cancer researchers. Both sets of people were asked to rate various cancer risks on a scale of 1–10, with 10 being the highest. Relative to expert judgments, environmentalists systematically overstated the risks of cancer from environmental causes.

| | RISK OF CANCER | |
CARCINOGEN	ENVIRONMENTALISTS	SCIENTISTS
Dioxin	8.1	3.7
Asbestos	7.8	6.5
EDB	7.3	4.2
DDT	6.7	3.8
Pollution	6.6	4.7
Dietary fat	6.0	5.4
Food additives	5.3	3.2
Nuclear power	4.6	2.5
Saccharin	3.7	1.6

SOURCE: Stanley Rothman and S. Robert Lichter, "Environmental Cancer: A Political Disease," *Annals of the New York Academy of Sciences* 775 (1996): 234–235.

female soldiers into combat, but activists pushing the ERA argued: "[C]ombat duty, horrendous as it might seem to all of us, must be assigned to persons on a gender-neutral basis."[82] Most Americans prefer a satisfactory compromise on abortion or the environment, not the extremes posed by the organizations they may join to promote one side or the other. In the end, the general interests of a moderate population can get lost amid the bitter fighting of intense and extreme special interests.

But what can be done? As the critics look over the experience of democratic governments, they see only one means of controlling group demands that is both democratic and effective. Ironically, it is the institution that George Washington warned the country about—political parties. Americans thus may face a difficult choice: finding the lesser evil between particularized groups that give more weight to those with money and general groups that distort individual influence in more haphazard ways.

CHAPTER SUMMARY

Although the Constitution makes no mention of them, political parties have been part of American politics from the beginning. Indeed, American political history often is told in terms of party systems, wherein each party has dependable support among particular social groups so that elections tend to be similar within each system. Such electoral eras end with critical or realigning elections that alter the group alignments and usher in new party systems.

The basic reason why parties have played such an important role in American history—as well as in the histories of all modern democracies—is that they perform organizing functions that are essential in large-scale representative democracies. Parties coordinate the actions of numerous officeholders, focus responsibility for their actions, and develop issues and recruit leaders. As a result, parties simplify choices when voters must select among numerous candidates for office.

Despite these important functions that parties perform, most Americans do not hold them in especially high regard. Parties struggle for power and, therefore, often act in self-interested ways contrary to the general interest. To prevent such behavior, the nation passed a series of reforms aimed at undercutting the power of political parties. Parties in the United States are not nearly so strong as they were in earlier periods. They have been democratized, with more openness to popular influence.

At present, the United States has a party system that is less stable and more confusing than most of those that have preceded it. Americans have turned to a different source of influence on government. They participate indirectly in politics by joining interest groups. In fact, compared to citizens of other democracies, Americans are more likely to participate indirectly and less likely to participate directly by voting.

There has been a major increase in the number of interest groups since 1960. Successful groups have found ways to overcome the free-rider problem—the tendency of people to benefit from group activity without contributing to its costs—using a mixture of selective benefits and a reliance on dedicated members who will keep the effort going. Yet these groups are an important mechanism for increasing popular influence, since more than ever they use strategies of electioneering, grassroots lobbying, and public persuasion.

Although interest-group activity is constitutionally protected, many worry about its effects. Special interests seem better represented than general interests. They sometimes offset each other, but the best policy for the nation may not merely be the sum of their demands—especially because interest groups seem to undermine democratic politics by expressing extreme demands rather than seeking compromise.

No doubt the United States could choose to reverse course, strengthening the political parties and weakening interest groups. The result would not be a return to some golden era of individualistic politics, though, since the parties did not give Americans equal influence any more than interest-group democracy does. But one thing is clear. Regardless of which mechanism for popular influence becomes the dominant one in the future, both of these institutions have become better at representing popular demands than they were in the past. The reliance on formal institutions to communicate with government may be regrettable, but those institutions opened up along with the rest of the political system to help form America's new democracy.

KEY TERMS

amicus curiae, p. 266
critical election,
    p. 239
direct action, p. 267
direct mail, p. 266
divided government,
    p. 248
free-rider problem,
    p. 257
grassroots lobbying,
    p. 262
iron triangle, p. 268
issue network, p. 268
lobbying, p. 260

lobbyist, p. 260
machine, p. 242
pluralism, p. 269
political action committee
    (PAC), p. 262
political entrepreneurs,
    p. 259
political parties, p. 236
proportional representation
    (PR), p. 239
public goods, p. 257
realignment, p. 239
selective benefits,
    p. 259

single-member, simple
    plurality (SMSP) system,
    p. 236
social movement, p. 260
ticket splitting, p. 245
two-thirds rule, p. 245

ON THE WEB

The Republican Party
www.rnc.org
The Internet home of the GOP, this site offers information on virtually all aspects of the Republican party—from its platform to its local, district organizations.

The Democratic Party
www.democrats.org
The Internet home of the Democratic party, this site offers information on virtually all aspects of the Democratic party—from its platform to its local, district organizations.

National Political Index
www.politicalindex.com/index.htm
The National Political Index is a Web site that provides an index of substantive political information for voters, political activists, political consultants, lobbyists, politicians, academicians, and media editors and has a wide range of products, information, services, simulations, games, and polling in an interactive communications environment.

National Lobbyist Directory
www.lobbyistdirectory.com/
This site provides a state-by-state directory of lobbyists, containing names, addresses, and phone numbers.

Online Pennsylvania Lobbyist Directory
www.penncen.com/palobby/
This site contains the names, phone numbers, and (where applicable) e-mail addresses and URLs for all registered Pennsylvania lobbyists.

SUGGESTED READINGS

Aldrich, John. *Why Parties?* Chicago: University of Chicago Press, 1995. Wide-ranging rational-choice account of how and why politicians form and transform political parties.

Baumgartner, Frank, and Beth Leech. *Basic Interests.* Princeton, NJ: Princeton University Press, 1998. Comprehensive review, critique, and synthesis of the interest-group literature.

Epstein, Leon. *Political Parties in the American Mold.* Madison: University of Wisconsin Press, 1986. Capstone work by a prominent student of American parties. Argues that modern parties have adapted and continue to play an important political role but that their future prospects are limited by ambivalent feelings in the American electorate.

Freeman, Jo, and Victoria Johnson. *Waves of Protest.* Lanham, MD: Rowman and Littlefield, 1999. Useful collection describing the social movements active since the 1960s.

Heinz, John, Edward Laumann, Robert Nelson, and Robert Salisbury. *The Hollow Core: Private Interests in National Policy Making.* Cambridge, MA: Harvard University Press, 1993. A recent, major study of the Washington interest-group scene. Principal focus is on the characteristics and activities of group representatives and lobbyists.

Jewell, Malcolm E., and Sarah M. Morehouse. *Political Parties and Elections in the American States,* Fourth Edition. Washington, DC: Congressional Quarterly, 2000. Textbook on parties and elections at the subnational level.

Key, V. O., Jr. *Southern Politics.* New York: Vintage, 1949. A classic. The material is dated, but the theoretical arguments about the nature of politics in systems with weak or nonexistent parties remain relevant today.

Lowi, Theodore. *The End of Liberalism.* New York: Norton, 1969. Noted critique of "interest-group liberalism." Argues that a government of laws has been superseded by a process of bargaining between organized groups and public officials.

Mayhew, David. R. *Placing Parties in American Politics.* Princeton, NJ: Princeton University Press, 1986. Comprehensive study of state party organization in the twentieth century.

Moe, Terry. *The Organization of Interests.* Chicago: University of Chicago Press, 1980. Analyzes the internal politics of groups and strategies used by political entrepreneurs for organizing and maintaining groups.

Sundquist, James. L. *Dynamics of the Party System,* Revised Edition. Washington, DC: Brookings, 1983. History of national politics since the 1840s told from a party-systems perspective.

Walker, Jack. *Mobilizing Interest Groups in America.* Ann Arbor: University of Michigan Press, 1991. Describes the state of the Washington interest-group universe. Noted for discussion of outside support for establishment of groups.

9

THE CONGRESS
AND ITS WORK

I n April 1992 a violent riot erupted in the city of Los Angeles, resulting in 60 deaths and a billion dollars of property damage. The media initially interpreted the event as a simple race riot, an explosion of rage after a jury acquitted police officers who had brutally beaten African American Rodney King. Blame for the riot shifted, however, when its multiethnic character became apparent. Experts eventually interpreted the rioting as a predictable release of tensions created by urban poverty, joblessness, and ethnic rivalries.

Many Americans turned to the national government to do something about "the crisis of the cities," and with an election only six months away lawmakers felt compelled to respond.[1] They eventually settled on a policy advocated by Jack Kemp, secretary of Housing and Urban Development in the George H. W. Bush administration—a policy that previously had received a cool reception from Democrats. Kemp's idea was to designate certain urban areas for favorable tax treatment. The goal of these "enterprise zones" would be to stimulate economic development in run-down neighborhoods that investors otherwise avoided.

Democratic legislators warmed to Kemp's proposal after the riots, adding in some extra spending for the designated areas. But when lawmakers actually turned to the task of identifying the zones, they wound up with a peculiar response to the crisis of the *cities*. The legislation that prevailed provided for 50 zones, but with half located in rural areas! The bulk of the direct spending was allocated to the urban zones, but much of it was earmarked for smaller cities rather than urban concentrations such as Los Angeles.

As it turned out, the odd priorities reflected in the legislation did not matter. Democratic strategists bundled the enterprise zones with a number of controversial pieces of legislation, and submitted them to then-President Bush in a massive tax bill a week before the elections. The legislative leadership had hoped to force Bush to accept programs he opposed, but the strategy backfired; he vetoed the bill. The crisis of the cities would have to wait.

THE ENTERPRISE-ZONE LEGISLATION MAY HAVE RESULTED IN NOTHING, but the episode itself reveals several characteristics of the national legislature that are worth understanding. On the one hand, individual members are quick to "do something" about societal problems. On the other hand, the body as a whole is slow to make decisions and often produces policies unlikely to alleviate the conditions that first motivated action. Members usually use their influence to seek particular benefits for constituents; they have little incentive to focus on the general interest. This seemingly perverse behavior explains why so many Americans can be disenchanted with an institution that works so hard to please them. Dedication

All politics is local?

Former Speaker Tip O'Neill symbolized the House of Representatives to many Americans in the 1980s. Despite his great influence, O'Neill believed that even national political leaders need a strong connection with their local constituents if they wish to retain office.

to satisfying popular constituencies, as America's new democracy requires, need not produce results that will gratify the nation as a whole.

CONGRESS—THE FIRST BRANCH

Article I of the Constitution sets out the structure and powers of a national elected assembly, called the Congress. The Congress differs from elected assemblies in most advanced nations. Most world democracies are *parliamentary* in form, with the elected assembly choosing a chief executive from among its members.* In parliamentary systems, the assembly usually does little more than rubber-stamp proposals from the executive they have selected. Indeed, assemblies generally are not called legislatures, because they do little legislating; instead they are called parliaments, because they do a lot of talking. The United States is one of

*A few countries, such as France, have hybrid systems.

the few world democracies with a *presidential* form of government—a government in which the chief executive is elected directly by the people rather than chosen by the legislature. Legislatures are more independent, and therefore ultimately more powerful, in presidential systems.

Like many of the world's parliaments, Congress is **bicameral,** consisting of two chambers. The relative importance of the Senate and House of Representatives has fluctuated over time. In the decades prior to the Civil War, the country's most prominent statesmen—Henry Clay, John C. Calhoun, Daniel Webster, and Stephen Douglas—were members of the Senate. After the Civil War, political leadership moved to the House, where shifting party control more accurately reflected national sentiments. Presidents of the period were undistinguished, and the public image of the Senate was poor, partly because the membership included numerous party bosses and millionaire industrialists. In this unusual context, a series of strong House Speakers, starting with Maine Republican James G. Blaine (1869–1875), organized their party members into energetic, cohesive lawmaking majorities.[2]

For most of the twentieth century the two chambers were equally important. Regardless of the political circumstances that gave prominence to one chamber, the other chamber always had the ability to check it. For example, after Republicans took over Congress in 1994, fewer than half of the 21 Contract with America provisions passed by the House won final congressional approval—a pointed reminder that the national legislature is genuinely bicameral. This balancing role creates a bit of a rivalry between the two chambers. A Speaker of the House once commented that "The Senate is a nice quiet place where good Representatives go when they die."[3] The Senate has a quick response to such jibes: Throughout the twentieth century, no one has ever given up a Senate seat to run for the House.

THE ORGANIZATION
OF CONGRESS

The House and Senate are not undifferentiated collections of people who sit in their seats all day debating and voting as the urge strikes them. Like other large decision-making bodies, the two chambers have developed traditions that advance their work: the committee system, which is an extensive division of labor, and a party leadership structure, which effectively organizes large numbers of people to make decisions. Both are more important in the House than in the Senate. The House is much larger, so it needs more internal organization to facilitate its work. The smaller Senate can afford to operate more informally.[4]

THE CONGRESSIONAL PARTIES

The principal organizing forces in the Congress are the parties, although they do not dominate Congress to the extent they dominate parliaments in other democracies.

SPEAKER OF THE HOUSE

The Constitution stipulates that the House shall elect a Speaker. Although technically a constitutional officer, in practice the **Speaker** is always the leader of the House's majority party. Until the late nineteenth century, the Speaker was the only formal party leader in the House. Indeed,

from the end of Reconstruction to the turn of the century, the Speaker often rivaled the president as the most powerful public official in the United States. Powerful Speakers awarded the chairmanships of important committees to their close allies, made all committee assignments, and punished disloyal members by removing them from committees on which they had previously served.[5] Moreover, as the presiding officer of the House and chairman of the Rules Committee—which determines legislative procedure—the Speaker controlled the **floor** of the chamber. Speakers ruled.

Big boss man
Joseph "Boss" Cannon, the last of the great House speakers, tightened his grip on Congress until it finally slipped through his fingers. A revolt from 1910 to 1911 weakened Cannon's hold over legislative rules and strengthened congressional committees at the Speaker's expense..

Republican Joseph "Boss" Cannon was the last of the great Speakers. Pushing the envelope of all the powers he had inherited, Cannon dominated the House in the first decade of the twentieth

century. But times were changing. The Republican party was split between regular and progressive wings, and maintaining party discipline led Cannon to an increasingly punitive use of his powers.[6] Dissident Republicans who chafed under the iron rule of the majority eventually joined with Democrats in a revolt that stripped the Speaker of his most important powers.[7] From 1910 to 1911, the

Speaker lost the power to make committee assignments and was removed from the Rules Committee. Procedural reforms also guaranteed ordinary members some right to have their proposals considered. The office of Speaker never regained the powers removed at this time.

PARTY LEADERSHIP: HOUSE   Next in line to the Speaker is the **majority leader,** who organizes the majority party on the floor. Majority leaders are elected by the members of their party. They are responsible for day-to-day operations: scheduling legislation; coordinating committee activity; and negotiating with the president, the Senate, and the minority. They play an important role in building the coalitions necessary to pass legislation, not simply by shoring up votes for a single bill, but also by maintaining "peace in the family." Different points of view flourish within parties, and it falls to the leadership to prevent minor spats and quarrels from developing into destructive feuds.[8]

The minority counterpart of the majority leader is the **minority leader,** the floor leader of the minority party. Both party leaders are assisted by **whips,** whose jobs are to communicate regularly with the parties' rank and file. The whip explains positions and strategies, counts votes, and carries rank-and-file views back to the leadership. The whip offices are rather large, with 25 whips in the Democratic party and 20 in the Republican party. Their title conjures up an image of party leaders whipping their members into line (the title derives from whippers-in of the hounds in a fox hunt), but in practice these officers seldom rely on coercion.

Others party members participate in leadership via steering committees, which are forums for discussing issues, developing party programs, and identifying committee heads.* Finally, all members belong either to their party *caucus* (if Democrats) or party *conference* (if Republicans). These meetings of the full party membership elect the leadership and vote on committee slates recommended by the steering committees. In Woodrow Wilson's time, they sometimes adopted resolutions requiring party members to support particular policy proposals—but this power is rarely used today.

PARTY LEADERSHIP: SENATE   With two members from each state—an even number—some tie-breaking mechanism is necessary, and the Constitution obliges by making the vice president the president of the Senate and giving him a tie-breaking vote. The Constitution also provides for a **president pro**

---

*The role of the steering committee differs depending upon whether the Democrats or the Republicans control the House.

tempore, who presides in the absence of the vice president, which is most of the time. This office is mainly honorific, without real power. Ordinarily, it goes to the most senior member of the majority party.

The Senate too has majority and minority leaders and whips, but Senate leaders today are not as strong as those in the House. Indeed, one of the main jobs of the leaders is to hammer out **unanimous-consent agreements**, so called because they are agreed to by all senators with any interest in proposals. Generally these agreements specify the terms of debate: what sort of amendments will be in order, how long they will be debated, when votes will be taken, and so forth.[9]

Agreements specifying the terms of debate are necessary because of the Senate's tradition of careful deliberation. According to present rules, a single member can talk for as long as desired—that is, **filibuster**—unless a **cloture** motion is adopted. A vote for cloture requires the support of 60 senators, so a coalition of 41 senators may stop the Senate from acting on any measure. The Senate is less of a majoritarian institution than the House.

motion to end debate

UPS AND DOWNS OF
THE CONGRESSIONAL PARTIES

Although the party leadership today is not as strong as it was in the period before the revolt against Boss Cannon, it is stronger than it was for half a century after the revolt. From the 1920s to the 1970s, Speakers were far weaker and less active than in the preceding half-century. Scholars refer to this midcentury period of weak party leadership as the era of "committee government," an allusion to the fact that committees operated much as they pleased with little constraint from the party leadership.[10] Beginning in the mid-1970s, however, a series of reforms and political developments strengthened the party leadership in general and the speakership in particular.

The Democrats picked up a large number of new seats in the wake of Watergate. The party caucus, fortified by this contingent of younger and more liberal members (the "class of '74"), deposed three standing committee chairmen. These older members were too moderate for the new party rank and file. Two of them were also known for overbearing and arbitrary styles of leadership that the newcomers found unacceptable. For example, when the chair of the Armed Forces Committee, F. Edward Hebert (D-LA), spoke before the freshmen, he was insulting, reportedly addressing them as "boys and girls."[11] His arrogance cost him his position.

Shortly thereafter, the party leadership regained influence. The power to make Democratic committee assignments was transferred to a steering committee in which the leadership was highly influential. Moreover, the Speaker was given the power to appoint the Democratic members of the Rules Committee, making it virtually part of his office. Figure 9.1 shows how increased party unity in roll-call voting accompanied these institutional changes.

When the Republicans took control of Congress in 1994, partisanship surged. They had chafed under Democratic control for decades, and now the time for payback was at hand. Democrats personally disliked Speaker Gingrich and bitterly opposed his program. Republicans, in turn, united in support of the leader who had brought them majority status. The congressional parties looked stronger in the mid-1990s than they had looked at any time since the late nineteenth century.

FIGURE 9.1

The congressional parties are more unified today than a generation ago

The graph shows the percentage of all recorded votes on which a majority of voting Democrats opposed a majority of voting Republicans. Numbers for each year have been averaged over each Congress.

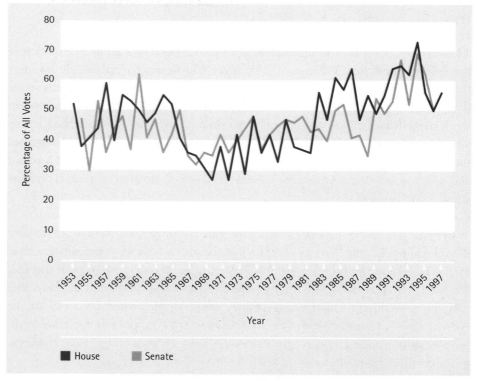

SOURCE: Norman Ornstein, Thomas Mann, and Michael Malbin, *Vital Statistics on Congress, 1999–2000* (Washington, DC: Congressional Quarterly, 2000), p. 201.

Why does party power rise and fall? Recent scholarship suggests that one reason is the homogeneity of the parties. If all party members agree about some issue, anyone can make decisions for the group. Members are willing to give more power to party leaders because they have little fear that the leaders will endanger their reelection prospects. But when the parties are more diverse, members are reluctant to give power to party leaders, who may act in ways that are electorally dangerous to them.[12]

Historical evidence backs up this supposition. The strong congressional parties of the late nineteenth century were a product of a time in which the two parties represented quite distinct interests.[13] Only when the Republican party split into progressive and regular wings did the movement to weaken the Speakership gain momentum. Conversely, the weak parties of the mid-twentieth century reflected their internal divisions. Numerous events undermined Democratic party cohesiveness, in particular: labor and liberal groups shaped presidential policy proposals during the New Deal, alienating moderates; civil rights split the party in the 1960s; and Vietnam and "social issues" continued dividing the party into the 1970s. Southern Democrats became especially unwilling to accept party leadership that would reflect the views of the northern majority.[14]

Parties are growing stronger again, in part because they are more uniform again. The civil rights revolution and the 1965 Voting Rights Act guaranteed everyone—particularly southern African Americans—the right to vote. As the electoral influence of southern African Americans increased, and as conservative whites started voting Republican, new Democrats elected in the South became much more liberal than their predecessors. Consequently, southern Democrats in the 1990s are not as different from northern Democrats as southern Democrats in the 1960s were. Especially in the House, the Democrats are now a liberal, urban party, whereas the Republicans are a conservative, suburban and rural party. So members have less to lose when they support strong leaders committed to particular national policies.[15]

Uniformity of beliefs may explain why strong leadership is less harmful to individual members, but it does not really explain why a member of Congress would accept it. What does a party member gain from cooperating with the team? Why are party switching and defections from the party line as rare as they are? Part of the explanation is that often strong leaders can help a party produce better outcomes than the party would get if they all worked independently. Passing an imperfect bill may be better than passing no bill at all, so members may sacrifice some influence over particular details.

Even when party members are unhappy with policies desired by their leaders, they have some incentive to stick together. Electoral success is partly linked to the successes of their political parties: the party images as a whole, as well as the performance of their presidential candidates. Congressional parties are also increasingly active in campaign funding, causing members to feel indebted to the leadership.[16] But members of Congress occasionally do tire of the compromises required by leadership, especially when the other party's beliefs seem more compatible (see the Election Connection, "The Jeffords Defection").

THE COMMITTEE SYSTEM

Congress does its work through its committees. Members introduce thousands of bills and resolutions every year. Nearly all are referred to committees for consideration, and most never emerge. Since 1980, for example, 6,000 to 8,000 bills have been introduced in each two-year session of the House of Representatives, but only 10 to 15 percent eventually passed. A few unsuccessful proposals died on the floor, but most of the 85 to 90 percent that failed never made it out of committee. Floor majorities can take a bill back from a recalcitrant committee via a rarely used "discharge petition," which requires 218 signatures, but in most cases favorable action by a committee is necessary for a proposal to become law.

To accomplish their work, both the House and the Senate utilize several kinds of committees. **Standing committees** have fixed memberships and jurisdictions, and they persist from one Congress to another. The Appropriations, Commerce, and Foreign Relations Committees are examples. **Select committees,** by contrast, are temporary committees created to deal with specific issues. Both houses of Congress had standing committee systems in place by 1825.[17] More than half a century later, the Legislative Reorganization Act of 1946 gave the committee system the shape it largely retains today. In the 106th Congress (1999–2000) there were 19 standing committees in the House and 17 in the Senate. These "full" committees are subdivided into more than 150 subcommittees. There also are 4 "joint" committees with membership from both houses, and a small number of select committees.

HOUSE COMMITTEES   House committees fall into three groups by level of importance. Both parties agree that the Rules, Appropriations, and Ways and Means Committees are highest in importance. The Rules Committee is the "right arm" of the Speaker. It controls the flow of legislation to the floor and the conditions of debate. The other two committees deal with spending and taxing, broad powers that enable them to affect nearly everything government does.

Committees at the second level of importance deal with nationally significant policy areas: agriculture, armed services, energy, and so forth. The least important committees include "housekeeping" committees, such as Government

The Jeffords Defection

Everyone suspected that GOP control of the U.S. Senate would not survive long after the 2000 elections. Democrats and Republicans had split the seats 50-50, leaving Vice President Dick Cheney to break ties. The loss of only one GOP senator would give Democrats organizational control over the chamber. A handful of elderly Republicans seemed likely candidates for the first departure. Most commentators guessed that the first to retire would be Strom Thurmond, a South Carolina Republican born in 1902.

No one suspected that Vermont moderate James Jeffords held the most vulnerable seat— at least not before rumors started circulating that the rangy maverick was upset with his party's leadership. Jeffords had never fit comfortably within the GOP, voting as often as not with the other party, but as the Republican center of gravity drifted in a southwesterly direction, the New England native felt less and less at home with its conservatism.[a]

Jeffords fought hard to liberalize the 2001 tax bill—and, because he was a swing vote, mostly got his way. He pushed making the child-care tax credit "refundable," so that people would get money back even if they had paid little or no taxes. He demanded that any drive to remove the "marriage penalty," a kink in the tax law that penalized married couples but not unmarried couples living together, also would provide extra benefits to poor married couples. And he insisted that the budget contain less of a tax cut and more money for special education.[b]

Jeffords accepted the eventual budget plan, but he was still unhappy with the treatment received from Republican leaders for charting his own course. Some say the final insult came when White House staffers neglected to invite Jeffords to a Teacher of the Year award ceremony, even though the guest of honor came from his state. Jeffords entered negotiations with Senate Minority Leader Tom Daschle, and also discussed his discontent with Nevada Senator Harry Reid—who was in line to chair the Environment and Public Works Committee if Democrats took over but offered to defer to Jeffords instead. Jeffords left the GOP in early June, ending six months of unified Republican government.

Only rarely does one person exercise so much influence. The Jeffords defection meant that the Judiciary Committee was under the control of one of the Senate's most liberal members, Patrick Leahy, who would be able to block Bush's judicial nominees. Armed Services switched to Carl Levin, an opponent of Bush's plan to develop antiballistic missile technology. West Virginia's Robert Byrd, considered a champion of pork-barrel spending, was again chair of Appropriations. Every committee except Ethics would have more Democrats than Republicans, rather than balanced memberships. Jeffords also raised the political stock of several senators considered possible 2004 presidential contenders—not only of Daschle but also of new Foreign Relations chair Joe Biden of Delaware and of 2000 vice presidential candidate Joe Lieberman of Connecticut, who took over Governmental Affairs.

Conservatives were livid at the Jeffords defection. The outgoing Republican Senate Majority Leader, Trent Lott of Mississippi, called it a "coup of one," an "impetuous decision of one man to undermine our democracy." In response, liberal columnists gleefully compared Lott's moral outrage to Al Gore's graceful surrender after losing the presidency to a Supreme

(continued)

(continued from previous page)

Court decision—they concluded that the Republicans were hypocrites.[c] However one interprets the Jeffords defection and the response to it, though, it reinforces the same message as the 2000 presidential election that preceded it: When the voting public is almost evenly divided between two parties in America's new democracy, minor fluctuations in the political system can make all the difference.

What do you think?
- Would Jeffords likely have left the GOP if his defection would not have switched control of the Senate or if the Democrats had not promised him leadership of an important committee?

- Who is responsible for keeping party members in Congress happy? the president? the congressional leadership? Or should legislators be expected to follow their own consciences?

- Do elected officials betray their constituents when they change partisan affiliations in the middle of a term?

[a]Karen Yourish and Bonnie Scranton, "Who's a Rock—and Who Rolls," *Newsweek* (June 4, 2001): 30–31.
[b]John F. Harris and Dan Balz, "A Delicate Balance: The Steady Courtship of Senate Moderates Was Key to the Passage of the Tax Bill," *Washington Post Weekly Edition* (June 4–10, 2001): 8–10.
[c]Michael Kinsley, "Trent Lott's Stages of Grief," *Washington Post Weekly Edition* (June 11–17, 2001): 27.

Reform and Oversight, and committees with narrow policy jurisdictions, such as Veterans' Affairs. The Budget Committee has a special status. Members can serve for only four years in any ten-year period, and its membership is drawn from other committees and from the leadership.

SENATE COMMITTEES   The Senate committee system is simpler than that of the House; it has only major and minor committees. Like their House equivalents, Appropriations and Finance are major committees, but the Senate Rules Committee is a minor committee with far less power than its House counterpart (the Senate leadership itself discharges the tasks performed by the House Rules Committee). Budget is also a major committee, as is Foreign Affairs, reflecting the Senate's constitutional responsibilities to advise on and consent to treaties and to confirm ambassadors.

Committee power in the Senate is widely distributed: Chairs of major committees cannot chair any other committee or subcommittee, and chairs of minor committees can chair only one other panel. Each senator serves on one minor and two major committees, and every senator gets to serve on one of the four major committees named above. On average, senators sit on more committees than representatives. In part this reflects a simple size difference: The Senate has nearly as many committees as the House but less than one-fourth as many members to staff them. But in addition, senators represent entire states, so many more issues concern their constituents. As a result, senators' legislative lives are not so closely tied to particular committees as are the lives of representatives.[18]

HOW COMMITTEES ARE FORMED   The committee system is formally under the control of the chamber's dominant party. Party committees nominate members for assignment, and party members gather in caucus to approve those assignments. Each committee thus has a partisan balance at least as favorable to the majority as the overall division of the chamber. The more important committees are especially stacked in favor of the majority party. In the 106th Congress, for example, the Republicans had a 9-to-4 advantage over the Democrats on the House Rules Committee, a ratio far greater than their 223-to-211 edge in the chamber. In contrast, the party ratio on the less important Judiciary Committee was 20 to 15.

Party influence over committee membership actually does not prevent individual committees from exercising a considerable degree of independence. Part of the reason is the use of **seniority** to choose committee chairs. Members generally are not removed from committees after their initial appointments, and the majority-party member with the longest continuous service on the committee is usually its chair. This norm for selecting committee chairs evolved in the Senate in the 1880s and migrated to the House after the 1910 revolt. It is rarely violated, although in 1994 Speaker Gingrich did pass up the most senior committee members when he named the Republican chairs of the Appropriations, Commerce, and Judiciary committees.[19] The seniority system gives chairs enough autonomy to resist the party leadership on occasion.

COMMITTEE REFORMS   By the 1950s, party leaders in Congress had become so weak that many observers believed committee chairs held the real power. A few of them behaved autocratically, closely controlling staff and budgets and even refusing to call meetings or to consider legislation they opposed. Some manipulated the subcommittee structure: creating and abolishing the smaller units, varying their jurisdictions, and monopolizing their chairmanships. To make matters worse, because members from safe southern seats had built up considerable seniority, Democratic chairs tended to be notably more conservative than their party's rank and file.[20]

Eventually, the Democratic party caucus injected more democracy into the system, weakening the chairs.[21] A caucus resolution passed in the early 1970s allowed House committee chairs to lead only one subcommittee. A "subcommittee bill of rights" protected the jurisdictions, budgets, and staff of the smaller units. The Senate moved in the same direction as the House, spreading power more evenly across the membership.

For more than a decade, political scientists debated the net impact of these reforms. Some questioned the wisdom of decentralizing power to 300 standing committees and subcommittees, many containing only eight or nine members. Today the prevailing view is that committees have been more subject to party influence in the last decade than they were a generation ago. An out-of-the-main-stream chair of an important committee or subcommittee would run a greater risk of being overthrown today than at any time since the revolt against Cannon. Moreover, when the Republicans took control in 1995, their leadership acted to restrict the independence of subcommittees.

THEORIES OF THE COMMITTEE SYSTEM

Why does the standing-committee system exist at all? Members of Congress are elected as equals. Why would the body give minorities—sometimes unrepresentative minorities—permanent influence over any policy area? Why not consider everything on the chamber floor (the so-called Committee of the Whole), where all members participate on an equal basis? And if the size of the membership would make that process too unwieldy, why not consider legislation in select committees specifically created for particular bills or resolutions? The various answers to these questions invoke different interpretations or theories of the committee system.

The **distributive theory** notes that members choose committees relevant to their districts. For example, members from urban districts seek membership on committees that deal with banking, housing, or labor; members from rural districts opt instead for committees that deal with agriculture and natural resources. The committee membership gets first crack at legislation in their issue area, and other members of the chamber go along with the committee in exchange for similar deference on bills they have shaped. This **logrolling** ensures that Congress will deliver benefits to each participant's constituency.[22] Studies document that districts and states receive a disproportionate share of government grants if their representatives sit on the relevant committees.[23]

An alternative interpretation is that committees primarily serve a knowledge-gathering function.[24] This **informational theory** stresses that members frequently are uncertain about the outcomes that proposed policies will produce. Hence they wish some members to become experts in each subject area and to reveal their knowledge to the broader membership. One way to do this is to give committees disproportionate influence, subject to the condition that they do their job conscientiously and do not abuse their power. Committee members can utilize their positions to gain a bit extra for themselves, but only to the extent that they specialize and give the chamber useful, reliable information.

These two theories are not incompatible. Each describes an important aspect of the committee system. Indisputably, members wish to serve their constituencies and regard committees as important means for doing so (although certainly not the *only* means). But just as certainly, members often are unsure exactly how they can best serve their constituencies, so they need and value information. If they adopt the wrong policy and the results are disastrous, it could come back to haunt them in a future campaign.[25]

The two theories probably apply differently to various committees. The distributive theory appears most relevant to committees responsible for straightforward matters, such as handing out money—subsidies, grants, and funding for projects. In these areas, members of Congress will allow interested colleagues to turn public institutions into private preserves, so long as they receive similar privileges in areas of importance to *their* constituencies. In contrast, where policy making involves great uncertainty or large costs and benefits—telecommunications regulation, for example—members will wish to have reliable information and will hold committees to a higher standard.

The distributive theory also seems somewhat less applicable today than in the period of so-called committee government. When government revenues were rising steadily and congressional party influence was weak, there was little to prevent members from using the committee system for their narrow ends. But with the budget deficits of the 1980s and 1990s, with stronger congressional parties, and with considerable uncertainty surrounding much of the policy agenda (health care, environmental protection, and the Internet revolution), committee members are less free to pursue their narrow constituency interests. The incentives still are present, but the opportunities are more limited.

THE STAFF

The legislative branch is much larger than the 535 elected members of the House and Senate. The members have personal staffs that total more than 7,000 in the House and 4,000 in the Senate, and each chamber hires thousands of staff members to support the committees. Many of these staffers are clerical workers, and others are policy experts who play an important role shaping legislation. Additional employees help coordinate partisan legislative proposals.

TABLE 9.1

THE LEGISLATIVE BRANCH

Members of Congress are only a fraction of the legislative branch.

EMPLOYEES			EMPLOYEES
House		**Joint Committee Staffs**	104
Committee staff	1,267	**Support Agencies**	
Personal staff	7,216	General Accounting Office	3,275
Leadership staff	179	Congressional Research Service	747
Officers of the House staff	974	Congressional Budget Office	232
Senate		**Miscellaneous**	
Committee staff	910	Architect	2,012
Personal staff	4,272	Capitol police	1,251
Leadership staff	219		
Officers of the Senate staff	990		

SOURCE: Norman Ornstein, Thomas Mann, and Michael Malbin, *Vital Statistics on Congress, 1999–2000* (Washington, DC: Congressional Quarterly, 2000), pp. 129–130.

Thousands of other staff members work in various support agencies of Congress. The Library of Congress employs thousands. So does the General Accounting Office (GAO), the watchdog agency of Congress that oversees the operation of the executive branch. A smaller number of people work for the Congressional Budget Office (CBO). This agency provides Congress with expert economic projections and budgetary information. In total, the legislative branch of government consists of some 24,000 people (see Table 9.1).

HOW A BILL BECOMES A LAW

Every civics class teaches that Congress "makes the law" governing the United States. However, this tidy phrase is inadequate to describe the complex process necessary for a bill to become a law. Passing a single statute requires steering it through two chambers organized into more than 250 committees and subcommittees, and usually requires the support of members of two political parties and numerous interest groups. Although no flowchart could possibly convey the complexity of getting a major bill through Congress, we will outline the stages through which important legislation must pass (see Figure 9.2).

FIGURE 9.2

How a bill becomes a law

There's a bit more detail involved than passage by Congress and a presidential signature.

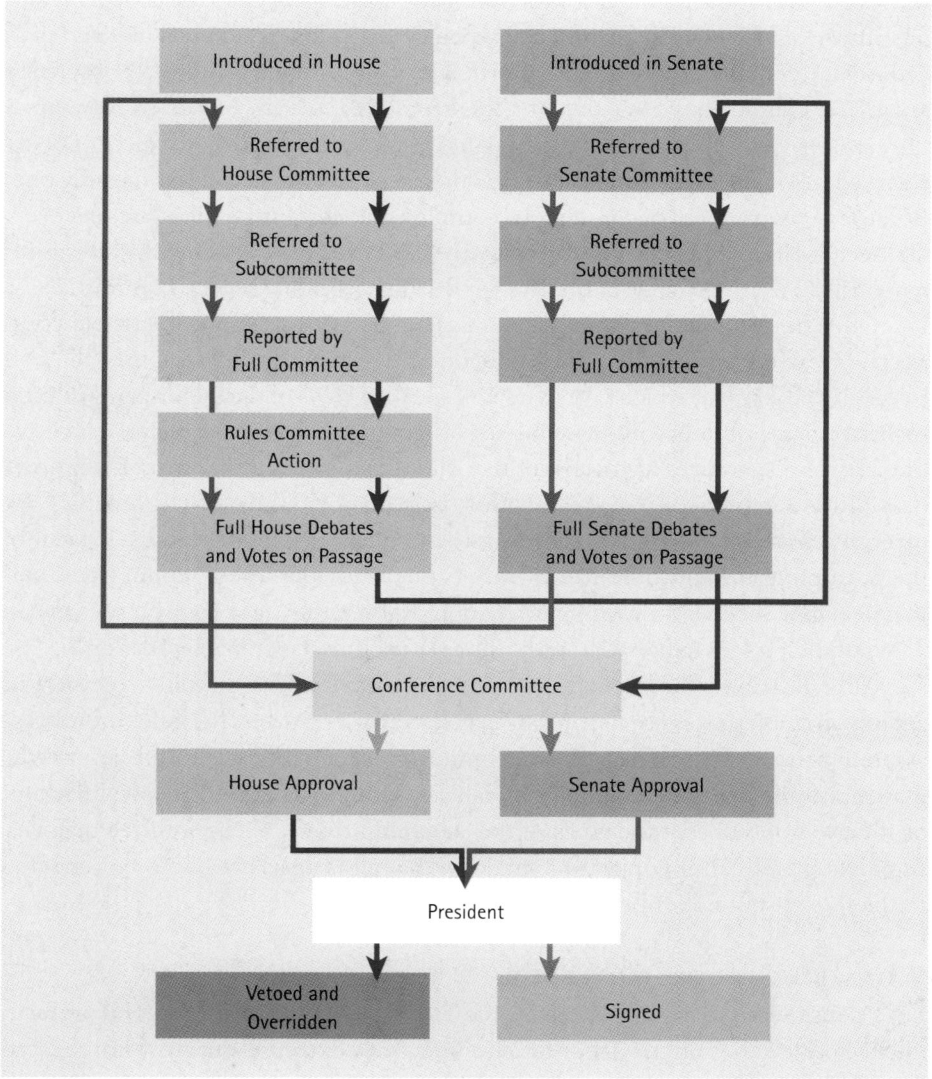

To start things off, a bill or resolution is introduced by a congressional **sponsor** and one or more cosponsors. The initial wording may be the legislator's own work, or a proposal offered by a constituent, but most likely it was provided by legislative staff at the member's direction. The House Speaker or the Senate presiding officer, advised by the chamber's parliamentarian (an expert on rules and procedures), refers the proposal to an appropriate committee. In some cases sponsors are not serious but are acting only to please some constituency or interest group. If they *are* serious, they may draft their bill in a way that increases its chances of being referred to a friendly committee—often theirs—rather than to a less friendly one. Because legislation has become more complex and committee jurisdictions overlap, recent House Speakers have used **multiple referrals,** sending the bill simultaneously to more than one committee or dividing it among several committees.

Once the bill goes to committee, the chair gives it to an appropriate subcommittee. Here the work begins. If the subcommittee takes the bill seriously, the staff schedules hearings at which witnesses will speak in favor of the bill or in opposition to it. Witnesses can be other members of Congress, members of the executive branch, representatives of groups and associations, or ordinary citizens. Sometimes hearings are genuine attempts to gather information. More often, hearings are carefully choreographed: The subcommittee staff stacks the witness list in favor of the position of the subcommittee chair. As one study observed, "committees neither seek nor receive complete information. Rather, they seek to promote certain views of their issues to bolster their abilities to produce favorable legislation."[26]

After hearings, the subcommittee begins **markup** of the bill—revising it, adding and deleting sections, and preparing it for report to the full committee, assuming that a majority of the subcommittee supports it. The full committee may repeat the process, holding its own hearings and conducting its own markup, or it may largely accept the work of the subcommittee.[27] If a committee majority supports the bill after committee markup, the bill is nearly ready to be reported to the floor—but not quite.

WHEN BILLS GO TO THE FLOOR

Let's consider first what happens in the House. Bills that are not controversial, either because they are trivial or because they have extremely narrow impact, can be called up at specified times and passed unanimously with little debate. Many somewhat more important bills are considered under a fast-track procedure called **suspension of the rules.** Upon being recognized, the committee chair moves to consider a bill under suspension. If a two-thirds majority of those voting agrees, the bill will be considered. Debate is limited to 40 minutes, no amendments are in order, and a two-thirds majority is required for passage. There is some risk in considering a bill under suspension: Even if a majority supports it, it could fail because the majority is smaller than two-thirds. Indeed, opponents of the bill sometimes support the motion to suspend the rules precisely in order to raise the threshold for passage to two-thirds.

Legislation that is important, and therefore usually controversial, goes to the Rules Committee before going to the floor. The Rules Committee, too, may hold hearings, this time on the type of **rule** it should grant. In these hearings only members of Congress may testify. The rule specifies the terms and conditions of debate. A rule specifies the time that the supporters and opponents will be allowed to speak, and it may prohibit any amendments (a *closed rule*), allow any amendments (an *open rule*), or specify the amendments that are in order (a *restrictive rule*). In recent years three-quarters of all bills coming from the Rules Committee have been granted restrictive rules.

Sometimes rules are unusual. For example, a *king-of-the-mountain rule* allows a number of (often conflicting) amendments to be offered but specifies that only the last amendment receiving a majority is adopted. Naturally, the committee orders the amendments so that the one it favors goes last. This kind of rule allows some members to play a little game with constituents and interest groups. The members can vote for several conflicting amendments, thereby satisfying each of their supporters, all the while knowing that the last vote is the only one that matters.

Assuming that the Rules Committee recommends a rule, the floor then chooses to accept or reject the rule. Rules rarely are rejected, but that does not mean that the floor goes along with anything the Rules Committee proposes. Rather, in shaping the rule, the committee anticipates the limits of what the floor will accept. Sometimes committee members miscalculate and are embarrassed when a floor majority rejects their rule. Most of the time the rule is approved, and the bill is finally under consideration by the chamber. After debating a proposal and voting on amendments, the floor then decides whether to adopt the bill.

In the Senate, the process is a bit simpler. For uncontroversial legislation, a motion to pass a bill by unanimous consent is sometimes all that is necessary. More important and controversial legislation will require the committee and party leaders to negotiate a unanimous-consent agreement, which is a complicated bargain analogous to a rule granted by the House Rules Committee. Assuming that they succeed and thereby avoid a filibuster, the bill eventually comes to a floor vote.

If a majority votes to adopt the bill, are we at the end of the process? Not at all. Before the bill can be sent for the president's signature, it must pass both chambers in identical form. But the bill may have started in one chamber before going to the other, or it may have proceeded simultaneously through both. In either case, it is extremely unlikely that the House and Senate will pass exactly the same bill. In fact, their versions of the legislation may be in serious conflict.

For major legislation, each chamber appoints conferees to participate in a **conference committee** that may reconcile the two versions of a bill. In theory, each chamber's conferees are committed to their chamber's version of the legislation and will negotiate a compromise as close as possible to their chamber's desired solution. In practice, this is not likely. Conferences for some complex bills involve hundreds of members who support some parts, oppose other parts, and care little about still other parts. This context makes the situation ideal for bargaining. When a majority of each chamber's conferees agree to the final compromise, the bill is reported back to the parent chambers, where another floor vote in each chamber is required for passage.[28]

Budgetary politics

Now, you may think that we have finally reached the end of the legislative process. Technically, this is true, but passage of a bill does not guarantee that it will be implemented. The reason is that we have been describing only the **authorization process.** Before the government actually can carry out the activities Congress authorizes, funding must be approved for them (see Chapter 15).

The Constitution grants Congress the power of the purse and makes the House the lead actor: All tax bills must originate in the House, and by custom and tradition, all appropriations bills do too. The **appropriations process** parallels the authorization process. Thirteen appropriations subcommittees in each chamber hold hearings and mark up a budget bill (the subcommittee chairs are commonly referred to as "the Cardinals of Capitol Hill").[29] The full committees may do the same, but usually they defer to their subcommittees.

In the House, appropriations bills are *privileged;* they take precedence over other legislation, and a motion to take up an appropriations bill can be offered at any time. But in practice, appropriations bills, too, usually pass through the Rules Committee. Thus, appropriations subcommittees in both chambers must report bills, the rank and file in both chambers must pass them, and a conference committee must agree on every dollar before the government actually has any money to spend.

Evaluating Congress

It is easy to get so wrapped up in the detail of Congress and its operations that we lose sight of the reason for our interest in the institution. The reason, of course, is that Congress is the first branch, arguably the most powerful and most important of the three branches of government. It is the branch that bears primary responsibility for representing the needs and values of the American public and for developing legislation to improve their well-being. How well does Congress meet its responsibilities?

CRITICISMS OF CONGRESS

The most common criticism of the congressional process is obvious: *It is lengthy and inefficient*. Legislation may take months or even years to wend its way through the process, and there is much duplication of effort—both within and between the chambers. Moreover, after all is said and done, Congress often produces a compromise that satisfies no one. To those who want quick, decisive action, Congress watching is enough to put their teeth on edge. Of course, that is what the framers intended. They wished to ensure that laws would pass only after thorough deliberation.

A congressional debate
Disrespect for Congress is nothing new, as this 1798 print of the congressional floor shows.

But that raises a second criticism: *The congressional process works to the advantage of policy minorities, especially those content with the status quo.* Proponents of legislation must build many winning coalitions—in subcommittee, full committee, appropriations committee, conference committee, and on the floor—in both chambers. Opponents have it much easier. A minority that controls only a single stage of the process may be able to frustrate the majority. Of course, a determined majority cannot be stopped indefinitely, except by a Senate filibuster, but it can be held at bay for a long time. Moreover, potential majorities sometimes decide not to act, calculating that the costs of overcoming all the obstacles are not worth the effort. Because changing the status quo requires positive action, the congressional process handicaps majorities who support change and helps minorities who are content to block change.

Two other criticisms focus on the policies Congress selects. Given that members are trying to please constituencies, *they constantly are tempted to use their positions to extract constituency benefits*, even when important national legislation is at stake. President Jimmy Carter got so upset trying to deal with Congress on national energy policy that he wrote in his diary, "Congress is disgusting on this particular subject."[30] President Clinton's lobbying on behalf of the North American Free Trade Agreement (NAFTA) was likened to an "oriental bazaar." Members not only demanded special treatment for constituency interests but even traded votes for concessions on unrelated issues. Besides appearing unseemly (unless *you* are part of the constituency getting the concession), Congress defeats, distorts, and otherwise damages national interests in pursuit of its members' parochial interests.

Finally, the nature of congressional procedure is such that *sometimes the very process of passing legislation ensures that it will not work.* This is especially true of proposals that target resources on small portions of the population. For example, in the aid-to-the-cities effort described in the introduction to this chapter, the process of getting the legislation through Congress spread the available resources across small cities and rural areas, leaving too little to make much difference to the major cities, even if the legislation had been enacted.[31]

Examples like these illustrate the charge that Congress regularly shows a **distributive tendency,** a tendency to spread program benefits widely. Every member wants a "fair" share of the federal pie for his or her district, and by *fair,* the legislators mean "as much as possible." Even if the district or state is relatively affluent or does not have the problem a program addresses, its representatives and senators are reluctant to pass up an opportunity to deliver local benefits. Some federal programs distribute money on the basis of complex formulas that include population, economic conditions, and characteristics of the people and area. These formulas are of great importance to members of Congress; staff members use state-of-the-art spreadsheets to show how much their districts would gain or lose under alternative formulas. All too often, those estimates become the basis for supporting or opposing policies.

Taken to extremes, this tendency can be almost comical. Consider, for example, the Economic Development Administration created in the 1960s to subsidize the construction of infrastructure—roads, utilities, industrial parks, and so forth—in depressed areas. By the time the program was killed by the Reagan administration, it had been repeatedly expanded by Congress to the point where more than 80 percent of all the counties in the United States were officially classified as "economically depressed" to make them eligible for federal subsidies.[32]

Bashing federal programs is a popular sport. Sometimes it is warranted—programs may be badly designed, poorly implemented, or incompetently administered. But federal programs often fail because they were born to fail: They are not focused on where they will do the most good, and resources are not sufficiently

Shoe on the other foot
Even members of Congress dedicated to the principle of smaller government are reluctant to give up money that might go to their own districts.

concentrated to have a major impact. Consequently, money is spent, and the citizenry has little to show for it. But this is not because of incompetence or corruption. It is because members of Congress, ostensibly working in their constituents' interest, spread resources so broadly and thinly that they have little impact.

WHY DO AMERICANS DISLIKE CONGRESS BUT LIKE THEIR MEMBERS?

More than people in other democracies, Americans are proud of their political institutions. They revere the Constitution, honor the law, and respect the presidency and the courts. But the prominent exception to this generalization is the Congress. Congress is often the butt of jokes. Humorist Mark Twain once observed that "it could probably be shown with facts and figures that there is no distinctly native American criminal class except Congress."[33] Congress has been defined as "a creature with 535 bellies, and no brain." Critics regularly remark that "the opposite of progress is Congress."

Disparaging quips like these reflect popular sentiments. As Figures 9.3 and 9.4 show, surveys report that only a minority of Americans trust the Congress to do what is right or have confidence in Congress, and they view members as having ethical standards only a bit higher than car salespersons. The reputation of Congress has been repeatedly tarnished by scandals. Ironically, this most electorally sensitive institution is the one whose image is the most negative.[34] Majorities of Americans doubt the competence and integrity of the Congress.[35]

This negative perception of Congress contrasts with the generally positive view Americans have of their particular senators and representatives. After all, at

FIGURE 9.3

Public confidence in Congress trails confidence in many other institutions

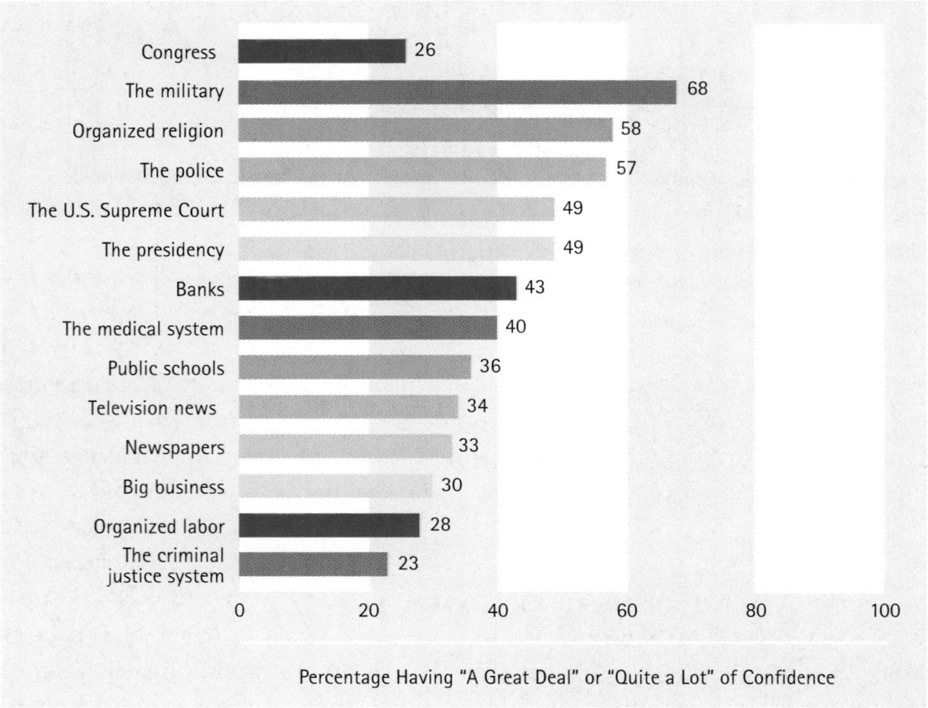

Institution	Value
Congress	26
The military	68
Organized religion	58
The police	57
The U.S. Supreme Court	49
The presidency	49
Banks	43
The medical system	40
Public schools	36
Television news	34
Newspapers	33
Big business	30
Organized labor	28
The criminal justice system	23

Percentage Having "A Great Deal" or "Quite a Lot" of Confidence

SOURCE: The Gallup Poll, June 10, 2000.

the same time that popular majorities express doubts about the collective Congress, they reelect 90 percent or more of all incumbents who run. This gap between electoral approval of individual members and unhappiness with the collective Congress is so striking that political scientists have given it a name: Fenno's paradox. Professor Richard Fenno first pointed out that citizens invariably rate their members of Congress far more favorably than the Congress as a whole (see Figure 9.5).[36] Members take advantage of this disparity by adopting an unusual electoral strategy: "Members run *for* Congress by running *against* Congress."[37] They criticize the institution and claim that they are different from the other members, who are the ones to blame for the things people dislike about Congress.

Fenno's observations are not puzzling in the light of a good understanding of the operation of Congress and the incentives underlying congressional operations. Americans dislike Congress but nevertheless reelect the great majority of

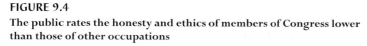

FIGURE 9.4

The public rates the honesty and ethics of members of Congress lower than those of other occupations

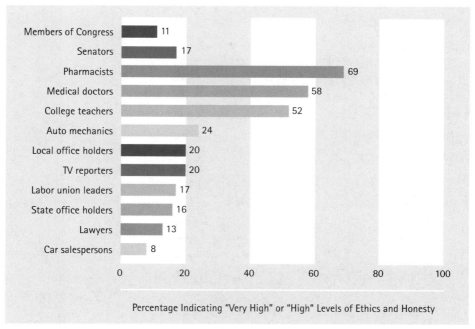

Percentage Indicating "Very High" or "High" Levels of Ethics and Honesty

SOURCE: The Gallup Poll, November 4–7, 1999.

their senators and representatives because they judge the collective Congress and the individual member by different standards.[38] They judge the Congress by how well it solves major problems and meets the serious challenges the country faces. Polls show that Americans generally take a dim view of how well the Congress solves those problems and meets those challenges. The Congress, they believe, rarely satisfies its collective responsibilities. Moreover, citizens take an equally dim view of how they think Congress operates—sluggishly, conflictually, inefficiently, and sometimes corruptly.

But citizens judge their representatives and senators positively for doing the very things that make the collective Congress perform poorly. Members respond to narrow—special—interests that are part of their constituencies, they look for opportunities to channel benefits to constituencies, they go to bat for constituents seeking exemptions from general policies, and they try to extract constituency concessions from major legislative efforts. Even though many of

FIGURE 9.5

**Americans rate their representatives much more positively
than the Congress**

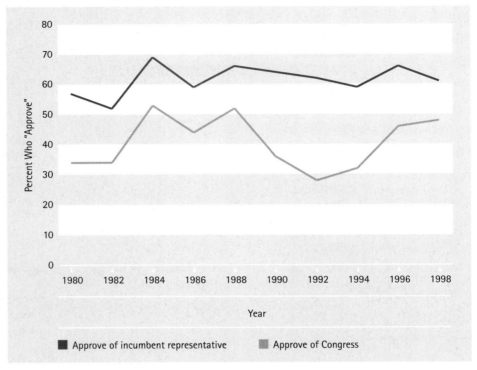

SOURCE: American National Election Studies Guide to Public Opinion and Electoral Behavior (http://www.umich.edu/~nes/nesguide/nesguide.htm)

these activities detract from the national good, local constituencies appreciate the willingness of their representatives to act as **delegates** to the federal government rather than **trustees** (see the Election Connection, "Delegates or Trustees?").

The collective good may suffer. An old country maxim states that "if you want to make an omelet, you've got to break some eggs." Constituencies want the omelet, but they oppose contributing any of their eggs—and indeed, they applaud when their members of Congress steal eggs from other districts and states. So widespread disgust with Congress stems not from a breakdown in the connection between constituents and representative; it grows from the responsiveness required by an especially strong connection.

Delegates or Trustees?

The debate over *whom* a representative should represent—the constituency or the whole country—goes back centuries in political philosophy. It is often intertwined with another debate about *how* the representative should act.[a] Political philosopher Edmund Burke posed the question most sharply in a classic speech in 1774.[b] Is it the representative's duty to act as a *delegate* of the constituency, who follows the wishes of voters, or as a *trustee,* who uses personal judgment to decide how to operate?

Many people have difficulty maintaining consistency when they think about this question. The type of representation they prefer often depends upon whether they agree with the majority's demands (in which case they favor greater responsiveness) or with the personal preferences of elected elites (in which case they favor strong leadership). The following thought experiment illustrates how hard it can be to stay loyal to a particular form of representation:

> *Representative A believes that the United States should constitutionally prohibit abortion, but she represents a suburban district with a pro-choice majority. Should she vote for or against a constitutional amendment prohibiting abortion?*

> *Representative B believes the Constitution implies a right to abortion, but she represents a Catholic district with a pro-life majority. Should she vote for or against a constitutional amendment prohibiting abortion?*

Our classroom experiments indicate that, on such a controversial and emotion-laden topic, many students do not remain consistent. They choose whichever form of representation will produce the policy in which they believe. Pro-choice students often would like the representatives to behave as a delegate in the first example and as a trustee in the second, whereas many pro-life students have the opposite preference.

What do you think?

- Should members of Congress generally act as delegates or as trustees?
- Does the issue under consideration make a difference? That is, should representatives behave as delegates on some issues and trustees on others?
- Should representatives behave differently from senators?

[a]Heinz Eulau, John Wahlke, William Buchanan, and Leroy Ferguson, "The Role of the Representative," *American Political Science Review* 53 (1959): 742–756.

[b]"Speech to the Electors of Bristol," Peter Standlis, ed., *Selected Writings and Speeches* (New York: Doubleday, 1963).

CHAPTER SUMMARY

The United States Congress is the world's most powerful legislature. It is also the most professionalized; its members are full-time, professional legislators. It has an extensive division of labor—the committee system—that is the envy of parliamentarians in other countries who have much less power and responsibility. Nevertheless, citizens hold Congress in much lower esteem than they hold their individual representatives and senators, whom they reelect regularly.

This discrepancy arises because members of Congress depend for their election on specific constituencies. Thus, they have strong incentives to serve those constituencies, and those incentives often are inconsistent with behavior that would best serve the larger interest of the nation. In particular, members organize the committee system not only to deal efficiently and effectively with major national problems but also to enable them to concentrate on issues important to their home districts. Members hesitate to give the party leadership enough power to mount efficient and effective responses to national problems in part because that power might be used to prevent them from serving constituency interests or even to force them to oppose constituency interests. The structure of Congress is an uneasy compromise between what it takes to get the job done and what it takes to get reelected.

The result is that Congress is slow and inefficient, and the laws that emerge from the complex legislative process may not be very effective policy. This makes citizens frustrated with Congress, but they fail to see that the problem is not a lack of democratic responsiveness but rather an excess of it. It is precisely the efforts of their own representatives to serve their specific interests that makes it so difficult for Congress as a whole to serve the national interest.

KEY TERMS

appropriations process, p. 294
authorization process, p. 294
bicameral, p. 278
cloture, p. 281
conference committee, p. 294
delegates, p. 300
distributive tendency, p. 296
distributive theory, p. 288
filibuster, p. 281
floor, p. 279

informational theory, p. 288
logrolling, p. 288
majority leader, p. 280
markup, p. 292
minority leader, p. 280
multiple referrals, p. 292
president pro tempore, p. 280
rule, p. 293
select committee, p. 284
seniority, p. 287

Speaker, p. 279
sponsor, p. 292
standing committee, p. 284
suspension of the rules, p. 292
trustees, p. 300
unanimous-consent agreement, p. 281
whips, p. 280

SUGGESTED READINGS

Arnold, R. Douglas. *The Logic of Congressional Action.* New Haven, CT: Yale University Press, 1990. An excellent discussion of how the incentives that motivate members interact with characteristics of public policy problems to shape legislation.

Deering, Christopher, and Steven Smith, *Committees in Congress.* Washington, DC: CQ Press, 1997. A thorough and up-to-date discussion of the congressional committee system.

Kingdon, John. *Congressmen's Voting Decisions,* Third Edition. Ann Arbor: University of Michigan Press, 1989. Classic study of how representatives decide to vote on the floor.

ON THE WEB

Roll Call Online
www.rollcall.com
Roll Call is widely regarded as the leading source for congressional news and information both inside the beltway and beyond. Since 1955, *Roll Call* has been the newspaper of Capitol Hill, giving members of Congress a way to communicate with one another across the aisle, between chambers, and beyond party affiliations.

THOMAS Online: Legislative Information on the Internet
thomas.loc.gov
Acting under the directive of the 104th Congress to make federal legislative information freely available to the Internet public, a Library of Congress team brought the THOMAS World Wide Web system online in January 1995. THOMAS is the most comprehensive congressional Web site on the net. It posts the full text of all congressional proceedings and contains historical information on Congress from its inception to the present.

Congressional Quarterly
www.cq.com
Congressional Quarterly is extremely successful in its mission to ". . . project the highest levels of accuracy, comprehensiveness, nonpartisanship, readability, timeliness and analytical rigor."

Legislative Histories
www.lib.umich.edu/libhome/ documents.center/legishis.html
A site designed by the University of Michigan for students doing research on the U.S. Congress. The site includes pointers to historical sources and present-day resources, and includes a concise tutorial on the legislative process.

The U.S. Government Legislative Branch Directory
leweb.loc.gov/global/legislative/ congress.html
A comprehensive list of Internet resources from and about the U.S. Congress, selected and organized by the Library of Congress.

Ornstein, Norman, Thomas Mann, and Michael Malbin. *Vital Statistics on Congress, 1999–2000*. Washington, DC: American Enterprise Institute, 2000. This biennial compilation of congressional statistics is to Congress watchers what *The Bill James Baseball Sourcebook* is to baseball fans.

Rohde, David. *Parties and Leaders in the Post-Reform House*. Chicago: University of Chicago Press, 1991. Important work that traces the strengthening of the congressional parties in recent decades.

Smith, Steven. *Call to Order: Floor Politics in the House and Senate*. Washington, DC: Brookings, 1989. Detailed study of the increasing importance of the chamber floors in the contemporary Congress.

10

❯─────◆─────❮

THE EXECUTIVE BRANCH

Campaigning for the presidency in 1992, Democrats Bill Clinton and Al Gore needed to overcome stereotypes that characterized their party as the champions of bureaucracy. To be tagged with a big-government label would have hurt their chances to oust the incumbent president, since perhaps 95 percent of the public believes that the federal government wastes "a great deal" or "quite a lot" of taxpayer money.[1] So Clinton and Gore emphasized their willingness to make changes. "We can no longer afford to pay more for—and get less from—our government," they declared to voters.[2]

The focus on streamlining federal agencies ended up being more than just campaign rhetoric; it produced what many call the longest sustained effort at institutional reform in the nation's history.[3] After the election, Vice President Gore spearheaded a Clinton administration initiative to "reinvent government." It was precisely the kind of policy area that appealed to the scholarly former senator: highly technical, and yet something he might reduce into terms understandable by regular Americans. He gathered an initial staff of 250 career bureaucrats into the National Partnership for Reinventing Government in 1993, and they quickly produced a report brimming with more than 1,200 proposals for change. The administration projected that the REGO efforts, as they are known, would save over $100 billion.

Gore worked hard to turn the complex policy issue into a political boon. The federal government would no longer order "designer bug sprays," he promised, or pay more for computer disks than those who buy at discount stores do.[4] When Gore's office needed a new electronic-mail program, employees did not go through a complicated procurement process; they simply drove to a nearby supplies store and bought the software. Gore appeared on the David Letterman show with a hammer and protective goggles to demonstrate the federally mandated procedure for safety regulators to test "ash receivers, tobacco desk type" (known to most of us as ashtrays). Gore eventually became so closely associated with the effort that he joked REGO was just "Gore spelled sideways."

President Clinton actively promoted the efforts of his second in command. "Make no mistake about this," Clinton said. "This is one report that will not gather dust in a warehouse."[5] Yet when the dust settled, the Clinton administration's efforts to make government "work better and cost less" returned little more than a mixed record. Only a third of federal bureaucrats surveyed in 1999 said their agencies treated reinvention as a priority. The federal workforce shrank by 300,000 employees, but only because of reductions growing out of the end of the Cold War. Otherwise the federal bureaucracy grew. The General Accounting Office studied cost reductions reported by Gore's office and found that it could not document billions of the claimed savings. Rather, Gore's budget analysts had

counted the same savings more than once, ignored expenses, and wrongly attributed savings created by other policy changes to the REGO effort.

Changes in employee policies or agency organizations seemed most threatening to civil servants and congressional factions, so these areas saw the least
progress. An illustrative example of the frustrations is Gore's proposal to "transfer law enforcement functions of the Drug Enforcement Administration [DEA]
and the Bureau of Alcohol, Tobacco and Firearms [ATF] to the Federal Bureau of
Investigation [FBI]." The missions of the three overlapped, and duplication of
efforts was not just inefficient; it was dangerous. "It is not uncommon for agents
from one … agency to believe the other to be the criminal element," said a draft
version of the Gore study.[6]

Despite the president's commitment to consolidating law enforcement,
Gore's proposal failed to get off the ground. Within days of its announcement,
critics in Congress and in government agencies scuttled the idea. ATF was located
within the Department of the Treasury, headed by Secretary Lloyd Bentsen, who
let it be known he did not want to give up part of his turf. The DEA also had its
supporters. Representative Charles Rangel, head of the House Caucus on Drugs,
said the merger "would be a monumental mistake."[7] Many government employees, familiar with the cultures of DEA and of the FBI, also considered a merger
between the two inconceivable. DEA agents often arrived at work in jeans, pony-
tails, and earrings, whereas their counterparts in the FBI dressed like Wall Street
bankers. Said one DEA agent, "An FBI guy's idea of undercover is to loosen his
tie."[8] In the end, the reorganization was abandoned.

EFFORTS TO REFORM THE STRUCTURE OF THE EXECUTIVE BRANCH ARE NOT
new and have generally met with little success. This long record of failure at com-
bating "unresponsive bureaucracies" often provokes frustration from regular citizens. The limited success of reform in the 1990s might appear to contradict the
central claim of this book—that elections give the public more influence over
government than ever before. But the persistence of bureaucracy is not incompatible with electoral responsiveness. Most elements of the Clinton–Gore rein-
venting-government story—an ambitious presidential agenda that conflicts with
vested political interests, executives with inadequate control over their policy
areas, and a bureaucracy tied down by rules that hamper efficiency—grew
directly out of America's new democracy.

These barriers to change generally result from public preferences expressed
through elections and through other forms of participation. Voters, seeking more
from their government, have required a more aggressive and politicized presidency to manage highly complex institutions. When Congress imposes public

demands on the bureaucracy, the result can be inefficiencies that slow down government action. As with so many institutions in the political system, therefore, the executive branch seems to frustrate popular will by failing to produce desirable results, but the cause of difficulty is often that the public got what it asked for.

THE EXECUTIVE BRANCH: MORE THAN THE PRESIDENT

For most Americans, one person embodies the entire executive branch: the president of the United States. Certainly the president is an influential public official, perhaps the most powerful individual in the world. But very few of the changes in culture, society, nature, or even government trace back to the decisions of single people. Markets follow their own economic logic, dictated by the behavior of numerous consumers, firms, and countries. Cultures evolve new habits, new tastes, and new modes of family or religious life through the individual decisions of millions. Climates fluctuate, diseases develop, the earth's crust shifts without asking permission of any mortal. Even the most powerful person in the world faces severe limits.

It may seem the national government should be different. The president is clearly at the top of any flowchart of power. Changes in government must be the ultimate responsibility of the "big boss," right? In theory, yes. But the federal government is a "12-million person operation," as executive-branch specialist Paul Light puts it; it is not just the combination of advisers, agency directors, and civil servants under a presidential administration, but also the "shadow government" of independent contractors and local government employees who carry out federally funded programs.[9] Such a massive and complicated executive branch would be beyond the close management of any one person, even if he or she did not have to share power with other public officials!

To characterize the frustrations of presidential power, political economists like to group them under a broader concept known to plague many complex organizations: the **principal-agent problem.** The idea is fairly simple. Whenever a boss (the "principal") wants her or his subordinate (the "agent") to do something, there is a tradeoff. The less detailed the instructions, the less likely the agent will carry them out exactly as desired. But more-detailed instructions reduce efficiency. Not only do the agent's own skills go to waste, because of a lack of discretion, but the principal has to spend more time gathering information on each task and formulating clear guidance.

Folk wisdom acknowledges the principal-agent problem in the old saying, "If you want something done right, you'd better do it yourself." But of course, a president cannot do the work of millions. One way to make the principal-agent dynamic become less problematic is to find employees who share the same values or possess clear professional norms. The more someone thinks as you do, the more you can trust that person to perform a task the way you would do it.

Within the executive branch, different sorts of government employees vary in how much the president influences their actions. The less control a president has over who holds a position, the less likely a particular government employee will share the goals of the boss—and thus the less true control the president is likely to exercise. Therefore, the remainder of this chapter deals with each portion of the exeutive branch separately: from the president to the closest advisers and finally to the far-flung bureaucracy.

THE PRESIDENCY

Presidents have a unique political asset: They fill the only position elected by a national constituency. Only presidents can claim to represent the country as a whole. This broad responsibility creates problems, however. In the eyes of the voters, presidents are the focal point of the U.S. government. The public routinely blames presidents for events and conditions over which they have little control. Presidents are expected to conduct foreign policy, promote desired legislation, respond to disasters, manage the government, and address an endless variety of real and imagined social problems.[10]

Although presidents sometimes take credit for prosperity and success, they more often attract the blame when things go bad. President George H. W. Bush, for example, enjoyed a succession of foreign policy triumphs equaled by few of his predecessors. He oversaw the fall of the Berlin wall, the collapse of the Soviet Union, and a spectacular victory in the Persian Gulf War. Yet when the economy faltered, Bush was drummed from office. Clinton presided over one of the longest periods of economic expansion in history, but his vice president, Albert Gore, still felt compelled to emphasize the economy's shortcomings during his presidential campaign.

Presidents also serve as the highest-ranking elected officials in their political parties. They must be sensitive to how their actions shape their parties' images. They must retain the support of their parties' most active members and contributors. If they do not satisfy their party constituencies, they may encounter difficulties with the party faithful in presidential primaries. In the 2000 primaries, when Democratic party activists considered Vice President Al Gore to be too moderate on health and environmental policies, many turned to Bill Bradley. This sort of defection is a common problem, since party activists are generally more extreme than typical voters are. Presidents have to find ways to balance the demands of their most ardent supporters with those of the electorate.

AN INVENTORY OF THE PRESIDENT'S LIMITED POWERS

Even if presidents can balance their national and party constituencies, they usually cannot take action on their pledges without considering their level of support in Congress. Accommodating congressional demands is particularly important because of the fundamental division of power between the executive and legislative branches written into the Constitution. Presidents are seldom in a position to force members of Congress to support them; they usually have to coax, beg, plead, and compromise to gain the necessary votes. Over 80 percent of the time, presidents either fail to secure passage of their major legislative agendas or must make important compromises to win congressional approval.[11]

Presidents find their positions particularly exasperating because the public expects them to take decisive action. The expectations they face have increased much more quickly than the powers they have to meet such expectations. Those who wrote the Constitution ensured that presidents would govern only with the help of Congress. The result is a government of "separated institutions sharing powers."[12] A thorough review of constitutional powers shows how little has changed to meet the increased expectations presidents face in America's new democracy, and how many powers rely on congressional cooperation (especially in domestic affairs.)

THE POWER TO PERSUADE   Perhaps the most important presidential power receives no direct mention in the Constitution. Modern presidents rely on hundreds of public speeches each year to set forth their visions of the country's future. They use their high profiles, as well as their responsibility to spread information about the government, as an opportunity to persuade Congress and the public at large to support their policies. Congress cannot check presidential propaganda, only reply to it—and members of Congress risk incurring either public or presidential wrath if they ignore the message.

The power to persuade is used much more publicly today than it was in the early years of the republic (see Figure 10.1). Early presidents seldom spoke in public, and when they did, their remarks were of a general nature. The Constitution requires that presidents report on the state of the union annually, but Thomas Jefferson and his immediate successors met this obligation through written messages to Congress. Early presidents usually avoided open involvement

FIGURE 10.1

Growth in presidential speech making

Presidents started giving more public addresses with the Progressive Era presidencies, from Theodore Roosevelt to Woodrow Wilson, but a big surge followed the spread of broadcast media.

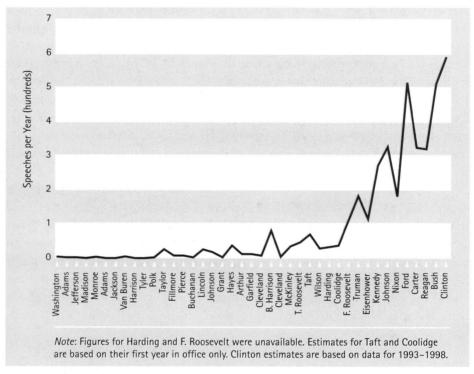

Note: Figures for Harding and F. Roosevelt were unavailable. Estimates for Taft and Coolidge are based on their first year in office only. Clinton estimates are based on data for 1993–1998.

SOURCES: Data on Washington through McKinley are taken from Jeffrey Tulis, *The Rhetorical Presidency* (Princeton, NJ: Princeton University Press, 1987), p. 64; for Theodore Roosevelt, see Robert V. Friedenberg, *Theodore Roosevelt and the Rhetoric of Militant Decency* (New York: Greenwood Press, 1990); for Taft, see *Presidential Addresses and State Papers of William Howard Taft*, Vol. 1, 1910 (New York: Doubleday); for Wilson, see Albert Shaw, ed., *Messages and Papers of Woodrow Wilson*, Vols. 1 and 2 (New York: Review of Reviews Corporation, 1924); for Coolidge, see Claude M. Feuss, *Calvin Coolidge: The Man from Vermont* (Hamden, CT: Archon Books, 1965); for Presidents Truman through Reagan, see Roderick Hart, *The Sound of Leadership* (Chicago: The University of Chicago Press, 1987); for Hoover, Bush, and Clinton, information is taken from *The Public Papers of the President*, various years.

in day-to-day politics, and when they did get involved, they seldom used public speeches to do so.[13] Jefferson, a master politician, invited members of Congress to the Executive Mansion (later called the White House) for dinners, at which he attempted to persuade them to support his political agenda.[14] He also communicated his views through friendly newspaper editors.

The first moves toward a vocal presidency came early in the twentieth century, during the Progressive Era (see Chapter 8). Perhaps more than any other president, Theodore ("Teddy") Roosevelt changed the definition of what was permissible in presidential rhetoric. Roosevelt liked to achieve results using what he called the **bully pulpit.*** Roosevelt suggested that, like a preacher, the president could use his position to move his "congregation"—the public—to action. Early efforts at public persuasion often failed, of course. As one historian has noted, "the number of laws [Roosevelt] inspired was certainly not in proportion to the amount of noise he emitted."[15] Yet Roosevelt's popular appeal ran high, so high that a cartoon depicting the president sparing the life of a bear cub resulted in the term "Teddy Bear."

A popular president
Although President Theodore Roosevelt was an avid hunter, it was his decision to spare the life of a bear cub in 1902 that led to the emergence of the term "Teddy Bear."

*Bully was nineteenth-century slang for "excellent."

Presidents since Teddy Roosevelt have increasingly used the bully pulpit to persuade others.[16] Woodrow Wilson addressed a joint session of both houses of Congress in 1913 to deliver a formal **State of the Union address,** a practice that has since become traditional in late January or early February.[17] Franklin Delano Roosevelt's "fireside chats" over the radio enabled him to sidestep the print media, which Republican publishers dominated.

President Reagan, the first president with experience as a professional actor, used television more effectively than any of his predecessors. He understood that there is but "a thin line between politics and theatricals."[18] Pictures were worth a thousand words, and body language spoke more convincingly than verbal formulations.[19] As Reagan once said, "I've wondered how people in positions of this kind ... manage without having had any acting experience."[20]

THE VETO POWER   Perhaps the most important *formal* presidential power is the **veto,** a limited ability to prevent bills passed by Congress from becoming law. The Constitution declared that, before any law "shall take effect," it must be "approved by" the president—whereas vetoed bills die unless "repassed by two-thirds of the Senate and House of Representatives." Before the Civil War, presidents seldom used the veto. President Washington cast only two. The average number cast by presidents between Madison and Lincoln was slightly more than four. Presidents from Franklin Roosevelt on have been much more willing to use the veto power (see Figure 10.2).

Congress usually fails to muster the necessary two-thirds vote in each chamber to **override** a veto. Since the Kennedy administration, Congress has overturned approximately 1 out of every 10.[21] Only 1 of President Clinton's 32 vetoes was overridden. The main check on the veto is simply its negative nature; it can stop policy change but not initiate it. During the energy crisis of the late 1970s, President Carter wanted an energy policy that was the "moral equivalent of war," but when confronted by opposition from oil-state senators, he was forced to sign a law much altered from his original proposals. Carter could have vetoed the legislation, but his desire for action required him to take what Congress was willing to give.

The veto gives presidents leverage when negotiating with Congress. In late 1999, even though President Clinton had suffered the disgrace of impeachment and was ineligible for reelection, he was able to use the veto to force Republicans to compromise with some of his policy objectives. Vetoes also allow presidents to define the terms of political conflict. Clinton both gained the upper hand in budget negotiations and increased his political support by vetoing a massive tax cut

FIGURE 10.2

Trends in presidential use of the veto power

Currently presidents use the veto less than they did at midcentury but more than they did in the 1800s. Why did presidents become more assertive?

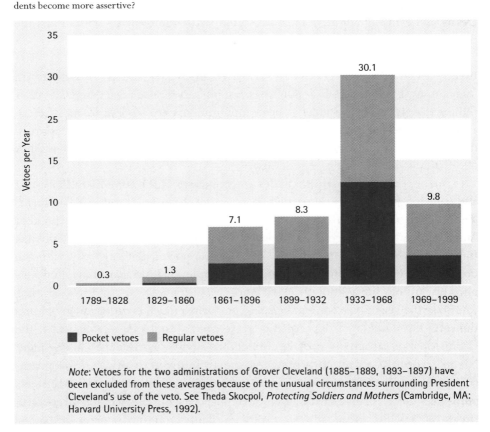

Note: Vetoes for the two administrations of Grover Cleveland (1885–1889, 1893–1897) have been excluded from these averages because of the unusual circumstances surrounding President Cleveland's use of the veto. See Theda Skocpol, *Protecting Soldiers and Mothers* (Cambridge, MA: Harvard University Press, 1992).

SOURCES: Figures from 1789–1996 are taken from Gary L. Galemore, "Presidential Vetoes, 1789–1996: A Summary Overview," Congressional Research Service Report for Congress, 97-163 GOV; figures from 1997–1999 are taken from Library of Congress, "Legislation: Bills, Amendments, and Laws," http://lcweb.loc.gov/global/legislative/bill.html, accessed December 7, 1999.

plan passed by Congress, for example. One GOP strategist acknowledged his advantages: "We've learned that it's nearly impossible to frame the national debate from the lower chamber of the legislative branch."[22]

If Congress enacts a law ten days before it adjourns, a president may exercise a **pocket veto** by simply not signing the bill into law. Nearly all of President Reagan's vetoes were pocket vetoes. Congress has no opportunity to override a pocket veto, so use of this power gave Reagan an aura of strength. The pocket-veto strategy works only at the very end of a congressional session, however; if Congress remains in session for more than ten days after passing a bill, the president must explicitly cast a veto to prevent the bill from becoming law. Congress remains in session virtually throughout the year, now that the lines between governing and campaigning have blurred, so the last few presidents seldom had the chance to cast pocket vetoes.

THE APPOINTMENT POWER   The Constitution allows presidents to "appoint Ambassadors, other public Ministers and Consuls . . . and all other Officers of the United States." These appointments are subject to the "Advice and Consent of the Senate," which is taken to mean that a majority must approve the nominations. The appointment power enables presidents to place thousands of officials in positions of responsibility.

The president's **Cabinet** includes key members of the administration. Most are heads of government departments and carry the title "secretary." The terms are left over from the days when a *secretary* was a confidential assistant who kept secrets under lock and key in a wooden *cabinet*. Originally, the president's Cabinet had but four departments, and the secretaries met regularly with the president. It was in Cabinet meetings, for example, that Abraham Lincoln developed his strategy for fighting the Civil War.

Over the years, government began to perform a much broader range of functions. As the number of departments grew from 4 to 14 (see Table 10.1), the Cabinet lost its capacity to provide confidential advice to presidents. In President Nixon's words, "Cabinet government is a myth and won't work. . . . No [president] in his right mind submits anything to his cabinet."[23] Today the Cabinet meets only occasionally, primarily for ceremonial purposes. But Cabinet jobs are still an excellent way for presidents to reward influential political supporters or to improve the administration's professional reputation by bringing in respected people.

INHERENT EXECUTIVE POWER   The Constitution declares that "the executive power shall be vested in a President." Some claim that this statement adds nothing to presidential power; it simply summarizes the specific rights granted to the president. But many presidents have found in this clause the basis for claims to additional rights and privileges. Presidential claims to inherent executive power have been invoked most frequently in making foreign policy, in part because the president is also recognized as **commander-in-chief** responsible for military matters and foreign affairs (see Chapter 15). But presidents have asserted inherent executive power on other occasions as well.

TABLE 10.1

ESTABLISHMENT YEAR AND INTEREST-GROUP ALLIES
OF EACH CABINET DEPARTMENT

Cabinet departments created after the nation's founding have specific issue domains and therefore fairly well-defined interest group constituencies. Why would outer Cabinet departments form alliances with interest groups?

DEPARTMENT	YEAR	INTEREST-GROUP ALLIES
Inner Cabinet		
State	1789	
Treasury	1789	
Justice (attorney general)	1789	
Defense	1789 (as War)	
Outer Cabinet		
Interior	1849	Timber, miners, ranchers
Agriculture	1889	Farm bureau, other farm groups
Commerce	1913	U.S. Chamber of Commerce, other business groups
Labor	1913	Labor unions
Health and Human Services	1953	American Association of Retired Persons
Housing and Urban Development	1965	National League of Cities, Urban League
Transportation	1966	Auto manufacturers, truckers, airlines
Energy	1977	Gas, oil, nuclear power interests
Education	1979	Teachers' unions
Veterans Affairs	1987	American Legion, Veterans of Foreign Wars
Environmental Protection Agency	Not an official department	Sierra Club, other environmental groups

One way in which presidents use their inherent executive powers is by issuing **executive orders**—directives to government employees that carry the weight of law even though they were not enacted by Congress. The Supreme Court ruled in 1936 that executive orders are constitutional, and since then they have increased in frequency and importance.[24] Truman used an executive order to desegregate the armed forces, Lyndon Johnson instituted the first affirmative action program, Ronald Reagan forbade homosexuality in the military, and Bill Clinton imposed sanctions on Haiti after a military coup in that country.

Executive orders may not run contrary to congressional legislation, and Congress may choose to overturn them after the fact. President Clinton decided not to issue an executive order removing the ban on gays in the military, for example, rather than face the threat of congressional action reversing him. However, presidents rarely worry about their executive orders being overturned, since passing a bill through Congress is so difficult and time-consuming (see Chapter 9). Figure 10.3 shows how sharply the use of executive orders has increased among modern presidents.

The most controversial invocation of inherent executive powers has been the doctrine of **executive privilege,** the right of the president to deny Congress information it requests. George Washington was the first to invoke executive privilege when he refused to provide Congress information about an ill-fated military expedition on the grounds that "disclosure . . . would injure the public."[25]

FIGURE 10.3

Significant executive orders, 1900–1996

A significant executive order *is defined as an order that receives mention in a Congressional hearing, on the floor of Congress, or in the pages of the* New York Times. Why do you think modern presidents have issued more executive orders than earlier presidents?

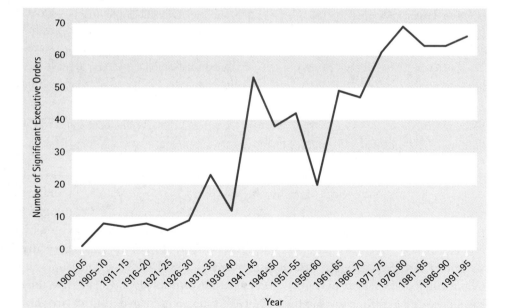

SOURCE: William Howell, "The President's Powers of Unilateral Action: The Strategic Advantages of Acting Alone." (Stanford University dissertation, 1999).

Ever since, presidents have claimed authority to withhold information on executive decision making from Congress.

The Watergate scandal brought this question before the Supreme Court. President Nixon had recorded extensive conversations with his aides and advisers. Prosecutors in the Watergate burglary case issued a subpoena to review the tapes, but Nixon refused to turn them over. The case quickly rose to the Supreme Court, but the Court's posture was rather confused. The justices could not agree on how much extra confidentiality a president needed.[26] They sanctioned the doctrine of executive privilege, saying that confidential conversations between the president and his aides were "fundamental to the operation of government and inextricably rooted in the separation of powers under the Constitution."[27] Yet they ruled unanimously against Nixon after reviewing the communications, explaining that he lacked sufficient privilege to frustrate a criminal investigation.

THE POWER AS CHIEF OF STATE Presidents often symbolize the United States to foreigners, including their political leaders. The Constitution anticipated this ceremonial role, indicating that presidents "shall receive Ambassadors and other public Ministers ... and shall Commission all the Officers of the United States." This clause seems to say little more than that presidents may welcome visitors and administer oaths of office. Yet the words endow presidents with an invaluable resource, the capacity to act with all the dignity countries accord heads of state.

According to Walter Bagehot, a nineteenth-century analyst of British politics, governments have both "efficient" and "dignified" aspects.[28] The efficient aspect of government involves setting policy, administering laws, and settling political disputes. This is the nuts and bolts of policy making, the kind of activity performed by prime ministers in England or France. It is also hard work that often generates conflict. But government has a dignified aspect equally important to its long-term effectiveness. Governments must express the unity of the people, their values and hopes. Monarchs often symbolize their nation, as in England, whereas in France an elected president (separate from the prime minister) serves this ceremonial role. In the American system, the executive must perform both jobs—as seen by President Bush's activities after terrorists attacked the United States, comforting the nation and formulating antiterrorism measures.

The dignified aspect of the presidency has always seemed somewhat inconsistent with America's egalitarian ideals. One of the issues discussed in the very first Congress was how to address George Washington. A Senate committee recommended "His Highness the President of the United States of America and

Protector of Their Liberties," whereas the House, objecting to royal language, pushed the simpler title preferred by Washington: "the President of the United States."[29]

Presidents differ in their level of comfort with the pomp and circumstance of office. Ronald Reagan emphasized the dignified aspect of the presidency—overseeing formal parties, appearing frequently at ceremonial events, but delegating day-to-day policy concerns. Bill Clinton initially took quite the opposite tack, becoming known as a "policy wonk." Eventually he distanced himself from the efficient side of governing, cultivating a strong but sympathetic image during national tragedies. The change helped him gather greater public support in subsequent years, until personal transgressions diminished some of his moral authority.

The balance presidents must seek between efficient and dignified activity changes with the times and with political events. Richard Nixon liked to listen to the presidential song, "Hail to the Chief," and to review ranks of marching soldiers at strict attention. His historical visit to China took on almost mythic proportions, leading composer John Adams to portray Nixon as an heroic figure in an English-language opera. After Watergate such pretensions began to look dangerous. Gerald Ford, a former college sports hero, distanced himself from his "imperial" predecessor by clowning on television. Jimmy Carter wore a sweater and carried his own suitcases; voters generally called him by his first name.

An informal president
President Jimmy Carter was uncomfortable with the dignified aspect of the presidency, adopting a casual style even when meeting with chiefs of state. He donned his trademark sweater for negotiations with Egyptian President Anwar Sadat.

As presidents have become increasingly engaged in policy, they have found it harder to maintain dignity—especially given increased media scrutiny. Some have received assistance from their families. First Lady Jacqueline Kennedy invigorated Washington art and culture and restored the White House. Barbara Bush's gray hair and unflappable demeanor gave her a matronly appeal that crossed political boundaries. Chelsea Clinton's maturity on trips to foreign nations, and her apparent devotion to her father even after the revelation of his affair with someone roughly her own age, may have helped Clinton survive his worst sex scandal.

But presidential family members can be a liability as well as an asset. George W. Bush's daughters, Jenna and Barbara, both faced busts for underage drinking—resulting in embarrassments for both Bush and the Secret Service. First Ladies Eleanor Roosevelt and Hilary Clinton angered conservatives by working for left-wing social policies,[30] and Nancy Reagan often attracted the scorn of liberals. Clinton in particular may have redefined the role of first lady, parlaying her position into a successful run for one of New York's U.S. Senate seats.[31] If their spouses continue to use their posts as political offices and their family members continue to face intimate media scrutiny, presidents will have to maintain dignity in some other fashion.

Similarly, the vice presidency once served a primarily ceremonial function, but the job has become more politicized in the last several decades. Perhaps

A mother's revenge
President George W. Bush's two daughters, Jenna and Barbara, created a minor scandal when they were accused of underage drinking. First Mother Barbara Bush, who had to grapple with the president's own disciplinary problems, quipped that "he is getting back some of his own."

because of the greater awareness that the vice president may one day gain the highest office, the role of the vice president has steadily broadened. For example, Vice President Albert Gore played a key role in shaping the Clinton administration's environmental policy. Richard Cheney, George W. Bush's vice president, was selected for his familiarity with national-security issues.

THE POWER TO RECOMMEND   Presidents who served before the Civil War seldom developed or promoted policies of their own.[32] They stayed out of the explosive slavery issue—a principle of silence that extended to other issues as well, especially after deliberations started on Capitol Hill.[33] Yet the Constitution explicitly encourages presidents to recommend for congressional "consideration such Measures as he shall judge necessary and expedient." This power expanded rapidly after the end of the Civil War. The country was growing swiftly, and many social and economic problems broadened in scope.

The power to recommend gives presidents the ability to initiate debate, to set the political agenda.[34] Presidents can shut down old policy options, create new possibilities, and change the political dialogue. Ronald Reagan placed defense increases and shrinking government on the policy agenda. Bill Clinton proposed broadening health care coverage, reforming welfare, and reducing class sizes in public schools. Theodore Roosevelt made conservation a major public concern. Franklin Roosevelt persuaded Congress to pass dozens of bills within 100 days of his inauguration.

However, this power does not go unchecked. Congress can—and often does—ignore or greatly modify presidential recommendations. Congress rejected Clinton's health care proposals and greatly modified his proposals on welfare reform. Nor is the power to initiate limited to the president. In 1994, congressional Republicans campaigned on what was called a Contract with America that set the policy agenda for the next two years, although only a small portion of the proposals became law.

Presidents have the best opportunity to initiate policy in the first months after their election. For this reason, presidents make most new proposals at the start of their terms (see Figure 10.4). "You've got to give it all you can that first year," one of Lyndon Johnson's top aides noted, "You've got just one year when they treat you right."[35] The 75-day **transition** period between election day and the inauguration of a new president is critical. Incoming presidents do not yet have the burdens of office, but they have the time, resources, and importance to prepare for power. The transition period is typically followed by the presidential **honeymoon**—the first several months of a presidency, when reporters are

FIGURE 10.4

The presidential legislative agenda

Presidents offer their largest agenda during their first terms. Why do presidents try to get the most done in their first year in office?

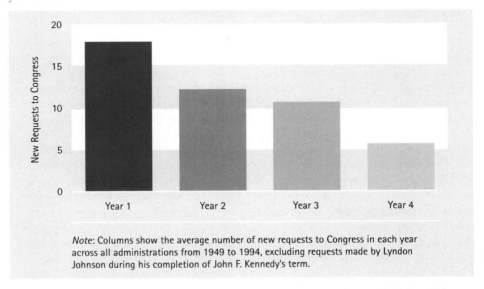

Note: Columns show the average number of new requests to Congress in each year across all administrations from 1949 to 1994, excluding requests made by Lyndon Johnson during his completion of John F. Kennedy's term.

SOURCE: Calculations are based on data drawn from Lyn Ragsdale, *Vital Statistics on the Presidency* (Washington, DC: CQ Press, 1996).

kinder than usual, Congress more inclined to be cooperative, and the public receptive to new approaches.[36] Presidential popularity is at its peak, and public interest is high. A crisis, such as the September 11 terrorist attack in 2001, also can give a president extra influence (see the Election Connection, "Unified in the Face of Terrorism").

THE BUDGETARY POWER Before 1921, every federal agency sent its own budget to Congress for examination by an appropriations subcommittee. No one, not even the president, knew whether agency requests exceeded government revenues. President Woodrow Wilson asked for a bureau to coordinate these requests, but Congress at first refused to create one, saying it would encroach on congressional authority. However, when federal deficits ballooned during World War I, Congress relented.

Originally known as the Bureau of the Budget, the agency is now called the **Office of Management and Budget (OMB),** a name that reflects its enlarged

ELECTION CONNECTION

Unified in the Face of Terrorism

Americans initially were divided over George W. Bush's presidency, with little more than half approving of his performance. Then, on September 11, 2001, terrorists hijacked airliners leaving three East Coast airports and targeted them at major American landmarks. Two struck Manhattan's World Trade Center, killing thousands and toppling twin towers that once dominated the urban skyline. Another struck the heart of the U.S. military, the famous five-sided Pentagon building in Washington, D.C.

All of a sudden everyone seemed happy with President Bush. Almost 9 out of 10 Americans reported to pollsters that they were satisfied with the job he was doing. Only two modern presidents have attracted such widespread popularity: Truman after World War II and Bush's father during the Gulf War. Nor was the wave of good feeling limited to regular folk. Democratic and Republican congressional leaders jointly pledged support for Bush and then broke into a chorus of "God Bless America." Congress voted almost unanimously to give the White House extensive power to fight terrorism and freed up $40 million for the crisis.

This wave of support may seem odd. President Bush played no role in the terrorist strike. Nor was his initial response extraordinary—he bounced around a few command centers before returning to the nation's capital to give a brief speech expressing his condolences and vowing to fight back. Why would Bush be so popular all of a sudden? Americans responded to the terrorist attack much as they respond to any other foreign policy crisis: they rally around the flag (see Chapter 15). Americans instinctively pull together to maintain a unified front against a hostile world, and do not criticize the resident of the Oval Office. For this reason, a national security threat can present the defining moment in any presidency. It allows leadership at a time when passions run high and political obstacles are minimal.

But with the new popularity comes a serious price: Americans expect to see quick performance. President Bush faced overwhelming expectations after the tragedy, including consoling the bereaved, increasing protections at home, exacting revenge abroad, shoring up the economy, and building international coalitions. Such demands are severe, almost certain to swamp other policy goals. Then, after a crisis is over, unity dissolves rapidly, and public attention wanders. Presidents rarely profit from disaster.

What do you think?
- Should presidents be judged by how they perform in extraordinary conditions or ordinary ones?
- Is Bush's situation similar to that faced by other wartime presidents, or does fighting terrorism require different presidential abilities?

SOURCES: Richard Morin and Claudia Deane, "Americans Approve of Bush's Handling of Crisis," *Washington Post* (September 13, 2001); Richard Benedetto and Patrick O'Driscoll, "Poll Finds a United Nation," *USA Today* (September 18, 2001).

responsibilities. Although development of the president's budget is still its most important job, OMB also sets personnel policy and reviews every piece of proposed legislation that the executive branch submits to Congress to ensure that it is consistent with the president's agenda. Agency regulations, too, must now get

Cartoon appeared in *Newsweek* (December 18, 2000), p. 23. © 2000 credited to Markstein, *Milwaukee Journal Sentinel.*

Battered but functional

Presidents usually enjoy a brief honeymoon period right after their elections, a time when the country is guardedly optimistic, public opinion embraces them, and Congress is more willing to pass their legislative agenda. This cartoon illustrates what many observers feared: The contentious 2000 election would leave a president with little honeymoon. Yet President Bush's approval ratings early in his term ended up reasonably high, and he was able to achieve his main policy goal in the first year: a significant tax cut.

OMB approval. One bureau chief claimed that OMB has "more control over individual agencies than . . . [the departmental] secretary or any of his assistants [do]."[37]

OMB was once considered a professional group of technicians, who searched for budget cuts. But OMB became more political as deficits took center stage in the electoral politics of the 1980s and 1990s.[38] Former Congressman David Stockman, Reagan's OMB director, led the fiscal side of the Reagan revolution.[39] Clinton's first OMB director, Leon Panetta, also came with congressional experience. The office has become a source of political power.

Congress created the Congressional Budget Office (CBO) in 1974 to counterbalance OMB's influence somewhat. The CBO evaluates presidential budgets as well as the budgetary implications of other legislation. CBO's sophisticated analyses of budget and economic trends have caused its influence in Washington to grow to the point where it now stands as a strong rival to OMB. In the health care policy debate, for example, it proved to be a "critical player in the game" whose estimates of the costs of health care reform doomed most proposals.[40]

THE IMPEACHMENT THREAT

Presidents may be impeached by a majority of the House for "high crimes and misdemeanors." The president leaves office if the Senate convicts by a two-thirds vote. Nothing makes more clear the subordination of presidents to Congress than the fact that legislators can remove the executive at will. Although seldom used, the constitutional power of **impeachment** is no dead letter. President Clinton's affair with a White House intern led to the first impeachment and trial of a president in over a century.

The President's sexual misconduct became a political issue when Paula Jones, an Arkansas public employee, sued Clinton for sexual harassment. She claimed that then-Governor Clinton had exposed himself to her in a Little Rock hotel room and requested sexual favors. Lawyers for Jones probed Clinton's romantic life while building their case, hoping to establish a pattern of sexual contact between Clinton and his employees and acquaintances. Under oath, Clinton denied having sexual relations with numerous women, including a young White House intern named Monica Lewinsky.

Evidence later appeared suggesting that Clinton and Lewinsky had indeed engaged in various forms of sexual conduct, including oral sex. Former solicitor general Kenneth Starr, who was investigating Clinton land deals, learned of this evidence contradicting the President's sworn testimony. So Starr expanded his investigation to include possible perjury and obstruction of justice charges, and eventually issued a report for Congress to use in impeachment hearings. The House voted (along mostly partisan lines) to impeach Clinton on December 19, 1998, making him only the second U.S. chief executive to face possible removal.

The Senate decided in early 1999 to acquit Clinton after his trial. The President eventually owned up to deception but claimed his denial was not official perjury because the Lewinsky affair did not include "sexual relations" as Clinton understood the term. Public reaction to the explanation was hard to read. Clinton remained popular, and some attributed Republican losses in the 1998 congressional elections to a perception that the GOP had tried to overturn the 1996 election. At the same time, Democrats apparently suffered in the 2000 elections because of the administration's poor image.

The Lewinsky scandal illustrates that Congress's impeachment power operates under an implicit check. The Constitution requires a two-thirds vote to remove a president after impeachment, thereby almost always requiring an overwhelming bipartisan effort. That effort will not arise in politically motivated impeachments, since members of Congress will not vote to remove an executive from their own party unless they feel they must. Impeachment is only feasible when a president's actions fundamentally violate the norms of American politics, as Richard Nixon's apparently did during the Watergate scandal.

Yet Clinton's scandals altered the American presidency in one important respect: They may have ended the use of **independent counsels** (also known as special prosecutors), investigators appointed to look into reports of executive-branch wrongdoing. Starr was able to spend huge sums of money investigating Clinton's sexual misdeeds because a judicial panel had appointed him in 1994 to look into an unrelated matter, the Whitewater land deals. Many observers decided afterward that giving roving investigators so much power and resources threatened the independence of the executive branch. The law expired in 1999, with few members of Congress favoring renewal and even Starr testifying against the law. Ethics investigations are now the province of the attorney general's office, part of the executive branch.[41] This change may make high-profile investigations less likely.

THE PRESIDENTIAL ADVISERS

The modern president's closest advisers are White House aides who deal in matters with utmost confidentiality. At one time the president's personal staff was small and informal. Abraham Lincoln had just two young assistants. Even President Franklin Roosevelt originally had only a handful of personal assistants.

To address organizational problems caused by the growing size of the federal government, Roosevelt in 1936 asked a committee of three specialists in public administration (headed by Louis Brownlow) to consider ways to improve federal government organization. Saying "the President needs help," the Brownlow Committee recommended sweeping changes throughout the government, including additional appointments to the president's personal retinue.

Congress rejected most of the Brownlow recommendations, but did agree to enlarge the White House staff.[42] The president's staff has steadily evolved in size and complexity.[43] The number of aides has grown from 48 in 1944 to over 400 today. These aides generally fill the **White House Office,** part of a much larger collection of presidential advisers and coordinating agencies called the **Executive Office of the President (EOP)** (see Table 10.2).

In Franklin Roosevelt's day, no single person headed the White House staff. Even as late as the Carter administration, White House aides worked together as

TABLE 10.2

EXECUTIVE OFFICE OF THE PRESIDENT,
BUDGET AND STAFF LEVELS

	BUDGET (MILLIONS)*	STAFF*
Office of Management and Budget	$60.6	518
White House Office	52.3	400
Office of National Drug Control Policy	48.0	124
Office of Administration	28.3	192
Office of the U.S. Trade Representative	24.2	178
White House Residence/Operating Expenses	8.1	91
National Security Council	6.8	60
Office of Policy Development	4.0	31
Office of Science and Technology Policy	5.0	39
Council of Economic Advisers	3.7	35
Office of the Vice-President	3.5	23
Council on Environmental Quality	2.7	22

*As of 1999.

SOURCE: Executive Office of the President, *Budget of the United States Government, Fiscal Year 2000,* Appendix.

"spokes in a wheel," each having direct access to the president. But today presidents usually place one person in charge.[44] This person, the **chief of staff,** meets with the president several times a day and communicates decisions to other staff, Cabinet officers, and members of Congress.

The best chiefs are usually Washington insiders. Although seldom acclaimed, Ronald Reagan's chief from 1987 to 1988, Howard Baker, was one of the most powerful and effective. A former Senate majority leader and presidential aspirant, Baker served at a time when he had forsaken all political ambition. Skilled at reaching compromises, Baker helped boost Reagan's popularity, despite the fact that the aging president had lost much of his former vitality.

Newcomers to Washington are usually less successful. Typically, they become lightning rods—people to be blamed when things go wrong. John Sununu, former governor of New Hampshire, was forced to leave the job of chief of staff when he was blamed for urging President Bush to sign an unpopular tax increase.[45] Thomas McLarty from Arkansas resigned when he was blamed for the Clinton administration's poor beginning.[46]

Although Brownlow expected White House aides to have "no power to make decisions," modern presidents regularly have used their staffs to shape their public policy proposals.[47] Within the White House staff, more than anywhere else, presidents can count on the loyalty of those around them simply because, unlike the careers of other bureaucrats, those of staff members are closely intertwined with those of the presidents.

The White House staff is more potent than ever in part because presidents have more need for political help. Presidents today need pollsters and consultants who can keep them in touch with changes in public opinion. Many observers criticized George W. Bush's early reliance on domestic-policy adviser Karl Rove, whose primary experience was in campaign politics. They attributed Bush's decision to halt Navy bombing on the Puerto Rican island of Viecques and his proposal to grant amnesty to as many as 3 million illegal Mexican immigrants to Rove's ambition to attract more of the Hispanic vote.[48] Presidents also need assistants who can help them communicate with the media, interest groups, and members of Congress. Once a major bill arrives for consideration on the chamber floor, White House aides are in regular contact with many legislators. In 1992, as part of the White House effort to enact legislation that would engage young people in a national service program, one aide personally contacted 67 Senate offices.[49] So intense is the work inside the White House that most staff jobs demand 7-day, 100-hour work weeks.

Quite apart from the president's genuine need for lots of political help, the White House staff is an excellent place to reward loyal supporters. Those who carry a candidate into office expect something in return after their candidate wins. The White House Office is a convenient place for the president to put campaign volunteers, because the president has exclusive control over appointments to his personal staff. None needs Senate confirmation, not even the chief of staff.

The number of people working at the White House sometimes provokes strong criticism from the opposition party, especially during presidential election years. When running for president, Bill Clinton promised to cut the White House staff by 25 percent. But when it came time to make the cuts, Clinton found his White House Office too valuable to be the target of cost-cutting efforts. Thus, the president made staff cuts elsewhere in the Executive Office of the President. The public's limited understanding of executive-branch organization prevented Republicans from getting much mileage out of Clinton's broken campaign promise.

Evaluating Presidents

Presidents are expected to be strong, yet presidential powers are limited. As a result, presidents seldom satisfy the hopes and aspirations of the voting public. Presidential successes are quickly forgotten, whereas their failures are often magnified by time. Presidents thus must work hard and exhibit impressive political acumen to convert their position into a source of continuing influence. Presidents add to their effectiveness by building up a strong professional reputation and extensive popular support—both more difficult to achieve, given the intrusive nature of presidential news coverage.

Presidents who are competent and reliable are more likely to gain the cooperation of Congress and other **beltway insiders,** the politically influential people who live inside the highway that surrounds Washington, D.C.[50] Presidents also need to maintain their popularity with the general public. As Abraham Lincoln shrewdly observed, "With public sentiment, nothing can fail; without it, nothing can succeed."[51] Popularity is now quite easy to assess; pollsters ask respondents about presidential performance every week!

All presidents experience fluctuations in their popularity over the course of their terms. Their support rises and falls with changes in economic conditions and in response to foreign policy crises. But in addition to these external factors, presidential popularity tends to decline over time as public expectations go unfulfilled.[52]

A study of the first term of eight recent presidents indicates that, apart from any specific economic or foreign policy events, their popularity on average fell by nearly 8 points in the first year and by 15 points by the middle of the third (see Figure 10.5). Their popularity recovered in the fourth year, when a presidential campaign was underway—either because presidents worked to communicate positive news about their administrations or because presidents start to look better when compared to their competition. Presidents regain popularity when reelected, but those bounces soon trail off.

Presidential Character

If presidential leadership is so difficult—requiring a strong professional reputation, robust public popularity, and the cooperation of numerous self-interested individuals—why are some past executives remembered as "Great Presidents"? What allows some presidents to succeed, even in periods of crisis, when most fail?

Political scientist James Barber traces success to the personality traits that make up presidential character (see Figure 10.6).[53] Effective presidents both like their job and readily adapt their policies to changing circumstances, Barber argues. Franklin Roosevelt was the ideal "active-positive" president. He loved his job and brought great energy to it.

FIGURE 10.5

Decline in presidential popularity over the first term

The president's popularity typically declines until the year before the next election.

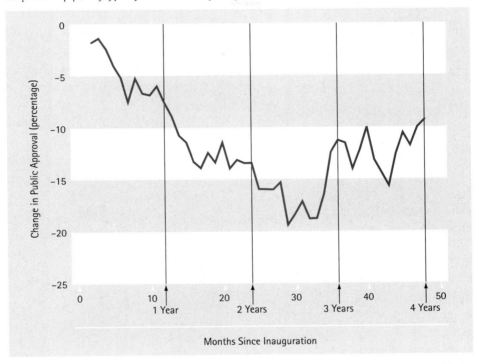

Source: This figure is taken from Paul Brace and Barbara Hinckley, *Follow the Leader: Opinion Polls and the Modern Presidents* (New York: Basic Books, 1992), p. 33, Figure 2.3.

Barber argues that most other modern presidents lacked one or the other of these two character traits. President Eisenhower brought a positive attitude, but he was passive, waiting for others to pose solutions to problems. Lyndon Johnson and Richard Nixon brought an "active-negative" attitude to the job. Both saw power as a burden and focused their energy on trudging through duties, which limited their adaptability. Each pursued a policy position long after "Great Presidents" would have changed course. Johnson led the country more deeply into the Vietnam War; Nixon tried to "cover up" Watergate misdeeds.

Critics of Barber's schema say he places too much emphasis on presidential activity.[54] Not everyone believes a president *should* be aggressive.[55] And the appearance of action is not the same thing as concrete performance. Bill Clinton was active, but he often failed to achieve policy goals. Eisenhower appeared passive, but presidential analyst Fred Greenstein shows that he governed with a

FIGURE 10.6

Presidential character

Political scientist James Barber popularized a typology that categorizes presidents according to their approach to the job. Great presidents, he says, are those with energy and a positive attitude. Does presidential effectiveness depend on each officeholder's personality?

	PRESIDENT HAS **HIGH** ENERGY LEVEL.	PRESIDENT HAS **LOW** ENERGY LEVEL.
PRESIDENT ENJOYS THE JOB.	Active-Positive Examples Thomas Jefferson Franklin Roosevelt	Passive-Positive Examples James Madison Dwight Eisenhower
PRESIDENT IS DISCOURAGED BY THE JOB.	Active-Negative Examples John Adams Lyndon Johnson	Passive-Negative Examples George Washington Calvin Coolidge

SOURCE: Adapted from James Barber, *The Presidential Character: Predicting Performance in the White House,* Fourth Edition. (Englewood Cliffs, NJ: Prentice-Hall, 1992).

"hidden hand."[56] Ike let others grab the headline, but steered the ship from behind; he stayed out of controversy and preserved his popularity. Reagan was hardly a detail man—on the contrary, he seldom let the presidency interfere with a good afternoon nap.[57] Yet his use of the power of the dignified presidency, together with his focus on fundamental goals, made him a powerful political force.

THE POLITICAL TIME

Presidential success may depend less on personality than on the circumstances, the "political time" in which they attain office.[58] According to presidential scholar Stephen Skowronek, most presidents are so hemmed in by the checks placed upon them that they simply cannot satisfy public expectations. As a result, presidents become "great" only when political circumstances allow them to move in a sharply different direction—usually in periods of crisis or right after an election that upsets the balance of political power (see Chapter 8).

Skowronek's model is not perfect. Many people think Theodore Roosevelt was one of the country's most successful presidents, but he did not become president through a pivotal election or at a time of crisis. And some people think other presidents—Eisenhower (for managing the Cold War) or Johnson (for initiating the Great Society)—deserve inclusion at the top of the list of presidents.

Nevertheless, dramatic presidential leadership generally seems to require strong party majorities in Congress.[59] On most issues, presidents gain more support from members of their own party than from the opposition. Members of a president's party in both the House and the Senate vote with their leader somewhere between 70 and 80 percent of the time. Opposition-party members vote with presidents somewhere between 40 and 50 percent of the time. Almost all the "great" presidents enjoyed an imbalanced Congress favoring their party.[60]

Recent events provide a clear illustration of the importance of congressional majorities. During the first two years of President Clinton's administration, he enjoyed a Democratic party majority in both the Senate and the House. During this time Congress approved several significant components of Clinton's election platform, including laws that eased voter registration requirements, provided medical and family leave for new parents, and reduced the budget deficit. After Democrats lost their majority in the 1994 elections, Clinton was forced to scale back his own agenda and accepted Republican welfare proposals with which he did not altogether agree. He even suffered impeachment by the House of Representatives as a result of the Lewinsky scandal.

SCANDALS IN THE WHITE HOUSE OFFICE

The highly personal and partisan nature of the White House staff can be a weakness as well as a strength. A White House full of personal friends and fellow partisans has at times so shielded presidents from external criticism that chief executives have lost touch with political reality. And sometimes staff members have used the power of the presidential office for improper, even illegal, purposes — paving the way for momentous scandals that tarnished both the sitting president's reputation and that of the presidency as an institution.

Scandals are hardly new to American politics. When lawmakers discovered that Abraham Lincoln's wife and her assistants outspent housekeeping funds, Lincoln successfully pleaded with Congress to appropriate more money secretly rather than to carry out an investigation.[61] But the intensity and significance of White House scandals have escalated in recent decades.[62] In addition to the Lewinsky scandal, two major and many more minor scandals have captured the attention of the nation and carried the potential for impeachment.

The most serious was the Watergate scandal during the Nixon administration. In 1972, at the instigation of members of the White House staff, five men broke into Democratic party headquarters at the Watergate condominium complex in Washington, D.C., apparently to obtain information on Democratic party campaign strategies. Nixon's chief of staff, Bob Haldeman, knew that the burglars had received "hush money" so that they would not reveal White House involvement. When tapes of Nixon's own conversations indicated that the president himself had been involved in the cover-up, the House initiated impeachment proceedings, which convinced the president to resign.

In the Iran–Contra scandal, staffers in the Reagan White House illegally sold arms to the Iranian government and gave the profits, also illegally, to a group of guerrillas known as Contras who were fighting to overthrow a left-wing government in Nicaragua. White House aides faced prosecution and some Democrats talked of impeachment, but no direct evidence implicating the president turned up.

THE BUREAUCRACY

Bureaucracies are essential to governmental action. Laws become effective only when an agency implements them. Without some kind of organization, government cannot build roads, operate schools, put out fires, fight wars, distribute social security checks, or do the thousands of other things Americans expect.

The federal government encompasses hundreds of agencies, most grouped under 1 of 14 **departments,** collections of federal agencies that report to a secretary who serves in the president's Cabinet. Some 63 **independent agencies,** such as the Central Intelligence Agency and the Environmental Protection Agency, are free-standing entities that report either to the president or to a board.[63] Finally, there are 27 **government corporations,** independent organizations that fulfill business-related functions.[64] Examples of government corporations include the Federal Deposit Insurance Corporation, which insures bank deposits, and the National Railroad Passenger Corporation, which runs Amtrak.

Americans often express frustration that the federal bureaucracy is arrogant and unresponsive. Three-fourths of all Americans think "people in the government waste a lot of money we pay in taxes" (see Figure 10.7). It is the big-government monolith that many disparage and some fear: the regulators, the tax collectors, and the social engineers. It is the villain of movies and television shows, such as *The X-Files.* Several presidents won office by campaigning against the government, promising to get the bureaucracy under control. Ronald Reagan's message was

FIGURE 10.7

The public thinks there is a lot of waste in government

Survey respondents were asked the following question: "Do you think that people in the government waste a lot of money we pay in taxes, waste some of it, or don't waste very much of it?" What do you think? Is the public justified in its belief that the government wastes a lot of money?

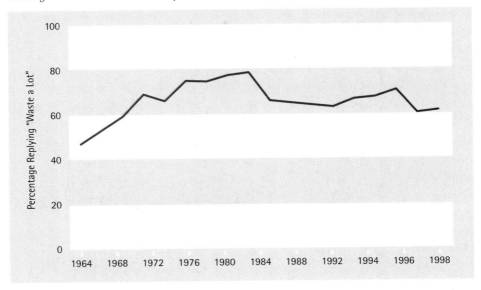

Source: National Election Study, 1948–1998 Cumulative Data File, conducted by the Center for Political Studies at the University of Michigan.

perhaps the most stark, as in this oft-quoted line: "Government is not the solution to our problem. Government *is* the problem."[65] But the size and power of government almost never shrinks; the sense of public vulnerability seldom diminishes.

Ironically, the public is partly to blame for their own sense of helplessness. The number of functionaries has greatly increased with the expansion of federal government responsibility, but few of these workers answer directly to elected national leaders. Most employment growth has occurred at state and local levels (see Figure 10.8). Since these positions often grow out of federal mandates or programs, the bureaucrats are not fully answerable to elected officials at any specific level of government. Many private contractors also perform tasks funded by government agencies. The decision to construct this "shadow government," over which elected federal officials exercise only indirect influence, is a policy choice resulting from conflicting public demands. The voting populace opposes growth in the federal bureaucracy, but expects national leaders to accomplish an increasing number of tasks.

FIGURE 10.8

Government employment, 1946–1997

The number of state and local employees has increased, but the number of federal employees has remained about the same. Note that federal government employment figures include civilians only. Military employment figures include only active-duty personnel.

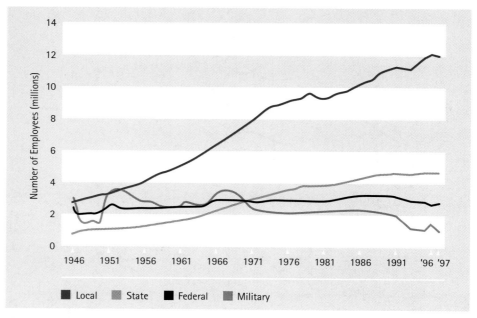

SOURCES: U.S. Bureau of the Census, *Historical Statistics of the United States: Colonial Times to 1970* (Washington, DC: GPO, 1975), pp. 1100, 1141; Advisory Commission on Intergovernmental Relations, *Significant Features of Fiscal Federalism, 1994* (Washington, DC: ACIR, 1994), Table E; Harold W. Stanley and Richard G. Niemi, *Vital Statistics on American Politics*, Fourth Edition. (Washington, DC: CQ Press, 1994), pp. 359–360; *Statistical Abstract of the United States, 1999*, Tables 534 and 578.

THE BUREAUCRACY PROBLEM

Ideally a bureaucracy is organized to achieve assigned tasks efficiently. Staff members are selected for their ability to do their jobs. Each reports to a superior, and ultimate authority is exercised by the head of the agency. The bureaucracy provides each worker with the supplies necessary to get the job done. The ideal is best exemplified by soldiers on parade, marching together in lockstep formation. When all works perfectly, bureaucracies exhibit unity, focus, and power.[66]

Although the ideal bureaucracy has tremendous potential, many forces inhibit perfection. Some of these flaws are inherent to all bureaucracies: they are slow to change, they have a tendency to expand, and performance is difficult to measure by outsiders. Other flaws, however, reflect the demands imposed on government bureaucrats through democratic elections: they often work under impossible expectations or debilitating limits. Taken together, these flaws create what is known as the "bureaucracy problem."[67]

SLOW TO CHANGE   Any large governmental organization has standard decision-making procedures. Standardization is essential if large numbers of people are to coordinate their work toward some common end. Otherwise, staff would be so confused they soon would be unable to do anything. Institutional habits are hard to break, though, making bureaucracies slow to adapt.[68] The U.S. Customs Service issued forms in the 1970s that "have not changed to any great extent since 1790, and merchant vessels today are required to report on the number of guns mounted."[69] As one humorist observed, "Bureaucracy defends the status quo long past the time when the quo has lost its status."[70]

EXPANSIONARY TENDENCIES   Once bureaucracies are created to address problems, they generally try to expand so they can address them better. Government agencies almost always feel they need more money, more personnel, and more time to perform effectively.[71] The head of the Forest Service once exclaimed to a congressional committee: "Mr. Chairman, you would not think that it would be proper for me to be in charge of this work and not be enthusiastic about it and not think that I ought to have more money, would you? I have been in it for thirty years, and I believe in it."[72]

DIFFICULTY MEASURING PERFORMANCE   Measuring the performance of government agencies from the outside is difficult, sometimes almost impossible.[73] One might observe the social conditions agencies must address, but it is hard to know either (1) what conditions would be like without the agency's actions or (2) what an agency reasonably could accomplish given its resources.

The streets and parks may be strewn with litter, but are garbage collectors to blame for performing badly? Is City Hall to blame for funding garbage collections inadequately (and if so, is the problem low taxes, or waste elsewhere in the budget)? Or are inconsiderate citizens to blame for spreading more trash than current cleaning efforts can handle? Not even an agency's immediate supervisors may be able to make these sorts of judgments without expensive studies, perhaps of garbage collection in other cities or of the citizenry's sanitation habits. An elected official even further removed from collection efforts, who has less familiarity with street-level behavior, is almost helpless when trying to force innovations. Any attempt likely would anger employee unions and politically connected supervisors more than it would please inattentive voters. As a result, bureaucracies often have a reputation for inefficiency.

IMPOSSIBILITY OF TASKS   Most governmental tasks are difficult to accomplish. If they were easy, someone other than the government would have undertaken the job! Tasks are usually complex, funds limited, and goals vague.[74] Schools are expected to teach students—but as society changes and knowledge expands, then the possible content outpaces the resources. Transportation agencies are expected to achieve smooth-flowing traffic—but so many people demand the right to drive that avoiding bottlenecks would require paving almost everything. The Environmental Protection Agency is supposed to combat pollutants—but nearly all human activity pollutes, and citizens resist inconveniences that limit their own waste. With such conflicting responsibilities, agencies may have no hope of satisfying everyone.

RED TAPE   British bureaucrats once bound government and legal documents in a sticky, reddish tape, so that anyone wishing to access a file would have to cut through the wrapping first. Today, the phrase "red tape" refers to any delay imposed by a government agency, the proverbial "forms filled out in triplicate" and "bureaucratic runaround" about which so many people complain.

Obviously, individual customers experience numerous delays and must surmount numerous barriers when they seek assistance from government. These inconveniences often lead regular citizens to conclude that agencies are unresponsive to the public, and perhaps even malicious. To an extent this perception may be correct. Certainly, there are times when an agency creates red tape to limit the number of people who take advantage of a program or so that individual officials can "cut through the tape" quickly in exchange for rewards ranging from gratitude or flirtations all the way to political favors or even bribes.

But this sort of chicanery is almost certainly the exception rather than the rule. Complaints overlook that most red tape comes from elected officials, who require detailed documentation to explain spending and who force elaborate agency practices to promote political goals. As one analyst has observed, "One person's red tape may be another's treasured procedural safeguard."[75] Bureaucracies seem unresponsive to individual members of the public precisely because they are excessively responsive to public demands expressed through elections.

People often complain, for example, that it takes forever to get a bridge repaired. But bridge repair can be politically complicated. The design of the replacement bridge must be acceptable to neighbors. If the bridge is classified an historical landmark—as are a surprising number of bridges—the local historical commission must approve. The agency, when letting contracts, must advertise the job and allow time for the submission of bids. To avoid accusations of political favoritism, published criteria must guide the choice of contractors. And regulators must supervise the repairs themselves—not only to ensure quality, but perhaps also to ensure worker safety or avoid environmental damage. Once again, a common bureaucratic problem is not caused by malice, but by political demands that trace back to the public.

AMERICAN BUREAUCRACIES: PARTICULARLY POLITICAL

The bureaucracy problem exists in all countries, but American bureaucracies have special problems that are rooted in the country's unusual political history. U.S. bureaucracies had a difficult beginning. They were built with patronage, and modernized slowly through "bottom-up" civil service reforms.

DIFFICULT BEGINNINGS   American bureaucrats lack the noble heritage of their counterparts in other industrialized countries, where government departments evolved out of the household of the king, queen, or emperor. The lineage of federal bureaucrats in the United States is less distinguished. Few American parents dream of the day when their children will grow up to be bureaucrats! The framers could not even agree on where to put the people who would run the new national government. Finally, as part of a compromise, they agreed to locate the home of the federal government, the District of Columbia, on the Maryland–Virginia border. The land Congress had chosen was swampy and miserable. Visitors complained that it was thick with "contaminated vapour," which produced "agues and other complaints."[76] If the government was to attract quality workers, location would not be its main selling point.

MOUNTAINS OF PATRONAGE   President Andrew Jackson's administration pioneered the use of federal jobs as a political reward, or source of **patronage,** for supporters (see the Election Connection, "The Election of 1828 and the Spoils System"). The practice of hiring workers on the basis of party loyalty became known as the **spoils system** when New York Senator William Marcy attacked Jackson for seeing "nothing wrong in the rule that to the victor belong the spoils."[77]

Politicians in both parties quickly saw that the spoils system suited their needs, because it allowed them to use tax revenue as an indirect payment for campaign workers who took on arduous jobs such as passing out pamphlets, organizing rallies, and getting people out to vote.[78] The New York machine politician George Washington Plunkitt explained the logic in this way: "You can't keep an organization together without patronage. Men ain't in politics for nothin'. They want to get somethin' out of it."[79]

The Election of 1828 and the Spoils System

Patronage became a staple of American national politics with the election of Andrew Jackson in 1828. Jackson replaced 2,000 government workers with his own supporters, creating what came to be known as the spoils system. Jackson saw patronage as critical for building a campaign organization, but he also elevated the practice to the level of political principle. In Jackson's view, one person was as good as the next. Almost anyone could do government work, and therefore everyone should take a turn. Government offices should rotate, giving new people a chance to learn the skills and duties of public service.

Jackson believed he was making government more democratic. The spoils system ensured that government administrators were in tune with the views of the people. It also got rid of malcontents in the bureaucracy who might frustrate the new government. But it often meant the appointment of unsavory political cronies to such positions as New York customs collector, a job with a wealth of opportunities for personal enrichment. Jackson's appointee absconded to England when it became clear that he could not account for a million dollars worth of fees.

What do you think?
- Corruption aside, do you believe expertise is the most important criterion for selection of a bureaucratic worker? Or did Jackson have a point when he argued that ordinary people should be represented in federal agencies?
- What sorts of jobs are best suited for experts, and what kinds for nonexperts?

Patronage also made it easier for parties to raise large amounts of cash to fund campaigns. Government workers would receive open requests for political donations, knowing that failure to contribute their share could result in dismissal.[80] Politicians considered these practices a natural and legitimate part of politics.

Looking back on American political history, many scholars have found much to praise in the old spoils system.[81] For one thing, it helped immigrants adjust to the realities of urban life in the United States. "I think there's got to be in every ward somebody that any bloke can come to—no matter what he's done—and get help," said one Boston politician. "Help, you understand; none of your law and your justice, but help."[82] Some help took the form of jobs. Irish immigrants were particularly good at using politics to get ahead. In Chicago, the percentage of public school principals of Irish background rose from 3 percent in the 1860s to 25 percent in 1914. In San Francisco, it climbed from 4 percent to 34 percent over a similar period.[83] Affirmative action programs work much the same way: they allow disadvantaged groups to use their political leverage to gain a toehold in the economic and social mainstream.[84]

The spoils system nonetheless undermined the image of American bureaucracies. Education, training, and experience counted for little, and jobholders changed each time a new party came to power. As one Democratic leader joked after his party had been in power for years, a bureaucrat was "a Democrat who holds some office that a Republican wants."[85] The many decades of patronage politics have left an antibureaucratic legacy that continues to the present day. Not only do Americans consider government wasteful (review Figure 10.7), they also do not grant federal workers much credibility (see Figure 10.9).

BOTTOM–UP REFORM   Civil service reformers gradually eroded the spoils system. In the 1880s, these reformers—a group of professors, journalists, clerics, and business leaders—went under the unflattering name **mugwumps.**[*]

FIGURE 10.9

Government workers are thought to be less credible than other occupational groups

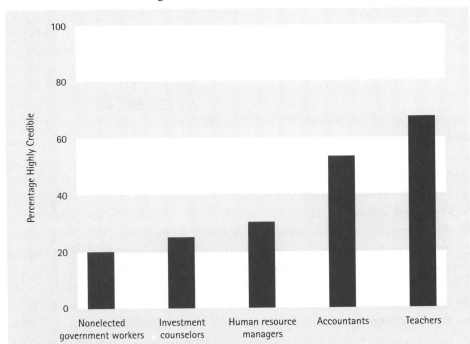

SOURCE: Gallup/Employee Benefit Research Institute Poll, April 1994 (USGALLUP.EBRI56).

[*]Originally a sarcastic term of abuse, the name is a modification of a Native American word meaning "great man" or "chief."

The reformers argued that government officials should be chosen on the basis of merit, not political connections. Mugwumps refused to back either political party, preferring to endorse reformers in both—leading to the quip that their "mugs" peered over one side of the fence while their "wumps" stuck out over the other.

The mugwumps won a succession of victories that gradually changed the system. Their first major breakthrough came in 1881 when President James Garfield was assassinated by a mentally disturbed man said to be a disappointed office seeker. Public scrutiny focused on the new president, Chester A. Arthur, who had once served as New York's customs collector and seemed to personify the spoils system. But the demand for reform swept the country, so Congress passed in 1883—and Arthur signed—the **Pendleton Act,** creating a Civil Service Commission to set up qualifications, examinations, and procedures for filling jobs.

Civil service reform occurred from the bottom up. Requirements initially applied mainly to lower-level, less-skilled jobs—those who swept the floors and typed government forms. Gradually, higher-level positions fell under the civil service system. Such additions were especially plentiful when the party in power expected defeat in the next election. By making a job part of the civil service, soon-to-be-ousted presidents blanketed in their position, making it impossible for their successors to replace unsupportive employees. Reform became nearly complete when, in 1939, Congress passed the **Hatch Act** barring federal employees from campaigning and solicitation. The mountains of patronage were all but worn away.

Patronage still survives in the American political system, but primarily among the most prestigious jobs. Those include most members of the White House staff, the heads of most departments and agencies, and the members of most government boards and commissions. Political appointees also predominate in the upper levels of individual agencies and departments, inhabiting offices bearing such titles as deputy secretary, undersecretary, deputy undersecretary, assistant secretary, deputy assistant secretary, and special assistant. The estimated number of these top-level agency appointees grew from less than 500 in 1960 to nearly 2,500 in 1998. Adding the White House staff, the total number of high-ranking patronage positions is estimated to be close to 3,000.[86]

The president's ability to recruit political allies for the top echelon of government has both advantages and disadvantages. On the positive side, it allows newly elected presidents to enlist people with innovative ideas, people who embrace their values and will lead agencies with these political goals in mind. For example, think-tank experts and business leaders helped design President Reagan's dramatic budget plans.

Yet the simultaneous arrival of so many new faces complicates the coordination of government. European and Japanese governments are marked by close, informal, long-time associations among leading administrators. In the United States, the average presidential appointee leaves office after only a little more than two years; almost a third leave in less than 18 months.[87] By the time they learn enough about an agency to lead it well, political appointees usually leave for other government posts or for better-paying jobs in the private sector. As public administration expert Leonard White once observed, "The previous experience of federal Secretaries does not usually prepare them to exercise quick and effective leadership."[88]

With rapid change in personnel, governmental memory becomes as limited as that of an antiquated computer. One Japanese trade specialist who negotiated with the United States observed that, "in the case of the United States, almost all of their negotiators seem like they came in just yesterday."[89] At one point in 1994, the differing styles of top Japanese and U.S. bureaucrats created a relationship so abrasive that the two countries broke off trade negotiations on the eve of a summit meeting.

Worst of all, the denial of most top-level positions to regular civil servants makes government work an unattractive career for intelligent, ambitious young people. In Japan, many of the top students graduating from the country's most prestigious law schools know that eventually they can reach the highest levels of government. But the peak of the U.S. government is not part of the bureaucratic career ladder.

PRESIDENTIAL CONTROL OVER THE BUREAUCRACY

An exasperated President Harry Truman once said, "All the president is, is a glorified public relations man who spends his time flattering, kissing, and kicking people to get them to do what they are supposed to do anyway." He was especially frustrated "when it comes to these bureaucrats."[90] The reason for Truman's frustration is clear: bureaucracies are generally difficult to maneuver, and the U.S. federal bureaucracy is even less maneuverable than most institutions because it operates under political constraints that limit effectiveness. The principal-agent problem is especially hard to master when the agents are either inexperienced political advisers or low-prestige civil servants.

Yet two other barriers stand in the way of presidential influence over the bureaucracy. First, by law many policy-making agencies in the executive branch need not answer directly to the president. Second, the president is seldom the only "boss" that bureaucrats have. They also answer to Congress, to special interests, and (at least indirectly) to the voting public. The principal-agent problem is mighty hard to solve when the agent can ignore the boss or play one boss off against the others.

INDEPENDENT REGULATORY AGENCIES

Not all agencies are part of Cabinet departments. Some of the most important, the independent agencies, have quasi-judicial regulatory functions meant to be carried out free from presidential interference. These agencies are generally headed by a board or commission appointed by the president and confirmed by the Senate. Independence from the president, which is considered desirable to insulate such agencies from partisan politics, is achieved by giving board members appointments that last for several years (see Table 10.3). For a number of agencies, a president may be unable to appoint a majority of board members until well into the second term.

Congress established most independent agencies in response to widespread public pressure to protect workers and consumers from negligent or abusive

TABLE 10.3

INDEPENDENT AGENCIES AND THEIR INTEREST-GROUP ALLIES

INDEPENDENT AGENCY	BOARD SIZE	LENGTH OF TERM (YEARS)	INTEREST-GROUP ALLIES
National Credit Union Administration	3	6	Credit unions
Federal Reserve Board	7	14	Banks
Consumer Product Safety Commission	5	5	Consumers Union
Equal Employment Opportunity Commission	5	5	Civil rights groups
Federal Deposit Insurance Corporation	5	3*	Banks
Federal Energy Regulatory Commission	4	4	Oil/gas interests
Federal Maritime Commission	5	5	Fisheries
Federal Trade Commission	5	7	Business groups
National Labor Relations Board	5	5	Unions
Securities and Exchange Commission	5	5	Wall Street
Tennessee Valley Authority	3	9	Regional farmers and utilities

*One member, the comptroller of the currency, has a 5-year term.

business practices. The Federal Trade Commission (FTC) was created in 1914 in response to the discovery of misbranding and adulteration in the meatpacking industry. The FTC was given the power to prevent price discrimination, unfair competition, false advertising, and other unfair business practices. Congress formed the Securities and Exchange Commission in 1934 to root out fraud, deception, and inside manipulation on Wall Street after the stock market crash of 1929 left many Americans suspicious of speculators and financiers.

When originally formed, most regulatory agencies aggressively pursued their reform mandates. But as the public's enthusiasm for reform faded, many agencies found that their most interested constituents were members of the very community they were expected to regulate. Thus the independent commissions have tended to become connected to organized interest groups.[91] In one instance, a regulator's legal fight to keep his job was financed by those subject to his regulation![92]

CONGRESS AND THE BUREAUCRACY

Everyone knows that no one should have more than one boss. When two or more people can tell someone what to do, signals get confused, delays ensue, and accountability suffers. It also becomes possible for employees to play one boss off against the other. However, the separation of powers ensures that every federal bureaucrat has many bosses. Presidents may appoint federal employees and otherwise execute policies, but Congress formally creates and funds government agencies. With Congress divided into House and Senate, and each chamber divided into many committees, bureaucrats often find themselves reporting to multiple bosses, all demanding and politically astute. This clamor for responsiveness from so many quarters means that the bureaucracy need not always give in to presidential demands or to congressional ones.

THE CONFIRMATION PROCESS   Congressional influence begins with the selection of executive department officers. The Senate's advice-and-consent power has long given Congress a voice in administrative matters. One mechanism for exercising influence is the practice of **senatorial courtesy,** an informal rule that sometimes allows senators to block potential nominees for positions within their states or regions. This practice allows senators to protect their political bases by controlling patronage and gives them indirect control over administrative practices.

Confirmation battles sometimes receive extensive media attention and so have become a new form of electioneering. Little-known senators can rise to national attention through their advocacy or opposition exhibited in confirmation hearings. Votes on whether to confirm a particular nominee also can become a campaign issue. For this reason, senators demand greater influence than that permitted by traditional courtesies. Senators now want public assurances that presidential nominees will take acceptable policy positions, do not have conflicts of interest that will prevent successful performance of their public duties, and have not acted contrary to laws or conventional moral norms.

The Senate rejected George H. W. Bush's nomination of John Tower as secretary of defense because of an acknowledged drinking problem. It forced Bill Clinton to withdraw the nomination of Zoe Baird as attorney general because she had not paid the required social security taxes for her housemaid. It denied confirmation of Henry Foster as Clinton's surgeon general because he had performed 39 abortions. George W. Bush's appointee for attorney general, former Missouri Senator John Ashcroft, endured intense scrutiny for exercising his senatorial courtesy power to slow the advancement of an African American judge he considered soft on capital punishment. Ashcroft also had to convince pro-choice senators that his strong pro-life stance would not prevent him from honoring the constitutional protections enjoyed by abortion clinics or their clients.

The Senate still rarely rejects presidential nominees. Yet the new, more election-driven confirmation process has had important consequences for administration. To decrease the likelihood of rejection, the White House must interview potential nominees at length, ask the FBI to undertake extensive background checks, and defend nominees against exhaustive senatorial scrutiny. When John Kennedy was president, the average nominee was confirmed in less than two and a half months. The confirmation of Bill Clinton's nominees required on average more than three times that long (see Figure 10.10).

AGENCY REORGANIZATION   Congress often interferes with agency organization, for example by opposing presidential proposals to reorganize executive departments. Congress resists change because each agency reports to a specific congressional committee, and these committees are frequently protective of their power, which allows them to serve constituencies back home. They therefore typically resist reorganization, no matter how redundant or antiquated existing organizational structures might be.[93] For example, Jimmy Carter proposed shifting worker training programs from the Department of Labor to the newly created Department of Education. But powerful senators defeated the proposal because they wanted to keep the programs within their committee's jurisdiction.[94] As seen at the beginning of this chapter, the same thing occurred when Vice President Gore proposed to move the DEA and ATF to the FBI.

FIGURE 10.10

Average time it takes presidential appointees to be confirmed

It has taken longer in recent years for presidential appointees to be confirmed. What role might elections have played in this trend?

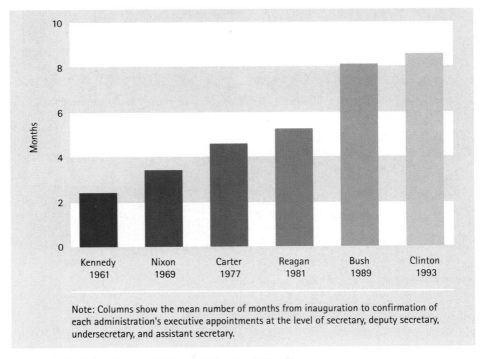

Note: Columns show the mean number of months from inauguration to confirmation of each administration's executive appointments at the level of secretary, deputy secretary, undersecretary, and assistant secretary.

SOURCE: Paul Light, *Thickening Government* (Washington, DC: Brookings, 1995), p. 68.

LEGISLATIVE DETAIL   Congress sometimes writes detailed legislation outlining an agency's specific legal responsibilities. Even legislation proposed by the president or by a specific agency will be revised extensively by Congress, mainly by the relevant committees.[95] Sometimes Congress invites an agency's clients to sue if they are discontented with their treatment. American bureaucracies therefore have limited authority over the jobs they do.

The issue of legislative detail is just another illustration of the principal-agent problem described earlier in the chapter. Members of Congress must balance their influence against administrative discretion: too many rules and opportunities for lawsuits will prevent bureaucrats from doing their jobs effectively; too few will allow either the president or the bureaucrats themselves to opt for policies different from what Congress prefers.

The industrial age's poison sniffers
The Environmental Protection Agency (EPA) faces the difficult task of protecting the environment from pollutants. What kinds of groups and individuals do you think might exert pressure on the EPA?

Legislative politics can produce absurd results. For over a decade, critics have ridiculed laws that give the Agriculture Department authority to regulate sausage pizzas but the Food and Drug Administration authority to regulate cheese pizzas. Agriculture receives its mandates from the House and Senate Agriculture committees, while the FDA operates under legislation authored by the House Commerce Committee and the Senate Human Resources Committee. No one wants to give up their slice of the pizza pie, so the odd division of agency responsibilities remains unresolved. The result, according to one report, "hinders the government's efforts to efficiently and effectively protect consumers from unsafe food."[96] The confusion also makes it rather difficult for a voter to figure out whom to blame if she gets sick after ordering a pan pizza with sausage and extra cheese!

BUDGETARY CONTROL   Every year each agency prepares a budget for the president to submit to Congress. That budget can go up or down at any stage in the legislative process, and with limited revenues, the fear is that it will drop substantially. One or two powerful congressional enemies can make an agency's experience unpleasant, and an agency whose budget request ignores the desires of important players in the appropriations process may jeopardize their funding. Congress therefore indirectly influences agency spending decisions.

Sometimes Congress will influence agency policies more directly. To ensure that agencies spend monies in ways consistent with congressional preferences, significant portions of many agency budgets are subject to an **earmark,** a very specific designation for how to spend funds. Some legislation even specifies particular congressional districts.

Earmarking seems to be on the increase. At one time Congress let the scientific community decide national research priorities, but between 1980 and 1995, the amount of research dollars earmarked for specific projects skyrocketed from $11 million to $875 million, often for pet projects at a representative's home university.[97] The greatest "earmarker" of all time may be the former chair of the Senate Appropriations Committee, Robert Byrd of West Virginia, beloved by constituents for his generosity with federal funds. For example, he once slipped into an emergency bill a provision that shifted the 2,600-employee FBI fingerprinting center from downtown Washington to Clarksburg, West Virginia.[98]

LEGISLATIVE OVERSIGHT Committees sometimes hold hearings to ensure that agencies are not straying from their congressional mandates. In recent decades the increase in such oversight hearings has expanded committee control over administrative practice. The number of days each year that committees hold oversight hearings nearly quadrupled between the 1960s and the 1980s.[99] At these hearings, members of the administration must testify about agency experiences and problems. Witnesses representing outside groups either praise or criticize the bureaucrats. Through the oversight process, committees decide whether to revise existing legislation or modify agency budgets.

Yet congressional influence is limited. Congress can enact general policies, but it cannot construct specific rules for every possible circumstance. Congress may decide to provide benefits to the disabled; but it is up to a bureaucrat to decide whether a particular handicap precludes employment, and it is up to the courts to determine whether the bureaucrat made the decision lawfully.[100] Often the difficulties of passing legislation will produce a bill even more vague than the policy area required. So Congress and the president both face the same problem when dealing with the federal bureaucracy: it is so large and complicated that exercising formal power can be terribly difficult. Bureaucracies will always exercise substantial influence over policy because of the need to grant them administrative discretion, the power to interpret mandates from elected officials.

INTEREST GROUPS AND THE BUREAUCRACY

The purpose of many Cabinet agencies is to provide interest-group access to the executive branch of government.[101] The Interior Department's job was originally to regulate the use of federal land, particularly in the West. Today, it maintains close ties to ranchers, timber companies, mining interests, and others who depend on federal lands for their livelihood. The Agriculture Department serves farmers; the Commerce Department helps business and industry, especially firms with overseas contracts; Labor defends unions; Health and Human Services heeds the American Association of Retired Persons; and Education pays attention to teacher organizations (review Table 10.1).

Presidents exercise their control over the Cabinet departments primarily by appointing political allies to top positions. But once they become agency heads, allies often identify more closely with their turf than with the president's program. This tendency to "go native" is particularly pronounced when an appointee already has close ties to interests connected to the department, when they are part of the issue network over which they suddenly gain responsibility (see Chapter 8).

ELECTIONS AND THE BUREAUCRACY

For more than a century, reformers have tried to separate politics from administration. Government should serve the people, they argue, not the special interests. Departments should make decisions according to laws and regulations, not in response to political pressure. Agencies should treat every applicant alike, not respond more favorably to those who contribute to political parties.

These reform principles are worthy of respect. When politics interferes, agencies can be inefficient and ineffective. The post office, long a patronage reserve, is said to deliver "snail mail." The customs service, its name once synonymous with political spoils, is still slow to report international economic transactions. The Department of Housing and Urban Development, always a political thicket, has at times so badly mismanaged property that it had to blow up buildings it constructed.[102]

Many of the more effective federal bureaucracies are less politically charged.[103] The National Science Foundation, protected from political pressures by an independent board, is known for the integrity with which it allocates dollars among competing scientific projects. The Federal Bureau of Prisons does a better job than many state prisons of maintaining security without depriving prisoners of rights; it has succeeded in part because members of Congress, respectful of prison leadership, have left the agency alone.[104]

But even though agency autonomy has worked in some instances, electoral pressures also have played a positive role and, in any case, are an essential feature of modern bureaucracies.[105] Public pressure exerted through elections has affected the way bureaucracies keep secrets, enforce the law, manage their budgets, and make decisions. In the end, elections create pressures that force many agencies to balance competing interests by striking compromises.

BUREAUCRATIC SECRECY   Bureaucracies like to protect their secrets. Inside knowledge is power. Secrecy can cover mistakes. Electoral pressures have sharply curtailed the amount of secrecy in American government. In the view of one specialist, "secrecy has less legitimacy as a governmental practice in the United States than in any other advanced industrial society with the possible exception of Sweden," in large part because "Congress has done a great deal to open up the affairs of bureaucracy to greater outside scrutiny."[106] Under the Freedom of Information Act of 1967, citizens have the right to inspect unprotected government documents. If the government believes the requested information needs to be kept secret, it must bear the burden of proof when arguing its case before a judge. The "sunshine law," passed in 1976, required that federal government meetings be held in public, unless they involve military plans, trade secrets, or personnel questions.

BUREAUCRATIC COERCION   Bureaucracies are often accused of using their coercive powers harshly and unfairly. Police officers stop young drivers for traffic violations that are often ignored when committed by older drivers. Bureaucratic zealots trick sales clerks into selling cigarettes to heavily bearded 17-year-olds. Disabled people are refused benefits because they do not fill out their applications correctly. Although such abuses occur, they happen less frequently because agencies are held accountable to the electorate.

In 1998, for example, Republican senators sensed popular discontent with the Internal Revenue Service (IRS), the government's tax collection agency. The agency's approval rating was an embarrassingly low 38 percent.[107] The Senate Finance Committee held a series of hearings that brought to light a litany of agency failings. The IRS had lost $150 billion in 1995 because of mistakes, unreported income, or improper deductions. Taxpayers were overbilled an average of $5 billion per year.[108] The technology the agency used was so outdated that even IRS Commissioner Charles Rossotti admitted, "I have never seen a worse situation in a large organization."[109] As a result of the hearings, Congress enacted a law restructuring the agency, making it harder for the IRS to accuse taxpayers of wrongdoing and bringing its tax collection systems up to date.[110]

AGENCY EXPANSION   Although agencies generally try to increase their budgets, elections brake such tendencies, if only because politicians get blamed for raising taxes. "As a general rule," says analyst Martha Derthick, "Congress likes to keep bureaucracy lean and cheap."[111] The number of people working for the federal government, as a percentage of the workforce, has declined (review Figure 10.8), in good part because elected officials are under public pressure to cut bureaucracy.

ADMINISTRATOR CAUTION   Federal agencies are sometimes accused of going beyond their legislative mandates. But most federal agencies err on the side of caution. The worst thing any agency can do is make a major mistake. As one official explained, "The public servant soon learns that successes rarely rate a headline, but government blunders are front-page news. This recognition encourages the development of procedures designed less to achieve successes than to avoid blunders."[112]

In 1962 doctors discovered that thalidomide, a sedative available to pregnant women in Europe, increased the probability that their babies would be born with serious physical deformities. Congress immediately passed a law toughening the Food and Drug Administration's procedures for regulating prescription drug distribution.[113] Two decades later, in keeping with this policy, the FDA refused to approve the sale of several experimental drugs to terminally ill people suffering from AIDS. When the FDA's refusal to allow experimentation became a public issue, the agency began to allow AIDS patients to try the untested drugs, this time loosening regulations in response to potential electoral pressures.

COMPROMISED CAPACITY   Agency effectiveness is often undermined by the very terms of the legislation that created it. For legislation to pass Congress, a broad coalition of support is necessary. To build this support, proponents must strike deals with those who are at best lukewarm to the idea. Such compromises, demanded by members of Congress to shore up their electoral support, can cripple a program.[114]

CHAPTER SUMMARY

Americans often wonder forlornly why the United States no longer elects great presidents who meet public expectations. They seem to believe that the failure is somehow one of insufficient public control over the political system. Yet most sources of frustration with the executive branch trace back to the demands of the public, or at least to the demands of elected officials who are then rewarded for their behavior.

One reason modern presidents fail is that they are expected to do so much. The institutions presidents must run and the problems they must solve have grown, yet their formal powers have changed very little. They still rely on cooperation from Congress. Passive presidents receive little praise but much scorn, and a president who preaches patience in the face of social problems risks reprisal from voters at the polls—even though presidents lack the opportunity to leave much of a stamp on government unless they are elected at the right political time.

Presidents oversee the federal bureaucracy, but their executive role confers problems as well as power. Not only do all bureaucracies exhibit certain operational flaws, American bureaucracies have specific troubles that can be attributed to the electoral climate in which they have evolved. Moreover, the president must share influence over the bureaucracy with numerous other actors, including Congress, interest groups, and the voting public. Most of these limitations ultimately derive from the elections so prominent in America's new democracy.

KEY TERMS

beltway insiders, p. 328

bully pulpit, p. 311

bureaucracies, p. 332

Cabinet, p. 314

chief of staff, p. 326

civil service, p. 340

commander-in-chief, p. 314

department, p. 332

earmark, p. 347

Executive Office of the
President (EOP),
p. 325

executive orders, p. 315

executive privilege, p. 316

government corporation,
p. 332

Hatch Act, p. 340

honeymoon, p. 320

impeachment, p. 324

independent counsel
(originally called special
prosecutor), p. 325

independent agencies,
p. 332

mugwumps, p. 339

Office of Management and
Budget (OMB), p. 321

override, p. 312

patronage, p. 337

Pendleton Act, p. 330

pocket veto, p. 313

principal-agent problem,
p. 307

senatorial courtesy, p. 343

spoils system, p. 337

State of the Union address,
p. 312

transition, p. 320

veto, p. 312

White House Office, p. 325

SUGGESTED READINGS

Barber, James. *The Presidential Character: Predicting Performance in the White House,* Fourth Edition. Englewood Cliffs, NJ: Prentice-Hall, 1992. Argues that presidential character affects presidential success.

Heclo, Hugh. "Issue Networks and the Executive Establishment," in Anthony King, ed. *The New American Political System.* Washington, DC: American Enterprise Institute, 1978. Describes the shift from iron triangles to issue networks.

ON THE WEB

The White House
www.whitehouse.gov
The official Web site of the White House offers current and historical information about U.S. presidents.

Center for the Study of the Presidency
www.thepresidency.org
The Center for the Study of the Presidency publishes *Presidential Studies Quarterly* and showcases academic information and links.

National Archives and Records Administration
www.nara.gov/nara/president/address.html
The National Archives and Records Administration provides information about and links to presidential libraries.

FedWorld
www.fedworld.gov
Most U.S. government agencies and departments have informative Web sites that can be reached through FedWorld.

Office of Management and Budget
www.whitehouse.gov/OMB/
The Office of Management and Budget offers copies of budget documentation, testimony before Congress, and regulatory information.

Congressional Budget Office
www.cbo.gov
The Congressional Budget Office provides copies of its reports on the economy, the budget, and current legislation.

General Accounting Office
www.gao.gov
The General Accounting Office, the investigative arm of Congress, assists Congress in its oversight of the executive branch.

National Performance Review
www.govinf.library.unt.edu/npr/default.html
The National Performance Review site provides information about the recent wave of "reinventing government" initiatives.

Jones, Charles O. *The Presidency in a Separated System.* Washington, DC: Brookings, 1994. Examines the role of the president under divided government.

Kernell, Samuel. *Going Public: New Strategies of Presidential Leadership,* Third Editon. Washington, DC: CQ Press, 1997. Describes the increasing tendency of presidents to use popular appeals to influence legislative processes.

Kettl, Donald F., and John J. DiIulio, Jr., eds. *Inside the Reinvention Machine: Appraising Governmental Reform.* Washington, DC: Brookings, 1995. Preliminary evaluation of the Clinton/Gore "reinventing government" initiative.

Korn, Jessica. *The Power of Separation: American Constitutionalism and the Myth of the Legislative Veto.* Princeton, NJ: Princeton University Press, 1996. Identifies the many ways in which power is shared between Congress and the executive.

Light, Paul. *Thickening Government: Federal Hierarchy and the Diffusion of Accountability.* Washington, DC: Brookings, 1995.

Identifies and explains the growth in higher-level governmental positions.

Morone, James A. *The Democratic Wish: Popular Participation and the Limits of American Government.* New York: Basic Books, 1990. Account of the ways in which democratic movements have shaped the development of public administration in U.S. history.

Neustadt, Richard E. *Presidential Power and the Modern Presidents.* New York: Free Press, 1990. Modern classic on the limits to presidential power.

Niskanan, William A. *Bureaucracy and Representative Government.* Chicago: Aldine-Atherton, 1971. Develops the argument that government bureaucracies seek to maximize their budgets.

Skowronek, Stephen. *The Politics Presidents Make: Leadership from John Adams to George Bush.* Cambridge, MA: Harvard University Press, 1993. Provocative analysis of the historical development of the presidency.

Tulis, Jeffrey. *The Rhetorical Presidency.* Princeton, NJ: Princeton University Press, 1987. Contrasts modern presidential rhetoric with that of early presidents. Argues against a rhetorical presidency.

Wilson, James Q. *Bureaucracy: What Government Agencies Do and Why They Do It.* New York: Basic Books, 1989. Comprehensive treatment of public bureaucracies.

Young, James. *The Washington Community 1800–1828.* New York: Harcourt, 1966. Engaging, insightful account of political and administrative life in Washington during the first decades of the nineteenth century.

11

THE JUDICIARY

T hurgood Marshall, the Supreme Court's first black justice, once jested, "I have a lifetime appointment and I intend to serve it. I expect to die at 110, shot by a jealous husband."[1] He nonetheless resigned in June 1991, reluctantly concluding that at age 83 he could no longer continue a civil rights struggle he had fought for decades. Asked by reporters why he was stepping down, an impatient Marshall declared, "I'm old! I'm getting old and coming apart."[2]

Marshall's retirement placed President George H. W. Bush in a bind. The Constitution allows presidents to appoint federal judges, but a majority of the Senate must confirm their choices. Most observers understood that, for symbolic reasons, President Bush would need to nominate an African American judge to replace Marshall. He could not afford to lose a confirmation battle in the Democrat-controlled Senate. But the pool of black conservatives from whom Bush might select was small, and almost any choice acceptable to a Republican president was bound to attract ire.

After days of media speculation, President Bush nominated Clarence Thomas, an African American with solid conservative credentials from his time as chair of the Equal Employment Opportunity Commission (EEOC). In stark contrast to the man he would replace, Thomas opposed affirmative action programs giving preferential treatment to minorities because "they assume that I am not the equal of someone else, and if I'm not the equal, then I'm inferior."[3] His general philosophy of constitutional interpretation also resembled that of the bench's most conservative members.

Democratic senators viewed the nominee with great suspicion, but at first it seemed that Thomas's political savvy would allow him to escape much criticism. For one thing, he had not publicly expressed his views on controversial constitutional issues, which made it more difficult for opponents to criticize his legal opinions. Thomas also realized that silence was golden during the nomination process. At the traditional confirmation hearings, members of Senate Judiciary Committee asked Thomas his opinion on the constitutionality of abortion bans no fewer than 70 times—but his replies were studiously vague.[4]

Liberal senators initially were easy on Thomas for another reason. Civil-rights groups had mixed feelings, disliking the nominee's views but encouraged that even a Republican president had heard their call for more blacks on the federal bench. They hesitated to oppose Thomas, whose defeat might give Bush an excuse to appoint a second judge of a different race. Moreover, opinion polls indicated that three-quarters of the black population, untroubled by his conservative opinions, supported Thomas' appointment.[5] Massachusetts Senator Edward Kennedy, opposed as he was to the Thomas nomination, had to admit, "In many ways he exemplifies the promise of the Constitution and the American ideal of equal opportunity."[6]

But Thomas ended up being the center of a political uproar after all—as the result of testimony by a soft-spoken young woman named Anita Hill. An attorney who once worked with the EEOC, Hill had left Washington politics to assume an academic position at the University of Oklahoma. She had left Washington, she told a friend, because Thomas had sexually harassed her.

Judiciary Committee staffers approached Hill, who told them her story. Within days, her accounts of sexual harassment leaked to the media. Liberal senators now had a legitimate justification for opposing Thomas, and they pounced. The committee scheduled televised hearings in which Hill described lewd and suggestive phrases she claimed to have heard from the mouth of a future justice of the Supreme Court. Thomas angrily denied all charges and called the televised Senate exploitation of Hill's allegations nothing less than a "high-tech lynching."[7]

The confirmation battle spilled out of the Washington beltway to involve men and women of all races and creeds all across the country. For the 14 Judiciary Committee senators forced to listen to the sensational testimony, it was a political nightmare. In some strange twist of politics, it was not just Thomas, but the Senate itself, that was on trial. When one senator explored Anita Hill's credibility through close questioning, women's groups attacked him for his aggressive style.

In the end, the Senate confirmed Thomas by a close vote. More Americans believed Thomas than believed Hill, and a clear majority continued to favor Thomas's confirmation.[8] The strong support Thomas received from black voters was particularly significant, since both Thomas and Hill were African Americans.[9] Yet the process had a dramatic effect on the next election. The more women thought about the outcome, the unhappier they became. The percentage of women who believed Thomas had harassed Hill increased from 27 to 51 percent over the following year, despite a lack of new information.[10]

Their anger led some women to run for Congress, and many others to support them. The number of women elected to the House of Representatives increased by almost 70 percent in 1992, from 28 to 47, and 4 new women were elected to the Senate. In the presidential election, Bush's support among women fell 5 percentage points lower than his support among men, enough of a difference to deny Bush reelection.[11] It was the costliest Supreme Court nomination a president had ever made.

IN RECENT DECADES, THE JUDICIARY HAS BECOME TIED MORE CLOSELY TO electoral influences. Presidents are more likely to consider policy goals when selecting their nominees. If Senate committee chairs dislike a president's choice, they are more likely to delay or even refuse to schedule confirmation hearings. Individual senators openly ask nominees about their likely rulings on various types of issues, even though no specific cases sit before the potential judges. If the nominee takes a clear position on a particular issue, or has written on the topic in law reviews and judicial rulings, senators mobilize opposition based upon their policy disagreements.

None of this maneuvering to influence the judiciary fits with how the framers viewed courts. They hoped that judges would remain free from public pressures, relative to other political institutions, so that they could interpret written law neutrally. Judges would protect individual citizens from governmental tyranny, even when an electoral majority endorsed restricting freedoms. But if current practices violate how the founders envisioned the political system functioning, they are fully consistent with trends in America's new democracy—which have spread public influence to even the most insulated institutions.

The federal court system

The Supreme Court provides the linchpin for the nation's judicial system, resolving difficult questions of federal law. (States have their own legal systems, which we discuss briefly at the end of this chapter.) Most of the day-to-day work of the federal judicial branch takes place at lower tiers. Indeed, the Supreme Court generally hears fewer than 100 cases per year, and the vast majority of those cases start in lower federal courts or in the state courts. These lower courts are less visible institutions, but they are no less affected by political and electoral forces. Understanding how elections influence the federal judiciary, as well as how they impact civil liberties (see Chapter 13) and civil rights (see Chapter 14), first requires understanding how the federal court system works.

ORGANIZATION OF THE FEDERAL COURTS

The Constitution established a Supreme Court but allowed Congress to decide on the shape of any lower courts. The first Congress enacted the Judiciary Act of 1789, which still provides the basic framework for the modern federal court system. Federal courts divide into three basic layers: trial courts, appeals courts, and the Supreme Court.

TRIAL COURTS Most federal cases initially appear in one of the 94 **federal district courts,** the lowest tier of the judicial system. There are also two specialized courts with nationwide jurisdiction over particular issues. The Court of International Trade handles cases concerning international trade and customs. And the U.S. Court of Federal Claims hears suits concerning federal contracts,

FIGURE 11.1
Federal and state court systems

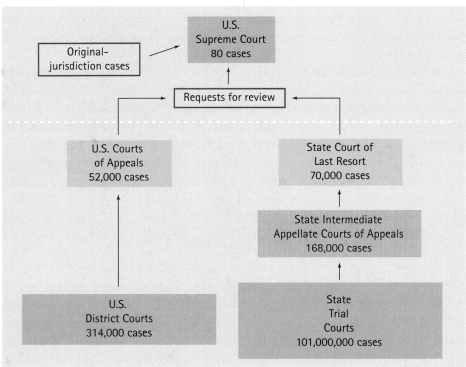

money damages against the United States, and other issues that involve the federal government. As Figure 11.1 shows, most federal cases end in these district courts, which are also called trial courts.

As their name suggests, the main responsibility of district courts is to hold trials. In all trials there are two sides: the **plaintiff,** the party bringing the suit, and the **defendant,** the party against whom the complaint is made. Trials settle alleged violations of the civil and criminal code.

The **civil code** regulates the legal rights and obligations of citizens with regard to one another. Individuals ask the court to award damages and otherwise offer relief for injuries they claim to have suffered. Medical malpractice suits are one example of a civil action; the patient sues a hospital or a doctor for improper treatment. People cannot be imprisoned for violating the civil code (although they can be imprisoned for not complying with a court order growing out of a civil suit).

Violations of the **criminal code** are offenses against society as a whole. The government enforces criminal law, acting as plaintiff and initiating charges against suspects. If convicted, the criminal owes a debt to society, not just to the injured party. The debt may be paid by fine, imprisonment, or, in the case of capital crimes, execution. Table 11.1 summarizes the differences between civil and criminal cases.

The same action can violate both codes simultaneously, so the defendant may have to fend off accusations more than once. After a jury acquitted former football star O. J. Simpson in the murder of his ex-wife, Nicole Brown Simpson, her relatives filed a suit seeking compensation for pain and suffering caused by her wrongful death. Their tactic might sound foolish. Why should Simpson pay Nicole's family for their loss if he did not murder her? The plaintiffs were hopeful that they might win a civil suit, despite losing the criminal trial, because the burden of evidence is weaker. In a criminal trial, one is "innocent until proven guilty" beyond a reasonable doubt, but in a civil suit the jury need only to decide whose case has the preponderance of supporting evidence. Also, a plaintiff cannot compel the accused to testify in a criminal trial because of the Fifth Amendment, but the accused in a civil action cannot refuse to respond without suffering consequences. The plaintiffs thus were able to secure a guilty verdict in the civil suit and a monetary award against Simpson of $33.5 million.

The Federal Bureau of Investigation usually looks into suspected violations of the federal criminal code, although other federal agencies, such as the Secret Service and the Bureau of Alcohol, Tobacco and Firearms, also exercise investigative powers. They turn over evidence to prosecutors in the office of a **U.S. attorney,** one of 93 litigators appointed by the president and confirmed by the

TABLE 11.1

DIFFERENCES BETWEEN CIVIL AND CRIMINAL TRIALS

	CRIMINAL TRIAL	CIVIL TRIAL
Plaintiff	The government	Private person or group
Issue	Duty of citizens to obey the law	Legal rights and obligations of citizens to one another
Type of wrongdoing	Transgression against society	Harm to private person or group
Remedy	Punishment (fine, imprisonment, etc.)	Compensation for damages
Standard of proof	Beyond a reasonable doubt	Preponderance of the evidence
Can defendant be forced to testify?	No	Yes

High-profile plaintiff

In 1997, several New York police officers tortured prisoner Abner Louima in a police station bathroom. After the officers were prosecuted in criminal court, Louima filed a civil suit against New York City, the police union, and his attackers.

Senate. If persuaded that a prosecution is warranted, the U.S. attorney asks a grand jury (consisting of 16 to 23 citizens) to indict, or bring charges against, the suspect. This stage is not a formal trial, just a decision to proceed with one, so the grand jury usually follows the U.S. attorney's advice. As one wit observed, "Under the right prosecutor, a grand jury would indict a ham sandwich."[12]

U.S. attorneys have a particularly high political profile. They usually share the president's party affiliation and may be sensitive to the needs of their political careers. U.S. attorneys do not handle routine law enforcement. Often they concentrate on attention-grabbing activities that can lead to a candidacy for higher office. New York Mayor Rudolph Giuliani achieved prominence as a federal attorney after successfully prosecuting Wall Street insider-trader Ivan Boesky and tax-evading hotel magnate Leona Helmsley. Thomas Dewey may have turned the office of U.S. attorney to greatest political advantage. After winning fame by prosecuting labor racketeers, he became governor of New York and, in 1948, won the Republican presidential nomination. He narrowly lost the election to Harry Truman.[13]

APPEALS COURTS Federal district courts are organized into 13 circuits, including 11 regional circuits, a District of Columbia circuit, and a federal circuit (which includes the specialized courts). Each has a **circuit court of appeals,** the court empowered to review all district rulings on appeal (see Figure 11.2).*

*Originally, appeals court judges literally traveled a circuit, going by stagecoach from district to district to hear appeals—thus, the name.

FIGURE 11.2
Courts of appeals circuit boundaries

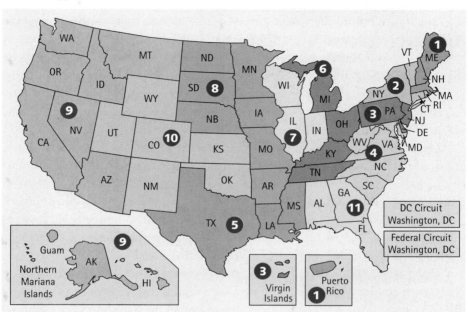

Source: Robert A. Carp and Ronald Stidham, *The Federal Courts,* Second Edition. (Washington, DC: CQ Press, 1991), p.18.

Appeals courts contain between 6 and 28 judges, depending on the size of the circuit. The senior appeals court judge assigns 3 judges, usually chosen by lot, to review each case. In exceptionally important cases, the appeals judges may participate in a **plenary session,** which includes all of them. Courts of appeals ordinarily take as given the facts of the case, as stated in the trial record and decided by district judges. They do not accept new evidence or hear additional witnesses but confine their review to points of law under dispute. Most appeals court decisions are final.

THE SUPREME COURT IN ACTION
The Supreme Court sits atop a massive pyramid of judicial activity. Each year prosecutors and private citizens bring more than 27 million criminal trials and civil suits before the state and federal courts.[14] Yet in the 1999–2000 term, the nation's high court heard only 80 cases. Through these few cases, the Court's **chief justice** and eight **associate justices** exert substantial influence.

CERTS   At one time the Supreme Court was, by law, forced to review many appeals. The workload became so excessive that, in 1925, Congress gave the Court power to refuse almost any case it did not want to consider. Today, nearly all cases argued before the Court arrive because at least four justices have voted to grant what is known as a **cert** (or **writ of *certiorari***).* When a cert is granted, it means the Court has agreed to consider the case and requests to be informed of the details.[15] The Court receives around 7,000 requests each year, denying approximately 95 percent of them. As one clerk for a Supreme Court justice put it, "You almost get to hate the guy who brings the cert petitions around. He is really a nice guy, but he gets abuse all the time."[16]

The number of certs granted by the Supreme Court has fallen markedly in recent years. In the 1970s the Supreme Court decided as many as 400 cases annually, including many controversial rulings.[17] The current Court seems to want to reduce its visibility in American politics. "Do I make policy?" asked Justice Anthony Kennedy. "Was I appointed for life to go around . . . suggesting answers to the Congress? That's not our function."[18] Certs are granted only for those cases that raise the most important legal or constitutional issues.

The case for cert is strongest if two lower courts have reached opposite conclusions on similar cases. The Supreme Court feels a responsibility to clarify and therefore standardize the law. In 1998, for example, the Supreme Court granted cert in a case involving media "ride-alongs" with law enforcement officials. The Fourth Circuit Court of Appeals had ruled in a Maryland case that police did not violate criminal defendants' privacy by bringing reporters along to witness an arrest. In a similar Montana case, however, the Ninth Circuit Court of Appeals ruled that the press should not be present when law enforcement officials search a private home. The Supreme Court eventually resolved the apparent contradiction between these two decisions: Police may not invite the press into private homes, but filming officers and suspects in public places is permissible.[19]

THE DECISION-MAKING PROCESS   Before reaching a decision, the Supreme Court considers **briefs,** written legal arguments submitted by the opposing sides. (Unfortunately for judges, briefs are seldom really brief!) The justices then listen to oral arguments from contending attorneys in a plenary session, attended by all nine justices, the chief justice presiding. Open to the public, these plenary sessions are held on Mondays, Tuesdays, and Wednesdays from October through May. During a controversial hearing, the courtroom overflows,

**Certiorari is a Latin phrase that means "to be informed of."

and outside "protesters square . . . off at the courthouse steps, chanting, singing and screaming at each other."[20]

During the half-hour allotted each side to present its case, attorneys often find themselves interrupted by searching questions from the bench. Former law professor Antonin Scalia is especially known for his willingness to turn the plenary session into a classroom seminar. Court reporters usually analyze the questions asked by justices to find clues indicating how each intends to vote on the case. Yet it is not always clear how closely the justices attend to the responses. As Chief Justice John Marshall said many years ago, "The acme of judicial distinction means the ability to look a lawyer straight in the eye for two hours and not hear a damned word he says."[21]

After hearing the oral arguments, the justices usually reach a preliminary decision the same week in a private conference presided over by the chief justice. There are "three levels of elbow room about the conference table." The most ample is for the chief justice and senior associate justice, who sit at opposite ends. The next best is grabbed by the three most senior justices sitting on one side, leaving the four most junior crowded together across from them. No outsiders, not even a secretary, are permitted to attend. The only record consists of handwritten notes taken by individual justices.

Justices use the private conferences as opportunities to signal where they stand on each case: which way they are leaning and which points of law or politics decided their position. The justices usually formalize their preferences in a vote, taken in order of seniority. When in the majority, the chief justice assigns authors to cases; otherwise the senior associate justice in the majority will do so.[22]

That the justices "vote" on the case does not mean they decide policy issues the same way a legislature might. Indeed, both clerks and justices become uncomfortable when their colleagues openly approach a decision with political considerations in mind.[23] Instead, courts are expected to follow the principle of *stare decisis.* The phrase is Latin for "let the decision stand." Judges should adhere to **precedents,** prior decisions, including written justifications known as **opinions of the court** that accompany them.

Stare decisis is a powerful judicial principle, ignored only at the risk of the legal system's stability and credibility. Consistent court decisions enable a country to live under a rule of law, because then citizens know what they are expected to obey. "We cannot meddle with a prior decision," one judge explained, unless it "strikes us as wrong with the force of a five-week-old unrefrigerated dead fish."[24] The principle also helps maintain the almost-sacred relationship between Americans and their Constitution. It preserves the image of judges as impersonal specialists applying a tangible body of law, rather than a tiny, unelected elite telling legislatures what they may or may not do.

When reaching a decision that seems contrary to a prior decision, courts try to find a legal distinction between the case at hand and earlier court decisions, usually by emphasizing how the facts of the current case differ. The process of drawing a legal distinction can in some cases become the refined art of perceiving a distinction when others can see no difference. As one wit has put it, the Supreme Court "could find a loophole in the Ten Commandments."[25] Or, as an attorney once bragged, "Law school taught me one thing: how to take two situations that are exactly the same and show how they are different."[26]

The justice assigned responsibility for preparing the court opinion circulates a draft version among the other eight. Comments received from them usually lead to revisions. Sometimes the comments are only suggestions, but sometimes they are demands; the justice will refuse to join the opinion unless certain changes appear in future drafts. On rare occasions, the justice writing the opinion has "lost a court"—that is, enough justices change their minds that the initial author no longer has a majority. To keep a majority, the justice writing the opinion may produce an extremely bland opinion that gives little guidance to lower-court justices. In a 1993 sexual harassment case, *Harris* v. *Forklift Systems*, for example, the majority hardly created any precedent at all, saying only that courts should look at the "totality of the circumstances" to decide whether harassment has occurred.[27]

Justices who vote against the majority may prepare a **dissenting opinion** that explains their disagreement. Any member of the majority who is unhappy with the Court opinion may write a **concurring opinion** providing different reasoning for the decision. Two hundred years ago, when John Marshall was chief justice, the court was usually unanimous, and the chief justice wrote most opinions. Today, the Court is seldom unanimous in its judgments; justices are sufficiently concerned with public policy that they choose to write either dissenting or concurring opinions explaining their own preferences. Often a case produces so many separate opinions that it is difficult to ascertain exactly what the majority has decided (see Figure 11.3). It is not uncommon for the Court's opinion to describe the full judgment of only one justice, with everyone else either dissenting or concurring.

Once the Court reaches a decision, it usually sends, or **remands,** the case to a lower court for implementation. Because the Supreme Court regards itself as responsible for establishing general principles and an overall framework, it seldom becomes involved in the detailed resolution of particular cases. This procedure leaves a great deal of legal responsibility in the hands of lower courts.

FIGURE 11.3

Number of Supreme Court dissents

This graph shows the rising number of dissenting opinions written by members of the Supreme Court over the decades. Why do you think dissents have increased? Do dissenting voices make the Court look more or less useful in your view?

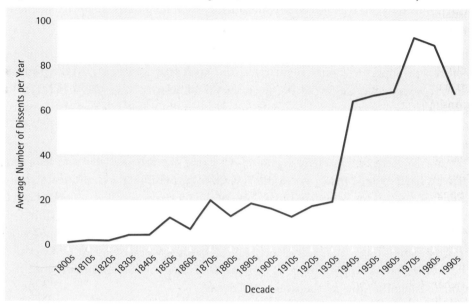

SOURCE: Data from Gregory Calderia and Christopher J. W. Zorn, *Of Time and Consensual Norms on the Supreme Court*, Inter-University Consortium on Political and Social Research, Study No. I01142; see Gregory Calderia and Christopher J. W. Zorn, "Of Time and Consensual Norms on the Supreme Court," *American Journal of Political Science* 42:3 (July 1998): 874–902.

If a court finds that an injury has been suffered, it is up to the court to fashion a **remedy,** the compensation for the injury. Often the remedy simply involves monetary compensation to the injured party. But a judge may also direct the defendant to alter future behavior. To overcome racial segregation in schools, courts have ordered school boards to institute magnet schools, to set up special compensatory programs, and to bus children from one part of a city to another. As a Nixon appointee, Justice Lewis Powell, once put it, courts have the right, if racial segregation is sufficiently severe, to "virtually assume the role of school superintendent and school board."[28]

THE ROLE OF THE CHIEF JUSTICE   Although the chief justice has only one vote and many of the chief's tasks are of a ceremonial or housekeeping nature, certain responsibilities give the office added influence. Perhaps the most important power is the one mentioned earlier: the power of the chief justice, if voting with a majority, to decide who will write the majority opinion. This assignment power can have far-reaching consequences, because it influences the explanations given for a ruling and the tone of the Court's judgment. The chief can frustrate a particular justice by refusing to give him or her important cases. Chief Justice Warren Burger often angered his colleagues by switching to the majority side late in a case, presumably so that he could choose the opinion author.[29]

THE ROLE OF THE SOLICITOR GENERAL   A powerful figure who appears before the Supreme Court regularly is the **solicitor general,** a government official responsible for airing the presidential administration's views before the Court. The solicitor general presents the government's case whenever it is party to a suit and, in other cases, may submit *amicus curiae* briefs—literally, briefs submitted by a "friend of the court" explaining its position.*

Involvement of the solicitor general is a signal that the president and attorney general have strong opinions on a subject, raising its visibility and political significance. Some call the occupant of this office "the tenth justice," because the Court accepts 70 percent of the solicitor general's cert petitions.[30] When the office of the solicitor general files an *amicus curiae* brief, its position is on the winning side approximately three-quarters of the time, a batting average envied by even the most successful private attorneys.[31] Some solicitor generals eventually join the Court, as did four during the twentieth century.

THE ROLE OF CLERKS   Much of the day-to-day work within the Supreme Court building is the job of **law clerks**—young, influential aides hired by each of the justices. Recently out of law school, most will have spent a year as a clerk with a lower court before being asked to help a Supreme Court justice. Each justice employs between two and four law clerks.[32]

The role of the law clerk has grown in recent years. Not only do clerks initially review certs, they also draft many opinions. Clerks have become so important to the Court's routine that some view the true "Supreme Court" of today as nothing more than a junior collection of bright but unseasoned attorneys, unconfirmed by the Senate or anybody else. Others reply that well-trained graduates of the country's most prestigious law schools may be better judges than aging titans who refuse to leave office well beyond the age of normal retirement. The truth probably lies between these two extremes: The brilliant energy of the young clerks and the experience of the justices are probably better in combination than either would be alone.[33]

Amicus curiae briefs can also be submitted by others who wish to inform the court of a legal issue presented by a particular case.

LITIGATION AS A POLITICAL STRATEGY

Interest groups increasingly use the federal court system to place issues on the political agenda, particularly when elected officials have not responded to group demands. Civil rights groups pioneered this strategy (see Chapter 14), but the technique has since spread.[34] Alexis de Tocqueville anticipated as much over a century and a half ago. He wrote that "there is hardly a political question in the United States which does not sooner or later turn into a judicial one."[35]

To advance an issue, advocacy groups often file **class action suits** on behalf of all individuals in a particular category, whether or not they actually participate in the suit. For example, in the late 1990s groups of former smokers in several states filed class action suits against the major tobacco companies for lying to consumers about the harms caused by smoking. In the first such case to reach a verdict favorable to plaintiffs, a jury ordered the five major tobacco companies to pay millions of dollars in damages to up to 500,000 ill Florida smokers.[36]

Class action suits are justified on the grounds that the issues affect many people in essentially the same way. It should not be necessary for each member of the class to bring an individual suit to secure relief. But often the main motive may be less to benefit the supposed clients and more to profit the attorneys. Actor Clint Eastwood, who served as mayor of Carmel, California, from 1986 to 1988, said in reference to suits growing out of the Americans with Disabilities Act: "Once they sue ya, you're screwed. They ride off in a Mercedes. The disabled ride off in a wheelchair." Critics of the judicial system's power also fear that class actions have become an indirect way to ban unpopular products such as cigarettes or handguns—driving up their costs or driving their manufacturers out of business—without having to follow democratic procedures.[37]

THE POLITICS OF JUDICIAL APPOINTMENTS

The judicial system is supposed to be politically blind. Justice, like the rain, is expected to fall equally on rich and poor, on Democrat and Republican, on all ethnic groups, and so forth. Judges are appointed for life so that they may decide each of their cases without concern for their political futures. Chief Justice Warren E. Burger expressed this ideal when he claimed that judges "rule on the basis of law, not public opinion, and they should be totally indifferent to pressures of the times."[38] At one level these ideals are clearly a myth in America's new democracy.

Political influences play a major role in the selection of federal judges. Most share the same partisan identifications as the presidents who nominate

FIGURE 11.4

Partisan affiliation of district judges

Republican presidents usually appoint Republican judges and Democratic presidents usually appoint Democratic judges.

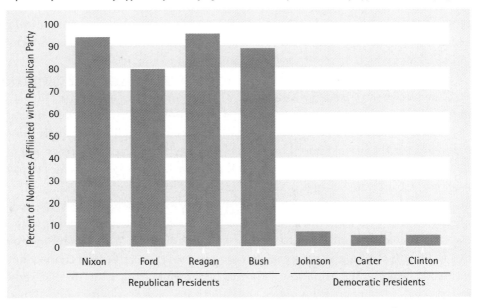

SOURCE: Sheldon Goldman, "Reagan's Judicial Legacy: Completing the Puzzle and Summing Up," *Judicature* 72 (April–May 1989): 321–322.

them; 94 percent of Ronald Reagan's nominees were Republican, and 90 percent of Jimmy Carter's nominees were Democrats (see Figure 11.4).[39] The convention known as **senatorial courtesy** requires that a judicial nominee be acceptable to the senior senator of the state or region involved who shares the president's political party.

Judicial decisions reflect the political orientation of the president who appointed each judge. According to one study, Reagan's district court appointees were significantly tougher toward those accused of crime than were Carter-appointed judges.[40] More generally, judges appointed by Democratic presidents are more likely than those appointed by Republican presidents to hand down liberal decisions (see Figure 11.5).

For at least the first half of the twentieth century, the idealistic view of judicial decision making guided the process through which the Senate confirmed nominees. Senators approved presidential selections as a matter of course. Most

FIGURE 11.5

Decision making by Democratic and Republican judges

Judges appointed by Democratic presidents make more liberal decisions.

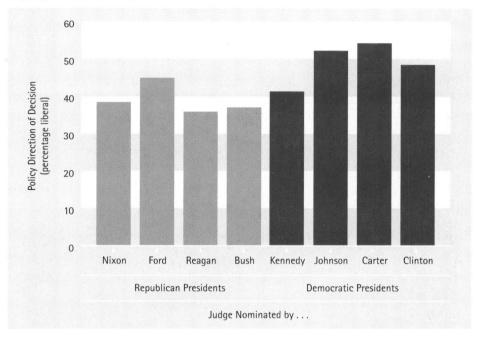

SOURCES: Robert A. Carp and Ronald Stidham, *The Federal Courts,* Second Edition. (Washington, DC: CQ Press, 1991), p.116; *U.S. News and World Report* (May 26, 1997): 24.

nominees did not even testify before congressional committees first. One of Harry Truman's nominees declined an explicit invitation to testify but was confirmed anyway.[41] Earl Warren, an Eisenhower appointee who dramatically changed the tenor of the Supreme Court as chief justice, also avoided testifying before confirmation.[42]

This long-time separation of Supreme Court nominations from political disputes owed a great deal to the efforts of William Howard Taft. Taft was the only person ever to serve both as president (1909–1913) and as chief justice of the Supreme Court (1921–1930). Before Taft, political factors openly affected the confirmation decisions; the Senate rejected a third of the presidents' nominees in the nineteenth century.[43] But Taft worked hard to enhance the quality of nominees, minimize the significance of confirmation procedures, and elevate the prestige of the Court. He also made sure that the new Supreme Court building, eventually completed in 1935, was designed to resemble a Greek temple, so that Americans would respect their laws with the same reverence with which the ancient Greeks venerated their gods.

Taft was so successful that until 1968, the Senate confirmed every twentieth-century nominee except one, most without significant dissent. The Senate has regained some of its power in the past 50 years, however, and the judicial-selection process has become increasingly political. Justices are nominated by the president, evaluated by the Senate Judiciary Committee, and confirmed by a vote of the full Senate based in large part on their policy views. The procedure guarantees numerous elected officials, interest groups, and the media a voice in who rises to the federal bench—and few are equipped to evaluate the nominees for their legal expertise. Instead, these players pay close attention to the electoral and policy consequences of judicial appointments.

Sacred justice
Originally conceived by President and Chief Justice William Howard Taft to instill public respect for the judicial branch, the Supreme Court building resembles a Greek temple built to house ancient gods or goddesses.

The Senate's propensity to reject presidential nominees has increased steadily (see Table 11.2). One of the most celebrated cases involved Robert Bork, a Reagan nominee rejected by the Senate in 1987. Bork had an extensive record of journal articles and speeches that identified him as an erudite legal scholar but a staunch conservative. Interest groups and Senate opponents used Bork's eccentric public record to attack him in a concerted national campaign, catching the Reagan administration off guard. "We didn't anticipate this would be conducted like a federal election," one aide complained.[44]

Most lower-court nominees win confirmation. Rejections usually result from financial or personal problems uncovered during the confirmation process. However, in recent decades even lower-court confirmations have become politicized. Opposition-party senators are most likely to exert their power by refusing to bring nominations to a vote. In the late 1990s, partisan conflict over judicial nominations became bitter and vocal, as President Clinton complained of congressional foot-dragging and Republicans criticized his judicial nominations as too liberal. The Senate approved only about 45 percent of Clinton's 1997 nominees (a 20-year low) and delayed action on the rest. Even conservative Chief Justice William Rehnquist issued a written statement pressing the Senate to act, arguing that "vacancies cannot remain at such high levels without eroding the quality of justice."[45]

TABLE 11.2

PRESIDENTIAL NOMINEES TO THE SUPREME COURT NOT CONFIRMED BY THE SENATE, 1900–2000

NOMINEE	YEAR	PRESIDENT	MAIN REASON FOR REJECTION/WITHDRAWAL
John Parker	1930	Hoover	Antilabor record
Abraham Fortas (sitting justice nominated to be chief justice)	1968	Johnson	Record too liberal; resigned from Court in 1969 over alleged financial abuses
Homer Thornberry	1968	Johnson	No vacancy when Fortas not confirmed for chief justice
Clement Haynesworth	1970	Nixon	Alleged financial abuses
G. Harrold Carswell	1970	Nixon	Racially conservative record
Robert Bork	1987	Reagan	Controversial conservative record
Douglas Ginsburg	1987	Reagan	Smoking of marijuana with students

Presidents sometimes avoid confirmation battles by choosing moderate judges or nominees with unknown views. In 1990 President Bush nominated David Souter, a New Hampshire state supreme court justice. Souter had never written an opinion or treatise on any major constitutional question. Most Supreme Court nominees also tell senators that they cannot comment on specific issues that might come before the Court. Legal scholars lament such conflict avoidance. One law professor protested that to sidestep a political firestorm, "no president will nominate anyone who has written anything very interesting."[46] Yet the strategy works; Washington insiders could not identify Souter's opinions and so the Senate confirmed him easily.

The United States is unlikely to go back to the apolitical way of selecting federal judges. Modern methods of communication—televised hearings, fax machines, toll-free numbers, radio talk shows, and the Internet—ensure that senators and interest groups can conduct detailed evaluations of each appointee. Presidents have no choice but to select judges with an eye to the public controversies they might create. Electoral considerations will continue to affect judicial selections.

The power
of judicial review

Policy-oriented senators scrutinize nominees closely because the Supreme Court's great political authority includes the power of **judicial review.** Federal courts regularly declare laws of both Congress and the state legislatures unconstitutional, meaning that they are null and void. The Supreme Court is the court of last resort on such judgments. Exercising this power is controversial because it gives judges, appointed for life, the authority to negate laws written by elected representatives. Senators hesitate to surrender so much power, and the public seems to share their caution. By a margin of 5 to 1, Americans agree that the "Senate should carefully scrutinize a presidential nominee."[47]

Although the Constitution claims to be the "supreme Law of the Land," it says nothing explicit about judicial review. From what little they said at the Constitutional Convention, it seems the delegates did not expect the Court to be powerful. Alexander Hamilton, writing as Publius in the 78th *Federalist Papers* essay, initially seemed to claim review powers for the judiciary, but then backed off his aggressive posture three essays later. As political scientist Robert McCloskey once observed, "The United States began its history . . . with a Supreme Court whose birthright was most uncertain."[48]

ORIGINS OF JUDICIAL REVIEW

The Supreme Court first asserted judicial-review powers in 1803, as part of the **Marbury v. Madison** judgment. Many consider this opinion the most significant Supreme Court decision ever rendered, so it is worth understanding how the case evolved and why even those skeptical of judicial review tolerated the ruling.[49]

Marbury v. *Madison* followed one of the most contentious elections in U.S. history and the first peaceful transition of power from a president of one political party to that of another. Federalist President John Adams lost the 1800 election to Thomas Jefferson, candidate of the arch-rival Democratic–Republicans (see Chapter 3). Congressional elections that year also produced widespread Federalist losses. Adams and his supporters feared that the Jeffersonians would usher in a period of dangerous radicalism. The Federalists therefore were determined to leave their mark on the U.S. government before stepping down.

Transfer of power

The first time the presidency changed parties, from Federalist John Adams to his rival Thomas Jefferson, the outgoing party feared a wave of dangerous radicalism. Adams feverishly appointed federal judges before his departure so that his allies could resist Jefferson from the bench. In other countries, upset elections sometimes can result in the end of democracy when leaders refuse to surrender power. Americans take for granted how casually power changes hands in their political system, even when rival leaders dislike or disrespect each other.

The best means of resistance seemed to be to stock the judiciary with Federalist sympathizers, who would enjoy lifetime appointments. So in the last days before Adams left office, he nominated numerous judges, including 42 new justices of the peace for Washington, D.C. The Senate approved the appointments a day afterward, and that evening, as the skies grew dark in the nation's capital, Secretary of State John Marshall stamped their official commissions with the Great Seal of the United States. The appointments had been arranged so hastily, however, that administration officials failed to deliver the commissions. The stack of documents remained lying on a table in the State Department. Jefferson's supporters found them when they arrived.

The Jeffersonians decided that appointees had no right to their posts until they received commissions, and so refrained from delivering them. But appointee William Marbury did not believe that the Jefferson administration could deny him a position simply because the official notification had not gone out. A law passed by Congress in 1789, the Judiciary Act, specified how jilted appointees might challenge denial of their posts. They could request a writ of *mandamus* (a court order) directly from the U.S. Supreme Court. So Marbury sued Jefferson's secretary of state, future president James Madison.

Ironically, John Marshall, who had prepared Marbury's commission, was the Court's chief justice by 1803. Indeed, it was a Federalist-dominated court. Yet Marshall saw a rare opportunity in the case. Installing a few extra justices of the peace might offer the Federalists a short-term victory, but nothing more. And there was no guarantee Madison would honor a Court ruling on Marbury's behalf. For Jefferson's administration to ignore the Court would weaken the judiciary over the long term. Instead, Marshall decided to give the administration its way, but to do so by declaring a constitutional principle that Jefferson opposed.

Marshall read his opinion to an anxious, crowded audience on February 24. His initial statement chastised the Jeffersonians for denying Marbury his rightful position. But then Marshall asked a crucial question: Was the Supreme Court the proper place to address Marbury's complaint? His stunning conclusion was that it was not. The Judiciary Act of 1789 had violated the Constitution by giving the Court original jurisdiction over judicial appointments. Marbury lost on a technicality.*

Marshall asserted the power of judicial review to explain why the Supreme Court could overturn offending portions of the Judiciary Act and deny Marbury's appeal. His reasoning was simple and straightforward: The Constitution is the

---

*One of the great mysteries of American history is why Marbury never tried to go through proper judicial channels to attain his commission. Marshall left no doubt that Marbury would win if he followed legal procedures.

highest law of the land, established by the people in convention before the national government even existed. No entity, not even Congress itself, can enact legislation that contravenes this higher law. Federal judges, who are responsible for interpreting the Constitution, are the ones who must declare when a law runs afoul of its restrictions. They could void unconstitutional laws.

Marshall's brilliant decision had transformed a situation sure to sap the Court's power into one that strengthened it tremendously. Madison and Jefferson could not refuse to win their own case, simply because they disliked the reasoning used to decide it! They would have lost credibility and likely looked ridiculous. So Marshall gained more power for the Court—a Federalist goal—through his willingness to lose a minor political battle. By invoking the power of judicial review for the first time, and in a manner that insulated it from challenge, Marshall ensured that the judiciary would always be an authoritative force.

THREE THEORIES OF CONSTITUTIONAL INTERPRETATION

The justification for judicial review makes sense when one views a court's role as a technical one. If someone must examine laws and compare them to a higher written law, reconciling situations in which two rules plainly contradict, then judges seem a logical choice for the task. They have the training to interpret legal phrasing and the political independence to do it fairly. However, very few judgments of constitutionality are simple, because few provisions are precise. What should justices do when a law seems as though it might violate the meaning of the Constitution but does not do so in a manner so plain that anyone schooled in the law would see it?

To address this dilemma, judges have developed three distinct theories of constitutional interpretation: the plain meaning of the text, the original intent of the text, and the living-constitution approach. The approach most appealing to common sense is to go by the *plain meaning* of a constitutional provision's words. The words are what people voted on, not anything else, so only they can lay out the law. Plain meaning has two clear advantages: (1) it is the approach least open to judicial abuse, because courts must restrict their attention to the laws before them, and (2) it calls upon judges to perform the task for which they are best trained, which is to decipher the meaning of legal language.

But plain-meaning theory has limitations. The Constitution is a very short document that left many issues undecided and phrases unexplained. The first amendment forbids Congress from passing any law "respecting an establishment of religion," but legal experts disagree over how to give teeth to this prohibition—since to do so requires figuring out what the framers actually banned.

What makes something a "religion" or not? At what point has a law moved too close to "establishing" one? And what does the "respecting" forbid that the word "establishing" alone might have allowed? The phrase is hardly plain, and the confusion it engenders is not just a rare exception.

Furthermore, words do not always have a clear legal definition. Vocabulary changes over time, and words that persist often alter in meaning. This transformation occurs regularly and swiftly in conversational English. The word "jazz" once served in New Orleans brothels to describe the transaction between prostitutes and their clients; now Martha Stewart might offer tips to help you "jazz up" a bedroom. A "cool" teacher may be friendly or laid back, not coldly formal and aloof as once was the meaning of the term. To be "jacked in" these days is to be on top of things, plugged in like a computer, whereas variants of that phrase once described heroin usage. Words used in legal terminology change in the same way, although perhaps more slowly. Just to take one example, the word "man" at various times has referred to a male of any age, to an adult male, to an adult of any gender, or to humankind.

Sometimes social changes take the law outside any context anticipated by those who first wrote the provisions. The Second Amendment may grant a "right to bear arms," but does this include nuclear bombs and tanks or only include hunting rifles? The word "arms" provides little guidance. Those who write laws often leave out details because they assume readers will understand what they mean, not anticipating that one day Americans will lack their cultural perspective. Early Americans may have understood what the Bill of Rights meant by "unreasonable" searches or "excessive" fines or "cruel and unusual" punishments, but today's readers lack the same point of reference.

A second approach, the theory of *original intent,* also tries to remain true to inherited law—but helps the authors a bit by filling in the meaning of words. Judges following this approach work to ascertain the intentions of those who approved constitutional provisions. Very little solid historical evidence exists to determine what the typical voter believed, but at least scholars can assess the intentions of the framers. Judges may examine such documents as the notes that James Madison wrote down at the Constitutional Convention, the *Federalist Papers,* and the speeches made during the ratifying campaign in 1787 and 1788. They also look at the laws commonly in effect when a provision originated. Justice Thomas, for example, favors overturning *Roe* v. *Wade* because the words used to justify a right to abortion joined the Constitution at a time when many states outlawed the practice.

Original-intent theory has its own problems. Those who wrote the Constitution did not contemplate many issues now before the courts. Nor could they anticipate the many social complexities added, for example, by advances in travel and communications. Judges can abuse the practice of determining intent. They may sift through the evidence selectively to find examples or arguments supporting their political preferences, and even a sincere judge is not trained in social science or historical methods. Furthermore, those who support provisions often do not agree on the meanings themselves, so not even trained historians can settle what voters thought they were endorsing in these instances.

Faced with the difficulty of figuring out what inherited words mean, or were supposed to mean, some judges prefer to assess the law according to the sentiments of their own time. Societies grow, and the law can evolve with this social change. This *living-constitution* theory allows judges to update the meaning of laws in light of the entire history of the United States as a nation. They can go beyond the literal meaning of laws or the opinions expressed at the time of their passage and incorporate the moral lessons Americans have learned since then. In the words of Justice Oliver Wendell Holmes, Jr., constitutional questions must be "considered in the light of our whole experience and not merely in that of what was said a hundred years ago."[50]

The living-constitution theory is practical in one important way: it provides a clear method for updating the law to include situations alien to the framers. Laws are slow to change, especially constitutional provisions (see Chapter 2). Judicial interpretation is a quicker method of adaptation. However, it is also the approach most susceptible to judicial abuse. One's reading of history's moral lessons is highly personal. It takes judges farthest from their area of expertise, requiring as it does insights drawn from numerous fields (including sociology, political science, psychology, history, theology, and perhaps natural science). Many question the wisdom of giving this power to judges—who are appointed for life almost solely from the legal profession.

These three approaches are useful conceptually. A justice occasionally will develop the reputation for espousing a particular view of constitutional interpretation. The late Justice Hugo Black endorsed a literal reading of the Constitution, refusing in principle either to read rights into the language or to water down those stated starkly in the document. The late Justice William O. Douglas emerged from the "realist" school of law, which endorsed incorporating a judge's observations of the real world when interpreting legal phrases.

The theories are also useful as a form of shorthand in political discussion. During the 2000 presidential election debates, President Bush promised to appoint "strict constructionists" to the bench—meaning judges who would stick to the plain meaning of written law. Listeners attuned to the political buzzwords knew that most judges fitting this description would oppose abortion rights and

loosen constitutional restrictions on government accommodation of religion. Vice President Gore, by contrast, said he would appoint judges likely to support abortion rights because they would believe in a living Constitution.

Concepts break down somewhat when describing the actual voting behavior of particular judges. Outsiders often point to Justice Antonin Scalia as the prime example of a strict-constructionist judge, but Scalia rejects the label. "I am not a strict constructionist," he told a law-school audience in Wisconsin. "You shouldn't be a strict constructionist—you should be reasonable."[51] He does tend to read the religious-freedom clauses of the First Amendment strictly, in that he allows the governmentwide latitude before finding a violation (see Chapter 13). But he allows occasional flexibility in the same amendment's free-expression clauses, for example including symbolic statements, such as burning flags or crosses, as instances of protected "speech." He considers free-speech rights to include an unwritten, but understood, "right to associate" with like-minded people in groups that exclude those who disagree. This principle led Scalia, in 2000, to forbid California's flexible primary rules (see Chapter 7) and to permit the Boy Scouts of America to exclude homosexual scout leaders.

VOTING ON THE SUPREME COURT

Justices of the Court fall into quite predictable voting blocs. Even Justice John Paul Stevens, "long . . . considered a maverick," has found himself consistently in dissent on the left in recent years. The most liberal justices, Stevens and Clinton-

The justices of the Supreme Court
In this composite, the justices of the Supreme Court are pictured from left to right according to their judicial philosophies. On the left are John Paul Stevens, Ruth Bader Ginsburg, Stephen Breyer, and David Souter. The two moderates are Sandra Day O'Connor and Anthony Kennedy. On the right are Chief Justice William H. Rehnquist, Antonin Scalia, and Clarence Thomas. Where do you think the next justice's picture will be positioned?

appointee Ruth Bader Ginsburg, favor a certain amount of **judicial activism,** meaning they are willing to overturn precedents to preserve fundamental freedoms that seem threatened by electoral majorities. They are willing to overrule legislatures aggressively to protect their vision of what the Constitution has come to mean. Souter and the other Clinton appointee, Stephen Breyer, usually join the liberal bloc, especially when it comes to continuing the enforcement of activist judicial precedents from the Warren and Burger eras.

A second bloc of conservative **restorationists**—Thomas, Scalia, and Chief Justice William Rehnquist—also frequently endorse overturning earlier court decisions. They think liberal activist judges have undermined the original meaning of the Constitution, and they will strike down precedents to restore that original intent. Although Scalia in particular often favors deferring to elected representatives, the conservative bloc also shows a certain willingness to strike down liberal-minded legislation that they see as invasive of the private spheres of American life: family, church, club, and neighborhood.

Sandra Day O'Connor and Anthony Kennedy usually serve as crucial swing votes on the Court. They often promote **judicial restraint,** forcing the majority to soften written opinions or weakening those opinions by writing a softer concurrence. They also write more than their share, since often the only way a majority can hold together is to conform to the preferences of their least-enthusiastic members. One outgrowth of O'Connor and Kennedy's restraint is that they avoid overturning prior court decisions, sometimes sticking with precedents contrary to their conservative inclinations. They emphasize the importance of maintaining the Supreme Court's integrity as a judicial body rather than a legislative one. If the law should change, that responsibility falls on the people's elected representatives or on the constitutional amendment process.

THE PROS AND CONS OF MODERATION   Ironically, it is often the moderates (and in particular O'Connor) who produce the decisions most frustrating to those who must stay within the bounds of constitutional law. "Ruling from the center" often requires rather fine legal distinctions. O'Connor allows government bodies to erect Christmas holiday displays, but only if they do not appear to endorse Christianity.[52] She considers nude dancing a protected form of expression, but allows a requirement that strippers wear partial covering as a means of limiting the negative social effects that crop up around strip clubs.[53] Sometimes the twists and turns of a moderate voting record can produce such a complicated body of constitutional law that it creeps disturbingly close to the type of detail customary in legislation.

Nevertheless, it is also striking how closely the Court's swing voters track the preferences of public opinion and how much their reasoning carries the flavor of common sense (although dressed up in a legalistic vocabulary). The moderate position on abortion, for example, matches surprisingly closely with the ambivalent opinions expressed by the American public (see Chapter 5). The moderates do not mind some religious influences in schools, as long as schools are not unfairly favoring religious organizations or pushing religion on students. They do not mind if legislatures consider race when designing legislative election districts, as long as the process does not produce obscenely shaped districts for which race was obviously the predominant factor determining their makeup (see Chapter 14). These are the sorts of compromises that one often hears proposed by regular voters seeking a resolution to public controversies.

PREDICTING IDEOLOGY   Most of the time, justices vote along lines anticipated by those who nominated and confirmed them. By the time lawyers rise in prominence sufficient to warrant Supreme Court appointments, they already have a fairly clear track record of opinions, speeches, law-review articles, and political activism to indicate likely future voting patterns. According to one study, information about the political views of Supreme Court justices at the time they were being confirmed allows one to anticipate the justices' decisions in civil liberties cases over 60 percent of the time.[54] This predictability allows elected officials—both presidents and senators—to shape the future direction of the Supreme Court, thereby maintaining some degree of popular control.

Not every prediction of future behavior is correct, however. Justices Felix Frankfurter and Robert Jackson, both New Deal insiders appointed by President Roosevelt, bitterly disappointed liberals by refusing to continue their progressive activism from the bench. President Nixon appointed Justice Harry Blackmun, expecting him to follow in the footsteps of fellow Minnesotan Warren Burger. Instead Blackmun delighted in the approval of his liberal colleagues on the Court and shifted decidedly to the left over the course of his career. On the present Court, Justice Souter also has disappointed conservatives, compiling a record as liberal as that of Clinton appointee Breyer.[55]

JUDICIAL REVIEW IN A DEMOCRATIC AGE

Disagreements about theories of judicial review or judicial activism are not just academic, despite the occasional inconsistency of particular judges. The manner in which the Court interprets the Constitution can have serious consequences. The second time the Supreme Court declared a law of Congress unconstitutional, the 1857 case *Dred Scott* v. *Sandford,* it helped precipitate the Civil War.

Liberals unhappy with the active application of judicial review like to point to the Supreme Court's role at blocking reform early in the twentieth century. *Lochner* v. *New York,* decided in 1905, struck down a New York state law limiting the number of hours bakers could work. A string of such decisions around that time helped limit state governments as a force for social change. After Franklin Delano Roosevelt became president in 1933, several conservative Supreme Court decisions helped slow the New Deal. *Schechter Poultry Corp.* v. *United States* (1935), for example, struck down the National Industrial Recovery Act, which managed labor and competition in the private sector.[56] The "sick chicken" case placed the Supreme Court squarely at odds with the president and Congress, creating a constitutional crisis (see the Election Connection, "Roosevelt's 1936 Reelection and the Supreme Court").

If anything, conservatives unhappy with an aggressive judiciary find even more to criticize. Earl Warren's tenure on the Supreme Court, from 1953 to 1969, offers numerous controversial applications of judicial review—especially in criminal justice and federalism. Many critics blame the 1973 abortion case, *Roe* v. *Wade,* for igniting a political controversy that has plagued American politics ever since and wreaked havoc in both electoral and judicial politics.

The many examples of failure and controversy have led some voices in both politics and academia to argue that the country should abandon judicial review as undemocratic. Despite the debate, however, judicial review has become a well-established practice in American government. It survives in part because it is seldom used to defy the strongly held views of national leaders. Between 1803

ELECTION CONNECTION

Roosevelt's 1936 Reelection and the Supreme Court

In 1936, seven of the nine Supreme Court justices had been appointed by Republican presidents. Most initially resisted President Franklin Roosevelt's efforts to expand federal power as part of the New Deal. As late as 1935, the Supreme Court, in *Schechter,* declared unconstitutional a federal regulation of economic activity within a state.[a]

The Roosevelt Democrats were furious at decisions that seemed to deny the country's elected officials their right to govern. Never before had judicial review placed the Supreme Court in such direct conflict with the president and Congress. But Roosevelt overplayed his hand. Instead of trying to change Court views gradually by appointing justices who shared his philosophy, he tried to "pack the Court" by adding six new justices over and above the nine already on the Court (one for each of those over 70 years old who refused to retire). Although the Constitution does not specify the number of justices that shall serve on the Supreme Court—its actual size has varied between five and ten—many believed the Court should not face such direct political manipulation. Roosevelt's court-packing scheme went nowhere in Congress.

Although Roosevelt lost the battle, he won the war. Shortly after his great reelection

victory in 1936, Chief Justice Charles Evans Hughes and Justice Owen Roberts, who had previously voted to restrict federal power, changed their views. This time the issue involved the recently passed Wagner Act, a New Deal law that protected union organizers.[b] Despite the fact that the new law regulated activities within a state, a Court majority, in a 5-to-4 vote, declared it constitutional.

Although judicial scholars note that the change of heart by Hughes and Roberts started before FDR challenged them, certainly the justices knew of the anger their rulings were causing. For this reason, the alteration in their jurisprudence has been called "the switch in time that saved nine." The New Deal majority that emerged on the Court was soon augmented and solidified by Roosevelt's own appointees.

What do you think?

- Should the Court respond to changing political conditions?

- Is it possible to alter the number of federal judges without engaging in political manipulation?

[a]*Schechter Poultry Corp.* v. *United States* 295 U.S. 495 (1935). Another rule, that Congress could not delegate its power over the executive branch without giving clear standards, also later fell.

[b]*NLRB* v. *Jones & Laughlin Steel Co.* 301 U.S. 1 (1937).

and 1999, the Supreme Court decided that a federal law was unconstitutional on only 143 occasions.[57] Most of these decisions affected old laws that were no longer supported either by a majority of Congress or by the president. The Supreme Court spends much more time striking down state laws unpopular with a large segment, if not a majority, of the American public.

Research indicates that changes in Supreme Court policy generally parallel swings in public opinion. These policy shifts are not so pronounced as those in

Congress, but justices still seem to pay "attention to what the public wants."[58] Unpopular decisions are the exception, not the rule. Bartender Mr. Dooley, an Irish cartoon figure, was not wide of the mark when he observed years ago that "th' supreme court follows th' illiction returns." Federal judges are key players in the election-driven political system.

STATUTORY INTERPRETATION

Judicial review is only the most sweeping and controversial of judicial powers. The courts also engage in **statutory interpretation,** the application of the laws of Congress to particular cases. American courts have great discretion in exercising this power. For example, in 1973 Congress passed a vague and general law protecting endangered species. It was the Supreme Court that gave this law sharp teeth, by saying that Congress intended to protect all species, the tiny snail darter as well as the eagle. Similarly, the precise requirements of 1991's Americans with Disabilities Act have emerged in the federal courts rather than through the legislative process itself.

Approaches to statutory interpretation parallel those for constitutional interpretation. Judges may stick to the written law, since this is what a legislature formally approved. They may use congressional speeches, the claims of a bill's authors, and the record of amendments accepted or rejected to determine a bill's intent. Or they may read legislation expansively, to keep the meaning current with modern sentiments. This latter approach is often as controversial as the parallel theory of constitutional interpretation, since it means that a bill can clear Congress with few members endorsing the sweeping application to which federal courts will put it. The difficult process for passing new legislation may allow faulty statutory interpretations to persist for decades (see Chapter 9).[59]

CHECKS ON COURT POWER

Although court decisions have great impact, their consequences can be limited by other political actors. As political scientist Jack Peltason has put it, "Judicial decision making is one stage, not the only nor necessarily the final one.[60] Other branches of government can alter or circumscribe court decisions in two important ways: by changing the laws that courts interpret or by neglecting to implement their rulings.

Changing the law is difficult in constitutional cases. It requires amending the U.S. Constitution, which is an arduous process (see Chapter 2). Troublesome statutory interpretations are easier to address, since Congress can simply change the law or clarify it. In the case of *Wards Cove Packing Co.* v. *Antonio,* for example, the Supreme Court narrowly interpreted a law banning race and gender discrimination—requiring those bringing a complaint to prove they suffered mistreatment. Congress responded in 1991 by passing a law shifting the burden of proof to the accused, effectively overturning the Court's judgment. Even this approach constraining court power is a limited one, however, since passing laws through Congress is not easy. Statutory interpretation favoring one side in a dispute gives that side the political advantage, because it is easier to block a bill than to pass one (see Chapter 9).

The political branches also can check court decisions by ignoring them. When told of a Supreme Court decision he did not like, President Andrew Jackson reportedly replied, "Justice Marshall has made his decision, now let him enforce it."[61] Although outright refusal to obey a judicial decision is unlikely today, legislatures may drag their feet on enforcing rulings. After the Supreme Court declared Bible reading in public schools unconstitutional, for example, the practice in many Southern school districts continued unchanged.[62]

To ensure implementation of judicial orders, courts sometimes appoint a **receiver,** an official who has the authority to see that judicial orders are carried out. For example, in 1996 a Massachusetts judge found the State Department of Mental Retardation guilty of willfully abusing its authority over a school that served severely disabled students. Because the state agency had a long history of misusing its authority over this school, the judge, to prevent future abuse, replaced state supervision of the school with that of a court-appointed receiver.

But elected officials can even check the court's monitoring power. For two decades, a court monitor oversaw the Correction Department in New York City, enforcing judicial orders ensuring respect for the civil rights of prisoners. Judge Harold Baer, Jr., reluctantly withdrew the monitor in 1995 after Congress and the president, concerned that the rights of the guilty were taking precedence over the rights of victims, enacted a law limiting court authority in such matters. "Although the court's [my] concerns with this new legislation are myriad," Judge Baer wrote, "I am constrained under the law to uphold it."[63]

STATE COURTS

Every state has its own judicial arrangements. In most states the basic structure has the same three tiers found in the federal system: trial courts, courts of appeals, and a court of last resort, usually called the state supreme court. State courts perform the same basic tasks as federal courts: interpreting state laws and determining when they contradict the state constitution. Decisions of state supreme courts may be appealed to federal courts, but generally only when a question of federal law appears in the case.

For the first few decades under the Constitution, the relationship between state and federal legal and judicial systems remained vague. Then, in an early key decision, *McCulloch* v. *Maryland* (1819), the Supreme Court made it clear that the power of judicial review applied to state laws as well (see Chapter 3).[64] However, federal courts usually defer to how states choose to interpret their own laws and constitutional provisions. They rule only on whether the state's approach squares with federal requirements.

The Supreme Court's power to review state laws and decisions of state courts is essential for maintaining basic uniformity in the laws of the United States. Over the decades, the Supreme Court has found more than 1,100 state statutes and state constitutional provisions contrary to the federal Constitution.[65] The judicial power to declare state laws unconstitutional is much less controversial than the power to declare laws of Congress unconstitutional. As Justice Holmes once said,

> I do not think the United States would come to an end if we lost our power to declare an act of Congress void. I do think the Union would be imperilled if we could not make that declaration as to the laws of the several states. For one in my place sees how often a local policy prevails with those who are not trained to national views.[66]

It is not hard to see why the Supreme Court would have an easier time overturning state laws. Congressional legislation generally enjoys the support of a national majority, or at least a majority among national political leaders. Court action casting out a recent law will anger a large segment of elites in the other branches of government. By contrast, state laws reflect the tastes or preferences of a state majority, but the nation as a whole may not think much of regional opinion. The Supreme Court can undo such laws without angering most of the country, and indeed may even please those outside the region in question. One reason the Supreme Court could take an active role promoting civil rights, for example, was that they primarily angered opinion leaders in the South; most of those elsewhere felt little attachment to the southern system of race relations.

STATE TRIAL COURTS: THE JUDICIAL WORKHORSES

Most judicial activity takes place within state trial courts under the control of state and local governments, which go by many different names in the various states (district courts, county courts, courts of common pleas, and so forth). In fact, 99 percent of all civil and criminal cases originate in these courts.

State courts are influenced by political factors at least as much as are federal courts. In 37 of the 50 states, both appellate and trial judges are subject to election. In the remaining states, judges are appointed by the state legislature, the governor, or a governmental agency. Exactly which judges are elected varies from state to state. In New York, trial court judges are elected but appellate judges are appointed.[67] In Georgia it is the reverse.

Although many state judges are subject to election, most judicial campaigns "are waged in obscurity, with the result that most voters are unfamiliar with the names, not to speak of the issues, involved in the campaign."[68] As a result, judicial elections have traditionally been dominated by organized groups and party politicians interested in controlling court patronage. During the 1960s, 73 out of Chicago's 80 circuit court judges were active in Democratic party politics.[69]

Interest groups have also had a growing influence on judicial elections, especially as the cost of running campaigns for judgeships has increased. In 1996, for example, the candidates for two Alabama supreme court seats spent a combined total of over $2 million on the race, nearly ten times what they likely would have spent only a decade earlier.[70] Much of the money to fund judicial races is donated by single-issue groups that may have an interest in the way certain cases are decided.

PROSECUTING STATE CASES

The process of bringing civil and criminal cases before state and local courts is comparable to the federal process. In civil cases, most states follow rules similar to the federal code of civil procedure. Upon receiving information from the police on criminal wrongdoing, prosecutors in the office of the local **district attorney** determine whether the evidence warrants presentation before a grand jury for prosecution. In large cities the district attorney has enormous responsibilities. In Los Angeles, for example, the district attorney's office prosecutes 300,000 cases a year.

Because they are responsible for the prosecution of all criminal cases, some of which have high visibility in local news media, many prosecutors earn recognition that wins them election or appointment to the judiciary. About 10 percent of all judges once worked in district attorney's offices.[71] Many local district attorneys are interested in moving to other elected offices as well.

In early 2000, Paul Howard, a Georgia district attorney, was up for reelection. He pressed for the arrest and trial of Baltimore Ravens football star Ray Lewis after two murders outside a suburban Atlanta bar. But prosecutors could find no evidence linking Lewis to the crime, and Lewis' attorney criticized them for "indicting before investigating."[72] After prosecutors dropped charges and released Lewis, some observers blamed the botched investigation on the district attorney's desire for notoriety. "Because Howard tried to ride to fame on the back of Ray Lewis," one critic wrote, "he has damaged—not enhanced—his chances for reelection."[73]

RELATIONS BETWEEN STATE AND FEDERAL COURTS

Most cases are heard in state courts, but any case can be shifted to a federal court if a federal law or constitutional principle is involved. The federal courts have higher prestige than state courts; to become a federal judge is to hold a position of great honor. But as Justice Sandra Day O'Connor, herself a former state judge, acutely observed, "When the state court judge puts on his or her federal court robe, he or she does not become immediately better equipped intellectually to do the job."[74]

The same act can simultaneously be a violation of both state and federal laws. Although the Fifth Amendment to the Constitution forbids **double jeopardy**—being tried twice for the same crime—something very close to double jeopardy can occur if a person is tried in both federal and state courts for the same action. In 1897 the Supreme Court permitted dual prosecutions, saying "an act denounced as a crime by both national and state sovereignties is an offense against the peace and dignity of both."[75] In recent years the chances for such prosecution have been rising, because Congress, under pressure to do something about crime, has passed new laws essentially duplicating state laws.

Despite the recent wave of anticrime legislation, dual state and federal prosecutions remain unusual. Most of the time, federal and state officials reach an agreement allowing one or the other to take responsibility. Generally speaking, the federal government takes over the prosecutions only when cases have national implications. (From this comes the popular phrase "Don't make a federal case out of it.") For example, the 1995 bombing of a federal building in Oklahoma, which killed 168 people, constituted a violation of both state and federal laws. Although state officials began the investigation, federal investigators quickly took charge, and the accused, Timothy McVeigh and Terry Nichols, were convicted in a federal courtroom. State prosecutors jumped back into the Nichols investigation only when he failed to receive the federal death penalty for his role in the crime.

If the state prosecution fails to result in a conviction in a sensational case where a federal law has been broken, the U.S. attorney may also bring charges. In 1992 the State of California was unable to win a conviction in the trial of four police officers charged with beating Rodney King, an event that had been videotaped. The failure to convict officers for what seemed to be a well-documented offense pro-voked three days of civil disorder in Los Angeles's minority communities. To help calm the city, the U.S. attorney decided to bring federal charges against the offi-cers, resulting in the conviction of two of them. The decision to hold a second trial was almost certainly affected by public and media pressure.

CHAPTER SUMMARY

The courts are the branch of government most removed from political influence. Federal judges are appointed for life. They are expected to rely on legal precedents when reach-ing their decisions, but they have been accused of using the power of judicial review to create new laws that frustrate the popular will.

Nevertheless, the courts are not immune to electoral pressures. The day-to-day work of the judiciary is carried out by state and lower federal court judges, who interpret the civil and criminal code. Many state judges and district attorneys are elected officials, and political factors also influence the operation of the lower courts in many other ways.

When justices are selected for federal courts, both presidents and Congress closely evaluate their judicial philosophies. Once appointed, most Supreme Court justices decide cases in ways that are consistent with views they were known to have at the time of their selection. Most of the time, court decisions are broadly responsive to contempo-rary political currents. If court decisions challenge deep-seated political views, they may be modified by new legislation, frustrated by nonimplementation, or even reversed by constitutional amendment. For all these reasons, the judiciary reinforce the role of popu-lar influence in America's new democracy.

KEY TERMS

associate justice, p. 361
briefs, p. 362
cert, p. 362
chief justice, p. 361
circuit court of appeals,
  p. 360
civil code, p. 358
class action suits, p. 367
concurring opinion, p. 364
criminal code, p. 359
defendant, p. 358
dissenting opinion, p. 364
district attorney, p. 386
double jeopardy, p. 387

federal district courts,
  p. 357
judicial activism, p. 379
judicial restraint, p. 379
judicial review, p. 372
law clerk, p. 366
Marbury v. *Madison,* p. 373
opinions of the court, p. 363
plaintiff, p. 358
plenary session, p. 361
precedents, p. 363
receiver, p. 384
remands, p. 364
remedy, p. 365

restorationists, p. 379
senatorial courtesy, p. 368
solicitor general, p. 366
stare decisis, p. 363
statutory interpretation,
  p. 383
U.S. attorney, p. 359
writ of *certiorari,* p. 362

On the Web

Supreme Court
www.supremecourtus.gov
The official Web site of the U.S. Supreme Court contains information on the Court's docket, the text of recent opinions, the rules of the Court, and links to related Web sites.

Legal Information Institute
www.law.cornell.edu
The Legal Information Institute at Cornell Law School includes information on federal and state laws, rules of civil and criminal procedure, and a searchable database of Supreme Court decisions.

Legal Information Site
www.findlaw.com
This all-purpose legal information site includes various searchable databases and links.

Federal Judiciary
www.uscourts.gov
The Federal Judiciary home page provides a concise guide to the federal court system, a regular newsletter, and annual reports on the state of the judiciary written by Chief Justice William Rehnquist.

Department of Justice
www.usdoj.gov/osg/
The Solicitor General's Office in the U.S. Department of Justice offers copies of briefs it has filed in federal court cases.

National Center for State Courts
www.ncsconline.org
The National Center for State Courts showcases statistical information on the caseload of state court systems, as well as links to state-level legal associations.

Suggested Readings

Agresto, John. *The Supreme Court and Constitutional Democracy.* Ithaca, NY: Cornell University Press, 1984. Makes a powerful case against judicial review.

Bronner, Ethan. *Battle for Justice: How the Bork Nomination Shook America.* New York: Norton, 1989. Fascinating case study of the Senate refusal to confirm Robert Bork's nomination to the Supreme Court.

Massaro, John. *Supremely Political: The Role of Ideology and Presidential Management in Unsuccessful Supreme Court Nominations.* Albany: State University of New York Press, 1990. Engaging account of the politics of Supreme Court nominations.

Melnick, R. Shep. *Between the Lines: Interpreting Welfare Rights.* Washington, DC: Brookings, 1994. Insightful analysis of the Court's role in the interpretation and elaboration of statutory law.

Perry, H. W., Jr. *Deciding to Decide: Agenda Setting in the United States Supreme Court.* Cambridge, MA: Harvard University Press, 1991. Comprehensive explanation of the process by which the Supreme Court decides whether to review a case.

Simon, James F. *The Center Holds: The Power Struggle Inside the Rehnquist Court.* New York: Simon & Schuster, 1995. Describes the recent split between conservative and moderate justices.

12

THE MEDIA

More than three decades ago, hundreds of thousands of young Americans fought in the Vietnam War. More than 58,000 died, and ten times that number were wounded. Vietnam has been called the first media war, because video footage from the conflict appeared regularly on television sets across the nation. Events associated with the war provide striking illustrations of the way the media affect public opinion.

A TALE OF TWO BATTLES
I: THE TET OFFENSIVE

In 1964, Democrat Lyndon B. Johnson (LBJ) ran as the peace candidate, promising to keep the United States out of growing hostilities in Vietnam. "Asian boys will fight Asian wars," he promised. This message soothed voters living under the shadow of the atom bomb, and LBJ routed Republican Barry Goldwater that year. Little by little, however, U.S. involvement deepened, and by late 1967 more than 500,000 troops were stationed in Vietnam.

The war began to distract members of LBJ's administration from their domestic policy agenda, including a celebrated "War on Poverty." Influential liberals who once praised LBJ's performance began to turn on him because of the war—including New York Senator Robert Kennedy, brother of the slain president that LBJ had replaced, and civil rights leader Martin Luther King, Jr.

To counter growing discontent, the administration launched what it called a "progress initiative," a public relations campaign intended to build support for the war. Top officials announced that they could see "light at the end of the tunnel." The commanding general predicted that troop withdrawals might begin within two years. But then came Tet.

On January 30, 1968, as the Vietnamese New Year (Tet) celebration began, North Vietnam's army and indigenous Viet Cong guerrillas launched offensives all across South Vietnam, attacking 36 provincial capitals, 64 district capitals, 5 of the 6 largest cities, and numerous hamlets. The surprise attacks initially rocked American forces. Even the U.S. embassy in Saigon nearly was overrun before the fighting petered out.

The American military tried to recover its stature afterward, calling Tet a defeat for the Vietnamese communists rather than a victory—but it was a public-relations disaster all the same. Criticism of the war had been confined to the political fringes before Tet, but now it spread to establishment circles. *Newsweek* published a "searching reappraisal," and editorial comment turned pessimistic in the aftermath of the offensive. Coverage began emphasizing low troop morale, drug abuse, and corruption in the South Vietnamese government.

Tet footage startled CBS anchorman Walter Cronkite—the most trusted man in America, according to polls. He resolved to go to Vietnam and observe the situation for himself. Upon his return, Cronkite broadcast a special report to the nation, contending that the war had become a bloody stalemate, with no military victory in sight:

> . . . it is increasingly clear to this reporter that the only rational way out . . . will be to negotiate, not as victors, but as an honorable people who lived up to their pledge to defend democracy and did the best they could.[1]

A journalist later wrote that "It was the first time in history that a war had been declared over by an anchorman."[2] LBJ apparently understood the significance of Cronkite's broadcast, telling aides afterward, "It's all over."[3] Johnson fell 8 points in the polls immediately after Tet and continued to slide for six weeks. Popular support for administration policy dropped from 60 percent to 40 percent. Optimism about victory faded.

The timing was not good for LBJ's presidency, for it was an election year. Less than two months after the offensive, Senator Eugene McCarthy (D-MN), a peace candidate, attracted 42 percent of the vote in New Hampshire's Democratic primary. Four days later Robert Kennedy, a much more influential antiwar candidate, entered the race. The incumbent was doomed. On March 31, LBJ announced that he would not seek reelection.

At first glance, this story is encouraging. Adverse developments occurred, the media reported the facts, and the public responded by replacing leaders who had failed—the system worked! But within a few years, some people took a second look and reached a different conclusion.[4] As emotions subsided, as documents were declassified, and as former enemies communicated, revisionists made a persuasive case that the media got Tet wrong. Tet in fact was exactly what the military had claimed: a major defeat for the enemy.[5]

Strategists had anticipated an attack.[6] Most initial Tet assaults were repulsed with heavy casualties for the attackers. The North Vietnamese and the Viet Cong suffered nearly 60,000 combat deaths, compared to 4,000 for the United States and 5,000 for the South Vietnamese. The Viet Cong, who bore the brunt of the fighting, were decimated. They had expected a popular uprising, but it did not occur; they were left exposed and outgunned. A stunning defeat.

But the U.S. media turned the Viet Cong's military losses into a major political victory. They horrified American voters by concentrating on the initial attacks, rather than the bloody Viet Cong retreats that followed. The media ignored the good performance of the South Vietnamese army, botched several big stories, and overlooked others. Flawed news coverage, by an ignorant and inexperienced press corps, significantly affected public opinion.[7]

The story seems to support those who believe in the awesome power of mass media to "create reality."[8]

A TALE OF TWO BATTLES
II: CHICAGO

Domestic politics grew increasingly turbulent after Tet. Elimination of graduate-student deferments in the spring meant that the **draft**—the involuntary induction of young men into the military—would catch up affluent youths rather than concentrate primarily on the working class. Partly in consequence, the antiwar movement grew rapidly, especially on college campuses.

As the Democratic convention drew near, activists planned to gather in Chicago and protest the impending presidential nomination of LBJ's vice president. Hubert Humphrey had not entered a single primary, but his influence within the Democratic party guaranteed that delegates would select him anyway. Most voters could not figure out exactly where Humphrey stood on the Vietnam

The 1968 Democratic convention in Chicago

The Democrats did not get a positive "bounce" from their 1968 national convention. Outside the convention hall, Chicago police wielded clubs, tear gas, and Mace in pitched battles with thousands of antiwar protesters. Contrast this picture with the more recent "infomercial" conventions. Why do parties work to script their conventions? Would a looser convention be interesting enough to risk another Chicago?

conflict by 1968 (see Chapter 7), but his previous support for the administration still angered the antiwar movement.

The level of tension that existed at that time exceeds anything familiar to observers of contemporary politics. Mayor Richard Daley and the Chicago police force fully expected widespread violence on the streets. Rumors flew among the cops and National Guard troops stationed outside that activists might lace the Convention water supply with hallucinogenic drugs or pose as cab drivers to kidnap Democratic officials.[9]

Daley refused to issue protest permits and warned that the city would deal harshly with those who spoiled the celebration. But some protest leaders were more than willing to provoke such reprisals.[10] A group calling themselves yippies even floated the rumor that they would fill a nearby lake with 10,000 nude bodies.[11] They never carried through on this threat, but did help fill Chicago with roughly that number of demonstrators.

Many protesters flooded into Chicago's Grant and Lincoln parks, despite the lack of permits. They milled about on the grass, danced to provocative rock music, or chanted Buddhist mantras.[12] After some preliminary skirmishes, Daley's storm troopers finally decided to flush them out of the parks. They bathed the assemblies with tear gas, forcing many into the streets, where more tear gas and more police waited. The harshest confrontation occurred outside the Hilton Hotel, where the convention delegates stayed. As a mostly college-age crowd gasped and choked, armored troops formed into attack wedges and surged into the crowd, flailing about with stout clubs. Other officers hid their identities and attacked news reporters.[13] Ultimately, more than 500 victims needed medical attention.

The attacks greatly disturbed many political elites. Inside and outside the convention, public figures used the harshest rhetoric. From the podium of the convention, on prime-time television, Senator Abraham Ribicoff of Connecticut accused Mayor Daley of using "Gestapo tactics" to quash dissent—eliciting a string of obscenities from the Mayor that media microphones could not pick up. Hard-bitten British reporters who had covered the civil war in Northern Ireland wrote that the Chicago police had gone berserk.[14] An investigative commission later described the explosion as a "police riot."

Many media reporters clearly sympathized with the protesters. As Tom Wicker of the *New York Times* put it, "These were our children in the streets, and the Chicago police beat them up."[15] Over the course of the evening, the media lost all semblance of balance. They allowed bleeding protesters to vent their spleens over the airwaves. Longtime NBC anchor Chet Huntley condemned the police. Walter Cronkite choked back tears.

It was exactly the sort of shocked reaction that many of the protesters had hoped to provoke when they exposed themselves to attack. They had uncovered the bankruptcy of "the establishment," which could combat disagreement only through brute force. As tear gas floated hazily before the cameras and sirens filled the background, the news footage carried a continuous taunt from the demonstrators: "The whole world is watching, the whole world is watching."

Indeed, much of the United States was watching. What neither the protesters nor the journalists realized was that most in the audience were cheering on the storm troopers! Poll results that followed the Democratic National Convention stunned American elites: Popular majorities thought Chicago police had acted appropriately. In fact, more believed that the police should have used greater force than considered their actions excessive.[16] In other words, the American people had tuned out the chatter, stared at their TVs, and rooted for the cops. So much for the awesome power of television.

HOW POWERFUL ARE THE MEDIA, THEN? Are they an overwhelming force that brings down presidents or a lot of sound and fury that ordinary Americans ignore? As this chapter explains, in certain circumstances both descriptions are accurate. The media can have extremely powerful effects on public opinion, even to the extent of determining who wins elections and what governments do. But under other conditions, media effects are sharply limited.

DEVELOPMENT OF THE MASS MEDIA

The term **mass media** refers to affordable communications technologies capable of reaching an extensive audience. Such resources have existed for less than two centuries. Their development is bound up with the evolution of America's new democracy. The more that voters know about the actions of their governmental leaders, the more they can exercise popular influence. Knowledge is power, and more political information is available now than ever before. Politicians must adapt to the information-rich environment, part of a never-ending struggle to shape how their constituents perceive them.

NEWSPAPERS

At the time of the American Revolution, most of the colonies' newspapers were weeklies; the first daily paper in the United States began publication in Philadelphia in 1783.[17] These early papers were published by printers who, like Benjamin Franklin, also published books, almanacs, and official documents. They

reprinted material from European newspapers and from each other, as well as letters and essays from their readers.

As party politics developed, both fledgling parties realized the importance
of having a means of communicating with their constituents. Hamilton and the
Federalists established a "house" paper, the *Gazette of the United States,* and the
Jeffersonians responded with the *National Gazette.* These newspapers were
unabashedly one-sided: they printed the party line, viciously attacked the opposition, and depended for economic survival on government printing contracts.
So although early presidents did not speak in their own voices, they have been
"going public" to the extent technology allowed since the beginning of the
republic.[18]

Improvements in the manufacturing of paper and type and the invention of
the steam-driven printing press made it cheaper and easier to publish papers. In
1833 the *New York Sun* began daily publication, selling for a mere penny. (Before
that time the going price for a newspaper was an exorbitant six cents!) The rise of
the penny press marks the birth of the mass media in the United States. Millions
of ordinary people could purchase and read newspapers. Within two years the
circulation of the *Sun* was third in the world, behind the two largest London
newspapers.

As readership expanded, newspapers began to acquire their modern characteristics. One is sensationalism. Then, as now, crime and sex sold newspapers.
Politics and economics were left to the older weeklies. Still, the new penny
papers were overwhelmingly partisan. According to the 1850 census, only 5 percent of the country's newspapers were neutral or independent.[19] Politicians
worked hand in hand with the editors of friendly papers and withheld information from those allied with the opposition.

After the Civil War, an independent press began to develop. One-sided editorial positions remained common, but many publishers saw little point in alienating a large portion of their potential audience. Nor did political leaders need
party organs any longer. This was the heyday of the political machine, when party
bosses used their own networks of volunteers to communicate with constituents
(see Chapter 8). Patronage jobs and government contracts cemented political
alliances, not editorials.

The trend toward independence continued into the turn of the century,
when many newspapers became large enterprises. Hearst, Scripps, and other
companies bought up independent papers and consolidated them into great
chains. Thus the typical paper no longer was the voice of a lone editor.
Journalists became more professional and even less partisan. Some newspapers

were important participants in the Progressive movement, publishing "muck-raking" exposés of shocking conditions in American industry and corruption in government.

The most important development in the modern newspaper industry is the decline in diversity. Afternoon newspapers have all but disappeared. Mergers have resulted in most cities being served by one or two papers, compared to several a half century ago, and chains such as Gannett have continued to gobble up independent newspapers. Moreover, some media conglomerates own TV and radio stations, even networks, not just newspapers. Some observers worry that the mass media are losing their value as they face increased pressure to generate corporate profit.

RADIO

In the 1930s, the print monopoly of mass communications began to erode. The first radio stations appeared in the 1920s, and the first radio news agencies, in the 1930s. Politicians quickly made use of this exciting new technology. President Coolidge (1924–1928) was known as "Silent Cal," but to reach voters he took to the airwaves. Franklin Roosevelt helped calm a worried nation in the 1930s with his famous "fireside chats." Radio demagogues, such as the anti-Semite Father Coughlin, exerted a less calming influence during the same period.

Radio spread rapidly throughout the country. Today, there are more than 14,000 stations that reach nearly 85 percent of the population at some time on an average day. Virtually every household has at least one radio; the average is more than five. And, of course, there are millions of cars on the road, nearly all of which contain radios. Because of its local orientation and because it is relatively cheap, radio continues to be an important way for lower-level public officials to reach people.

Probably the most important recent development in radio communications is the rapid increase in talk shows. Talk shows have existed for half a century, but until recently most were local productions. The development of satellite technology and the lowering of long-distance telephone rates removed the geographic limits on such shows, and today many of them are syndicated by large networks. Rush Limbaugh's show is perhaps the best-known example. This conservative commentator began broadcasting nationally in 1988, and, as of 2000, his program reaches about 20 million listeners on more than 600 stations.[20] Liberals have tried to compete in this medium as well, although conservative viewpoints continue to have a wide edge. The talk format is a very popular radio format, trailing only country-western and adult contemporary music programs.[21]

TELEVISION

To most people today, the term "mass media" means television. There are more than 1,500 television stations in the United States, and about 99 percent of all households have at least one TV set, the average being four. Like radio, TV is close to being a universal medium of communications.

The first TV station went on the air in 1939, but TV grew very slowly during World War II. Afterward it spread rapidly; by 1960, 90 percent of all households had TVs. Three large networks initially dominated the industry: NBC, CBS, and ABC. The networks pay local affiliates to carry programs the networks offer. The affiliates, in turn, make advertising time available for the networks to sell. Of course, the profit that networks make from their advertising time depends critically on the popularity of their shows—which is why ratings are such an important consideration when it comes to programming decisions.

The Eisenhower campaign was the first to take advantage of TV for communicating political messages, producing simple commercials that are amusing when viewed today. But it was the Kennedy administration that elevated TV above the print medium and used it effectively (see the Election Connection, "TV and the 1960 Presidential Election"). During his short presidency, Kennedy held regularly televised press conferences that enabled him to go over the heads of the media and communicate directly with voters. Kennedy once commented to a reporter, "When we don't have to go through you bastards we can really get our story to the American people."[22]

When network TV reached its height in the 1980s, about 85 percent of all the commercial TV stations in the country were affiliated with one of the big-three networks: ABC, CBS, or NBC. But the network system began to fray after government deregulated the cable industry in the 1970s. The percent of households with cable increased from 20 percent in 1980 to 67 percent in 2000. Prime-time network programming has lost more than a quarter of its audience, as cable stations have proliferated.[23] Still, although the combined ratings of the big-three evening news telecasts have fallen by 30 percent since the mid-1980s, they continue to draw an audience of about 70 million people on an average weekday.[24] Network TV remains the largest single source of information available to Americans.

NEW MEDIA

During the 1992 campaign, Bill Clinton and Ross Perot irritated the establishment media by appearing on nontraditional outlets, such as *Larry King Live!* and the *Arsenio Hall Show,* and even on cable station MTV. Clinton played his sax for

TV and the 1960 Presidential Election

As Dwight Eisenhower's second term drew to a close, it was unclear whether the presidency would revert to Democratic control—as was the norm during the New Deal party system—or continue under a Republican administration. The prospective Republican candidate was Richard Nixon, Eisenhower's vice president. On the Democratic side, the identity of the nominee was much less certain. One of the aspiring Democrats was John Kennedy, a young Massachusetts senator.

Kennedy had several liabilities. By the standards of the time, he was relatively inexperienced, especially in foreign affairs, and he had few legislative accomplishments to show for his years in the Senate. In addition, Kennedy was a Catholic. Every president (and vice president) prior to 1960 had been a Protestant. The only previous Catholic nominee, Al Smith in 1928, had lost badly—even in some states in the Democratic "solid South." Although Kennedy was a personable, attractive candidate, many in the party feared that nominating a Catholic was a losing proposition.

To convince party leaders of his viability, Kennedy took his case to the people, previewing the kind of campaign that is now the norm. In 1960 only 16 states held primaries, and these chose only a small fraction of the convention delegates. Primaries were mostly beauty contests in which candidates could show strength and indirectly influence the professionals who would choose the nominee. Yet Kennedy entered seven primaries.

In Wisconsin, Kennedy beat Senator Hubert Humphrey, who also had decided to take the primary route, but the voting pattern was troublesome. Kennedy lost the Protestant congres-

sional districts and won Catholic districts, fueling fears that a Catholic still could not win a national election in a heavily Protestant country. This set up West Virginia, 95-percent Protestant, as the critical battleground.

Kennedy took the direct approach and discussed the religion issue in a half-hour statewide telecast. Never giving up the offensive, Kennedy barnstormed the state, but according to Theodore White,

> Above all, over and over again there was the handsome, open-faced candidate on the TV screen, showing himself, proving that a Catholic wears no horns. The documentary film on TV opened with a cut of a PT boat spraying a white wake through the black night, and Kennedy was a war hero; the film next showed the quiet young man holding a book in his hand in his own library receiving the Pulitzer Prize, and he was a scholar; then the young man held his golden-haired daughter of two, reading to her as she sat on his lap, and he was the young father; and always, gravely, open-eyed, with a sincerity that could not be feigned, he would explain his own devotion to the freedom of America's faiths and the separation of church and state.[a]

Kennedy beat Humphrey in Protestant West Virginia and went on to win the nomination. TV was not the only explanation for his victory—he had the Kennedy family fortune behind him and, by all accounts, used it freely—but more than any previous candidate, he had used TV as a critical part of the campaign.

The next task was to defeat a more formidable foe, Vice President Nixon—viewed by

(continued)

(continued from previous page)

many as more knowledgeable and experienced than Kennedy. Nixon and Kennedy agreed to a series of four debates to be carried by radio and, for the first time, TV. The audience for the debates was huge, approaching World Series figures. A mythology has grown up about the debates. It is too much to say that they were the key to Kennedy's winning the election, although in what was to be the closest election in American history, everything was critical.

Both candidates performed creditably, and the discussion was more substantive than TV debates generally are today. But winning debating points was not Kennedy's aim. By showing him side by side with Nixon, the debates helped Kennedy establish that he belonged in the race. He projected a cool, confident image that contrasted favorably with Nixon's more-nervous, less-comfortable appearance. Through the debates, Kennedy was able to offset Nixon's perceived advantage in maturity and experience. He overcame the hesitation of some Democrats previously reluctant to vote for him.[b]

In November, Kennedy's Catholicism cost him votes in some areas and gained him votes in others, but the losses concentrated in the South where the Democrats had plenty of votes to spare. On the plus side, religion may have gained him the critical states of New Jersey and Illinois, the latter by a thin 9,000-vote margin.[c] Kennedy became the first Catholic president, and the religion issue—at least in its Protestant versus Catholic form—was laid to rest.

What do you think?

• Is religion irrelevant when judging the values of a presidential candidate? Should voters ignore when a candidate holds different religious beliefs from theirs, or is that a fair criterion when deciding whom to support?

• Which aspects of a religious creed matter to political life? Which aspects bear no relation to politics?

• When public officials promise that their religious beliefs will not influence the performance of their duties, how would you interpret this guarantee? Does it mean that religion is not important to them, or is there an alternative meaning?

[a]Theodore H. White, *The Making of the President, 1960* (New York: Signet, 1961), p. 128.

[b]Nelson Polsby and Aaron Wildavsky, *Presidential Elections: Strategies of American Electoral Politics* (New York: Scribner, 1964), pp. 119–121.

[c]Angus Campbell, Philip Converse, Warren Miller, and Donald Stokes, "Stability and Change in 1960: A Reinstating Election," in *Elections and the Political Order* (New York: Wiley, 1966), Ch. 5.

Arsenio and discussed his underwear preferences on MTV. Perot virtually announced his candidacy on *Larry King Live!* Even President Bush felt compelled to appear on *Larry King Live!* and MTV to compete for attention. National politicians now avoid popular programs at their peril.

Cable TV is the most widespread example of the **new media,** although the term also includes VCRs, fax machines, cellular phones, satellite dishes, CDs, and especially anything connected with the Internet.[25] The Cable News Network (CNN) only appeared in 1979. Aside from cable TV, few Americans use the new media for political information. Surveys indicate that only half of the American population had access to the Internet by the summer of 2000.[26] Few of those with Internet access pay much attention to political Web sites. One survey during the height of the 2000 primary season found that only 11 percent of Internet users had ever visited a candidate's Web site, a figure far lower than the number who had seen a candidate on network TV's evening news or even CNN.[27]

But radio and TV also started small, and given the explosive growth of the Internet, it is likely that after another election cycle or two, the Internet will be a true mass medium. Consider that in 1992 neither presidential candidate had an official Web site; by 2000, Web sites were standard in campaigns as far down as the local level. Use of the Web for raising money grew rapidly in the recent primary campaigns as well. In absolute terms the amount raised was small: The four leading presidential candidates (Bradley, Bush, Gore, and McCain) raised a total of $139 million in 1999, less than 3 percent of which came from online contributions.[28] But the proportion raised online increased over the course of the year. Moreover, after McCain's upset victory in the New Hampshire primary, online contributions soared—he raised $5.6 million in the month after New Hampshire, a quarter of his total fund-raising.[29] Given the ease of contributing online, especially after so-called e-check technology becomes widespread, such fund-raising no doubt will grow.[30]

Network TV has a large, diverse audience. Thus it encourages politicians to make general appeals. In contrast, the newer media allow politicians to communicate more specific information to targeted audiences. Once again, an innovation in the media realm is altering the existing equilibrium between politicians and the media, this time apparently in favor of politicians. The new media give them a greater capacity to communicate to voters without having their messages constrained and edited by the traditional mass media. The struggle for control of information continues.

WHICH INFORMATION SOURCES DO AMERICANS USE?

Communication is a two-way street. No one can make people read newspapers, listen to radio, watch TV, or visit a home page. Citizens are free to consume or ignore any message. These choices guide the information that becomes available, since media companies are profit-making enterprises. Their growth or decline reflects the tastes of the popular audience.

Surveys show that TV supplanted newspapers as the public's principal source of information in the early 1960s. Nearly 50 percent of Americans today rely primarily on television (see Figure 12.1). A much smaller 20 percent rely primarily

FIGURE 12.1

TV is the primary source of news for contemporary Americans

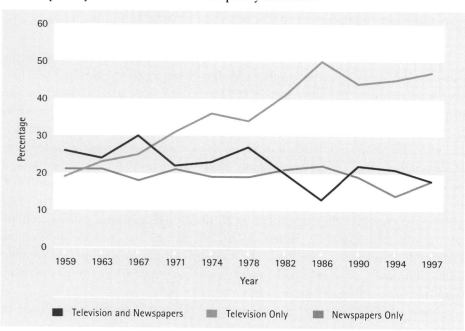

SOURCE: Data are taken from the Roper Organization, *America's Watching: Public Attitudes Toward Television* (1997).

on newspapers, and the remaining 20 percent use both. Figure 12.2 shows that a comparable percentage reports TV to be the most credible source of information. In short, TV is America's dominant information provider.

Newspapers have slightly more influence over politics than over society as a whole.[31] In presidential campaigns, people rely more on TV than on newspapers by a margin of 3 to 1. But in statewide races for governor and senator, TV's edge is only 5 to 3. And in local election contests, newspapers have an edge over TV as the principal source of information. The national networks do not cover local races in small cities and towns, except under unusual circumstances. Whether newspapers can maintain their importance in this niche as local cable stations proliferate remains to be seen.

Individuals vary in their absorption of information.[32] Well-educated or older individuals are particularly likely to rely on newspapers, as are whites. Newspaper supporters argue that print is more informative than TV, but research

FIGURE 12.2

Contemporary Americans consider TV their most credible source of news

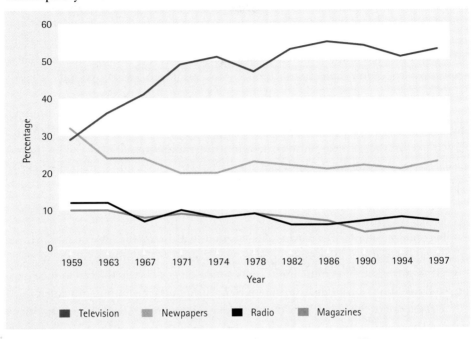

SOURCE: Data are taken from the Roper Organization, *America's Watching: Public Attitudes Toward Television* (1997).

fails to support that argument once the characteristics of the audience (such as education) are taken into account.[33] That is, people of comparable background tend to learn about the same amount, whether they rely on print or television.

MEDIA EFFECTS

People once feared the mass media as a great danger to democratic politics. The rapid spread of radio in the 1930s coincided with the rise of fascism in Europe. Some worried that this was more than coincidence. Before 1930, political leaders had communicated with constituencies indirectly, speaking and writing to lower-level leaders who in turn communicated with the grassroots. But demagogues like Hitler and Mussolini spoke directly to their audience, sparking fears that radio created a "mass society" of lonely individuals susceptible to charismatic hate mongerers.[34]

Stimulated by such concerns, researchers conducted numerous studies of the media's ability to persuade. Contrary to expectations, research on the effects of mass communication turned up negative results. Americans, at least, were remarkably resistant to propaganda; media messages seldom altered the audience's views. Listeners apparently engaged in selective perception, absorbing information consistent with their predispositions and discounting the rest. Thus, exposure to communications tended to reinforce what people already believed.[35]

By 1960, many scholars accepted the idea that mass media had a minimal impact on American public opinion.[36] Younger generations of researchers took a new look at the subject, however, after the rapid spread of TV. This newer research has documented important media effects, more subtle than the kind of mass persuasion earlier studies had sought to document.

AGENDA SETTING

Public-opinion scholar Bernard Cohen argued that the media may not tell people *what* to think but do tell people what to think *about*.[37] The media set the agenda, even if they do not determine how issues get resolved. The media can induce people to think about a particular problem by focusing on it, whipping up concern.

Catastrophes in Third World countries, for example, largely go unnoticed unless the media — particularly television — turn their attention to such events. Famine struck Ethiopia in 1984, resulting in numerous front-page articles in powerful U.S. newspapers such as the *New York Times* and the *Washington Post*. The Associated Press (AP) wire service carried 228 stories.[38] But it was not until television stations carried heartrending footage into their living rooms that a great number of Americans became aware of the problem and supported governmental efforts to help.[39] Similar responses followed media coverage of Somalia, Rwanda, and Kosovo. Media analysts have even given government responses like these a nickname, the "CNN effect," after the tendency for a problem to be addressed once CNN covers it.

Agenda setting is well documented, although much of the evidence is inconclusive.[40] Researchers face a dilemma trying to sort out what causes what. Do worries prompt the coverage, does coverage create the worries, or do real experiences produce both? Some careful studies conclude that the independent impact of the media has been exaggerated; astute government officials use the media to place problems on the national and international agendas.[41] Nevertheless, experimental studies that raise viewer concern about subjects *not* high on the national agenda have been able to provide some evidence of agenda setting.[42]

PRIMING AND FRAMING

As we relate in Chapter 5, President Bush's approval ratings soared in 1991 after an American ground offensive drove Iraqi forces out of Kuwait. His popularity ratings reached unprecedented levels (near 90 percent). Yet within a year they had plummeted. What happened? Journalists turned to other stories after the war ended, chiefly the struggling economy. Gradually, Bush's ratings became dependent on his handling of the economy, which was viewed far less positively than his handling of the war.[43]

Bush's fall from favor is an example of **priming**—news coverage primed people to evaluate him according to his handling of the war in February 1991, but later coverage primed people to evaluate him in terms of the economy. Obviously, the media do not have full control over which criteria Americans use to evaluate their presidents. War pushes everything else off the agenda of public opinion: All other concerns seem minor when husbands and wives and sons and daughters are in danger. Still, studies suggest that the media overemphasized economic difficulties in the early 1990s, heightening public pessimism as well as the attention people paid to an issue on which President Bush was vulnerable.[44]

Framing and priming are related notions.[45] In Chapter 5 we explain that Americans tend to shift their opinions on abortion depending upon how pollsters frame the question. How issues are framed shapes more than just survey results, however; it also molds how public opinion thinks about issues more generally. For example, if crime is framed as a problem that presidents can and should do something about, it is more likely to have a political impact than if it is framed as an uncontrollable by-product of social breakdown.

HOW STRONG ARE MEDIA EFFECTS?

The view that the mass media would enable demagogues to manipulate public opinion clearly overstated media's influence. Yet the initial social-science research that rejected media influence went too far in the opposite direction. The truth appears to be somewhere in between. Media can affect the political agenda—what people think about. They can prime people to think about certain issues and frame how they evaluate them. But the strength of these media effects depends on both the audience and the message.

People who are uninterested in and uninformed about politics are most susceptible to agenda setting. For example, political independents differ from partisans. Independents are more likely to be uninformed, so their concerns shift from one issue to another with the intensity of media coverage. On the other hand, partisans are more easily primed to think in terms of issues at the core of their party's concerns.[46]

The characteristics of information being communicated is at least as important. When a problem or event is far away—well beyond personal experience—the mass media provide the only information available. Their influence diminishes when information is closer to home and people have some personal basis for arriving at opinions.[47] The Tet and Chicago examples illustrate this phenomenon. The media provided almost the only available information about the events in South Vietnam, so they influenced the public's view considerably. Protesters of the sort demonstrating in Chicago, on the other hand, were familiar sights on college campuses, at public buildings such as draft offices, and in city streets. Many people had developed strong views about protesters; there was little opportunity for the media's interpretation of the events in Chicago to alter such predispositions.

MEDIA BIASES

Modern journalists purport to be objective. They are supposed to report events and describe conflicts accurately so that voters can make informed judgments about their government. If reporters and editors usually lived up to this ideal, then media effects would not be much cause for concern. But news organizations and other media corporations represent an important player in the political system, essentially an institution with its own interests, values, and operating procedures. The mass media might threaten democracy's operation if they use the powers of agenda setting, priming, and framing in a biased manner.

Many observers believe that the media do skew the news. The most common charge is that the media show political bias, but most academic critics believe that other sorts of bias are even more serious.

IDEOLOGICAL BIAS   Conservatives often complain about the "liberal media." There is no doubt that liberal viewpoints are overrepresented among practicing journalists. Numerous studies report that journalists are more Democratic than the population at large: Even George McGovern and Walter Mondale received strong majorities of the vote among journalists despite popular landslides in favor of their opponents. More recently, a survey of Washington bureau chiefs and congressional correspondents reported that, in 1992, 89 percent voted for Clinton, compared to 43 percent of the electorate that did.[48] More detailed analyses indicate that journalists hold views that are even more liberal than those of other college-educated professionals, especially on social issues such as abortion, crime, and gay rights.[49]

But do such biases show through in the news? Some studies find evidence of partisan bias on the part of reporters. For example, a team of researchers carefully watched tapes of the network evening news programs broadcast during the 1984 campaign. Their aim was to evaluate the **spin**—the positive or negative slant—that reporters and anchors put on their reports. They found that President Reagan got 10 seconds of bad spin for every second of good spin. In contrast, the Democratic candidate, Walter Mondale, had a 3-to-2 ratio of good spin to bad.[50] On a less serious note, a study of the jokes told by late-night TV talk show hosts during the 1988 campaign found that Republicans were skewered twice as often as Democrats.[51] As for the 2000 election, by mid-September George W. Bush had been the butt of 50 percent more late night jokes than Al Gore.[52]

Sometimes the journalistic hostility against Republicans shows through in small ways. During President Reagan's farewell address at the 1988 Republican National Convention, his speech followed a repetitive structure. Reagan would claim an accomplishment for the outgoing administration, one that Democrats might wish to deny, and end the item by admonishing, "But facts are stubborn things." Part way through the list, a loud crack shattered Reagan's concentration. The noise probably came from the stage sound system, or perhaps a balloon, but it resembled a gunshot—at least enough to rattle Reagan, who had already survived one assassination attempt. The next time he returned to the refrain, Reagan flubbed the line, saying "Facts are stupid things." A friendlier press corps might have described the speaker's mistake as a very human reaction to fear. Instead, national journalists did not even mention the loud noise; they portrayed Reagan's gaffe as symbolic of the conservative administration's scorn for truth.

Although journalists do deviate from objectivity and Republicans suffer more than Democrats, lapses are not as common as media critics imply. Newspaper readers do not perceive consistently liberal viewpoints.[53] More than three-fourths of the presidential election coverage on television in 1984 had no spin at all. In the 2000 elections Democrat Al Gore received a fair bit of negative coverage, interrupted only during the couple of weeks immediately following his selection of Connecticut Senator Joseph Lieberman as a running mate. The media tend to be hard on incumbents, losers, and those caught up in scandals—even when they are Democrats. Similarly, late-night TV hosts usually focus on whoever offers the best material.

Although they are less vocal, critics on the left of the political spectrum also charge that the media are ideologically biased—only they see a conservative slant. Whatever the personal views of rank-and-file journalists, they work for profit-making enterprises reliant on corporate advertising. They cannot afford to emphasize ethical or environmental abuses perpetuated by business because to do so would offend potential advertisers. Media celebrities also attract generous honoraria from corporate interests who invite them to give speeches, leading critics to call them "buckrakers" rather than muckrakers.

Some defenders of the journalistic profession point to the contradictory critiques as evidence that no real ideological bias exists. If one group says the news is too liberal and another says it is too conservative, they imply, then coverage must be just right. This response rules out the possibility that *both* criticisms may be correct. News professionals resemble others who share their social status: progressive reformers with left-wing social views who nevertheless reap the solid incomes and generous retirement benefits provided by a corporate payroll.[54] Just as Al Gore in 2000 could be both too left-wing for the Republicans but too comfortable with big business for the Greens, so it is possible for the typical journalist to be biased in a way that will prompt different critics to use different terminology.

The weakening of the dominance of the big-three networks should reduce any existing progressive bias. Local news and public affairs programs are more likely to reflect community sentiments and less likely to represent the biases of network news operations headquartered in New York, Washington, and Los Angeles. Cable channels broadcast programs produced by conservative and evangelical groups. Talk radio has a conservative slant. The Internet is open to all points of view, and libertarians are especially well represented there. In short, the communications channels of the future should be more open to alternative points of view than were the airwaves in the past.

SELECTION BIAS   Periodically, frustrated citizens write to editors to complain that all their newspapers ever print is bad news. They are criticizing the professional norms that journalists use to define what is "newsworthy."[55] People working hard and contributing to their communities are not news; one sociopath who runs amok is. A government program that works well is not news; one that is mismanaged, corrupt, or a failure is news. An elected official who works diligently and avoids conflict is not newsworthy; those who stoke controversy or become mired in scandal are.

Professor Larry Sabato argues that the negative tone of the media has become much more prominent in recent decades. He contends that presidents from Franklin Roosevelt to John Kennedy enjoyed the support of a press with a "lapdog" mentality. Johnson and Nixon were subject to far greater scrutiny from a press with a "watchdog" mentality. Succeeding presidents, he maintains, suffer mean treatment from a press with a "junkyard dog" mentality—attacking anyone

Dogbert news network

Americans generally get "bad" rather than "good" news, though they often express a preference for positive stories. Why do the media lead with controversy and mayhem? Is it what the people really want?

who comes in range.[56] Some observers believe that the negative tone of modern press coverage has contributed to the American public's increased cynicism.[57]

Newsworthiness also favors things that are new, especially those that are exciting and unusual. Sudden events make better news than gradual developments or persistent conditions. A crisis lends itself to the kind of hit-and-run coverage favored by contemporary media. Heroes and villains, not abstract social and economic developments, form the ingredients of a good story. This bias is particularly characteristic of TV, which is even more fast-paced than print. TV needs dramatic events, colorful personalities, bitter conflicts, short and snappy comments (sound bites), and, above all, compelling pictures. A frequently heard maxim is "If it bleeds, it leads."

A media tendency to favor sudden, short-term developments can have serious political implications. Stories that do not fit media needs may receive insufficient, or at least distorted, treatment.[58] A favorite example is the largest economic policy debacle in recent American history: the savings and loan (S&L) disaster of the 1980s. This one event cost taxpayers a total of $200 billion.[59]

As early as 1981, accountants, prominent economists, and a top government regulator began to issue warnings about the troubled S&L industry—but media outlets paid little attention. As one journalist commented, "It was a 'numbers' story, not a 'people' story."[60] Most reporters lacked the training to handle such a complex issue, and anyway it was hard to cram into 30-second news segments. The government waited until 1989 to close down insolvent S&Ls, after years of reckless operation. At this point the crisis started generating catchy stories: indictments of executives, investigations of members of Congress, and housing developments auctioned off for a song. But the news coverage came a little too late for American taxpayers; they covered the S&L losses through the Federal

Savings and Loan Insurance Corporation. And even the stories that did emerge concentrated on a few instances of corruption rather than on the government policies that led to the crisis.[61]

PROFESSIONAL BIAS   A third kind of media bias arises from the demands of the journalism profession itself. A few journalists are experts who work specific beats—business reporters, education reporters, health reporters, Supreme Court reporters, and so on. But most reporters and journalists are generalists who lack specific substantive expertise. They operate on tight deadlines and must start from scratch on each new story. Thus, on many subjects more complex than scandals and conflicts, they are dependent on experts and other outside sources for information and interpretation.

Ironically, despite the familiar image of the investigative reporter, reporters uncover only a small fraction of the scandals they report — probably less than one-quarter.[62] Government agencies expose the lion's share, and they generally do so officially, not through surreptitious leaks. Moreover, as journalists themselves recognize, the news media have increased their emphasis on entertainment.[63] Especially in the case of TV, looks and personalities are more important today than a generation ago. Network news becomes more like "infotainment" (a mixture of news and entertainment), and major newspapers become more like tabloids.

The lack of internal expertise and the competitive pressure for ratings and sales contribute to an unattractive feature of modern political coverage: "pack journalism," in which reporters unanimously decide something is "The Big

Lowest common denominator
As the public gets more reports of scandal, some worry that the electorate grows more cynical. Do feeding frenzies "packaged as a soap opera and horse race" lead the public to distrust government?

Story" and gravitate to it as a herd. When a scandal arises, the group mentality becomes even more extreme; Larry Sabato calls the typical response to scandal a "feeding frenzy" because reporters leap upon the victim like sharks tearing apart wounded prey.[64]

People who observe this feeding frenzy may be puzzled by the media's obsession with seemingly minor matters, but journalists enjoy safety in numbers. One can hardly be faulted for working on the same story as other prominent journalists. Far better to focus on what turns out to be an overblown, inconsequential story than "run the risk of going down in history as 'the reporter who missed the next Watergate.'"[65] Indeed, every news show or newspaper fears missing a big story.

PROSPECTS FOR CHANGE   Americans are not happy with the press corps. Popular evaluations of the media have declined sharply since the mid-1980s. Growing percentages believe that the media are unprofessional, uncaring, immoral, and even harmful to democracy (see Table 12.1).

However justified, criticisms of the media's coverage of politics and government miss an important point. The American public gets what it pays for. News

TABLE 12.1

NEGATIVE EVALUATIONS OF THE MEDIA ARE ON THE INCREASE

NEWS ORGANIZATIONS GENERALLY ARE	1985	1999
Moral	54%	40%
Immoral	13%	38%
Caring about people they report on	35%	21%
Uncaring about people they report on	48%	67%
Highly professional	72%	52%
Not professional	11%	32%
Protecting democracy	54%	45%
Hurting democracy	23%	38%
Caring about how good a job they do	79%	69%
Uncaring about how good a job they do	11%	22%

SOURCE: "Big Doubts About New Media's Values," The Pew Research Center for the People & the Press (http://www.people-press.org , posted February 1999).

executives use focus groups and other measures of audience interest to determine what impresses their consumers: what they will read, what they will watch, what they will buy.[66] As one journalist commented, "The purpose of the media is not to educate; it is to impress—to make an impression. There isn't the time or space to educate."[67] News coverage may fall short of what public-spirited critics would like to see, but only because it provides more of the sort of "news" that the audience wants.

Columnist Dave Barry once gently mocked his readers for the hypocrisy revealed by their complaints:

> *Probably, if anybody asks you what you think of the news media, you say, "I think they go too far. They should stop covering sex and go back to covering important issues, such as the economy." You make a strong point. Let me respond by saying this: Liar, liar, pants on fire. You don't want to read about the economy. You love to read about sex. Everybody does.*
>
> *Let's consider two headlines. FIRST HEADLINE: "Federal Reserve Board Ponders Reversal of Postponement of Deferral of Policy Reconsideration." SECOND HEADLINE: "Federal Reserve Board Caught in Motel with Underage Sheep."*
>
> *Be honest, now. Which of these two stories would you read? There's no need to answer: We in the newspaper business already know.* [68]

Perhaps the main hope of media critics is that executives underestimate their audience. People in the media were stunned by the ratings Ross Perot's "infomercials" earned during the 1992 presidential campaign—as many as 10 million households tuned in.[69] TV producers defend sound-bite journalism with the observation that the average voter has an attention span of less than 30 seconds, but Perot treated voters as intelligent adults and held the interest of many for 30 minutes with lengthy expositions accompanied by charts and figures!

As the network system declines, as more independent stations begin operating, and as the new media continue to advance, we may see the development of numerous specialized informational channels able to tap into the interest in public affairs that Perot uncovered. Yet the growth of better information sources may only widen the knowledge gap dividing an attentive elite from those who would just as soon spend their evening watching sitcoms or drinking in a bar. The effects on American democracy may not be as positive as reformers might hope.

THE MEDIA AND ELECTORAL POLITICS

The mass media play an important role in democratic politics. Ideally, they transmit information about problems and issues, helping voters make intelligent choices about the candidates who compete for their votes. Many critics believe that the general biases we have discussed can cause media coverage of elections to fall far short of the ideal.

CAMPAIGN COVERAGE

Nowhere do critics of the mass media find more to criticize than in the media's coverage of political campaigns. The media provide little coverage of policy issues: the nature of social and economic problems, the contrasts among programs the candidates advocate, unbiased appraisals of officials' performance, and so forth. Instead, critics charge, the media devote too much attention to "character" issues that have little to do with the ability of the candidates to govern. Thus, the press dwells on whether a candidate was suspended from school, had an extramarital affair, or once worked for a company with interest in government contracts.

Not only do the media concentrate on seemingly frivolous matters at the expense of genuine policy debates, their interest in such issues stems primarily from a wish to handicap the race. Coverage focuses on which candidate is leading, which candidate is dropping back, which one is coming up on the rail, what the latest polls say, who got what endorsement, and how a new announcement on a key issue will affect the polls. Candidate qualifications receive little attention, and issue positions are evaluated for their success as tactical moves. Critics thus assail the media for treating democratic elections as little more than horse races.

This tendency toward horse-race coverage has become much more pronounced over the past generation, and the attention devoted to substance has declined.[70] Increasingly, journalists interpret what candidates say rather than allow candidates to speak for themselves. One study that compared network newscasts in 1968 with those in 1988 found that the average sound bite for presidential candidates who appeared on the news had fallen from 42 seconds to less than 10.[71] Although the media consciously tried to make sound bites longer in 1992 and 1996, the situation has improved little, and candidates still do not get enough time to explain their positions on complex issues.

Observers of contemporary political campaigns are not the only ones critical of media coverage. The candidates themselves are unhappy—so much so that they are finding ways to get around the news media. Not only do they turn to television talk shows to reach voters, their campaigns have also invested heavily in other forms of media such as Web pages and phone banks. Establishment reporters complain that candidates are trying to insulate themselves from the hard questioning of seasoned political reporters. But if "hard questioning" is only going to produce snippets on the evening news, then it cannot be doing much for the democratic process. Candidates may simply value the opportunity to talk about issues rather than the trivia so fascinating to journalists.

THE CONVENTIONS

Before voters chose presidential candidates in party primaries, the national conventions were important political events. Party leaders came together, made deals, hammered out a platform, nominated candidates, and (if successful) left with a unified party prepared to battle the opposition. In recognition of the importance of the conventions, CBS and NBC provided gavel-to-gavel coverage from 1956 to 1976 and regularly assigned their top anchors and reporters to the events.

The conventions have not been nearly so important since the development of primaries, institutionalized in 1972. Media coverage has dropped accordingly (see Figure 12.3). The parties now treat the conventions as huge infomercials in an attempt to take advantage of their diminishing time on the screen. Planners slot the most attractive speakers for prime time and arrange the entire convention schedule with the media in mind.

The parties showcase their candidates in hopes of producing a "bounce" upward in the polls, as happened after the 1988 Republican convention (for Bush) and the 2000 Democratic convention (for Gore).[72] Media coverage is a double-edged sword, however; if coverage emphasizes a divided party or unpopular ele-

FIGURE 12.3

The networks increasingly ignore the national political conventions

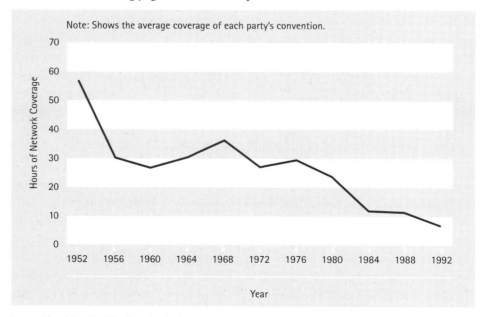

Note: Shows the average coverage of each party's convention.

Year

Hours of Network Coverage

SOURCE: Adapted from Harold Stanley and Richard Niemi, *Vital Statistics of American Politics*, Fifth Edition. (Washington, DC: CQ Press, 1995), p. 69.

ments of the party, it will cause the candidate to drop in the polls. The 1968 Chicago Democratic convention is perhaps the classic example, but a strident speech by Pat Buchanan to the 1992 Republican convention turned off many moderates and hurt President Bush's chances for reelection.

THE PRESIDENTIAL DEBATES

One of the high points of modern presidential campaigns is the series of debates between the two—sometimes three—major candidates. No other campaign events earn such high ratings. In fact, more people watch the debates than vote.

The first televised debates were held during the 1960 campaign between candidates Richard Nixon and John Kennedy. One of the surprising findings in studies of the debates was that people who listened to them on the radio evaluated Nixon's performance more favorably than people who watched them on TV did, an indication that visual images could influence voter perception.[73] No debates took place in 1964, 1968, or 1972, but they have been held in every election since. The format and arrangements continue as matters of considerable controversy, but presidential debates have become an institution.

Studies show that performance in the debates can sway the undecided voter. For example, in 1984 President Reagan appeared tired and confused in his first debate with Walter Mondale. His unexpectedly poor performance raised the issue of his age (then 73) and resulted in a slight drop in the polls. Knowing how important the next encounter was, Reagan came in alert, prepared, and full of good humor. He dispelled the concerns raised in the first debate and gained 4 points in the polls.[74]

As in campaign coverage generally, the first question journalists raise about debates is "Who won?" Most observers agree that Vice President Gore flubbed *something* during the 2000 debates, although they disagree on exactly what or how many votes it cost him. Several minor falsehoods, uttered in the heat of debate, attracted a journalistic feeding frenzy.[75] Gore also wavered between an arrogant and combative style (in the first and third debates) and smarmy ineffectiveness (in the second debate), some combination of which apparently alienated important swing voters.[76] But even his drop in the polls eventually dissipated.

MEDIA COVERAGE OF GOVERNMENT

Media coverage of government exhibits problems and biases analogous to those evident in media coverage of campaigns. From the standpoint of the mass media, much of the routine work of government is dull; hence, the media focus on what they consider more exciting.

EMPHASIS ON THE PRESIDENT
(AND OTHER PERSONALITIES)

The president is a single individual with personality and character; therefore, he (no woman has thus far been president) is inherently more interesting than a collective like Congress or an abstraction like the bureaucracy. The president receives the lion's share of evening news coverage.[77] And not only does Congress play second fiddle, but coverage of the institution has declined in recent decades.[78]

The problem, of course, is that the president is only one part of the government, a part with fairly limited powers (see Chapter 10). Thus the media prime citizens to focus on the president to a degree that is disproportionate to his powers and responsibilities. The exception to this generalization is one that proves the rule. For six months after the 1994 elections, the media virtually forgot about President Clinton as pack journalists turned their attention to House Speaker Newt Gingrich and the new Republican majority in Congress. For once, the media could represent Congress via a single personality. If the Republican takeover of Congress had not been associated with a colorful individual like Gingrich, the media, in all likelihood, would have devoted less attention.

This focus of the media on personalities seems to be a universal tendency. Note that it is similar to building sports coverage around superstars, such as baseball sluggers Barry Bonds, Mark McGwire, and Sammy Sosa. An effective governmental team, like a winning sports team, requires a strong group, but the media find individual heroics and failures more compelling. Unfortunately, this sort of personal coverage probably discourages teamwork, reinforcing grandstanding tendencies already present in the political system. Moreover, such media coverage primes citizens to think about government in terms of the heroic exploits and tragic failures of individuals rather than in terms of institutions and processes that are operating effectively or less well.[79]

EMPHASIS ON CONFLICT

Every time Speaker Gingrich made a controversial comment, he was assured of media coverage. Indeed, Gingrich's rise in national politics in part grew from his willingness to make the kind of comments that reporters love, and to offer them up in convenient sound bites.

In 1995, President Clinton and Speaker Gingrich appeared on the same platform in New Hampshire and engaged in an intelligent, mature discussion. Citizens were very receptive, and even Clinton and Gingrich seemed to enjoy it. Journalists found it dull. How could they report an intelligent discussion? They would have preferred the Speaker to level a serious charge or offer a personal criticism that could have provided a 10-second sound bite. According to David Broder, the dean of American political commentators,

> *It is conflict—not compromise—that makes news. A piece of videotape showing Democratic Rep. Pete Stark of California denouncing the Republicans for "cutting" Medicare will play over and over. Tape of a Democrat praising a Republican for the successful "culmination of a long, bipartisan effort to reexamine and refocus the federal role in the education and training of America's workers" will never make it out of the editing room.* [80]

EMPHASIS ON SCANDALS AND GAFFES

However favorable the coverage of Clinton's election, his honeymoon with the media ended quickly. In the first months of his presidency, the public was bombarded with stories about the Whitewater land deal, aide Vince Foster's suicide, $200 haircuts, parties with actress Sharon Stone, turmoil in the White House travel office, Hillary Clinton's investments, and numerous other matters that you probably do not remember. The reason you most likely do not remember them is that, however important these matters were to the individuals involved at the time, they were not important for the overall operation of government. Hence, they have been appropriately forgotten.

The focus of congressional coverage has changed. From 1972 to the mid-1980s, policy stories outnumbered scandal stories by 13 to 1, but since then the ratio has plunged to 3 to 1. [81] It is doubtful that either Congress or the White House has gotten that much worse.

GOVERNMENT REGULATION OF THE ELECTRONIC MEDIA

Freedom of the press is closer to being an absolute doctrine in the United States than in other countries. In theory the press has wide latitude in its ability to report on and even criticize government. Few media outlets receive direct public funding, and politicians do not regularly dictate policy to any significant media outlet—contrary to the situation in some democracies (see the Election Connection, "Television and the 2000 Russian Presidential Election").

Radio and TV, however, lack some press freedoms because they use the public airwaves. Government has used its power to regulate broadcast media, embodied in the Federal Communications Commission (FCC), as a justification for weighing in on media content—an argument accepted by federal courts.

One outgrowth of this regulatory power is that politicians have ensured that media owners cannot use their property to favor some candidates over others.

ELECTION CONNECTION

Television and the
2000 Russian Presidential Election

Skeptics of publicly owned or operated media can point out disturbing examples of abuse when government is involved with operation of the news media. In the 2000 Russian elections, for example, supporters of acting President Vladimir Putin were determined to ensure that he receive an absolute majority in the first round of voting so that he could claim a popular mandate.[a] On the eve of the election, the ORT television network, 51 percent of which is owned by the government, broadcast a series of damaging reports against candidate Grigori Yavlinsky, most of whose support was thought to overlap with Putin's.

The broadcasts exploited prejudices still widespread in Russia: anti-Semitism, distrust of foreigners, and intolerance of gays. One broadcast alleged that Yavlinsky's campaign was bankrolled by rich Jewish businessmen (he is half-Jewish and has dual Russian and Israeli citizenship). A second reported on gay support for Yavlinsky. A third alleged, without evidence, that Yavlinsky was supported by German think tanks.

The Putin campaign denied any involvement and suggested that ORT was merely reporting facts that the Russian people had a right to know. Disinterested observers believed otherwise, especially because another one of the network's principal owners, Boris Berezovsky, is a major Putin supporter. Although the effects of the broadcasts cannot be measured, Putin won his majority and was elected to a full term as president. This extreme example raises disturbing questions about government involvement in the media.

What do you think?

- Is this kind of heavy-handed government interference in media operations likely in a developed democracy, such as the United States, or is it a concern only in a new democracy like Russia?
- Are there institutional or constitutional safeguards that could prevent this kind of abuse from occurring in the United States?

[a]This account is drawn from Michael R. Gordon, "Russian TV Assails Putin Rival," *San Francisco Chronicle* (March 26, 2000): A13.

Legislation creating the FCC established an **equal-time rule** specifying that if a station sells time to a legally qualified candidate, it must be willing to sell time to all such candidates. Later, the rule was expanded so that, for example, when the networks carry the president's State of the Union speech, they also must carry a reply from the opposition.

From 1949 to 1987, the FCC also enforced a **fairness doctrine** that required stations to devote a reasonable amount of time to matters of public importance and to air contrasting viewpoints on those matters. Eventually, the doctrine also required stations to give public figures who were attacked an opportunity to reply. But communications technologies expanded so much that, by the

1970s, it undercut some of the rationale for government regulation. In 1987 an FCC staffed by Reagan appointees repealed the fairness doctrine. And more deregulation was to come, as Congress encouraged competition between telephone and cable television companies.

Despite this general trend toward deregulation, recent years have seen a rise in the number of proposals for regulation of the Internet. Some people would like to regulate content, making it difficult for children to reach pornographic, hate-filled, violent, or otherwise objectionable Web sites, for example. The courts probably will rule against most such attempts to restrict content transmitted over the Internet. Various others would like to regulate so-called e-commerce. For example, many state governors are unhappy that purchases made over the Internet are often not subject to state sales tax, which has the effect of denying their states revenue and putting state merchants at a competitive disadvantage. This is a touchy subject, and both George W. Bush and Al Gore finessed it during the 2000 campaign by supporting a moratorium on Internet taxation that expired in October 2001.

CHAPTER SUMMARY

Although the mass media do influence public opinion, such effects are not automatic. They depend on people's predispositions and their outside sources of knowledge. Nevertheless, the media can set the political agenda by focusing Americans' attention on particular issues. They can prime the audience to think about politicians in a certain way or frame political issues in a manner that influences public opinion.

Frequently, critics charge the media with one or another form of bias. Journalists certainly appear to be establishment liberals, progressive reformers who support capitalism but endorse liberal social change. More importantly, norms of newsworthiness and pressures on the news-gathering process distort coverage of political issues, prompting critics to assail how the news industry presents both elections and the process of governance.

Nevertheless, the mass media are less than two centuries old, and the spread of political knowledge permits voters more influence over their government. Government-regulated TV and radio stations dominate mass communications, but recent technological and legal developments have promoted numerous alternate media. Outlets such as cable TV and the Internet are weakening the traditional broadcast system, and they are expanding the number and the diversity of information sources. If knowledge really is power, then media organizations form an important political institution that has expanded popular influence in America's new democracy.

KEY TERMS

agenda setting, p. 404

draft, p. 393

equal-time rule, p. 418

fairness doctrine, p. 418

framing, p. 405

mass media, p. 395

new media, p. 400

priming, p. 405

spin, p. 407

SUGGESTED READINGS

Davis, Richard. *The Web of Politics: The Internet's Impact on the American Political System.* New York: Oxford University Press, 1999. A first look at how the Internet is changing American politics.

Iyengar, Shanto, and Donald Kinder. *News That Matters.* Chicago: University of Chicago Press, 1987. An exemplary experimental study that demonstrates the existence of agenda setting and priming.

Jamieson, Kathleen. *Packaging the Presidency.* New York: Oxford University Press, 1996. Critical survey of the evolution of presidential campaign advertising from the Eisenhower years to the present.

Neumann, W. Russell. *The Future of the Mass Audience.* Cambridge, England: Cambridge University Press, 1991. Thoughtful examination of the effects of technological change on mass communications. Concludes that new media will not fragment the audience as much as many think.

Patterson, Thomas. *Out of Order.* New York: Vintage, 1994. A critical discussion of the way the print media define news when they cover presidential campaigns. Recommended by President Clinton.

Sabato, Larry. *Feeding Frenzy: Attack Journalism and American Politics.* Baltimore: Lanahan, 1991. New edition. Entertaining critique of the most extreme manifestations of "pack journalism."

ON THE WEB

ABC News Political Nation
abcnews.go.com/sections/politics

This industry leader provides news, campaign coverage, chat rooms, and multimedia reports.

The Pew Research Center for the People and the Press
www.people-press.org

The site reports on surveys of American public opinion, particularly as related to the media and the way the media cover campaigns and government.

Politics Now
www.politicsnow.com

Newsweek, ABC News, the *Washington Post,* the *National Journal,* the *Los Angeles Times,* and the *Associated Press* collaborate to offer this political-affairs Web site.

CNN and Time AllPolitics
www.cnn.com/ALLPOLITICS/

This online portal contains breaking news, features, documents, quizzes, and links to other Internet resources from AOL Time Warner.

Part Four

Outputs from the Political System

13

CIVIL LIBERTIES

Timothy McVeigh drove up to the Alfred P. Murrah Federal Building in a bright yellow Ryder truck. A 7,000-pound bomb sat just two feet behind him, fuses already burning. The 26-year-old McVeigh did not hesitate. He parked beside the structure's north side and then walked swiftly but steadily into the streets of Oklahoma City to escape the imminent blast.[1]

It was 9 A.M. on a busy workday. This was no accident; the Gulf War Army veteran had planned his arrival with military precision to ensure an impressive number of victims. Lights already burned inside office windows. Pedestrians already coursed the sidewalks. Parents were already arriving to leave their children at America's Kids Day Care Center, which sat on the second floor just above the smoking weapon.

The date—April 19, 1995—was also no accident. Exactly two years previously, law-enforcement agents had ended an armed standoff with the Branch Davidian cult by storming their compound in Waco, Texas. Eighty-six cultists, including children, had died in fires linked to the assault. Like many fringe activists, McVeigh blamed the carnage on federal agents intoxicated by power. He viewed his own lethal mission as a sensible counterstrike, a "legit tactic." McVeigh's target was not the individuals who happened to fall within his blast radius, whom he had never met, but the government offices that many of them staffed.

The explosion struck a couple of minutes later, after McVeigh had jogged to safety. It ripped off the concrete structure's face, reducing most of the offices to rubble. Surrounding buildings shuddered, sending plate glass cascading into the streets. Automobiles crumpled and caught flame. Even people hundreds of yards away felt the concussion.

It was the "worst act of domestic terrorism in American history" to date (although dwarfed by the terriorist strikes in 2001). Rescue workers would spend more than a month ministering to the living and extracting the 168 dead, sometimes battling against cold wind and rain. The debris that remained behind would require even longer to clean up. So would the nation's emotional wounds. Gory photos of dead infants—19 children perished in the attack—shocked and horrified viewers across the United States. Americans cried for swift justice. They wanted the culprit identified, tried, and punished. Most wanted him executed.[2]

Catching the perpetrator, at least, did not take very long. An Oklahoma highway patrolman nabbed him just 90 minutes after the explosion. The officer saw McVeigh's Mercury Marquis speeding north on an interstate highway 75 miles from Oklahoma City. The vehicle bore no license plate, and McVeigh had stuffed his unregistered Glock pistol in a shoulder holster where the patrolman could see it. While McVeigh sat in jail on charges stemming from the traffic stop, investigators closed in on his identity. Witnesses in Kansas described his face to a police sketch artist as the man who had rented the Ryder truck, and a former coworker identified the terrorist from his sketch. Right before McVeigh was due for release, law-enforcement officials realized that his name matched that of the suspected bomber.

Once McVeigh's name rose to the top of the suspect list, numerous indicators pointed to his guilt. His reported obsessions and his loose affiliation with right-wing militia groups indicated a strong dislike for the federal government. Agents found bomb residue on McVeigh's clothing. His fingerprint appeared on a receipt for ammonium nitrate fertilizer, one of the bomb ingredients. A former associate and even McVeigh's sister provided damaging testimony against him. Thus, detailed evidence abounded that the feds already had their man.

Resolution of the atrocity was far, far slower in arriving. The Justice Department could not afford to lose a prosecution in such a sensitive case, so the FBI launched an investigation (code-named OKBOMB) that assembled millions of documents. FBI computers contained 26 separate databases to keep track of an effort that, by December 2000, had compiled 23,290 pieces of evidence, 28,000 interview transcripts, and 238,000 photographs. U.S. attorneys eventually compiled this record into what ABC anchor Tom Brokaw called "the single most effective prosecution case I've ever seen."[3] McVeigh's defense team successfully requested that the trial be held outside Oklahoma so that they might find impartial jurors. In June 1997, a 12-person federal jury finally convicted McVeigh on 11 counts of murder and conspiracy, and sentenced him to die.

McVeigh might have dragged the case on even longer with numerous appeals.* Instead, he soon shut down the legal maneuvering, admitted his guilt openly, and claimed sole responsibility for the explosion. "I bombed the Murrah Building. It was my choice, and my control, to hit that building when it was full," he boasted. "It was just me." McVeigh's celebrity status translated his death-row cell into a soapbox. He granted two reporters with the *Buffalo News* 75 hours of interview time so that they could write a book telling his story. The quotes they attributed to McVeigh revealed a remorseless murderer, who dismissed the young casualties as "collateral damage" in a battle that he had won 168 to 1.[4]

Neither McVeigh's decision to suspend legal appeals nor his taunting confessions ended the Oklahoma City saga. While awaiting execution, McVeigh sat contentedly in Colorado's Supermax facility, holed up in a 9-by-12-foot concrete bunker with reading material and a simple television.[5] Prison officials loosened regulations so that he could exercise outdoors with cell-block mates as well as talk with them across cages.†

---

*State-level capital crimes generally take 8 to 12 years to resolve, although the federal process is more streamlined.

†The prison is hardly a luxury resort. Inmates call it the "Hellhole of the Rockies." But McVeigh apparently was content there.

McVeigh reportedly traded "smut books" with Luis Felipe (also known as King Blood), a founder of New York City's Latin Kings gang, whom the feds had prosecuted for ordering beatings, murders, and even a beheading from his state prison cell. Ramzi Yousef, the terrorist whose 1993 World Trade Center bombing killed six people and injured a thousand, apparently tried to convert McVeigh to Islam. But his true kindred spirit was Theodore Kaczynski, known as the Unabomber because he mailed booby-trapped packages to 16 people over the course of two decades. The two antiauthoritarians discussed politics and traded books about the criminal-justice system.[6]

Just days before McVeigh's scheduled demise, yet another obstacle slowed the process. The FBI suddenly revealed that roughly 4,500 pages of documents from their OKBOMB investigation had gone unreported. Attorney General John Ashcroft had to postpone the execution yet another month while McVeigh's lawyers reviewed the allegedly inconsequential paperwork. His defense team appealed to the federal courts for even more time, but McVeigh instructed them to give up after the Tenth Circuit Court of Appeals judged that they had "utterly failed to demonstrate substantial grounds" why the execution should not immediately take place.

Finally, on Monday, June 11, 2001—more than six years after he had wrecked hundreds of lives—the Oklahoma City bomber ate his last meal: two pints of mint chocolate chip ice cream. He walked into an Indiana execution chamber and cooperated calmly as executioners prepared him for lethal injection, strapping him to a table and inserting an intravenous needle into his right leg. He spoke no last words.* He stared at the ceiling. Tubes emerging from a slot in the wall soon fed the needle. A toxic cocktail of three chemicals pulsed into his bloodstream, and the life passed out of Timothy James McVeigh at 7:14 A.M. central daylight time. For the first time in almost 40 years, the U.S. government had executed a criminal.

THE CRIMINAL-JUSTICE SYSTEM'S SLUGGISHNESS, EVEN WHEN FACED WITH an individual clearly responsible for a terrible atrocity, exemplifies why many Americans are impatient with their country's approach to civil liberties. The presumption of innocence makes proving guilt so difficult that they suspect the system lets many dangerous criminals go free. The American system sets such a high barrier against tyranny that even the easy cases exact serious costs—whether measured in time, money, or emotional trauma. Voters also dislike the tendency to "coddle" criminals who do face justice.

---

*McVeigh allowed a poem to speak for him. It was "Invictus," by William Ernest Henley, which he had copied by hand.

During the six years between McVeigh's crime and his punishment, the thousands he had injured emotionally and physically faced repeated reminders of their losses. McVeigh was able to publicize his beliefs widely, issuing several statements painful and offensive to his living victims. Some descended into depression, lost their marriages, or took their lives. Patti Hall, whose injuries from the bombing required repeated operations and extensive physical therapy, sighed before the cameras on the day of the execution, "People have been waiting for this for so long."

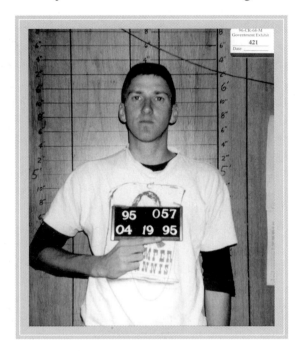

Dead man talking

The federal government's effort to execute Timothy McVeigh for blowing up a federal building in Oklahoma City took more than six years and cost millions of dollars. McVeigh thus encapsulates the American debate over civil liberties: Some thought he was able to abuse his rights, and other considered his trial and execution an abuse of the government's law-enforcement powers. McVeigh's T-shirt, at the time of his arrest, ironically pictured Abraham Lincoln over the Latin phrase for "Always there will be tyrants."

At the same time, other critics draw the opposite conclusion: The United States no longer respects civil liberties adequately. Constitutional rights no longer seem to inhibit governmental abuse of law-enforcement powers. They point to the blunders committed by overzealous federal agents, in the so-called drug war as well as during the crackdown on right-wing groups that spurred McVeigh to violence. They point to the federal government's growing role in law enforcement, which has taken authority away from state officials. Only eight of McVeigh's victims were federal agents, but it was for their deaths that the national government executed him, not for the other 160.

Both conspiracy theorists and death-penalty opponents interpreted the temporary loss of 4,500 pages of FBI documents as an indication of how the criminal-justice system can tyrannize people caught in its web.[7] "The FBI proved his case for him—that the system is hopelessly corrupt," argued Bob Papovich, one of McVeigh's friends. Many Europeans and some Americans consider the revitalization of America's death penalty as a sign of its commitment to violent barbarism.[8]

This debate over one aspect of liberty—the treatment of the accused—matches the debate over civil liberties more generally. Some critics complain that judges undermine popular will by abusing the Constitution's freedoms. They allow individuals to exploit their rights. However, others argue that constitutional rights seldom protect individuals from a committed majority. Rights can deteriorate in response to political demands. Federal judges often shift the meaning of constitutional guarantees to suit the times. Especially in America's new democracy, courts seldom step far out of line from what American culture and society expect from government. The judiciary rarely does more than remind a freedom-loving people when their laws are in danger of undermining the liberties they hold so dear.

ORIGINS OF CIVIL LIBERTIES IN THE UNITED STATES

The U.S. Constitution never mentions the concept of **civil liberties,** fundamental freedoms that protect a people from tyranny. But specific protections appear in the Bill of Rights—the first ten amendments to the Constitution—and again in amendments added after the Civil War. The Supreme Court has shaped the evolution of these freedoms, as have political debates and election outcomes. Usually civil liberties reflect basic values shared by most citizens (see Chapter 4).

Although conversational English sometimes refers to these fundamental freedoms as "rights," as does the term Bill of Rights, do not confuse them with *civil rights* (considered in Chapter 14). Civil liberties promise *freedom from government interference,* while civil rights guarantee *equal treatment by the government.*

ORIGINS OF THE BILL OF RIGHTS

"Liberty" was one of the American Revolution's rallying words. Not only did the Declaration of Independence assert fundamental rights to "Life, Liberty and the pursuit of Happiness," but many states incorporated similar principles into their laws. For example, the Virginia assembly passed a bill of rights that pronounced freedom of the press "one of the great bulwarks of liberty."[9] American patriots revered the idea of creating a free people.

Nevertheless, the colonial revolutionaries did not always live up to their ideals. They trampled on the liberties of the Tories, who opposed the revolution. They closed Tory newspapers, threatened well-known editors, confiscated their property, and intimidated the royalists so much that more than 80,000 people fled to Canada, England, and the West Indies.[10]

James Madison's House Campaign and the Bill of Rights

Despite harboring doubts about the necessity of the Bill of Rights, James Madison emerged in the first Congress as the driving force behind its passage. Madison's willingness to defer to the desire of others can be explained by the same constituency pressures that shape the views of modern-day members of Congress. Although a Federalist, Madison came from Virginia, home state of the acclaimed Virginia Bill of Rights and of the country's most influential Anti-Federalists, George Mason and Patrick Henry. Henry had successfully fought to prevent Madison from being selected as one of Virginia's two senators, and Madison had won a seat in the House of Representatives only by promising to work for the passage of a Bill of Rights.

That Madison was influenced more by election pressures than by constitutional scruples is evident from the fact that at the Constitutional Convention itself, he had seen little need for such a document. Even after the convention, Madison wrote, "I have never thought the omission [of a bill of rights] a material defect, nor been anxious to supply it even by subsequent amendment, for any other reason than that it is anxiously desired by others."

In Madison's hands, the meaning of the Bill of Rights underwent a significant transformation. Whereas the Anti-Federalists had wanted amendments to protect state governments, Madison's amendments focused on individual liberties. Only two amendments addressed state prerogatives. Madison thus was able to avoid the central issue of contention between Federalists and Anti-Federalists—the balance of power between levels of government. The ten amendments Congress eventually agreed upon were quickly and quietly ratified in 1791 by all but two states, apparently because few people thought the amendments would have much practical effect.

What do you think?

- If, as historians believe, Madison promoted the Bill of Rights under electoral pressure, should this change our understanding of these rights?
- Should it change how the courts interpret them today?

SOURCES: Robert A. Rutland, *The Birth of the Bill of Rights* (Chapel Hill: University of North Carolina Press, 1955); Stanley Elkins and Eric McKitrick, *The Age of Federalism* (New York: Oxford University Press, 1993); Thornton Anderson, *Creating the Constitution: The Convention of 1787 and the First Congress* (University Park, PA: Pennsylvania State University Press, 1993), p. 176.

Nor did those who drafted the Constitution include explicit protection for individual civil liberties. When delegate Charles Pinckney offered a motion at the Constitutional Convention to guarantee freedom of the press, the Federalist majority voted the measure down—on the grounds that states should be responsible for regulating speech and the press.[11] Only when ratification of the Constitution seemed in danger did Federalists agree to add a Bill of Rights after it passed (see Chapter 2). In 1790, at James Madison's insistence, the first Congress approved the ten amendments making up the Bill of Rights, thinking they would have little effect (see the Election Connection, "James Madison's House Campaign and the Bill of Rights").

FEW LIBERTIES BEFORE THE CIVIL WAR

Initially, the Bill of Rights applied only to the national government, not to the states. The First Amendment, for example, focused solely on the national government, saying that "Congress shall make no law" abridging speech or religious practice. State governments could do whatever their voters permitted. As a result, the Episcopal Church remained the official state church in Virginia, and the Puritan religion remained the established religion in Massachusetts.

Many of the other provisions in the Bill of Rights did not specifically mention either the national or the state governments and left open the possibility that they applied to both. For example, the Fifth Amendment said that "no person shall ... be deprived of life, liberty, or property, without due process of law." But in 1833, when the owner of Barron's Wharf complained that the city of Baltimore had deprived his company of property by filling the water with debris, the Supreme Court ruled that the Fifth Amendment limited the powers of the federal government but not those of the states. The Bill of Rights, wrote Chief Justice John Marshall, "contain[s] no expression indicating an intention to apply them to the state governments. This court cannot so apply them."[12]

APPLYING THE BILL OF RIGHTS
TO STATE GOVERNMENTS

The Civil War transformed the spirit, meaning, and application of the Bill of Rights. Judges began interpreting constitutional law differently, and the Constitution picked up three new amendments: the Thirteenth, Fourteenth, and Fifteenth. These **civil rights amendments** abolished slavery, redefined civil rights and liberties, and guaranteed voting rights to all adult male citizens, respectively.*

Of all the provisions in the civil rights amendments, the one that has had the greatest significance for civil liberty is the **due process clause** of the Fourteenth Amendment. According to this clause, *states* cannot "deprive any person of life, liberty, or property, without due process of law." By carrying over the language of the Fifth Amendment, this provision gave federal courts a strong new weapon to wield against state laws unpopular elsewhere in the country.

---

*Southern voters likely would not have passed these amendments given the choice; but ratification was one condition for rejoining the union, and occupation governments controlled many southern states.

Of course, the due process clause is rather vague. Judges cannot agree how one takes away rights *with* due process. Some read the words literally; they require a fair procedure to remove freedoms. Others give them political substance; they think a fair system may never revoke certain freedoms. Judges also do not agree what "liberty" encompasses. Some argue that the phrase means the freedoms guaranteed elsewhere in the Bill of Rights. Others prefer to shape a judicial understanding of liberty, based on legal traditions or the spirit of the times.

Generally the Supreme Court has hedged on these questions. The Court has never accepted the theory that states must follow the Bill of Rights, but over time it has incorporated most of those constitutional guarantees into the due process clause's definition anyway (an approach known as **selective incorporation**). One major exception is the Second Amendment's guarantee that "the right of the people to keep and bear arms shall not be abridged," which states need not honor.

FREEDOM OF SPEECH, PRESS, AND ASSEMBLY

Of all the liberties listed in the Bill of Rights, one trio is paramount: freedom of speech, press, and assembly. These three rights to free expression, although distinct, are closely intertwined. They all promise that Americans may express political ideas freely. Despite the First Amendment's promise, however, people have been jailed for expressing controversial thoughts—as long ago as 1798 and as recently as 1968.

FREE SPEECH AND MAJORITARIAN DEMOCRACY

Free speech is vital to the workings of free elections in a democratic society. Otherwise the government could manipulate public opinion without fear of contradiction, and consolidate its power over the people. Yet the people themselves also sometimes threaten liberty. The larger a majority, the more certain it becomes that its views are correct, and the easier it becomes to silence dissenters. For this reason James Madison thought liberty's greatest threat came from **tyranny of the majority**—the suppression of minority opinions by those voted into power.[13] The founders enshrined free expression in the Constitution so that the government would have to tolerate disagreement.

The classic defense of free speech was provided by the English civil libertarian John Stuart Mill, who insisted that in the free exchange of ideas, truth eventually would triumph over error. But must society even tolerate offensive and vicious ideas? For example, it is not easy to accept allowing people to spread doctrines of racial hatred. Are not their beliefs immoral and therefore obviously wrong? Even in such cases Mill defends free expression—both to prevent scurrilous ideas from gaining strength under the cloak of secrecy and to remind people why they believe what they do.

THE EVOLUTION OF FREE SPEECH DOCTRINE

The Supreme Court generally has not protected speakers and writers from tyranny of the majority, contrary to the initial hopes of those who wrote the Bill of Rights. Instead, the Supreme Court's view of what free speech entails has moved along at about the same speed as—or perhaps a little slower than—that of the rest of the country.

Initially, free expression guaranteed only that a speaker or writer could deliver a message without officials censoring it first (the **prior restraint doctrine**). Nothing prevented the government from punishing messages after the fact. Indeed, the source of a hostile message could be convicted for bringing the government's "dignity into contempt," even if criticisms were true!

CLEAR AND PRESENT DANGER   The first major Supreme Court decision affecting freedom of speech arose when the United States started conscripting soldiers to fight in World War I. Charles Schenck, a socialist, distributed a mailing urging draft-age men to resist their conscription into the armed forces. A jury convicted Schenck for violating the 1917 Espionage Act, which made it illegal to obstruct military recruitment. A unanimous Supreme Court, in *Schenck* v. *United States* (1919), accepted Schenck's conviction. Justice Oliver Wendell Holmes explained that free speech did not extend to messages posing a "clear and present danger" to the U.S. war effort. To justify his ruling, Holmes drew a famous analogy: no person, he explained, has the right falsely to cry "Fire" in a crowded theater.

Although the **clear and present danger doctrine** initially developed to justify censorship, it also implicitly limited what government might do. Congress could not regulate speech *unless* it posed a clear and present danger. The doctrine thus provided a foundation on which a tradition of free expression could build. Indeed, Holmes was one of the first to liberalize his views, after facing widespread criticism for *Schenck*. The Court heard a parallel case called *Abrams* v. *U.S.* (1919) less than a year later. Left-wing protesters, angry at the United States for intervening in Russia's revolution, had thrown leaflets from an upper-story window to munitions workers. This time Holmes split with the majority, no longer seeing sufficient danger in a "silly leaflet by an unknown man."

During the 1930s, when the public became more tolerant of dissenting opinion, the Supreme Court changed with the political climate. Two cases decided in

1931, *Stromberg* v. *California* and *Near* v. *Minnesota*, were particularly important in this respect. Yetta Stromberg had encouraged children attending a camp operated by the Young Communist League to pledge allegiance to the flag of the Soviet Union, a violation of California's "red-flag" law.[14] And the Minnesota legislature had shut down a newspaper for publishing "malicious, scandalous and defamatory" material. In both cases the Court endorsed free expression. Neither Stromberg nor the Minnesota newspaper constituted a clear and present danger, the Court explained.

FIGHTING WORDS The toleration that emerged during the 1930s did not survive World War II (see the Election Connection, "America's Concentration Camps"). Congress responded to public outrage against fascism by enacting a new censorship law in 1940, the Smith Act. Instead of acting as a bulwark against majority tyranny, the Supreme Court again started endorsing limitations on free speech.

In *Chaplinsky* v. *New Hampshire* (1942), the court enunciated the **fighting words doctrine** defining some words as inherently harmful, violent acts. Walter Chaplinsky, a member of the Jehovah's Witnesses religious group, tried to give a pacifist speech. A threatening crowd gathered, but when he asked a policeman for protection, the officer cursed him and asked him to "come along." Chaplinsky responded in kind, calling the policeman "a God damned racketeer" and "a damned Fascist"—for which he was arrested.

The Supreme Court upheld Chaplinsky's conviction on the grounds that he had used words that are not speech but "by their very utterance inflict injury or intend to incite an immediate breach of the peace."[15] In other words, personal insults do not always enjoy First Amendment protection. This ruling would worry courts in later years, and although *Chaplinsky* has never been overturned, it is also seldom used. Not even burning a cross on someone's lawn qualifies as "fighting words," despite the dual risk of violence from or against the homeowner.[16]

BALANCING DOCTRINE The end of World War II did not automatically restore civil liberties. Instead, the nation went through a "Red scare." People regarded as sympathetic to the Soviet Union suffered harassment by government officials. Senator Joseph McCarthy of Wisconsin gained political popularity by accusing artists, teachers, and government officials of having ties to the Communist party. Anyone who wished to receive a student loan or work for the federal government had to take an oath swearing loyalty to the United States.

It was not judges, but elected leaders, who resisted the threat that McCarthyism posed to the country's civil liberties. A disgusted President

ELECTION CONNECTION

America's Concentration Camps

Responding to public concern that Japanese Americans might spy for Japan during World War II, President Franklin Roosevelt approved a military order requiring 70,000 Japanese American citizens and another 40,000 resident Japanese to leave their homes and live in "relocation centers." Those who swore loyalty to the United States could leave the camps, but if they lived on either coast could not return home. Earl Warren, the California attorney general and later chief justice of the Supreme Court, gave a racial rationale for these actions: "When we are dealing with the Caucasian race we have methods that will test the loyalty of them. . . . But when we deal with the Japanese . . . we cannot form any opinion that we believe to be sound."[a]

Discriminatory actions by elected officials at a time when the nation was at risk and popular opinion was ferociously anti-Japanese may be perhaps understandable. More difficult to rationalize is the inability of the Supreme Court to protect this minority against the tyranny of the majority. In *Korematsu v. United States* (1944), the Court deferred to the military's expertise on evaluating national security and declared the relocation centers constitutional. But in his dissent from the Court's decision, Justice Frank Murphy condemned the relocation as "one of the most sweeping and complete deprivations of constitutional rights in the history of this nation."[b] To rectify the injustice, Congress in 1988 finally voted to compensate many Japanese Americans who had been relocated.

What do you think?

- Most people agree that the detention and relocation of Japanese Americans during World War II was unjust. But are there circumstances under which concerns for public safety should override liberties?
- How high must the probability of guilt be before members of a group may be singled out for distinct treatment? How severe the risk?
- Who ought to have the authority to decide when such action can be taken? the courts? the president? Congress?

[a]Robert Goldstein, *Political Repression in Modern America: 1870 to the Present* (New York: Schenkman, 1978), pp. 266–267.
[b]*Korematsu v. United States* 323 US 244 (1944).

Eisenhower refused to act on McCarthy's most outrageous accusations, and McCarthy's Senate colleagues finally inquired into the senator's methods of operation, later censuring him for his inappropriate conduct.

The courts, on the other hand, showed little interest in protecting minority dissidents. Instead, the Supreme Court enunciated a **balancing doctrine,** which allowed courts to balance freedom of speech against other public interests. In *Dennis v. United States* (1951), 11 nonviolent Communist party leaders faced prison sentences for spreading writings that espoused the revolutionary overthrow of government. The Court ruled their convictions constitutional, arguing that the "balance . . . must be struck in favor" of the governmental interest in resisting subversion.

Modern witch hunt
Senator Joseph McCarthy built a career in the 1950s on investigating alleged Communist sympathizers. His methods
outraged many and frightened many more, but should civil liberties be balanced against other important governmental interests, such as national security?

FUNDAMENTAL FREEDOMS DOCTRINE Public opinion eventually became
more supportive of free-speech rights, even for radicals and Communists (see
Figure 13.1). Reflecting these changes in public opinion, the Supreme Court
gradually developed the **fundamental freedoms doctrine,** the principle that
some civil liberties are basic to the functioning of a democratic society and
require vigorous protection.

The doctrine had rather modest origins. It appeared, almost as an aside, in
the footnote of an unrelated 1938 Supreme Court opinion written by Justice
Harlan Stone. His *Carolene Products* footnote said that some freedoms, such as
freedom of speech, might deserve a "preferred position" in the Constitution
because of their central importance to an electoral democracy. Any law threatening these freedoms should receive strict scrutiny from the Supreme Court.[17]

The fundamental freedoms doctrine became the Supreme Court's governing
principle during the Vietnam War. Under its guidance, the Court was more effective at defending dissenters against government repression than it was in any previous war. As one civil libertarian wrote in 1973, "The truly significant thing in recent

years has not been the attempt of the current administration to suppress criticism, but rather the marked inability of the administration to do so effectively."[18]

In virtually every case that came before it, the Court ruled against efforts to suppress free speech. For example, it would not allow the University of Missouri to expel a student for distributing a picture of a policeman raping the Statue of Liberty. Said the Court: "The mere dissemination of ideas—no matter how offensive to good taste—on a state university campus may not be shut off" in the name of decency.[19]

The Nixon administration inadvertently helped expand civil liberties by trying to grab too much power. It tried to justify censoring publication of a Defense Department report criticizing the war effort, but could not convince a single Supreme Court justice that national security required prior restraint of the document.[20] Commonly called the *Pentagon Papers case,* this decision greatly advanced freedom of the press. In subsequent years, the Nixon administration's

FIGURE 13.1

Percentage opposed to allowing communists to make a speech

The public has become more willing to grant rights even to extremists. Do you believe that this is a sign that people are becoming more tolerant? Or is their changed attitude merely a reflection of the end of the Cold War?

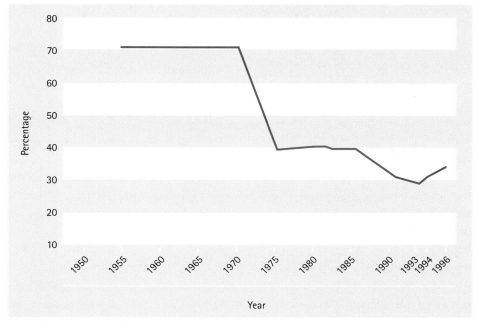

SOURCES: Benjamin L. Page and Robert Y. Shapiro, *The Rational Public: Fifty Years of Trends in Americans' Policy Preferences.* (Chicago: University of Chicago Press, 1992), p. 87; National Opinion Research Center, General Social Survey.

entanglement in the Watergate scandal served to reinforce both public and judicial support of civil liberties (see the Election Connection, "Watergate and the Elections of 1972, 1974, and 1976").

SYMBOLIC SPEECH   Nothing better illustrates the contemporary Supreme Court's strong commitment to fundamental freedoms than its flag-burning decisions, which have enjoyed the support of both liberal and conservative justices.[21]

Flammable cloth; indestructable symbol
Gregory Johnson's 1984 conviction for torching the American flag was overturned by the Supreme Court. Is flag burning legitimate protest, as the Court argued, or is the flag a unique national symbol that requires special protection?

During the 1984 Republican national convention in Dallas, a young radical named Gregory Johnson was arrested for burning an American flag to protest Reagan administration policies. Five years later, Johnson's case came before the Supreme Court. The Court, in *Texas* v. *Johnson* (1989), overturned his conviction, saying the principal purpose of free speech is to invite dispute; the mere burning of the flag was "expressive conduct" that did not breach the peace.[22]

Unlike earlier court decisions, the Supreme Court in the flag-burning case went well beyond popular opinion of the day. President George H. W. Bush angrily called for a constitutional amendment to prohibit flag desecration, and over 70 percent of the public supported him. Almost immediately, Congress passed a law making it a federal offense to burn the flag. The very day the law took effect, however, activists set fire to flags in Seattle and Washington, D.C.—and within a year the Supreme Court reaffirmed its defense of symbolic protest.[23]

LIMITATIONS ON FREE SPEECH
Although free speech has now been firmly established as one of the country's fundamental freedoms, this does not mean that all speech is free of government control. Government certainly may regulate the time, place, and manner in which one speaks. One does not have the right to express political views with a bullhorn

ELECTION CONNECTION

Watergate and the Elections of 1972, 1974, and 1976

Many consider civil liberties fundamental to a democracy because fair elections require freedom of expression. The Watergate scandal that destroyed Richard Nixon's presidency reinforced how important civil liberties are to elections—and how dangerous executive power can be to fundamental freedoms.

As part of its campaign for reelection in 1972, the Nixon administration engaged in a wide variety of activities that violated the privacy of prominent opponents and undermined the electoral process. Nixon operatives tapped telephones without court authorization, scrutinized income tax returns for politically motivated reasons, and broke into a psychiatrist's office to gather dirt on the insider who had leaked the controversial Pentagon Papers. One aide even suggested firebombing the Brookings Institution, a Washington think tank, to cover up a political burglary there.

Later, police apprehended five burglars breaking into Democratic party headquarters at the Washington, D.C., Watergate apartment and office complex. When it became clear that the president and his top aides had authorized the burglary, Nixon was forced to resign as president of the United States. Public outrage over Watergate placed civil liberties on more solid ground than ever before. Nixon's party suffered overwhelming defeat in the 1974 congressional elections, and it lost control of the White House in 1976. Elected officials became aware that serious violations of civil liberties could provoke adverse electoral consequences.

What do you think?

- What safeguards can prevent the U.S. president, who holds the country's most powerful office, from violating civil liberties?
- If fair elections themselves are undermined by such behavior, can other governmental institutions check the presidency?

SOURCE: Fred Emery, *Watergate: The Corruption of American Politics and the Fall of Richard Nixon* (New York: Simon & Schuster, 1994).

at 3 A.M. in a residential neighborhood. Three particular types of speech also lack full protection: commercial speech, libel, and obscenity.

Government may regulate advertising to protect consumers from false or misleading information, or to discourage the consumption of harmful products such as cigarettes. False speech defaming someone's reputation also lacks constitutional protection, although the standard depends upon whether the victim is a private or a public figure. For public figures, a **libel** conviction requires that the source made false statements knowingly or with reckless disregard for the truth—a strong protection of free expression announced in *New York Times* v. *Sullivan* (1964).

And the Court gives relatively little protection to sexual expression—which American culture finds more disturbing than, for example, violent images. Often sexual expression falls under the Supreme Court's 1973 definition of

obscenity—offensive communications with no redeeming social value other than titillation. This determination, according to *Miller* v. *California* (1973), depends in part upon local community standards.[24]

But the Court frequently finds other legal justifications for allowing government to regulate indecency. For example, Justice O'Connor decided in *Erie* v. *Kandyland* (2000) that cities could ban nude dancing by requiring strippers to wear "pasties" and G-strings—even though dancing naked is not obscene. Her justification was that cities might choose to target the "secondary effects" that spring up around strip clubs, such as drug use and prostitution.

On the other hand, the Court does not accept government regulations simply because they target sexual expression. Congress tried to halt the proliferation of sexually explicit material on the Internet by passing the Communications Decency Act in 1996, ostensibly to protect minors. The Supreme Court struck this law down the following year, arguing that its restrictions were too broad. Congress could not require such dramatic changes in adult behavior when less restrictive methods of protecting minors existed.[25] Since the ruling, pornography's opponents have concentrated on promoting software to screen out objectionable sites.

FREEDOM OF RELIGION

Two clauses in the First Amendment guarantee religious freedom. Both appear in the same sentence: Congress shall make no law (a) respecting an establishment of religion, or (b) prohibiting the free exercise thereof. The **establishment clause** denies government the power to push religious practices on the citizenry. The **free exercise clause** protects the right of individuals to practice their religion.

How the Supreme Court interprets these guarantees often depends upon the political and electoral context in which it makes decisions. During the 1960s, when Americans began experimenting with a large number of eastern and New Age religions, liberal judges formulated an aggressive approach to protecting religious freedom. They would subject laws to a particular test to determine when government infringed on a religious freedom. But the rise of born-again Christianity and the so-called Religious Right corresponded to a reversal on the Court, shaping the current state of case law.

THE ESTABLISHMENT CLAUSE

Few constitutional phrases have caused more difficulty than the ban on laws "respecting an establishment of religion." As discussed in Chapter 11, the language simply does not convey a clear meaning; judicial interpretation is necessary for the words to offer any protection at all. Perhaps for this reason, the relationship between church and state reveals numerous inconsistencies. The motto "In God We Trust" appears on U.S. currency, yet courts have ruled against nativity scenes in village squares. Each session of Congress opens with a prayer, but public schools cannot begin their days in a similar fashion.

The main source of inconsistency is that judges disagree on how to interpret the establishment clause and therefore cannot settle on a specific rule for determining when laws cross the line. Liberal judges generally embrace Thomas Jefferson's call for a strict **separation of church and state.** They prefer to keep government as far away from religion as possible, believing that to overlap the spheres would (1) corrupt churches by introducing political ambitions and (2) invite public officials to legislate moral codes, bullying those of different faiths.

THE LEMON TEST   In the late 1940s, when the Supreme Court first began probing the meaning of the establishment clause, liberals dominated the bench. Over the next 25 years the Court evolved a particular test for determining whether laws violate the Constitution. It is usually called the **Lemon test** after a 1971 case, *Lemon* v. *Kurtzman,* although the heart of the rule dates from earlier decisions. The Court (a) required all laws to have clear secular (that is, not religious) purposes, (b) did not permit laws to advance or inhibit either one religion or religion in general, and (c) considered as one sign of a religious establishment if the law entangled public officials with religious institutions or activities.*

Few people openly endorse the Lemon test these days. Even those who prefer a strong division between church and state recognize that the federal courts have not done a very good job applying *Lemon*.[26] Furthermore, liberals have become a minority on the Court; most justices disparage their approach as overly hostile to religion. Yet no ruling has ever cast out *Lemon* entirely, since its detractors cannot agree on a replacement. Instead, the evolution of case law has forced repeated modifications to how and when federal courts use the test.

THE COERCION TEST   Conservative judges generally read the establishment clause very narrowly: Government may not coerce citizens into pursuing religious practices. Permitting, encouraging, or even indirectly rewarding religion does not "establish" anything, so the Constitution does not forbid it. Some conservatives, such as Justice Antonin Scalia, openly embrace when a government uses moral judgments to construct law.[27] But religious conservatives have never been

---

*The significance of the Lemon test's third "prong" has varied over time. Recent modifications have demoted it from the Court's central approach to the establishment clause.

able to form a Court majority, so they win establishment clause cases only when they are willing to compromise with more moderate justices.

The closest conservatives have ever come to replacing the Lemon test may have been a 1992 case called *Lee* v. *Weisman*. Deborah Weisman's middle school, like so many public schools around the nation, permitted a prayer at the beginning of its graduation ceremony. Deborah objected to the practice, since it required her either (1) to skip the ceremony, despite having earned her place there; (2) to rise and pray with everyone else, contrary to her religious beliefs; or (3) to opt out of the ceremony's prayer, in full view of her fellow students. She argued the Constitution did not allow a public school to place her in this position.

Conservatives seemed poised to win their long-running battle to constrict the establishment clause. So many schools featured graduation prayers, and had been doing so for such a long time, that public opinion weighed heavily against Deborah's complaint. Furthermore, they apparently had the votes lined up. Thomas, a strong conservative, had recently joined three committed opponents of the Lemon test: Rehnquist, Scalia, and White. And just three years before, Justice Anthony Kennedy had written that "policies of accommodation, acknowledgment, and support for religion are an accepted part of our political and cultural heritage." Any test that consistently "would invalidate longstanding traditions cannot be a proper reading of the [establishment] clause," he wrote.[28]

Imagine their dismay when Kennedy decided to abandon his conservative allies and write a 5-to-4 opinion against them! Kennedy ignored the Lemon test, explaining that Deborah's middle school had failed even the **coercion test** implied by a narrower reading of the establishment clause. Avoiding the religious exercise would bring damaging peer pressure down on her, either because she skipped graduation or because she did not pray. Kennedy agreed with Deborah: A public institution could not coerce a young girl using the force of local opinion.

Justice Scalia could hardly restrain his bitterness in the dissenting opinion, calling Kennedy's reasoning "psychology practiced by amateurs." Establishing religion requires *physical* punishment of dissenters, he argued, not simply hurt feelings:

> In holding that the Establishment Clause prohibits invocations and benedictions at public school graduation ceremonies, the Court—with nary a mention that it is doing so—lays waste a tradition that is as old as public school graduation ceremonies themselves. . . . As its instrument of destruction, the bulldozer of its social engineering, the Court invents a boundless, and boundlessly manipulable, test of psychological coercion.[29]

But no amount of bile could erase the fact that religious conservatives on the Court had lost their chance to unify behind a coercion test to replace *Lemon*. Justice White retired, replaced by a Clinton appointee, and in 2000 another "longstanding American tradition" fell to the establishment clause in a 6-to-3 vote: the practice of school-sponsored prayer at athletic events.[30]

RELIGION IN SCHOOLS   Many religious people believe that worship should be an ongoing part of a child's life, rather than just a diversion compartmentalized to evenings or weekends. They view education as going beyond teaching reading and arithmetic to include teaching morality and values as well. Yet parents often cannot afford to take their children out of public schools, where children of diverse faiths must mingle. No one has found a feasible way for public schools to accommodate religious exercises without favoring particular forms of religion. Government-run institutions cannot promote the multitude of religions that various parents may select, nor is it clear that they are equipped for the task of spiritual guidance. Public education thus especially aggravates the controversy surrounding church–state relations.

Those who demand a strict wall between church and state generally fear that allowing religion in public schools will become an invitation for communities to push their preferred faiths. This fear is not ungrounded. Massachusetts passed the nation's first compulsory schooling law in 1852, largely because many Protestants feared the waves of Catholic immigrants pouring into Boston from Ireland and Germany. The Boston School Committee openly declared that its purpose was to reform Catholics, to "keep them in the right path amid the moral darkness which is their daily and domestic walk."[31] As recently as 2000, the Supreme Court prevented a school district in Texas from hosting prayers before sporting events, in part because the District reportedly had worked to convert students by "promoting attendance at a Baptist revival meeting, encouraging membership in religious clubs, chastising children who held minority religious beliefs, and distributing Gideon Bibles on school premises."[32]

Evangelical religious groups, concerned by the growing secularization of society, have reacted to Court decisions by advocating an amendment to the Constitution that would allow prayer in schools. A majority of the public have said they support such an amendment,[33] and Republican presidential candidates have generally campaigned in favor of its adoption. But supporters have been unable to win the necessary two-thirds vote in Congress. The Supreme Court has been more responsive, ruling in 1990 that students may form Bible-reading or school prayer clubs if other clubs are allowed to use school property.[34] Banning religious groups while allowing secular ones to organize infringed upon students' rights to free exercise of their religion, the Court explained.

Other recent decisions have also opened up windows in the wall of separation between church and state. In 2000 the Supreme Court ruled that states could provide private religious schools with computer equipment.[35] More importantly, in *Agostini* v. *Felton* (1997) the Supreme Court ruled that public school teachers could provide specialized, nonreligious instruction in religious schools, so long as religious schools did not have an advantage at getting the assistance and any aid to students occurred "only as a result of the genuinely independent and private choices of individuals." By justifying its decision in terms of private choice, the Court once again showed a concern for the right to the free exercise of religion, the subject to which we now turn.

THE FREE EXERCISE CLAUSE

If the establishment clause seems to bar state involvement in religion, the free exercise clause seems to instruct states to accommodate religious practices. This mandate is equally hard to apply, however, for three rough reasons: (1) Someone has to decide when a set of beliefs qualifies as a "religion" rather than just a personal preference; (2) someone has to decide when a law really infringes on core

An education of the spirit
Many parents want religion to be a central part of their children's lives but cannot afford parochial-school tuition after already having paid taxes for public educational institutions. To what extent should the Constitution permit government-funded institutions to promote religious exercises? How can schools offer meaningful religious guidance without discriminating against members of minority religions (or those with no religion at all)?

religious exercises rather than just customs; and (3) someone has to decide what to do when religious beliefs interfere with governmental efforts to protect other constitutional values.

Sorting out these three dilemmas places federal courts in quite a quandary. They are not qualified to define religions. Yet allowing public officials to pick them could undercut constitutional protections: popular faiths would be "religions" while unpopular faiths would be "cults" or merely "philosophies." Allowing individuals to define their own religions, meanwhile, could turn every disagreeable law into a constitutional violation. Imagine the religions that would appear! The Church of No Taxes, the Church of Marijuana Smoking, the Church of Running Red Lights—the possibilities are endless. And the same difficulty appears when determining a religion's core practices. Courts are not qualified to define the central tenets of a faith, but they cannot trust elected officials, church leaders, or individual worshipers to do so either.

THE SHERBERT TEST On the matter of balancing religious free exercise against other governmental interests, liberals and conservatives once again differ on how stringently to apply the First Amendment. Around the same time they developed the core of the Lemon test, liberals formulated another three-prong formula—the **Sherbert test**—to determine when a law unconstitutionally violates the free exercise clause. The test took formal shape in *Sherbert* v. *Verner* (1963), a case that focused on whether laborers could apply for unemployment benefits if they gave up work because it fell on a holy day. Limits on religiously motivated action, or compulsions to engage in religiously prohibited action, had (a) to promote a secular (that is, nonreligious) goal that was (b) a compelling governmental interest and to do so (c) in the manner least restrictive to religious practices.[36]

THE NEUTRALITY TEST Conservatives have been more successful at narrowing the free exercise clause than the establishment clause. Writing for a conservative majority in *Oregon* v. *Smith* (1990), Justice Scalia threw out *Sherbert* to rule that the free exercise clause did not protect ritual use of the drug peyote by members of the Native American Church. When government passes a neutral, generally applicable law to prevent criminal behavior, Scalia explained, individuals cannot claim a religious exemption. Scalia recognized that his **neutrality test** places minority religions "at a relative disadvantage," since laws will seldom interfere with mainstream religions. But he preferred to accept that inconvenience as "an unavoidable consequence of democratic government" rather than contemplate the alternative: "a system in which each conscience is a law unto itself."

FREE EXERCISE AND PUBLIC SCHOOLS   Once again, religious freedom often arises in the context of education policy. The Court protects private religious schools from hostile action by state legislatures. But popular impulses sometimes push the Court to allow interference with religious practices.

Two flag-salute cases provide a good example of how the Court shifts with the times. In 1940, with war breaking out in Europe and patriotic fervor on the rise, the Court upheld a Pennsylvania statute requiring that Jehovah's Witnesses salute the American flag in public school ceremonies, even though their religion forbids revering a government symbol. The Court said that schools could interfere with religious liberty in this case, because saluting the flag promoted "national unity, [which] is the basis of national security."[37] Only one justice dissented.[38]

Just three years later, times had changed. Not only did the earlier flag-salute case stir up extensive mob violence against Jehovah's Witnesses, which brought shame on the Court, but experiences with Nazism lessened American ardor for forced patriotism. "Compulsory unification of opinion," wrote Justice Robert Jackson, when reversing the previous flag-salute ruling, "achieves only the unanimity of the graveyard."[39] Behind him were three justices who had ruled on the opposite side just three years before.

The debate over school choice, which divided presidential candidates in 2000, sets the establishment clause against the free exercise clause.[40] Republican candidate George W. Bush favored giving families vouchers that would allow parents to choose among public schools and religious private schools. Democrat Al Gore argued that choice should be limited to public schools. A key point of contention was whether allowing parents to use public funding at religious schools would violate the Constitution's establishment clause or help reinforce its free exercise clause. The Supreme Court has yet to decide between these two interpretations. In 1998 it allowed a Milwaukee private-school voucher program to continue by refusing to review a lower-court case, a good sign for voucher supporters.[41] But some observers argue that Court opinion is so evenly divided that the outcome will hinge on President Bush's appointments to the Supreme Court. If so, the voucher issue demonstrates once again how closely court rulings track political changes.

THE RIGHT TO PRIVACY

The civil liberties discussed so far in this chapter—freedom of expression and freedom of religion—each trace back to a specific provision in the Bill of Rights. Not all freedoms recognized by the courts appear in the Constitution, however.

Indeed, the Ninth Amendment explicitly recognizes that the people retain rights not listed in the document. The most controversial unlisted right recognized by the Supreme Court is the **right to privacy.**

Privacy, as a legal concept, has evolved over time. Originally, the right to privacy represented an ability to prevent others from publicizing details about one's private life. The word's meaning changed as judges sought a concept to defend personal autonomy, which Americans increasingly valued after World War II. Privacy now means the right to be free of public interference in personal life choices.

The modern right to privacy owes its genesis to the Supreme Court's ruling in *Griswold* v. *Connecticut* (1965).[42] Estelle Griswold, executive director of Planned Parenthood, was fined $100 for violating a Connecticut law prohibiting contraceptives. Justice William O. Douglas did not see any way for government to enforce such a law without intruding on the relationship between husbands and wives, and so declared the law unconstitutional based on "a right of privacy older than the Bill of Rights." His approach to privacy was similar to the old-fashioned concept, because it emphasized keeping personal details out of the public eye. "Would we allow the police to search the sacred precincts of marital bedrooms for telltale signs of the use of contraceptives?" asked Douglas. "The very idea is repulsive to the notions of privacy surrounding the marriage relationship."[43]

A second contraceptives case represented an even bigger jump. This time the Court faced a Massachusetts law that banned contraceptives sales rather than use. The old notion of privacy could not apply here. Governments may not be able to regulate the personal relationships inside a family, but they regulate what businesses sell all the time. So Justice Brennan, assigned the case, sought a new reason for striking down laws against contraception. His solution in *Eisenstadt* v. *Baird* (1972) was to adapt the notion of privacy: It no longer prevented government from exposing private details but actually prevented government from trying to influence those details. Privacy had changed to mean personal autonomy rather than just secrecy.[44]

ABORTION RIGHTS When Brennan wrote his *Eisenstadt* opinion, he was thinking about more than just condoms and the pill. He also had his eye turned toward a related set of cases on the Supreme Court docket: those dealing with abortion. Chief Justice Warren Burger had assigned the abortion cases to newly appointed Justice Harry Blackmun, an expert in medical law thought to be mildly conservative. Brennan did not wish to steal the chore away from Blackmun; as the Court's high-profile Catholic justice, he knew that someone else had better announce abortion rights. But Brennan did want to help steer Blackmun to a strong ruling in favor of the right to choose. Brennan's approach to privacy in *Eisenstadt* was tailor-made for the abortion issue.[45]

Blackmun's *Roe* v. *Wade* (1973) decision appeared the next year, guaranteeing at least a partial right of abortion. The case arose out of a request from Norma McCorvey, who used the pseudonym Jane Roe. She asked for a judgment declaring Texas antiabortion laws unconstitutional. Blackmun grouped the decision whether to give birth to a fetus under the privacy rubric created by Douglas and Brennan, and allowed state interference only when public interest in the potential life became compelling— that is, when the pregnant woman was close to term.

Before the remorse
Shown here in 1973, when Roe v. Wade *was decided, Norma McCorvey (whose privacy at the time was protected via the pseudonym Jane Roe) in 1995 made the surprise announcement that she had become a pro-life advocate.*

The *Roe* decision arrived at the tail end of America's "sexual revolution," and so enjoyed substantial support from parts of the U.S. population. Many others ardently opposed the Supreme Court's decision, which had struck down antiabortion laws across the nation. *Roe* v. *Wade* launched a powerful political crusade, the right-to-life movement, dedicated to banning abortion again. Supporters became actively engaged in state and national politics, lobbying legislatures and courts to impose as many restraints on abortion as the courts would allow.

Responding to right-to-life groups, Congress in 1976 enacted legislation preventing coverage of abortion costs under government health insurance programs, such as Medicaid. In 1980 the Republican party promised to restore the "right to life," and in subsequent years, Republican presidents began appointing Supreme Court justices expected either to reverse *Roe* v. *Wade* or to limit its scope.

The Court did begin accepting some restrictions on abortion. For example, the Court upheld the congressional act prohibiting abortion funding in 1980.[46] In 1989 it ruled that states could require the doctor to ascertain the viability of a fetus before permitting an abortion, if the woman were 20 or more weeks pregnant.[47] By 1990 judicial observers believed that four justices on the Supreme Court were prepared to overturn *Roe* and that any new appointment by a Republican president would create the majority needed.

Opposition to right-to-life groups was at first weak and uncertain, mainly because many of those who supported a woman's constitutional "right of choice" thought they had won. But as the right-to-life movement gained momentum and it became more likely that *Roe* v. *Wade* would be overturned, the right-to-choose movement also gained strength and aggressiveness. By 1984 it was able to secure the Democratic party's commitment to the right-to-choose principle.

Both sides of the controversy waited anxiously for the 1992 court decision in *Planned Parenthood* v. *Casey*.[48] The organization had challenged a Pennsylvania law that restricted abortion in numerous ways. Right-to-life groups hoped and right-to-choose groups feared that the Court would return authority for abortion law to the states. The majority ultimately decided against taking such a dramatic step, however. Justice O'Connor's opinion explicitly refused to overturn *Roe* v. *Wade* but did allow numerous restrictions on and regulations of the abortion procedure as long as they did not place an "undue burden" on women trying to exercise their constitutional right. In 2000, the Court reaffirmed its position when it ruled that states could not simply ban a particular type of abortion, in this case the so-called partial-birth abortion procedure.[49]

Either by accident or design, the Court majority once again adopted a position very close to that of the average American voter. It permitted restrictions endorsed by a majority of voters (such as a requirement that a teenager obtain parental consent) but rejected those most people consider unwarranted (such as a requirement that a married woman obtain the consent of her husband). Even in matters as sensitive as the right of privacy, the Court seems to be influenced by majority opinion, as expressed in the outcome of recent elections.

GAY RIGHTS   There is little doubt that most Americans thought a married couple should be able to use contraceptives, and a large chunk of the U.S. population wanted liberalized access to abortion. Early privacy cases therefore did not require the Supreme Court to stand alone against a large popular majority. In 1986, however, *Bowers* v. *Hardwick* confronted the Court with a more difficult constitutional claim: the claim that the right to privacy prevented Georgia from prohibiting sodomy between two consenting homosexuals.

The Court declined to buck popular hostility to homosexuality, even though the logic used to allow contraceptives and abortions seemed to apply to intercourse between same-sexed adults. Noting that laws against sodomy—that is, anal or oral sex—existed at the founding, the Court majority found no rea-

son to think that privacy rights exempted homosexual behavior from state regulation. Not every state has taken advantage of the Court's weakened stance on privacy rights. Louisiana, Kentucky, Maryland, and even Georgia itself have decided that their state constitutions offer a stronger right to privacy than that found in the U.S. Constitution.[50] But the Court's decision has allowed various sexual regulations to stand on the law books, including bans on sodomy of any sort (even between married couples) in 13 states.

Although these rulings may appear inconsistent with one another, they are consistent with one measure: public opinion. In 1986, when *Bowers* was decided, a

Going to the chapel?
A couple celebrates after the Vermont legislature voted to legalize gay civil unions in April 2000. Should the right to privacy include gay marriage?

majority of those surveyed believed that homosexual relations should be outlawed. But by 1999, polls found that Americans favored legalizing homosexual behavior by a margin of 50 to 43 percent. Similarly, 83 percent of people thought gays and lesbians should have equal rights in the workplace—a figure up nearly 25 percentage points from the early 1980s. If the Supreme Court accepts recent lower-court decisions, it will once again have shifted with changing public sentiment.[51]

LAW, ORDER, AND THE RIGHTS OF SUSPECTS

We end where we began: with the criminal-justice system. Elections also affect court interpretations of the procedural rights of the accused. Rights of the accused vary with social currents, with the dictates of public opinion. Barriers to criminal arrest and prosecution emerged during a period in which Americans were terribly suspicious of authority, but then have broken down again as the American public tires of the impositions that criminal behavior can impose on their lives.

CRIME RATES

Politics affects criminal justice routines, because almost everyone worries about being a victim of a crime. According to the Federal Bureau of Investigation, 83 percent of all Americans will become crime victims at some point in their lives.[52] Most of these crimes—thefts, burglaries, and robberies—take place in the United States at more or less the same rate as that in other major industrial countries. But many people in the United States today are especially afraid of personal injury and violent death, and their fears are not unfounded. The U.S. murder rate far exceeds that found in most other countries (see Figure 13.2).

In recent years, the news media have magnified public concern about crime. Coverage of murders, rapes, carjackings, and muggings surged in the mid-1990s. Even if these stories do not touch most people directly, they create an atmosphere in which many believe they are witnessing a crime rate escalating out of control. In response to public demands to solve the problem, politicians often believe they must "do something." As one senator remarked, "There is a mood here that if someone came to the floor and said we should barbwire the ankles of anyone who jaywalks, I suspect it would pass."[53]

Whether crime rates are actually rising or falling is not so easy to determine, because many crime statistics are notoriously unreliable. The best evidence on trends in crime rates comes from statistics on homicides, because most murders are reported and are correctly classified. Most victims of homicides are men. Black men are more likely to be murdered than white men. But for older men, both black and white, the murder rate has been falling since the 1980s. On the other hand, the murder victimization rate among younger men, especially younger black men, rose steeply in the early 1990s (see Figure 13.3) and then declined noticeably in the late 1990s.

Even declines in the crime rate may not represent a clear improvement, however, because they do not factor in the steps Americans have taken to prevent their own victimization: the extra time lost locking doors or taking indirect routes when traveling; the costs associated with alarms and bars on windows; the social risks that come when more people choose to arm themselves or train themselves for self-defense; and the simple human freedoms sacrificed when one must be cautious to avoid dangerous places or potentially risky situations.

FIGURE 13.2

A violent nation

Most rates of criminal activity are the same in the United States as those in other nations. The one exception is violent crime: the United States apparently is a much more violent society than are other industrialized nations. Do these violent crime statistics indicate that the United States should erect more severe gun-control laws? Or do they prove that Americans are more violent, and would find a way to commit murder even if they did not have access to guns?

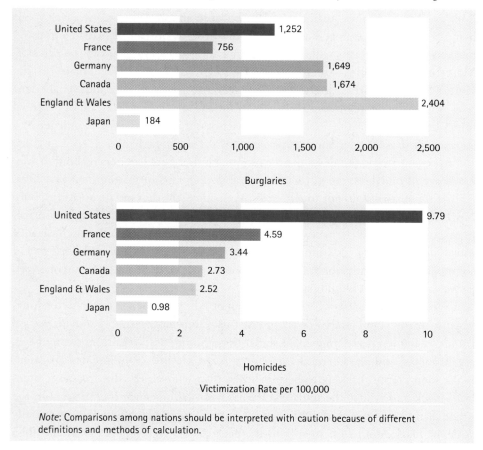

Burglaries

Homicides

Victimization Rate per 100,000

Note: Comparisons among nations should be interpreted with caution because of different definitions and methods of calculation.

SOURCE: International Criminal Police Organization (Interpol), 1991.

RIGHTS OF THE ACCUSED

The way the criminal-justice system treats suspects underwent radical alteration during the 1960s. Influenced by political currents at the time, the Supreme Court, under the leadership of Chief Justice Earl Warren, issued a series of decisions that substantially extended the meaning of the Bill of Rights. It specifically broadened the interpretation of five constitutional provisions, discussed in this

FIGURE 13.3

Homicide rates in the United States

Rates rose in the 1980s and early 1990s but fell in the latter half of the 1990s.

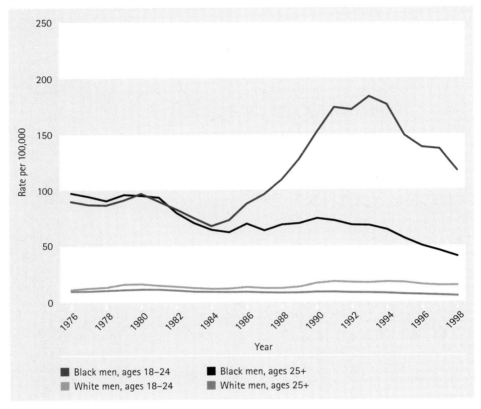

SOURCES: Bureau of Justice Statistics, *Homicide Trends in the U.S.* (www.ojp.usdoj.gov/bjs/homicide/homtrnd.htm contents, accessed March 24, 2000).

section: (1) protection from unreasonable search and seizure, (2) immunity against self-incrimination, (3) right to an impartial jury, (4) right to legal counsel, and (5) protection from double jeopardy.

Law-enforcement officials often did not appreciate these rulings, claiming that the Court had become contemptuous of both the rights of victims and the difficulties of enforcing laws in a complex society. Eventually the Warren Court provoked a backlash among voters, who were angry about criminals "getting off on technicalities." An increasing number of voters began to favor rigorous enforcement of laws and harsh punishments for criminals, including the death penalty (see Figure 13.4).

FIGURE 13.4

Most people think courts should be tougher on criminals

Although still strongly in favor of law and order, Americans no longer support tough criminal penalties at the rate they did a decade ago. Why has support for the death penalty dropped in recent years?

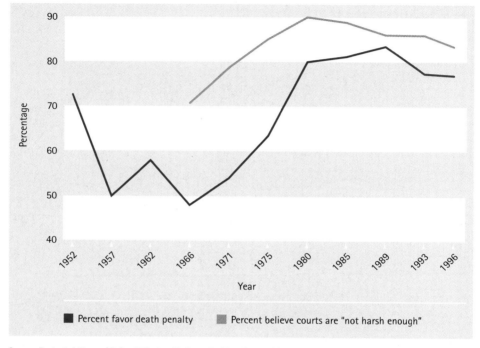

- Percent favor death penalty
- Percent believe courts are "not harsh enough"

SOURCE: Benjamin I. Page and Robert Y. Shapiro, *The Rational Public: Fifty Years of Trends in Americans' Policy Preferences.* (Chicago: University of Chicago Press, 1992), p. 92; General Social Survey.

Court procedures soon became a campaign issue, and many who sought office called for tougher law enforcement. Richard Nixon's successful 1968 campaign was the first to provoke what has become known as a "law and order" election. Since then, the issue has arisen in both national and local campaigns. In the 2000 presidential race, both George W. Bush and Al Gore campaigned as law-and-order candidates. Bush, as governor of Texas, allowed the executions of a number of death row inmates during the presidential campaign, including born-again Christian Karla Faye Tucker and great-grandmother Betty Lou Beets. Although activist groups denounced Bush's failure to grant clemency in these cases, Gore did not. The Supreme Court has responded to changing political circumstances, tempering its decisions on the rights of the accused without actually overturning them (see Table 13.1).

TABLE 13.1

KEY CHANGES IN THE RIGHTS OF THE ACCUSED

CONSTITUTIONAL PROVISION	AMENDMENT	EXTENSIONS BY WARREN COURT	LIMITATION BY POST-WARREN COURT
Search and seizure	4	*Mapp* v. *Ohio*, 1961 Improperly collected evidence cannot be introduced in court.	*Washington* v. *Chrisman*, 1982 But campus dorm rooms can be searched.
Self-incrimination	5	*Miranda* v. *Arizona*, 1966 Officers must tell suspects their rights before questioning.	*Harris* v. *NewYork*, 1971 But if suspects testify, evidence obtained without "reading them their rights" can be introduced. *Dickerson* v. *U.S.*, 2000 *Miranda* reaffirmed.
Impartial jury	6	*Sheppard* v. *Maxwell*, 1966 Ruling establishes guidelines to protect jurors from biased news coverage.	*Nebraska Press Association* v. *Stuart*, 1976 But pretrial publicity does not necessarily preclude a fair trial.
Legal counsel	6	*Gideon* v. *Wainwright*, 1963 Poor defendants are guaranteed legal counsel.	No limitation
Double jeopardy	5	*Benton* v. *Maryland*, 1969 Provision applies to state as well as federal trials.	No limitation

SEARCH AND SEIZURE   Police may not search your home without a court first granting them a search warrant, based on evidence that a crime has probably been committed. The Warren Court established an **exclusionary rule** in *Mapp* v. *Ohio* (1961): Improperly obtained evidence cannot appear during a trial.[54]

More recently, conservatives on the Court have limited the scope of the exclusionary rule. In *Washington* v. *Chrisman* (1982), for example, the Court exempted college dormitories from the rule's protection.[55] The Court has also ruled that workplace urine tests and police roadblocks may not constitute unreasonable searches. In early 2000, a unanimous Court ruled that officers sometimes may stop and search people because they run when they see police approaching. Running away, argued the Court, created enough "reasonable suspicion" to justify a search. "Headlong flight—whenever it occurs—is the consummate act of evasion," Chief Justice William Rehnquist wrote in his opinion. "It is not necessarily indicative of wrongdoing, but it is certainly suggestive of such."[56]

SELF-INCRIMINATION The Fifth Amendment protects individuals from torture and coerced confessions by exempting accused persons from testifying against themselves. For this reason, defendants in courtroom dramas often "take the Fifth," refusing to answer questions on grounds of possible self-incrimination.

At one time law-enforcement officials could take advantage of ignorance of civil liberties by tricking or scaring suspects into confessing after their arrests. The Warren Court therefore put teeth into the Fifth Amendment in *Miranda* v. *Arizona* (1966), requiring police officers to alert suspects of their rights before questioning them. This decision produced the **Miranda warning** so familiar in cop shows, such as *NYPD Blue,* which begins: "You have the right to remain silent . . ." If suspects are not so informed, then any information obtained may not be presented in court.

Father of a new right
Ernesto Miranda, namesake of the warning that is read to all suspects before questioning. The Supreme Court ruled that Miranda's confession was inadmissible in court because he had not been advised of his right to remain silent. Is the Miranda warning now part of American culture?

After Richard Nixon made the *Miranda* decision an issue in his 1968 presidential campaign, the Supreme Court softened the ruling. It decided, in *Harris* v. *New York* (1971), that information gathered in violation of the *Miranda* decision may be introduced in evidence when defendants testify on their own behalf. But the Supreme Court declined to throw out *Miranda* in a 2000 decision authored by Chief Justice Rehnquist, usually a hard-liner against rights of the accused. Rehnquist's 7-to-2 decision pointed out that "*Miranda* has become embedded in routine police procedure to the point where the warnings have become part of our national culture."

IMPARTIAL JURY The requirement that a jury be impartial is difficult to meet when crimes become newsworthy, because most potential jurors witness media accounts of the alleged crime before and during the trial. The Warren Court considered these issues in *Sheppard* v. *Maxwell* (1966), a case in which police accused an influential medical doctor of murdering his wife. (The story became the basis for two television shows as well as a movie, all called *The Fugitive*.)

Sam Sheppard complained about the excessive news coverage jurors witnessed. The media even sat in the courtroom where they could listen in on Sheppard's conversations with his attorneys.[57] The Supreme Court overturned his conviction and provided guidelines to ensure impartial juries in the future. Judges can postpone trials or transfer them far away from the initial crime to lower public awareness. McVeigh's trial, for example, changed **venue** from Oklahoma to Colorado. Judges can **sequester** juries during a trial—that is, keep them from external sources of information—as happened with jurors in the O. J. Simpson murder trial. Jurors also should be questioned to screen out those with fixed opinions and should be instructed to rule out any prejudices in the case derived apart from evidence presented in a trial.[58]

Although the Supreme Court has never reversed these constitutional safeguards designed to prevent a biased jury, some later decisions weakened the legal onus against pretrial publicity. The Court's decision in *Nebraska Press Association* v. *Stuart* (1976) is just one example of how criminal-justice law has reflected the country's more conservative mood. It ruled that "pre-trial publicity—even pervasive, adverse publicity—does not inevitably lead to an unfair trial."[59]

LEGAL COUNSEL   The Warren Court ruled in *Gideon* v. *Wainwright* (1963) that all citizens accused of serious crimes, even the indigent, must have access to proper advice. When the accused are too poor to hire attorneys, then the Sixth Amendment right to counsel requires courts to appoint legal representation.

It was easier to enunciate this right than to put it into practice. At one time, courts asked private attorneys to donate their services in order to defend the poor. But donating time to help suspected crooks was not popular among members of the legal profession. As a result, most states have created the office of **public defender,** an attorney whose full-time responsibility is to provide for the legal defense of indigent criminal suspects.

This solution has its own problems, though. For one thing, the job of a public defender is thankless, pay is low, and defenders must deal with "rotten case after rotten case."[60] From the perspective of the police, defenders simply throw up roadblocks to prevent conviction of the guilty. The public trend toward strong anticrime views therefore undercuts the right to counsel directly by influencing the budgets and prestige that accompany the job. One of the public defenders' biggest problems is winning respect from those with whom they work—including from the suspects they represent. Defendants, like most other people, think that anything free probably is not worth much. One felon, when asked by a judge whether he had been represented by an attorney, replied, "No, I had a public defender."[61]

DOUBLE JEOPARDY   The Warren Court ruled in *Benton v. Maryland* (1969) that states cannot try a person twice for the same offense, thereby placing the defendant in **double jeopardy.** The purpose was to prevent law-enforcement officials from wearing someone down by repeated prosecutions.

This rule does not prevent prosecution in both federal and state courts for the same act, as long as it violates multiple laws. Prosecution by both levels of government is most likely in high-visibility cases, in which political considerations may play a role. For example, when the state of California could not win a conviction of the four police officers charged with beating Rodney King, federal prosecutors went after the officers and won two convictions. Oklahoma courts tried to pin murder charges on Timothy McVeigh's co-conspirator, Terry Nichols, because a federal jury gave him only life imprisonment for his lesser role in the Oklahoma City bombing.[62]

RIGHTS IN PRACTICE: THE PLEA BARGAIN

If a case is newsworthy, constitutional procedures are generally observed: The public is looking on, and those participating in the trial must take political pressures into account. But the reality of justice in most criminal cases is very different. Hardly anyone accused of a crime is actually tried by a jury, and nearly all those convicted of a crime testify against themselves. The accused have their rights, to be sure, but very few of the accused actually choose to exercise them. Most of the time, it is to their advantage *not* to do so.[63]

Trial court judges depend on the willingness of prosecutors and defenders to settle cases before going to trial. The number of people accused of crimes is high, the list of cases on court dockets is seemingly endless, court personnel resources are limited, and court time is precious. Judges must preside over efficient courtrooms, settle cases quickly, and keep dockets short. To speed the criminal justice process, a defender and a prosecutor usually arrange a **plea bargain**—an agreement between prosecution and defense that the accused will admit to having committed a crime, provided that other charges are dropped and a reduced sentence is recommended. That is, suspects "cop a plea."

Extensive use of the plea bargain has become an issue in electoral politics, with many candidates insisting that those convicted should serve longer sentences. One popular proposal, enacted in a number of states, is known as "three strikes and you're out." Criminals must receive life imprisonment after their third felony conviction; prosecutors cannot offer them lighter sentences. As a result of these tough new laws, incarceration rates are rising, and prison costs are becoming one of the fastest growing items in state budgets. The United States now has one of the largest incarceration rates in the world (see Figure 13.5).

FIGURE 13.5

A "lock 'em up" mentality?

The United States imprisons a far larger portion of its citizenry than most other industrialized countries do. Arrests in the so-called drug war are a major source of America's large prison population; even limited drug possession can lead to years of incarceration. Does the United States imprison so many people because law-enforcement officials catch more criminals or because the United States is less tolerant toward deviant behavior?

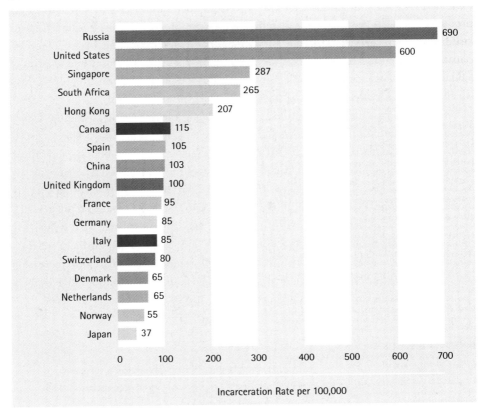

Incarceration Rate per 100,000

SOURCE: Marc Mauer, *Americans Behind Bars: U.S. and International Use of Incarceration, 1995* (Washington, DC: The Sentencing Project, 1997).

CHAPTER SUMMARY

The Bill of Rights remained a dead letter until the Civil War ended slavery, because state governments did not have to honor the Constitution's civil liberties protections. Only after the due process clause of the Fourteenth Amendment joined the Constitution did civil liberties become an effective component of the country's constitutional makeup.

Although the founders hoped courts would protect individual rights against majority tyranny, most of the time the Supreme Court follows public opinion. This is true in most areas of constitutional law: free expression, religious freedom, privacy rights, and protection of the accused. Some examples of Court sensitivity to public opinion date back to the early twentieth century and include the Court's fluctuations on the clear and present danger doctrine between war time and peace time and the Court's rapid reversal in the flag-salute cases. But sensitivity to public opinion seems heightened in America's new democracy.

The Warren and early Burger Courts responded to America's postwar liberalism and expanded civil liberties in multiple areas. The Court embraced free expression as a fundamental freedom central to the democratic system. It evolved three-prong tests to determine when laws violated the First Amendment's establishment or free exercise clauses. It altered the meaning of privacy to increase personal autonomy and to protect individual decisions from public intervention. And it sought mechanisms to give teeth to constitutional provisions protecting those accused of criminal behavior.

The public has since become more conservative in various respects, and the Court has responded by pulling back somewhat from Warren Court precedents. This retreat is least pronounced for free speech, because several prominent Republican appointees (especially Scalia and Kennedy) continue to defend political expression. But current law on religious freedom no longer follows the Warren Court approach, perhaps most easily remembered as the "Lemon Sherbert" era (after the two tests that dominated the period). Now, the United States is stuck with the Lemon, and a modified one at that. Privacy rights provide less protection for abortion than they once did, and do not shield consenting adults who engage in sodomy. Finally, law-enforcement officials enjoy increasing power over those suspected of criminal behavior. The country's definition of civil liberties seems to depend as much on the thinking of its citizens as on judicial principles.

KEY TERMS

balancing doctrine,
  p. 433
civil liberties,
  p. 427

civil rights amendments,
  p. 429
clear and present danger doctrine, p. 431

coercion test, p. 440
double jeopardy, p. 456
due process clause,
  p. 429

Suggested Readings

Friedman, Lawrence M. *Crime and Punishment in American History.* New York: Basic Books, 1993. Readable overview of the changing nature of the American system of criminal justice.

Garrow, David J. *Liberty and Sexuality.* New York: Macmillan, 1994. Comprehensive account of the legal debate over abortion before and after *Roe.*

Goldstein, Robert. *Saving "Old Glory": The History of the Desecration Controversy.* Boulder, CO: Westview, 1995. Authoritative political and constitutional history of the flag-burning controversy.

Lewis, Anthony. *Make No Law: The Sullivan Case and the First Amendment.* New York: Random House, 1992. Excellent, readable case study of the politics of the *Sullivan* decision and the evolution of free speech doctrine.

Macedo, Stephen. *The New Right* v. *The Constitution.* Washington, DC: Cato Institute, 1987. Thoughtfully asserts the responsibility of the courts to protect all liberties, not just fundamental freedoms, from legislative intrusion.

McIntyre, Lisa J. *The Public Defender: The Practice of Law in the Shadows of Repute.* Chicago: University of Chicago Press, 1987. Careful sociological study of this little-appreciated courtroom player.

Rosenberg, Gerald N. *The Hollow Hope: Can Courts Bring About Social Change?* Chicago: University of Chicago Press, 1991. Casts doubt on the proposition that the courts play a major, independent role in shaping policy.

Sandel, Michael J. *Democracy's Discontent: American in Search of a Public Philosophy.* Cambridge, MA: Belknap Press of Harvard, 1996. A readable but sophisticated book arguing that the Supreme Court's approach to civil liberty overemphasizes individual autonomy at the expense of republican principles favoring a community's right to self-government.

Wilson, James Q. *Thinking About Crime.* New York: Basic Books, 1975. Makes a persuasive, realistic, and conservative case for ways of controlling crime.

ON THE WEB

American Civil Liberties Union
www.aclu.org
The sometimes controversial American Civil Liberties Union has a detailed Web site outlining its agenda for promoting civil liberties as well as describing the history and present status of the law.

Freedom Forum
www.freedomforum.org
The Freedom Forum is an international foundation that promotes freedom of the press and of religion.

Electronic Frontier Foundation
www.eff.org
The Electronic Frontier Foundation follows issues and provide information about free speech and privacy.

Center for Democracy and Technology
www.cdt.org
The Center for Democracy and Technology follows issues and provide information about free speech and privacy.

Program on Educational Policy and Governance
data.fas.harvard.edu/pepg
Harvard University's Program on Educational Policy and Governance provides reports of studies on existing school-choice programs.

CIVIL RIGHTS

The scene reminded observers of a 1960s protest. On a cool Wednesday night in November 1996, hundreds of University of California (UC) students gathered in the center of the Berkeley campus for an angry rally. Sixty then marched to the university's Campanile clock tower and occupied the structure, some chaining themselves to its stone walls. Meanwhile, 300 UC–Santa Cruz students surrounded their registrar's office, forcing its closure. The next day, a group of San Francisco State University students blocked traffic on a crowded city street. Less than a week later, UC–Riverside protesters stormed the administration building, shackled the doors shut from inside, and presented a list of demands.[1]

What prompted the wave of protests was not a war or even an autocratic university decision, but a popular vote. The day before the first rumblings in Berkeley, voters statewide had passed Proposition 209, an amendment to the state constitution that banned giving preferential treatment to "any individual or group on the basis of race, sex, color, ethnicity or national origin in the operation of public employment, public education, or public contracting."[2] Although at first glance those words may appear uncontroversial—an affirmation of long-standing American values, such as equality and fairness—the measure actually represented a dramatic policy change. It dismantled a series of California programs that explicitly took race into consideration, including those for university admissions.

Many minority college students feared that, because of the vote, future graduating classes would be less diverse than theirs. "I've made it through UC, but I have little brothers and sisters that could be denied access," said one protester.[3] But supporters of the proposition argued that policies favoring minority groups were insulting and damaging. Ward Connerly, an African American member of the UC Board of Regents, backed the constitutional amendment. "For decades we have relied on government to secure our rights. . . . The time has indeed come to let go. We cannot forever look through the rearview mirror at America's mistakes."[4]

New admissions policies took effect at UC in 1997. Instead of scoring minority students differently during the admissions process, UC concentrated on recruiting more minority applicants, increasing the size and quality of the admissions pool. Results have been mixed. In early 2000, University officials trumpeted statistics showing that the number of minority applicants increased after the new policy. Many of the applicants were strong candidates, who had no trouble getting into UC even without preferential treatment. "Underrepresented groups" made up 17.6 percent of the 2000 incoming UC class, just short of the 18.8 percent before the change.

Their distribution across individual campuses was less clear.[5] It is still too soon to judge what lasting impact the new admissions system will have on California's university system.

THE DEBATE OVER PROPOSITION 209 RAISES A BROADER QUESTION ABOUT America's new democracy. Popular influence may have surged in the U.S. political system, but what does the change mean for people who are members of a minority because of their race, ethnicity, primary language, or sexuality? On the one hand, when elections drive policy, voters decide the nation's future. Minorities are, by definition, smaller than majorities—and so elections could place them at a political disadvantage.* They may exercise influence only when resources and interests mobilize them disproportionately.

On the other hand, elections could favor tightly knit groups whose common concerns prompt them to participate as a bloc. Politicians usually construct their electoral coalitions from multiple factions; they seldom appeal to voters as an undifferentiated mass. Minority-group leaders who can sway the behavior of a large chunk of voters receive disproportionate influence. They are valuable allies and worrisome enemies. For candidates and policy makers, it may be easier to accommodate the passionate demands of a unified and vocal minority than to worry about the mild or divided preferences of a numerical majority. America's new democracy therefore may expand minority influence, compared to a system more insulated from voters.

This chapter grapples with the difficult question of where minorities stand in a system that enhances popular influence. The reality is complex: Sometimes minorities thrive in election-driven politics, and sometimes their political goals suffer when the majority rules. Elected officials and ballot-box policies sometimes reflect the preferences, interests, and prejudices of those who enjoy strength in numbers. But sometimes the sensibilities and values of common voters prove friendlier to minorities than what elites or interest groups might have endorsed. And sometimes minorities can operate as swing voters in elections and force public officials to pay heed.

Conversely, the least democratic American institution—the judicial branch—occasionally stands up for minority groups against discriminatory policies. But in most cases the Supreme Court's approach to civil rights follows trends initiated by

---

*This generalization refers to a "minority" in a statistical sense. Sometimes people use the term "minority" in a political sense, to mean a disadvantaged or less-powerful group, in which case women are a "minority" with greater numbers than men.

the public debates and coalition building that make up electoral politics. As Justice Ruth Bader Ginsburg once observed, "With prestige to persuade, but not physical power to enforce, and with a will for self-preservation, the Court generally follows, it does not lead, changes taking place elsewhere in society."[6] Usually, the Court does little more than codify existing policy preferences into constitutional doctrine. Sometimes it even lags behind the times.

CIVIL RIGHTS: MORE THAN JUST A RACE THING

The terms *civil rights* and *civil liberties* are similar but not identical. Civil liberties are fundamental freedoms that preserve the rights of a free people. **Civil rights** embody the American guarantee to equal treatment under the law—not just for racial groups, as students often assume, but more generally. In Chapter 13 we emphasize how important the due process clause of the Fourteenth Amendment has been to the protection of civil liberties in the United States. An equally important provision in the Fourteenth Amendment guards civil rights. According to the **equal protection clause,** states must give everyone equal protection of the law.

The equal protection clause is no plainer in meaning than the due process clause. Choice of the word "protection" might suggest that the language only applies to law-enforcement officials and the courts, requiring that the justice system defend everyone equally. Yet most interpreters emphasize the word "equal" instead. They read the clause to imply that laws should not make categorical distinctions. Everyone must receive equal *treatment* when government formulates public policy.

But even given this wider understanding, it is not clear exactly how "equal" everyone must be. Almost every law treats some people in one way and others in a different way. Laws regularly distinguish people based upon age, income, health, wealth, criminal history, or place of residence. Some distinguish people based upon race, gender, or sexuality. Obviously, some sorts of categories are acceptable some of the time, and federal judges are the ones who decide (sometimes receiving indirect guidance from civil rights legislation).

Generally, the courts distinguish various sorts of unequal treatment according to the level of "scrutiny" they deserve. Most legal distinctions need only pass a *rational basis test*—the law must offer a reasonable way to promote some legitimate government purpose. Laws receive *strict scrutiny* when they distinguish people according to a **suspect classification**—which is to say, according to some grouping that has a long history of being used for purposes of discrimination, such as race. State governments or federal agencies responsible for unequal treatment must provide a compelling reason for the differentiation and must explain why their goals were unreachable using less group-conscious legislation. Certain groupings, such as gender, fall between these two extremes. Compared to regular laws, laws distinguishing people according to these categories receive *heightened scrutiny*, but they need not clear the steep hurdle that suspect-class legislation does. In all instances, though, the process is the same: Judges decide whether government has good reasons for the categories it uses.

Few voices criticize either the looser interpretation of the word "protection" or varying application of the word "equal" (although the three-tiered "scrutiny" system does have its detractors).[7] Two other questions about how to interpret the Fourteenth Amendment generate much more controversy.[8] The first is over how actively laws must distinguish people before they fall under scrutiny. A government policy with no direct reference to race—say, for example, a performance test for police academy recruits—might impact two races differently. How should courts decide when indirect sources of unequal treatment represent unconstitutional discrimination? Answers differ. And when individuals or private groups behave in a way that distinguishes people, how aggressively must government pressure them to select new forms of behavior? If government allows a social condition to persist, does that violate the Constitution? Again, answers differ.

The second major controversy over the equal protection clause is how to deal with a law that distinguishes people according to a suspect class but does so to favor rather than harm a minority group. It may be unconstitutional to establish university scholarships available only to Asians or whites.* But can a public university offer money only for blacks, Hispanics, or Native Americans? It may be unconstitutional to shut minority businesses out of receiving government contracts. But can a state government set aside some of its projects exclusively for minority contractors? People clash angrily over whether equal treatment must go both ways when American society itself contains deep inequalities.

The stakes are high in these various debates over the equal protection clause. Many minority group members rely on constitutional guarantees to assure that they obtain equal opportunity. Those outside a minority group, meanwhile, must be on guard to ensure that the claim to equal treatment does not become an excuse for special interests to encroach on their liberties or their own equality before the law. Thus, the struggle over civil rights is shaped as much by majority

---

*The term "white" used in spoken English has no basis in genetic traits such as skin, hair, or eye color. Anglo-Saxons, Nordics, Slavs, Arabs, Jews, and many other groups all fall into the "white majority" of the U.S. population.

opinion as by minority demands. Elected leaders, although occasionally sensitive to the rights of minorities, cannot forget that they are elected by majorities.

Because minorities seldom control the outcome of elections, they have often pursued a legal strategy, bringing apparent civil rights violations to the attention of the courts. But litigation does not always work. Judges, too, are concerned about preserving credibility with majorities. If judges defy public opinion regularly, they may undermine confidence in the courts—and eventually elected officials will replace them.

AFRICAN AMERICANS AND THE IMPORTANCE OF VOTING RIGHTS

At the end of the Civil War, some southern states passed "black codes," restrictive laws that applied to newly freed slaves but not to whites. "Persons of color . . . must make annual written contracts for their labor," one of the codes said, adding that if blacks ran away from their "masters," they had to forgo a year's wages.[9] Other codes denied African Americans access to the courts or the right to hold property, except under special circumstances.

Northern abolitionists urged Congress to override these black codes, which they considered thinly disguised attempts to continue slavery. Congress responded by passing the Civil Rights Act of 1866, which gave all citizens "the same right . . . to full and equal benefit of all laws." Both the sentiment and some of the words carried over to the equal protection clause of the Fourteenth Amendment, which won final ratification two years later.

The federal government promoted its civil rights stance during **Reconstruction,** a period after the Civil War when the federal military still occupied southern states. During this period, blacks exercised their right to vote, a right many white Confederate veterans lacked. In addition, Congress established a Freedman's Bureau, designed to provide blacks with education, immediate food relief, and inexpensive land from former plantations.[10]

The close election of 1876 brought Reconstruction to an end. Republican presidential candidate Rutherford B. Hayes claimed victory, but the outcome depended on fraudulent vote counts reported by several states, including three in the South. Politicians trying to resolve the disputed election worked out a compromise. Republicans won the presidency; Democrats won removal of federal troops from the South and control of future southern elections.

Within a generation the South had restored many of its old racial patterns.[11] One critical change was that black citizens lost their voting rights, a process that disturbed the electoral connection between blacks and their government. State

Under the shadow of Jim Crow

Within a generation after the end of Reconstruction, southern states erected strict social barriers between blacks and whites, as did many states outside the South. People of different races could not attend the same schools, use the same public transportation, or mingle in the same public facilities (such as theaters). Would Jim Crow laws have been more difficult to maintain if blacks had been able to vote?

legislatures enacted laws requiring voters to pass literacy tests, meet strict residency requirements, and pay poll taxes to vote. Although the laws themselves used general words, and therefore did not seem to violate equal protection of the law, they clearly targeted blacks and the poor whites who might have allied with them in elections.

These laws became even more discriminatory once local officials began applying them. As the chair of the suffrage committee in Virginia bluntly admitted, "I expect the [literacy] examination with which the black men will be confronted to be inspired by the same spirit that inspires every man in this convention. I do not expect an impartial administration of this clause."[12] States also enacted what became known as a **grandfather clause,** a law that exempted men from voting restrictions if their fathers and grandfathers had voted before the Civil War. Of course, only whites benefited from this exemption.

The most successful restriction on the right to vote was the *white primary,* a nomination election held by the Democratic party that excluded nonwhites from participation. Republicans almost never won southern elections at the time, because of the party's tie to Reconstruction, so Democratic primary winners almost always took office.[13] This practice, combined with the various voting restrictions, denied former slaves or their descendants a meaningful vote. Only 10 percent of adult African American males were registered in most states of the old Confederacy by 1910.[14]

African Americans also faced **Jim Crow laws,** state laws that segregated the races from each other.* Jim Crow laws required African Americans to attend segregated schools, sit in separate areas in public trains and buses, eat in different restaurants, and use separate public facilities. These laws were almost universal in the South but appeared in numerous states outside that region as well. So, those of African descent entered the twentieth century lacking most privileges enjoyed by other Americans, including the electoral connection that usually requires government to heed citizen demands.

EARLY COURT INTERPRETATIONS OF CIVIL RIGHTS

The Supreme Court initially took a very restrictive view of the Fourteenth Amendment's equal protection clause. Two rulings held particular significance. In a decision given the ironic title the *Civil Rights Cases* (1883), the Court declared the Civil Rights Act of 1875 unconstitutional.[15] This law abolished segregation in restaurants, train stations, and other public places. But the Supreme Court ruled that only government policies must comply with federal equal rights law, not the actions of private individuals (a position called the **state action doctrine**). Congress had no constitutional authority to tell private individuals who could use their property.

The second major decision by the courts, *Plessy* v. *Ferguson* (1896), had even more sweeping consequences. It developed the **separate but equal doctrine,** the principle that segregated facilities passed constitutional muster as long as they were equivalent. Homer Plessy had challenged Louisiana's law requiring racial segregation in buses, railroad cars, and waiting rooms. Plessy argued that his inability to use white facilities denied him equal protection before the law. But the Supreme Court upheld Louisiana's statute, explaining that separating races did

---

*The name comes from a stereotypical, belittling characterization of African Americans in minstrel shows popular at the time.

not stamp either with a "badge of inferiority." Only one justice, a Kentuckian, dissented. Justice John Marshall Harlan protested that "our Constitution is color-blind, and neither knows nor tolerates classes among citizens." Laws enforcing segregation, Harlan argued, clearly violate this ideal.[16]

BLACKS GAIN ELECTORAL POWER

Legally sanctioned segregation remained intact well into the twentieth century. During that time, however, African Americans gained electoral clout by migrating north, to states where they could vote. During both world wars, in particular, northern industrial cities filled labor shortages with blacks from the rural South (see Figure 14.1). Northerners were not much more tolerant of blacks than were southerners. But machine politicians who dominated big city politics were not fussy about the color or religion of the voters they organized. Any warm body who could walk into a voting booth was worth courting.[17]

FIGURE 14.1

Percentage of African Americans living outside the South, by decade, 1910 to 1999

The northern migration of African Americans greatly increased their electoral clout. What explains the northern migration of blacks from 1910 to 1970, and their recent return to the South?

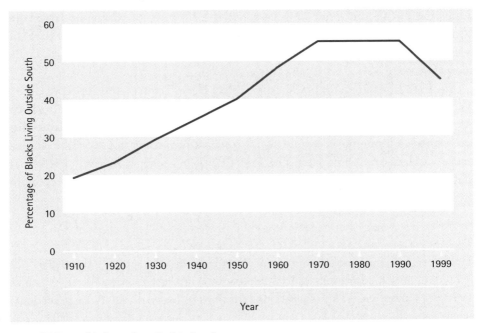

SOURCE: U.S. Bureau of the Census, *Current Population Survey Reports.*

By the 1930s, African Americans used their votes to win small places in the politics of a few big cities. But the biggest political breakthrough for African Americans occurred in 1948, when they appeared to cast the decisive votes electing Harry Truman president (see the Election Connection, "Blacks Helped Elect Harry Truman in 1948"). This clout, and the increased rhetorical support President Truman gave to civil rights, lent added force to civil rights lawsuits that activists began bringing before the Supreme Court.

WEAKENING THE STATE ACTION DOCTRINE

The legal case against segregation was developed gradually by the National Association for the Advancement of Colored People (NAACP). Formed in 1909, the NAACP chose a courtroom strategy because its leaders feared the inadequacy of black electoral strength. Only 12 percent of the southern black adult population could vote in 1947.[18] Yet a legal strategy without electoral leverage could not be very effective. The NAACP's lead attorney, Thurgood Marshall (who later became the first black Supreme Court justice), initially had few successes.

The NAACP's efforts gained potency as blacks moved north. Their earliest advances involved the state-action doctrine. The Court was willing to expand its definition of state activity to protect the political and legal rights of African Americans. In an important 1944 case, *Smith* v. *Allwright,* the Court outlawed the white primary, saying parties were not private organizations but integral parts of a state electoral system.[19] After this decision, black voting in the South gradually increased.

In 1948, the same year blacks helped elect Harry Truman, the Supreme Court took a major step against residential segregation. One tool whites used to keep African Americans out of their neighborhoods was the **restrictive housing covenant;** a home buyer would sign a contract promising not to sell the property to a black household later. The Court ruled in *Shelley* v. *Kraemer* (1948) that states could not give legal standing to such private agreements and enforce them without violating the equal protection clause.[20]

TAKING THE "SEPARATE" OUT OF "EQUAL"

The Supreme Court moved much more slowly against the separate but equal doctrine, which helped preserve social inequalities, not just political ones. As late as 1950 the Court passed up several opportunities to overrule the *Plessy* precedent, sensing that the time was not right to take such a controversial stand.[21] The problem was not a lack of sympathetic justices. Rather, the Court feared stepping too far beyond public opinion and losing the policy battle.

Blacks Helped Elect Harry Truman in 1948

For most of the early twentieth century, African Americans favored the Republican party, largely because Republican President Abraham Lincoln had ended slavery. But the Republican stranglehold on black votes began to loosen during the 1930s. Franklin Delano Roosevelt's New Deal programs induced many black voters to switch parties. By 1948 it was no longer clear which party would win black electoral support.

The presidential election that year was hotly contested. President Harry Truman, who had risen to his office after FDR's death, was struggling. Advisers pushed him to court the black vote aggressively. In the words of his top analyst, "the northern Negro vote today holds the balance of power in Presidential elections for the simple arithmetical reason that the Negroes not only vote in a block but are geographically concentrated in the pivotal, large and closely contested electoral states such as New York, Illinois, Pennsylvania, Ohio, and Michigan."

Truman himself had never been known as a civil rights enthusiast. On the contrary, he came from Missouri, a former slave state, and his private language was sprinkled with racial slurs. But Truman possessed exceptional political instincts. He called for the abolition of poll taxes, more effective protection of black voting rights, the creation of a Fair Employment Practices Commission with authority to stop racial discrimination, and an end to racial segregation within the armed forces.

Truman's civil rights strategy may have secured his reelection. Just a few thousand votes decided the victor. The two-thirds support he received from African Americans helped him carry the "large, pivotal" states of Ohio by 7,000 votes, Illinois by 33,000, and California by 17,000. Had he lost these states, his Republican opponent, Thomas Dewey, would have been elected. Although no single factor determines the outcome of any presidential election, African Americans had become a significant force in national politics for the first time since 1876. Significantly, it was in that same year the NAACP began to win key Supreme Court decisions. And since then, Democrats have received overwhelming majorities of the black vote.

What do you think?

- Does black loyalty allow Democrats to take black voters for granted?

- Would blacks gain more influence if Republicans had a chance of winning their votes?

SOURCES: David McCullough, *Truman* (New York: Simon & Schuster, 1992), pp. 586–590; Patricia Gurin, Shirley Hatchett, and James S. Jackson, *Hope and Independence: Blacks' Response to Electoral and Party Politics* (New York: Russell Sage, 1989), pp. 36–38.

NAACP attorneys continued seeking cases that might prompt the Court to overturn *Plessy*. Of the handful they moved to the Court's docket in 1952, one from Kansas eventually took center stage: ***Brown v. Board of Education of Topeka*** (1954). Oliver Brown had filed a suit arguing that his daughter Linda's all-black school denied her equal protection of the law. The fact that Topeka funded white and black education equivalently made no difference, NAACP lawyers argued; separation was inherently unequal. The Justice Department's Civil Rights Division backed the NAACP's claim, using strategies developed in

collaboration with Justice Felix Frankfurter, a former director of the NAACP.*
The Court agreed to hear their arguments and did so in December 1952.

The Supreme Court was still skittish, though. Chief Justice Fred Vinson, a conservative Democrat, did not consider *Plessy* a bankrupt precedent. Three other justices also hesitated to overturn it. The Court scheduled a second round of arguments in 1953. Before they could take place, however, Vinson died of a heart attack. Frankfurter called Vinson's death "the first indication I have ever had that there is a God."[22] President Eisenhower turned to a popular former governor, Earl Warren, to lead the Court.

Dramatic changes followed Warren's appointment. The Californian approached his appointment not as a former attorney or judge, concerned with refining points of law, but as a politician determined to set public policy.[23] To Warren, the South's racial caste system represented an evil that most American voters were willing to exorcise; the Court should not hesitate to alter constitutional law as a means of promoting this moral goal. He decided to write the *Brown* opinion himself.

Warren realized how risky it was for the Court to abolish segregated institutions with long histories. He wanted a unanimous judgment, to give the ruling additional authority. He delayed voting on the issue for four months while he worked to persuade reluctant justices. He made compromises: limiting the judgment to schools and leaving flexibility in the ways a school district might remedy a segregated system. Eventually, every justice agreed to sign on—no dissents and no concurrences.

Warren's opinion in *Brown* built less from law than from social science. Warren cited psychological studies claiming that segregation created a sense of inferiority among black children. One study showed, for example, that black children favored white dolls over black ones.[24] Warren therefore overturned *Plessy* only in the field of education, and did not embrace Harlan's *Plessy* dissent declaring the Constitution "color-blind." The Court still hesitated to take on social arrangements that dated back to the earliest colonial settlements.

CIVIL RIGHTS AFTER *BROWN*

The *Brown* decision energized civil rights activists around the country. The impact on young people and church leaders was particularly noticeable; they formed numerous civil rights organizations and adopted more militant techniques.[25] NAACP activist Rosa Parks, of Montgomery, Alabama, engaged in an extraordi-

---

*For a justice to collaborate with interested parties in a Supreme Court appeal clearly violates today's ethical standards, but there is no indication that Frankfurter saw any problem with sharing notes on an important case. See Howard Ball and Phillip J. Cooper, *Of Power and Right* (New York: Oxford, 1992), p. 177.

narily successful act of **civil disobedience**—a peaceful violation of a law, designed to dramatize that law's injustice. She refused to vacate her seat in a segregated bus when the driver attempted to expand the white section past her spot. The standoff prompted a bus boycott led by a young Baptist minister, Martin Luther King, Jr., who had recently earned his Ph.D. in theology. He was only 27 years old at the time, but he had the resourcefulness necessary to give the event national significance.[26]

The civil rights movement won overwhelmingly sympathetic coverage in the northern press, but it met intense opposition from regional officials.[27] In March 1956, nearly every southern member of Congress signed the Southern Manifesto, committing each official to resist implementation of the *Brown* decision by "all lawful means."[28] Southern resistance was so consistent and complete that, in the states of the Old Confederacy, few schools desegregated. In the fall of 1964, ten years after *Brown*, only 2.3 percent of black students in former Confederate states attended integrated schools.[29]

Civil rights workers
Tear-gas clouds, laid by the Mississippi Highway Patrol, rained confusion on early civil rights marchers in Canton, Mississippi. Did these marchers or the courts contribute more to the end of formal segregation?

Content of his character
Martin Luther King, Jr., delivers his "I Have a Dream" speech at the 1963 March on Washington. Why did the civil rights movement lose support just a few years later?

Yet the protests and demonstrations gradually had their effect. For one thing, southern blacks were registering to vote. From 1947 to 1960, the percentage more than doubled from 12 percent to 28 percent. At the same time, African Americans were becoming a more powerful political force in the large industrial states of the North. Presidential candidates had to balance southern resistance against their need for black votes.

John Kennedy's victory over Richard Nixon in the breathtakingly close election of 1960 owed much to his success attracting the black vote. When the 1960 election campaign began, Kennedy realized that he needed to improve his civil rights credentials, especially because he had won the Democratic nomination by defeating two candidates with stronger records: Hubert Humphrey and Adlai Stevenson. A golden opportunity arose when Birmingham authorities jailed

Martin Luther King, Jr. Kennedy placed a well-publicized phone call to Coretta Scott King, expressing sympathy for the plight of her husband. That phone call took on great symbolic significance and helped mobilize Kennedy's supporters in the black community. He captured enough black votes to win such crucial states as Ohio, Michigan, and Illinois.

Once in office, Kennedy introduced civil rights legislation. To support his efforts, 100,000 black and white demonstrators marched on the Washington Mall in the summer of 1963. Others organized the event, but King emerged as the star, delivering his moving "I Have a Dream" oration from the steps of the Lincoln Memorial. Suddenly, a plurality of Americans viewed civil rights as the country's most important problem.[30] A few months later, Kennedy's assassination generated an unprecedented outpouring of moral commitment to racial justice (see Figure 14.2).

FIGURE 14.2

Evaluation of civil rights as the country's most important problem

Many people saw civil rights as an important problem in the wake of the Kennedy assassination and civil rights demonstrations. Today (not shown) only around 3 percent view race relations as the most important problem. Does this change reflect real progress or a lack of attention to current problems?

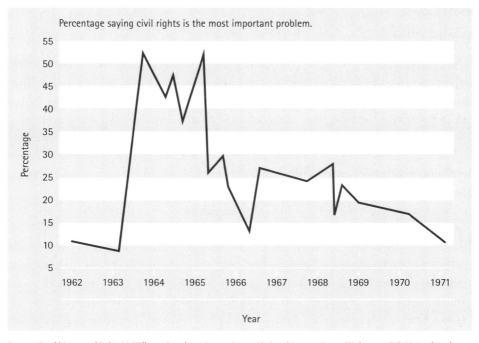

SOURCE: Gerald Jaynes and Robin M. Williams, Jr., eds., *A Common Destiny: Blacks and American Society* (Washington, DC: National Academy Press, 1989), p. 224.

Elected political leaders responded quickly to this transformation in the nation's mood. The new president, Lyndon Baines Johnson (LBJ) of Texas, knew that he had to dispel public doubts about his commitment to racial change. The southerner called upon Congress to memorialize his dead predecessor by enacting civil rights legislation stalled in the Senate since the previous summer. After intense debate, majorities of both Republican and Democratic members of Congress voted to pass the legislation in 1964. This act banned segregation in all places of public accommodation, prohibited federal money from being used to support segregated programs, and created the Equal Employment Opportunity Commission (EEOC) to guard against employment discrimination. From 1964 to 1972, the percentage of black students in southern schools that included whites increased dramatically from 2.3 percent to 91.3 percent.

Buoyed by economic prosperity and his civil rights achievements, LBJ won a sweeping election victory in the fall of 1964. He followed this success by engineering congressional passage of the Voting Rights Act of 1965, which guaranteed that more black voters would be able to turn out for Democratic candidates in the future.[31] The percentage of voters among southern black adults jumped upward; by 1992 they were as likely to vote as northern blacks.[32] From 1965 to 1998, the number of black elected officials rose from less than 500 to over 8,800.[33]

DECLINE OF THE CIVIL RIGHTS MOVEMENT

Segregation and discrimination did not stop at the South's borders. Most northern blacks lived in racially isolated neighborhoods, sent their children to predominantly black schools, and struggled to get good jobs. Martin Luther King shifted his focus northward after the successes in 1964 and 1965 by mounting a series of demonstrations in Chicago.[34] King broadened his issue concerns, protesting poverty and criticizing the Vietnam War. At the same time, new black leaders such as Malcolm X took a more militant position, affirming black culture and denying the value of integration.

Increasing assertiveness by black leaders changed how the public viewed civil rights. Support for protests dwindled.[35] At the same time, African Americans grew increasingly disenchanted with the slowness of racial change. Leaders began calling for **affirmative action** policies, which are programs designed to enhance opportunities for race- or gender-based groups by giving them extra consideration in recruitment and promotion decisions. Riots broke out in minority neighborhoods, beginning in Los Angeles in 1964 and spreading to other cities over the next three years. King's assassination in the spring of 1968 again set off

Defending Dixie

Symbolizing Southern pride to some and racial hatred to others, South Carolina's practice of flying a Confederate flag over the statehouse became an issue in the 2000 presidential campaign. The flag was later moved elsewhere as part of a compromise.

violent racial disturbances in dozens of cities throughout the country. National guard and army units had to quell wholesale theft and property destruction. The civil rights movement lost its moral authority, and whites began to lose interest in the cause (review Figure 14.2).

Racial issues began to divide the two political parties. When Arizona Senator Barry Goldwater voted against the Civil Rights Act of 1964, he was among a minority of Republicans to do so. But by 1968, his party started pursuing a "southern strategy" by appealing to those who thought civil rights legislation had gone too far. Meanwhile, blacks solidified their allegiance to the Democratic party.[36] Between 1968 and 1972, the percentage of delegates attending the

FIGURE 14.3

**Percentage of African American delegates
to the Republican and Democratic national conventions**

The shifting racial characteristics of party activists reflect similar changes in voter loyalties. Why has African American participation in Democratic party politics risen dramatically?

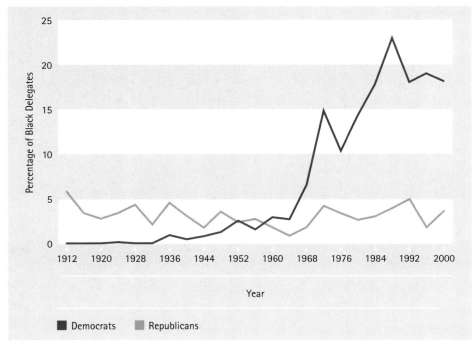

Sources: "The Democratic Delegates," *San Francisco Examiner* (August 27, 1996): A9; Robert Zauser, "Small Number of Black Delegates Illustrates Problem for Republicans," *Philadelphia Inquirer* (August 16, 1996): A22.

Democratic convention who were black grew from 6.7 to 14.6 percent (see Figure 14.3).

THE SUPREME COURT STOPS AT THE SOUTH'S BORDERS

African American leaders hoped the federal courts would remain a bulwark against popular sentiment, but they did not. The Supreme Court mostly tracked public opinion. It distinguished between two types of segregation: *de jure* **segregation,** the legal separation of races as practiced in the South, and *de facto* **segregation,** separation occurring as the result of private decisions made by individuals. The equal protection clause forbade only southern-style segregation, the Court decided.

In *Milliken* v. *Bradley* (1974), the Supreme Court considered the constitutionality of *de facto* segregation plaguing northern urban school districts.[37] A ring of all-white suburban districts surrounded the heavily black city of Detroit, leaving school systems racially distinct. No law required racially segregated schools—they were a product of (1) district borders drawn with no apparent discriminatory intent and (2) residential decisions made by private individuals. Four justices tried to persuade their brethren that the state of Michigan still held responsibility for district borders; federal courts could force them to consolidate systems. But the Court majority, led by Nixon appointee Warren Burger, would not expand the definition of state action to include *de facto* social conditions. The Chief Justice wrote that the Constitution forbids discriminatory policy; it "does not require any particular racial balance."

The Supreme Court also considered the constitutionality of affirmative action programs in a 1978 case, *Regents of the University of California* v. *Bakke*. Recruitment policies favoring minorities or women vary in their size and significance. In some cases, these programs may consist of nothing more than special advertising and counseling designed to inform disadvantaged groups about available opportunities. At the opposite extreme, some policies establish inflexible **quotas,** or specific numbers of positions, reserved for members of disadvantaged groups. The policy under review in *Bakke* was a quota system; the UC–Davis medical school required 16 percent of its entering class to be minority students. Allen Bakke, a Norwegian American, sued after falling just short of admission two years in a row—despite a stronger record than minorities who were admitted.[38]

The Supreme Court could not agree on an opinion. Four justices rejected Bakke's claim, arguing that institutions with no history of discrimination could still formulate policies to remedy "societal discrimination." Four other justices would not allow policies that judged applicants differently based on race—whether to help or hurt disadvantaged groups. They declared all forms of affirmative action illegal, a violation of either the equal protection clause or the Civil Rights Act of 1964. This left the Court in a 4-to-4 tie, with Justice Lewis Powell sitting in the middle.

Powell, a moderate southerner appointed by President Nixon, supported active attempts to create diversity but knew that explicit quotas lacked public support. He ended up writing an opinion fully supported by no other member of the Court, yet one that defined constitutional doctrine for decades. It allowed race to play a role in university admissions decisions, with minority applicants favored over others, but forbade unseemly quota systems. Bakke won his case, but California's universities retained strong affirmative action programs until the 1990s.

ELECTIONS, COURTS, AND CIVIL RIGHTS: AN APPRAISAL

Significant problems still beset U.S. blacks. Chief among them is the persistence of unemployment,[39] which creates a high poverty rate in the black community.[40] Teen pregnancy and infant mortality rates are far higher among African Americans than among others.[41] But there is reason for increasing optimism. The percentage of black men and women in professional and managerial positions increased markedly in the decades following the civil rights acts.[42] From 1975 to 1997, the percentage of blacks between the ages of 18 and 24 who have dropped out of high school fell from 27 percent to 17 percent. And between 1980 and 1990, the test scores of black high school seniors improved by 9 percent (compared with negligible gains among whites).[43] Blacks have also made electoral gains, winning an increasing number of political offices—sometimes with the help of "affirmative-action redistricting" (see the Election Connection, "Affirmative-Action Redistricting") and sometimes without it.[44] Half a century is a long time to allow injustices to persist in a democratic society, but few nations have moved so quickly to address deep-seated social inequalities.

THE CIVIL RIGHTS OF ETHNIC MINORITIES

Congress framed 1960s civil rights legislation to redress unique historical grievances growing out of slavery and the Jim Crow system, and so it dwelt on the position of African Americans. Meanwhile, the Supreme Court has never specifically delineated requirements for a minority group to be eligible for government protection. But after the civil rights movement altered equal protection law, groups representing other ethnic minorities began to make similar civil rights claims. Both Congress and the courts often give recognition to these groups.

Not every ethnic minority enjoys the same political standing in American law. For much of U.S. history, Jews faced virulent prejudice and crippling discrimination, including lynchings and synagogue bombings in the twentieth century.[45] Yet Jewish people receive no affirmative protections from government. The degree to which each ethnic minority gains political clout depends in large part on how effectively it mobilizes members in elections. Hispanics and Asian Americans represent influential voting blocs in several large states crucial during presidential elections and, so, can exert disproportionate influence on national politics. Only Native Americans rely on their legal position to issue demands on government.

Affirmative-Action Redistricting

Civil rights laws guarantee minority-group access to most jobs. One important exception is elected office. Neither Congress nor the courts may throw out election results by claiming that voters "discriminated." No one has a "right" to hold office unless they win the most votes. Nevertheless, activists claim that the electoral system does not give minority candidates a fair shake. They seek a form of affirmative action for public service, so that the country will not suffer from a lack of diversity in the halls of government.

Policy makers have targeted legislative offices as the best opportunity to increase minority representation. District borders change regularly, in part based on political motives. The right district borders virtually can assure the election of African American or Hispanic politicians by grouping voters according to race or ethnicity. Furthermore, the Voting Rights Act of 1965 (VRA) gives the Justice Department influence over how some states draw their legislative maps—so the national government is in a position to push affirmative-action districts. And 1982 amendments to the VRA have been interpreted by the courts to require creation of districts dominated by a minority wherever possible.

The Bush administration Justice Department aggressively promoted affirmation-action districts after the 1990 census, and the strategy worked. In the 103rd Congress, for example (the first Congress after the most recent redistricting), 32 of the 39 black members came from districts in which African Americans had a majority, and in 5 of the remaining 7 districts, African Americans plus Hispanics made up a majority. Similarly, 15 of the 17 Hispanic members in the 103rd Congress came from majority-Hispanic districts; none came from districts with a white majority. Similar successes resulted in state legislatures around the country.

It may seem puzzling that a Republican administration would promote minority representation, when most minority legislators are Democrats. But the costs were low. Creating majority–minority enclaves requires pulling hordes of Democratic voters from surrounding districts, leaving the remainder much more favorable to the GOP. Many white Democrats found themselves defending legislative districts filled with conservative suburban voters. The Democratic party lost around 11 seats in Congress as a result of the 1990 redistricting round, contributing to their minority status in the House. They also lost seats in almost every Southern state legislature, including control of two lower chambers.[a]

Some voters asked the courts to declare race-conscious map making a violation of their equal protection guarantees. Conservative

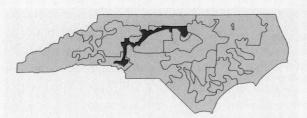

North Carolina's I-95 congressional district

(continued)

(continued from previous page)

federal judges ended up less concerned with the practical political advantages of racial redistricting than other conservative public officials were. They reacted negatively to the unseemly district shapes necessary to pack minority voters into single legislative districts.

The U.S. Supreme Court first faced the question in a case from North Carolina. One congressional district followed Interstate 95 across the state to pick up black residential areas in the state's major cities (see the accompanying graphic). A splintered Court ruled in *Shaw* v. *Reno* (1993) that creative electoral maps had limits: A district created on no basis other than to include a majority of minorities might raise constitutional questions. The Court went further in *Miller* v. *Johnson* (1995). By a 5-to-4 majority, the Court ruled that Georgia's plan was a "racial gerrymander" that violated the equal protection clause of the Constitution.[b] Although the Court has not explicitly rejected the use of racial considerations in redistricting, the current Court rejects plans that use race as a "predominant factor" when picking district borders.

Changes mandated by federal courts initially had little effect. Both minority and Republican legislators first elected because of

affirmative-action districting usually were able to survive despite changes in their district borders. In particular, southern white voters proved willing to vote for black Democrats at the same rate they support other candidates from that party. Sanford Bishop, a member of Congress from Georgia, was able to hold on to his heavily rural district despite a new constituency that was only 26.8% black.[c] Less clear is whether minorities will continue to be competitive in such districts after the current incumbents step down.

What do you think?

- Could election districts intended to increase minority representation actually harm their interests?
- How does the equal protection clause of the Constitution support arguments both for and against majority-minority districts?

[a]David Lublin and D. Stephen Voss, "Racial Redistricting and Realignment in Southern State Legislatures," *American Journal of Political Science*, 2000, 44 (October): 792–810; Lublin and Voss, "Boll-Weevil Blues: Polarized Congressional Delegations into the 21st Century," *American Review of Politics*, forthcoming.

[b]Holly Idelson, "Court Takes a Harder Line on Minority Voting Blocs," *Congressional Quarterly Weekly Report* (July 1, 1995): 1944–1946.

[c]D. Stephen Voss and David Lublin, "Black Incumbents, White Districts: An Appraisal of the 1996 Congressional Elections," *American Politics Research*, 2001, 29 (March): 141–82.

HISPANICS

Hispanics (or Latinos) are the fastest-growing minority group in the United States.* In 1980 they made up only 6.4 percent of the U.S. population, but by 2000 they surpassed African Americans as the nation's largest minority group: 12.5 percent to 12.3 percent.[46] Yet Hispanics are only starting to make a significant political impact. Previously, language barriers and the large number of immigrants without citizenship limited their influence. Many new Hispanic

---

*Following author Geoffrey Fox, we opt for the less politicized term "Hispanic" rather than "Latino," although we realize the imperfection in either label. See Geoffrey Fox, *Hispanic Nation: Culture, Politics, and the Constructing of Identity* (Secaucus, NJ: Birch Lane, 1996), pp. 9–14.

immigrants also plan to return to their countries of origin and, therefore, stay out of U.S. politics.[47]

Hispanic voters are much less likely than African Americans to vote as a bloc. Whereas 85 percent of blacks consider themselves Democrats, only 55 percent of Hispanics do.[48] This political diversity is a natural outgrowth of real social and cultural diversity within "the Hispanic nation."[49] Some Hispanics have been Americans for many generations; others are recent arrivals speaking little English. Some are affluent and respected members of their communities; others are migrant laborers living on a pittance. Hispanics come from many different countries. Mexican Americans concentrate in California and Texas. Puerto Ricans concentrate in northern industrial cities, such as New York. Cuban Americans concentrate in Florida. These disparate groups have little in common, so they share few political concerns.

Activists have worked hard to construct an Hispanic identity. One of the earliest groups to do so was the Mexican American Legal Defense and Education Fund (MALDEF), which has focused on voting, education, and immigration issues. In 1974, in response to MALDEF complaints, the Supreme Court interpreted the 1964 Civil Rights Act to mean that schools must provide special educational programs for those not proficient in the English language.[50] MALDEF and other advocacy groups also argued that voting materials discriminated against linguistic minorities because they appeared only in English. Congress responded in 1982 by requiring foreign-language ballots for any linguistic minority constituting more than 5 percent of a county's population.[51]

Cuban politics took center stage in 1999 when fishermen off the Florida coast rescued six-year-old Elian Gonzalez and brought him to Miami. Elian had escaped Cuba with his mother, but she had perished in an accident at sea. Elian's uncle and other relatives in Miami embraced the boy and sought to become his legal guardians. But the U.S. Immigration and Naturalization Service (INS) insisted Elian return to his father in Cuba, a position the Justice Department enforced aggressively—angering activists who have long fought the island's dictatorial Castro regime. This event underscored the strength of Cuban voters in an important swing state: Vice President Gore broke with the Clinton administration position; and he took the side of Elian's Miami relatives rather than risk giving south Florida to George W. Bush.

Both presidential candidates worked hard to court the Latino vote in 2000. George W. Bush repeatedly repudiated anti-immigration laws and cited his moderate record on immigration in Texas. He also stressed his support for some bilingual education programs and his opposition to English-only mandates. Bush's Hispanic nephew, George P. Bush, made pleas on his uncle's behalf. Both Al Gore

Courting the Latino vote
George P. Bush, whose mother is of Mexican descent, campaigned for his uncle, George W. Bush, in the Latino community in 2000. Why has the importance of the Latino vote lagged behind that of blacks?

and George Bush peppered their speeches with Spanish while campaigning in such key states as California, Florida, and NewYork.

ASIAN AMERICANS

Asian Americans only recently gained a voice in national electoral politics. They constitute only 4 percent of the population, and over 60 percent are foreign born.[52] Like Hispanics, they represent many different nationalities and have differing, even conflicting, foreign policy concerns. Asians vote Republican more often than other minorities do, and are more likely to oppose affirmative-action programs that promote other ethnic groups at their expense.[53]

In 1996 activists in the Asian American community flexed their political muscle by mounting a coordinated fund-raising and voter-registration drive.[54] That year, Gary Locke of Washington state was elected the first Asian American governor of a state other than Hawaii. Yet many Asian Americans worry about anti-immigration sentiment among U.S. voters. Initiatives to require English for government business or to cut off immigrant welfare benefits frequently appear on state ballots. In 1996 a Chinese American scientist was jailed, and even placed in isolation, for alleged spying—even though the government eventually dropped all serious charges against him. Activists worry that a growth in stereotyping could produce a "chilling effect" on Asian American political participation.[55]

NATIVE AMERICANS

The Bill of Rights does not protect the rights and liberties of Native Americans. At the time of the Constitution's ratification, descendants of indigenous tribes were considered citizens of foreign nations. As one authority on Indian rights put it, "No constitutional protections exist for Indians in either a tribal or an individual sense."[56]

Instead, relations between Native Americans and the government operate under federal laws and treaties signed with American Indian tribes. Over the long course of U.S. history, the government, facing political pressure from those migrating westward, ignored or broke many of the treaties it made with these tribes. Still, the Supreme Court today interprets some of these treaties as binding.[57] As a result, tribal members have certain rights and privileges not available to other groups. For example, Court rulings have given tribes in the Pacific Northwest special rights to fish for salmon.

One economically significant right recognized in recent years has been the authority to provide commercial gambling on tribal property. The Court has said that tribal grounds are governed by federal, not state, law. Federal law does not disallow gambling on tribal grounds except if it is forbidden everywhere within a state. In several cases, tribes have secured political influence using proceeds from gambling operations.

Congressional legislation has applied most of the Bill of Rights to tribe members. To protect religious freedom, for example, Congress passed the 1978 American Indian Religious Freedom Resolution. Tribal leaders have argued that the resolution gives them special access to traditional religious sites in national parks and other government lands. But the federal courts have interpreted the resolution narrowly, saying it does not make indigenous Americans "supercitizens." Rather, it gives them religious freedoms comparable to those granted other citizens.[58]

GENDER, SEXUALITY, AND CIVIL RIGHTS

"It is in the very nature of ideas to grow in self-awareness, to work out all their implications over time," one constitutional scholar writes. "The very content of the great clauses of the Constitution, their coverage, changes."[59] So it has been with the equal protection clause of the Fourteenth Amendment. Although gender is not mentioned anywhere in the clause, its meaning has evolved to include equal rights for women. But these changes did not take place entirely within the confines of federal courtrooms. They were part of a broad struggle for women's rights, played out as much among the electorate as in the legal arena.

The first struggle for women's rights focused on voting. Once the Nineteenth Amendment passed in 1920, the women's movement fell dormant for nearly 50 years.[60] Women's groups grew more active in the 1960s, and since then have achieved three civil rights objectives: equal treatment before the law, protection against sexual harassment, and access to state-funded military academies.

THE RIGHT TO EQUALITY
BEFORE THE LAW

As unlikely as it may seem, a conservative southerner, Howard Smith of Virginia, proposed amending Title VII of the Civil Rights Act of 1964 to prohibit discrimination on the basis of sex as well as race, religion, or national origin. The amendment passed overwhelmingly, but activists formed the National Organization for Women (NOW) to ensure that courts would enforce it. They also pushed to ensconce equal treatment in the Constitution, backing the **Equal Rights Amendment (ERA),** a failed amendment that would have banned gender discrimination.

At first, the ERA seemed destined to sail through the ratification process; it seemed an easy way for politicians to win female votes. Overwhelming congressional majorities passed the ERA in 1972. Within a year a majority of states voted to ratify it.[61] But just before the ERA could join the U.S. Constitution, a resistance movement led by groups of conservative women derailed the effort. Aware of unpopular policies mandated by federal courts in the name of racial equality, the ERA's opponents warned that judges would do the same with constitutional language promising gender equality. They would require government funding of abortions, coed bathrooms, and women in combat.[62] The ERA fell three state legislatures short of the three-fourths required to ratify a constitutional amendment.

As discouraging as the ERA defeat was for its supporters, in retrospect it seems that they won the war by losing the battle. The Supreme Court had done little, if anything, to prevent gender discrimination before the ERA campaign. Court opinions changed after the Congress voted overwhelmingly in favor of the ERA's passage. Gender equality gained recognition. In *Craig v. Boren* (1976), the Supreme Court declared unconstitutional an Oklahoma law that allowed women to drink at 18 but denied that privilege to men until the age of 21. Oklahoma defended the law on the grounds that young men were more likely to drive when drunk. But the Supreme Court rejected Oklahoma's statistical evidence as irrelevant.* The law embodied "invidious gender-based discrimination" that constituted "a denial of equal protection of the laws."[63]

Categorizing people by their sex does not receive the same strict scrutiny that racial categories do. Nevertheless, the Supreme Court has ruled that gender discrimination violates the equal protection clause, so gender distinctions receive heightened scrutiny compared to most other legal categories. The Court will rule against a law unless its gender distinctions have "a substantial relationship to an important objective."[64] Partly, the Court's cautiousness reflects mixed public feelings about feminism.

The Supreme Court accepted gender distinctions within the military in *Rostker v. Goldberg* (1981). Congress holds broad constitutional powers in military matters, Justice William Rehnquist explained, and "the lack of competence on the part of the courts is marked."[65] The ruling was consistent with the view of a majority of the voters, who favor restricting female participation in combat.[66]

The Supreme Court also has allowed firms some latitude when they do not recruit and retain women, as long as a "business necessity" explains their imbalanced personnel practices.[67] The Court initially required those claiming discrimination to disprove the business-necessity argument. Justice Byron White argued in *Ward's Cove Packing Co. v. Antonio* (1989) that Title VII of the Civil Rights Act gave claimants the burden of proof.[68] Women's organizations opposed the ruling, because it is hard for plaintiffs to characterize conclusively what a business needs. The Civil Rights Act of 1991, signed by President George H. W. Bush, shifted the burden of proof to businesses. It was elected officials, not the Court, who took the lead on this issue.

SEXUAL HARASSMENT

The Supreme Court did not rule on the meaning of sexual harassment in the workplace until *Meritor Savings Bank v. Vinson* (1986).[69] In this case, Michelle Vinson said that sexually abusive language used in her presence had left her psychologically damaged. Justice Rehnquist decided in Vinson's favor, but wrote a narrow opinion implying that harassment would be considered illegal only if it caused real harm. Afterward, sexual harassment became a major political issue,

---

*Oklahoma subsequently made 21 the legal drinking age for both men and women.

resulting in a large crop of new female elected officials in 1992, the "year of the woman" (see Chapter 12). Responding to the change in the political atmosphere, the Supreme Court expanded its definition of sexual harassment in the unanimous decision *Harris* v. *Forklift Systems* (1993).[70]

Teresa Harris worked at Forklift Systems, Inc., a heavy equipment rental firm. Her employer called her derogatory terms, such as "dumb ass woman." Although Harris complained and her boss promised to restrain his remarks, he subsequently suggested in front of other employees that Harris had slept with a client to obtain a contract. She quit and sued. Although Harris could not show serious psychological damage, Justice Sandra Day O'Connor wrote that Title VII of the Civil Rights Act "comes into play before harassing conduct leads to a nervous breakdown." Justice Ruth Bader Ginsburg went further, arguing in her concurring opinion that discrimination exists whenever it is more difficult for a person of one gender to perform well on a job. Once again, the Supreme Court moved forward in the wake of public pressure.

SINGLE-SEX SCHOOLS

Single-sex schools have long been a significant part of American education. As late as the 1950s, well-known private colleges, such as Princeton and Yale, limited their admissions to men. Although these colleges now admit approximately equal numbers of men and women, single-sex education survives at many private women's colleges. These colleges assert that women learn more in an environment where many can assume leadership roles. Hillary Rodham Clinton, who graduated from a Massachusetts women's college, once said: "I am so grateful that I had the chance to go to college at a place where women were valued and nurtured and encouraged."[71] All-male education also has supporters, especially for African American boys who frequently suffer low attendance and test scores in conventional school programs.[72]

Despite the claims of those who favor single-sex education, many believe that education separated by gender cannot be equal. The Supreme Court cast doubt on its constitutionality in 1996. In *United States* v. *Virginia*, the Court ruled that women must be admitted to Virginia Military Institute (VMI), even though the state had recently established a separate military training program for women.[73] The Court said the newly established program for women did not match the history, reputation, and quality of VMI. Justice Scalia, in his dissent, recognized the importance of public opinion on the Court's ruling. He lambasted "this most illiberal Court" because it had "embarked on a course of inscribing one after another of the current preferences of the society . . . into our Basic Law."

THE FUTURE OF WOMEN'S RIGHTS: AN APPRAISAL

Despite many gains, the women's movement has not yet realized all of its civil rights agenda. Sexual harassment remains a burning issue within the military and in many business firms. Only a few women have broken through what is known as the glass ceiling—the invisible barrier that has limited their opportunities for advancement to the highest ranks of politics, business, and the professions. Very few women serve as college presidents, as corporate heads, or as partners in major law firms. And although women held many important political posts in 2000—including 2 on the Supreme Court, 9 in the Senate and 56 in the House—no woman has yet received a major-party nomination for president.

The changing American family has also left many women in difficult circumstances. The percentage of children raised in single-parent families headed by a woman has increased sharply in the past quarter-century, and these households are much more likely to be poor than households headed by males or couples. Women's issues are likely to remain an important feature in American politics in the twenty-first century.

GAYS AND LESBIANS

Some of the most contentious political debates in the late 1990s surrounded the rights of gays and lesbians. It is no accident that, at the same time, homosexuals engaged in electoral politics more than ever before—especially as campaign contributors. Gay and lesbian donors gave an estimated $3.5 million to the 1992 Clinton campaign, leading Clinton to flirt with ending a ban on gays in the military.[74] Since the early 1990s, according to one estimate, the number of openly gay government officials has tripled.[75]

At the same time, the country is undergoing an increasingly vocal debate over gay rights, a debate being fought in election and referendum campaigns. The American public believes that gays should have equal rights and in particular equal job opportunities, a belief that is a recent development (see Figure 14.4). Laws barring employment discrimination on the basis of sexual orientation have passed in 11 states and have bipartisan support in Congress.[76] In 2000 Vermont became the first state to recognize same-sex civil unions.

But public opinion remains conservative on other issues regarding homosexuality. Large majorities disapprove of same-sex marriages. Thirty-two states have passed laws banning same-sex marriages. In Hawaii, where a state court decision had legalized such unions in 1993, voters overwhelmingly passed a constitutional amendment five years later outlawing them again. Americans also have serious reservations when asked whether gays should be allowed to serve as teachers or

FIGURE 14.4

**Public opinion on gay rights has changed as gay
and lesbian political activism increased**

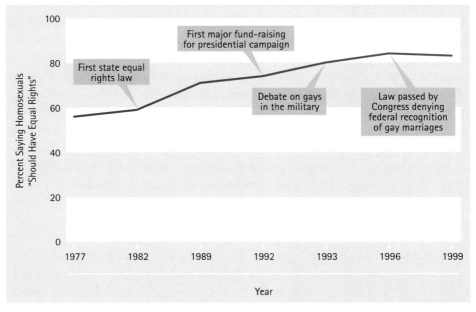

SOURCE: The Gallup Poll, www.gallup.com, accessed April 12, 2000.

youth leaders. Elected officials must struggle to reconcile the confusing signals
public opinion sends on the place of homosexuals in American society.

RIGHTS OF AMERICANS
WITH DISABILITIES

Disabled people constitute about 9 percent of the working-age population.[77]
They have an important political advantage that other minorities lack: Every person risks becoming disabled someday, so the rights of disabled people have broad
appeal. Yet a troublesome drawback offsets this advantage: The cost of helping
people with disabilities can be exorbitant. The estimated annual cost of disability
payments and health care services for this group exceeds $275 billion, for exam-
ple.[78] Even those sympathetic to the handicapped may not like paying for the services needed to help them "live normal lives."

Government began concerning itself with the quality of life for disabled people in the 1960s, around the same time other minority groups gained their voice

in American politics. Previously, programs for the disabled were seen as charitable activities to be supported by private donations. Mentally disabled people were closeted away in "insane asylums" and "homes for the incurable." Americans held many stereotypes about the extent to which handicaps limited one's abilities.

Rights of the disabled received their first big push not from an interest group, but from one individual. Hugh Gallagher, a wheelchair-bound polio victim, served as a legislative aide to Alaska Senator E. L. Bartlett in the mid-1960s. Gallagher constantly faced great difficulty using public toilets and gaining access to buildings, such as the Library of Congress. At his prodding, Congress in 1968—just four years after the Civil Rights Act—enacted a law requiring that all future public buildings constructed with federal money provide access for the disabled. Similar language appeared in a transportation act in 1970.[79]

Once elected officials responded to the demands of the disabled, the courts became more sensitive. Previously, school officials had denied "retarded" children access to public education on the grounds that they were not mentally competent. But in the early 1970s, federal courts in Pennsylvania and the District of Columbia required that states provide disabled children with equal educational opportunity.[80] These decisions generated a nationwide movement for disabled children, culminating in the passage in 1975 of federal legislation that guaranteed all handicapped children educational access.[81]

Encouraged by both judicial and legislative victories, groups representing the physically and mentally challenged became increasingly assertive. They discovered that politicians did not wish to appear insensitive; guarantees of rights for the disabled were much less controversial than those for other minorities. A series of legislative victories in education, transportation, and construction of public buildings finally culminated in the Americans with Disabilities Act of 1991, signed by President George H. W. Bush. This act made it illegal to deny someone employment because of a handicap. Workplaces must adapt to the capacities of disabled persons, when feasible.

These legislative and judicial mandates have produced a sharp change in American society. Twenty years ago, public toilets for the disabled hardly existed. Sidewalks and staircases had no ramps. Buses and trains were inaccessible to those in wheelchairs. College and university campuses did not accommodate attendance by the physically challenged. Unlike President Franklin Roosevelt, who 50 years ago avoided being photographed in his wheelchair, Robert Dole referred constantly to his disabled arm during his 1996 presidential campaign. Meanwhile, Georgia voters elected wheelchair-bound Vietnam veteran Max Cleland to the Senate, and President Clinton appointed David Tatel, who is blind, to a federal appeals court.

Max Cleland
*U.S. Senator from
Georgia.* Are courts
or elected officials
more likely to pro-
tect the rights of
the disabled? Why?

Yet the disabled rely on goodwill from other voters to enhance their political strength, and resistance is growing as Americans gain a sense of the social costs. Educators complain that the investment required to teach a handful of disabled students extracts too many dollars from pinched school budgets. Architectural changes in public buildings and adaptations in transportation are said to be far too expensive to justify the limited amount of usage they receive. Ordinary citizens grumble as they drive past empty handicapped-parking spots. The disabled soon could lose their status as the minority group that legislators fear most.

CHAPTER SUMMARY

African Americans achieved most of their advances through electoral politics—either directly by exercising their voting rights or indirectly by attracting political support through nonviolent demonstrations.[82] The most notable progress toward racial desegregation occurred as the result of legislation passed in the mid-1960s by bipartisan majorities in Congress. By contrast, the Supreme Court has usually followed the nation's popular moods: denying rights claims late in the nineteenth century, recognizing them after blacks moved north and acquired voting rights, then pulling back after the civil rights movement itself headed north (see Figure 14.5).

FIGURE 14.5

Important events of the civil rights and women's movements

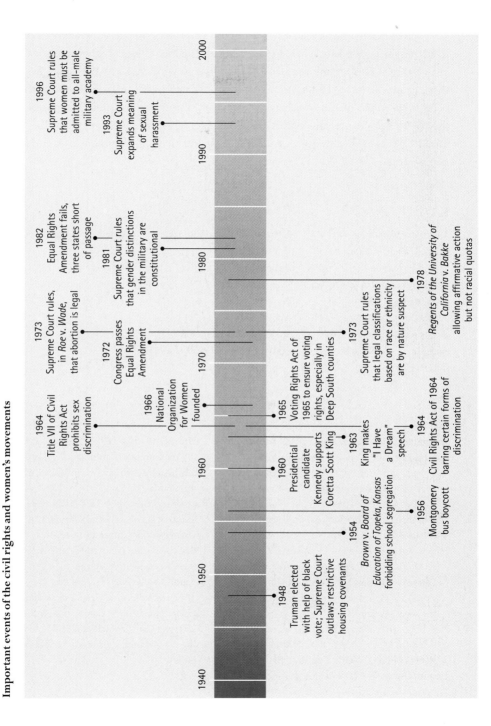

Warren Court decisions redefined the equal protection clause, which eventually led to a stronger legal position for Hispanics, Asians, and members of other minority groups. Yet getting courts to enforce legal rights relies in part on a group's clout. In general, these groups have only begun to exert their strength in national elections, so they have been slower than blacks to achieve recognition. Often congressional measures, such as the ERA or the Americans with Disabilities Act, signal to the courts when the political mood has changed. So, even civil rights respond to public opinion in America's new democracy.

KEY TERMS

affirmative action, p. 476

Brown v. Board of Education of Topeka, Kansas, p. 471

civil disobedience, p. 473

civil rights, p. 464

de facto segregation, p. 478

de jure segregation, p. 478

equal protection clause, p. 464

Equal Rights Amendment, p. 486

grandfather clause, p. 467

Jim Crow laws, p. 468

quota, p. 479

Reconstruction, p. 466

restrictive housing covenant, p. 470

separate but equal doctrine, p. 468

state action doctrine, p. 468

suspect classification, p. 464

SUGGESTED READINGS

Browning, Rufus, Dale Rogers Marshall, and David H. Tabb. *Protest Is Not Enough: The Struggle of Blacks and Hispanics for Equality in Urban Politics.* Berkeley, CA: University of California Press, 1984. Excellent analysis of the importance of electoral politics for black advances.

Higgenbotham, A. Leon, Jr. *Shades of Freedom: Racial Politics and Presumptions of the American Legal Process.* New York: Oxford University Press, 1996. A sharp critique of racial bias in the legal system.

Key, V. O., Jr. *Southern Politics.* New York: Random House, 1949. Classic study of the effects of racial conflict on southern politics.

Lublin, David. *The Paradox of Representation: Racial Gerrymandering and Minority Interests in Congress.* Princeton, NJ: Princeton University Press, 1997. Shows that increasing the number of minority legislators actually decreases the policy influence of minorities.

Rosenberg, Gerald N. *The Hollow Hope: Can Courts Bring About Social Change?* Chicago: University of Chicago Press, 1991. Argues that courts are generally unable to act contrary to majority opinion.

Skocpol, Theda. *Protecting Soldiers and Mothers: The Political Origins of Social Policy in the United States.* Cambridge, MA: Harvard University Press, 1992. Analyzes the way women's groups have influenced policy.

ON THE WEB

U.S. Department of Justice
www.usdoj.gov
The U.S. Department of Justice's Civil Rights division provides information on its enforcement of existing civil rights law.

U.S. Commission on Civil Rights
www.usccr.gov
Established in 1957, the U.S. Commission on Civil Rights monitors discrimination in many sectors of American society.

Martin Luther King, Jr., Papers Project
www.stanford.edu/group/King/
The Martin Luther King, Jr., Papers Project at Stanford University maintains a Web site with many of King's speeches and sermons, as well as several scholarly articles and book chapters.

National Association for the Advancement of Colored People (NAACP)
www.naacp.org
The NAACP is the nation's oldest civil rights organization.

National Organization for Women (NOW)
www.now.org
The country's largest feminist organization, NOW seeks "to take action to bring about equality for all women."

National Council of La Raza
www.nclr.org
The National Council of La Raza monitors issues of concern to Hispanic Americans.

Human Rights Campaign
www.hrc.org
This is the official Web site for the Human Rights Campaign (a leading gay rights organization).

Leadership Education for Asian Pacifics, Inc.
www.leap.org
Leadership Education for Asian Pacifics, Inc. (LEAP) houses the Asian Pacific American Public Policy Institute, which authors numerous reports on Asian Americans.

National Council on Disability
www.ncd.gov
The National Council on Disability is an independent federal agency that makes recommendations to the president and Congress regarding Americans with disabilities. The agency's site provides links to other relevant federal agencies, press releases, and in-depth reports.

15

PUBLIC POLICY

For decades the U.S. government spent much more than it earned in tax revenue. Controversy swirled around tough political questions, such as how much to raise taxes and which program budgets to limit. But suddenly, in 1998, a budget surplus appeared—almost out of nowhere. The growing economy had allowed expected resources to outpace planned spending. By the summer of 2000, the expected ten-year surplus topped $2 trillion!

Unanticipated revenues are a true bonanza for elected officials, because of the possibilities they present. Politicians quickly began jockeying to hand out the extra money. Some advocated helping the needy, arguing that national prosperity had left too many people behind. They wanted to increase welfare funding and expand health care coverage for the indigent. Others recommended shoring up programs oriented toward senior citizens before the baby boom generation retired. Those concerned with the severity of past budget cuts in defense pushed investing in military supplies and equipment. Yet another group interpreted the excess revenue as a sign that early-1990s tax hikes had gone too far. They called for returning some of the largesse to taxpayers before the economy slowed down. "Let's give this money back to the people who earned it," they said.

By the time politicians aired all of their various proposals, not a single area of public policy had been overlooked. Every political interest entered the ring to get a piece of that $2-trillion prize. Whoever won the contest would realize a massive victory, influencing the shape of governmental policies for years to come. If politics is the game of "who gets what," as some simple definitions suggest, then this debate was more than just a casual discussion of priorities. The conflict would expose the very soul of American politics.

The 2000 elections served as the arena for this policy battle. Presidential and congressional candidates committed their support to particular proposals, which voters and interest groups could use to help identify their selections. The differences between Democrats and Republicans offered useful grounds for choosing a party. Democrats wanted more spending, Republicans, more tax cuts. Democrats talked more about increasing welfare, promoting health care, and protecting the environment. The GOP talked more about quality education, military preparedness, and improving the transportation infrastructure.

Because Republicans won the White House, held the House of Representatives, and temporarily controlled the Senate, it may seem as though their priorities won—a victory for taxpayers, families, and the military. Not so. Rather, the 2000 election illustrated an old insight: The true sign of power is not which side wins a battle, but which side can stay off the battlefield altogether.[1] More important than how Republicans differed from Democrats is how they agreed. Neither side could afford to challenge spending on behalf of the elderly.

Both the Bush and Gore campaigns loudly stressed the need to shore up programs that help senior citizens. Indeed, they promised new resources, including expensive proposals to cover prescription drugs—even though the elderly already receive far more of the national government's domestic spending than any other group. Programs catering to older voters therefore locked up the lion's share of the surplus before even a single vote was cast. Everyone else was simply fighting for a place in line to get some of the leftovers.

IF THE 2000 ELECTION PROVIDED A TRUE TEST OF AMERICA'S NEW democracy, then senior citizens passed with flying colors. Why did the elderly win the bulk of the projected surplus with little more than a tussle, trumping other important areas of public policy? The answer lies in the growing importance of popular influence, and especially elections, in America's new democracy. Not only do the elderly vote in large numbers, but opinion supports their claims on the public till.

Other policy areas must struggle to attract voter sympathy. Unlike the elderly, families and children seeking government assistance usually receive the cold shoulder. Voters rarely worry about the national debt and show only lukewarm interest in tax cuts. Defense industries once received top dollar, but the end of the Cold War undercut their claims to public revenues (although terrorist attacks in 2001 may have reversed their fortunes once again). And Americans overwhelmingly dislike the idea of foreign aid. None of these policy areas can compete politically with programs for the elderly in times of peace. Elections mold priorities in America's new democracy, and in the electoral arena, the elderly reign supreme.

SETTING PUBLIC POLICY

All government programs and regulations are examples of public policy. Policies generally break down into three types: (1) domestic policy, which consists of all government programs and regulations that directly affect those living within the country; (2) economic policy, which indirectly affects those within the country by changing government budgets and the value of a nation's currency; and (3) foreign and defense policy, which involves relations with other nations to preserve national security. However, the distinctions among these three areas of policy is not always sharp and clear. Some domestic policies, such as immigration policy, affect relations with other countries. Some foreign policies, such as trade regulations, have major domestic consequences.

Policy making is a complex, never-ending round of events. To clarify what is often a very messy process, political scientists have divided the policy-making round into six stages (see Figure 15.1):

- *Agenda setting*, deciding which issues government must address.[2] Issues enter the agenda when they reach the notice of public officials. Those issues serious enough to influence voters are most likely to grab attention.

- *Policy deliberation*, the debate over how government should deal with an issue on the agenda.[3] At this stage, groups try to convince leaders that their proposals will win favor with the electorate.

- *Policy enactment*, the passage of a law by public officials at either the national, state, or local level. Elected officials who support a law usually expect that doing so will enhance their popularity, although there are celebrated instances when political leaders knowingly sacrificed their careers to take an unpopular stand.

- *Policy implementation*, the translation of a law into specific government programs.[4] Most laws are flexible, but bureaucrats seldom stray from the intentions of the legislative branch when doing so might evoke a public backlash.

FIGURE 15.1
Policy-making stages
Political scientists break the policy process into six stages.

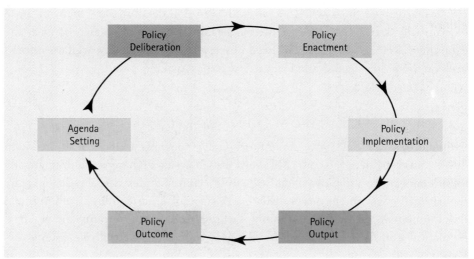

- *Policy outputs*, the rules and regulations growing out of a program. Beneficiaries usually think well of those responsible for helpful outputs and support them politically. Those who are hurt or neglected by a program's specifics may punish the elected officials responsible.
- *Policy outcomes*, the effect of a policy on American society, the economy, or the international sphere.[5] These outcomes often give rise to new issues, which in turn join the policy agenda.

The political forces at work differ from one policy to the next, but electoral incentives almost always influence how policies pass through the six stages of development. The enactment of the 1996 welfare reform law, **Temporary Assistance for Needy Families (TANF)**, provides one example of the policy process at work.

Bill Clinton placed reform on the policy *agenda* in his 1992 presidential campaign by promising to "end welfare as we know it." Interest groups, policy experts, members of Congress, and the media began *deliberating* how the United States might redesign welfare policy. Congress then *enacted* a law shifting responsibility for welfare policy to state governments, and President Clinton signed the bill. State governments *implemented* new welfare programs in early 1997. Many families left or were removed from the welfare rolls as one *output* of the new programs.

The *outcome* of welfare reform is only now becoming clear. Welfare rolls have declined dramatically; about half as many people received assistance in 1999 as in 1994. Many of these former welfare recipients found jobs because the economy was growing rapidly at the time. Others shifted to programs serving the disabled. However, many of those with few job skills were left destitute, and many of those who initially found jobs left them within a year.[6] These numbers may grow as the economy falters. If this problem becomes severe, it could place welfare reform back on the policy agenda and force a new policy-making round.

DOMESTIC POLICY

Although the national government originally concentrated on relations with other countries, over the course of more than 200 years it has grown dramatically to influence more and more of daily life in the United States. Social policies set by the national government now impact every stage of American life, from prenatal development in the mother's womb (through nutrition programs and medical regulations) all the way through to death (or even after death if one counts survivor's benefits).

A HEALTHY PLACE TO GROW OLD

The generosity of national social policies varies significantly over the course of a lifetime. Domestic policy's primary focus has been to enhance the income and medical care enjoyed by senior citizens, while relatively little money has gone toward Americans in the youngest age ranges. The effect of this policy choice shows up in the nation's poverty statistics. From 1970 to 1988, poverty among senior citizens fell from 25 percent to 10.5 percent (see Figure 15.2). During the same period, poverty among families with children increased from 15 percent to 20 percent, a rate twice as high as that in most other advanced industrial societies.[7]

Poverty is not just a matter of money; it is a matter of life and death. Of the seven countries with the largest economies, the United States has the highest infant mortality rate but the longest life span among senior citizens. As one

FIGURE 15.2

U.S. poverty rates for senior citizens and children, 1970–1998

Poverty rates have fallen for seniors and risen for children.

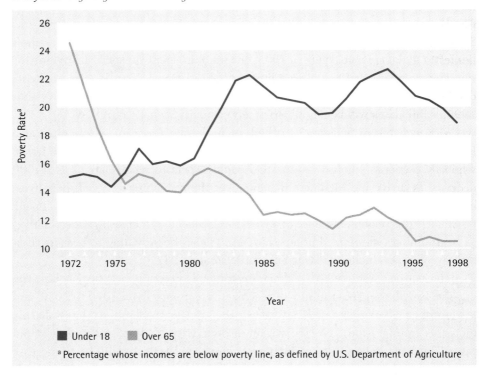

Year

■ Under 18   ■ Over 65

[a] Percentage whose incomes are below poverty line, as defined by U.S. Department of Agriculture

SOURCE: U.S. Census Bureau, *Historical Poverty Tables—People,* Table 3: Poverty Status by Age, Race and Hispanic Origin, www.census.gov/hhes/poverty/histpob/hstpov3.html, accessed July 24, 2000.

analyst put it, the United States is the "healthiest place to grow old but the riskiest [in which] to be born."[8]

BENEFITS FOR SENIOR CITIZENS   The national government has not always worked so hard to finance retirements and medical care for seniors. Poverty among the elderly was so acute during the Great Depression that Congress enacted the Social Security Act of 1935. This legislation created a broad range of social programs, including a social insurance program for senior citizens generally known as Social Security.[9]

The Social Security program initially cost the government very little. Benefits were low, and life expectancy short. Those reaching age 65 on average lived only 12.6 years. Over time both medical improvements and policy changes caused the costs to leap upward. A typical worker retiring at 65 today lives more than 17 years. Congress expanded the number of people covered. Benefits have increased in size and cost, including a large hike in 1972 that linked future benefits to the inflation rate. If inflation goes up 10 percent, so does the paycheck.[10] And the national government took another substantial step in 1965 by setting up **Medicare**, a program to subsidize health costs for Social Security recipients.

The result is that spending on the elderly has grown to dominate the nation's domestic budget. From 1960 to 1995, the amount spent on social programs for senior citizens quadrupled after adjusting for inflation.* Nor do these benefits depend upon need. Upon reaching the age of 65, even billionaire Microsoft founder Bill Gates will be eligible to receive a Social Security check.

Although Social Security is called an insurance program, it operates at a loss—giving people more in benefits than they contribute in payroll taxes. Typically, a couple who retired in 1995 could expect to receive about $471,000 in Social Security and Medicare benefits over the remaining years of their lives, even though the family's worker contributed only $184,000.[11] How is this magic possible?[12] It is possible because of a workforce that (1) is increasingly productive, (2) outnumbers the retired population, and (3) has been willing to bear increasing payroll taxes, including large hikes in 1977 and 1982.[13]

The nation's approach to old-age insurance is probably not sustainable. The massive baby boom generation will reach retirement age from 2010 to 2030, and the number of workers will not keep pace (unless the United States sharply increases immigration). Nor is worker productivity likely to increase at rapid rates. Thus, the only way to maintain retirement programs would be to increase payroll taxes sharply.

---

*Spending grew from under $4,000 per senior citizen to more than $16,500 in 1995 (based on 1999 dollars).

But will the workers of the future be willing to bear taxes sufficient to subsidize retirees at the same level of material comfort as the United States does today?
Figure 15.3 illustrates how improbable that is. It projects the payroll tax rates that
would be required to sustain current benefits into the future. By 2040, years
before today's college students will be old enough to retire, benefits already
would demand around 40 percent of taxable payroll. Pessimistically, the price tag
could rise to more than half of all payroll money. Will the workers of 2040 give up
half of their potential salaries just to take care of the elderly? Not likely.

So, it is not surprising that political leaders were grateful for an unanticipated budget surplus in the late 1990s. The surplus allowed leaders to maintain
today's generous senior-citizen benefits without accelerating the day of reckon-
ing. However, a stalled economy has lessened optimism about future surpluses,

FIGURE 15.3

Projected cost of social insurance for senior citizens

Costs of programs for senior citizens will rise rapidly in the coming years.

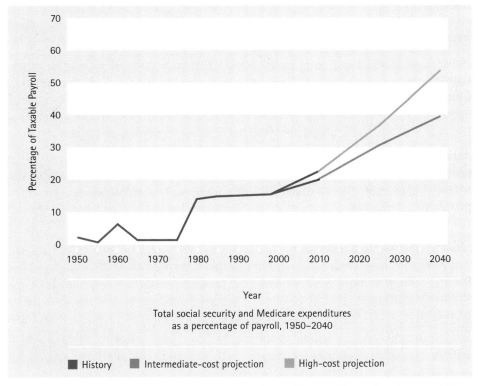

Total social security and Medicare expenditures
as a percentage of payroll, 1950–2040

■ History ■ Intermediate-cost projection ■ High-cost projection

SOURCE: Neil Howe and Richard Jackson, *The Graying of theWelfare State* (Washington, DC: National Taxpayers Union Foundation, 1999).

and security and reconstruction needs after the 2001 terrorist attacks are laying claim to the rest.[14]

SENIOR-CITIZEN BENEFITS AND THE PERMANENT CAMPAIGN Most public officials know better than to question the Social Security program, even though it is the most costly single item in the entire federal budget. In 1981 President Ronald Reagan suggested offhandedly that Congress might need to place limits on the program's growth. The public backlash was swift and angry, prompting every single senator to condemn the president's idea two days later. Even so, Reagan's remark contributed to his party's loss of the U.S. Senate. For this reason, both Democratic President Clinton and Republican House Speaker Newt Gingrich insisted that Social Security would be "off the table" when they started imposing massive budget cuts in 1995.

The politics of Medicare are much the same, making it difficult to hold down program costs. Medicare cost little more than $30 billion in 1970, but by 1999 it had grown to nearly $212 billion.[15] It pays for cutting-edge medical techniques—such as magnetic resonance imaging, bone marrow transfusions, and other high-tech, high-cost procedures. Adding to the costs are the exorbitant penalties that lawsuits extract from doctors who make mistakes, which drive up the fees doctors must charge to cover their insurance.

Congress contained costs in the late 1990s, but costs will rise again as the baby boom generation ages—leading many to fear that Medicare is doomed.[16] Recognizing this concern, Republicans in 1995 proposed raising insurance premiums and requiring patients to pay a larger share of the costs. They suffered for the attempt. President Clinton and his Democratic allies in Congress gleefully noted that the Medicare savings Republicans wanted roughly equaled the cost of a tax cut "for the rich" that they also proposed.[17] Clinton was able to exploit the issue so successfully that he carried Florida, a normally Republican state to which many retirees have migrated.

Politicians operate in fear of senior citizens because the electoral cost of pleasing them is much lower than the cost of resisting. At a time when overall voter turnout has been declining, senior-citizen turnout rates are high and have been climbing. Sixty percent of Americans over 65 said they voted in the 1998 congressional elections, but only 17 percent of those between the ages of 18 and 24 reported voting.[18] Children cannot vote at all. Senior citizens are also much more likely than young people to back up their votes by other political actions, such as writing letters to officials and contributing money to campaigns.[19]

Upon reaching the age of 50, any person can become a member of the American Association of Retired Persons (AARP) for $8 per year. Members qualify for a wide range of discounts worth much more than their annual dues, so more than 33 million people have joined—making AARP the largest interest group in the United States. AARP employs more than 1,100 people, works with over 160,000 volunteers, and has an annual budget that exceeds $500 million.[20]

Few voters punish elected officials for accommodating AARP demands. In fact, young people are just about as likely to support Social Security as those over the age of 65. They know others who are receiving benefits and hope to do the same some day. Many believe, fallaciously, that the elderly are simply receiving funds they originally contributed—and they think that the government is saving their own contributions for them. Only 7 percent of younger adults say that the elderly are getting more than their fair share of government benefits, and 48 percent think the elderly are getting less than their fair share.[21]

A RISKY PLACE TO BE BORN

Poor families with children do not receive very good representation in America's new democracy. No association comparable to AARP defends their interests, and neither political party shows much concern for their programs. As a result, government aid to poor families is neither as lavish nor as easy to obtain as that intended for the elderly.

BENEFITS FOR THE POOR   More programs assist households with limited income than assist the elderly, although these programs are rarely as generous. Public assistance programs include TANF, food stamps, the Earned Income Tax Credit (EITC), rent subsidies, and Medicaid.

TANF maintains the incomes of poor families. It varies by state but always limits aid to no more than two years in a row and to no more than five years altogether. It took the place of a costlier, and highly unpopular, program called **Aid to Families with Dependent Children (AFDC),** which most Americans knew simply as "welfare." After the end of AFDC, some beneficiaries switched to Supplemental Security Income (SSI). Created in 1972, SSI provides financial assistance to disabled people of low income. As of January 2000, the average monthly benefit for SSI's 6.6 million recipients was $377.27.

The **Earned Income Tax Credit (EITC)** returns taxes to those who have little income. Initially proposed by Republicans in the early 1970s as a tax rebate that would reward the working poor, EITC expanded early in the Clinton administration so that even those who have not paid taxes can receive checks. In 1999, a family of four could receive a credit of as much as $3,800 a year. Some critics suggest that the Clinton-era EITC improperly turns the Internal Revenue Service into a mechanism for redistributing wealth—that is, into a sneaky replacement for welfare. But EITC enjoys firm support from many politicians.[22]

The national government also provides more focused benefits to needy families. **Food Stamps** are coupons that can be used to purchase edibles. Enacted by Congress on an experimental basis in the early 1970s, the program has expanded gradually—in part because it is popular with agricultural interests who grow American produce. Low-income families also may receive rent subsidies if they live in designated residences. By helping with housing needs, the program has helped many minority families leave crime-ridden inner cities and move to the suburbs.

Medicaid covers medical services for the poor. A person becomes eligible only if he or she has no more than a minimal income and few assets other than a home. Medicaid costs have risen almost as rapidly as those for Medicare—from around $12 billion in 1970 to $108 billion in 1999. Since the program covers poor families regardless of age, however, the elderly benefit from Medicaid too. More than one-quarter of all Medicaid costs go to low-income seniors.[23]

SENIORS VS. CHILDREN: A COMPARISON   The list of public assistance programs helping poor families seems impressive, but actual expenditures are only one-tenth as much as what is spent on the elderly. Federal social programs for the elderly amounted to over $13,000 per person in 1990, whereas public assistance programs for families with children amounted to little more than $1,300 per capita (see Figure 15.4).

Programs for families with children are also more restrictive than programs for senior citizens.[24] They are less likely to provide flexible cash benefits and more likely to provide inflexible goods and services. In 1990 the elderly received nearly 67 percent of their benefits in cash,[25] whereas poor families received only 41 percent that way.[26] Nearly all benefits to the elderly are tied to changes in the cost of living. By contrast, welfare spending generally fails to keep pace with inflation. Between 1975 and 1993, AFDC benefits fell by 43 percent, on average, across the states. Following welfare reform and the switch to TANF in 1996, average benefit levels dropped another 7 percent.[27]

The benefits that families receive vary from one state to another. Only EITC benefits are uniform throughout the country. For the other major programs—TANF, food stamps, SSI, housing assistance, and Medicaid—eligibility rules and benefit levels vary from state to state. Variation makes using the programs more confusing and may limit the mobility of the poor.[28] For example, TANF benefits

FIGURE 15.4

Federal entitlement expenditures by beneficiary age group, per capita, 1960–1996

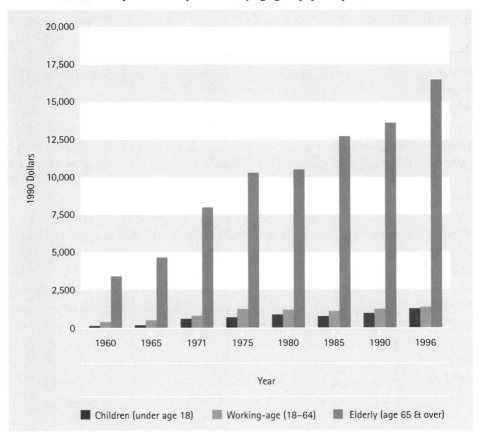

NOTE: Figures in constant 1996 dollars.

SOURCE: Neil Howe and Richard Jackson, *1998 Chartbook: Entitlement and the Aging of America* (Alexandria, VA: National Taxpayers Union Foundation, 1998), Chart 3-3, p. 35.

can be eight times as much in one state as in another.[29] Senior citizens, by contrast, can move from New Jersey to Florida (or even overseas) without jeopardizing the amount or delivery of their Social Security checks.

The benefits that poor families with children receive are substitutes for other income. In most states, a family is not eligible for assistance if it has savings of more than $1,000, a car worth more than $1,500, or anything other than a very modest home. The head of the household must visit a government agency and reveal to a government official the family's complete fiscal record. Benefits drop swiftly as a family starts to climb from poverty.[30]

By comparison, senior-citizen benefits supplement the recipient's own resources. Senior citizens may receive their Medicare and Social Security benefits even if they are working full time, have savings, earn dividends and interest on their investments, and are homeowners. Before the year 2000, Social Security recipients between 65 and 69 years old lost some benefits if they earned more than $17,000 per year. But Republicans and Democrats in Congress, eager to please elderly voters in an election year, repealed this "earnings penalty" unanimously.[31]

WELFARE AND THE PERMANENT CAMPAIGN   Children and the poor exercise little power, so they rely on others to defend their political interests. However, analysts disagree about the causes of poverty and, therefore, disagree over how generous government benefits should be. So do interest groups who influence domestic policy. Liberal voices generally criticize low benefit levels, pointing out that European countries lower their poverty rates more actively.[32] But they are counterbalanced by others skeptical of welfare expenditures.

Conservatives usually deride a "culture of poverty" that encourages young people to place short-term pleasures ahead of long-term goals. Flashy clothes, adventure, crime, and sexual promiscuity thrive in poor communities and are subsidized in part by government programs.[33] Out-of-wedlock births and absentee fathers especially aggravate social conditions, since two-thirds of all impoverished children live in female-headed households.[34] Between 1970 and 1991, the percentage of women with children who were living without a mate more than doubled—from 11 percent to 27 percent. Given this analysis, conservatives do not look to generous government benefits as a solution. They look to moral and cultural changes, including a system that encourages discipline, patience, and the hard work necessary for long-term success.

Sociologist William J. Wilson points out that the culture of poverty feeds off of a weak blue-collar economy. Young men without high school degrees have a much harder time finding work than they once did.[35] According to Wilson, when young men cannot find work, they refuse to take on the responsibilities of marriage and child rearing. Young women, meanwhile, are reluctant to marry men with few prospects. Trends in the late 1990s seem to reinforce Wilson's view. When the economy blossomed, less-educated males found new job opportunities—and marriage rates climbed at the same time.

The general public wavers between liberal and conservative explanations for rising poverty rates. Generally, when the economy is strong, they are more likely to blame the poor and less likely to attribute poverty to circumstances beyond a person's control.[36] Public opinion also shifts with the current policies. In particular, the welfare issue has become less controversial since the end of AFDC.

Political parties fluctuate on welfare policy in step with public opinion. When the country was building the Great Society in the 1960s and 1970s, Democrats took the lead, but Republicans were not far behind. Republican presidents signed into law several welfare programs for children. President Nixon proposed the food stamp and SSI programs. Republicans proposed, and President Ford signed, the law creating EITC. Republicans in Congress initiated the Medicaid program. As the public mood shifted in a conservative direction, the positions of both parties changed accordingly. In 1995 it was the Republicans who took the lead, proposing cuts in many of the programs they had once sponsored.[37] Although some Democrats opposed the cuts, a majority voted in favor of welfare reform, and President Clinton signed the bill.

EDUCATION POLICY

Historically, Americans have supported a large, well-financed education system. This solicitude seems to contradict their relative stinginess toward other programs for young people. However, education differs in many ways from other programs oriented toward children. It is not restricted to the poor and so attracts middle-class support. It promotes "equal opportunity" rather than a "culture of poverty" and so coincides with America's political values (see Chapter 4). It cultivates good workers who generate profits and who are less likely to become criminals, and so benefits society as a whole. To the extent public schools fall short of expectations, however, the weaknesses in the educational system reflect the same handicaps that hold back other programs intended to help the young: few budgetary assurances, limited growth in funding, and low flexibility.

Primary responsibility for education resides at the state and local level. This decentralization means that taxes for education often go straight to the local community and so are not as unpopular as many other taxes. Today, 95 percent of the cost of public education is paid for out of state and local budgets, each contributing approximately half the cost (though the exact percentage paid varies widely from one state to another). Nevertheless, elderly voters often defeat bond issues intended to increase school funding.[38]

The public's commitment to schooling is historically rooted. As early as 1785, Congress set aside the revenue from the sale of one-sixteenth of the land west of the Appalachian Mountains to help pay for "the maintenance of public schools."[39] Support for public schools intensified with the flood of immigrants that arrived in the nineteenth century, because the institutions helped build American democracy. Public schools fostered a common language among people from disparate parts of the world and reinforced a common American identity.

They also educated the workforce to operate the new machines that eventually turned the country into an industrial power.

Nevertheless, public schools are not as popular as they once were. From 1973 to 1999, the percentage of Americans expressing "a good deal" or "quite a lot" of confidence in the public schools dropped from 58 percent to 34 percent (see Figure 15.5).[40] Critics argue that public institutions are local monopolies that perform badly, pointing to weak performance by American students in reading, science, math, and geography.[41] Schools serve the interests of the adults teaching in and administering them, they say, not those of the students. Modern educators are more interested in making every child equal than they are in helping children achieve the limits of their potential. They no longer unify American children, instead pushing a multicultural agenda that undermines the nation's individualism. All of these criticisms have added up to a loss of faith.

FIGURE 15.5

Fewer Americans have confidence in public schools

Widespread criticism of public schools seems to have influenced public opinion. What accounts for the decrease in confidence in public schools over the last few decades?

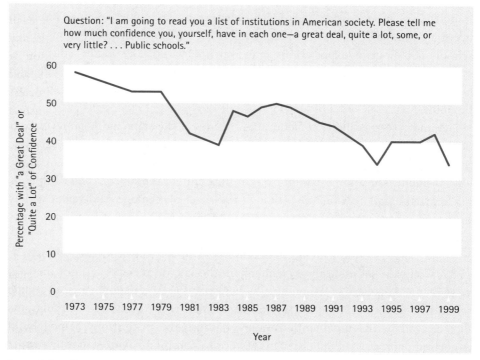

Question: "I am going to read you a list of institutions in American society. Please tell me how much confidence you, yourself, have in each one—a great deal, quite a lot, some, or very little? . . . Public schools."

SOURCE: Gallup Poll, various years.

Public schools suffered financially as popular attitudes turned against them. The share of resources dedicated to elementary and secondary education has increased only slightly over the past 25 years.[42] Between 1985 and 1995, spending inched upward from 4.7 percent to 5 percent of the country's gross domestic product (a measure of economic productivity).[43] Teacher salaries, relative to salaries in other occupations, have hardly improved at all.[44] By contrast, between 1985 and 1995 government spending on health care jumped 50 percent—from 4.2 to 6.3 percent of GDP.[45] In other words, government has committed itself to extending the last years of life rather than enhancing capacities in the first years of life.

As with other programs for children, educational policies do not provide cash benefits. Children must attend the schools provided for them. The public programs available will not supplement family resources, only substitute for them. Citizens lose all the taxes they pay into the school system if they choose to send their children to private schools. Some critics recommend breaking the local monopolies held by public schools by promoting competition among educational institutions. They advocate redesigning the educational system so that students and parents have their choice of schools, just as Medicare recipients have their choice of doctors and hospitals.[46]

One controversial option is the voucher plan. Government would give each family a voucher, which could then be used to purchase education from any school the family preferred. Opposition from the educational profession is intense. Teachers' unions argue that vouchers would enhance ethnic, class, and religious divisions.[47] Thus far, voucher supporters have won only a few victories, such as in Milwaukee, Cleveland, and Florida. But already their drive has pushed governments to innovate—for example, by chartering institutions that are not subject to the same state regulations or union rules as those governing traditional public schools. In 2000, there were over 1,600 charter schools operating in 34 states, although less than 2 percent of public school students attended them.

REGULATION

Not all domestic policy involves redistributing tax dollars. The national government also imposes numerous rules—called regulations—on private companies (as well as on lower levels of government). Regulations are attractive to politicians because their costs do not come out of the federal budget. They usually come indirectly, through higher prices paid by consumers (or through taxes paid to state and local governments). Voters reward elected officials for promoting social goals and blame someone else for the costs.

The breadth of regulations often outpaces what federal bureaucrats can enforce, since members of Congress are more eager to approve rules than they are to fund regulatory agencies. The result can be a false sense of security. Americans think that government is protecting them from a particular catastrophe when, practically speaking, their only guarantee consists of rules on paper.

The 110 people who boarded ValuJet's Flight 592 from Miami to Atlanta on May 11, 1996, are one example. These customers, many of them students returning from spring break, boarded a craft that regulations did not allow to carry hazardous materials.[48] Yet they were sitting on top of a potential bomb: 100 oxygen generators, mislabeled as empty, that had been loaded into the cargo hold. Shortly after takeoff the jet exploded and nose-dived into the Florida Everglades, killing everyone aboard. A Federal Aviation Administration (FAA) regulator was fired and ValuJet's 51 aircraft grounded. Congress launched a massive investigation. But this activity after the fact no doubt provided little consolation for the tragedy.

THE HISTORY OF REGULATION   The basis for federal regulation is found in the U.S. Constitution, which gives Congress authority "to regulate Commerce." The first commerce clause regulations targeted the railroad industry. They expanded briskly during three periods in the country's history: the Progressive Era, from the 1890s to the early 1900s, when muckraking journalists aggressively exposed the abuses of industrialization; the New Deal period, when the national government targeted practices thought to have caused the Great Depression; and the Great Society period, when the national government expanded its scope to influence numerous areas of American life.

Since the New Deal, the Supreme Court has generally found regulatory policies constitutional.[49] Regulations now influence everything from civil rights to national insurance standards. Three situations frequently motivate policy makers to regulate industries: (1) a situation in which small numbers of companies provide products or services and could take advantage of their market dominance at the expense of consumers; (2) a situation in which companies might be tempted to engage in undesirable actions that would not cost them anything, such as polluting the environment to reduce production costs; and (3) a situation in which evaluating the quality of products or services would require more time or expertise than regular consumers are likely to bring to the task.

THE POLITICS OF REGULATION   Electoral pressures influence when and how regulations are imposed. Members of Congress often create regulatory agencies to escape criticism when things go wrong. For example, the *Exxon Valdez* oil spill in 1989 polluted the pristine waters of an Alaskan sound. Congress responded with the Oil Pollution Act of 1990, which established rules for avoiding future oil spills and requiring a rapid cleanup when they do occur. The need to respond to each high-profile crisis often results in overlapping or even contradictory regulations.[50]

Because telling people what to do can upset or anger them, members of Congress usually try to disguise their actions. Congress may not write a detailed set of rules, instead passing the job to an agency. The Clean Air Act of 1990, for example, did not raise gasoline taxes or alter emissions standards for high-pollution vehicles; it simply stated goals for eliminating air pollution and let the Environmental Protection Agency (EPA) figure out how to get there. Forcing agencies to determine regulations lets legislators distance themselves from rules that prove unpopular.[51]

The autonomy afforded to regulatory agencies is not limitless. There exists a zone of acceptance—a range within which Congress will accept whatever an agency decides is the correct interpretation of the statutes.[52] When an agency extends beyond what Congress will permit, political opposition arises, and the agency backtracks.

Although regulatory policies are enacted by Congress and executed by agencies, federal courts interpret the meaning of congressional statutes and decide whether agencies apply them properly. Courts exercise considerable discretion when performing this role, because they are often asked to interpret vague laws.

Court interpretations of the 1973 Endangered Species Act illustrate how federal judges influence public policy. The law protects any species (on federal lands) that the U.S. Fish and Wildlife Service considers in risk of extinction. The species' natural habitats must be safeguarded from threatening human activity, no matter the economic consequences. The political push for this legislation grew from concern about large animals, such as wolves, whooping cranes, and eagles. However, the Fish and Wildlife Service declared nearly 1,000 species to be in danger of extinction, including such little-known species as desert kangaroo rats, tiny snail darters, and spotted owls—an interpretation that federal courts have upheld (see the Election Connection, "The Spotted Owl Dispute").

DEREGULATION   Regulation is expensive. Salaries for bureaucrats, lawyers, and investigators generate an annual price tag that runs to billions of dollars. Regulatory policies also may limit the ability of businesses to compete effectively. The additional paperwork, inspections, procedures, and mandates imposed by regulatory agencies can make the difference between a business that thrives and provides good jobs to Americans and one that cannot compete with foreign firms.

The Spotted Owl Dispute

One of the most controversial examples of statutory interpretation involved the northern spotted owl. This small creature lives in the Pacific Northwest's old-growth forests. Some 3,000 pairs remain. The species can be saved from extinction only by preserving a habitat dark enough to allow it to evade its main predator, the great horned owl.

Environmentalists called for the protection of the spotted owl partly because they can, at the same time, preserve old-growth forests from logging. Only 10 percent of the original forests remain, with their marvelous redwoods, cedars, and Douglas firs. To safeguard these, environmentalists asked the Fish and Wildlife Service to declare the spotted owl an endangered species. After extensive investigation, the Fish and Wildlife Service announced that logging on federally owned ancient forests would have to be reduced by 50 percent.

Timber interests prized these great trees for the quality of their wood. The industry saw little need to protect an owl that few had ever seen. "There are millions of owls in the world," said their political ally, Oregon Republican Representative Denny Smith. "This little puppy just happens to be a passive kind of owl that's being run over." The thousands of workers in the industry cherished not only their jobs but also the logging way of life. Bumper stickers appeared, calling on the reader to "Save a Logger. Kill a Spotted Owl." Local taverns advertised "Spotted Owl Stew" for dinner.

The dispute went before a federal judge, William Dwyer, who issued an injunction halting all logging on federally owned, old-growth forests until the government offered a clear plan that would protect the spotted owl. This became a major campaign issue in the 1992 presidential election, in part because

Washington and Oregon were important swing states. Bush called the Endangered Species Act a "broken law," asserting "it's time to put people ahead of owls." Governor Clinton sought votes from both environmentalists and loggers by criticizing the Bush administration for failing to resolve the conflict.

After Clinton won the presidency (and both Oregon and Washington), officials in his administration reduced logging operations by two-thirds and restricted logging entirely in over 3 million acres of ancient forests. At the same time, the federal government allocated more than $1 billion to retrain loggers and to stimulate the economy of distressed logging communities. Both sides found it difficult to accept the compromise. Environmentalists condemned loopholes in the plan, and timber interests claimed the aid was simply a way of paying off displaced loggers. But Judge Dwyer found the compromise consistent with the requirements of the Endangered Species Act.

Subsequently, a Republican Congress voted in favor of allowing the timber industry to carry out a two-year program that salvaged fallen trees. Despite the intense opposition of environmentalists, who said fallen trees were part of the ecology, Clinton signed the bill—a decision he later reported regretting.

What do you think?

- Should courts have the power to safeguard a small animal in danger of extinction? Or should such issues be left to Congress?

- How would regulations change if Congress had to approve each regulatory decision?

SOURCES: Timothy Egan, *The Good Rain* (New York: Random House, 1991); *New York Times* (June 23, 1990): A1; *New York Times* (January 9, 1992): A14; *New York Times* (May 22, 1990): A20; and *New York Times* (September 15, 1992): A25. See also Kathie Durbin, *Tree Huggers* (Seattle, WA: Mountaineers Books, 1996).

Regular voters usually do not connect higher costs and business failures to government action, but sometimes policy analysts do—and they frequently join businesses in calling for a reduction in regulation. Congress sometimes responds to their calls by backing off from rules that govern industries. It has systematically authorized the partial deregulation of the trucking, banking, and communications industries.[53]

Perhaps the most celebrated deregulation occurred in the airline industry. At one time, a government agency oversaw the airfare set for every route commercial planes flew. Critics charged that the regulators used their authority to limit price competition for customer fares, driving up profits for the few carriers in the industry. Alfred Kahn pushed the issue forward when President Carter appointed him chair of the Civil Aeronautics Board. Kahn stripped away many of the pricing regulations that had governed the airline industry for decades.[54] His initiative led to enactment of the Airline Deregulation Act. Many of the policy outcomes were favorable: lower fares, more service to remote areas, and fewer deaths per passenger mile.

DOMESTIC POLICY IN AMERICA'S NEW DEMOCRACY: A SUMMARY

Many domestic policies divide the two political parties, but parties usually follow the dictates of popular influence. The elderly possess the most clout, and public opinion favors their demands, so government benefits for seniors are generous, flexible, and beyond political challenge. Poor families, and especially children, lack either influence or much public sympathy. As a result, programs to help the poor are decentralized, hard to use, and relatively stingy. Politicians often attract voter support by promising to cut these programs. Partly as a result, seniors live longer but babies die more often in the United States than they do in other industrialized countries.

Even public education, the one policy for children that receives generous funding, still shares traits with other domestic policies oriented toward the younger population. Schools are decentralized, with institutions varying widely in quality and funding from place to place. Beneficiaries generally have no choice of what schools they attend; teachers' unions have fought off voucher programs in most places. And political support for the policy has been declining.

Regulations also reveal the important role of popular influence on domestic policy. Congress passes many regulations because they are a cheap way to curry favor with voters. When an industry's performance becomes unpopular, Congress can respond by adding rules for which consumers must pay. But most laws expanding the government's regulatory power are vague enough that Congress need not take responsibility for their implementation. On the few occasions when poor industry performance clearly stems from government involvement, Congress responds to the public clamor by deregulating.

ECONOMIC POLICY

The U.S. economy is one of the strongest in the world, allowing Americans good wages and a high standard of living. Nevertheless, even wealthy countries experience **business cycles**—periods of economic expansion and rising prices alternating with occasional slowdowns in economic activity called **recessions** (see Figure 15.6). Governments seek economic policies that minimize disruptions such as inflation and unemployment.

FIGURE 15.6

Long-term growth and the business cycle in the United States

Although the general economic trend may be upward over the long run, expansions and recessions that characterize the business cycle can—in the short term—harm both citizens and elected officials.

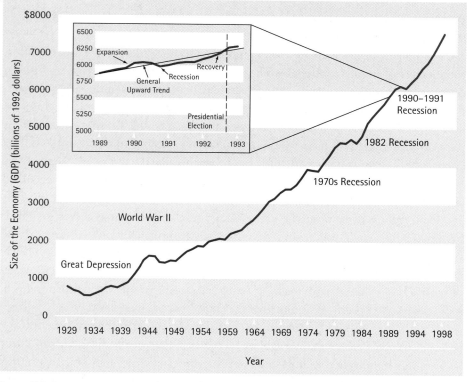

SOURCES: U.S. Census Bureau, *Statistical Abstract of the United States: 1999*, p. 881, Table 1434; U.S. Department of Commerce, Economics and Statistics Administration, "National Income and Product Accounts," www.bea.doc.gov/bea/dn/gdplev.htm, accessed July 27, 2000.

ELECTION CONNECTION

The Miserable Voter

In 1980 Jimmy Carter became the first elected president since Herbert Hoover to lose his bid for reelection. Ironically, the struggling economy that helped him win office in 1976 led to his defeat four years later.

In 1976 Carter had added together the inflation and unemployment rates and named the resulting sum the "misery index," suggesting that it was a measure of the misery suffered by the average American. The misery index was 12.5 in 1976, up from 8.9 in 1972. Partly as a result of the poor economic conditions summarized by the index, Carter narrowly defeated the unelected incumbent, Gerald Ford.

Carter was unlucky enough to hold office in the 1970s, an era of stagflation—low growth (economic stagnation) and high inflation. During his administration, inflation raged at double-digit levels, interest rates exceeded 15 percent, and even the unemployment rate seemed stuck at a relatively high level. In the late 1970s, the Gallup Poll reported that the Democrats had lost their traditional advantage of being perceived as the party best able to keep the country prosperous. In 1980, the misery index stood at 18.2, one-third higher than it was when Carter defeated Ford.

Ronald Reagan campaigned across the country asking crowds, "Are you better off today than you were four years ago?" And the crowds yelled back, "No!" In the final days of the campaign, undecided voters moved decisively to Reagan, and he won easily. In the next few years, stern decisions by the Federal Reserve smashed inflation. In 2000, the misery index had fallen to 7.7.

What do you think?

- Is it fair to judge a president's performance on the basis of the misery index?

- Why do many voters place economic issues ahead of other issues in evaluating candidates?

SOURCE: Data are taken from *OECD Economic Outlook*, no. 58, December 1995 (Paris: Organisation for Economic Cooperation and Development).

Inflation—a rise in the price level—makes consumers pay more money for an equal amount of goods and services, thereby undermining the value of personal savings. **Unemployment**, which occurs when people willing to work at prevailing wages cannot find jobs, harms a smaller number of people—but in ways that can be severe. For a long time, economists thought the two conditions were closely related; lower unemployment eventually created higher inflation, and vice versa.[55] But economists no longer believe the relationship is so close. In fact, President Carter had the misfortune to run for reelection at a time of stagflation, when both inflation and unemployment were high. He suffered a humiliating defeat (see the Election Connection, "The Miserable Voter").

As Carter's experience shows, people tend to blame those in charge when times are hard. President George H. W. Bush's popularity ratings plummeted 40 percentage points over two years because of unemployment increases.

Eisenhower, Nixon, and Reagan all lost public support when recessions struck on their watches.[56] Terrible economic times produce massive election losses for the president's party. The depression of the 1890s ushered in an era of Republican dominance, and the Great Depression of the 1930s did the same for the Democrats. Indeed, Republican President Herbert Hoover (1929–1933) became one of history's most unpopular presidents simply because he was in office when the Great Depression began.

Prosperity, in contrast, strengthens a president's position for reelection (see Figure 15.7). Riding booming economies, Lyndon Johnson trampled Barry Goldwater in 1964, Richard Nixon crushed George McGovern in 1972, and Ronald Reagan trounced Walter Mondale in 1984. Of course, a healthy economy does not guarantee presidential popularity. For example, prosperity in 1968 did not protect Johnson from the Vietnam War's unpopularity. Nonetheless, presidents usually do better electorally when the economy is strong—results that spill over to influence both congressional and state elections.[57]

FIGURE 15.7

Retrospective voting

How Americans feel about the economy influences what they think about the president. When does the economy not have a major impact on the public's view of the president?

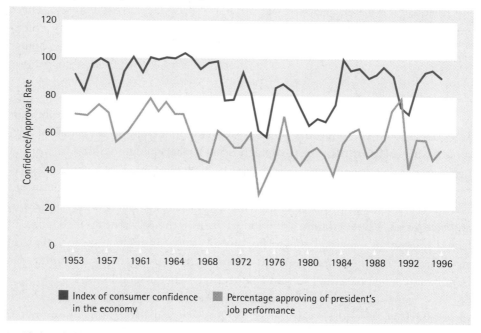

Index of consumer confidence in the economy

Percentage approving of president's job performance

Note: The figure displays data for the first quarter of each year.

FISCAL POLICY

Because so much rides on national economic performance, presidents pay close attention to economic policy. Traditionally, they try to improve conditions by using two major policy tools: fiscal policy and monetary policy. A government's **fiscal policy,** the sum total of taxation and spending in its budget, influences how money passes through a nation's economic system. Sometimes government spending exceeds revenue, producing a *deficit*. Other times revenue outpaces spending, producing a *surplus*. In either case, fiscal policy influences the speed at which a nation's financial resources exchange hands.

According to an influential English economist of the 1920s and 1930s, John Maynard Keynes, budget deficits can lift an economy out of a recession. Government spending jump-starts the economy by giving consumers extra money with which to buy goods and services. Following this line of reasoning, which came to be called **Keynesianism,** Franklin Delano Roosevelt broke with the traditional belief in a balanced budget and embraced large deficits during the Great Depression. The flip side of Keynesianism is that, if government grabs up more money than it spends, then consumers lack sufficient cash to drive up prices and fuel inflation. Congress passed a tax increase in 1968 intended to limit inflation, although the tactic failed.[58]

Administrations today are much less likely to use fiscal policy as a tool for managing the economy than they were immediately after FDR's New Deal. Three reasons explain the movement away from using fiscal-policy tools: the complexity of the budgetary process, the tendency of elected officials to put off unpopular choices, and the impotence of fiscal tools in the face of a globalized economy.

THE BUDGETARY PROCESS The federal budgetary process is long and complicated. It starts within the executive branch a year and a half before the beginning of the fiscal year.* Federal agencies submit their budget requests during the summer to the Office of Management and Budget (OMB). During the fall the OMB reviews requests and modifies them through negotiations with the departments (perhaps under the president's supervision). The Budget and Accounting Act of 1921 requires that Congress receive the president's budget no later than the first Monday in February.

No law requires Congress to pay any attention to what the president recommends. To construct its own budget, Congress generally follows the procedures laid down in the 1974 Budget and Impoundment Control Act. Two budget

---

*By law, fiscal years and calendar years do not overlap completely. Fiscal year 2000, for example, started on October 1, 1999.

committees—one in the Senate, one in the House—collect budget proposals from the other congressional committees and construct a resolution specifying the overall amount that the government will raise and spend in each of the next five years. This stage can be quite controversial because, since 1990, Congress has operated under a pay-as-you-go rule; any proposal to cut taxes or increase spending must show where the money will originate. Congress has only met the April 15 deadline for approving a budget resolution once since the deadline went into effect in 1974.[59]

Once the budget resolution is enacted, appropriations subcommittees use the budget resolution's funding targets as a framework for writing 13 detailed appropriations bills. Congress has until October 1, the start of the new fiscal year, to pass these bills. In practice, passage almost never happens on schedule, and parts of the government must operate under continuing resolutions, temporary funding measures passed by Congress to keep the government operating.

In 1999, the Republican Congress had passed only 5 of the 13 appropriations bills by October, and Clinton vetoed one of these. The president also rejected a Republican-sponsored $800-billion, ten-year tax-cut bill. In addition, congressional Republicans wanted to delay payment of the earned income tax credit, a benefit for lower-income families (although they backed off after Republican presidential candidate George W. Bush objected to their proposal).[60] Resolving these differences of opinion required weeks of continuing resolutions and late-night negotiations over budget targets, and involved partisan acrimony. Clinton signed the bill into law on November 29, 1999—two months after the fiscal year started.

This example may seem extreme in the amount of bickering that occurred, but in reality it is about average. Worse conflicts and delays occurred in 1985, 1987, and 1990. In 1995, partisan battles forced two extended government shutdowns and left the nation without a budget for nearly four months. In 1998, Congress skipped the budget-resolution stage, technically violating the law.

Given this complicated process, it is not difficult to understand why fiscal policy is a blunt tool for addressing economic troubles. Fiscal policy changes slowly, especially when different political parties must agree on a budget, whereas economic conditions can fluctuate rapidly.[61] For example, the national government approved a tax increase in 1990 to check inflation, but it did not take effect until the country faced just the opposite problem: unemployment growing out of a recession.

SHORT-SIGHTED BUDGETING   Fiscal policy operates under long-term limits. Several years of deficit spending can run up a serious *debt*—the total quantity of money a government owes. Not only does a large debt tie up lots of borrowed money that otherwise might go toward productive investments, it also commits the government to increasing interest payments on the loans. These sorts of obligations limit how much flexibility the government has to pump up the economy with direct spending. The more debt a nation carries, other things being equal, the higher interest rates that investors demand before they will loan more.

Furthermore, elected officials are quick to spend money they do not have, but are much less eager to take away taxpayer money without a better justification than the need to slow down the economy! As a result, beginning in the early 1950s, the U.S. government ran up higher and higher deficits, and did not reverse the trend until the 1990s when the national debt's economic impact became too serious to ignore (see Figure 15.8). Policy makers cannot turn to deficit spending to help the economy if they are already running up a large deficit before the economy sours.

FIGURE 15.8

The federal deficit or surplus, 1950–2005

The last several decades witnessed unprecedented deficit spending for peacetime, a pattern that reversed during the Clinton administration. What accounts for the large deficits of the 1980s and the sudden surpluses of the late 1990s?

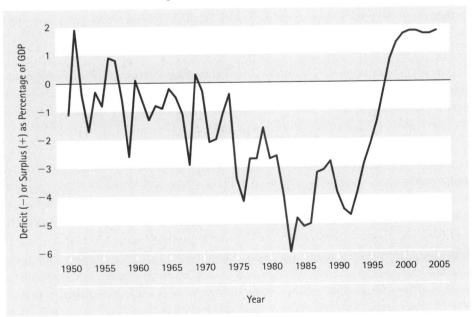

SOURCE: Office of Management and Budget, *The Budget of Fiscal Year 2001, Historical Tables,* p. 22, Table 1.2.

GLOBALIZATION Fiscal policy rarely seems to work in a globalized economy. Budgetary changes cannot compensate for swings in the value of a nation's currency. The value of money determines the exchange of goods across national borders. When the dollar is particularly valuable, Americans import more. Deficit spending cannot increase the circulation of money if the cash it pumps into the economy leaks across national borders. When the dollar is weak, foreigners buy more American goods. High taxes cannot limit inflation if consumers in other countries pump their own assets into the U.S. economy. Investors can shift their assets back and forth in a similar fashion, using their knowledge of a country's economic policies.

MONETARY POLICY

Fiscal policy's limited usefulness as an economic tool has led to a school of economic thinking called **monetarism**, which stresses the importance of the money supply. **Monetary policy,** adjusting interest rates and varying the supply of money, is now the government's most important economic tool. When money is cheap, with low interest rates, people borrow more. They invest or spend the money, spurring new productivity and lower unemployment. The weak dollar attracts foreign spending and investments. Conversely, when money is expensive, with high interest rates, people hold on to their money and borrow less. Inflationary pressures ease. Foreign goods become cheaper for American consumers, siphoning cash out of the overheated economy.

HOW THE FED WORKS The **Federal Reserve System** (or "the Fed") manages the government's monetary policy. Created in 1913, the Fed is headed by a board consisting of seven governors appointed by the president and confirmed by the Senate. Each Fed governor holds office for 14 years. The chair of the system serves for a four-year term. The Fed acts on the economy through the operations of its 12 regional banks, each of which oversees member banks in its part of the country.

The agency is formally independent of both politics and external pressure groups.[62] Long terms assure that presidents may not be able to appoint chairs until late in their administrations, and may not appoint majorities of the board until they have been in office six years. Members of Congress also seldom get a crack at the Fed's board members. Furthermore, monetary policy is too arcane to engage the general public, so Fed-bashing is not a very effective campaign tactic. The Fed maintains a professional image, not a political one—a self-preservation tactic enhanced by the tendency to hire qualified specialists to staff the agency.

Second most powerful man in America?
Greenspan's role as chairman of the Federal Reserve Board gives him great independent influence. What are the sources of his sway over economic policy?

Because the Fed is small and relatively independent of other government officials, it can change monetary policy quickly—interest rates can fluctuate on a monthly, weekly, or even daily basis if the need arises (although the policy outcomes may take months to appear). The most important decisions affecting the day-to-day workings of the economy are made by the Fed's Open Market Committee (FOMC). This committee considers whether interest rates are too high or too low and what adjustments should be made. The committee consists of the 7 governors, all of whom vote, and the 12 regional bank presidents, only 5 of whom have votes (the New York bank president always has a vote; the remaining 4 votes rotate among the other 11 banks). When the national economy slowed early in 2001, and then confidence collapsed after the September 11 terrorist attacks, the FOMC responded with a series of nine interest-rate cuts by October 2.[63]

The chair of the Federal Reserve Board ranks among the most powerful persons in government. The chair's great power derives from close ties to the president, direct access to up-to-date economic information supplied by Fed staff, and the power to approve the appointment of the 12 presidents of the Federal Reserve banks (upon the recommendation of the member banks in each region). The current Fed chair, Alan Greenspan, has been particularly successful at wielding power and improving his reputation. Greenspan's management of the economy during the Clinton administration won him such universal acclaim that 2000 presidential candidate John McCain quipped, "If Mr. Greenspan were to die, God forbid, I would do like in the movie *Weekend at Bernie's* and stuff him and prop him up."[64]

WHO CONTROLS THE FED? Buying Treasury bonds is a necessary part of the Fed's job. It is one way the Fed influences the amount of money in the economy. Fed investments earn billions of dollars (nearly $27 billion in 1998). The Fed keeps about a tenth of this money for its own operations, turning the rest over to the Treasury.[65] This economic independence means that Congress cannot pressure the Fed using its budgetary powers. Once the Senate approves nominees to the Fed, they become insulated from electoral pressures expressed through the legislative branch.[66]

The president—who appoints or reappoints the Fed's members, including the chair—has a great deal more influence than Congress.[67] The Fed must not stray too far from presidential demands, or it might tarnish its apolitical image. Ironically, this sensitivity to appearances causes politics to influence monetary policy. Republicans tend to dislike inflation, so the Fed attacks it more aggressively when Republicans hold the presidency. Democratic constituencies include lots of working-class voters whose jobs are insecure, so the Fed combats unemployment more aggressively when Democrats sit in the White House.[68]

Nevertheless, few citizens like either inflation or unemployment, so Fed behavior does not fluctuate very much with the party of the president. Presidents particularly dislike economic troubles during an election years. Some skeptics even argue that presidents deliberately manipulate the economy to engineer their reelections. They tolerate slow growth, even recessions, early in their terms of office so they can step on the gas and "rev up" the economic engine when payoffs are greatest. Richard Nixon's 1972 reelection campaign provides the classic example; his administration pulled out all the stops to achieve a huge increase in household income that year.[69] Yet neither Jimmy Carter nor George H. W. Bush presided over active economies during their reelection campaigns. At best, economic growth picks up only slightly in an election year, calling into question the extent to which presidents really manipulate monetary policy.

Many liberal critics argue that the banking industry controls the Fed and leads its members to fight inflation much more vigorously than they combat unemployment.[70] When jobs are plentiful and people are spending freely, the Fed typically responds by raising interest rates and slowing down the economy. As one critic put it, "Just when the party gets going, the Fed takes away the beer."[71] Certainly bankers enjoy some influence over monetary policy. They influence the appointment of the Board of Governors, and they nominate the Federal Reserve bank presidents, who cast five votes on the FOMC. But the Fed has not consistently fought inflation, as indicated by the 1970s when it mistakenly allowed inflation to get out of control.

THE FED'S HOLD ON MONETARY POLICY   The Fed is able to operate with a considerable amount of independence in large part because it tries to achieve what nearly everyone desires: steady, stable economic growth. The president, in particular, requires solid economic performance and therefore usually can afford to leave the Fed alone. A case in point is the relationship President Clinton had with Fed chair Alan Greenspan. Ronald Reagan first appointed Greenspan as Fed chair, but Clinton retained him in 1996 to reassure financial markets.[72] Members of Congress also know that they would undermine confidence in the U.S. economy if they encroached too closely upon the Fed's domain.

The position of the Federal Reserve System in America's new democracy therefore is a rare case in which popular moods play little role in determining policy. Yet it is "the exception that proves the rule" of public opinion's influence. The election connection usually does not sway monetary policy precisely because of a conscious choice to insulate the money supply from the tides of political fortune. Just as a dieter might padlock the refrigerator as a defense against moments of weakness, Americans apparently do not trust themselves to weigh in on monetary policy. They respect—and even revere—the distant body of experts who try to fine-tune the economy without giving in to shortsighted impulses.

THE POLITICS OF TAXATION

During the 1980s and most of the 1990s, the budget deficit was a major issue in American politics. Voters wanted to reduce the deficit without raising taxes or cutting spending—contradictory demands that elected officials struggled to reconcile. The task suddenly became possible due to surprisingly high economic growth, which produced a surge in expected government revenue.[73] The projected surplus grew so large that President George W. Bush was even able to convince Congress to cut taxes in 2001 and carry out one of his campaign pledges.

WHY CUT TAXES?   The drive to cut taxes puzzled many observers. After so many years operating on lean budgets, why wouldn't Americans use their sudden windfall to bolster national programs or start new ones? The answer lies in the popular preference for limited government in the United States, a core part of the nation's political culture (see Chapter 4). Most people think that their tax bills are too high. As a result, tax policy is a major topic of public concern, eliciting heated debate.[74]

The total level at which Americans are taxed by the federal government, called the federal tax burden, has risen substantially since World War II. Entering the war, only the wealthiest American families paid income taxes, whereas afterward only the poorest third of the workforce escaped the tax collector.[75] Federal individual income tax receipts rose by over 60 percent between 1950 and 1970, relative to the nation's productivity, after which personal income stagnated.[76] Many Americans came to feel that they were paying too much, even though their combined tax burden is still low by international standards (see Figure 15.9).

Nor is opposition to taxation simply a matter of values. For some it is a matter of good sense. Free-market economists, as well as many regular Americans, believe that taxes damage economic performance over the long term. Taxes lessen

FIGURE 15.9

U.S. tax burden less than in many other democracies

No one likes taxes, but low rates in the United States reflect the American political culture.

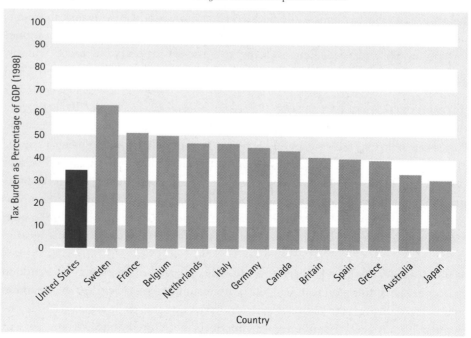

the incentive that workers and businesses have to increase productivity. Taxes draw wealth out of productive sectors of the economy and distribute it according to political considerations that may have nothing to do with efficiency, logic, or fairness. To antitax thinkers, then, the best way for government to improve social conditions is to stand out of the way of economic progress.

Certainly, many Americans disagree with the belief in limited government and yearn for national institutions that take a more active role in shaping society and directing economic development. Yet the cultural tendency against concentrated power is strong enough, when combined with a natural tendency to resent one's own tax burden, to inspire occasional responses from elected officials. Both major-party candidates advocated tax cuts during the 2000 presidential race.

TAX PREFERENCES Very few Americans endorse cutting national taxes altogether. The debate revolves instead around which taxes to permit and which to scale back or abolish. Many economists argue that taxes are less intrusive if they are broad-based—that is, imposed on all economic activity at the same rate. Thus, the amount one pays in income taxes should depend only on the amount of income, not on the source. Nor should sales taxes vary depending on whether one buys groceries, cars, beer, or medical insurance. If everything is taxed alike, then the policy will not distort economic decisions or otherwise sway the choices people make. Special interests will not be able to manipulate the tax code.

Broad-based taxes are difficult to defend in the political arena, however. Organized groups work hard to convert public opinion over to their pet causes. They call on elected officials to use the tax code to encourage some behaviors and discourage others. In response to these pressures, national and state legislators have enacted thousands of **tax preferences,** special treatment that exempts particular types of activity from taxation.

Tax preferences cost the government billions of dollars in forgone revenue, but they often are extremely popular with the public or with attentive interest groups. Popular tax preferences include credits for college tuition and deductions for home mortgages and charitable contributions. Analysts have pointed to problems with each of these credits. They fault tuition credits for driving up education costs at the expense of the poor, mortgage deductions for funding oversized homes at the expense of the environment, and charitable deductions because it is hard to tell when a "charity" in fact is providing donors with some kind of hidden product or service. Yet no amount of criticism has dampened enthusiasm for these sacred cows of the tax code.

Furthermore, tax preferences are the classic "slippery slope." Once government grants one to any group, it abandons the principle of neutral taxation and

Dogbert's tax plan
Elected officials curry favor and influence social behavior by raising taxes to high levels and then exempting particular constituencies with tax preferences.

confuses tax law. The policy encourages other groups to lobby for their own preferences, sometimes outside the view of public scrutiny. Moreover, granting preferences to some activities requires higher taxes on everyone else. This dynamic played out in the 2000 presidential campaign. Vice President Al Gore proposed extensive tax breaks for favored activities, leading George W. Bush—who preferred lowering overall tax rates—to dismiss him as "a picker and a chooser."

Not all special treatment is favorable. The government also sometimes imposes **sin taxes,** taxes intended to make money from people who engage in unpopular behavior. The most prominent sin taxes target cigarettes and alcohol. Critics of such measures argue that they fall primarily on the poorest segments of the population and fail to have a significant impact on the consumption of addictive products. But governments scrambling for revenue seldom pass up sin taxes as a politically popular source of money.

One more general form of unequal taxation is the *progressive tax*, which describes any tax that impacts people more severely as they become more affluent. The most important progressive tax is the federal income tax, which applies different rates depending upon family income. As with other tax inequalities, progressive taxation attracts criticism for distorting economic behavior. Conservatives claim that progressive rates punish investment and hard work contributed by the most productive members of society. Liberals, by contrast, oppose narrowing differences in rates because to do so lessens the tax burden carried by the affluent.

Other taxes are *regressive*, hitting low-income people harder. The payroll tax in 2000 applied only to the first $76,200 a person earned, so the overall tax rate actually decreased as income climbed past that limit. For this reason, when all taxes levied by federal, state, and local governments—including numerous exceptions and exemptions—are taken into account, it is difficult to say whether the tax structure in the United States is progressive or not.[77]

In recent years, both presidential candidate Steve Forbes and many members of Congress have proposed a sweeping income-tax reform called the *flat tax*—a proposal that would eliminate progressive rates and tax everyone above a certain minimum income at the same rate.[78] Supporters of a flat tax defend it on the grounds of efficiency. The more progressive that taxes are, the more time and money must go into documenting income for the government, and the greater the incentive for wealthy households to find loopholes in tax law to reduce their payments. Their claims are not frivolous; taxpayers spend at least $75 billion a year on record keeping, filling out forms, complying with audits, and paying for professionals to figure out their tax obligations.[79] But the flat tax has not generated much popularity outside conservative circles.

AN INTERNATIONAL COMPARISON   Compared to other democracies, the United States is doing a decent job dealing with its economic difficulties. Five and one-half trillion dollars, the size of the national debt in 2000, may be almost unimaginable. Relative to the size of the economy, though, the public debt in the United States is moderate. For example, relative to their productivity, France, Germany, and Japan all have larger national debts than the United States does. Italy's debt is more than twice as large (see Figure 15.10).

The United States has done a better job than most countries of incorporating new workers into the economy. In 2000, for example, the unemployment rate in Western Europe hovered around 10 percent—more than twice the U.S. rate. European countries kept their unemployment rates as low as they did only by using policies that would be unacceptable in the United States. For example, Germany and Switzerland induced so-called guest workers to return to their countries of origin. The United States, by contrast, increased immigration during the 1980s. Limited regulations and low taxation combined to encourage innovation—including development of the high-tech industries that fueled prosperity in the 1990s.

The price of limited government seems to be greater social inequality than found in other advanced democracies. After declining between 1930 and 1970, inequality rose until, in the 1990s, it was higher than at any time since the 1930s. Yet public demand for income distribution is low.[80] The explanation may lie in the necessary tradeoff between encouraging prosperity and mandating equality. Americans do not wish to kill the goose that lays the golden eggs. At some point, being relatively poor in a strong economy becomes better than being equal in a weak one.

FIGURE 15.10

U.S. debt is smaller than the debt of other countries

The U.S. debt exceeds $5 trillion, but this figure (as a proportion of national productivity) is moderate by international standards.

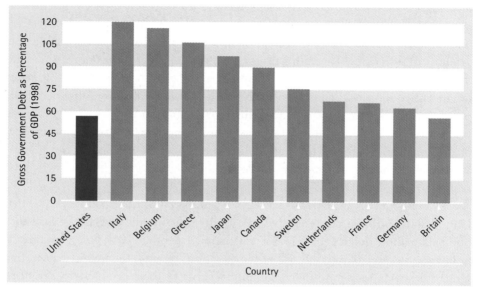

SOURCE: U.S. Bureau of the Census, *Statistical Abstract of the United States, 1999,* Table 1372.

ECONOMIC POLICY IN AMERICA'S NEW DEMOCRACY: A SUMMARY

People care whether they can find jobs and what they have to pay for the things they buy. When times are bad, the president takes the blame. When times are good, the president usually—but not always—gets the credit. National economic conditions significantly influence the president's popular standing. To a lesser extent, this is also true of members of Congress and even state-level officials.

Given these political facts of life, presidents give economic policy top priority. They give the agency responsible for monetary policy, the Federal Reserve, a good deal of independence. For half a century, presidents also tried to use fiscal policy to manage the economy. But this approach has lost popularity, in part because it is hard to manipulate, but more so because it seldom works.

The American tax system generally reflects American political culture. The tax system includes numerous progressive taxes as well as tax breaks for people who pursue politically popular or influential activities. Yet candidates who push equalizing income attract limited support. Americans seem pleased with the balance in their system between rewarding success and eliminating inequalities—

which has helped produce an adaptive economic system with less debt and lower unemployment rates.

Foreign and defense policy

Put foreign affairs first, the sixteenth-century Italian thinker Nicolò Machiavelli advised his prince. If you fail at foreign policy, nothing you do in the domestic sphere will matter. American presidents often wish to ignore foreign affairs, because voters pay more attention to domestic policies that influence their daily lives. Yet international politics has a way of forcing itself onto a president's policy agenda, and domestic successes generally will not save a president who flubs a foreign-policy crisis. Machiavelli's advice still holds in America's new democracy.

At the same time, foreign and defense policies provide a rare opportunity for presidents. They exercise more authority and more independence when dealing with other nations than when dealing with domestic or economic policy. Many foreign-policy duties are ceremonial and therefore allow the executive chances to look presidential—while avoiding the political squabbles that often plague domestic policy. A crisis can increase presidential popularity and influence (see Chapter 10). Foreign affairs allow an executive to tap into deep-seated patriotic emotions, to inspire deep loyalty in voters with military ties, and to gain respect worldwide. The government's international performance can play a significant role in electoral calculations.

Foreign policy in the Constitution

The Constitution declares the president "commander in chief of the army and navy," which added to the usual executive power conveys significant authority over foreign affairs. The Constitution does give Congress power to declare war, to approve treaties, and to govern the armed forces. But presidents have found ways to exercise great power, even when it comes to making war or negotiating international agreements.

WAR POWER   The Constitution did not settle which branch would control the nation's war power. Prior to the Civil War, presidents seldom acted on their own in military matters. President James Madison refused to attack Great Britain in 1812 until Congress declared war. And in 1846, although President James K. Polk provoked war by placing troops in disputed territory, he still waited on Congress before ordering troops into battle against Mexico.

Faced with a national emergency, Abraham Lincoln was the first to give an expanded interpretation to the role of commander in chief. When the southern states seceded from the Union, Lincoln proclaimed a blockade of southern ports and enlisted 300,000 volunteers before Congress convened. A few decades later, Theodore Roosevelt acted similarly, and in a much less urgent situation. He sent naval ships to Japan even when Congress refused to appropriate money for the trip. Congress, if it wished, could appropriate enough funds to get them back. Congress did. Following the lead of Lincoln and Roosevelt, modern presidents often initiate military action without congressional approval. President Truman fought the Korean War without any congressional declaration whatsoever. More recently, President Clinton ordered the bombing of Kosovo without securing congressional approval.

Two major Supreme Court decisions have set the boundaries within which presidents exercise their authority as commanders in chief. In *U.S.* v. *Curtiss-Wright* (1936), the Court considered whether Congress could delegate to the president power over arms sales. Justice George Sutherland wrote that presidents were "the sole organ of the federal government in the field of international relations." The president has "a degree of discretion and freedom," he wrote, "which would not be admissible were domestic affairs alone involved."[81]

The Court limited presidential power in a later case, *Youngstown Sheet and Tube Co.* v. *Sawyer* (1951). Trade unions in the steel industry had gone on strike during the Korean War. Claiming that the industry was crucial for national defense, President Truman ordered the federal government to seize control of the steel mills and commanded the strikers to return to work. In doing so, Truman ignored alternative procedures for handling strikes recently enacted by Congress, thereby attracting a constitutional challenge from the steel companies. Justice Robert Jackson wrote that presidents could not use their foreign-policy authority to grab power at home. When a president "takes measures incompatible with the expressed or implied will of Congress, his power is at its lowest ebb," Jackson explained.[82]

The issue of executive authority arose again during the Vietnam War. In the summer of 1964, North Vietnamese torpedo boats attacked several U.S. destroyers stationed in Tonkin Bay off the coast of Haiphong, Vietnam's second largest city. President Lyndon Johnson denounced the action as an unlawful attack on U.S. ships sailing in international waters.* Congress overwhelmingly passed the **Tonkin Gulf Resolution,** which effectively entered the United States into war with Vietnam by giving the president authority to "take all necessary measures" to repel any attacks and to "prevent further aggression."[83]

The experience of a long and discouraging war in Vietnam prompted Congress to rethink the president's authority over military action. In 1973 Congress passed,

---

*Only much later was it revealed that Johnson had misled Congress; the destroyers had invaded North Vietnam's territorial waters.

A slow buildup
Initially serving as military advisers, U.S. soldiers gradually became more involved in the fight against communism in Southeast Asia. Why did this war induce Congress to pass the War Powers Resolution?

over President Nixon's veto, the **War Powers Resolution,** which required that a president formally notify Congress any time U.S. troops engage in military action. The resolution further specifies that troops must withdraw unless Congress approves the presidential decision within 60 days after receiving notification. Presidents generally question the War Powers Resolution's legal standing. Other than George H. W. Bush, who asked Congress to authorize the Persian Gulf War, no president has sought approval for military action. On five separate occasions, individual members of Congress sued in federal courts to enforce the resolution. In each case, however, judges dismissed the suits, and Congress has never been willing to take more drastic steps while troops were in the field.[84]

TREATY POWER   Presidents may negotiate **treaties**—official agreements with foreign countries—but they do not take effect without approval by a two-thirds Senate vote. This supermajority requirement limits presidential flexibility when negotiating with foreign countries. Prior to 1928, the Senate rejected or withheld approval of 14 percent of the treaties brought before it.[85] A president who cannot get Congress to approve a treaty after negotiations conclude loses credibility in international politics.

No president was more frustrated by this constitutional check on presidential power than Woodrow Wilson. During negotiations to end World War I, President Wilson pursued one objective above all others: establishment of the **League of Nations,** an international organization to settle international disputes. Wilson believed that such an organization could prevent future world wars. But the Senate perceived the League of Nations as a threat to U.S. sovereignty and voted against joining. Shocked and dismayed, Wilson lost both his political efficacy and his personal health.

Eighty years later, President Clinton faced similar difficulties with Congress. In October 1999, the Senate considered the Comprehensive Nuclear Test Ban Treaty, negotiated three years earlier. The multinational agreement would have prohibited testing nuclear weapons and enacted more stringent monitoring systems to ensure compliance. Proponents of the treaty argued that it was essential to slowing the spread of nuclear weapons around the world. But critics, including many Senate Republicans, doubted its effectiveness and worried that it would hamper the nation's ability to modernize its armed forces. After negotiations broke down between Republican leaders and the Clinton administration, the Senate voted against ratification, 51 to 48.

Because a small number of senators can block a treaty, presidents often negotiate **executive agreements,** legal contracts with foreign countries that require only a presidential signature. Nothing in the Constitution explicitly gives the president power to make executive agreements, but the practice has a long history. President James Monroe signed the first executive agreement with Great Britain in 1317, limiting the size of both countries' naval forces on the Great Lakes.

The Supreme Court affirmed the constitutionality of executive agreements in 1937.[86] Since then, presidents have turned to the device regularly. Most executive agreements either are extensions of treaties ratified by the Senate or involve routine presidential actions otherwise authorized by Congress. But presidents sometimes use executive agreements to implement major foreign policy decisions. For example, President Clinton relied on an executive agreement to coax newly independent Ukraine into giving up its nuclear arsenal in exchange for economic aid.[87] In recent years, about 20 executive agreements have been signed for every treaty submitted to the Senate (see Figure 15.11).

THE PRESIDENT AS COMMANDER IN CHIEF

Just as the public demands a strong economy and punishes the president for failing to provide one, the public also expects the president to keep the nation strong internationally. The policy areas differ in one important respect, however. The president clearly must share power with Congress on fiscal policy and must work through an independent Fed to influence monetary policy, but in foreign affairs the president exercises more personal influence. The main limits on presidential action come from foreign leaders and global trends, not from U.S. politicians.

In a classic essay, political scientist Aaron Wildavksy developed the **two-presidency theory,** which explains why presidents exercise greater power over foreign affairs.[88] Foreign policy requires fast action and focused responsibility, and neither interest groups nor members of Congress conflict as much over foreign affairs.

FIGURE 15.11

Growing presidential power

Executive agreements are replacing treaties. Why have presidents increasingly turned to executive agreements? Does this behavior deny the Senate its constitutional role in foreign policy?

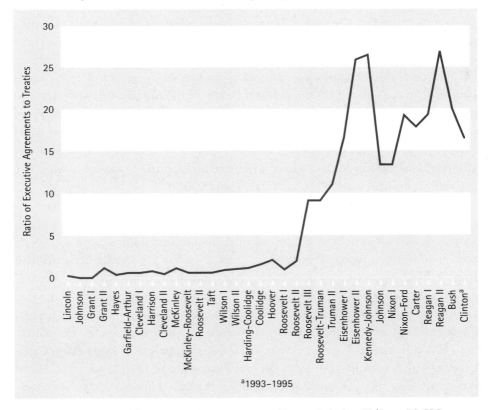

SOURCES: Gary King and Lyn Ragsdale, *The Elusive Executive: Discovering Statistical Patterns in the Presidency* (Washington, DC: CQ Press, 1988), pp. 131–140; U.S. Bureau of the Census, *Statistical Abstracts of the United States* (U.S. Government Printing Office, 1996), Table 1294, 792; and fax from Randall J. Snyder, Law Librarian, Office of the Legal Advisor, Department of State, Washington, DC, December 1996.

THE NEED FOR SPEED Foreign policy questions often require a rapid response, and not only because voters demand it. Sometimes options disappear as a crisis develops. Sometimes, sluggishness at resolving a conflict can allow disputes among nations to escalate, for example if foreign powers misunderstand a nation's position. Moreover, foreign-policy success often relies on secrecy. Attacks are more successful when they are surprises, and sometimes ignorance of a nation's strategic position can lead foreign negotiators to give up more than necessary. Presidents are better equipped to streamline foreign-policy decisions for speed and secrecy. Partly for this reason, members of Congress sometimes follow a "self-denying ordinance" on foreign policy. They may not think it is their job to determine the nation's defense posture.[89] This was particularly true in the years immediately after World War II.[90]

LOBBYING IN FOREIGN AFFAIRS Special interests occasionally influence American foreign policy. For example, the United States has refused to recognize the legitimacy of Cuba's regime, in part because hundreds of thousands of people who live in Florida come from families who had to flee Castro's revolutionary government in the 1950s. The conflict between Israel and Palestine is "a perpetual fixture of domestic politics," according to former Secretary of State James Baker, in part as a result of "the political power of the American Jewish community."[91] Israel receives 20 percent of all U.S. foreign aid.[92] Yet few areas of foreign policy contain such strong and vitally interested domestic constituencies. Most nationality groups are not large enough, concentrated enough, or sufficiently attentive to events overseas to have a decisive effect on U.S. foreign policy. The interest group structure is "weak, unstable, and thin."[93]

RALLYING AROUND THE FLAG In the early days of a foreign-affairs crisis, voters usually fall in behind the commander in chief and ignore those who criticize presidential actions. This tendency, often called the **"rally 'round the flag" effect,** shows up in opinion polls in almost every foreign policy emergency.[94] Between 1950 and 1999, public support for presidents increased by an average of 8 percentage points in the month after a crisis (see Figure 15.12). President Bush experienced the largest popularity increase ever recorded after the 2001 terrorist attacks; his ratings rivaled Roosevelt's after Pearl Harbor (see Chapter 10). Yet failure to resolve the crisis can erase or even reverse this initial sympathy (see the Election Connection, "The Iran Hostage Crisis" on page 539).[95] President Carter's popularity dropped significantly when he could not get American hostages back from Iran (see Figure 15.13).

FIGURE 15.12

"Rally 'round the flag" effects

Presidents' gains in popularity average 8 percentage points in the months following crises. Why do you think President Clinton did not experience as large a boost in public support after foreign policy crises as his predecessors?

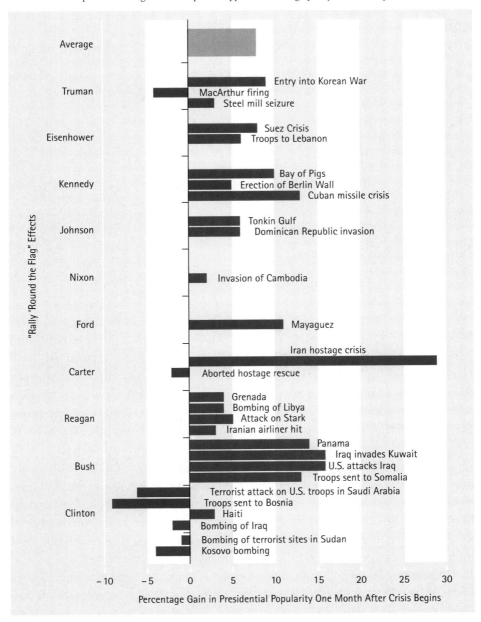

FIGURE 15.13

Shifts in Carter's popularity during the hostage crisis

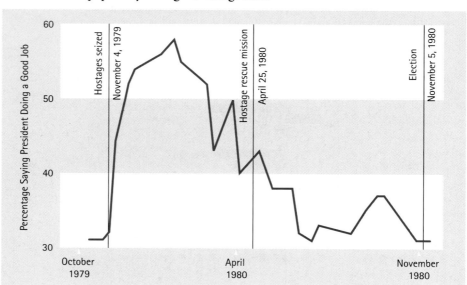

SOURCE: Michael Nelson, ed., *Congressional Quarterly Guide to the Presidency, 1989*, (Washington, DC: CQ Press), 1471.

The public seems especially ready to hold presidents accountable when war breaks out and American casualties mount. The public supported U.S. entry into both the Korean and Vietnam Wars. But when the conflicts dragged on, both Harry Truman and Lyndon Johnson lost so much public support that they decided against running for reelection. The opposition party won the next election in each instance.[96] The Clinton administration provides a more-recent example. After Clinton kept troops in Somalia for more than a year, the deaths of 18 soldiers cost the president public support, resulting in troop withdrawal.

Media coverage shortens the time presidents have to respond to a crisis and how many international events demand attention in the first place. Satellite television and the Internet supply details about international events to a broader public audience than ever before. Struggles that might have been unknown or ignored in the past are now served regularly on the nightly news. Americans can view intense images of conflict and suffering from anywhere on the planet.

President George W. Bush sent troops to Somalia to end internal warfare there, in part because television stations confronted American voters with "the sight of the suffering of the starving people."[97] Similarly, President Clinton felt

The Iran Hostage Crisis

Leaders not only must succeed in foreign policy, they must do so quickly, as the following story illustrates. Muslim fundamentalists, led by Ayatollah Ruhollah Khomeini, overran Iran in the late 1970s. Ayatollah Khomeini's supporters believed that Iran's leadership was too supportive of the United States and not sufficiently respectful of the country's religious traditions. They held ever-larger demonstrations in the streets of Tehran, the Iranian capital, and finally seized power in 1979.

For hundreds of years, countries have established diplomatic ties with one another so that they can learn about each other, communicate about differences, and reach agreements. The residence and offices of the ambassador, known as the embassy, are respected as the sovereign territory of the guest nation. Even when war breaks out between two countries, each side breaks diplomatic relations formally and allows the other's ambassador and staff to depart peacefully. Yet Iran's extremist revolutionaries violated this ancient and fundamental principle of international law. On the night of November 4, demonstrators stormed into the U.S. embassy in Tehran, taking more than 60 American officials hostage. Khomeini supported their action.

President Jimmy Carter imposed a trade embargo on Iran and froze all of the nation's economic assets in the United States, expecting that these strong actions would prompt the return of the hostages. But after five months passed and the American public grew restless, Carter ordered a secret rescue operation. The mission wound up a severe embarrassment: one helicopter crashed and three broke down in a desert sandstorm. Carter again decided to wait out the captors.

The president suffered for his patience. At the beginning of the crisis, public opinion rallied around the president. His standing in the polls jumped by as much as 27 percentage points. But as the crisis persisted, public concern with Carter's immobility rose. Television networks began counting the number of days of captivity. Stations aired interviews with the hostages' families. Yellow ribbons, banners, and bumper stickers began appearing across the nation. Carter's support fell dramatically. Eventually, Carter's image as a weak leader cost him the presidency. The hostages were released on the day President Carter stepped down, as newly elected President Ronald Reagan viewed his inaugural parade.

What do you think?

- Does the president have enough influence over foreign powers to answer for a hostage crisis?
- Would Carter have recovered from the hostage crisis if Iran had released American captives before the 1980 presidential election?

responsible for resolving the political disorder that was causing widespread suffering in Haiti. He sent in troops to enforce a plan to restore democracy. In the words of one commentator, decisions such as these are "less the result of a rational weighing of need or what is remediable than . . . of what gets on nightly news shows."[98]

INSTITUTIONS RESPONSIBLE
FOR FOREIGN POLICY

The institutions responsible for American foreign policy took shape in the early years of the **Cold War** (1946–1989). This conflict between the United States and the Soviet Union sprang up in the wake of World War II. The Soviets first took over East Germany. In short order, they also converted Poland, Hungary, Bulgaria, and Romania into satellite nations. Finally, in 1948, Soviet-backed communists seized control of Czechoslovakia. Together, these East European countries formed a buffer between the Soviet Union and Western Europe. Armed barriers prevented movement across borders—a line that came to be called the **iron curtain.**

Berlin remained a sticking point. After the Third Reich fell, the Allies divided Germany's former capital into four quadrants ruled by different countries: France, Britain, the United States, and the Soviet Union. People passed freely across quadrants, so East Germans wishing to flee communist tyranny could do so very easily. Approximately 2.7 million people made this choice between 1949 and 1961. One night in 1961, the East German government closed this last gap in the iron curtain, erecting fortifications through the center of Berlin. A huge concrete rampart, known as the Berlin Wall, eventually replaced the temporary partition. It dramatically symbolized the world's division into communist and western spheres of influence.

President Truman mobilized bipartisan support for a strategy of **containment.** This policy, designed by a State Department specialist named George Kennan, called for stopping the *spread* of communism but otherwise allowing the ill-considered system to collapse on its own.[99] The Truman administration greatly modernized and expanded America's diplomatic and espionage capabilities. Truman also assembled an impressive team of foreign policy advisers to help the United States resist Soviet expansion.

STATE DEPARTMENT   The Cold War forced the United States to modernize its diplomatic institutions. Ever since then, the **secretary of state** usually has been the president's central foreign policy adviser and chief diplomat. For example, the secretary of state during the first term of the Clinton administration, Warren Christopher, played a major role in negotiating a peace agreement between Israel and the Palestinians.

Reporting to the secretary of state are **ambassadors,** who head the diplomatic delegations to major foreign countries. Ambassadors manage U.S. **embassies,** which house diplomatic delegations in the capital cities of foreign countries. Consulates are maintained in important cities that are not foreign capitals. Although embassies and consulates help American tourists and businesses, their most important political responsibility is to gather detailed information on the government, politics, and social conditions of the host country. The ambassador also conveys to the host country the views of the U.S. government, as instructed by the State Department.

Negotiating with foreign powers is extremely challenging. As former Secretary of State George Marshall once commented, "In diplomacy, you never can tell what a man is thinking. He smiles at you and kicks you in the stomach at the same time."[100] Or as one pundit put it, "Diplomacy is the art of saying 'nice doggie' until you can find a rock."[101] Because the diplomatic corps is critical to American foreign policy, the staff managing U.S. embassies and consulates is organized into the **foreign service.** Dean Acheson, President Truman's secretary of state, worked hard to improve the service's professional caliber. A reporter at the time declared, "For the first time in the memory of living man, the American foreign office comes somewhere near being adequate to the needs of the country."[102]

DEFENSE DEPARTMENT Since the first decades of the country's independence, Americans worried about the ill effects of a large military. Congress and the president have always made certain that the military was controlled by civilian appointees. As one analyst puts it, freedom "demands that people without guns be able to tell people with guns what to do."[103] The Cold War posed new challenges for this ideal of civilian control. To ensure the country's continued international leadership and carry out the policy of containment, Congress provided for the largest military establishment in the nation's history.

The military went through several major organizational changes. The 1947 National Security Act created a single **Department of Defense** that contained within it the departments of Army, Navy, and Air Force, each with its own civilian secretary appointed by the president. The secretaries for the army and the air force are each responsible for their respective branches of the armed services. The secretary of the navy is responsible for both the naval forces and the marines. All three secretaries report to the **secretary of defense,** the president's chief civilian adviser on defense matters and overall head of all three departments.

Subordinate to the civilian leadership of the secretary of defense and the other three appointed secretaries, military professionals direct the armed forces. At one time, each armed force had its own leadership, and they acted more or less independently of each other. To achieve better coordination, Congress formally created the **Joint Chiefs of Staff** in 1947. The Joint Chiefs consist of the heads of all the military services—the army, navy, air force, and marine corps—together with a chair and vice-chair nominated by the president and confirmed by the Senate.

The end of the Cold War offers a number of serious challenges for the Defense Department. Some experts worry that the military has become so large and institutionalized that it is slow to adapt to the changing world. Most of the armed forces are operating with weapons systems and technology designed to battle the Soviet Union rather than to engage in smaller regional conflicts or to protect the United States against global terrorist networks.[104]

In part, the military has been slow to change because of congressional resistance. Many military facilities appear in key congressional districts. These key members of Congress resist any change that might mean a loss of jobs. With increasing frequency, the Defense Department is in the awkward position of receiving ample funds for projects that no longer need the money and of getting insufficient resources for important new weapons systems. At a congressional hearing in 1998, Chairman of the Joint Chiefs of Staff Henry Shelton scolded Congress for not closing enough military bases.[105] Defense Secretary Donald Rumsfeld met severe resistance when he tried to reorganize the military early in George W. Bush's administration.

Accentuating these specific funding issues has been the fact that the overall military budget declined significantly in the 1990s. At the beginning of the Cold War, the United States invested heavily in its armed forces. Throughout the 1950s, approximately 10 percent of the nation's productivity was devoted to defense. The figure reached as high as 14 percent during the Korean War and was 6 percent as recently as the mid-1980s. After the fall of the Berlin Wall, Congress began to cut the defense budget, responding to a decline in public concern. In 1998 and 1999, defense expenditures plummeted to 3.2 percent of economic activity (see Figure 15.14).

CENTRAL INTELLIGENCE AGENCY   "I only regret that I have but one life to lose for my country," the Revolutionary War hero Nathan Hale reportedly said, after he had been caught spying and was about to be hanged by the British. A statue in Hale's memory stands at the entrance of the main offices of the **Central Intelligence Agency (CIA),** the agency primarily responsible for gathering and analyzing information about the political and military activities of other nations. The subject of many a spy novel, it is lovingly referred to as "the Company" or "the Pickle Factory" by members of the intelligence community.[106]

FIGURE 15.14
Budgets after the Cold War
Defense expenditures have declined as a percentage of GDP from 1950 to 1999.

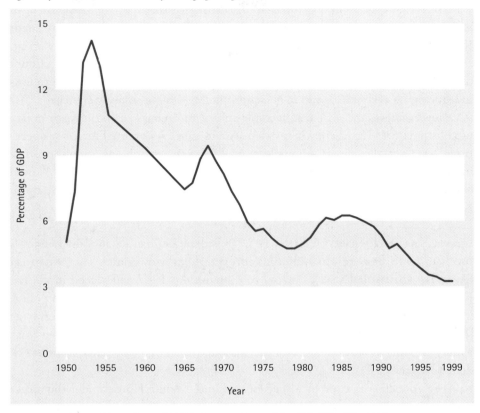

SOURCE: *Statistical Abstract of the United States, 1999* (U.S. Government Printing Office, 1999), Tables 574 and 1444.

But if spying is an ancient and honorable practice, its organization into an independent agency that reports directly to the president is of fairly recent vintage. The need for better-organized intelligence became clear during World War II, but it was not until the Cold War began that Congress established a systematic, centralized system of intelligence gathering. The National Security Act of 1947 created the CIA as a separate agency, independent of both the Department of State and the Department of Defense. Although State and Defense (as well as other departments) continue to have their own sources of intelligence, the 1947 law made the CIA the main intelligence collection agency.

It also gave the CIA the authority to conduct secret operations abroad at the request of the president, a controversial mandate. One especially notorious covert operation was an ill-fated attempt to dislodge communist leader Fidel Castro from Cuba.[107] In an effort to overthrow Castro, the CIA helped Cuban exiles plan a 1961 invasion on the shores of the Cuban **Bay of Pigs.** President Kennedy approved the invasion, hoping that it might foment a popular insurrection, but refused to give it naval or air support. The effort failed, leaving in doubt the CIA's ability to conduct large-scale military operations. CIA covert operations in Chile in the early 1970s and in Nicaragua in the 1980s also drew criticism.

Nevertheless, the CIA has become one of the pillars of the foreign policy establishment.[108] The agency helps identify and squelch potential terrorist operations, assesses the threat of nuclear proliferation, and helps monitor other nations' compliance with arms control agreements. In 1999, the CIA even assisted in efforts to document war crimes committed by the Serbian military in Kosovo.[109]

NATIONAL SECURITY COUNCIL   President Truman decided he needed a mechanism to help resolve different foreign-policy viewpoints. The **National Security Council (NSC),** created by Congress in 1947 and placed inside the Executive Office of the President, is responsible for coordinating foreign policy. Meetings of the NSC are generally attended by the president, the vice president, the secretaries of state and defense, the head of the CIA, the chair of the Joint Chiefs of Staff, the president's chief of staff, and such other persons as the president designates.[110]

The council is assisted by a staff located in the White House under the direction of the National Security Adviser (NSA). The NSA has often played a coordinating role, reconciling interagency disagreements or, if that proves impossible, reporting them to the president. But inasmuch as the NSA has more access to the president than any member of the foreign policy team, the adviser can wield great influence. During the Nixon administration, National Security Adviser Henry Kissinger even overshadowed the secretary of state.

The NSA has not escaped controversy. The most notorious scandal is called the **Iran–Contra affair.** The NSA office attempted to conduct a covert operation, selling arms to Iran and then diverting the funds to rebels in Nicaragua known as the Contras. Since Congress had forbid such aid, the Iran–Contra affair developed into a bitter confrontation with President Ronald Reagan, who had privately asked National Security Adviser Robert McFarlane to "assure the Contras of continuing administration support."[111] Hearings and investigations followed, although no convictions withstood court appeals.

IDEALS AND INTERESTS
IN AMERICAN FOREIGN POLICY

The way the president and his advisers resolve foreign policy questions is shaped by a long-standing tension that exists between American philosophical ideals and the country's practical need to defend itself. Alexander Hamilton, in the *Federalist Papers,* made the best case for placing the highest priority on practical interests: "No Government [can] give us tranquility and happiness at home, which [does] not possess sufficient stability and strength to make us respectable abroad."[112] The idealist point of view was best expressed by Abraham Lincoln, who reminded his fellow citizens that one purpose of the American experiment was to spread liberty throughout the world "for all future time."[113]

NATIONAL IDEALS   Over the course of its history, the United States has not been so naïve or innocent that it ignored underlying national interests. The country acquired land and possessions when opportunities were ripe. But more than most nations, the United States has expressed its international goals in missionary language. Liberty, democracy, and inalienable rights are so important to the country's self-definition that they cannot be ignored when framing its relations with other nations. The **Monroe Doctrine,** declaring the Western Hemisphere free from European colonial influence, provides an early statement of U.S. foreign policy ideals. In 1823, at a time when European countries were establishing colonies throughout the world, President Monroe declared that "The American continents . . . are henceforth not to be considered as subjects for future colonization by any European power."[114]

A century later, the United States fought in two world wars in the name of freedom. When asking Americans to enter World War I, President Woodrow Wilson claimed it was necessary because "the world must be made safe for democracy."[115] He promised, rather idealistically, that it would be the war to end all wars. When World War II broke out, President Roosevelt asked Americans to fight for four freedoms: free speech, religious freedom, freedom from want, and freedom from fear.[116]

NATIONAL INTERESTS   Ideals may structure American foreign policy, but that policy also reflects the country's practical self-interests. One of the oldest U.S. foreign policy principles, **isolationism,** is in fact explicitly self-centered. According to this principle, the United States should remain separate from the conflicts taking place among other nations. Isolationists often quote a phrase from George Washington's Farewell Address, made when he retired from the presidency: "Tis our true policy to steer clear of permanent alliances."[117] For more than a century after Washington made this speech, the United States was, in the words of Winston Churchill, "splendidly isolated."

Isolationism is not entirely a philosophy of weakness or of fear, so much as a lack of concern. The United States has always sat an ocean away from the world's major powers. Wars take place far away. The U.S. mainland last faced foreign invasion in 1814—unless one counts recent terrorist attacks. Limited interest in international affairs has been fed by the country's wartime successes, which have fostered a sense of invincibility. After the War of 1812 and until the Vietnam War, the United States had an impressive military record. Most wars ended in overwhelming victories. The United States has suffered few casualties in foreign wars (see Figure 15.15).

Such a large proportion of Americans sympathized with the isolationist argument that the United States became involved in World Wars I and II only reluctantly and belatedly. World War I broke out in August 1914, but the United States stayed out of it for more than two years. In language reminiscent of Washington's, President Wilson initially called for the United States to be "neutral in fact as well as in name."[118] The United States did not declare war until well after the Germans began torpedoing U.S. commercial ships.

At the beginning of World War II, the United States once again declared its neutrality. In his 1940 campaign for reelection, President Roosevelt promised "mothers and fathers" that the country's neutrality would be preserved: "I shall say it again and again and again: Your boys are not going to be sent into any foreign wars."[119] But soon after the election, Roosevelt began preparing for war, declaring "we must be the great arsenal of democracy."[120]

ISRAEL AND THE ISLAMIC WORLD   Terrorists hijacked four airliners on September 11, 2001, and converted them into weapons of mass destruction. Two jets destroyed the twin towers of New York City's World Trade Center. One demolished a side of the Pentagon in Washington, D.C. The fourth crashed into the Pennsylvania countryside, apparently thanks to heroism displayed by the jet's passengers. The death toll exceeded 6,000 people, including hundreds of British citizens and foreign nationals from more than 50 countries. Early evidence suggested that the perpetrators were Islamic extremists associated with a wealthy terrorist leader, based in Afghanistan, named Osama bin Laden—who had declared war on Americans because of U.S. foreign policy in the Middle East.

The devastating cost of this tragedy caused many Americans to wonder why the United States was even involved in such a volatile region. In particular, many began to question the U.S. alliance with Israel, a beleaguered Jewish state on the

FIGURE 15.15
United States lucky in war

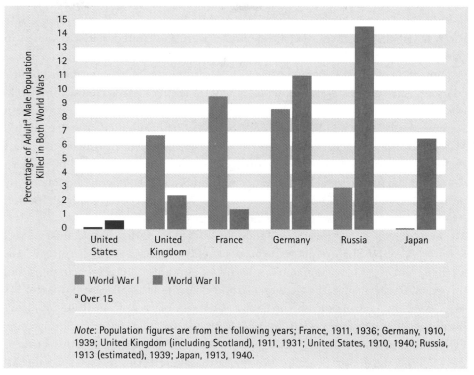

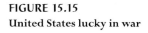

Note: Population figures are from the following years; France, 1911, 1936; Germany, 1910, 1939; United Kingdom (including Scotland), 1911, 1931; United States, 1910, 1940; Russia, 1913 (estimated), 1939; Japan, 1913, 1940.

SOURCES: R. Ernest Dupy and Trevor N. Dupuy, *The Harper Encyclopedia of Military History: From 3500 B.C. to the Present* (New York: HarperCollins, 1993); Y. Takenob, *The Japan Year Book: 1919–1920* (Tokyo: Japan Year Book Office, 1921); B. R. Mitchell, *International Historical Statistics: Europe 1750–1988* (New York: Stockton Press, 1992); B. R. Mitchell, *International Historical Statistics of the Americas: 1750–1988* (New York: Stockton Press, 1993); B. R. Mitchell, *International Historical Statistics: Africa and Asia* (New York: New York University Press, 1982); and Raymond E. Zickel, ed., *Soviet Union: A Country Study* (Washington, DC: U.S. Government Printing Office, 1991).

eastern shore of the Mediterranean—asking whether an idealistic consideration, such as loyalty to a small and distant ally, was worth the risk.[121] The connection between Israel and the terrorist strike is actually rather thin, since bin Laden is a native of Saudi Arabia and appears primarily to be upset with the U.S. military presence in his home country and with the nation's strong-arm treatment of Iraq. Nevertheless, the perception that relations between the United States and Israel have brought on terrorist reprisals is strong—and it does contain an element of truth because American support for Israel infuriates many Arab and Islamic militants. The United States provides Israel with extensive foreign aid and stands by its ally in the chambers of international governance. So the combination of ideals and interests underlying that relationship is worth reviewing.

The United States shares responsibility for the existence of Israel. Zionist Jews began returning to their holy land in the nineteenth century to find a safe haven from anti-Semitism, which was prevalent in the United States as well as in Europe.[122] After World War I, American President Woodrow Wilson joined the League of Nations to encourage Jewish resettlement of the territory. Industrialized democracies watched with delight as settlers converted an impoverished, neglected, and war-torn land into a thriving mix of agricultural and urban communities.[123] The resolve to establish a Jewish state solidified after the United States and other world powers shut their borders to refugees during the Nazi Holocaust.[124] The society Israelis created in 1948 is heavily influenced by western values. In particular, Israel is a democratic country in a region dominated by monarchies and by religious and military dictatorships. Guilt and admiration compel American support for Israel on idealistic grounds.

Less clear is how Americans should evaluate the conflict between Israel and Palestinian Arabs. Surrounding nations declared war on Israel the day after it was formed, and they have supported a series of sporadic military excursions and terrorist attacks against the fledgling nation over the last half-century. Israel has responded by expanding its territory. One six-day clash in June of 1967 prompted Israel to seize two neighboring pieces of territory inhabited by Palestinians: the West Bank of the Jordan River and the Gaza Strip that borders the Mediterranean Sea. Israeli possession of these territories poses a special challenge to American ideals. Palestinian Arabs claim that the Israelis are an abusive "occupying power," a posture endorsed by many neighboring governments. Israeli officials have violated civil liberties while attempting to preserve order, occasionally shooting protestors armed only with rocks and a few times even resorting to assassination or torture of suspected terrorists.[125] These acts offend American values.

By contrast, when Palestinians ask for the right to form their own democratic government in the occupied territories, the request sounds consistent with American ideals (as well as American interests in stability). Indeed, the Clinton administration joined a chorus of outsiders who have pushed Israel to return the land, resulting in a series of accords starting in 1993 that passed partial control of the occupied territories over to a "Palestinian Authority" led by Yassir Arafat. That transition process broke down in the fall of 2000, in the face of violence sponsored by Arab organizations (such as Hamas) that are dedicated to the destruction of Israel. Palestinian terrorists repeatedly murdered civilians using suicide bombs and other bloody methods, a behavior that Arafat seldom inhibits and sometimes exploits.[126] Nor has the hatred faced from nearby Islamic countries abated (although two governments, those in Egypt and Jordan, have signed peace treaties with Israel). The West Bank's border and the Mediterranean's shore are less than 10 miles apart, leaving a strip of land so narrow that it is almost indefensible against a divide-and-conquer strategy. Asking any people to sacrifice their buffer against attack from sworn enemies, and therefore to expose themselves to severe security risks of a sort the United States would not accept, does not seem compatible with American "common sense."

Meanwhile, Americans have practical reasons for involvement in Israel's future. Most obvious is concern with national security. Regional conflict can lead to nuclear strikes or out-of-control biological warfare that indirectly would impact the United States. The intelligence apparatus necessary to watch for (and perhaps undermine) the development of deadly weapons is costly and complex, but Israel bears much of that burden for the other industrialized democracies. Economic concerns may be more immediate. The Arab world contains a majority of the globe's petroleum reserves, which the United States consumes in large quantities. Low-cost oil purchased from the Middle East fuels factories and powers generators and vehicles. The price of oil is significant economically because it dictates the cost of American mobility, of food and goods transported to stores, and of petroleum-based products such as detergents, plastics, and fabrics. Any threat to the Middle Eastern oil trade in turn threatens the U.S. economy. Having a strong ally in the region therefore takes on great significance.

Obviously, the situation is complex, so America's relationship with Middle Eastern governments must be complicated as well. Both ideals and interests pull the United States into the region and compel a friendship with Israel, and yet the various impulses are often contradicted once the U.S. government becomes involved. Future terrorist strikes may punish Americans for sticking with their besieged ally. The United States also one day may reassess the military and diplomatic costs associated with its consumption of foreign oil. Only one fact about the situation is clear: There is no quick and easy foreign policy solution to protect the United States from the politics of the Middle East.

THE POLITICS OF WORLD TRADE: NEW ALLIANCES?

When the Cold War began, U.S. foreign policy makers were concerned with economic as well as political and military questions. Believing that stable economies and the growth of free markets would aid in the effort to contain communism, the Truman administration helped negotiate a new international economic system. International banks were created to loan money to needy countries, United Nations organizations handled world health and refugee problems, and an international trade agreement reduced tariffs around the world. In late 1947, for example, 23 countries founded the General Agreement on Tariffs and Trade (GATT).

During the Cold War, most of the public saw trade policy as arcane and uncontroversial. But in the 1990s, trade became a much more contentious issue. First came the 1993 battle over the North American Free Trade Agreement (NAFTA), which eliminated trade barriers among the United States, Canada, and Mexico. Negotiated by President Bush and promoted by President Clinton, NAFTA won only a narrow majority in Congress after fierce lobbying by all sides. It linked Republican business groups and Democrats active in international affairs, who supported NAFTA, against Republican isolationists and such Democratic special-interest constituencies as labor unions and environmental groups.

The battle over NAFTA proved to be only the beginning of a very public debate over the status of world trade. In 1994, negotiators from 104 nations officially transformed GATT into the World Trade Organization (WTO), a more powerful trade body. Opposition to the organization was led by the same groups that opposed NAFTA. Tens of thousands of protesters disrupted a meeting of WTO trade ministers in Seattle in 1999, blocking streets and preventing delegates from attending the meetings. World trade shows signs of creating new political coalitions and invoking more conflict than a foreign policy issue typically would. Trade issues seem sure to define a major part of post–Cold War American foreign policy.

FOREIGN POLICY IN AMERICA'S NEW DEMOCRACY: A SUMMARY

Electoral considerations help account for the fact that presidents dominate policy making on foreign policy questions more than on domestic ones. Voters expect presidents to take the lead, and support presidents early in a crisis regardless of the actions taken. Only later, if things do not turn out well, do voters penalize poor choices. Voters defer to the president on foreign policy for good reason. The president has an expansive array of analysts and advisers from whom to draw advice. Leaders of the three agencies that shape U.S. foreign policy—State, Defense, and the CIA—all sit on the National Security Council. A national security adviser coordinates decisions through this body. So much help allows the president to move quickly and secretly to resolve a crisis.

Both idealistic and realistic factors help shape American foreign policy. On the one hand, the United States feels responsible for promoting the democratic experiment abroad. Voters do not appreciate presidential sluggishness when children are starving or people are being massacred. On the other hand, the United States, like any other country, has its own interests to protect. Voters become unhappy when the nation enters unnecessary conflicts or appears weak on the world stage. They reward elected officials who, because of their foreign policy activities, achieve important goals—not the least of which is prosperity.

Chapter Summary

Elderly voters initially won the battle of the budget surplus because of their indomitable political power. But domestic policy is not the only area influenced by popular preferences. Fiscal policy does not work in part because politicians often do not believe they can raise taxes or cut programs to eliminate national debt without suffering electorally. The Fed conducts monetary policy with little interference, but only because regular Americans seem to revere experts pursuing shared economic goals. Tax law reflects basic American values, including a preference for prosperity over equality. Presidents must attend to foreign affairs even when they wish to concentrate on domestic policy; voters will punish them if they fail to resolve an international crisis swiftly. The whole scope of public policy illustrates quite starkly this book's central theme: In America's new democracy, elections (or at least the anticipation of them) matter more than they do in most countries and more than they have for most of the nation's history.

Key Terms

Aid to Families with Dependent Children (AFDC), p. 505
ambassador, p. 540
Bay of Pigs, p. 544
business cycle, p. 516
Central Intelligence Agency (CIA), p. 542
Cold War, p. 540
containment, p. 540
Department of Defense, p. 541

Earned Income Tax Credit (EITC), p. 505
embassy, p. 540
executive agreement, p. 534
Federal Reserve System, p. 522
fiscal policy, p. 519
food stamps, p. 506
foreign service, p. 541
inflation, p. 517
Iran–Contra affair, p. 544
iron curtain, p. 540

isolationism, p. 545
Joint Chiefs of Staff, p. 541
Keynesianism, p. 519
League of Nations, p. 534
Medicaid, p. 506
Medicare, p. 502
monetarism, p. 522
monetary policy, p. 522
Monroe Doctrine, p. 545

SUGGESTED READINGS

Birnbaum, Jeffrey H., and Alan S. Murray. *Showdown at Gucci Gulch.* New York: Random House, 1987. Fast-paced case study of the passage of the 1986 tax reforms.

Bradford, David F. *Untangling the Income Tax.* Cambridge, MA: Harvard University Press, 1986. Everything you ever wanted to know about income taxes, presented in a reasonably comprehensible fashion.

Huntington, Samuel. *The Clash of Civilizations.* New York: Simon & Schuster, 1996. Argues that future world conflicts will occur between clusters of nations that share a common cultural heritage.

Johnson, Loch K. *America's Secret Power: The CIA in a Democratic Society.* New York: Oxford University Press, 1989. Informed critique of CIA power and tactics.

Kingdon, John. *Agenda, Alternatives and Public Policies.* Boston: Little, Brown, 1984. Discusses the policy-making process, paying special attention to how problems become issues on the political agenda.

Koh, Harold Hungju. *The National Security Constitution: Sharing Power after the Iran–Contra Affair.* New Haven, CT: Yale University Press, 1990. Analyzes the distribution of constitutional authority in foreign policy.

Leffler, Melvyn P. *A Preponderance of Power: National Security, the Truman Administration, and the Cold War.* Stanford, CA: Stanford University Press, 1992. Historical account of Cold War strategy.

Melnick, R. Shep. *Regulation and the Courts.* Washington, DC: Brookings, 1983. Case studies of the central role the courts play in interpreting government regulations.

Pierson, Paul. *Dismantling the Welfare State? Reagan, Thatcher and the Politics of Retrenchment.* New York: Cambridge University Press, 1994. Insightful analysis of political battles over cuts in welfare expenditure.

Weaver, R. Kent. *Automatic Government: The Politics of Indexation.* Washington, DC: Brookings, 1988. Explains policy changes that have allowed government entitlements to become increasingly expensive.

Weir, Margaret. *Politics and Jobs: The Boundaries of Employment Policies in the United States.* Princeton, NJ: Princeton University Press, 1992. Broad historical and political analysis of government efforts to guarantee jobs.

Wilson, James Q. *The Politics of Regulation.* New York: Basic Books, 1980. Comprehensive text on regulatory politics and policy.

Wilson, William J. *The Truly Disadvantaged: The Inner City, the Underclass, and Public Policy.* Chicago: University of Chicago Press, 1987. Argues that poverty has been caused by the globalization of the economy and the disappearance of blue-collar jobs.

ON THE WEB

Social Security Administration
www.ssa.gov
The Social Security Administration (SSA) Web site provides information on the characteristics of the Social Security program.

Health Care Financing Administration
www.hcfa.hhs.gov
The Health Care Financing Administration (HCFA) administers the Medicare and Medicaid programs.

American Association of Retired People
www.aarp.org
The American Association of Retired People (AARP) maintains a large Web site describing its volunteer programs and lobbying efforts and offering health and recreation tips for seniors.

Harvard University Program on Education Policy and Governance
data.fas.harvard.edu/pepg/
Harvard's Program on Education Policy and Governance researches issues of school choice and vouchers.

Public Citizen
www.publiccitizen.org
Ralph Nader's Public Citizen lobbies for consumer protection regulations. The site contains facts and figures and links to papers and other publications.

Heritage Foundation
www.regulation.org
This, the conservative Heritage Foundation's regulation Web site, advocates decreased regulation. The site contains facts and figures and links to papers and other publications.

The Federal Reserve
www.federalreserve.gov
The Federal Reserve System maintains an informative Web site, complete with publications, congressional testimony, and economic data.

Department of State
Department of Defense
Central Intelligence Agency
www.state.gov
www.defenselink.mil
www.odci.gov
The Web sites of the Department of State, the Department of Defense, and the CIA provide publications and other information about the structure and conduct of U.S. foreign policy.

United Nations
World Trade Organization
www.un.org
www.wto.org
Learn about the United Nations and the World Trade Organization at their Web sites.

Council on Foreign Relations
www.cfr.org
Founded in 1921, the Council on Foreign Relations promotes understanding of international politics and publishes the journal *Foreign Affairs*.

Senate Committee on Foreign Relations
www.senate.gov/~foreign/
The U.S. Senate's Committee on Foreign Relations provides information on treaties presented to the Senate for its approval as well as on nominations and hearings on foreign policy.

APPENDIX

The Declaration of Independence

The Constitution of the United States of America

The Federalist No. 10

The Federalist No. 51

Presidents of the United States

The Declaration of Independence
In Congress, July 4, 1776

The Unanimous Declaration
of the Thirteen United States of America

WHEN IN THE COURSE of human events it becomes necessary for one people to dissolve the political bonds which have connected them with another, and to assume, among the powers of the earth, the separate and equal station to which the Laws of Nature and of Nature's God entitle them, a decent respect to the opinions of mankind requires that they should declare the causes which impel them to the separation.

We hold these truths to be self-evident, that all men are created equal, that they are endowed by their Creator with certain unalienable Rights, that among these are Life, Liberty and the pursuit of Happiness. That to secure these rights, Governments are instituted among Men, deriving their just powers from the consent of the governed. That whenever any Form of Government becomes destructive of these ends, it is the Right of the People to alter or to abolish it, and to institute new Government, laying its foundation on such principles and organizing its powers in such form, as to them shall seem most likely to effect their Safety and Happiness. Prudence, indeed, will dictate that Governments long established should not be changed for light and transient causes; and accordingly all experience hath shown that mankind are more disposed to suffer, while evils are sufferable, than to right themselves by abolishing the forms to which they are accustomed. But when a long train of abuses and usurpations, pursuing invariably the same Object evinces a design to reduce them under absolute Despotism, it is their right, it is their duty, to throw off such Government, and to provide new Guards for their future security.

Such has been the patient sufferance of these Colonies; and such is now the necessity which constrains them to alter their former Systems of Government. The history of the present King of Great Britain is a history of repeated injuries and usurpations, all having in direct object the establishment of an absolute Tyranny over these States. To prove this, let Facts be submitted to a candid world.

He has refused his Assent to Laws, the most wholesome and necessary for the public good.

He has forbidden his Governors to pass Laws of immediate and pressing importance, unless suspended in their operation till his Assent should be obtained; and when so suspended, he has utterly neglected to attend to them.

He has refused to pass other Laws for the accommodation of large districts of people, unless those people would relinquish the right of Representation in the Legislature, a right inestimable to them and formidable to tyrants only.

He has called together legislative bodies at places unusual, uncomfortable, and distant from the depository of their Public Records, for the sole purpose of fatiguing them into compliance with his measures.

He has dissolved Representative Houses repeatedly, for opposing with manly firmness his invasions on the rights of the people.

He has refused for a long time, after such dissolutions, to cause others to be elected; whereby the Legislative Powers, incapable of Annihilation, have returned to the People at large for their exercise, the State remaining in the meantime exposed to all the dangers of invasion from without, and convulsions within.

He has endeavored to prevent the population of these States; for that purpose obstructing the Laws of Naturalization of Foreigners; refusing to pass others to encourage their migration hither, and raising the conditions of new Appropriations of Lands.

He has obstructed the Administration of Justice, by refusing his Assent to Laws for establishing Judiciary powers.

He has made Judges dependent on his Will alone, for the tenure of their offices, and the amount and payment of their salaries.

He has erected a multitude of New Offices, and sent hither swarms of Officers to harass our people, and eat out their substance.

He has kept among us, in times of peace, Standing Armies without the Consent of our legislatures.

He has affected to render the Military independent of and superior to the Civil power.

He has combined with others to subject us to a jurisdiction foreign to our constitution, and unacknowledged by our laws, giving his Assent to their Acts of pretended Legislation:

For quartering large bodies of armed troops among us:

For protecting them, by a mock Trial, from punishment for any Murders which they should commit on the Inhabitants of these States:

For cutting off our Trade with all parts of the world:

For imposing Taxes on us without our Consent:

For depriving us in many cases, of the benefits of Trial by Jury:

For transporting us beyond Seas to be tried for pretended offences:

For abolishing the free System of English Laws in a neighboring Province, establishing therein an Arbitrary government, and enlarging its Boundaries so as to render it at once an example and fit instrument for introducing the same absolute rule into these Colonies:

For taking away our Charters, abolishing our most valuable Laws, and altering fundamentally the Forms of our Governments:

For suspending our own Legislatures, and declaring themselves invested with power to legislate for us in all cases whatsoever.

He has abdicated Government here, by declaring us out of his Protection and waging War against us.

He has plundered our seas, ravaged our Coasts, burnt our towns, and destroyed the lives of our people.

He is at this time transporting large Armies of foreign Mercenaries to compleat the works of death, desolation and tyranny, already begun with circumstances of Cruelty and perfidy scarcely paralleled in the most barbarous ages, and totally unworthy the Head of a civilized nation.

He has constrained our fellow Citizens taken Captive on the high Seas to bear Arms against their Country, to become the executioners of their friends and Brethren, or to fall themselves by their Hands.

He has excited domestic insurrections amongst us, and has endeavored to bring on the inhabitants of our frontiers, the merciless Indian Savages, whose known rule of warfare, is an undistinguished destruction of all ages, sexes and conditions.

In every stage of these Oppressions We have Petitioned for Redress in the most humble terms: Our repeated Petitions have been answered only by repeated injury: A Prince, whose character is thus marked by every act which may define a Tyrant, is unfit to be the ruler of a free people.

Nor have We been wanting in attention to our British brethren. We have warned them from time to time of attempts by their legislature to extend an unwarrantable jurisdiction over us. We have reminded them of the circumstances of our emigration and settlement here. We have appealed to their native justice and magnanimity; and we have conjured them by the ties of our common kindred to disavow these usurpations, which would inevitably interrupt our connections and correspondence. They too have been deaf to the voice of justice and consanguinity. We must, therefore, acquiesce in the necessity, which denounces our Separation, and hold them, as we hold the rest of mankind, Enemies in War, in Peace Friends.

We, therefore, the Representatives of the United States of America, in General Congress, Assembled, appealing to the Supreme Judge of the world for the rectitude of our intentions, do, in the Name, and by Authority of the good People of these Colonies, solemnly publish and declare, That these United Colonies are, and of Right ought to be Free and Independent States; that they are Absolved from all Allegiance to the British Crown, and that all political connection between them and the State of Great Britain, is and ought to be totally dissolved: and that as Free and Independent States, they have full power to levy War, conclude Peace, contract Alliances, establish Commerce, and to do all other Acts and Things which Independent States may of right do. And for the support of this Declaration, with a firm reliance on the protection of divine Providence, we mutually pledge to each other our Lives, our Fortunes and our sacred Honor.

JOHN HANCOCK

NEW HAMPSHIRE
Josiah Bartlett,
Wm. Whipple,
Matthew Thornton.

MASSACHUSETTS BAY
Saml. Adams,
John Adams,
Robt. Treat Paine,
Elbridge Gerry.

RHODE ISLAND
Step. Hopkins,
William Ellery.

CONNECTICUT
Roger Sherman,
Samuel Huntington,
Wm. Williams,
Oliver Wolcott.

NEW YORK
Wm. Floyd,
Phil. Livingston,
Frans. Lewis,
Lewis Morris.

NEW JERSEY
Richd. Stockton,
In. Witherspoon,
Fras. Hopkinson,
John Hart,
Abra. Clark.

PENNSYLVANIA
Robt. Morris,
Benjamin Rush,
Benjamin Franklin,
John Morton,
Geo. Clymer,
Jas. Smith,
Geo. Taylor,
James Wilson,
Geo. Ross.

DELAWARE
Caesar Rodney,
Geo. Read,
Tho. M'kean.

MARYLAND
Samuel Chase,
Wm. Paca,
Thos. Stone,
Charles Caroll of
Carollton.

VIRGINIA
George Wythe,
Richard Henry Lee,
Th. Jefferson,
Benjamin Harrison,
Thos. Nelson, jr.,
Francis Lightfoot Lee,
Carter Braxton.

NORTH CAROLINA
Wm. Hooper,
Joseph Hewes,
John Penn.

SOUTH CAROLINA
Edward Rutledge,
Thos. Heyward, Junr.,
Thomas Lynch, jnr.,
Arthur Middleton.

The Constitution of the United States of America

PREAMBLE

WE THE PEOPLE of the United States, in Order to form a more perfect Union, establish Justice, insure domestic Tranquility, provide for the common defence, promote the general Welfare, and secure the Blessings of Liberty to ourselves and our Posterity, do ordain and establish this Constitution for the United States of America.

ARTICLE 1

Section 1

All legislative Powers herein granted shall be vested in a Congress of the United States, which shall consist of a Senate and House of Representatives.

Section 2

The House of Representatives shall be composed of Members chosen every second Year by the People of the several States, and the Electors in each State shall have the Qualifications requisite for Electors of the most numerous Branch of the State Legislature.

No person shall be a Representative who shall not have attained to the Age of twenty five Years, and been seven Years a Citizen of the United States, and who shall not, when elected, be an Inhabitant of that State in which he shall be chosen.

Representatives and direct Taxes shall be apportioned among the several States which may be included within this Union, according to their respective Numbers which shall be determined by adding to the whole Number of free Persons, including those bound to Service for a Term of Years, and excluding Indians not taxed, three fifths of all other Persons. The actual Enumeration shall be made within three Years after the first Meeting of the Congress of the United States, and within every subsequent Term ten Years, in such Manner as they shall by Law direct. The Number of Representatives shall not exceed one for every thirty Thousand, but each State shall have at Least one Representative; and until such enumeration shall be made, the State of New Hampshire shall be entitled to chuse three, Massachusetts eight, Rhode-Island and Providence Plantations one, Connecticut five, New-York six, New Jersey four, Pennsylvania eight, Delaware one, Maryland six, Virginia ten, North Carolina five, South Carolina five, and Georgia three.

When vacancies happen in the Representation from any State, the Executive Authority thereof shall issue Writs of Election to fill such Vacancies.

The House of Representatives shall chuse their speaker and other Officers; and shall have the sole Power of Impeachment.

Section 3

The Senate of the United States shall be composed of two Senators from each State chosen by the Legislature thereof, for six Years; and each Senator shall have one Vote.

Immediately after they shall be assembled in Consequence of the first Election, they shall be divided as equally as may be into three Classes. The Seats of the Senators of the first Class shall be vacated at the Expiration of the second year, of the second Class at the Expiration of the fourth Year, and of the third Class at the Expiration of the sixth Year, so that one third may be chosen every second Year and if Vacancies happen by Resignation, or otherwise, during the Recess of the Legislature of any State, the Executive thereof may make temporary Appointments until the next Meeting of the Legislature, which shall then fill such Vacancies.

No Person shall be a Senator who shall not have attained to the Age of thirty Years, and been nine Years a Citizen of the United States, and who shall not, when elected, be an Inhabitant of that State for which he shall be chosen.

The Vice President of the United States shall be President of the Senate, but shall have no Vote, unless they be equally divided.

The Senate shall chuse their other Officers, and also a President pro tempore, in the Absence of the Vice President, or when he shall exercise the Office of President of the United States.

The Senate shall have the sole Power to try all Impeachments. When sitting for that Purpose, they shall be on Oath or Affirmation. When the President of the United States is tried, the Chief Justice shall preside: And no Person shall be convicted without the Concurrence of two thirds of the Members present.

Judgment in Cases of Impeachment shall not extend further than to removal from Office, and disqualification to hold and enjoy any Office of honor, Trust or Profit under the United States; but the Party convicted shall nevertheless be liable and subject to Indictment, Trial, Judgment and Punishment, according to Law.

Section 4

The Times, Places and Manner of holding Elections for Senators and Representatives, shall be pre-scribed in each State by the Legislature thereof; but the Congress may at any time by law make or alter such Regulations, except as to the Places of chusing Senators.

The Congress shall assemble at least once in every Year, and such Meeting shall be on the first Monday in December, unless they shall by Law appoint a different Day.

Section 5

Each House shall be the Judge of the Elections, Returns and Qualifications of its own Members, and a Majority of each shall constitute a Quorum to do Business; but a smaller Number may adjourn from day to day, and may be authorized to compel the Attendance of absent Members, in such Manner, and under such Penalties as each House may provide.

Each House may determine the Rules of its Proceedings, punish its Members for disorderly Behaviour, and with the Concurrence of two thirds, expel a Member.

Each House shall keep a journal of its Proceedings, and from time to time publish the same, excepting such Parts as may in their judgment require Secrecy; and the Yeas and Nays of the Members of either House on any question shall, at the Desire of one fifth of those present, be entered on the Journal.

Neither House, during the Session of Congress, shall, without the Consent of the other, adjourn for more than three days, nor to any other Place than that in which the two Houses shall be sitting.

Section 6

The Senators and Representatives shall receive a Compensation for their Services, to be ascertained by Law, and paid out of the Treasury of the United States. They shall in all Cases, except Treason, Felony and Breach of the Peace, be privileged from Arrest during their Attendance at the Session of their respective Houses, and in going to and returning from the same; and for any Speech or Debate in either House, they shall not be questioned in any other Place.

No Senator or Representative shall, during the Time for which he was elected, be appointed to any civil Office under the Authority of the United States, which shall have been created, or the Emoluments whereof shall have been encreased during such time; and no Person holding any Office under the United States, shall be a Member of either House during his Continuance in Office.

Section 7

All Bills for raising Revenue shall originate in the House of Representatives; but the Senate may propose or concur with Amendments as on other Bills.

Every Bill which shall have passed the House of Representatives and the Senate, shall, before it become a Law, be presented to the President of the United States; If he approves he shall sign it, but if not he shall return it, with his Objections to that House in which it shall have originated, who shall enter the Objections at large on their journal, and proceed to reconsider it. If after such Reconsideration two thirds of that House shall agree to pass the Bill, it shall be sent, together with the Objections, to the other House, by which it shall likewise be reconsidered, and if approved by two thirds of that House, it shall become a Law. But in all such Cases the Votes of both Houses shall be determined by Yeas and Nays, and the Names of the Persons voting for and against the Bill shall be entered on the Journal of each House respectively. If any Bill shall not be returned by the President within ten Days (Sundays excepted) after it shall have been presented to him, the Same shall be a Law, in like Manner as if he had signed it, unless the Congress by their Adjournment prevent its Return, in which Case it shall not be a Law.

Every Order, Resolution, or Vote to which the Concurrence of the Senate and House of Representatives may be necessary (except on a question of Adjournment) shall be presented to the President of the United States; and before the Same shall take Effect, shall be approved by him, or being disapproved by him, shall be repassed by two thirds of the Senate and House of Representatives, according to the Rules and Limitations prescribed in the Case of a Bill.

Section 8

The Congress shall have Power To lay and collect Taxes, Duties, Imposts and Excises, to pay the Debts and provide for the common Defence and general Welfare of the United States; but all Duties, Imposts and Excises shall be uniform throughout the United States;

To borrow Money on the credit of the United States;

To regulate Commerce with foreign Nations, and among the several States, and with the Indian Tribes;

To establish a uniform Rule of Naturalization, and uniform Laws on the subject of Bankruptcies throughout the United States;

To coin Money, regulate the Value thereof, and of foreign Coin, and fix the Standard of Weights and Measures;

To provide for the Punishment of counterfeiting the Securities and current Coin of the United States;

To establish Post Offices and post Roads;

To promote the Progress of Science and useful Arts, by securing for limited Times to Authors and Inventors the exclusive Right to their respective Writings and Discoveries;

To constitute Tribunals inferior to the supreme Court;

To define and punish Piracies and Felonies committed on the high Seas, and Offences against the Law of Nations;

To declare War, grant Letters of Marque and Reprisal, and make Rules concerning Captures on Land and Water;

To raise and support Armies, but no Appropriation of Money to that Use shall be for a longer Term than two Years;

To provide and maintain a Navy;

To make Rules for the Government and Regulation of the land and naval Forces;

To provide for calling forth the Militia to execute the Laws of the Union, suppress Insurrections and repel Invasions;

To provide for organizing, arming, and disciplining, the Militia, and for governing such Part of them as may be employed in the Service of the United States, reserving to the States respectively, the Appointment of the Officers, and the Authority of training the Militia according to the discipline prescribed by Congress;

To exercise exclusive Legislation in all Cases whatsoever, over such District (not exceeding ten Miles square) as may, by Cession of particular States, and the Acceptance of Congress, become the Seat of the Government of the United States, and to exercise like Authority over all Places purchased by the Consent of the Legislature of the State in which the Same shall be for the Erection of Forts, Magazines, Arsenals, dock-Yards, and other needful Buildings;—And

To make all Laws which shall be necessary and proper for carrying into Execution the foregoing Powers, and all other Powers vested by this Constitution in the Government of the United States, or in any Department or Officer thereof.

Section 9

The Migration or Importation of such Persons as any of the States now existing shall think proper to admit, shall not be prohibited by the Congress prior to the Year one thousand eight hundred and eight, but a Tax or duty may be imposed on such Importation, not exceeding ten dollars for each Person.

The Privilege of the Writ of Habeas Corpus shall not be suspended, unless when in Cases of Rebellion or Invasion the public Safety may require it.

No Bill of Attainder or ex post facto Law shall be passed.

No Capitation, or other direct, Tax shall be laid, unless in Proportion to the Census or Enumeration herein before directed to be taken.

No Tax or Duty shall be laid on Articles exported from any State.

No Preference shall be given by any Regulation of Commerce or Revenue to the Ports of one State over those of another; nor shall Vessels bound to, or from, one State, be obliged to enter, clear, or pay Duties in another.

No Money shall be drawn from the Treasury, but in Consequence of Appropriations made by Law; and a regular Statement and Account of the Receipts and Expenditures of all public Money shall be published from time to time.

No Title of Nobility shall be granted by the United States: And no Person holding any Office of Profit or Trust under them, shall, without the Consent of the Congress, accept of any present, Emolument, Office, or Title, of any kind whatever, from any King, Prince, or foreign State.

Section 10

No state shall enter into any Treaty, Alliance, or Confederation; grant Letters of Marque and Reprisal; coin Money; emit Bills of Credit; make any Thing but gold and silver Coin a Tender in Payment of Debts; pass any Bill of Attainder, ex post facto Law, or Law impairing the Obligation of Contracts, or grant any Title of Nobility.

No State shall, without the Consent of the Congress, lay any Imposts or Duties on Imports or Exports, except what may be absolutely necessary for executing its inspection Laws: and the net Produce of all Duties and Imposts, laid by any State on Imports or Exports, shall be for the Use of the Treasury of the United States, and all such Laws shall be subject to the Revision and Control of the Congress.

No State shall, without the Consent of Congress, lay any Duty of Tonnage, keep Troops, or Ships of War in time of Peace, enter into any Agreement or Compact with another State, or with a foreign Power, or engage in War, unless actually invaded, or in such imminent Danger as will not admit of delay.

ARTICLE II
Section 1

The executive Power shall be vested in a President of the United States of America. He shall hold his Office during the Term of four Years, and, together with the Vice President, chosen for the same Term, be elected as follows.

Each State shall appoint, in such Manner as the Legislature thereof may direct, a Number of Electors, equal to the whole Number of Senators and Representatives to which the State may be entitled in the Congress; but no Senator or Representative, or Person holding an Office of Trust or Profit under the United States, shall be appointed an Elector.

The Electors shall meet in their respective States, and vote by Ballot for two Persons, of whom one at least shall not be an Inhabitant of the same State with themselves. And they shall make a List of all the Persons voted for, and, of the Number of Votes for each; which List they shall sign and certify, and transmit sealed to the Seat of the Government of the United States, directed to the President of the Senate. The President of the Senate shall, in the Presence of the Senate and House of Representatives, open all the Certificates, and the Votes shall then be counted. The Person having the greatest Number of Votes shall be the President, if such Number be a Majority of the whole Number of Electors appointed; and if there be more than one who have such Majority, and have an equal Number of Votes, then the House of Representatives shall immediately chuse by Ballot one of them for President; and if no Person have a Majority, then from the five highest on the List the said House shall in like Manner chuse the President. But in chusing the President, the Votes shall be taken by States, the Representation from each State having one Vote; A quorum for this Purpose shall consist of a Member or Members from two thirds of the States, and a Majority of all the States shall be necessary to a Choice. In every Case, after the Choice of the President, the Person having the greatest Number of Votes of the Electors shall be the Vice President. But if there should remain two or more who have equal Votes, the Senate shall chuse from them by Ballot the Vice President.

The Congress may determine the Time of chusing the Electors, and the Day on which they shall give their Votes; which Day shall be the same throughout the United States.

No Person except a natural born Citizen, or a Citizen of the United States, at the time of the Adoption of this Constitution, shall be eligible to the Office of President; neither shall any Person be eligible to that Office who shall not have attained to the Age of thirty five Years, and been fourteen Years a Resident within the United States.

In Case of the Removal of the President from Office, or of his Death, Resignation, or Inability to discharge the Powers and Duties of the said Office, the Same shall devolve on the Vice President, and the Congress may by Law provide for the Case of Removal, Death, Resignation or Inability, both of the President and Vice President, declaring what Officer shall then act as President, and such Officer shall act accordingly, until the Disability be removed, or a President shall be elected.

The President shall, at stated Times, receive for his Services, a Compensation, which shall neither be encreased nor diminished during the Period for which he shall have been elected, and he shall not receive within that Period any other Emolument from the United States, or any of them.

Before he enter on the Execution of his Office, he shall take the following Oath or Affirmation—"I do solemnly swear (or affirm) that I will faithfully execute the Office of President of the United States, and will to the best of my Ability, preserve, protect and defend the Constitution of the United States."

Section 2

The President shall be Commander in Chief of the Army, and Navy of the United States, and of the Militia of the several States, when called into the actual Service of the United States; he may require the Opinion, in writing, of the principal Officer in each of the executive Departments, upon any Subject relating to the Duties of their respective Offices, and he shall have Power to grant Reprieves and Pardons for Offences against the United States, except in Cases of Impeachment.

He shall have Power, by and with the Advice and Consent of the Senate, to make Treaties, provided two thirds of the Senators present concur; and he shall nominate, and by and with the Advice and Consent of the Senate, shall appoint Ambassadors, other public Ministers and Consuls, Judges of the supreme Court, and all other Officers of the United States, whose Appointments are not herein otherwise provided for, and which shall be established by Law: but the Congress may by Law vest the Appointment of such inferior Officers, as they think proper, in the President alone, in the Courts of Law, or in the Heads of Departments.

The President shall have Power to fill up all Vacancies that may happen during the Recess of the Senate, by granting Commissions which shall expire at the end of their next Session.

Section 3

He shall from time to time give to the Congress Information of the State of the Union, and recommend to their Consideration such Measures as he shall judge necessary and expedient; he may, on extraordinary Occasions, convene both Houses, or either of them, and in Case of Disagreement between them, with Respect to the Time of Adjournment, he may adjourn them to such Time as he shall think proper; he shall receive Ambassadors and other public Ministers; he shall take Care that the Laws be faithfully executed, and shall Commission all the Officers of the United States.

Section 4

The President, Vice President and all civil Officers of the United States, shall be removed from Office on Impeachment for, and Conviction of, Treason, Bribery, or other high Crimes and Misdemeanors.

ARTICLE III
Section 1

The judicial Power of the United States, shall be vested in one supreme Court, and in such inferior Courts as the Congress may from time to time ordain and establish. The Judges, both of the supreme and inferior Courts, shall hold their Offices during good Behaviour, and shall, at stated Times, receive for their Services, a Compensation, which shall not be diminished during their Continuance in Office.

Section 2

The judicial Power shall extend to all Cases, in Law and Equity, arising under this Constitution, the Laws of the United States, and Treaties made, or which shall be made, under their Authority;—to all Cases affecting Ambassadors, other public Ministers and Consuls;—to all Cases of admiralty and maritime Jurisdiction;—to Controversies to which the United States shall be a Party;—to Controversies between two or more States;—between a State and Citizens of another State;—between Citizens of different States,—between Citizens of the same State claiming Lands under Grants of different States,—and between a State, or the Citizens thereof, and foreign States, Citizens of Subjects.

In all Cases affecting Ambassadors, other public Ministers and Consuls, and those in which a State shall be Party, the supreme Court shall have original Jurisdiction. In all the other Cases before mentioned, the supreme Court shall have appellate Jurisdiction, both as to Law and Fact, with such Exceptions, and under such Regulations as the Congress shall make.

The Trial of all Crimes, except in Cases of Impeachment, shall be by Jury; and such Trial shall be held in the State where the said Crimes shall have been committed; but when not committed within any State, the Trial shall be at such Place or Places as the Congress may by Law have directed.

Section 3

Treason against the United States, shall consist only in levying War against them, or in adhering to their Enemies, giving them Aid and Comfort. No Person shall be convicted of Treason unless on the Testimony of two Witnesses to the same overt Act, or on Confession in open Court.

The Congress shall have Power to declare the Punishment of Treason, but no Attainder of Treason shall work Corruption of Blood, or Forfeiture except during the Life of the Person attainted.

ARTICLE IV
Section 1

Full Faith and Credit shall be given in each State to the public Acts, Records, and judicial Proceedings of every other State. And the Congress may by general Laws prescribe the Manner in which such Acts, Records and Proceedings shall be proved, and the Effect thereof.

Section 2

The Citizens of each State shall be entitled to all Privileges and Immunities of Citizens in the several States.

A Person charged in any State with Treason, Felony, or other Crime, who shall flee from Justice, and be found in another State, shall on Demand of the executive Authority of the State from which he fled, be delivered up, to be removed to the State having Jurisdiction of the Crime.

No Person held to Service or Labour in one State under the Laws thereof, escaping into another, shall, in Consequence of any Law or Regulation therein, be discharged from such Service or Labour, but shall be delivered up on Claim of the Party to whom such Service or Labour may be due.

Section 3

New States may be admitted by the Congress into this Union; but no new State shall be formed or erected within the Jurisdiction of any other State; nor any State be formed by the Junction of two or more States, or Parts of States, without the Consent of the Legislatures of the States concerned as well as of the Congress.

The Congress shall have Power to dispose of and make all needful Rules and Regulations respecting the Territory or other Property belonging to the United States; and nothing in this Constitution shall be so construed as to Prejudice any Claims of the United States, or of any particular State.

Section 4

The United States shall guarantee to every State in this Union a Republican Form of Government, and shall protect each of them against Invasion, and on Application of the Legislature, or of the Executive (when the Legislature cannot be convened) against domestic Violence.

ARTICLE V

The Congress, whenever two thirds of both Houses shall deem it necessary, shall propose Amendments to this Constitution, or, on the Application of the Legislatures of two thirds of the several States, shall call a Convention for proposing Amendments, which, in either Case, shall be valid to all Intents and Purposes, as Part of this Constitution, when ratified by the Legislatures of three fourths of the several States, or by Conventions in three fourths thereof, as the one or the other Mode of Ratification may be proposed by the Congress; Provided that no Amendment which may be made prior to the Year One thousand eight hundred and eight shall in any Manner affect the first and fourth Clauses in the Ninth Section of the first Article; and that no State, without its Consent, shall be deprived of its equal Suffrage in the Senate.

ARTICLE VI

All Debts contracted and Engagements entered into, before the Adoption of this Constitution, shall be as valid against the United States under this Constitution, as under the Confederation.

This Constitution, and the laws of the United States which shall be made in Pursuance thereof; and all Treaties made, or which shall be made, under the Authority of the United States, shall be the supreme Law of the Land; and the Judges in every State shall be bound thereby, any Thing in the Constitution or Laws of any State to the Contrary notwithstanding.

The Senators and Representatives before mentioned, and the Members of the several State Legislatures, and all executive and judicial Officers, both of the United States and of the several States, shall be bound by Oath or Affirmation, to support this Constitution; but no religious Test shall ever be required as a Qualification to any Office or public Trust under the United States.

ARTICLE VII

The Ratification of the Conventions of nine States, shall be sufficient for the Establishment of this Constitution between the States so ratifying the Same.

Done in Convention by the Unanimous Consent of the States present the Seventeenth Day of September in the Year of our Lord one thousand seven hundred and Eighty seven and of the Independence of the United States of America the Twelfth. In witness whereof we have hereunto subscribed our Names,

Go. WASHINGTON
Presid't. and deputy from Virginia

Attest
WILLIAM JACKSON
Secretary

Articles in addition to, and amendment of the Constitution of the United States of America, proposed by Congress and ratified by the Legislatures of the several states, pursuant to the Fifth Article of the original Constitution.

(The first ten amendments were passed by Congress on September 25, 1789, and were ratified on December 15, 1791.)

AMENDMENT I

Congress shall make no law respecting an establishment of religion, or prohibiting the free exercise thereof; or abridging the freedom of speech, or of the press; or the right of the people peaceably to assemble, and to petition the Government for a redress of grievances.

AMENDMENT II

A well regulated Militia, being necessary to the security of a free State, the right of the people to keep and bear Arms, shall not be infringed.

AMENDMENT III

No Soldier shall, in time of peace be quartered in any house, without the consent of the Owner, nor in time of war, but in a manner to be prescribed by law.

AMENDMENT IV

The right of the people to be secure in their persons, houses, papers, and effects, against unreasonable searches and seizures, shall not be violated, and no warrants shall issue, but upon probable cause, supported by Oath or affirmation, and particularly describing the place to be searched, and the persons or things to be seized.

AMENDMENT V

No person shall be held to answer for a capital, or otherwise infamous crime, unless on a presentment or indictment of a Grand Jury, except in cases arising in the land or naval forces, or in the Militia, when in actual service in time of War or public danger; nor shall any person be subject for the same offence to be twice put in jeopardy of life or limb; nor shall be compelled in any criminal case to be a witness against himself, nor be deprived of life, liberty, or property, without due process of law; nor shall private property be taken for public use, without just compensation.

AMENDMENT VI

In all criminal prosecutions, the accused shall enjoy the right to a speedy and public trial, by an impartial jury of the State and district wherein the crime shall have been committed, which district shall have been previously ascertained by law, and to be informed of the nature and cause of the accusation; to be confronted with the witnesses against him; to have compulsory process for obtaining witnesses in his favor, and to have the assistance of counsel for his defence.

AMENDMENT VII

In Suits at common law, where the value in controversy shall exceed twenty dollars, the right of trial by jury shall be preserved, and no fact tried by a jury, shall be otherwise re-examined in any Court of the United States, than according to the rules of the common law.

AMENDMENT VIII

Excessive bail shall not be required, nor excessive fines imposed, nor cruel and unusual punishments inflicted.

AMENDMENT IX

The enumeration in the Constitution, of certain rights, shall not be construed to deny or disparage others retained by the people.

AMENDMENT X

The powers not delegated to the United States by the Constitution, nor prohibited by it to the States, are reserved to the States respectively, or to the people.

AMENDMENT XI
[RATIFIED ON FEBRUARY 7, 1795]

The Judicial power of the United States shall not be construed to extend to any suit in law or equity, commenced or prosecuted against one of the United States by Citizens of another State, or by Citizens or Subjects of any Foreign State.

AMENDMENT XII
[RATIFIED ON JUNE 15, 1804]

The Electors shall meet in their respective states, and vote by ballot for President and Vice-President, one of whom, at least, shall not be an inhabitant of the same state with themselves; they shall name in their ballots the person voted for as President, and in distinct ballots the person voted for as Vice-President, and they shall make distinct lists of all persons voted for as President, and of all persons voted for as Vice-President, and of the number of votes for each, which lists they shall sign and certify, and transmit sealed to the seat of the government of the United States, directed to the President of the Senate;—The President of the Senate shall, in the presence of the Senate and House of Representatives, open all the certificates and the votes shall then be counted;—The person having the greatest number of votes for President, shall be the President, if such number be a majority of the whole number of Electors appointed; and if no person have such majority; then from the persons having the highest numbers not exceeding three on the list of those voted for as President, the House of Representatives shall choose immediately, by ballot, the President. But in choosing the President, the votes shall be taken by states, the representation from each state having one vote; a quorum for this purpose shall consist of a member or members from two-thirds of the states, and a majority of all the states shall be necessary to a choice. And if the House of Representatives shall not choose a President whenever the right of choice shall devolve upon them, before the fourth day of March next following, then the Vice-President shall act as President, as in the case of the death or other constitutional disability of the President.——The person having the greatest number of votes as Vice-President, shall be the Vice-President, if such number be a major-ity of the whole number of Electors appointed, and if no person have a majority, then from the two highest numbers on the list, the Senate shall choose the Vice-President; a quorum for the purpose shall consist of two-thirds of the whole number of Senators, and a majority of the whole number shall be necessary to a choice. But no person constitutionally ineligible to the office of President shall be eligible to that of Vice-President of the United States.

AMENDMENT XIII
[RATIFIED ON DECEMBER 6, 1865]
Section 1

Neither slavery nor involuntary servitude, except as a punishment for crime whereof the party shall have been duly convicted, shall exist within the United States, or any place subject to their jurisdiction.

Section 2

Congress shall have power to enforce this article by appropriate legislation.

AMENDMENT XIV
[RATIFIED ON JULY 9, 1868]
Section 1

All persons born or naturalized in the United States, and subject to the jurisdiction thereof, are citizens of the United States and of the State wherein they reside. No State shall make or enforce any law which shall abridge the privileges or immunities of citizens of the United States; nor shall any State deprive any person of life, liberty, or property, without due process of law; nor deny to any person within its jurisdiction the equal protection of the laws.

Section 2

Representatives shall be apportioned among the several States according to their respective numbers, counting the whole number of persons in each State, excluding Indians not taxed. But when the right to vote at any election for the choice of electors for President and Vice President of the United States, Representatives in Congress, the Executive and Judicial offi-cers of a State, or the members of the Legislature thereof, is denied to any of the male inhab-itants of such State, being twenty-one years of age, and citizens of the United States, or in any way abridged, except for participation in rebellion, or other crime, the basis of representation therein shall be reduced in the proportion which the number of such male citizens shall bear to the whole number of male citizens twenty-one years of age in such State.

Section 3

No person shall be a Senator or Representative in Congress, or elector of President and Vice President, or hold any office, civil or military, under the United States, or under any State, who, having previously taken an oath, as a member of Congress, or as an officer of the United States, or as a member of any State legislature, or as an executive or judicial officer of any State, to support the Constitution of the United States, shall have engaged in insurrection or rebellion against the same, or given aid or comfort to the enemies thereof. But Congress may by a vote of two-thirds of each House, remove such disability.

Section 4

The validity of the public debt of the United States, authorized by law, including debts incurred for payment of pensions and bounties for services in suppressing insurrection or rebellion, shall not be questioned. But neither the United States nor any State shall assume or pay any debt or obligation incurred in aid of insurrection or rebellion against the United States, or any claim for the loss or emancipation of any slave, but all such debts, obligations and claims shall be held illegal and void.

Section 5

The Congress shall have power to enforce, by appropriate legislation, the provisions of this article.

AMENDMENT XV
[RATIFIED ON FEBRUARY 3, 1870]

Section 1

The right of citizens of the United States to vote shall not be denied or abridged by the United States or by any State on account of race, color, or previous condition of servitude.

Section 2

The Congress shall have power to enforce this article by appropriate legislation.

AMENDMENT XVI
[RATIFIED ON FEBRUARY 3, 1913]

The Congress shall have power to lay and collect taxes on incomes, from whatever source derived, without apportionment among the several States, and without regard to any census or enumeration.

AMENDMENT XVII
[RATIFIED ON APRIL 8, 1913]

The Senate of the United States shall be composed of two Senators from each State, elected by the people thereof, for six years; and each Senator shall have one vote. The electors in each State shall have the qualifications requisite for electors of the most numerous branch of the State legislatures.

When vacancies happen in the representation of any State in the Senate, the executive authority of such State shall issue writs of election to fill such vacancies: Provided, That the legislature of any State may empower the executive thereof to make temporary appointments until the people fill the vacancies by election as the legislature may direct.

This amendment shall not be so construed as to affect the election or term of any Senator chosen before it becomes valid as part of the Constitution.

AMENDMENT VXIII
[RATIFIED ON JANUARY 16, 1919]

Section 1

After one year from the ratification of this article the manufacture, sale, or transportation of intoxicating liquors within, the importation thereof into, or the exportation thereof from the United States and all territory subject to the jurisdiction thereof for beverage purposes is hereby prohibited.

Section 2

The Congress and the several States shall have concurrent power to enforce this article by appropriate legislation.

Section 3

This article shall be inoperative unless it shall have been ratified as an amendment to the Constitution by the legislatures of the several States, as provided in the Constitution, within seven years from the date of the submission hereof to the States by the Congress.

AMENDMENT XIX
[RATIFIED ON AUGUST 18, 1920]

The right of citizens of the United States to vote shall not be denied or abridged by the United States or by any State on account of sex.

Congress shall have power to enforce this article by appropriate legislation.

AMENDMENT XX
[RATIFIED ON FEBRUARY 6, 1933]

Section 1

The terms of the President and Vice President shall end at noon on the 20th day of January, and the terms of Senators and Representatives at noon on the 3d day of January, of the years in which such terms would have ended if this article had not been ratified; and the terms of their successors shall then begin.

Section 2

The Congress shall assemble at least once in every year, and such meeting shall begin at noon on the 3d day of January, unless they shall by law appoint a different day.

Section 3

If, at the time fixed for the beginning of the term of the President, the President elect shall have died, the Vice President elect shall become President. If a President shall not have been chosen before the time fixed for the beginning of his term, or if the President elect shall have failed to qualify, then the Vice President elect shall act as President until a President shall have qualified; and the Congress may by law provide for the case wherein neither a President elect nor a Vice President elect shall have qualified, declaring who shall then act as President, or the manner in which one who is to act shall be selected, and such person shall act accordingly until a President or Vice President shall have qualified.

Section 4

The Congress may by law provide for the case of the death of any of the persons from whom the House of Representatives may choose a President whenever the rights of choice shall have devolved upon them, and for the case of the death of any of the persons from whom the Senate may choose a Vice President whenever the right of choice shall have devolved upon them.

Section 5

Sections 1 and 2 shall take effect on the 15th day of October following the ratification of this article.

Section 6

This article shall be inoperative unless it shall have been ratified as an amendment to the Constitution by the legislatures of three-fourths of the several States within seven years from the date of its submission.

AMENDMENT XXI
[RATIFIED ON DECEMBER 5, 1933]
Section 1

The eighteenth article of amendment to the Constitution of the United States is hereby repealed.

Section 2

The transportation or importation into any State, Territory, or possession of the United States for delivery or use therein of intoxicating liquors, in violation of the laws thereof, is hereby prohibited.

Section 3

This article shall be inoperative unless it shall have been ratified as an amendment to the Constitution by conventions in the several States, as provided in the Constitution, within seven years from the date of the submission hereof to the States by the Congress.

AMENDMENT XXII
[RATIFIED ON FEBRUARY 27, 1951]

No person shall be elected to the office of the President more than twice, and no person who has held the office of President, or acted as President, for more than two years of a term to which some other person was elected President shall be elected to the office of the President more than once. But this Article shall not apply to any person holding the office of President when this Article was proposed by the Congress, and shall not prevent any person who may be holding the office of President, or acting as President, during the term within which this Article becomes operative from holding the office of President or acting as President during the remainder of such term.

AMENDMENT XXIII
[RATIFIED ON MARCH 29, 1961]

Section 1

The District constituting the seat of Government of the United States shall appoint in such manner as the Congress may direct:

A number of electors of President and Vice President equal to the whole number of Senators and Representatives in Congress to which the District would be entitled if it were a State, but in no event more than the least populous State; they shall be in addition to those appointed by the States, but they shall be considered, for the purposes of the election of President and Vice President, to be electors appointed by a State; and they shall meet in the District and perform such duties as provided by the twelfth article of amendment.

Section 2

The Congress shall have power to enforce this article by appropriate legislation.

AMENDMENT XXIV
[RATIFIED ON JANUARY 23, 1964]

Section 1

The right of citizens of the United States to vote in any primary or other election for President or Vice President, for electors for President or Vice President, or for Senator or Representative in Congress, shall not be denied or abridged by the United States or any State by reason of failure to pay any poll tax or other tax.

Section 2

The Congress shall have power to enforce this article by appropriate legislation.

AMENDMENT XXV
[RATIFIED ON FEBRUARY 10, 1967]
Section 1

In case of the removal of the President from office or of his death or resignation, the Vice President shall become President.

Section 2

Whenever there is a vacancy in the office of the Vice President, the President shall nominate a Vice President who shall take office upon confirmation by a majority vote of both Houses of Congress.

Section 3

Whenever the President transmits to the President pro tempore of the Senate and the Speaker of the House of Representatives his written declaration that he is unable to discharge the powers and duties of his office, and until he transmits to them a written declaration to the contrary, such powers and duties shall be discharged by the Vice President as Acting President.

Section 4

Whenever the Vice President and a majority of either the principal officers of the executive departments or of such other body as Congress may by law provide, transmit to the President pro tempore of the Senate and the Speaker of the House of Representatives their written declaration that the President is unable to discharge the powers and duties of his office, the Vice President shall immediately assume the powers and duties of the office as Acting President.

Thereafter, when the President transmits to the President pro tempore of the Senate and the Speaker of the House of Representatives his written declaration that no inability exists, he shall resume the powers and duties of his office unless the Vice President and a majority of either the principal officers of the executive department or of such other body as Congress may by law provide, transmit within four days to the President pro tempore of the Senate and the Speaker of the House of Representatives their written declaration that the President is unable to discharge the powers and duties of his office. Thereupon Congress shall decide the issue, assembling within forty-eight hours for that purpose if not in session. If the Congress, within twenty-one days after receipt of the latter written declaration, or, if Congress is not in session, within twenty-one days after Congress is required to assemble, determines by two-thirds vote of both Houses that the President is unable to discharge the powers and duties of his office, the Vice President shall continue to discharge the same as Acting President; otherwise, the President shall resume the powers and duties of his office.

AMENDMENT XXVI
[RATIFIED ON JULY 1, 1971]
Section 1

The right of citizens of the United States, who are eighteen years of age or older, to vote shall not be denied or abridged by the United States or by any State on account of age.

Section 2

The Congress shall have power to enforce this article by appropriate legislation.

AMENDMENT XXVII
[RATIFIED ON MAY 7, 1992]

No law varying the compensation for the services of Senators and Representatives shall take effect until an election of Representatives shall have intervened.

The Federalist No. 10
November 22, 1787
James Madison

TO THE PEOPLE OF THE STATE OF NEW YORK.

Among the numerous advantages promised by a well constructed Union, none deserves to be more accurately developed than its tendency to break and control the violence of faction. The friend of popular governments, never finds himself so much alarmed for their character and fate, as when he contemplates their propensity to this dangerous vice. He will not fail therefore to set a due value on any plan which, without violating the principles to which he is attached, provides a proper cure for it. The instability, injustice and confusion introduced into the public councils, have in truth been the mortal diseases under which popular governments have every where perished; as they continue to be the favorite and fruitful topics from which the adversaries to liberty derive their most specious declamations. The valuable improvements made by the American Constitutions on the popular models, both ancient and modern, cannot certainly be too much admired; but it would be an unwarrantable partiality, to contend that they have as effectually obviated the danger on this side as was wished and expected. Complaints are every where heard from our most considerate and virtuous citizens, equally the friends of public and private faith, and of public and personal liberty; that our governments are too unstable; that the public good is disregarded in the conflicts of rival parties; and that measures are too often decided, not according to the rules of justice, and the rights of the minor party; but by the superior force of an interested and over-bearing majority. However anxiously we may wish that these complaints had no foundation, the evidence of known facts will not permit us to deny that they are in some degree true. It will be found indeed, on a candid review of our situation, that some of the distresses under which we labor, have been erroneously charged on the operation of our governments; but it will be found, at the same time, that other causes will not alone account for many of our heaviest misfortunes; and particularly, for that prevailing and increasing distrust of public engagements, and alarm for private rights, which are echoed from one end of the continent to the other. These must be chiefly, if not wholly, effects of the unsteadiness and injustice, with which a factious spirit has tainted our public administrations.

By a faction I understand a number of citizens, whether amounting to a majority or minority of the whole, who are united and actuated by some common impulse of passion, or of interest, adverse to the rights of other citizens, or to the permanent and aggregate interests of the community.

There are two methods of curing the mischiefs of faction: the one, by removing its causes; the other, by controlling its effects.

There are again two methods of removing the causes of faction: the one by destroying the liberty which is essential to its existence; the other, by giving to every citizen the same opinions, the same passions, and the same interests.

It could never be more truly said than of the first remedy, that it is worse than the disease. Liberty is to faction, what air is to fire, an aliment without which it instantly expires. But it could not be a less folly to abolish liberty, which is essential to political life, because it nourishes faction, than it would be to wish the annihilation of air, which is essential to animal life, because it imparts to fire its destructive agency.

The second expedient is as impracticable, as the first would be unwise. As long as the reason of man continues fallible, and he is at liberty to exercise it, different opinions will be formed. As long as the connection subsists between his reason and his self-love, his opinions and his passions will have a reciprocal influence on each other; and the former will be objects to which the latter will attach themselves. The diversity in the faculties of men from which the rights of property originate, is not less an insuperable obstacle to a uniformity of interests. The protection of these faculties is the first object of Government. From the protection of different and unequal faculties of acquiring property, the possession of different degrees and kinds of property immediately results: and from the influence of these on the sentiments and views of the respective proprietors, ensues a division of the society into different interests and parties.

The latent causes of faction are thus sown in the nature of man; and we see them every where brought into different degrees of activity, according to the different circumstances of civil society. A zeal for different opinions concerning religion, concerning Government and many other points, as well of speculation as of practice; an attachment to different leaders ambitiously contending for pre-eminence and power; or to persons of other descriptions whose fortunes have been interesting to the human passions, have in turn divided mankind into parties, inflamed them with mutual animosity, and rendered them much more disposed to vex and oppress each other, than to cooperate for their common good. So strong is this propensity of mankind to fall into mutual animosities, that where no substantial occasion presents itself, the most frivolous and fanciful distinctions have been sufficient to kindle their unfriendly passions, and excite their most violent conflicts. But the most common and durable source of factions, has been the various and unequal distribution of property. Those who hold, and those who are without property, have ever formed distinct interests in society. Those who are creditors, and those who are debtors, fall under a like discrimination. A landed interest, a manufacturing interest, a mercantile interest, a monied interest, with many lesser interests, grow up of necessity in civilized nations, and divide them into different classes, actuated by different sentiments and views. The regulation of these various and interfering interests forms the principal task of modern Legislation, and involves the spirit of party and faction in the necessary and ordinary operations of Government.

No man is allowed to be a judge in his own cause; because his interest would certainly bias his judgment, and, not improbably, corrupt his integrity. With equal, nay with greater reason, a body of men, are unfit to be both judges and parties, at the same time; yet, what are many of the most important acts of legislation, but so many judicial determinations, not indeed concerning the rights of single persons, but concerning the rights of large bodies of citizens, and what are the different classes of legislators, but advocates and parties to the causes which they determine? Is a law proposed concerning private debts? It is a question to which the creditors are parties on one side, and the debtors on the other. Justice ought to hold the balance between them. Yet the parties are and must be themselves the judges; and the most numerous party, or, in other words, the most powerful faction must be expected to prevail. Shall domestic manufactures be encouraged, and in what degree, by restrictions on foreign manufactures? are questions which would be differently decided by the landed and the manufacturing classes; and probably by neither, with a sole regard to justice and the public good. The apportionment of taxes on the various descriptions of property, is an act which seems to require the most exact impartiality; yet, there is perhaps no legislative act in which greater opportunity and temptation are given to a predominant party, to trample on the rules of justice. Every shilling with which they over-burden the inferior number, is a shilling saved to their own pockets.

It is in vain to say, that enlightened statesmen will be able to adjust these clashing interests, and render them all subservient to the public good. Enlightened statesmen will not always be at the helm: Nor, in many cases, can such an adjustment be made at all, without taking into view indirect and remote considerations, which will rarely prevail over the immediate interest which one party may find in disregarding the rights of another, or the good of the whole.

The inference to which we are brought, is, that the causes of faction cannot be removed; and that relief is only to be sought in the means of controlling its effects.

If a faction consists of less than a majority, relief is supplied by the republican principle, which enables the majority to defeat its sinister views by regular vote: It may clog the administration, it may convulse the society; but it will be unable to execute and mask its violence under the forms of the Constitution. When a majority is included in a faction, the form of popular government on the other hand enables it to sacrifice to its ruling passion or interest, both the public good and the rights of other citizens. To secure the public good, and private rights, against the danger of such a faction, and at the same time to preserve the spirit and the form of popular government, is then the great object to which our enquiries are directed: Let me add that it is the great desideratum, by which alone this form of government can be rescued from the opprobrium under which it has so long labored, and be recommended to the esteem and adoption of mankind.

By what means is this object attainable? Evidently by one of two only. Either the existence of the same passion or interest in a majority at the same time, must be prevented; or the majority, having such co-existent passion or interest, must be rendered, by their number and local situation, unable to concert and carry into effect schemes of oppression. If the impulse and the opportunity be suffered to coincide, we well know that neither moral nor religious motives can be relied on as an adequate control. They are not found to be such on the injustice and violence of individuals, and lose their efficacy in proportion to the number combined together; that is, in proportion as their efficacy becomes needful.

From this view of the subject, it may be concluded, that a pure Democracy, by which I mean, a Society, consisting of a small number of citizens, who assemble and administer the Government in person, can admit of no cure for the mischiefs of faction. A common passion or interest will, in almost every case, be felt by a majority of the whole; a communication and concert results from the form of Government itself; and there is nothing to check the inducements to sacrifice the weaker party, or an obnoxious individual. Hence it is, that such Democracies have ever been spectacles of turbulence and contention; have ever been found incompatible with personal security, or the rights of property; and have in general been as short in their lives, as they have been violent in their deaths. Theoretic politicians, who have patronized this species of Government, have erroneously supposed, that by reducing mankind to a perfect equality in their political rights, they would, at the same time, be perfectly equalized and assimilated in their possessions, their opinions, and their passions.

A republic, by which I mean a government in which the scheme of representation takes place, opens a different prospect, and promises the cure for which we are seeking. Let us examine the points in which it varies from pure democracy, and we shall comprehend both the nature of the cure and the efficacy which it must derive from the union.

The two great points of difference, between a democracy and a republic, are, first, the delegation of the government, in the latter, to a small number of citizens, elected by the rest; secondly, the greater number of citizens, and greater sphere of country, over which the latter may be extended.

The effect of the first difference is, on the one hand, to refine and enlarge the public views, by passing them through the medium of a chosen body of citizens, whose wisdom may best discern the true interest of their country, and whose patriotism and love of justice, will be least likely to sacrifice it to temporary or partial considerations. Under such a regulation, it may well happen, that the public voice, pronounced by the representatives of the people, will be more consonant to the public good, than if pronounced by the people themselves, convened for the purpose. On the other hand the effect may be inverted. Men of factious tempers, of local prejudices, or of sinister designs, may by intrigue, by corruption, or by other means, first obtain the suffrages, and then betray the interest of the people. The question resulting is, whether small or extensive republics are most favorable to the election of proper guardians of the public weal, and it is clearly decided in favor of the latter by two obvious considerations.

In the first place, it is to be remarked that, however small the republic may be, the representatives must be raised to a certain number, in order to guard against the cabals of a few; and that however large it may be, they must be limited to a certain number, in order to guard against the confusion of a multitude. Hence, the number of representatives in the two cases not being in proportion to that of the constituents, and being proportionally greatest in the small republic, it follows, that if the proportion of fit characters be not less in the large than in the small republic, the former will present a greater option, and consequently a greater probability of a fit choice.

In the next place, as each Representative will be chosen by a greater number of citizens in the large than in the small Republic, it will be more difficult for unworthy candidates to practise with success the vicious arts, by which elections are too often carried; and the suffrages of the people being more free, will be more likely to center on men who possess the most attractive merit, and the most diffusive and established characters.

It must be confessed, that in this, as in most other cases, there is a mean, on both sides of which inconveniences will be found to lie. By enlarging too much the number of electors, you render the representatives too little acquainted with all their local circumstances and lesser interests; as by reducing it too much, you render him unduly attached to these, and too little fit to comprehend and pursue great and national objects. The Federal Constitution forms a happy combination in this respect; the great and aggregate interests being referred to the national, the local and particular, to the state legislatures.

The other point of difference is, the greater number of citizens and extent of territory which may be brought within the compass of Republican, than of Democratic Government; and it is this circumstance principally which renders factious combinations less to be dreaded in the former, than in the latter. The smaller the society, the fewer probably will be the distinct parties and interests composing it; the fewer the distinct parties and interests, the more frequently will a majority be found of the same party; and the smaller the number of individuals composing a majority, and the smaller the compass within which they are placed, the more easily will they concert and execute their plans of oppression. Extend the sphere, and you take in a greater variety of parties and interests; you make it less probable that a majority of the whole will have a common motive to invade the rights of other citizens; or if such a common motive exists, it will be more difficult for all who feel it to discover their own strength, and to act in unison with each other. Besides other impediments, it may be remarked, that where there is a consciousness of unjust or dishonorable purposes, communication is always checked by distrust, in proportion to the number whose concurrence is necessary.

Hence it clearly appears, that the same advantage, which a Republic has over a Democracy, in controlling the effects of faction, is enjoyed by a large over a small Republic—is enjoyed by the Union over the States composing it. Does this advantage consist in the substitution of Representatives, whose enlightened views and virtuous sentiments render them superior to local prejudices, and to schemes of injustice? It will not be denied, that the Representation of the Union will be most likely to possess these requisite endowments. Does it consist in the greater security afforded by a greater variety of parties, against the event of any one party being able to outnumber and oppress the rest? In an equal degree does the increased variety of parties, comprised within the Union, increase this security? Does it, in fine, consist in the greater obstacles opposed to the concert and accomplishment of the secret wishes of an unjust and interested majority? Here, again, the extent of the Union gives it the most palpable advantage.

The influence of factious leaders may kindle a flame within their particular States, but will be unable to spread a general conflagration through the other States: a religious sect, may degenerate into a political faction in a part of the Confederacy but the variety of sects dispersed over the entire face of it, must secure the national Councils against any danger from that source: a rage for paper money, for an abolition of debts, for an equal division of property, or for any other improper or wicked project, will be less apt to pervade the whole body of the Union, than a particular member of it; in the same proportion as such a malady is more likely to taint a particular county or district, than an entire State.

In the extent and proper structure of the Union, therefore, we behold a Republican remedy for the diseases most incident to Republican Government. And according to the degree of pleasure and pride, we feel in being Republicans, ought to be our zeal in cherishing the spirit, and supporting the character of Federalists.

PUBLIUS

The Federalist No. 51
February 6, 1788
James Madison

TO THE PEOPLE OF THE STATE OF NEW YORK.

To what expedient then shall we finally resort for maintaining in practice the necessary partition of power among the several departments, as laid down in the constitution? The only answer that can be given is, that as all these exterior provisions are found to be inadequate, the defect must be supplied, by so contriving the interior structure of the government, as that its several constituent parts may, by their mutual relations, be the means of keeping each other in their proper places. Without presuming to undertake a full development of this important idea, I will hazard a few general observations, which may perhaps place it in a clearer light, and enable us to form a more correct judgment of the principles and structure of the government planned by the convention.

In order to lay a due foundation for that separate and distinct exercise of the different powers of government, which to a certain extent, is admitted on all hands to be essential to the preservation of liberty, it is evident that each department should have a will of its own; and consequently should be so constituted, that the members of each should have as little agency as possible in the appointment of the members of the others. Were this principle rigorously adhered to, it would require that all the appointments for the supreme executive, legislative, and judiciary magistracies, should be drawn from the same fountain of authority, the people, through channels, having no communication whatever with one another. Perhaps such a plan of constructing the several departments would be less difficult in practice than it may in contemplation appear. Some difficulties however, and some additional expense, would attend the execution of it. Some deviations therefore from the principle must be admitted. In the constitution of the judiciary department in particular, it might be inexpedient to insist rigorously on the principle; first, because peculiar qualifications being essential in the members, the primary consideration ought to be to select that mode of choice, which best secures these qualifications; secondly, because the permanent tenure by which the appointments are held in that department, must soon destroy all sense of dependence on the authority conferring them.

It is equally evident that the members of each department should be as little dependent as possible on those of the others, for the emoluments annexed to their offices. Were the executive magistrate, or the judges, not independent of the legislature in this particular, their independence in every other would be merely nominal.

But the great security against a gradual concentration of the several powers in the same department, consists in giving to those who administer each department, the necessary constitutional means, and personal motives, to resist encroachments of the others. The provision for defense must in this, as in all other cases, be made commensurate to the danger of attack. Ambition must be made to counteract ambition. The interest of the man must be connected with the constitutional right of the place. It may be a reflection on human nature, that such devices should be necessary to control the abuses of government. But what is government itself but the greatest of all reflections on human nature? If men were angels, no government would be necessary. If angels were to govern men, neither external nor internal controls on government would be necessary. In framing a government which is to be administered by men over men, the great difficulty lies in this: You must first enable the government to control the governed; and in the next place, oblige it to control itself. A dependence on the people is no doubt the primary control on the government; but experience has taught mankind the necessity of auxiliary precautions.

This policy of supplying by opposite and rival interests, the defect of better motives, might be traced through the whole system of human affairs, private as well as public. We see it particularly displayed in all the subordinate distributions of power; where the constant aim is to divide and arrange the several offices in such a manner as that each may be a check on the other; that the private interest of every individual, may be a sentinel over the public rights. These inventions of prudence cannot be less requisite in the distribution of the supreme powers of the state.

But it is not possible to give to each department an equal power of self defense. In republican government the legislative authority, necessarily, predominates. The remedy for this inconveniency is, to divide the legislature into different branches; and to render them by different modes of election, and different principles of action, as little connected with each other, as the nature of their common functions, and their common dependence on the society, will admit. It may even be necessary to guard against dangerous encroachments by still further precautions. As the weight of the legislative authority requires that it should be thus divided, the weakness of the executive may require, on the other hand, that it should be fortified. An absolute negative, on the legislature, appears at first view to be the natural defense with which the executive magistrate should be armed. But perhaps it would be neither altogether safe, nor alone sufficient. On ordinary occasions, it might not be exerted with the requisite firmness; and on extraordinary occasions, it might be perfidiously abused. May not this defect of an absolute negative be supplied, by some qualified connection between this weaker department, and the weaker branch of the stronger department, by which the latter may be led to support the constitutional rights of the former, without being too much detached from the rights of its own department?

If the principles on which these observations are founded be just, as I persuade myself they are, and they be applied as a criterion, to the several state constitutions, and to the federal constitution, it will be found, that if the latter does not perfectly correspond with them, the former are infinitely less able to bear such a test.

There are moreover two considerations particularly applicable to the federal system of America, which place that system in a very interesting point of view.

First. In a single republic, all the power surrendered by the people, is submitted to the administration of a single government; and usurpations are guarded against by a division of the government into distinct and separate departments. In the compound republic of America, the power surrendered by the people, is first divided between two distinct governments, and then the portion allotted to each, subdivided among distinct and separate departments. Hence a double security arises to the rights of the people. The different governments will control each other; at the same time that each will be controlled by itself.

Second. It is of great importance in a republic, not only to guard the society against the oppression of its rulers; but to guard one part of the society against the injustice of the other part. Different interests necessarily exist in different classes of citizens. If a majority be united by a common interest, the rights of the minority will be insecure. There are but two methods of providing against this evil: The one by creating a will in the community independent of the majority, that is, of the society itself, the other by comprehending in the society so many separate descriptions of citizens, as will render an unjust combination of a majority of the whole, very improbable, if not impracticable. The first method prevails in all governments possessing an hereditary or self appointed authority. This at best is but a precarious security; because a power independent of the society may as well espouse the unjust views of the major, as the rightful interests, of the minor party, and may possibly be turned against both parties. The second method will be exemplified in the federal republic of the United States. While all authority in it will be derived from and dependent on the society, the society itself will be broken into so many parts, interests and classes of citizens, that the rights of individuals or of the minority, will be in little danger from interested combinations of the majority. In a free government, the security for civil rights must be the same as for religious rights. It consists in the one case in the multiplicity of interests, and in the other, in the multiplicity of sects. The degree of security in both cases will depend on the number of interests and sects; and this may be presumed to depend on the extent of country and number of people comprehended under the same government. This view of the subject must particularly recommend a proper federal system to all the sincere and considerate friends of republican government: Since it shows that in exact proportion as the territory of the union may be formed into more circumscribed confederacies or states, oppressive combinations of a majority will be facilitated, the best security under the republican form, for the rights of every class of citizens, will be diminished; and consequently, the stability and independence of some member of the government, the only other security, must be proportionally increased. Justice is the end of government. It is the end of civil society. It ever has been, and ever will be pursued, until it be obtained, or until liberty be lost in the pursuit. In a society under the forms of which the stronger faction can readily unite and oppress the weaker, anarchy may as truly be said to reign, as in a state of nature where the weaker individual is not secured against the violence of the stronger: And as in the latter state even the stronger individuals are prompted by the uncertainty of their condition, to submit to a government which may protect the weak as well as themselves: So in the former state, will the more powerful factions or parties be gradually induced by a like motive, to wish for a government which will protect all parties, the weaker as well as the more powerful. It can be little doubted, that if the state of Rhode Island was separated from the confederacy, and left to itself, the insecurity of rights under the popular form of government within such narrow limits, would be displayed by such reiterated oppressions of factious majorities, that some power altogether independent of the people would soon be called for by the voice of the very factions whose misrule had proved the necessity of it. In the extended republic of the United States, and among the great variety of interests, parties and sects which it embraces, a coalition of a majority of the whole society could seldom take place on any other principles than those of justice and the general good; and there being thus less danger to a minor from the will of the major party, there must be less pretext also, to provide for the security of the former, by introducing into the government a will not dependent on the latter; or in other words, a will independent of the society itself. It is no less certain than it is important, notwithstanding the contrary opinions which have been entertained, that the larger the society, provided it lie within a practicable sphere, the more duly capable it will be of self government. And happily for the republican cause, the practicable sphere may be carried to a very great extent, by a judicious modification and mixture of the federal principle.

PUBLIUS

Presidents of the United States

PRESIDENT	YEAR	PARTY	MOST NOTEWORTHY EVENT
George Washington	1789–1797	Federalist	Establishment of Federal Judiciary
John Adams	1797–1801	Federalist	Alien-Sedition Acts
Thomas Jefferson	1801–1809	Dem.-Republican	First President to Defeat Incumbent/Louisiana Purchase
James Madison	1809–1817	Dem.-Republican	War of 1812
James Monroe	1817–1825	Dem.-Republican	Monroe Doctrine/ Missouri Compromise
John Quincy Adams	1825–1829	Dem.-Republican	Elected by "King Caucus"
Andrew Jackson	1829–1837	Democratic	Set up Spoils System
Martin Van Buren	1837–1841	Democratic	Competitive Parties Established
William H. Harrison	1841	Whig	Universal White Male Suffrage
John Tyler	1841–1845	Whig	Texas Annexed
James K. Polk	1845–1849	Democratic	Mexican-American War
Zachary Taylor	1849–1850	Whig	California Gold Rush
Millard Fillmore	1850–1853	Whig	Compromise of 1850
Franklin Pierce	1853–1857	Democratic	Republican Party Formed
James Buchanan	1857–1861	Democratic	Dred Scott Decision
Abraham Lincoln	1861–1865	Republican	Civil War
Andrew Johnson	1865–1869	Dem. (Unionist)	First Impeachment of President
Ulysses S. Grant	1869–1877	Republican	Reconstruction of South
Rutherford B. Hayes	1877–1881	Republican	End of Reconstruction
James A. Garfield	1881	Republican	Assassinated by Job-seeker
Chester A. Arthur	1881–1885	Republican	Civil Service Reform
Grover Cleveland	1885–1889	Democratic	Casts 102 Vetoes in One Year
Benjamin Harrison	1889–1893	Republican	McKinley Law Raises Tarrifs
Grover Cleveland	1893–1897	Democratic	Depression/Pullman Strike

(continued)

Presidents of the United States
(continued)

PRESIDENT	YEAR	PARTY	MOST NOTEWORTHY EVENT
William McKinley	1897–1901	Republican	Spanish-American War
Theodore Roosevelt	1901–1909	Republican	Conservation/Panama Canal
William H. Taft	1909–1913	Republican	Judicial Reform
Woodrow Wilson	1913–1921	Democratic	Progressive Reforms/World War I
Warren G. Harding	1921–1923	Republican	Return to Normalcy
Calvin Coolidge	1923–1929	Republican	Cuts Taxes/Promotes Business
Herbert C. Hoover	1929–1933	Republican	Great Depression
Franklin D. Roosevelt	1933–1945	Democratic	New Deal/World War II
Harry S. Truman	1945–1953	Democratic	Beginning of Cold War
Dwight D. Eisenhower	1953–1961	Republican	End of Korean War
John F. Kennedy	1961–1963	Democratic	Cuban Missile Crisis
Lyndon B. Johnson	1963–1969	Democratic	Great Society/Vietnam War
Richard M. Nixon	1969–1974	Republican	Watergate Scandal
Gerald R. Ford	1974–1977	Republican	War Powers Resolution
James Earl Carter	1977–1981	Democratic	Iranian Hostage Crisis
Ronald Reagan	1981–1989	Republican	Tax Cut/Expenditure Cuts
George Bush	1989–1993	Republican	End of Cold War/Persian Gulf War
William J. Clinton	1993–2001	Democratic	Deficit Reduction

NOTE: Refer to www.ablongman.com/fiorina

GLOSSARY

A

advice and consent   Support for a presidential action by a designated number of senators. (Chapter 2)

affirmative action   Programs designed to enhance opportunities for groups that have suffered discrimination in the past. (Chapter 14)

agenda setting   Occurs when the media affect the issues and problems people think about. (Chapter 12)

Aid to Families with Dependent Children (AFDC)   Public assistance program established in 1935 as part of the Social Security Act and replaced in 1996. (Chapter 15)

ambassador   The head of a diplomatic delegation to a major foreign country. (Chapter 15)

amicus curiae   Latin term meaning "friend of the court." It refers to legal briefs submitted by interested groups who are not directly party to a court case. (Chapter 8)

Annapolis Convention   Meeting in 1786 to discuss constitutional reform. (Chapter 2)

Anti-Federalists   Those who opposed ratification of the Constitution. (Chapter 2)

appropriations process   Process of providing funding for governmental activities and programs that have been authorized. (Chapter 9)

associate justice   One of the eight justices of the Supreme Court who are not the chief justice. (Chapter 11)

authorization process   Term given to the process of providing statutory authority for a government program activity; does not provide funding for the project. (Chapter 9)

B

balancing doctrine   The principle enunciated by the courts that freedom of speech must be balanced against other competing public interests. (Chapter 13)

Bay of Pigs   Location of CIA-supported effort by Cuban exiles in 1961 to invade Cuba and overthrow Fidel Castro. (Chapter 15)

beltway insider   Person living in the Washington metropolitan area who is engaged in, or well informed about, national politics and government. (Chapter 10)

bicameral   A legislature that contains two chambers. (Chapter 9)

block grant   Federal grant to a state and/or local government that imposes minimal restrictions on the use of funds. (Chapter 3)

brief   Written arguments presented to a court by lawyers on behalf of clients. (Chapter 11)

Brown v. Board of Education of Topeka, Kansas   Supreme Court decision (1954) declaring racial segregation in schools unconstitutional. (Chapter 14)

retrospective voting   Voting on the basis of the past performance. (Chapter 7)

bully pulpit   A description of the presidency emphasizing opportunities to preach to voters on behalf of good policy. (Chapter 10)

bureaucracy   Hierarchical organization designed to perform a particular set of tasks. (Chapter 10)

business cycle   The alternation of periods of economic growth with periods of economic slowdown. (Chapter 15)

C

Cabinet   Top administration officials; mostly heads of executive branch departments. (Chapter 10)

categorical grant   Federal grant to a state and/or local government that imposes programmatic restrictions on the use of funds. (Chapter 3)

caucus   Either a meeting to choose delegates to a state or national convention or a collection of like-minded legislators. (Chapters 7, 9)

Central Intelligence Agency (CIA)   Agency responsible for analyzing the political and military activities of other nations. (Chapter 15)

cert   See writ of *certiorari.*

checks and balances   Limits that one branch of government places on another because they have different interests, preventing an abuse of power. (Chapter 1)

chief justice   Head of the Supreme Court. (Chapter 11)

chief of staff   Head of White House staff usually in continuous contact with the president. (Chapter 10)

circuit court of appeals   Court to which decisions by federal district courts are appealed. (Chapter 11)

civic republicanism   A political philosophy that emphasizes the obligation of citizens to act virtuously in pursuit of the common good. (Chapter 4)

civil code   Laws regulating relations among individuals. Alleged violators are sued by presumed victims, who ask courts to award damages and otherwise offer relief. (Chapter 11)

civil disobedience   A peaceful violation of law designed to dramatize injustice. (Chapter 14)

civil liberties   Fundamental freedoms that protect a people from their government. (Chapter 13)

civil rights   Guarantees to equal treatment under the law. (Chapter 14)

civil rights amendments   The Thirteenth, Fourteenth, and Fifteenth Amendments to the U.S. Constitution, designed to abolish slavery and secure rights for freemen. (Chapter 13)

civil service   A system that protects government employees from losing their jobs when elected offices change hands. (Chapter 10)

class action suit   Suit brought on behalf of all individuals in a particular category, whether or not they are actually participating in the suit. (Chapter 11)

clear and present danger doctrine   The principle that people should have freedom of speech unless their language poses a direct threat that lawmakers have the authority to prevent. (Chapter 13)

closed primaries   Primaries in which only party members can vote—and vote only in the party in which they are registered. (Chapter 7)

cloture   Motion to end debate; requires 60 votes to pass. (Chapter 9)

coattails   Positive electoral effect of a popular presidential candidate on congressional candidates of the party. (Chapter 7)

coercion test   Alternative to the Lemon test preferred by conservative judges defining a religious establishment as an instance when government coerces citizens into following religious practices or punishes those who do not. (Chapter 13)

Cold War   The 43-year period (1946–1989) during which the United States and the Soviet Union threatened one another with mutual destruction. (Chapter 15)

commander in chief   The president in his role as head of the military. (Chapter 10)

commerce clause   Constitutional provision that gives Congress power to regulate commerce "among the states." (Chapter 3)

compositional effect   A change in the behavior of a group that arises from a change in membership rather than a change in the behavior of individuals in the group. (Chapter 6)

concurring opinion   A written opinion prepared by judges who vote with the majority but who wish to disagree with or elaborate on some aspect of the majority opinion. (Chapter 11)

conference committee   Group of representatives from both the House and the Senate who iron out the differences between the two chambers' versions of a bill or resolution. (Chapter 9)

constituency   Those legally entitled to vote for a public official. (Chapter 1)

constituency service   The work a member of Congress performs to win federal funds for the state or district and to help constituents deal with federal agencies. (Chapter 7)

containment   U.S. policy that attempted to stop the spread of communism in the expectation that this system of government would eventually collapse on its own. (Chapter 15)

cooperative federalism   See *marble-cake federalism.*

criminal code   Laws regulating relations between individuals and society. Alleged violators are prosecuted by government. (Chapter 11)

critical election   Election that marks the emergence of a new, lasting alignment of partisan support within the electorate. (Chapter 8)

D

Declaration of Independence   Document signed in 1776 declaring the United States to be a country independent of Great Britain. (Chapter 2)

de facto **segregation**   Segregation that occurs as the result of private decisions. (Chapter 14)

defendant   One accused of violating the civil or criminal code. (Chapter 11) *de jure* **segregation**   Segregation that is legally sanctioned. (Chapter 14)

delegate   Role a representative plays when following voters' wishes. (Chapter 9)

democracy   System in which governmental power is widely shared. (Chapter 1)

department   Organizational unit into which many federal agencies are grouped. (Chapter 10)

Department of Defense   Cabinet department responsible for the U.S. armed forces. (Chapter 15)

devolution   Return of governmental responsibilities to states and localities. (Chapter 3)

direct action   Informal political activism ranging from peaceful sit-ins and demonstrations to riots and even rebellion. (Chapter 8)

direct democracy   System in which ordinary people make all the laws themselves. (Chapter 1)

direct mail   Computer-generated letters, faxes, and other communications to people who might be sympathetic to an appeal for money or support. (Chapter 8)

dissenting opinion   Written opinion presenting the reasoning of judges who vote against the majority. (Chapter 11)

distributive tendency   Tendency of Congress to spread the benefits of any program widely and thinly across the districts of the members. (Chapter 9)

distributive theory   Theory predicting that a legislature's members will serve on the committees most important for delivering benefits to their constituents. (Chapter 9)

district attorney   Person responsible for prosecuting criminal cases. (Chapter 11)

diversity   Describes when many different sorts of people coexist in the same society or institution; relative to time and place. (Chapter 4)

divided government   Said to exist when no single party controls the presidency and both houses of Congress. (Chapter 8)

divine right   Doctrine that says God selects the sovereign for the people. (Chapter 2)

double jeopardy   Fifth Amendment provision that prohibits prosecution for the same offense twice. (Chapters 11, 13)

draft   Also called conscription, the involuntary induction of citizens into military service. (Chapter 12)

dual sovereignty   A theory of federalism by which both the national and state governments have final authority over their own policy domains. (Chapter 3)

due process clause   Clause found in the Fifth and Fourteenth Amendments to the Constitution that forbids deprivation of life, liberty, or property without due process of law. (Chapter 13)

E

earmark   A specific congressional designation of the way money is to be spent. (Chapter 10)

Earned Income Tax Credit (EITC)   Provision that returns tax payments to those who have little income. (Chapter 15)

electoral incentive   Desire to obtain or retain elected office. (Chapter 1)

electoral vote   Votes cast for a presidential candidate, with each state receiving one vote for each of its members of the House of Representatives and one vote for each of its senators. (Chapter 7)

embassy   The structure that houses ambassadors and their diplomatic aides in the capital cities of many foreign countries. (Chapter 15)

equal protection clause   Fourteenth Amendment clause specifying that no state can deny any of its people equal protection under the law. (Chapter 14)

Equal Rights Amendment (ERA)   Failed constitutional amendment to ban gender discrimination. (Chapter 14)

equality of opportunity   The notion that individuals should have an equal chance to advance economically through individual talent and hard work. (Chapter 4)

equality of results   The notion that all individuals have a right to a more or less equal part of the material goods that society produces. (Chapter 4)

equal-time rule   Promulgated by the FCC, rule that required any station selling time to a candidate to sell time to other candidates at comparable rates. (Chapter 12)

establishment clause   Clause that denies government the power to favor religion or to establish any single religious practice as superior. (Chapter 13)

exclusionary rule   The rule that evidence obtained improperly may not be introduced in a trial. (Chapter 13)

executive agreement   Agreement with foreign countries that requires only a presidential signature. (Chapter 15)

Executive Office of the President (EOP)   Agency that houses both top coordinating offices closely connected to the president; contains the White House office. (Chapter 10)

executive order   A presidential directive that has the force of law. (Chapter 10)

executive privilege   The right of members of the executive branch to have private communications among themselves that need not be shared with Congress. (Chapter 10)

F

fairness doctrine   Promulgated by the FCC, policy that required stations to carry some public affairs programming and to balance the points of view expressed. (Chapter 12)

federal district courts   The lowest level of the federal court system and the courts in which most federal trials are held. (Chapter 11)

Federal Reserve System   The country's central bank, which executes monetary policy by manipulating the supply of funds that lower banks can lend. (Chapter 15)

federalism   Division of sovereignty between at least two different levels of government. (Chapter 3)

Federalist Papers   Essays that were written in support of the Constitution's ratification and have become a classic argument for the American constitutional system. (Chapter 2)

Federalists   Those who campaigned on behalf of the Constitution. (Chapter 2)

fighting words doctrine   The principle that some words constitute violent acts and therefore do not enjoy First Amendment protection. (Chapter 13)

filibuster   Delaying tactic by which senators refuse to allow legislation to be considered, usually by speaking indefinitely. (Chapter 9)

filing deadline   The latest date on which a candidate for office may file official papers or pay required fees to state election officials. (Chapter 7)

First Continental Congress   The first quasi-governmental institution that spoke for nearly all the colonies (1774). (Chapter 2)

First Lady   Traditional title of the president's spouse. (Chapter 10)

fiscal policy   The sum total of government taxing and spending decisions. (Chapter 15)

floor   Term for an entire congressional chamber; usually used when bills have left committee and moved to a vote of the full membership. (Chapter 9)

food stamps   Public assistance program providing recipients with stamps that can be used to purchase food. (Chapter 15)

foreign service   Diplomats who staff U.S. embassies and consulates. (Chapter 15)

framing   Stating of an argument in such a way as to emphasize one set of considerations and deemphasize others. (Chapters 5, 12)

franchise   The right to vote. (Chapter 6)

frank   Free mailing privileges enjoyed by members of Congress when communicating with constituents. (Chapter 7)

free exercise clause   Clause that protects the right of individuals to practice their religion. (Chapter 13)

free-rider problem   Barrier to collective action that arises when people can enjoy the benefits of group activity without contributing their limited share of the costs. (Chapter 8)

fundamental freedoms doctrine (preferred freedoms doctrine)   Court doctrine stating that some liberties are fundamental to the preservation of democratic practice—the freedoms of speech, press, assembly, and religion—are to be scrutinized by the courts more closely than other legislation. (Chapter 13)

G

general election   Final election that selects the office holder. (Chapter 1)

general revenue sharing   The most comprehensive of block grants, which gives money to state and local governments to be used for any purpose whatsoever. (Chapter 3)

gerrymandering   Drawing of boundary lines of congressional districts in order to confer an advantage on some partisan or political interest. (Chapter 7)

government   The institution in society that monopolizes the legitimate use of physical force. (Chapter 1)

government corporation   Independent organization created by Congress to fulfill functions related to business. (Chapter 10)

grandfather clause   Racially restrictive provision of certain southern laws after Reconstruction permitting a man to vote if his grandfather could have voted. (Chapter 14)

grassroots lobbying   Efforts by groups and associations to influence elected officials indirectly, by arousing their constituents. (Chapter 8)

H

Hatch Act   Law enacted in 1939 prohibiting federal employees from engaging in political campaigning and solicitation. (Chapter 10)

honeymoon   The first several months of a presidency, when reporters are more forgiving than usual, Congress more inclined to be cooperative, and the public receptive to new approaches. (Chapter 10)

I

ideology   System of beliefs in which one or more organizing principles connect the individual's views on a wide range of issues. (Chapter 5)

impeachment   Recommendation by a majority of the House of Representatives that a president, other executive-branch official, or judge of the federal courts be removed from office; removal depends on a two-thirds vote of the Senate. (Chapter 10)

implementation   The way in which grant programs are administered at the local level. (Chapter 3)

incumbency advantage   The electoral advantage a candidate enjoys by virtue of being an incumbent, over and above his or her other personal and political characteristics. (Chapter 7)

independent agencies   Agencies that have quasi-judicial responsibilities. (Chapter 10)

independent counsel   Originally called special prosecutor, legal officer appointed by a court to investigate allegations of criminal activity against high-ranking members of the executive branch. Law expired in 1999. (Chapter 10)

inflation   A sustained rise in the price level such that people need more money to purchase the same amount of goods and services. (Chapter 15)

information cost   The time and mental effort required to absorb and store information, whether from conversations, personal experiences, or the media. (Chapter 5)

informational theory   Theory that sees committees as means of providing reliable information about the actual consequences of the legislation that members could adopt. (Chapter 9)

initiative   Proposed laws or state constitutional amendments placed on the ballot via citizen petition. (Chapter 1)

Iran–Contra affair   An allegedly illegal diversion of funds from the sale of arms to Iran to a guerrilla group in Nicaragua. (Chapter 15)

iron curtain   Armed barrier during the Cold War that prevented movement across national borders between communist Eastern Europe and democratic Western Europe. (Chapter 15)

iron triangle   A congressional committee, bureaucratic agency, and allied interest groups who combine to dominate policy making in some specified policy area. (Chapter 8)

isolationism   A foreign policy that keeps the United States separate from the conflicts taking place among other nations. (Chapter 15)

issue network   A loose constellation of larger numbers of committees, agencies, and interest groups active in a particular policy area. (Chapter 8)

issue public   Group of people particularly affected by or concerned with a specific issue. (Chapter 5)

J

Jim Crow laws   Segregation laws passed after Reconstruction. (Chapter 14)

Joint Chiefs of Staff   The heads of all the military services, together with a chair and vice-chair nominated by the president and confirmed by the Senate. (Chapter 15)

judicial activism   Doctrine that indicates the principles of *stare decisis* and legislative deference should sometimes be sacrificed in order to adapt the Constitution to changing conditions. (Chapter 11)

judicial restraint   Doctrine that indicates courts should, if at all possible, avoid overturning a prior court decision or legislative act. (Chapter 11)

judicial review   Court authority to declare null and void laws of Congress and of state legislatures on the grounds that they violate the Constitution. (Chapters 2, 11)

K

Keynesianism   Economic policy based on the belief that governments can control the economy by running deficits to expand it and surpluses to contract it. (Chapter 15)

L

law clerk   Young, influential aide to a Supreme Court justice. (Chapter 11)

League of Nations   International organization created after World War I to settle international disputes; precursor of the United Nations. (Chapter 15)

Lemon test   Three-part test developed in the early 1960s and formalized in 1971; determines whether a law violates the Constitution's establishment clause. (Chapter 13)

libel   False statement damaging to someone's reputation. (Chapter 13)

liberalism   A philosophy that elevates and empowers the individual as opposed to religious, hereditary, governmental, or other forms of authority. (Chapter 4)

line item veto   Power of most governors to reject specific components of legislation rather than reject entire bills. (Chapter 3)

lobbying   Attempts by interest group representatives to influence the decisions of government officials directly. (Chapter 8)

lobbyist   One who engages in lobbying. (Chapter 8)

logrolling   Colloquial term given to politicians' trading of favors, votes, or generalized support for each other's proposals. (Chapter 9)

M

machine   A highly organized party under the control of a boss, based on patronage and control of government activities. (Chapter 8)

Marbury* v. *Madison   Supreme Court decision (1803) in which the court first exercised the power of judicial review. (Chapter 11)

majority leader   The Speaker's chief lieutenant in the House and the most important officer in the Senate. He or she is responsible for managing the floor. (Chapter 9)

marble-cake federalism (cooperative federalism)   The theory that all levels of government can work together to solve common problems. (Chapter 3)

markup   Process in which a committee or subcommittee considers and revises a bill that has been introduced. (Chapter 9)

mass media   Means of communication that are technologically capable of reaching most people and economically affordable to most. (Chapter 12)

mass public   Ordinary people for whom politics is a peripheral concern. (Chapter 5)

matching funds   Public moneys (from $3 checkoffs on income tax returns) that the FEC distributes to primary candidates. (Chapter 7)

Mayflower Compact   First document in colonial America in which the people gave their expressed consent to be governed. (Chapter 2)

McCulloch* v. *Maryland   Decision of 1819 in which the Supreme Court declared unconstitutional the state's power to tax a federal government entity. (Chapter 3)

measurement error   Polling error that arises from questioning rather than sampling. (Chapter 5)

Medicaid   Program that provides medical care to those of low income. (Chapter 15)

Medicare   Program that provides medical benefits to Social Security recipients. (Chapter 15)

midterm loss   When the president's party loses seats in Congress during the off-year election, which failed to happen only twice in the twentieth century: 1934 and 1998. (Chapter 7)

minority leader   Leader of the minority party in the House or Senate. (Chapter 9)

Miranda warning   The specific words used by police officers to inform accused persons of their constitutional rights; necessary before questioning suspects. (Chapter 13)

mobilization   The efforts of parties, groups, and activists to encourage their supporters to participate in politics. (Chapter 6)

monetarism   An economic school of thought that rejects Keynesianism, arguing that the money supply is the most important influence on the economy. (Chapter 15)

monetary policy   The actions taken by government to affect the level of interest rates by varying the supply of money. (Chapter 15)

Monroe Doctrine   Policy (1819) that declared the Western Hemisphere to be free of European colonial influence. (Chapter 15)

mugwumps   A group of civil service reformers organized in the 1880s who maintained that government officials should be chosen on a merit basis. (Chapter 10)

multiculturalism   The idea that ethnic and cultural groups should maintain their identity within the larger society and respect one another's differences. (Chapter 4)

multiple referrals   Practice of party leaders who give more than one committee responsibility for considering a bill. (Chapter 9)

N

National Security Council (NSC)   White House agency responsible for coordinating U.S. foreign policy. (Chapter 15)

necessary and proper clause   Constitutional clause that gives Congress the power to take all actions that are "necessary and proper" to the carrying out of its delegated powers. Also known as the *elastic clause*. (Chapters 2, 3)

neutrality test   Test allowing restrictions on the exercise of religion when they are part of a neutral criminal law generally applied to the population. Replaced the Sherbert test. (Chapter 13)

New Deal   Programs created by Franklin Roosevelt's administration that expanded the power of the federal government over economic affairs. (Chapter 3)

new media   Cable and satellite TV, the fax, e-mail, and the Internet—the consequences of the technological advances of the past few decades. (Chapter 12)

NIMBY problem   The problem that results when everyone wants the problem solved, but "Not In My Back Yard." (Chapter 3)

nullification   A doctrine that gives states the authority to declare acts of Congress unconstitutional. (Chapter 3)

O

obscenity   Publicly offensive language or portrayals with no redeeming social value. (Chapter 13)

Office of Management and Budget (OMB)   Agency responsible for coordinating the work of departments and agencies of the executive branch. (Chapter 10)

open primaries   Primaries in which any registered voter can vote in any party's primary. (Chapter 7)

open seat   A House or Senate race with no incumbent (because of death or retirement). (Chapter 7)

opinion of the court   A court's written explanation for its decision. (Chapter 11)

Order of the Cincinnati   Secret society of Revolutionary War officers, nominally led by George Washington, active in politics under the Articles of Confederation. Also known as the Society of Cincinnati. (Chapter 2)

override   Congressional passage of a bill by a two-thirds vote over the president's veto. (Chapter 10)

P

party identification   A person's subjective feeling of affiliation with a party. (Chapter 7)

patronage   Jobs, contracts, or favors in exchange for their political support. Widely practiced in the eighteenth and nineteenth centuries and continues to present day. (Chapters 2, 10)

Pendleton Act   Legislation in 1881 creating the Civil Service Commission. (Chapter 10)

permanent campaign   Term describing the tendency for election campaigns to begin as soon as the last election has ended and for the line between electioneering and governing to disappear. (Chapter 1)

plaintiff   One who brings legal charges against another. (Chapter 11)

plea bargain   Agreement between prosecution and defense that the accused will admit having committed a crime, provided that other charges are dropped or the recommended sentence shortened. (Chapter 13)

plenary session   Activities of a court in which all judges participate. (Chapter 11)

pluralism   A school of thought holding that politics is the clash of groups that represent all important interests in society and check and balance each other. (Chapter 8)

pocket veto   Presidential veto after congressional adjournment, executed merely by not signing a bill into law. (Chapter 10)

political action committee (PAC)   Specialized organization for raising and contributing campaign funds. (Chapter 8)

political culture   Collection of beliefs and values about government. (Chapter 4)

political efficacy   The belief that one can make a difference in politics. (Chapter 5)

political elite   Activists and officeholders who are deeply interested in and knowledgeable about politics. (Chapter 5)

political entrepreneurs   People willing to assume the costs of forming and maintaining an organization even when others may free ride on them. (Chapter 8)

political parties   Groups of like-minded people who band together in an attempt to take control of government. (Chapter 8)

political socialization   The set of psychological and sociological processes by which societal units inculcate beliefs and values in their members. (Chapter 4)

popular vote   The total vote cast for a presidential candidate nationwide. (Chapter 7)

precedent   Previous court decision or ruling applicable to a particular case. (Chapter 11)

president pro tempore   Leader of the Senate, who presides in the absence of the vice president. (Chapter 9)

primary election   Preliminary election that narrows the number of candidates by determining who will be the party nominees in the general election. (Chapters 1, 7)

priming   What occurs when the media affect the standards people use to evaluate political figures or the severity of a problem. (Chapter 12)

principal-agent problem A phenomenon that plagues bureaucracies. Bosses must balance between controlling subordinates and allowing them discretion to work efficiently. (Chapter 10)

prior restraint doctrine Legal doctrine that gives individuals the right to publish without prior restraint—that is, without first submitting material to a government censor. (Chapter 13)

proportional representation (PR) An electoral system that assigns legislative seats in a manner roughly proportional to the number of votes each party received. (Chapters 7, 8)

proprietary colony Colony governed either by a prominent English noble or by a company. (Chapter 2)

psychic benefits of voting Intangible rewards of voting, such as satisfaction with doing one's duty and feelings of solidarity with the community. (Chapter 6)

public defender Attorney whose full-time responsibilities are to provide for the legal defense of indigent criminal suspects. (Chapter 13)

public goods Goods that you can enjoy without contributing. (Chapter 8)

Q

quorum Number of members of a council or legislative body who must be present for official business to take place. (Chapter 2)

quota Specific number of positions set aside for a specific group; said by the Supreme Court to be unconstitutional. (Chapter 14)

R

"rally 'round the flag" effect The tendency for the public to back presidents in moments of crisis. (Chapters 10, 15)

random sample A representative subset of a larger group, chosen in such a way that each member of the group had roughly the same chance of being selected. (Chapter 5)

realignment Arrangement that ccurs when the pattern of group support for political parties shifts in a significant and lasting way, such as in the latter half of the twentieth century, when the white South shifted from Democratic to Republican. (Chapter 8)

reapportionment The allocation of House seats to the states after each decennial census. (Chapter 7)

recall election Attempt to remove an official from office before the completion of the term. (Chapter 1)

receiver Court official who has the authority to see that judicial orders are carried out. (Chapter 11)

recession A slowdown in economic activity, officially defined as a decline that persists for two quarters (six months). (Chapter 15)

Reconstruction Period after the Civil War when southern states were subject to a federal military presence. (Chapter 14)

redistricting Drawing of new boundaries of congressional districts. (Chapter 7)

referendum A law or state constitutional amendment that is proposed by a legislative body but does not go into effect unless the required number of voters approve it. (Chapter 1)

registered voters Those legally eligible to vote who have registered in accordance with the requirements prevailing in their states and localites. (Chapter 6)

remand To send a case to a lower court to determine the best way of implementing the higher court's decision. (Chapter 11)

remedy Court-ordered action designed to compensate plaintiffs for wrongs they have suffered. (Chapter 11)

representative democracy (republic) An indirect form of democracy in which the people choose representatives who determine what government does. (Chapter 1)

republic See *direct democracy.* (Chapter 1)

restorationist Judge who thinks that the only way the original meaning of the Constitution can be restored is by overturning prior liberal rulings. (Chapter 11)

restrictive housing covenant Legal promise by home buyers that they would not resell to black households; enforcement declared unconstitutional by Supreme Court. (Chapter 14)

right to privacy Right to keep free of government interference those aspects of one's personal life that do not affect others. (Chapter 13)

roll-call vote A congressional vote in which the specific choice of each member is recorded, allowing constituents to learn how their representative voted. (Chapter 7)

royal colony Colony governed by the king's representative. (Chapter 2)

rule Specification of the terms and conditions under which a bill or resolution will be considered on the floor of the House—in particular, how long debate will last, how time will be allocated, and the number and type of amendments that will be in order. (Chapter 9)

S

safe seat A congressional district almost guaranteed to elect either a Democrat or a Republican because the distribution of partisans is so lopsided. (Chapter 7)

sampling error The error that arises in public opinion surveys as a result of relying on a representative but small sample of the larger population. (Chapter 5)

Second Continental Congress Political authority that directed the struggle for independence beginning in 1775. (Chapter 2)

secretary of defense The president's chief civilian adviser on defense matters and overall head of the army, navy, and air force. (Chapter 15)

secretary of state Officially, the president's chief foreign policy adviser and head of the Department of State, the agency responsible for conducting diplomatic relations. (Chapter 15)

select committee Temporary Congressional committee appointed to deal with a specific issue or problem. (Chapter 9)

selection bias The error that occurs when a sample systematically includes or excludes people with certain attitudes. (Chapter 5)

selective benefits   Side benefits of belonging to an organization that are limited to contributing members of the organization. (Chapter 8)

selective incorporation   The case-by-case incorporation, by the courts, of the Bill of Rights into the due process clause of the Fourteenth Amendment. (Chapter 13)

senatorial courtesy   An informal rule that the Senate will not confirm nominees within or from a state unless they have the approval of the senior senator of the state from the president's party. (Chapters 10, 11)

seniority   Congressional practice by which the majority party member with the longest continuous service on a committee becomes the chair. (Chapter 9)

separate but equal doctrine   Obsolete rule stating that racial segregation did not violate the equal protection clause as long as the facilities were equivalent. (Chapter 14)

separation of church and state doctrine   The principle that a wall should separate the government from religious activity. (Chapter 13)

separation of powers   A system of government in which different institutions exercise different components of governmental power. (Chapter 2)

sequester   To house jurors privately, away from any information other than that presented in the courtroom. (Chapter 13)

Shays's Rebellion   Uprising in western Massachusetts in 1786 led by Revolutionary War captain Daniel Shays. (Chapter 2)

Sherbert test   Three-part test formalized in the early 1960s but overruled in 1990 that determined whether a law violates the Constitution's free exercise clause. (Chapter 13)

sin tax   Tax intended to discourage unwanted behavior. (Chapter 15)

single-issue voter   Voter for whom one issue is so important that it determines which political candidates attract his or her votes or campaign activism. (Chapters 1, 5)

single-member, simple plurality (SMSP) system   Electoral system in which the country is divided into geographic districts, and the candidates who win the most votes within their districts are elected. (Chapter 8)

social connectedness   The degree to which individuals are integrated into society—families, churches, neighborhoods, groups, and so forth. (Chapter 6)

social issues   Issues such as obscenity, feminism, gay rights, capital punishment, and prayer in schools that reflect personal values more than economic interests. (Chapter 6)

social movement   Broad-based demand for government action on some problem or issue, such as civil rights for blacks and women or environmental protection. (Chapter 8)

socializing agent   A person or institution that teaches social values and political attitudes. (Chapter 5)

soft money   Campaign funds that are spent on a candidate's behalf by an interest group or political party but that the candidate does not receive or coordinate directly. (Chapter 7)

solicitor general   Government official responsible for presenting before the courts the position of the presidential administration. (Chapter 11)

sovereignty Fundamental governmental authority. (Chapter 3)

Speaker The presiding officer of the House of Representatives; normally, the Speaker is the leader of the majority party. (Chapter 9)

spending clause Constitutional provision that gives Congress the power to collect taxes to provide for the general welfare. (Chapter 3)

spin The positive or negative slant that reporters or anchors put on their reports. (Chapter 12)

spoils system A system of government employment in which workers are hired on the basis of party loyalty. (Chapter 10)

sponsor Representative or senator who introduces a bill or resolution. (Chapter 9)

Stamp Act Passed by Parliament in 1765, it required people in the colonies to purchase a small stamp to be affixed to a legal or other document. (Chapter 2)

standing committee Committee with fixed membership and jurisdiction, continuing from Congress to Congress. (Chapter 9)

stare decisis In court rulings, remaining consistent with precedents. (Chapter 11)

state action doctrine Rule stating that only the actions of state and local governments, not those of private individuals, must conform to the equal protection clause. (Chapter 14)

State of the Union address Annual speech delivered by the president in fulfillment of the constitutional obligation of reporting to Congress on the state of the Union. (Chapter 10)

statutory interpretation The judicial act of applying laws to particular cases. (Chapter 11)

suffrage Another term for the right to vote. (Chapter 6)

supremacy clause Part of the Constitution that says the Constitution is the "supreme Law of the Land," to which all judges are bound. (Chapters 2, 3)

suspect classification Categorization of a particular group that will be strictly scrutinized by the courts to see whether its use is unconstitutional. (Chapter 14)

suspension of the rules Fast-track procedure for considering bills and resolutions in the House; debate is limited to 40 minutes, no amendments are in order, and a two-thirds majority is required for passage. (Chapter 9)

T

tax preferences Special tax treatment received by certain activities, property, or investments. (Chapter 15)

Temporary Assistance for Needy Families (TANF) Reformed welfare program established by Congress in 1996. (Chapter 15)

three-fifths compromise Constitutional provision that counted each slave as three-fifths of a person when calculating representation in the House of Representatives; repealed by the Fourteenth Amendment. (Chapter 2)

ticket splitting Occurs when a voter chooses candidates from multiple parties. (Chapter 8)

Tonkin Gulf Resolution Congressional resolution giving the president the authority to send troops to Vietnam. (Chapter 15)

Tories   Those colonists who opposed independence from Great Britain. (Chapter 2)

transition   The period after a presidential candidate has won the November election but before the candidate assumes office as president on January 20. (Chapter 10)

treaties   Official agreements with foreign countries ratified by the Senate. (Chapter 15)

trustee   Role a representative plays when using his or her own judgment. (Chapter 9)

turnout   Defined officially by the Census Bureau as the number of people voting divided by the size of the voting-age population. (Chapter 6)

two-thirds rule   Rule governing Democratic national conventions from 1832 to 1936. It required that the presidential and vice presidential nominees receive at least two-thirds of the delegates' votes. (Chapter 8)

two-presidency theory   Idea that a president has so much more power in foreign affairs than in domestic policy that there are two presidencies. (Chapter 15)

tyranny of the majority   Stifling of dissent by those voted into power by the majority. (Chapter 13)

U

U.S. attorney   Person responsible for prosecuting violations of the federal criminal code. (Chapter 11)

unanimous-consent agreement   Agreement that sets forth the terms according to which the Senate will consider a bill; these are individually negotiated by the leadership for each bill. (Chapter 9)

unemployment   When people who are willing to work at the prevailing wage cannot get jobs. (Chapter 15)

unfunded mandates   Federal regulations that impose burdens on state and local governments without appropriating enough money to cover costs. (Chapter 3)

unitary government   System under which national government holds all authority. (Chapter 3)

V

venue   Place where a trial is held. (Chapter 13)

veto   Executive rejection of legislation, which usually may be overridden by a supermajority in the legislature. (Chapter 10)

voting-age population   All people in the United States over the age of 18. (Chapter 6)

W

War on Poverty   One of the most controversial of the Great Society programs, it was designed to enhance the economic opportunity of low-income citizens. (Chapter 3)

War Powers Resolution   Congressional resolution in 1973 requiring the president to notify Congress formally upon ordering U.S. troops into military action. (Chapter 15)

Whigs   Political opposition to royal power in eighteenth-century England. (Chapter 2)

whips   Members of Congress who serve as informational channels between the leadership and the rank and file. (Chapter 9)

White House Office   Political appointees who work directly for the president, many of whom occupy offices in the White House. (Chapter 10)

winner-take-all voting   Any voting procedure in which the side with the most votes gets all of the seats or delegates at stake. (Chapter 7)

writ of *certiorari* (cert)   A document issued by the Supreme Court indicating that the Court will review a decision made by a lower court. (Chapter 11)

ENDNOTES

PREFACE

1. On the limited importance of elections, see for example the string of works by Benjamin Ginsberg, including an influential book with Martin Shefter, *Politics By Other Means: The Declining Importance of Elections in America* (New York: Basic, 1990). On the dominance of elites, see the running textbook series by Thomas R. Dye, including—listed in their first editions—*Who's Running America?* (Englewood Cliffs, NJ: Prentice-Hall, 1976) and, with L. Harmon Ziegler, *The Irony of Democracy* (Belmont, CA: Wadsworth, 1970).

2. Consider, for example, the Pew Charitable Trust's "Transition to Governing Project," directed by Norman Ornstein and Thomas Mann.

3. Morris P. Fiorina and Paul E. Peterson, *The New American Democracy,* Second Edition (New York: Longman, 2001).

CHAPTER 1

1. David Bauder (Associated Press), "TV Networks Lambasted for Election Coverage," *Lexington Herald-Leader* (February 3, 2001): A7.

2. On Republican reliance on the South, see Earl Black and Merle Black, *The Vital South* (Cambridge, MA: Harvard University Press, 1992).

3. All election-night quotations come from ABC-NEWS television coverage presented the night of the election through the following morning.

4. Henry E. Brady, Michael C. Herron, Walter R. Mebane, Jr., Jasjeet Singh Sekhon, Kenneth W. Shotts, and Jonathan Wand, "Law and Data: The Butterfly Ballot Episode," *PS: Political Science and Politics* 34 (2001): 59–69.

5. Manny Garcia and Tom Dubocq, "Unregistered Voters Cast Ballots in Dade," *Miami Herald* (December 24, 2000); and David Kidwell, Phil Long, and Geoff Dougherty, "Hundreds of Felons Cast Votes Illegally," *Miami Herald* (December 1, 2000).

6. James Laxer, "Supreme Court Stole U.S. Election," *Toronto Star* (December 20, 2000); Solita Collas-Monsad, "Stolen Fair and Square," *Philippine Daily Inquirer* (December 16, 2000); Erdrol Miller, "Politics and Principles," *Jamaica Gleaner* (Kingston, December 15, 2000); "A Diminished Democracy," *Hindu* (India, December 14, 2000); and "Damaged and Devalued: The Presidency Is Now in Danger of Both," *Statesman* (India, December 11, 2000).

7. Joseph S. Nye, Jr., Philip D. Zelikow, and David C. King, eds., *Why People Don't Trust Government* (Cambridge, MA: Harvard University Press, 1997).

8. H. H. Gerth and C. W. Mills, trans., *From Max Weber* (New York: Oxford University Press, 1946), p. 78.

9. Chuck Henning, *The Wit and Wisdom of Politics: Expanded Edition* (Golden, CO: Fulcrum, 1992), p. 91.

10. Thomas Hobbes, *Leviathan* (New York: Dutton, 1973), p. 65.

11. "Federalist No. 51," *The Federalist Papers.*

12. Henning, *Wit and Wisdom,* p. 89.

13. "How to Run a Referendum," *The Economist* (November 23, 1996): 66.

14. Good surveys of democratic theory include J. Roland Pennock, *Democratic Political Theory* (Princeton, NJ: Princeton University Press, 1979); Giovanni Sartori, *The Theory of Democracy Revisited* (Chatham, NJ: Chatham House, 1987); and Carole Pateman, *Participation and Democratic Theory* (New York: Cambridge University Press, 1970). A critical summary appears in James Marone, *The Democratic Wish: Popular Participation and the Limits of American Government* (New York: Basic Books, 1990), p. 5.

15. Paul F. Lazarsfeld, Bernard Berelson, and Hazel Gaudet, *The People's Choice: How the Voter Makes Up His Mind in a Presidential Campaign*, Second Edition (New York: Columbia University Press, 1948); Bernard Berelson, Paul F. Lazarsfeld, and William McPhee, *Voting* (Chicago: University of Chicago Press, 1954); Angus Campbell, Philip E. Converse, Warren E. Miller, and Donald E. Stokes, *The American Voter* (New York: Wiley, 1960); Deborah R. Hensler and Carl P. Hensler, *Evaluating Nuclear Power: Voter Choice on the California Nuclear Energy Initiative* (Santa Monica, CA: Rand Corporation, 1979), p. 106; David Magleby, *Direct Legislation: Voting on Ballot Propositions in the United States* (Baltimore: Johns Hopkins University Press, 1984), p. 144; Barbara S. Gamble, "Putting Civil Rights to a Popular Vote." *American Journal of Political Science* 41 (1997): 245–269; and D. Stephen Voss and Penny Miller, "The Phantom Segregationist: An Aggregate-Data Analysis of Kentucky's 1996 Constitutional Amendment Vote," paper presented at the annual meeting of the Kentucky Political Science Association, Lexington, KY, March 5–6, 1999.

16. John Adams, *The Political Writings of John Adams,* George Peek, Jr., ed. (New York: Macmillan, 1985), p. 89.

17. Alexis de Tocqueville, *Democracy in America,* Second Edition, Henry Reeve, trans., 2 vols. (Cambridge, MA: Sever & Francis, 1863), I, pp. 318–319, as quoted in Marone, *The Democratic Wish*, p. 86.

18. "Federalist No. 51."

19. "Half a Million Voters' Choices," *Governing* (April 1995): 15.

20. Herbert Jacob and Kenneth Vines, "Courts," in Virginia Gray, Herbert Jacob, and Kenneth Vines, eds., *Politics in the American States: A Comparative Analysis*, Fourth Edition. (Boston: Little, Brown, 1983), p. 238.

21. Professor Richard Murray, as reported by Professor Jay Greene, personal communication, April 10, 1997.

22. Thomas Cronin, *Direct Democracy* (Cambridge, MA: Harvard University Press, 1989); and Magleby, *Direct Legislation.*

23. For an analysis of the 1995 Canadian referendum, see David Lublin and D. Stephen Voss, "Context and Francophone Support for Sovereignty: An Ecological Analysis," *Canadian Journal of Political Science* (forthcoming).

24. Anthony King, *Running Scared: Why America's Politicians Campaign Too Much and Govern Too Little* (New York: Free Press, 1996), pp. 2–3.

25. Susan A. Macmanus, *Young v. Old: Generational Combat in the 21st Century* (Boulder, CO: Westview Press, 1996), Ch. 2.

26. Sidney Blumenthal, *The Permanent Campaign* (New York: Simon & Schuster, 1982).

27. Hugh Heclo, "The Permanent Campaign: A Conspectus," in *Campaigning to Govern or Governing to Campaign?* Thomas Mann and Norman Ornstein, eds. (Washington, DC: Brookings, 2000).

28. Woodrow Wilson, *Congressional Government* (Cleveland, OH: Meridian Books, 1956), p. 39.

29. Richard Boyd, "Decline of U.S. Voter Turnout: Structural Explanations," *American Politics Quarterly* 9 (1981): 133–159.

30. Frank Sorauf, *Political Parties in the American System* (Boston: Little, Brown, 1964); and Martin Wattenberg, *The Decline of American Political Parties, 1952–1984* (Cambridge, MA: Harvard University Press, 1986).

31. Gary Jacobson finds that national swings in House elections are much more heterogeneous than at midcentury. See "The Marginals Never Vanished: Incumbency and Competition in Elections to the U.S. House of Representatives, 1952–1982," *American Journal of Political Science* 31 (1987): 126–141.

32. Norman Ornstein, Thomas Mann, and Michael Malbin, *Vital Statistics on Congress, 1997–1998* (Washington, DC: Congressional Quarterly, Inc., 1998), Table 3.1.

33. John Broder, "Governors Join Ranks of Full-Time Campaign Money-Raisers," *New York Times* (December 5, 1999): 22.

34. John Alford and John Hibbing, "Electoral Convergence of the Two Houses of Congress," paper presented at the Norman Thomas Conference on Senate Exceptionalism, Vanderbilt University, Nashville, TN, October 21–23, 1999.

35. Ginsberg and Shefter, *Politics by Other Means*; and Terry Moe, "The Politics of Bureaucratic Structure," in John Chubb and Paul Peterson, eds., *Can the Government Govern?* (Washington, DC: Brookings, 1989), pp. 267–329.

36. John Dewey, as quoted in Marone, *The Democratic Wish*, p. 322.

37. Marone, *The Democratic Wish*.

38. R. Douglas Arnold, *The Logic of Congressional Action* (New Haven, CT: Yale University Press, 1990).

39. Henning, *Wit and Wisdom*, p. 58.

40. Henning, *Wit and Wisdom*, p. 94.

41. "A League of Evil," *The Economist* (September 11, 1999): 7.

42. Charles Masters, "Riviera Tramps Run Risk of 'Tourist Cleansing' Round-Ups," *Daily Telegraph*, (July 27, 1996, International Section): 15.

CHAPTER 2

1. Stanley M. Elkins and Eric McKitrick, *The Age of Federalism* (New York: Oxford University Press, 1993), Ch. 1.

2. Warren E. Burger, *It Is So Ordered: A Constitution Unfolds* (New York: William Morrow & Co., 1995), p. 7.

3. Herbert J. Storing, ed., *The Complete Anti-Federalist: Maryland and Virginia and the South,* Volume 5 (Chicago: University of Chicago Press, 1981), p. 210.

4. James W. Loewen, *Lies My Teacher Taught Me* (New York: New Press, 1995), Ch. 3.

5. Thomas A. Bailey, *The American Pageant: A History of the Republic* (Boston: D. C. Heath, 1956).

6. Gordon S. Wood, *The Radicalism of the American Revolution* (New York: Knopf, 1992), p. 80.

7. Jack P. Greene, "The Role of the Lower Houses of Assembly in Eighteenth-Century Politics," in Jack P. Greene, ed., *The Reinterpretation of the American Revolution, 1763–1789* (New York: Harper & Row, 1968), pp. 86–109.

8. Merrill D. Peterson, *Thomas Jefferson and the New Nation* (New York: Oxford University Press, 1970), pp. 22–23.

9. Wood, *Radicalism,* p. 55.

10. J. Franklin Jameson, *The American Revolution Considered As a Social Movement* (Princeton, NJ: Princeton University Press, 1926).

11. Thomas Hobbes, *Leviathan* (New York: Oxford University Press, 1996). Originally published in 1651.

12. John Locke, *Two Treatises on Civil Government* (London: Dent, 1924). Originally published in 1690.

13. J. H. Plumb, *The Origins of Political Stability* (Boston: Houghton Mifflin, 1967).

14. For a discussion of the influence of James Harrington on colonial thought, see Samuel H. Beer, *To Make a Nation: The Rediscovery of American Federalism* (Cambridge, MA: Harvard University Press, 1993).

15. Thomas Paine, *Common Sense* (New York: Penguin, 1986). Originally published in 1776.

16. Edmund S. Morgan and Helen M. Morgan, *The Stamp Act Crisis: Prologue to Revolution* (Chapel Hill, NC: University of North Carolina Press, 1953), p. 106.

17. Morgan and Morgan, *Stamp Act Crisis,* p. 106.

18. Bernard Bailyn, *The Origins of American Politics* (New York: Knopf, 1968), p. 12.

19. C. L. Becker, *Freedom and Responsibility in the American Way of Life* (New York: Knopf, 1945), p. 16, as quoted by Louis Hartz, *The Liberal Tradition in America* (New York: Harcourt, 1955), p. 61.

20. Robert J. Dinkin, *Voting in Revolutionary America: A Study of Elections in the Original Thirteen States, 1776–1789* (Westport, CT: Greenwood Press, 1982); and Robert J. Dinkin, *Voting in Provincial America: A Study of Elections in the Thirteen Colonies, 1689–1776* (Westport, CT: Greenwood Press, 1977).

21. Willi Paul Adams, *The First American Constitutions: Republican Ideology and the Making of the State Constitutions in the Revolutionary Era* (Chapel Hill, NC: University of North Carolina Press, 1980), pp. 245, 308–311.

22. Adams, *First American Constitutions,* p. 207.

23. Bailey, *American Pageant,* p. 136.

24. Gordon S. Wood, *The Creation of the American Republic, 1776–1787* (Chapel Hill, NC: University of North Carolina Press, 1969), pp. 396–403.

25. Merrill Jensen, *The New Nation: A History of the United States During the Confederation, 1781–1789* (New York: Vintage, 1965), p. 33.

26. Charles A. Beard, *An Economic Interpretation of the Constitution of the United States* (New York: Free Press, 1913).

27. Robert E. Brown, *Charles Beard and the Constitution* (Princeton, NJ: Princeton University Press, 1956); and Forrest McDonald, *We the People* (Chicago: University of Chicago Press, 1958).

28. John P. Roche, "The Founding Fathers: A Reform Caucus in Action," *American Political Science Review* 55 (December 1961): 799–816.

29. Winton U. Solberg, ed., *The Federal Convention and the Formation of the Union of the American States* (New York: Bobbs-Merrill, 1958), p. 78.

30. Solberg, *Federal Convention,* p. 79.

31. Solberg, *Federal Convention,* pp. 131–134.

32. Max Farrand, *The Framing of the Constitution of the United States* (New Haven, CT: Yale University Press, 1913), p. 113.

33. Thornton Anderson, *Creating the Constitution: The Convention of 1787 and the First Congress* (University Park, PA: Pennsylvania State University Press, 1993).

34. Arthur M. Schlesinger, Jr., ed., *History of American Presidential Elections, 1789–1968,* Vol. 2 (New York: McGraw-Hill, 1971), p. 1244.

35. Anderson, *Creating the Constitution,* p. 148.

36. Anderson, *Creating the Constitution,* p. 148.

37. Jane Mansbridge, *Why We Lost the ERA* (Chicago: University of Chicago Press, 1986).

38. Owen S. Ireland, *Religion, Ethnicity and Politics: Ratifying the Constitution in Pennsylvania* (University Park, PA: Pennsylvania State University Press, 1995).

39. Henry Steele Commager, ed., *Documents of American History* (New York: Appleton-Century-Crofts, 1958), p. 104; and Adams, *First American Constitutions.*

40. Arthur M. Schlesinger, *Prelude to Independence* (New York: Knopf, 1958), p. 299.

41. C. M. Kenyon, "Men of Little Faith: The Anti-Federalists on the Nature of Representative Government," in Jack P. Greene, *The Reinterpretation of the American Revolution, 1763–1789* (New York: Harper & Row, 1968), pp. 526–567; and Herbert J. Storing, ed., *The Anti-Federalist* (Chicago: University of Chicago Press, 1986).

42. John Jay, Alexander Hamilton, and James Madison, writing under the pseudonym Publius, *The Federalist Papers* (New York: New American Library, 1961).

43. Beard, *An Economic Interpretation of the Constitution of the United States.*

44. Bernard Bailyn, *The Ideological Origins of the American Revolution* (Cambridge, MA: Harvard University Press, 1967); and Wood, *Creation of the American Republic.*

45. Second Inaugural Address, 1865, as quoted in John Bartlett, *Familiar Quotations,* Sixteenth Edition. (Boston: Little, Brown, 1992), p. 450.

CHAPTER 3

1. Candy Lightner's story comes from Jay Mathews, "One California Mother's MADD Drive to Bar Highways to Drunken Killers," *Washington Post* (June 16, 1984):A2; and John J. O'Connor, "'MADD' Drama Fights Drunken Driving," *New York Times* (March 14, 1983): C14.

2. Jane Perlez, "Teen-Age Drinking Vote: Crusader is 'Delighted,'" *New York Times* (June 9, 1984):5.

3. David G. Savage, "Justices Support Move for Drinking Age of 21: High Court Rules Congress May Curb Highway Funds to States That Refuse to Raise Minimum," *Los Angeles Times* (June 24, 1987): 15.

4. The story of the National Minimum Drinking Age Act of 1984 comes primarily from two sources: Perlez, "Teen-Age Drinking Vote," and Douglas B. Feaver, "Reagan Now Wants 21 As Drinking Age," *Washington Post* (June 14, 1984): A1.

5. Martin Tolchin, "Senate Votes Bill Aimed at Forcing Drinking Age of 21," *New York Times* (June 27, 1984): 1.

6. Al Kamen, "High Court Upholds Law Linking U.S. Highway Funds, State Drinking Age," *Washington Post* (June 24, 1987): A8.

7. Lu Ann Snider, "The Politics and Consequences of the New Drinking Age Law," *Florida State University Law Review* 13 (Fall 1985): 847–861.

8. Stuart Taylor, Jr., "Justices Back Use of Aid to Get States to Raise Drinking Age," *New York Times* (June 24, 1987): 20.

9. Savage, "Justices Support Move."

10. South Louisiana differs from the rest of the southern United States in other ways as well, including political preferences and approaches to race. See D. Stephen Voss, "Beyond Racial Threat: Failure of an Old Hypothesis in the New South," *Journal of Politics* 58 (1996): 1156–1170;

James G. Dauphine, *A Question of Inheritance: Religion, Education, and Louisiana's Cultural Boundary, 1880–1940.* (Lafayette, LA: Center for Louisiana Studies, 1993); and John H. Fenton and Kenneth N. Vines, "Negro Registration in Louisiana," *American Political Science Review* 51 (1957): 704–713.

11. Details on Louisiana's battle to keep its lower drinking age come from: Bill Voelker and Susan Finch, "21-Year Limit Discriminates, High Court Says," *New Orleans Times-Picayune* (March 9, 1996): A1; Bruce Alpert, "Drinking Age Ruling May Slash Road Aid," *New Orleans Times-Picayune* (March 15, 1996): A1; Susan Finch and Ed Anderson, "Court Reverses on Age to Drink; It's 21 to Imbibe or to Buy Liquor," *New Orleans Times-Picayune* (July 3, 1996): A1; and Joe Gyan, Jr., "Drinking Age Revived," *Baton Rouge Advocate* (July 3, 1996): 1A.

12. James Gill, "Court Tampers with Drinking Age," *New Orleans Times-Picayune* (March 13, 1996): B7.

13. Doug Myers, "Poll Shows Voters Want Drinking Age Set at 21," *New Orleans Times-Picayune* (March 17, 1996): 1A. Despite the mixed feelings of Louisiana men and the strong feelings of the state's young adults, the statewide results supported a higher drinking age because women overwhelmingly endorsed the higher limit. It is unclear how much of the position reflected sincere policy preferences and how much represented desire for the "blackmail portion" of the funds.

14. Ed Anderson, "Gamblers, Drinkers Still Must Be 21," *New Orleans Times-Picayune* (June 5, 1999): A2. At least some members of the House said they opposed the bill not because it would lower the drinking age, but because it would also lower the gambling age and might prevent companies from giving senior citizens special discounts.

15. Manuel Roig-Franzia and Ed Anderson, "Lower Alcohol Limit Clears Hurdle, but Drinking Age Measure Blocked," *New Orleans Times-Picayune* (April 3, 1998): A1; and Sherry Sapp, "Try Fails to Close Drinking Age Law Loophole," *Baton Rouge Advocate* (April 4, 1998): 8A.

16. Associated Press, "Law Doesn't Stop Teen Drinkers," *Dubuque Telegraph Herald* (August 12, 1996): B10.

17. John Bartlett, *Familiar Quotations: Revised and Enlarged,* Fifteenth Edition. (Boston: Little, Brown, 1980), p. 452.

18. Alexis de Tocqueville, *Democracy in America,* Vol. I, Philips Bradley, ed. (New York: Knopf, 1945), p. 169.

19. Jean E. Smith, *John Marshall: Definer of a Nation* (New York: Henry Holt, 1996), pp. 440–446.

20. *McCulloch* v. *Maryland* (1819), 4 Wheaton 316, as reprinted in Henry Steele Commager, ed., *Documents of American History,* Sixth Edition. (New York: Appleton-Century-Crofts, 1949), p. 217.

21. *McCulloch* v. *Maryland* (1819), as reprinted in Commager, p. 217.

22. *United States* v. *E. C. Knight Co.,* 156 U.S. 1 (1895).

23. *NLRB* v. *Jones & Laughlin Co.,* 317 U.S. 111 (1937).

24. *Wickard* v. *Filburn,* (1942).

25. *Helvering* v. *Davis,* 301 U.S. 548, 599 (1937).

26. *South Dakota* v. *Dole,* 483 U.S. 203 (1987).

27. Barry Friedman, "The Law and Economics of Federalism: Valuing Federalism," *Minnesota Law Review* 82 (December 1997): 317.

28. Lynn A. Baker, "Conditional Federal Spending and States' Rights," *Annals of the American Academy of Political and Social Science* 574 (March 2001): 105.

29. Morton Grodzins, *The American System: A New View of Government in the United States,* Daniel J. Elazar, ed. (Chicago: Rand McNally, 1966).

30. Calculated from data in Ester Fuchs, *Mayors and Money* (Chicago: University of Chicago Press, 1992), p. 210.

31. Chuck Henning, *The Wit and Wisdom of Politics: Expanded Edition.* (Golden, CO: Fulcrum, 1992), p. 208.

32. James M. Perry, "GOP Congressman Shows How to Keep Power, Even While Under Indictment for Corruption," *Wall Street Journal* (June 14, 1994): A16.

33. Jeffrey L. Pressman and Aaron Wildavsky, *Implementation,* Third Edition. (Berkeley, CA: University of California Press, 1984); Martha Derthick, *New Towns in Town: Why a Federal Program Failed* (Washington, DC: Urban Institute, 1972); and Eugene Bardach, *The Implementation Game,* Fourth Edition. (Cambridge, MA: MIT Press, 1982).

34. Derthick, *New Towns in Town.*

35. Pressman and Wildavsky, *Implementation,* p. 118.

36. Timothy Conlan, *New Federalism: Intergovernmental Reform from Nixon to Reagan* (Washington, DC: Brookings, 1988).

37. Executive Office of the President, Office of Management and Budget, *Budget for Fiscal Year 2000, Historical Tables,* Table 12.3.

38. David McKay, *Domestic Policy and Ideology: Presidents and the American State, 1964–1987* (New York: Cambridge University Press, 1989), Ch. 4.

39. Peter J. Howe, "State's Share of Federal Dollars Drops," *Boston Globe* (July 2, 1994): 17.

40. Lynda McDonnell, "Will Our State Be a Magnet for Poor from Across Nation?" *Pioneer Press* (December 31, 1995): 1A, 10A.

41. Timothy Conlan, "And the Beat Goes On: Intergovernmental Mandates and Preemption in an Era of Deregulation," *Publius* 21 (Summer 1991): 57. On the costs of environmental mandates, see Richard C. Feiock, "Estimating Political, Fiscal and Economic Impacts of State Mandates: A Pooled Time Series Analysis of Local Planning and Growth Policy in Florida," paper prepared for the annual meeting of the American Political Science Association, 1994; Colleen M. Grogan, "The Influence of Federal Mandates on State Policy Decision-Making," paper prepared for the annual meeting of the American Political Science Association, 1994; Teresa Coughlin, Leighton Ku, and John Holahan, *Medicaid Since 1980* (Washington, DC: Urban Institute, 1994); and John Holahan et al., "Explaining the Recent Growth in Medicaid Spending," *Health Affairs* 12 (Fall 1993): 177–193.

42. Gregory S. Lashutka, "Local Rebellion: How Cities Are Rising Up Against Unfunded Mandates," *Commonsense* 1 (Summer 1994): 66.

43. Dan M. Berkovitz, "Waste Wars: Did Congress 'Nuke' State Sovereignty in the Low-Level Radioactive Waste Policy Amendments Act of 1985?" *Harvard Environmental Law Review* 11 (1987): 437–440.

44. *New York Times* (January 18, 1991).

45. *New York v. U.S.,* 112 *Supreme Court Reporter,* 2414-47, 301 U.S. 1 (1991).

46. James Bryce, *Modern Democracies* (New York: Macmillan, 1921), Vol. I, p. 132.

47. Robert R. Alford and Eugene C. Lee, "Voting Turnout in American Cities," *American Political Science Review* 62 (1968): 796–813.

48. Village politics are well described in A. J. Vidich and J. Bensman, *Small Town in Mass Society* (New York: Harper & Row, 1972). For descriptions of courthouse gangs in the county politics of the South, see V. O. Key, *Southern Politics* (New York: Random House, 1949).

49. Paul E. Peterson, *City Limits* (Chicago: University of Chicago Press, 1981).

50. *Statistical Abstract of the United States,* 1992, Table 22.

51. Greta Anand, "Circling of the Welcome Wagons: Selectman Candidates Rip Social Programs," *Boston Globe* (West Weekly Section, March 19, 1995): 1, 8.

52. "Money to Burn," *The Economist* (August 14, 1993): 23.

53. Steve Rushin, "The Heart of a City," *Sports Illustrated* (December 4, 1995).

54. Morris Fiorina, *Divided Government* (New York: Macmillan, 1992).

55. Calculated from U.S. Bureau of the Census, *State and Local Finance Estimates by State: 1995–1996* (accessed at www.census.gov/govs/www/esti96.html on November 11, 1999). Data on state expenditures combine expenditures by state and local governments. Because the sharing of responsibilities by state and local governments varies widely from state to state, any interstate comparison that looks at state government expenditures alone can be quite misleading.

56. Paul E. Peterson, *The Price of Federalism* (Washington, DC: Brookings Institution, 1995), p. 105.

57. The Council of State Governments, *The Book of the States: 1996–97 Edition* (Lexington, KY: Council of State Governments).

58. Thad Beyle, "Being Governor," in Carl E. Van Horn, ed., *The State of the States,* Second Edition. (Washington, DC: Brookings, 1993).

59. George Skelton, "Lessons from an Earlier Foreign Journey," *Los Angeles Times* (October 25, 1999).

CHAPTER 4

1. Joseph B. Mitchell, *Military Leaders of the American Revolution* (McLean, VA: EPM Publications, 1967), pp. 138–149.

2. Jan Stanislaw Kopczewski, *Kosciuszko and Pulaski* (Warsaw, Poland: Impress Publishers, 1976).

3. Louis des Cognets, Jr., *Black Sheep and Heroes of the American Revolution* (Princeton, NJ: Cognets, 1965), Ch. 15.

4. See Alvin Rabushka and Kenneth Shepsle, *Politics in Plural Societies* (Columbus, OH: Merrill, 1972).

5. Carl J. Friedrich, *Problems of the American Public Service* (New York: McGraw-Hill, 1935), p. 12.

6. John A. Garrity and Peter Gay, eds., *The Columbia History of the World* (New York: Harper & Row, 1972), p. 673.

7. Garrity and Gay, eds., *Columbia History of the World,* pp. 669–670.

8. Israel Zangwill, *The Melting Pot* (New York: Macmillan, 1912, ©1909).

9. Quoted in Marc Shell, "Babel in America; or, The Politics of Language Diversity in the United States," *Critical Inquiry* 20 (1993): 109.

10. Richard McCormick, "Ethno-Cultural Interpretations of Nineteenth-Century American Voting Behavior," *Political Science Quarterly* 89 (1974): 351–377.

11. Richard Wayman, "Wisconsin Ethnic Groups and the Election of 1890," *Wisconsin Magazine of History* 51 (1968): 273. More generally, see Paul Kleppner, *The Third Electoral System, 1853–1892: Parties, Voters, and Political Cultures* (Chapel Hill, NC: University of North Carolina Press, 1979).

12. J. Morgan Kousser, *The Shaping of Southern Politics* (New Haven, CT: Yale University Press, 1974).

13. John Miller, "Chinese Exclusion Act," *Congressional Record–Senate 1882,* 13, Pt. 2: 1484–1485.

14. This is Oscar Handlin's sardonic characterization. See his *Race and Nationality in American Life* (Boston: Little, Brown, 1957), p. 95.

15. Madison Grant, *The Passing of the Great Race* (New York: Scribner's, 1916), pp. 80–81.

16. *Abstracts of Reports of the Immigration Commission* (Washington, DC: Government Printing Office, Vol. 1, 1911). See pp. 229, 244–265.

17. Henry Cabot Lodge, "Immigration Restriction," *Congressional Record—Senate 1896*, 28, Pt. 3: 2817.

18. "Emergency" immigration restrictions passed in 1921 were fine-tuned and formalized in the National Origins Act of 1924 and the National Origins Quota Act of 1929.

19. Seymour Martin Lipset and Earl Raab, *The Politics of Unreason* (New York: Harper & Row, 1970), p. 111.

20. Alan Lichtman, *Prejudice and the Old Politics: The Presidential Election of 1928* (Chapel Hill, NC: University of North Carolina Press, 1979).

21. Spencer Rich, "A 20-Year High Tide of Immigration," *Washington Post National Weekly Edition* (September 4–10, 1995): 30.

22. Caroline J. Tolbert and Rodney E. Hero, "Race/Ethnicity and Direct Democracy: An Analysis of California's Illegal Immigration Initiative," *Journal of Politics* 58 (1996): 806–818.

23. George Borhas, "The New Economics of Immigration," *The Atlantic Monthly* (November 1996): 72–80.

24. National Research Council, *The New Americans: Economic, Demographic, and Fiscal Effects of Immigration.* (Washington, DC: National Academy Press, 1977), Chs. 4–6.

25. Brad Knickerbocker, "Environment vs. Immigrants," *Christian Science Monitor* (April 27, 1998): 3; and William Branigin, "Sierra Club Votes for Neutrality on Immigration; Population Issue 'Intensely Debated,'" *Washington Post* (April 26, 1998): A16.

26. David Kennedy, "Can We Still Afford to Be a Nation of Immigrants?" *The Atlantic Monthly* (November 1996): 67.

27. Arthur Schlesinger, Jr., *The Disuniting of America* (Knoxville, TN: Whittle, 1991).

28. Louis Hartz, *The Liberal Tradition in America* (New York: Harcourt, 1955).

29. On Madison's pessimistic view of human nature, see Richard Matthews, *If Men Were Angels* (Lawrence, KS: University of Kansas Press, 1995), especially Ch. 3.

30. Ayn Rand, *The Virtue of Selfishness: A New Concept of Egoism*, New American Library (New York: Signet, 1964), pp. 80–91.

31. Bernard Bailyn, *The Ideological Origins of the American Revolution* (Cambridge, MA: Harvard University Press, 1967).

32. Gordon Wood. *The Creation of the American Republic* (New York: Norton, 1972), and J. G. A. Pocock, *The Machiavellian Moment* (Princeton, NJ: Princeton University Press, 1975).

33. Michael J. Sandel, *Democracy's Discontent: American in Search of a Public Philosophy* (Cambridge, MA: Belknap Press of Harvard, 1996).

34. Rogers Smith, "Beyond Tocqueville, Myrdal and Hartz: The Multiple Traditions in America," *American Political Science Review* 87 (1993): 549–566. These inconsistencies were not lost on earlier thinkers, to be sure. Recall Jefferson's pessimistic predictions in his *Notes on the State of Virginia 1781–1785*. Also see Alexis de Tocqueville, *Democracy in America,* J. P. Mayer, ed. (New York: Harper, 1969), pp. 340–363.

35. Samuel Huntington, *American Politics: The Promise of Disharmony* (Cambridge, MA: Harvard University Press, 1981).

36. I. A. Lewis and William Schneider, "Hard Times: The Public on Poverty," *Public Opinion* (June/July 1985): 2–8, 59–60.

37. "Income Tax Irritation." *Public Perspective* (July/August, 1990): 86.

38. Stanley Feldman, "Structure and Consistency in Public Opinion: The Role of Core Beliefs and Values," *American Journal of Political Science* 32 (1988): 416–440.

39. Paul Krugman, *Peddling Prosperity* (New York: Norton, 1994), Ch. 5.

40. Madison, "Federalist No. 10," *The Federalist Papers*.

41. Everett Carll Ladd, *The American Ideology* (Storrs, CT: The Roper Center, 1994), pp. 56–57.

42. Sidney Verba and Gary Orren, *Equality in America* (Cambridge, MA: Harvard University Press, 1985).

43. Bailyn, *Ideological Origins*, pp. 257–268.

44. Seymour Martin Lipset, *American Exceptionalism* (New York: Norton, 1996).

45. Mariana Servin-Gonzalez and Oscar Torres-Reyna, "Trends: Religion and Politics," *Public Opinion Quarterly* 63 (1999): 613–614.

46. Robert Booth Fowler, *Religion and Politics in America* (Metuchen, NJ: American Theological Library Association, 1985), p. 27.

47. Huntington, *American Politics*.

48. Frederick Jackson Turner, *The Frontier in American History* (New York: Holt, 1920).

49. Hartz, *The Liberal Tradition*, p. 89.

50. For a discussion, see Seymour Martin Lipset, "Why No Socialism in the United States?" in Seweryn Bialer and Sophia Sluzar, eds., *Sources of Contemporary Radicalism* (New York: Westview Press, 1977).

51. Sven Steinmo, "American Exceptionalism Reconsidered," in Larry C. Dodd and Calvin Jillson, eds., *The Dynamics of American Politics* (Boulder, CO: Westwood, 1994), pp. 106–131.

52. For a sympathetic description of the trials and ordeals of the immigrants, see Oscar Handlin, *The Uprooted*, Second Edition. (Boston: Little, Brown, 1973).

53. Hartz, *The Liberal Tradition*, p. 18.

54. *Abstracts of Reports of the Immigration Commission*, p. 170.

55. William Bennett and Jack Kemp, "The Fortress Party?" *Wall Street Journal* (October 21, 1994): A14.

56. David Firestone, "Mayor Seeks Immigration Coalition," *New York Times* (October 11, 1996): B-3.

57. "The Effects of Ethnicity on Political Culture," in Paul Peterson, ed., *Classifying by Race* (Princeton, NJ: Princeton University Press, 1995), pp. 351–352.

58. Rodolfo de la Garza, Angelo Falcon, and F. Chris Garcia, "Will the Real Americans Please Stand Up: Anglo and Mexican American Support of Core American Political Values," *American Journal of Political Science* 40 (1996): 335–351.

59. Lydia Saad, "Immigrants See United States as Land of Opportunity," *The Gallup Poll Monthly* (July 1995): 19–33.

60. Gregory Rodriguez, quoted in Patrick McDonnell, "Immigrants Quickly Becoming Assimilated, Report Concludes," *San Francisco Chronicle* (July 7, 1999): A4.

61. Philip Martin and Elizabeth Midgley, "Immigration to the United States" (Washington, DC: Population Reference Bureau, June 1999): 37.

CHAPTER 5

1. For background on the Gulf War, see "Gulf Crisis Grows into War with Iraq," *1990 Congressional Quarterly Almanac* (Washington, DC: Congressional Quarterly, Inc., 1991): 717–756; and "1991 Begins with War in the Mideast," *1991 Congressional Quarterly Almanac* (Washington, DC: Congressional Quarterly, Inc., 1992): 437–450.

2. Jon Krosnick and Laura Brannon, "The Impact of the Gulf War on the Ingredients of Presidential Evaluations," *American Political Science Review* 87 (1993): 963–975.

3. V. O. Key, *Public Opinion and American Democracy* (New York: Knopf, 1961).

4. Carl Friedrich, *Man and His Government* (New York: McGraw-Hill, 1963), pp. 19–215.

5. Robert Hess and Judith Horney, *The Development of Political Attitudes in Children* (Garden City, NY: Doubleday, 1967).

6. Elizabeth Cook, Ted Jelen, and Clyde Wilcox, *Between Two Absolutes: Public Opinion and the Politics of Abortion* (Boulder, CO: Westview Press, 1992).

7. David Leege, Kenneth Wald, and Lyman Kellstedt, "The Public Dimension of Private Devotionalism," in David Leege and Lyman Kellstedt, eds., *Rediscovering the Religious Factor in American Politics* (Armonk, NY: Sharpe, 1993), pp. 139–156; and Alan Hertzke and John Rausch, "The Religious Vote in American Politics: Value Conflict, Continuity, and Change," in Stephen Craig, ed., *Broken Contract* (Boulder, CO: Westview Press, 1996), p. 188.

8. Warren Miller and Santa Traugott, *American National Election Studies Data Sourcebook, 1952–1986* (Cambridge, MA: Harvard University Press, 1990), pp. 316, 332.

9. For a survey of positive and negative findings, see Jack Citrin and Donald Green, "The Self-Interest Motive in American Public Opinion," *Research in Micropolitics,* Vol. 3 (Greenwich, CT: JAI Press, 1993), pp. 1–28.

10. Douglas Hibbs, *The American Political Economy* (Cambridge, MA: Harvard University Press, 1987), Ch. 5.

11. David Sears and Jack Citrin, *Tax Revolt* (Cambridge, MA: Harvard University Press, 1985), Chs. 6–7.

12. Norman Nie, Jane Junn, and Kenneth Stehlik-Barry, *Education and Democratic Citizenship in America* (Chicago: University of Chicago Press, 1996).

13. Larry Bartels, "Messages Received: The Political Impact of Media Exposure," *American Political Science Review* 87 (1993): 267–285.

14. John G. Geer, *From Tea Leaves to Opinion Polls: A Theory of Democratic Leadership* (New York: Columbia University Press, 1996).

15. Details on how these polls are conducted appear in D. Stephen Voss, Andrew Gelman, and Gary King, "Preelection Survey Methodology: Details from Eight Polling Organizations, 1988 and 1992," *Public Opinion Quarterly* 59 (Spring 1995): 98–132.

16. Don Van Natta, Jr., "Polling's 'Dirty Little Secret': No Response," *New York Times* (November 21, 1999, Sect. 4): pp. 1, 16.

17. John Brehm, *The Phantom Respondents* (Ann Arbor, MI: University of Michigan Press, 1993), Ch. 2.

18. Everett Ladd, "The Pollsters' Waterloo," *Wall Street Journal* (November 19, 1996).

19. "Poll Leaves Democrats with Red Faces," (Reuters, January 5, 2000).

20. For a full discussion, see David Moore and Frank Newport, "Misreading the Public: The Case of the Holocaust Poll," *Public Perspective* : March/April 1994): 28–30; and Tom Smith, "Review: The Holocaust Denial Controversy," *Public Opinion Quarterly* 59 (1995): 269–295. D. Stephen Voss and Penny Miller present two other instances in which a double negative apparently caused many people to misreport their policy preferences in "Following a False Trail: The Hunt for White Backlash in Kentucky's 1996 Desegregation Vote," *State Politics and Policy Quarterly* 1 (2001): 63–82.

21. Tom Smith, "Public Support for Public Spending, 1973–1994," *The Public Perspective* 6 (April/May 1995): 2.

22. Jon Krosnick and Matthew Barent, "Comparisons of Party Identification and Policy Preferences: The Impact of Survey Question Format," *American Journal of Political Science* 37 (1993): 941–964.

23. On these topics, see Howard Schuman and Stanley Presser, *Questions and Answers in Attitude Surveys* (New York: Harcourt, Academic Press, 1981); and the essays in Thomas Mann and Gary Orren, eds., *Media Polls in American Politics* (Washington, DC: Brookings, 1992).

24. Tamar Lewin, "Study Points to Increase in Tolerance of Ethnicity," *New York Times* (January 8, 1992): A12.

25. For a comprehensive breakdown of federal spending, see "Where the Money Goes," *Congressional Quarterly* (December 11, 1993).

26. Anthony Downs, *An Economic Theory of Democracy* (New York: Harper & Row, 1957), Chs. 11–13.

27. Morris P. Fiorina, "Information and Rationality in Elections," in John Ferejohn and James Kuklinski, eds., *Information and Democratic Processes* (Urbana, IL: University of Illinois Press, 1990), pp. 329–342.

28. John Krosnick, "Government Policy and Citizen Passion: A Study of Issue Publics in Contemporary America," *Political Behavior* 12 (1990): 59–92; and Peter Natchez and Irvin Bupp, "Candidates, Issues, and Voters," *Public Policy* 1 (1968): 409–437.

29. Anthony Downs, "Up and Down with Ecology—The Issue Attention Cycle," *The Public Interest* 28 (1972): 38–50.

30. Fiorina, "Information and Rationality."

31. Anthony King, "Names and Places Lost in the Mists of Time," *Daily Telegraph* (August 26, 1997): 4.

32. Philip Converse, "The Nature of Belief Systems in Mass Publics," in David Apter, ed., *Ideology and Discontent* (New York: Free Press, 1964), pp. 206–261.

33. There is a huge literature debating the size of the increase in ideological thinking. See inter alia, Norman Nie and Kristi Andersen, "Mass Belief Systems Revisited: Political Chance and Attitude Structure," *Journal of Politics* 36 (1974): 540–580; John Field and Ronald Anderson, "Ideology in the Public's Conceptualization of the 1964 Election," *Public Opinion Quarterly* 33 (1969): 380–398; and John Sullivan, James Piereson, and George Marcus, "Ideological Constraint in the Mass Public: A Methodological Critique and Some New Findings," *American Journal of Political Science* 22 (1978): 233–249.

34. Miller and Traugott, *American National Election Studies Data Sourcebook,* p. 94.

35. Vernon Van Dyke, *Ideology and Political Choice* (Chatham, NJ: Chatham House Publishers, 1995), Chs. 3–5.

36. James A. Davis, "Changeable Weather in a Cooling Climate Atop the Liberal Plateau," *Public Opinion Quarterly* 56 (1992): 261–306; and Morris P. Fiorina, "The Reagan Years: Turning to the Right or Groping Toward the Middle?" in Barry Cooper, Allan Kornberg, and William Mishler, eds., *The Resurgence of Conservatism in Anglo-American Democracies* (Durham, NC: Duke University Press, 1988), pp. 430–459.

37. "Public Expects GOP Miracles," *Times-Mirror News Release* (December 8, 1994).

38. Samuel Stouffer, *Communism, Conformity, and Civil Liberties* (New York: Doubleday, 1955); and James Prothro and Charles Grigg, "Fundamental Principles of Democracy: Bases of Agreement and Disagreement," *Journal of Politics* 22 (1960): 176–194.

39. For evidence that people's opinions reflect a smaller number of "core beliefs" that may conflict with each other or situational characteristics, see Stanley Feldman, "Structure and Consistency in Public Opinion: The Role of Core Beliefs and Values," *American Journal of Public Opinion* 32 (1988): 416–440; and Stanley Feldman and John Zaller, "A Simple Theory of the Survey Response: Answering Questions versus Revealing Preferences," *American Journal of Political Science* 36 (1992): 579–616.

40. On the effects of posing political conflicts as matters of conflicting rights, see Mary Anne Glendon, *Rights Talk: The Impoverishment of Political Discourse* (New York: Free Press, 1991).

41. Cook, Jelen, and Wilcox, *Between Two Absolutes,* Ch. 2.

42. "Abortion: Overview of a Complex Opinion," *The Public Perspective* (November/December, 1989): 19, 20.

43. Ibid., 20.

44. "Abortion," *The American Enterprise* (July/August 1995): 107.

45. Cites from John F. Harris, "Campaign Promises Aside, It's Politics as Usual: Policy Shifts, Internal Debates—The Bush White House Looks a Lot Like the Clinton One," *Washington Post Weekly Edition* (July 2–8, 2001): 11.

46. Dan Carney, "House GOP Embrace of Gun Curbs Not Yet Lock, Stock and Barrel, *CQ Weekly* (May 29, 1999): 1267.

47. Dan Carney, "Beyond Guns and Violence: A Battle for House Control," *CQ Weekly* (June 1999): 1426–1432.

48. Kathy Keily, "After Failed Gun Legislation, Political Finger Pointing Begins," *USA Today,* June 21, 1999: 14A.

49. ABC News/Washington Post poll of August 30–September 2, 1999.

50. James Stimson, "A Macro Theory of Information Flow," in John Ferejohn and James Kuklinski, eds., *Information and Democratic Processes* (Urbana, IL: University of Illinois Press, 1990), pp. 345–368.

51. James Stimson, *Public Opinion in America: Moods, Cycles, and Swings* (Boulder, CO: Westview Press, 1991).

52. Benjamin Page and Robert Shapiro, *The Rational Public* (Chicago: University of Chicago Press, 1992).

53. Christopher Wlezien, "The Public as Thermostat: Dynamics of Preferences for Spending," *American Journal of Political Science* 39 (1995): 981–1000.

CHAPTER 6

1. Jeff Jacoby, "Making It Too Easy to Vote," *Boston Globe* (July 18, 1996): A15.

2. Benjamin Barber, *Strong Democracy: Participatory Politics for a New Age* (Berkeley and Los Angeles, CA: University of California Press, 1984), p. xiii.

3. John Aldrich, *Why Parties?* (Chicago: University of Chicago Press, 1995), pp. 106–107.

4. "18-Year-Old Vote: Constitutional Amendment Cleared," *Congressional Quarterly Almanac* (Washington, DC: Congressional Quarterly, 1972), pp. 475–477.

5. For a comparative study of the American and Swiss suffrage movements, see Lee Ann Banaszak, *Why Movements Succeed or Fail* (Princeton, NJ: Princeton University Press, 1996).

6. Howard Rosenthal and Subrata Sen, "Electoral Participation in the French Fifth Republic," *American Political Science Review* 67 (1973): 29–54.

7. Raymond E. Wolfinger and Steven J. Rosenstone, *Who Votes?* (New Haven, CT: Yale University Press, 1980), p. 116.

8. Ruy Teixeira, *The Disappearing American Voter* (Washington, DC: Brookings, 1992), p. 10.

9. Martha Angle, "Low Voter Turnout Prompts Concern on Hill," *Congressional Quarterly Weekly Report* (April 2, 1988): 864; and Stephen Bennett, "The Uses and Abuses of Registration and Turnout Data," *PS: Political Science and Politics* 23 (1990): 166–171.

10. Stephen Knack, "Drivers Wanted: Motor Voter and the Election of 1996," *PS: Political Science and Politics* 32 (1999): 237–243; and Michael Martinez and David Hill, "Did Motor Voter Work? *American Politics Quarterly* 27 (1999): 296–315.

11. Wolfinger and Rosenstone, *Who Votes?* p. 88.

12. Richard Hasen, "Voting Without Law," *University of Pennsylvania Law Review* 144 (1996): 2135–2179.

13. Mark Franklin, "Electoral Engineering and Cross-National Turnout Differences: What Role for Compulsory Voting? *British Journal of Political Science* 29 (1999): 205.

14. Richard Boyd, "Decline of U.S. Voter Turnout: Structural Explanations," *American Politics Quarterly* 9 (1981): 133–159.

15. Stephen Knack, "The Voter Participation Effects of Selecting Jurors from Registration Lists," Working Paper No. 91–10, University of Maryland, Department of Economics; and J. Eric Oliver and Raymond Wolfinger, "Jury Aversion and Voter Registration," paper presented at the 1997 Annual Meeting of the American Political Science Association, Washington, DC.

16. G. Bingham Powell, "American Voter Turnout in Comparative Perspective," *American Political Science Review* 80 (1986): 17–43; and Robert Jackman, "Political Institutions and Voter Turnout in the Industrial Democracies," *American Political Science Review* 81 (1987): 405–423.

17. Steven J. Rosenstone and John Mark Hansen, *Mobilization, Participation, and Democracy* (New York: Macmillan, 1993), pp. 63–70. There is some conflict between their figures and those reported by Sidney Verba, Kay Lehman Schlozman, and Henry E. Brady in *Voice and Equality: Civic Volunteerism in American Politics* (Cambridge, MA: Harvard University Press, 1995), pp. 69–74. Part of the explanation may be that the survey items relied on by Rosenstone and Hansen generally have more specific referents (such as this year's elections), whereas the items relied on by Verba, Schlozman, and Brady ask more generally about activity in the last year or two years. Thus, the Verba, Schlozman, and Brady figures may reflect the increasing number of opportunities.

18. Jack Citrin, "Comment: The Political Relevance of Trust in Government," *American Political Science Review* 68 (1974): 973–988.

19. Teixeira, *The Disappearing American Voter,* p. 49.

20. "Politics Brief: Is There a Crisis?" *The Economist* (July 17, 1999): 50.

21. Rosenstone and Hansen, *Mobilization, Participation, and Democracy,* Ch. 2.

22. Jeffrey Jones, "Does Bringing Out the Candidate Bring Out the Votes?" *American Politics Quarterly* 26 (1998): 406.

23. John Milholland, "The Danger Point in American Politics," *North American Review* 164 (1897).

24. Wolfinger and Rosenstone, *Who Votes?* p. 101.

25. John Ferejohn and Morris Fiorina, "The Paradox of Not Voting: A Decision Theoretic Analysis," *American Political Science Review* 68 (1974): 525–535.

26. Anthony Downs, *An Economic Theory of Democracy* (New York: Harper & Row, 1957), Ch. 14.

27. Richard Brody, "The Puzzle of Political Participation in America," in Anthony King, ed., *The New American Political System* (Washington, DC: American Enterprise Institute, 1978),

pp. 287–324; and Paul Abramson and John Aldrich, "The Decline of Electoral Participation in America," *American Political Science Review* 76 (1982): 502–521.

28. Rosenstone and Hansen, *Mobilization, Participation, and Democracy,* p. 183.

29. Ibid., Ch. 7, p. 175.

30. Marshall Ganz, "Motor Voter or Motivated Voter," *The American Prospect* (September–October, 1996): 46–48; and Marshall Ganz, "Voters in the Crosshairs," *The American Prospect* (Winter 1994): 100–109.

31. Stephen Knack, "Civic Norms, Social Sanctions, and Voter Turnout," *Rationality and Society* 4 (1992): 133–156.

32. Warren Miller, "The Puzzle Transformed: Explaining Declining Turnout," *Political Behavior* 14 (1992): 1–43.

33. Robert Putnam, "Tuning In, Tuning Out: The Strange Disappearance of Social Capital in America," *PS: Political Science and Politics* 28 (1995): 664–683.

34. Rosenstone and Hansen, *Mobilization, Participation, and Democracy*, Ch. 7; and Teixeira, *The Disappearing American Voter*, Ch. 2.

35. Laura Stoker and M. Kent Jennings, "Life-Cycle Transitions and Political Participation: The Case of Marriage," *American Political Science Review* 89 (1995): 421–433.

36. For detailed analyses of the relationship between demographic characteristics and voting, see Wolfinger and Rosenstone, *Who Votes?*, and Rosenstone and Hansen, *Mobilization, Participation, and Democracy*, Ch. 5.

37. Sidney Verba and Norman Nie, *Participation in America: Political Democracy and Social Equality* (New York: Harper & Row, 1972), pp. 170–171; and Wolfinger and Rosenstone, *Who Votes?* p. 90.

38. Rosenstone and Hansen, *Mobilization, Participation, and Democracy in America*, Ch. 5.

39. Katherine Tate, "Black Political Participation in the 1984 and 1988 Presidential Elections," *American Political Science Review* 85 (1991): 1159–1176.

40. On language and political participation, see Verba, Schlozman, and Brady, *Voice and Equality*.

41. Russell Dalton, *Citizen Politics in Western Democracies* (Chatham, NJ: Chatham House, 1988), pp. 51–52.

42. Herbert Tingsten, *Political Behavior: Studies in Election Statistics* (London: King & Son, 1937), pp. 225–226.

43. "The Democratic Distemper," *The Public Interest* 41 (1975), pp. 36–37.

44. Quoted in Seymour Martin Lipset, *Political Man* (New York: Anchor, 1963), p. 228, note 90.

45. George Will, "In Defense of Nonvoting," in George Will, ed., *The Morning After* (New York: Free Press, 1986), p. 229.

46. Political theorist Benjamin Barber refers to the former as an example of "strong democracy" and to the latter as an example of "thin democracy." See Barber, *Strong Democracy* (note 2).

47. Stephen Bennett and David Resnick, "The Implications of Nonvoting for Democracy in the United States," *American Journal of Political Science* 34 (1990): 771–802.

48. U.S. Bureau of the Census, *Current Population Reports*, P20–485, Table B. For a general discussion, see Peverill Squire, Raymond Wolfinger, and David Glass, "Residential Mobility and Voter Turnout," *American Political Science Review* 81 (1987): 45–65.

49. Teixeira, *The Disappearing American Voter*, p. 92.

50. Rosenstone and Hansen, *Mobilization, Participation, and Democracy*, p. 51.

51. David Nexon, "Asymmetry in the Political System: Occasional Activists in the Democratic and Republican Parties, 1956–1964," *American Political Science Review* 65 (1971): 716–730; and Warren Miller and M. Kent Jennings, *Parties in Transition* (New York: Russell Sage, 1986), Ch. 2.

CHAPTER 7

1. For a fuller discussion, see Barbara Sinclair, "Trying to Govern Positively in a Negative Era: Clinton and the 103rd Congress," in Colin Campbell and Bert Rockman, eds., *The Clinton Presidency: First Appraisals* (Chatham, NJ: Chatham House, 1996), pp. 101–109.

2. Dana Milbank, "Staring History in the Face: The Past is Passe When It Comes to Predicting the Winner of the Presidential Race," *Washington Post Weekly Edition* (October 30, 2000): 21–22; David Stout, "Experts, Once Certain, Now Say Gore is a Maybe," *New York Times* (November 7, 2000); Richard Morin, "It's Not Easy to Pick a Winner: The Gore–Bush Presidential Race is So Close that the Experts Say All Bets are Off," *Washington Post Weekly Edition* (September 11, 2000): 34; and Karl Eisenhower and Pete Nelson, "The Phony Science of Predicting Elections: Who'll Win in November? The Experts' Guess is as Good as Yours," (Slate Archives, http://slate.msn.com/Features/forecast/forecast.asp, accessed August 15, 2001).

3. Hanna Rosin, "Personal Faith and Public Policy," *Washington Post Weekly Edition* (September 11, 2000): 10–11.

4. Nina J. Easton, "For Now, Silence is Golden: The Political Right is Maintaining a Low Profile, Waiting for a GOP President," *Washington Post Weekly Edition* (October 9, 2000): 21; Richard L. Berke, "A Race in Which Candidates Clung to the Center," *New York Times* (November 7, 2000); and George Stephanopoulos, "Clinton's Long Shadow," *Newsweek* (August 21, 2000): 35.

5. David Brooks, "The Revenge of the Liberals: A Conservative Argues the Left is Really Writing Gore's Script," *Newsweek* (October 30, 2000): 39; David S. Broder, "Still the Economy, Stupid," *Washington Post Weekly Edition* (September 18, 2000): 4; Sebastian Mallaby, "The Paradox of Prosperity," *Washington Post Weekly Edition* (September 18, 2000): 29; George Packer, "Gore Says He'll Protect the Middle Class, but His Rhetoric is 100 Years Out of Date," *Washington Post Weekly Edition* (November 6, 2000): 21–22; and Richard Morin and Claudia Deane, "The Nader Factor: Some Last-Minute Voting Decisions are Likely Among Green Party Supporters," *Washington Post Weekly Edition* (November 6, 2000): 34.

6. Dan Balz, "Still Neck-and-Neck: With No Major Errors, The First Debate Nonetheless Exposed Weaknesses in Both Candidates," *Washington Post Weekly Edition* (October 9, 2000): 14; Dan Balz, "Tests Passed, but Questions Remain: Bush Showed a Mastery of Foreign Policy, and Gore Appeared Tentative in the Second Debate," *Washington Post Weekly Edition* (October 16, 2000): 14; David von Drehle, "The Candidates, Great and Small: Gore Looms Large in the 3rd Debate, But Is That Good?" *Washington Post Weekly Edition* (October 23, 2000): 11; Richard Morin, "For Better and For Worse: Post-Debate Polls Show No Clear-Cut Winner, with Good and Bad News for Both Candidates," *Washington Post Weekly Edition* (October 23, 2000): 34; and "Face to Face Combat," *Newsweek* (November 20, 2000): 102.

7. David von Drehle and Ceci Connolly, "The Truth About Gore's Credibility: Republicans Are Trying to Use the Tall Tales He Tells on the Stump to Trip Him Up," *Washington Post Weekly Edition* (October 16, 2000): 11; Jim Hoagland, "The 'BS' Factor," *Washington Post Weekly Edition* (October 2, 2000): 5; Jonathan Alter, "Al Gore and the Fib Factor," *Newsweek* (October 16, 2000): 43; and "Face to Face Combat," *Newsweek* 94, 102–103.

8. Andrew Gelman and Gary King, "Why Are American Presidential Election Campaign Polls So Variable When Votes Are So Predictable?" *British Journal of Political Science* 23 (1993): 409–451; Dan B. Thomas and Larry R. Baas, "The Postelection Campaign: Competing Constructions of the Clinton Victory in 1992," *Journal of Politics* 58 (1996): 309–331; and Richard Morin, "The True Political Puppeteers: Pocketbooks and Partisan Ways," *Washington Post Weekly Edition* (February 20–26, 1989): 37.

9. Although the general notion of "partisanship" has been around for centuries, the social-psychological concept of party ID was advanced in the pioneering work of Angus Campbell, Philip Converse, Warren Miller, and Donald Stokes, *The American Voter* (New York: Wiley, 1960), Chs. 6–7.

10. Donald Philip Green and Bradley Palmquist, "Of Artifacts and Partisan Instability," *American Journal of Political Science* 34 (1990):872–902; Donald Philip Green and Bradley Palmquist, "How Stable is Party Identification?" *Political Behavior* 16 (1994): 437–466; and Donald Green, Bradley Palmquist, and Eric Schickler, "Macropartisanship: A Replication and Critique," *American Political Science Review* 92 (1998): 883–899.

11. Morris Fiorina, *Retrospective Voting in American National Elections* (New Haven, CT: Yale University Press, 1981); and Michael MacKuen, Robert Erikson, and James Stimson, "Macropartisanship," *American Political Science Review* 83 (1989): 1125–1142.

12. Bruce E. Keith, David B. Magleby, Candice J. Nelson, Elizabeth Orr, Mark C. Westlye, and Raymond E. Wolfinger, *The Myth of the Independent Voter* (Berkeley, CA: University of California Press, 1992).

13. Jane Mansbridge, "Myth and Reality: The ERA and the Gender Gap in the 1980 Election," *Public Opinion Quarterly*, 49 (1985): 164–178.

14. Emily Stoper, "The Gender Gap Concealed and Revealed," *Journal of Political Science* 17 (1989): 50–62; and Tom Smith, "The Polls: Gender and Attitudes Toward Violence," *Public Opinion Quarterly* 48 (1984): 384–396.

15. For discussions, see Pamela Conover, "Feminists and the Gender Gap," *Journal of Politics* 50 (1988): 985–1010; and Elizabeth Cook and Clyde Wilcox, "Feminism and the Gender Gap—A Second Look," *Journal of Politics* 53 (1991): 1111–1122.

16. This was first noted by Herbert Weisberg, "The Demographics of a New Voting Gap: Marital Differences in American Voting Behavior," *Public Opinion Quarterly* 51 (1987): 335–343.

17. "Where the Parties Are," *The Public Perspective* (March/April 1994): 78–79; and "Which Party Is Better on Which Issues?" *The Public Perspective* (June/July 1996): 65.

18. Fiorina, *Retrospective Voting.*

19. Scott Teeter, "Public Opinion in 1984," and Gerald Pomper, "The Presidential Election," both in Gerald Pomper et al., *The Election of 1984* (Chatham, NJ: Chatham House, 1985).

20. Samuel Popkin, *The Reasoning Voter* (Chicago: University of Chicago Press, 1991), pp. 60–67.

21. The classic demonstration appears in Chapter 8 of Campbell et al., *The American Voter*, although there is general agreement that the picture presented there is overstated. For balanced treatments of policy issues in recent campaigns, see the series of *Change and Continuity* volumes by Paul Abramson, John Aldrich, and David Rohde, published by CQ Press. Angus Campbell, Philip Converse, Warren Miller, and Donald Stokes, *The American Voter* (New York: Wiley, 1960).

22. Benjamin Page and Richard Brody, "Policy Voting and the Electoral Process: The Vietnam War Issue," *American Political Science Review* 66 (1972): 979–995.

23. Edward Carmines and James Stimson, "The Two Faces of Issue Voting," *American Political Science Review* 74 (1980): 78–91.

24. Donald Stokes, "Some Dynamic Elements of Contests for the Presidency," *American Political Science Review* 60 (1966): 19–28.

25. Fiorina, *Retrospective Voting,* pp. 150–153; and Andrew Kohut, "The Vox Pop on Malaprops," *Washington Post Weekly Edition* (October 2, 2000): 22.

26. Stokes, "Some Dynamic Elements," p. 222.

27. Indeed, by some calculations, Kennedy's results were worse than those of a "generic" Democrat for that time. See Angus Campbell, Philip Converse, Warren Miller, and Donald Stokes, "Stability and Change in 1960; and A Reinstating Election," in *Elections and the Political Order* (New York: Wiley, 1966), pp. 78–95.

28. On the failure of incumbency to provide a complete explanation of Democratic dominance during this era, see Morris Fiorina, *Divided Government*, Second Edition. (Boston: Allyn & Bacon, 1996), pp. 18–23. For an example of a member of Congress wrongly attributing her electoral success to incumbency, see the analysis of U.S. Representative Cynthia McKinney of Georgia in D. Stephen Voss and David Lublin, "Black Incumbents, White Districts: An Appraisal of the 1996 Congressional Elections," *American Politics Research* 29 (2001):141–182.

29. Norman Ornstein, Thomas Mann, and Michael Malbin, *Vital Statistics on Congress, 1998–2000* (Washington, DC: American Enterprise Institute, 2000).

30. Robert Erikson, "Malapportionment, Gerrymandering and Party Fortunes in Congressional Elections," *American Political Science Review* 66 (1972): 1234–1245. Gary King and Andrew Gelman, "Systemic Consequences of Incumbency Advantage in U.S. House Elections," *American Journal of Political Science* 35 (1991): 110–138.

31. James Young, *The Washington Community, 1800–1828* (New York: Harcourt, 1966), Ch. 2.

32. The South was primarily agricultural and had fewer high-status career opportunities outside of politics. From the very beginning, southern members of Congress stayed longer than northerners. Morris Fiorina, David Rohde, and Peter Wissel, "Historical Change in House Turnover," in Norman Ornstein, ed., *Congress in Change* (New York: Praeger, 1975), pp. 34–38.

33. Robert Struble, Jr., "House Turnover and the Principle of Rotation," *Political Science Quarterly* 94 (1979–1980): 660.

34. Douglas Price, "The Congressional Career—Then and Now," in Nelson Polsby, ed., *Congressional Behavior* (New York: Random House, 1971), pp. 14–27.

35. Douglas Arnold, *The Logic of Congressional Action* (New Haven, CT: Yale University Press, 1990), Ch. 2.

36. Glenn Parker, *Homeward Bound* (Pittsburgh, PA: University of Pittsburgh Press, 1986).

37. John G. Geer, *From Tea Leaves to Opinion Polls: A Theory of Democratic Leadership* (New York: Columbia University Press, 1996).

38. Ornstein, Mann, and Malbin, *Vital Statistics*, pp. 67–68.

39. John Ferejohn, "On the Decline of Competition in Congressional Elections," *American Political Science Review* 71 (1977): 172–174.

40. Gary Jacobson, *The Politics of Congressional Elections*, Fourth Edition. (New York: Longman, 1997).

41. Heinz Eulau, "Changing Views of Representation," in Heinz Eulau and John Wahlke, eds., *The Politics of Representation* (Beverly Hills, CA: Sage, 1978), pp. 31–53.

42. Morris Fiorina, *Congress—Keystone of the Washington Establishment*, Second Edition. (New Haven, CT: Yale University Press, 1989).

43. Ibid., Ch. 10. See also Bruce Cain, John Ferejohn, and Morris Fiorina, *The Personal Vote* (Cambridge, MA: Harvard University Press, 1987), Ch. 2.

44. Burdett Loomis, "The Congressional Office as a Small Business: New Members Set Up Shop," *Publius* 9 (1979): 35–55.

45. Ornstein, Mann, and Malbin, *Vital Statistics*, pp. 126, 130.

46. Walter Gellhorn, *Ombudsmen and Others: Citizens' Protectors in Nine Countries* (Cambridge, MA: Harvard University Press, 1966).

47. Morris Fiorina, "Congressmen and Their Constituents: 1958 and 1978," in Dennis Hale, ed., *The United States Congress: Proceedings of the Thomas P. O'Neill, Jr., Symposium* (Leominster, MA: Eusey Press, 1982), pp. 33–64.

48. Richard H. Shapiro, *Frontline Management* (Washington, DC: Congressional Management Foundation, 1989), p. 94.

49. David Brady and Morris Fiorina, "Ruptured Legacy: Presidential Congressional Relations in Historical Perspective," in Larry Berman, ed., *Looking Back on the Reagan Presidency* (Baltimore, MD: Johns Hopkins University Press, 1989), pp. 268–287.

50. John Ferejohn and Randall Calvert, "Presidential Coattails in Historical Perspective," *American Journal of Political Science* 28 (1984): 127–146.

51. Morris Fiorina, *Divided Government*, Second Edition. (Boston: Allyn & Bacon, 1996), p. 14.

52. Ibid., pp. 135–139.

53. Ronald Keith Gaddie and Charles S. Bullock, III, *Elections to Open Seats in the U.S. House: Where the Action Is* (Lanham, MD: Rowman and Littlefield, 2000), pp. 4–5, 24–35; and David Lublin and D. Stephen Voss, "Boll-Weevil Blues," *American Review of Politics* (forthcoming).

54. Jon Healey, "'Projects' Are His Project," *Congressional Quarterly Weekly Report* (September 21, 1996): 2672. Also see Jonathan Salant, "Some Republicans Turned Away from Leadership," *Congressional Quarterly Weekly Report* (December 7, 1996): 3352–3354; and Andrew Taylor, "GOP Pet Projects Give Boost to Shaky Incumbents," *Congressional Quarterly Weekly Report* (August 3, 1996): 2169–2173.

55. Karen Foerstel, "Slouching Toward Election Day, Democrats Are Anxious and Angry," *Congressional Quarterly Weekly Report* (September 12, 1998): 2383–2385.

56. www.commoncause.org

57. David Rohde, *Parties and Leaders in the Postreform House* (Chicago: University of Chicago Press, 1991).

58. Donna Cassate, "'Independent Groups' Ads Increasingly Steer Campaigns," *Congressional Quarterly Weekly Report* (May 2, 1998): 1114.

59. Max Farrand, ed., *The Records of the Federal Convention of 1787* (New Haven, CT: Yale University Press, 1966), Vol. 1, p. 151.

60. James Campbell, "When Have Presidential Campaigns Decided Election Outcomes?" paper presented at the 1999 Annual Meeting of the American Political Science Association, Atlanta.

61. See Thomas Holbrook, *Do Campaigns Matter?* (Thousand Oaks, CA: Sage, 1996).

62. For a discussion, see Marjorie Hershey, "The Campaign and the Media," in Gerald Pomper et al., *The Election of 1988* (Chatham, NJ: Chatham House, 1989), Ch. 3.

63. See, for example, Adam Nagourney and Elizabeth Kolbert, "Missteps Doomed Dole from the Start," *New York Times* (November 8, 1996): A1.

64. Jim Drinkard, "Let the Fundraising Begin—Again," *USA Today* (March 10, 2000): 14A.

65. Elizabeth Shogren, "Bush Cracks Records for Campaign Spending," *USA Today* (March 21, 2000): 13A.

66. During the last two months of the presidential campaigns of 1976 to 1988, about 40 percent of the lead stories on the CBS evening news were about the election, as were 20 percent of all the stories reported. See Steven J. Rosenstone and John Mark Hansen, *Mobilization, Participation, and Democracy in America* (New York: Macmillan, 1993), p. 178, n. 26.

67. Anthony Corrado, "Financing the 1996 Presidential General Election," in John Green, *Financing the 1996 Election* (Armonk, NY: M.E. Sharpe, 1999), pp. 84–85.

68. Thomas Patterson and Robert McClure, *The Unseeing Eye: The Myth of Television Power in National Elections* (New York: Putnam, 1976); and Stephen Ansolabehere and Shanto Iyengar, *Going Negative: How Attack Ads Shrink and Polarize the Electorate* (New York: Free Press, 1995).

69. Darrel West, *Air Wars: Television Advertising in Election Campaigns, 1952–1992* (Washington, DC: Congressional Quarterly, 1993).

70. Edwin Diamond and Stephen Bates, *The Spot,* Third Edition. (Cambridge, MA: MIT Press, 1992).

71. Craig Brians and Martin Wattenberg, "Campaign Issue Knowledge and Salience: Comparing Reception from TV Commercials, TV News, and Newspapers," *American Journal of Political Science* 40 (1996): 172–193.

72. Federal Election Commission (www.fec.gov).

73. Gary Jacobson, "Practical Consequences of Campaign Finance Reform: An Incumbent Protection Act?" *Public Policy* 42 (1976): 1–32.

74. Gary Jacobson, *Money in Congressional Elections* (New Haven, CT: Yale University Press, 1980).

75. Jacobson, *Politics of Congressional Elections*, p. 40.

76. Kenneth Bickers and Robert Stein, "The Electoral Dynamics of the Federal Pork Barrel," *American Journal of Political Science* 40 (1996): 1300–1326.

77. Dave Barry, "Direct Deposit," *Boston Globe Magazine* (November 30, 1997): 12–13.

78. Charles Lane, "Kohl Train," *The New Republic* (February 14, 2000): 17.

79. Richard Katz, "Party Organizations and Finance," in Lawrence LeDuc, Richard Niemi, and Pippa Norris, eds., *Comparing Democracies* (Thousand Oaks, CA: Sage, 1996), pp. 129–132.

80. Howard Margolis, "The Banzhaf Fallacy," *American Journal of Political Science* 27 (1983): 321–326; George Rabinowitz and Stuart Elaine MacDonald, "The Power of the States in U.S. Presidential Elections," *American Political Science Review* 80 (1986): 65–87; and James C. Garand and T. Wayne Parent, "Representation, Swing, and Bias in U.S. Presidential Elections, 1872–1988," *American Journal of Political Science* 35 (1991): 1011–1031.

81. For a discussion, see Nelson Polsby and Aaron Wildavsky, *Presidential Elections,* Tenth Edition. (Chatham, NJ: Chatham House, 2000), pp. 245–253.

82. Frederick D. Weil, "The Sources and Structure of Legitimation in Western Democracies," *American Sociological Review* 54 (1989): 682–706; and Frederick D. Weil, "Political Culture, Political Structure and Democracy: The Case of Legitimation and Opposition Structure," in Frederick D. Weil, ed., *Research on Democracy and Society, Vol. 2, Political Culture and Political Structure: Theoretical and Empirical Studies* (Greenwich, CT: JAI Press, 1994).

83. "Fresh Light on Primary Colors," *The Economist* (February 24, 1996): 23.

84. A good current description of the caucus system can be found in William Mayer, "Caucuses: How They Work, What Difference They Make," in William Mayer, ed., *In Pursuit of the White House* (Chatham, NJ: Chatham House, 1996).

85. On the history of the presidential primary, see James Davis, *Springboard to the White House* (New York: Crowell, 1967).

86. John Kessel, *The Goldwater Coalition* (Indianapolis, IN: Bobbs-Merrill, 1968), Ch. 3.

87. Nelson Polsby, *Consequences of Party Reform* (New York: Oxford University Press, 1983), Ch. 1.

88. For a participant observer's account of the post-1968 reforms, see Austin Ranney, *Curing the Mischiefs of Faction* (Berkeley, CA: University of California Press, 1975).

89. On primary dynamics, see John Aldrich, *Before the Convention* (Chicago: University of Chicago Press, 1980); and Larry Bartels, *Presidential Primaries and the Dynamics of Public Choice* (Princeton, NJ: Princeton University Press, 1988).

90. John Haskell, *Fundamentally Flawed* (Lanham, MD: Rowman and Littlefield, 1996).

91. Pew Research Center for the People and the Press, "It's Still Too Early for the Voters," http://www. peoplepress.org/june99rpt.htm.

92. Kathy Kiely, "Wealth of Debates Keeps the Hopefuls Talking," *USA Today* (January 26, 2000): 8A.

93. Larry Sabato, "Presidential Nominations: The Front-Loaded Frenzy of '96," in Larry Sabato, ed., *Toward the Millennium: The Elections of 1996* (Boston: Allyn & Bacon, 1997), pp. 37–91.

94. "A Good Fight Draws a Crowd," *New York Times* (March 12, 2000): 5.

95. See John G. Geer, *Nominating Presidents* (New York: Greenwood Press, 1989), Ch. 2; and Barbara Norander, "Nomination Choices: Caucus and Primary Outcomes, 1976–1988," *American Journal of Political Science* 37 (1993): 343–364.

96. On presidential fund-raising, see Clifford Brown, Lynda Powell, and Clyde Wilcox, *Serious Money* (Cambridge, England: Cambridge University Press, 1995).

97. Thomas Patterson, *Out of Order* (New York: Vintage, 1994), p. 74.

98. "Once Again, 2 Small States Warp Political Process, *USA Today* (January 24, 2000): 18A.

99. Patterson, *Out of Order*, p. 82.

100. Most research finds only small electoral impacts for the vice presidential nominees. See Steven Rosenstone, *Forecasting Presidential Elections* (New Haven, CT: Yale University Press, 1983), pp. 64–66, 87–88.

101. "Congressional Primary Schedule," *Congressional Quarterly Weekly Report* (January 1, 2000): 16–17.

102. Michael Kinsley, as quoted by Howard Kurtz, "The Premature Post-Mortems Are Starting," *Washington Post* (online extras, October 31, 2000).

CHAPTER 8

1. The following account is based on Phil Kunz, "Home Schooling Movement Gives House a Lesson," *Congressional Quarterly Weekly Report* (February 26, 1994): 479–480.

2. This short account is based on James MacGregor Burns, *The Deadlock of Democracy* (Englewood Cliffs, NJ: Prentice-Hall, 1964), Ch. 2.

3. Jackson Turner Main, *Political Parties Before the Constitution* (New York: Norton, 1973).

4. Steven Rosenstone, Roy Behr, and Edward Lazarus, *Third Parties in America* (Princeton, NJ: Princeton University Press, 1981).

5. Maurice Duverger, *Political Parties: Their Organization and Activity in the Modern State* (New York: Wiley, 1963), Book II, Ch. 1.

6. Ibid. For elaboration, see Thomas Palfrey, "A Mathematical Proof of Duverger's Law," in *Models of Strategic Choice in Politics,* Peter Ordeshook, ed. (Ann Arbor, MI: University of Michigan Press, 1989), pp. 69–91.

7. Douglas Rae, *The Political Consequences of Electoral Laws,* Revised Edition. (New Haven, CT: Yale University Press, 1971), p. 98. Compare Arend Lijphart, who argues that Rae's figures exaggerate the difference; see Lijphart, "The Political Consequences of Electoral Laws, 1945–1985," *American Political Science Review* 84 (1990): 481–496.

8. The seminal contribution was V. O. Key, Jr., "A Theory of Critical Elections," *Journal of Politics* 17 (1955): 3–18. The most influential elaborations and extensions of the idea are Walter Dean Burnham, *Critical Elections and the Mainsprings of American Politics* (New York: Norton, 1970) and James Sundquist, *Dynamics of the Party System,* Revised Edition. (Washington, DC: Brookings, 1983).

9. Robert Remini, *Martin Van Buren and the Making of the Democratic Party* (New York: Columbia, 1959); and Donald Cole, *Martin Van Buren and the American Political System* (Princeton, NJ: Princeton University Press, 1984).

10. For a recent history of the period, see Paul Kleppner, *The Third Electoral System, 1853–1892: Parties, Voters, and Political Cultures* (Chapel Hill, NC: University of North Carolina Press, 1979).

11. Charles Stewart and Barry Weingast, "Stacking the Senate, Changing the Nation: Republican Rotten Boroughs, Statehood Politics, and American Political Development," *Studies in American Political Development* 6 (1992): 223–271.

12. Michael McGerr, *The Decline of Popular Politics* (New York: Oxford University Press, 1986).

13. Harold Gosnell provides a classic study of a machine. See his *Machine Politics: Chicago Model* (Chicago: University of Chicago Press, 1937). For a more recent study, see M. C. Brown and C. N. Halaby, "Machine Politics in America, 1870–1945," *Journal of Interdisciplinary History* 17 (1987): 587–612.

14. John D. Hicks, *The Populist Revolt* (Minneapolis, MN: University of Minnesota Press, 1931).

15. E. E. Schattschneider, "United States: The Functional Approach to Party Government," in Sigmund Neumann, ed. *Modern Political Parties* (Chicago: University of Chicago Press, 1956), pp. 194–215.

16. Alan Lichtman, *Prejudice and the Old Politics* (Chapel Hill, NC: University of North Carolina Press, 1979).

17. Stanley Lebergott, *The Americans: An Economic Record* (New York: Norton, 1984), Ch. 34.

18. Joel Silbey, "Beyond Realignment and Realignment Theory," in Byron Shafer, ed., *The End of Realignment?* (Madison, WI: University of Wisconsin Press, 1991), pp. 3–23.

19. Martin Wattenberg, *The Decline of American Political Parties, 1952–1992* (Cambridge, MA: Harvard University Press, 1994).

20. E. E. Schattschneider, *Party Government* (New York: Farrar and Rinehart, 1942), p. 1.

21. American Political Science Association, "Toward a More Responsible Two-Party System: A Report of the Committee on Political Parties," *Supplement to the American Political Science Review* 44 (1950).

22. John Aldrich, *Why Parties?* (Chicago: University of Chicago Press, 1995), Ch. 2.

23. See, for example, James Campbell, *The Presidential Pulse of Congressional Elections* (Lexington, KY: University Press of Kentucky, 1993).

24. Richard Fenno, *Home Style* (Boston: Little, Brown, 1978), Ch. 3.

25. V. O. Key, Jr., *Southern Politics* (New York: Knopf, 1949).

26. Anthony Downs, *An Economic Theory of Democracy* (New York: Harper & Row, 1957).

27. R. Michael Alvarez and Jonathan Nagler, "Economics, Issues, and the Perot Candidacy: Voter Choice in the 1992 Presidential Election," *American Journal of Political Science* 39 (1995): 714–744.

28. Morris Fiorina, *Divided Government,* Second Edition. (Boston: Allyn & Bacon, 1996), pp. 107–110.

29. Julius Turner, *Party and Constituency: Pressures on Congress* (Baltimore, MD: Johns Hopkins University Press, 1951).

30. Burns, *Deadlock of Democracy.*

31. Writing in the 1970s, Hugh Heclo put the number at 3,000. See his *A Government of Strangers* (Washington, DC: Brookings, 1977). By 1992, Thomas Weko put the number at about 3,700. See *The Politicizing Presidency* (Lawrence, KA: University of Kansas Press, 1995), p. 161.

32. Stephen Skowronek, *Building a New American State* (New York: Cambridge University Press, 1992), p. 69.

33. Stephen Frantzich, *Political Parties in the Technological Age* (New York: Longman, 1989).

34. Gordon Baker, *The Reapportionment Revolution* (New York: Random House, 1966).

35. Austin Ranney, *Curing the Mischiefs of Faction* (Berkeley, CA: University of California Press, 1975); and Nelson Polsby, *Consequences of Party Reform* (New York: Oxford University Press, 1983).

36. Cornelius Cotter, James Gibson, John Bibby, and Robert Huckshorn, *Party Organizations in American Politics* (New York: Praeger, 1984).

37. Ibid.

38. John Coleman, "Resurgent or Just Busy? Party Organizations in Contemporary America," in John Green and Daniel Shea, eds., *The State of the Parties,* Second Edition. (Lanham, MD: Rowman and Littlefield, 1996), pp. 312–326.

39. David Hosansky, "House Torn on Agriculture; Senate Makes Progress," *Congressional Quarterly Weekly Report* (September 30, 1995): 2980–2984.

40. Robert Dahl, *Dilemmas of Pluralist Democracy* (New Haven, CT: Yale University Press, 1982).

41. There is some controversy about how to measure group membership and consequently about the exact figures. For differing viewpoints, see Frank Baumgartner and Jack Walker, "Survey Research and Membership in Voluntary Associations," *American Journal of Political Science* 32 (1988): 908–928; Tom Smith, "Trends in Voluntary Group Membership: Comments on Baumgartner and Walker," *American Journal of Political Science* 34 (1990): 646–661; and Baumgartner and Walker, "Response to Smith's 'Trends in Voluntary Group Membership,'" *American Journal of Political Science* 34 (1990): 662–670.

42. Alexis de Tocqueville, *Democracy in America*, ed. J. P. Mayer (New York: HarperPerennial, 1969), p. 513.

43. Kay Schlozman and John Tierney, *Organized Interests and American Democracy* (New York: Harper & Row, 1981), p. 75.

44. Robert Wiebe, *The Search for Order, 1877–1920* (New York: Hill and Wang, 1967).

45. Jack Walker, *Mobilizing Interest Groups in America* (Ann Arbor, MI: University of Michigan Press, 1991), p. 10.

46. Jeffrey Berry, *Lobbying for the People* (Princeton, NJ: Princeton University Press, 1977).

47. An excellent source of basic information about groups and associations in the United States is the *Encyclopedia of Associations,* Carol Schwartz and Rebecca Turner, eds. (Detroit, MI: Gale Research, Inc., annual editions).

48. James Q. Wilson, *Political Organizations* (New York: Basic Books, 1973), Ch. 3.

49. Mancur Olson, *The Logic of Collective Action* (Cambridge, MA: Harvard University Press, 1965).

50. The term is from Richard Wagner, "Pressure Groups and Political Entrepreneurs," *Papers in Nonmarket Decision Making* 1 (1966): 161–170. For extended discussions, see Norman Frolich, Joe Oppenheimer, and Oran Young, *Political Leadership and Collective Goods* (Princeton, NJ: Princeton University Press, 1971); and Terry Moe, *The Organization of Interests* (Chicago: University of Chicago Press, 1980), Chs. 3–4.

51. Walker, *Mobilizing Interest Groups,* pp. 98–99.

52. Expenditures were $1.4 billion in 1998, the latest year for which we have figures. "Spending on Lobbying Rises," *USA Today* (November 16, 1999): 11A.

53. Carl Weiser, "Enforcement of Law Almost Non-existent," *USA Today* (November 16, 1999): 11A.

54. *American Lobbyists Directory,* Robert Wilson, ed. (Detroit, MI: Gale Research Inc., 1995). The estimate of Washington lobbyists is that of James Thurber, cited in Burdett Loomis, *The Contemporary Congress* (New York: St. Martin's, 1996), p. 35.

55. Lobbyist Michael Bromberg, quoted in Eleanor Clift and Tom Brazaitis, *War Without Bloodshed: The Art of Politics* (New York: Scribner, 1996), p. 100.

56. Peter Odegard, *Pressure Politics: The Story of the Anti-Saloon League* (New York: Columbia University Press, 1928), p. 76.

57. Frank Sorauf, *Inside Campaign Finance* (New Haven, CT: Yale University Press, 1992), Ch. 4. A basic reference on PACs is *The PAC Directory* (Cambridge, MA: Ballinger, various editions).

58. Ross Baker, *The New Fat Cats: Members of Congress as Political Benefactors* (New York: Priority Press, 1989); and Eliza Carney, "PAC Men," *National Journal* (October 1, 1994): 2268–2273.

59. See Edward Epstein, "Business and Labor Under the Federal Election Campaign Act of 1971," in Michael Malbin, ed., *Parties, Interest Groups, and Campaign Finance Laws* (Washington, DC: American Enterprise Institute, 1980), pp. 107–151.

60. Thomas Ferguson and Joel Rogers, *Right Turn: The Decline of the Democrats and the Future of American Politics* (New York: Hill and Wang, 1986).

61. For a discussion, see Richard Hall and Frank Wayman, "Buying Time: Moneyed Interests and the Mobilization of Bias in Congressional Committees," *American Political Science Review* 84 (1990): 797–820.

62. Jim Drinkard, "Issue Ads Crowd Airwaves Before 2000 Election," *USA Today* (November 29, 1999): 11A.

63. R. Kenneth Godwin, *One Billion Dollars of Influence* (Chatham, NJ: Chatham House, 1988).

64. Andrew McFarland, *Common Cause: Lobbying for the People* (Chatham, NJ: Chatham House, 1984), pp. 74–81.

65. For an analysis of the expansion by the judiciary of federal programs for the handicapped and the poor, see R. Shep Melnick, *Between the Lines* (Washington, DC: Brookings, 1994).

66. For elaboration, see Hugh Graham and Ted Gurr, *The History of Violence in America* (New York: Bantam, 1969).

67. Jonathan Rauch, *Demosclerosis* (New York: Random House, 1994).

68. Philip Stern, *The Best Congress Money Can Buy* (New York: Pantheon, 1988).

69. John Heinz, Edward Laumann, Robert Nelson, and Robert Salisbury, *Representing Interests: Structure and Uncertainty in National Policy Making* (in press).

70. J. Leiper Freeman, *The Political Process*, Revised Edition. (New York: Random House, 1965); Grant McConnell, *Private Power and American Democracy* (New York: Knopf, 1966); and Theodore Lowi, *The End of Liberalism* (New York: Norton, 1969).

71. David Hosansky, "House and Senate Assemble Conflicting Farm Bills," *Congressional Quarterly Weekly Report* (February 3, 1996): 298.

72. Hugh Heclo, "Issue Networks and the Executive Establishment," in Anthony King, ed., *The New American Political System* (Washington, DC: Brookings, 1978), pp. 87–124.

73. Robert Salisbury, John Heinz, Robert Nelson, and Edward Laumann, "Triangles, Networks, and Hollow Cores: The Complex Geometry of Washington Interest Representation," in Mark Petracca, ed., *The Politics of Interests* (Boulder, CO: Westview Press, 1992), pp. 130–149.

74. John Chubb, *Interest Groups and the Bureaucracy* (Stanford, CA: Stanford University Press, 1983), pp. 249–265; and Richard Harris, "Politicized Management: The Changing Face of Business in American Politics," in Richard Harris and Sidney Milkis, eds., *Remaking American Politics* (Boulder, CO: Westview Press, 1989), pp. 261–286.

75. Schlozman and Tierney, *Organized Interests and American Democracy*, pp. 314–317.

76. Henry Brady, Sidney Verba, and Kay Schlozman, "Beyond SES: A Resource Model of Political Participation," *American Political Science Review* 89 (1995): 271–294.

77. John Hibbing and Elizabeth Theiss-Morse, *Congress as Public Enemy* (New York: Cambridge University Press, 1995), pp. 63–65, 147.

78. Earl Latham, *The Group Basis of Politics* (New York: Cornell University Press, 1952); and David Truman, *The Governmental Process* (New York: Knopf, 1958).

79. E. E. Schattschneider, *The Semisovereign People* (New York: Holt, 1960), pp. 34–35.

80. Peter Aranson and Peter Ordeshook, "A Prolegomenon to a Theory of the Failure of Representative Democracy," in Aranson and Ordeshook, eds., *American Re-evolution* (Tucson, AR: University of Arizona, 1977), pp. 23–46.

81. "The Gerontocrats," *The Economist* (May 13, 1995): 32.

82. Jane Mansbridge, *Why We Lost the ERA* (Chicago: University of Chicago Press, 1986), p. 73.

CHAPTER 9

1. The blow-by-blow account appears in various issues of *Congressional Quarterly Weekly Report* published in 1992. See pages 1605, 1860, 1927, 2154, 2251, 2354, 2435, 3020, 3134, and 3556.

2. For colorful accounts of these congressional leaders, see Neil McNeil, *Forge of Democracy* (New York: McKay, 1963).

3. Speaker Thomas Reed, as quoted in Neil McNeil, *Forge of Democracy* (New York: McKay, 1963).

4. Richard Fenno, *The United States Senate: A Bicameral Perspective* (Washington, DC: American Enterprise Institute, 1982).

5. Nelson Polsby, Miriam Gallagher, and Barry Rundquist, "The Growth of the Seniority System in the U.S. House of Representatives," *American Political Science Review* 63 (1969): 787–807.

6. Ibid.

7. Charles Jones, "Joseph G. Cannon and Howard W. Smith: An Essay on the Limits of Leadership in the House of Representatives," *Journal of Politics* 30 (1968): 617–646.

8. Barbara Sinclair, *Majority Leadership in the U.S. House* (Baltimore, MD: Johns Hopkins University Press, 1983).

9. For a full discussion, see Steven S. Smith and Marcus Flathman, "Managing the Senate Floor: Complex Unanimous Consent Agreements Since the 1950s," *Legislative Studies Quarterly* 14 (1989): 349–374.

10. Lawrence Dodd and Richard Schott, *Congress and the Administrative State* (New York: Wiley, 1979), Ch. 3. For further discussion, see Kenneth Shepsle, "The Changing Textbook Congress," in John Chubb and Paul Peterston, eds., *Can the Government Govern?* (Washington, DC: Brookings, 1989).

11. "Democrats Oust Hebert, Poage; Adopt Reforms," *Congressional Quarterly Weekly Report* (January 18, 1975): 114.

12. Barbara Sinclair, *Legislators, Leaders, and Lawmaking: The U.S. House of Representatives in the Postreform Era* (Baltimore, MD: Johns Hopkins University Press, 1995).

13. David Brady, *Congressional Voting in a Partisan Era* (Lawrence, KA: University of Kansas Press, 1973).

14. Gary Cox and Mathew McCubbins, *Legislative Leviathan* (Berkeley, CA: University of California Press, 1993).

15. David Rohde, *Parties and Leaders in the Postreform House* (Chicago: University of Chicago Press, 1991).

16. Jim Drinkard, "Confident Candidates Share Campaign Wealth," *USA Today* (April 19, 2000): 10A.

17. Gerald Gamm and Kenneth Shepsle, "Emergence of Legislative Institutions: Standing Committees in the House and Senate, 1810–1825," *Legislative Studies Quarterly* 14 (1989): 39–66; and Joseph Cooper, *The Origins of the Standing Committees and the Development of the Modern House* (Houston, TX: Rice University Studies, 1970).

18. Richard Fenno, *Congressmen in Committees* (Boston: Little, Brown, 1973), p. 172.

19. Karen Foerstel, "Gingrich Flexes His Power in Picking Panel Chiefs," *Congressional Quarterly Weekly Report* (November 19, 1994): 3326.

20. Mark Ferber, "The Formation of the Democratic Study Group," in Nelson Polsby, ed., *Congressional Behavior* (New York: Random House, 1971), pp. 249–267.

21. Norman Ornstein, "Causes and Consequences of Congressional Change: Subcommittee Reforms in the House of Representatives, 1970–1973," in Norman Ornstein, ed., *Congress in Change* (New York: Praeger, 1975), pp. 88–114; and Roger Davidson and Walter Oleszek, *Congress Against Itself* (Bloomington, IN: Indiana University Press, 1977).

22. Barry Weingast and William Marshall, "The Industrial Organization of Congress," *Journal of Political Economy* 91 (1988): 132–163.

23. John Ferejohn, *Pork Barrel Politics* (Stanford, CA: Stanford University Press, 1974); and R. Douglas Arnold, *Congress and the Bureaucracy* (New Haven, CT: Yale University Press, 1979).

24. Keith Krehbiel, *Information and Legislative Organization* (Ann Arbor, MI: University of Michigan Press, 1991).

25. Morris Fiorina, *Representatives, Roll Calls, and Constituencies* (Lexington, MA: D. C. Heath, 1974), Chs. 2–3; and R. Douglas Arnold, *The Logic of Congressional Action* (New Haven, CT: Yale University Press, 1990), Chs. 2–4.

26. Jeffrey Talbert, Bryan Jones, and Frank Baumgartner, "Nonlegislative Hearings and Policy Change in Congress," *American Journal of Political Science* 39 (1995): 391–392.

27. For a detailed study of how and why individual members participate at these various stages of the legislative process, see Richard Hall, *Participation in Congress* (New Haven, CT: Yale University Press, 1996).

28. On the conference committee in recent years, see Stephen Van Beek, *Post-Passage Politics: Bicameral Relations in Congress* (Pittsburgh, PA: University of Pittsburgh Press, 1995).

29. Richard Munson, *The Cardinals of Capitol Hill* (New York: Grove Press, 1993).

30. Quoted in Stephen Skowronek, *The Politics Presidents Make* (Cambridge, MA: Harvard University Press, 1993), p. 389.

31. The Model Cities case provides an older, similar example. See Arnold, *Congress and the Bureaucracy*, Ch. 8.

32. Harrison Donnelly, "Reagan Opposition Threatens EDA Development Program," *Congressional Quarterly Weekly Report* 40 (1982): 2295–2296.

33. Chuck Henning, *The Wit and Wisdom of Politics* (Golden, CO: Fulcrum, 1992), p. 39.

34. For institutional comparisons, see John Hibbing and Elizabeth Theiss-Morse, *Congress as Public Enemy* (New York: Cambridge University Press, 1995), Ch. 2.

35. Kelly Patterson and David Magleby, "Trends: Public Support for Congress," *Public Opinion Quarterly* 56 (1992): 539–551.

36. Richard Fenno, "If, as Ralph Nader Says, Congress is the 'Broken Branch,' How Come We Love Our Congressmen So Much?" in Norman Ornstein, ed., *Congress in Change* (New York: Praeger, 1975), pp. 277–287.

37. Richard Fenno, *Home Style: House Members in Their Districts* (Boston: Little, Brown, 1978), p. 168.

38. Glenn Parker and Roger Davidson, "Why Do Americans Love Their Congressman So Much More Than Their Congress? *Legislative Studies Quarterly* 4 (1979): 52–61.

CHAPTER 10

1. *New York Times* (September 8, 1993): B10.

2. Bill Clinton and Al Gore, *Putting People First: How We Can All Change America* (New York: Times Books, 1992).

3. Sources for reinventing government story include Lisa Getter, "GAO Report Disputes Gore Claims on Red-Tape Cuts," *Los Angeles Times* (August 14, 1999): A6; Stephen Barr, "Some Pessimism on 'Reinvention,' " *Washington Post* (March 31, 2000): A27; Tome Brune and William Douglas, "Reinvention Reality: Gore Boasts REGO Success, But Critics See New Problems," *Newsday* (July 17, 2000): A5; Stephen Barr, "Reinventing Government Is an Idea Whose Time Has Come—Again," *Washington Post* (October 22, 2000): C2; Jonathan Weisman, "Gore Misstates Job-Cutting Role: 'Reinventing' Results Do Not Match Claims, Many Analysts Say," *Baltimore Sun* (October 27, 2000): 1A; and Stephen Barr, "Members of Campaign to Reinvent Government Packing Up, Not Giving Up," *Washington Post* (January 14, 2001): C2.

4. *New York Times* (September 9, 1993): D20.

5. *New York Times* (September 8, 1993): B10.

6. *Washington Post* (August 12, 1993): A6.

7. *New York Times* (September 5, 1993, Sec. I): 39.

8. *New York Times* (September 5, 1993, Sec. I): 39.

9. Brune and Douglas, "Reinvention Reality."

10. Terry Moe, "The Politicized Presidency," in John Chubb and Paul E. Peterson, eds., *The New Direction in American Politics* (Washington, DC: Brookings, 1985).

11. Mark Peterson, *Legislating Together: The White House and Capitol Hill from Eisenhower to Reagan* (Cambridge, MA: Harvard), p. 157.

12. Richard E. Neustadt, *Presidential Power and the Modern Presidents* (New York: Free Press, 1990), p. 29.

13. James S. Young, *The Washington Community 1800–1828* (New York: Columbia University Press, 1966).

14. Benjamin Ginsberg and Martin Shefter, *Politics by Other Means: The Declining Importance of Elections in America* (New York: Basic Books, 1990).

15. Thomas Bailey, *The American Pageant* (Boston: D. C. Heath, 1956), p. 669.

16. Samuel Kernell, *Going Public* (Washington, DC: CQ Press, 1986).

17. Daniel Stid, *The Statesmanship of Woodrow Wilson: Responsible Government under the Constitution* (Lawrence, KS: University Press of Kansas, 1998), Ch. 6.

18. Neustadt, *Presidential Power,* p. 274.

19. Denis G. Sullivan and Roger D. Masters, "Happy Warriors: Leaders' Facial Displays, Viewers' Emotions and Political Support," *American Journal of Political Science* 32 (1988): 345–368.

20. Chuck Henning, *The Wit and Wisdom of Politics* (Golden, CO: Fulcrum, 1992), p. 240.

21. Norman C. Thomas, Joseph A. Pika, and Richard A. Watson, *The Politics of the Presidency,* Third Edition. (Washington, DC: CQ Press, 1993), p. 204.

22. John F. Harris, "Both Sides Frustrated as Budget Wars End," *Washington Post* (November 15, 1999): A1.

23. As quoted in James P. Pfiffner, *The Modern Presidency* (New York: St. Martin's, 1994), p. 114.

24. *United States* v. *Belmont* 301 US 324 (1936); Harold Bruff and Peter Shane, *The Law of Presidential Powers: Cases and Materials* (Durham, NC: Carolina Academic Press, 1988), p. 88; and Joseph Paige, *The Law Nobody Knows: Enlargement of the Constitution—Treaties and Executive Orders.* (New York: Vantage Press, 1977), p. 63.

25. Louis Fisher, *Constitutional Conflicts Between Congress and the President,* Third Edition, Revised. (Lawrence, KA: University of Kansas, 1991), p. 154.

26. Bob Woodward and Scott Armstrong, *The Brethren: Inside the Supreme Court* (New York: Simon and Schuster, 1979), Ch. 5 (1973 Term), especially p. 365.

27. *United States* v. *Nixon,* 418 US 683, 709 (1974).

28. Walter Bagehot, *The English Constitution* (London, England: Fantana, 1993).

29. Stanley Elkins and Eric McKitrick, *Age of Federalism* (New York: Oxford University Press, 1993), p. 48.

30. Doris Kearns Goodwin, *No Ordinary Time: Franklin and Eleanor Roosevelt: The Home Front in World War II* (New York: Simon & Schuster, 1994).

31. Bert Rockman, "Leadership Style and the Clinton Presidency," in Colin Campbell and Bert Rockman, eds., *The Clinton Presidency: First Appraisals* (Chatham, NJ: Chatham House, 1996), p. 334–336.

32. Jeffrey Tulis, *The Rhetorical Presidency* (Princeton, NJ: Princeton University Press, 1987), Ch. 3.

33. Ibid.

34. John W. Kingdon, *Agendas, Alternatives and Public Policies* (Boston: Little, Brown, 1981).

35. Harry McPherson, *A Political Education* (Boston: Little, Brown, 1972), p. 268, as quoted in Paul C. Light, *The President's Agenda: Domestic Policy Choice from Kennedy to Reagan* (Baltimore, MD: Johns Hopkins University Press, 1991), p. 13.

36. Stephen Hess, *Organizing the Presidency* (Washington, DC: Brookings, 1988), pp. 11–18.

37. Herbert Kaufman, *The Administrative Behavior of Federal Bureau Chiefs* (Washington, DC: Brookings, 1981), p. 183, n. 8.

38. Hugh Heclo, "OMB and the Presidency—the Problem of 'Neutral Competence,'" *Public Interest* 38 (Winter 1975): 80–98; and Karen Hult, "Advising the President," in George C. Edwards, John H. Kessel, and Bert A. Rockman, *Researching the Presidency: Vital Questions, New Approaches* (Pittsburgh, PA: University of Pittsburgh Press, 1992), p. 126.

39. David Stockman, *The Triumph of Politics* (New York: Harper & Row, 1986).

40. Haynes Johnson and David Broder, *The System: The American Way of Politics at the Breaking Point* (Boston: Little Brown, 1996), p. 116.

41. David Johnston, "With Counsel Law Expiring, Attorney General Takes Reins," *New York Times* (June 30, 1999).

42. John Hart, *The Presidential Branch: From Washington to Clinton,* Second Edition. (Chatham, NJ: Chatham House, 1995), pp. 26–30.

43. See Matthew Dickinson, *Bitter Harvest: FDR, Presidential Power, and the Growth of the Presidential Branch* (New York: Cambridge University Press, 1997).

44. Paul Quirk, "Presidential Competence," in Michael Nelson, ed., *The Presidency and the Political System,* Fourth Edition. (Washington, DC: CQ Press, 1994), pp. 171–221; and John P. Burke, *The Institutional Presidency* (Baltimore, MD: Johns Hopkins University Press, 1992), pp. 40–42.

45. Colin Campbell, "Management in a Sandbox," in Campbell and Rockman, *The Clinton Presidency*, p. 60.

46. Charles O. Jones, "Campaigning to Govern: The Clinton Style," in Campbell and Rockman, *The Clinton Presidency,* p. 16.

47. Terry Moe, "The Politicized Presidency," in Chubb and Peterson, *New Direction in American Politics*; and Andrew Rudalevige, "The President's Program and the Politicized Presidency," paper presented at the Annual Meeting of the American Political Science Association, Atlanta, GA, September 2–5, 1999.

48. Bruce E. Altshuler, *LBJ and the Polls* (Gainesville, FL: University of Florida Press, 1990); and Lawrence R. Jacobs, "The Recoil Effect: Public Opinion in the U.S. and Britain," *Comparative Politics* 24 (1992): 199–217. On the importance of political consultant Karl Rove to George W. Bush's White House, see Dana Milbank, "The White House Lightning Rod: If Sparks are Flying, Karl Rove Is Probably at the Center," *Washington Post Weekly Edition* (July 23–29, 2001): 13–14; and Thomas B. Edsall, "Bush's Big Gamble: An Amnesty Proposal for Illegal Immigrants Angers GOP Conservatives," *Washington Post Weekly Edition* (July 23–29, 2001): 14.

49. *Wall Street Journal* (December 22, 1993): A4.

50. Neustadt, *Presidential Power,* Ch. 4.

51. As quoted in Henning, *Wit and Wisdom,* p. 222

52. The effect of time on presidential support is stressed by Paul Brace and Barbara Hinckley, "The Structure of Presidential Approval: Constraints Within and Across Presidencies," *Journal of Politics* 53 (1991): 993–1017; and John Mueller, "Presidential Popularity from Truman to Johnson," *American Political Science Review* 64 (1970): 18–34. For contrasting views, which stress events rather than time, see Richard A. Brody, *Assessing the President: The Media, Elite Opinion, and Public*

Support (Stanford, CA: Stanford University Press, 1991); and Samuel Kernell, "Explaining Presidential Popularity," *American Political Science Review* 72 (1978): 506–522. Also see Michael MacKuen, "Political Drama, Economic Conditions, and the Dynamic of Public Popularity," *American Journal of Political Science* 27 (1983): 165–192; Charles Ostrom and Dennis Simon, "Promise and Performance: A Dynamic Model of Presidential Popularity," *American Political Science Review* 79 (1985): 334–358; and James Stimson, "Public Support for American Presidents," *Public Opinion Quarterly* 40 (1976): 401–421.

53. James Barber, *The Presidential Character: Predicting Performance in the White House* (Englewood Cliffs, NJ: Prentice-Hall, 1972).

54. For criticism of Barber's analysis, see Michael Nelson, "The Psychological Presidency," in Michael Nelson, ed., *The Presidency and the Political System,* Fourth Edition. (Washington, DC: CQ Press, 1994), pp. 198–224; Alexander George, "Assessing Presidential Character," *World Politics* 26 (January 1974): 234–282; Jeffrey Tulis "On Presidential Character," in Jeffrey Tulis and Joseph M. Bessette, eds., *The Presidency in the Constitutional Order* (Baton Rouge, LA: Louisiana State University Press, 1981); and Erwin C. Hargrove, "Presidential Personality and Leadership Style," in George C. Edwards III, John H. Kessel, and Bert A. Rockman, eds., *Researching the Presidency: Vital Questions, New Approaches* (Pittsburgh, PA: Pittsburgh University Press, 1993), pp. 93–98.

55. George Will, "In Praise of Inactivity: Congress, Far from Doing Too Little, Is Doing Enough to Stir Nostalgia for Calvin Coolidge," *Newsweek* (June 22, 1998): 90.

56. Fred Greenstein, *The Hidden-Hand Presidency: Eisenhower as Leader* (New York: Basic Books, 1982).

57. Charles O. Jones, "The Separated Presidency—Making It Work in Contemporary Politics," in Anthony King, ed., *The New American Political System,* Second Version (Washington, DC: American Enterprise Institute, 1990), p. 24.

58. Stephen Skowronek, *The Politics Presidents Make.*

59. Mark Peterson, *Legislating Together: The White House and Capitol Hill from Eisenhower to Reagan* (Cambridge, MA: Harvard University Press, 1990), Ch. 6; and Jon R. Bond and Richard Fleisher, *The President in the Legislative Arena* (Chicago: University of Chicago Press, 1990), Ch. 4.

60. Charles O. Jones, "Separating to Govern: The American Way," in Byron E. Shafer, ed., *Present Discontents: American Politics in the Very Late 20th Century* (Chatham, NJ: Chatham House, 1997), pp. 56–59.

61. Jack Mitchell, *Executive Privilege: Two Centuries of White House Scandals* (New York: Hippocrene Books, 1992), p. 89–90.

62. John Farrell, "Embattled Security Official Quits, Calls Getting FBI Files a 'Mistake,'" *Boston Globe* (June 27, 1996): 12.

63. Committee on Government Reform and Oversight, U.S. House of Representatives, *U.S. Government Policy and Supporting Positions ("Plum Book")* (Washington, DC: U.S. Government Printing Office, 1996).

64. General Accounting Office, *Government Corporations: Profiles of Existing Government Corporations*, (GAO/GGD-96-14) (Washington, DC: General Accounting Office, 1995).

65. Henning, *Wit and Wisdom,* p. 92.

66. Max Weber, *Essays in Sociology* (New York: Oxford University Press, 1958); and Max Weber, *Economy and Society* (Berkeley, CA: University of California Press, 1978).

67. James Q. Wilson, "The Bureaucracy Problem," *The Public Interest* (Winter 1967): 3–9.

68. Graham Allison, *Essence of Decision: Explaining the Cuban Missile Crisis* (Boston: Little, Brown, 1971), Ch. 3.

69. Herbert Kaufman, *Red Tape: Its Origins, Uses and Abuses* (Washington, DC: Brookings, 1977), as reprinted in Francis E. Rourke, *Bureaucratic Power in National Policy Making,* Fourth Edition. (Boston: Little, Brown, 1986), p. 442.

70. Laurence J. Peter, as quoted in Chuck Henning, *The Wit and Wisdom of Politics: Expanded Edition* (Golden, CO: Fulcrum Publishing, 1992), p. 16.

71. William A. Niskanen, *Bureaucracy and Representative Government* (Chicago: Aldine-Atherton, 1971), Chs. 2–4.

72. Aaron Wildavsky, *The New Politics of the Budgetary Process* (Boston: Little, Brown, 1988), pp. 84–85.

73. Michael Lipsky, *Street-Level Bureaucracy: Dilemmas of the Individual in Public Services* (New York: Russell Sage, 1980).

74. Ibid.

75. Kaufman, *Red Tape*, p. 434.

76. James Young, *The Washington Community 1800–1828* (New York: Harcourt, 1966), p. 49. Ellipses deleted.

77. John Bartlett, *Familiar Quotations: Revised and Enlarged,* Fifteenth Editon. (Boston: Little, Brown, 1980), p. 455.

78. Seymour J. Mandelbaum, *Boss Tweed's New York* (New York: Wiley, 1965).

79. As quoted in Henning, *Wit and Wisdom*, p. 11.

80. A. James Reichley, *The Life of the Parties* (New York: Free Press, 1992), pp. 157–158.

81. Robert Dahl, *Who Governs?* (New Haven, CT: Yale University Press, 1961); Raymond E. Wolfinger, *The Politics of Progress* (Englewood Cliffs, NJ: Prentice-Hall, 1974), Ch. 4; Edward Banfield and James Q. Wilson, *City Politics* (New York: Random House, 1963); and Robert K. Merton, *Social Theory and Social Structure* (Glencoe, IL: Free Press, 1957), pp. 71–81.

82. Quoted in Reichley, *Life of the Parties,* p. 212.

83. Paul E. Peterson, *The Politics of School Reform, 1870–1940* (Chicago: University of Chicago Press, 1985), pp. 86–87.

84. Rufus P. Browning, Dale Rogers Marshall, and David H. Tabb, *Protest Is Not Enough: The Struggle of Blacks and Hispanics for Equality in Urban Politics* (Berkeley, CA: University of California Press, 1984), Ch. 5.

85. Alben W. Barkley, vice president of the United States, 1949–1953, as quoted in Henning, *Wit and Wisdom,* p. 17.

86. Paul Light, *Thickening Government: Federal Hierarchy and the Diffusion of Accountability* (Washington, DC: Brookings, 1995), Ch. 1.

87. G. Calvin MacKenzie, "The Presidential Appointment Process: Historical Development, Contemporary Operations, Current Issues," background paper for the Twentieth Century Fund Panel on Presidential Appointments, March 1, 1994, p. 1.

88. Leonard White, *Introduction to the Study of Public Administration,* Fourth Edition. (New York: Macmillan, 1955), p. 80.

89. *Wall Street Journal* (February 9, 1994): 1.

90. Lyn Ragsdale, "Studying the Presidency: Why Presidents Need Political Scientists," in Michael Nelson, ed., *The Presidency and the Political System*, Fifth Edition. (Washington, DC: CQ Press 1998), p. 50.

91. Marver H. Bernstein, *Regulating Business by Independent Commission* (Princeton, NJ: Princeton University Press, 1955); Harold Seidman, *Politics, Position and Power: The Dynamics of Federal Organization*, Second Edition. (New York: Oxford University Press, 1975); George J. Stigler, "The Theory of Economic Regulation," *Bell Journal of Economics and Management Science* 2 (Spring 1971): 3–21; Terry Moe, "Regulatory Performance and Presidential Administration," *American Journal of Political Science* 16 (1982), 197–224; and B. R. Weingast and M. J. Moran, "Bureaucratic Discretion or Congressional Control? Regulatory Policymaking by the Federal Trade Commission," *Journal of Political Economy* 91 (1983): 765–800; and B. R. Weingast, "The Congressional-Bureaucratic System: A Principal—Agent Perspective (with Application to the SEC)," *Public Choice* 44, 1 (1984): 147–191.

92. Robyn Meredith, "Credit Unions Help Finance a Bid for Reinstatement by a Dismissed Federal Regulator," *New York Times* (July 20, 1996): 7; and United States Court of Appeals for the District of Columbia Circuit, November 22, 1996, No. 96–5193.

93. President George W. Bush's nominations began running into trouble soon after the Senate switched to Democratic control.

94. David King, "The Nature of Congressional Committee Jurisdictions," *American Political Science Review* 88 (March 1995): 48–62.

95. Beryl A. Radin and Willis D. Hawley, *The Politics of Federal Reorganization: Creating the U.S. Department of Education* (New York: Pergamon Press, 1988).

96. R. Shep Melnick, *Regulation and the Courts: The Case of the Clean Air Act* (Washington, DC: Brookings, 1983).

97. Dick Kirschten, "Slicing the Turf," *Government Executive* (April 1999).

98. Graeme Browning, "Fiscal Fission," *National Journal* (June 8, 1996): 1259.

99. Bill McAllister, "Byrd's Big Prize: Bringing Home the FBI," *Washington Post* (March 13, 1991): A1.

100. Joel Aberbach, *Keeping a Watchful Eye* (Washington, DC: Brookings, 1990), p. 38.

101. Martha Derthick, *Agency Under Stress: The Social Security Administration in American Government* (Washington, DC: Brookings, 1990).

102. Jefferson Cohen, *The Politics of the U.S. Cabinet* (Pittsburgh, PA: University of Pittsburgh Press, 1988).

103. Paul E. Peterson, Barry G. Rabe, and Kenneth K. Wong, *When Federalism Works* (Washington, DC: Brookings, 1986), Ch. 8; John J. Harrigan, *Political Change in the Metropolis,* Second Edition. (Boston: Little, Brown, 1981), pp. 267–268, 350–351; and Rochelle L. Stanfield, "Communities Reborn," *National Journal* (June 22, 1966): 1371.

104. Patrick Wolf, "What History Advises About Reinventing Government," Ph.D. dissertation, Department of Government, Harvard University, 1996.

105. John DiIulio, *No Escape: The Future of American Corrections* (New York: Basic Books, 1991), pp. 19–26.

106. James A. Morone, *The Democratic Wish: Popular Participation and the Limits of American Government* (New York: Basic Books, 1990).

107. Francis Rourke, "Executive Secrecy: Change and Continuity," in Rourke, *Bureaucratic Power in National Policy Making,* pp. 536–537.

108. Jeffrey Birnbaum, Eileen Gunn, et al., "Unbelievable! The Mess at the IRS *Is* Worse Than You Think" *Fortune* (April 13, 1998).

109. Birnbaum, Gunn, et al.

110. Birnbaum, Gunn, et al.

111. Albert B. Crenshaw, "IRS Overhaul Set for Passage; Measure Gives Taxpayers New Rights, Includes Capital Gains Break," *Washington Post* (June 25, 1998): A1.

112. Martha Derthick, *Agency Under Stress,* p. 87.

113. Former Bureau of the Budget Director Kermit Gordon, as quoted in Kaufman, *Administrative Behavior,* p. 443.

114. Paul J. Quirk, "Food and Drug Administration," in James Q. Wilson, *The Politics of Regulation* (New York: Basic Books, 1980), p. 199.

115. Terry Moe, "The Politics of Bureaucratic Structure," in John E. Chubb and Paul E. Peterson, *Can the Government Govern?* (Washington, DC: Brookings, 1988).

CHAPTER 11

1. As quoted in Chuck Henning, *The Wit and Wisdom of Politics* (Golden, CO: Fulcrum Publishing, 1992), p. 250.

2. Ruth Marcus, "Plain-Spoken Marshall Spars with Reporters," *Washington Post* (June 29, 1991): A1.

3. David Brock, *The Real Anita Hill: The Untold Story* (New York: Free Press, 1993), p. 66. On the understanding that Bush would appoint an African American, see, for example, David G. Savage, "Court Nominee Warfare Opens," *Los Angeles Times* (July 6, 2001): A18.

4. Paul Simon, *Advice and Consent* (Washington, DC: National Press Books, 1992), p. 89.

5. Ibid., p. 93.

6. Bob Dart, "Abortion Key to Hearing Today," *Atlanta Journal and Constitution* (September 11, 1991): A1.

7. Simon, *Advice and Consent,* Chs. 5–6.

8. Ibid., p. 122.

9. Ibid., p. 122.

10. Brock, *The Real Anita Hill,* p. 17.

11. Gerald Pomper, "The Presidential Election," in Gerald M. Pomper et al., *The Election of 1992: Reports and Interpretations* (Chatham, NJ: Chatham House, 1993), p. 138.

12. Henning, *Wit and Wisdom,* p. 108.

13. Richard N. Smith, *Thomas E. Dewey and His Times* (New York: Simon & Schuster, 1982), Chs. 5–9.

14. Linda Greenhouse, "Legacy of a Term," *New York Times* (July 3, 1996): A1.

15. H. W. Perry, Jr., *Deciding to Decide: Agenda Setting in the United States Supreme Court* (Cambridge, MA: Harvard University Press, 1991), p. 27.

16. Ibid., pp. 218–219.

17. Ibid., p. 99.

18. Joan Biskupic, "The Rehnquist Court: Justices Want to Be Known as Jurists, Not Activists," *Washington Post* (January 9, 2000): B3.

19. Joan Biskupic and Howard Kurtz, "Police Can Be Sued for Letting Media See Raids," *Washington Post* (May 25, 1999): A8.

20. Simon, *Advice and Consent,* p. 128.

21. As quoted in Henning, *Wit and Wisdom,* p. 106.

22. John C. Jeffries, Jr., *Justice Lewis F. Powell, Jr: A Biography* (New York: Scribner, 1994), pp. 245–247.

23. Bob Woodward and Scott Armstrong, *The Brethren: Inside the Supreme Court* (New York: Simon and Schuster, 1979), pp. 126, 286–287, 297–298, 311.

24. *Parts and Electric Motors* v. *Sterling Electric* 866 F 2d 288 (1988).

25. Henning, *Wit and Wisdom,* p. 213.

26. Hart Pomerantz, as quoted in Henning, *Wit and Wisdom,* p. 250.

27. *Harris* v. *Forklift* 508 US 938 (1993).

28. Jeffries, *Justice Lewis F. Powell, Jr.*, p. 323

29. Woodward and Armstrong, *The Brethren*, pp. 71, 199.

30. This was true for the period 1958–1967; with the reduction in the number of certs accepted, this percentage has undoubtedly declined. Robert Scigliano, *The Supreme Court and the Presidency* (New York: Free Press, 1971), as quoted in Rebecca M. Salokar, *The Solicitor General: The Politics of Law* (Philadelphia, PA: Temple University Press, 1992), p. 3.

31. Jeffrey A. Segal, "*Amicus Curiae* Briefs by the Solicitor General During the Warren and Burger Courts: A Research Note," *Western Political Quarterly* 41 (March 1988): 135–144.

32. Perry, *Deciding to Decide,* p. 71.

33. Perry, *Deciding to Decide*; and Bernard Schwartz, *A History of the Supreme Court* (New York: Oxford University Press, 1993), Ch. 16.

34. Abram Chayes, "The Role of the Judge in Public Law Litigation," *Harvard Law Review* 89 (May 1976): 1281–1316.

35. Alexis de Toqueville, *Democracy in America*, J. P. Mayer, ed. (New York: Harper, 1988), p. 270.

36. Myron Levin and Henry Weinstein, "Big Tobacco Must Pay Damages in Florida Case," *Los Angeles Times* (April 8, 2000): A1.

37. Robert J. Samuelson, "Delegating Democracy: Government by Litigation Has Become Increasingly Popular," *Newsweek* (June 12, 2000): 59; and "Perspectives," *Newsweek* (May 29, 2000): 19.

38. As quoted in Henning, *Wit and Wisdom,* p. 107.

39. David O'Brien, "Background Paper," in Twentieth Century Fund, *Judicial Roulette* (New York: Priority Press, 1988), p. 37.

40. C. K. Rowland, Donald Songer, and Robert Carp, "Presidential Effects on Criminal Justice Policy in the Lower Federal Courts: The Reagan Judges," *Law and Society Review* 22/1 (1988): 191–200.

41. Carl B. Swisher, *American Constitutional Development,* Second Edition. (Boston: Houghton Mifflin, 1954), pp. 1075–1079.

42. Simon, *Advice and Consent,* p. 275.

43. Henry J. Abraham, *Justices and Presidents: A Political History of Appointments to the Supreme Court,* Third Edition. (New York: Oxford University Press, 1992).

44. Gloria Borger with Kenneth T. Walsh, Ted Gest, and Sharon Golden, "Going . . . Going: How the White House Booted the Nomination of Judge Robert Bork," *U.S. News and World Report* (October 12, 1987): 20.

45. Thomas B. Edsall, "Clinton Plans Judicial Offensive; Administration Will Hit GOP Efforts to Thwart Nominees," *Washington Post* (January 16, 1998): A1.

46. Stephen L. Carter, "Looking for Law in All the Wrong Places," *Manhattan Lawyer* (September 1990): 20.

47. Ethan Bronner, *Battle for Justice: How the Bork Nomination Shook America* (New York: Norton, 1989), pp. 158–59.

48. Robert G. McCloskey, *The American Supreme Court* (Chicago: University of Chicago Press, 1960), p. 14.

49. Marbury's story is drawn primarily from Jean Edward Smith, *John Marshall: Definer of a Nation* (New York: Holt, 1996), Ch. 13, as well as the case itself, *Marbury v. Madison* 5 U.S. 137 (1803).

50. *Lochner v. New York* 195 US 45 (1905).

51. University of Wisconsin Law School, "Supreme Court Justice Scalia Speaks at Law School," *Law School News* (March 2001, accessed at http://www.law.wisc.edu/news/main.asp on July 30, 2001).

52. *Lynch v. Donnelly* 465 US 668 (1984); and *County of Allegheny v. ACLU* 492 US 573 (1989).

53. *City of Erie v. Pap's A. M., "Kandyland"* 98–1161 (2000).

54. Jeffrey A. Segal and Albert D. Cover, "Ideological Values and the Votes of U.S. Supreme Court Justices," *American Political Science Review 83* (June 1989): 557–565.

55. Institute for Justice, *State of the Supreme Court 2000: The Justices' Record on Individual Liberties* (Washington, DC: Institute for Justice, 2000, accessed at http://www.ij.org/PDF_folder/supreme_court_report.pdf on August 13, 2001).

56. *Schechter Poultry Corp. v. United States* 295 US 495 (1935).

57. Congressional Research Service, Library of Congress, *The Constitution of the United States of America: Analysis and Interpretation, 1998 Supplement* (Washington, DC: Government Printing Office, 1999).

58. James A. Stimson, Michael B. Mackuen, and Robert S. Erikson, "Dynamic Representation," *American Political Science Review* 89 (1995): 555. Also see William Mishler and Reginald S. Sheehan, "The Supreme Court as a Counter-Majoritarian Institution? The Impact of Public Opinion on Supreme Court Decisions," *American Political Science Review* 87 (1993): 87–101; and Helmut Norpoth and Jeffery Segal, "Popular Influence on Supreme Court Decisions," *American Political Science Review* 88 (1994): 711–724.

59. R. Shep Melnick, *Between the Lines* (Washington, DC: Brookings, 1994), Ch. 1.

60. As quoted by Austin Ranney, "Peltason Created a New Way to Look at What Judges Do," Public Affairs Report, Institute of Governmental Studies, Vol. 36, No. 6, November 1995, p. 7.

61. C. Herman Pritchett, *The American Constitution* (New York: McGraw-Hill, 1959), p. 99.

62. Lee Epstein and Thomas G. Walker, *Constitutional Law for a Changing America: Rights, Liberties, and Justice,* Third Edition (Washington, DC: Congressional Quarterly, Inc., 1998), pp. 200–201.

63. Steven Lee Myers, "U.S. Judge Upsets Rules to Control How Jails Are Run," *New York Times* (July 24, 1996): B2.

64. As quoted in Pritchett, *The American Constitution*, pp. 65, 215.

65. Congressional Research Service, Library of Congress, *The Constitution of the United States of America: Analysis and Interpretation, 1998 Supplement* (Washington, DC: Government Printing Office, 1999).

66. Pritchett, *American Constitution*, p. 134.

67. Herbert Jacob and Kenneth Vines, "Courts," in Virginia Gray, Herbert Jacob, and Kenneth Vines, eds., *Politics in the American States: A Comparative Analysis*, Fourth Edition. (Boston: Little, Brown, 1983), p. 238.

68. Jacob and Vines, "Courts," p. 239.

69. Excerpted with ellipses deleted. Milton Rakove, *Don't Make No Waves; Don't Back No Losers* (Bloomington, IN: Indiana University Press, 1975), pp. 223–225.

70. Mark Hansen, "A Run for the Bench," *ABA Journal* (October 1998): 68.

71. John Paul Ryan, Allen A. Ashman, Bruce D. Sales, and Sandra Shane-Dubow, *American Trial Judges* (New York: Free Press, 1980), p. 125.

72. "Investigate, Then Prosecute; Bungled Lewis Trial: Atlanta Prosecutors, Police Rushed to Indict Before They Had All the Evidence," *Baltimore Sun* (June 14, 2000): 22A.

73. Cynthia Tucker, "My Opinion; Murder Acquittals: Running for Glory, Fulton DA Fumbles." *Atlanta Constitution* (June 14, 2000): 14A.

74. Henning, *Wit and Wisdom,* p. 187.

75. *In re Chapman* 16 US 661 (1897).

CHAPTER 12

1. Quoted in Peter Braestrup, *Big Story,* Abridged Edition (New Haven, CT: Yale University Press, 1983), p. 134.

2. David Halberstam, *The Powers That Be* (New York: Knopf, 1979), p. 514.

3. Austin Ranney, *Channels of Power: The Impact of Television on American Politics* (New York: Basic Books, 1983), p. 4.

4. Don Oberdorfer, *Tet!* (New York: Doubleday, 1971).

5. Braestrup provides the most ambitious account, comparing, in *Big Story,* the reality of the war to the news coverage.

6. In December, the chairman of the Joint Chiefs of Staff noted the possibility of an all-or-nothing offensive such as the Battle of the Bulge launched by the Germans as they retreated during World War II, ibid., p. 54.

7. For a thoughtful treatment of the media's impact, see Braestrup, *Big Story,* pp. 505–507.

8. David Altheide, *Creating Reality: How TV News Distorts Events* (Beverly Hills, CA: Sage, 1976).

9. Allen J. Matusow, *The Unraveling of America: A History of Liberalism in the 1960s* (New York: Harper and Row, 1984), p. 413; Jules Witcover, *The Year the Dream Died: Revisiting 1968 in America* (New York: Warner Books, 1997), p. 321; and Todd Gitlin, *The Sixties: Years of Hope, Days of Rage* (New York: Bantam, 1987), p. 322.

10. Ronald Radosh, *Divided They Fell: The Demise of the Democratic Party, 1964–1996* (New York: Free Press, 1996), 123; and Gitlin, *The Sixties,* p. 320.

11. Matusow, *Unraveling of America,* p. 413; and Gitlin, *The Sixties,* p. 322.

12. Radosh, *Divided They Fell,* pp. 124–128; and Matusow, *Unraveling of America,* pp. 418–419.

13. Witcover, *The Year the Dream Died,* p. 327; and Matusow, *Unraveling of America,* p. 418

14. On the British reporters, see Lewis Chester, Godfrey Hodgson, and Bruce Page, *An American Melodrama* (New York: Viking, 1969), p. 582. For an attempt to interpret Daley's verbal abuse of Ribicoff, see Gitlin, *The Sixties,* p. 334.

15. Chester, Hodgson and Page, *An American Melodrama,* p. 592.

16. John Robinson, "Public Reaction to Political Protest: Chicago 1968," *Public Opinion Quarterly* 34 (1970): 1–9.

17. Frank Luther Mott, *American Journalism* (New York: Macmillan, 1950).

18. Samuel Kernell, *Going Public: New Strategies of Presidential Leadership* (Washington, DC: CQ Press, 1986). Compare Mel Laracey, "The Presidential Newspaper: The Forgotten Way of Going Public," manuscript, Harvard University, 1993.

19. Mott, *American Journalism,* p. 216.

20. Personal communication of Premier Radio, which manages and distributes the Limbaugh show, with research assistant Sam Abrams, March 28, 2000.

21. The 1999 annual radio station survey by M Street Corporation of Nashville (http://www.mstreet.net).

22. Mary Ann Watson, *The Expanding Vista: American Television in the Kennedy Years* (New York: Oxford University Press, 1990), p. 76.

23. Austin Ranney, "Broadcasting, Narrowcasting, and Politics," in Anthony Kind, ed., *The New American Political System,* Second Version (Washington, DC: AEI Press, 1990), pp. 175–201.

24. Pew Research Center for the People and the Press (http://www.peoplepress.org/med98rpt.htm); and Mediamark Research Inc., "Multimedia Audiences," 1999.

25. William Mayer, "The Rise of the New Media," *Public Opinion Quarterly* 58 (1994): 124–146.

26. www.nua.ie/surveys/how_many_online/index.html

27. Mark Gillespie, "'Cyber-Politics' May be More Hype Than Reality . . . So Far," Gallup Poll Release, February 25, 2000.

28. Jim Puzzanghera, "Candidates Rake in Funds on Internet, *San Jose Mercury News* (January 5, 2000).

29. Jeff Glasser, "Virtual Campaign Pays Off,"*U.S. News and World Report* (March 6, 2000).

30. Eve Gerber, "Six Arguments for Online Fund Raising," *Slate* (January 18, 2000); and Lindsey Arent, "Candidates Eye Check Republic," *Wired News* (January 13, 2000).

31. William Mayer, "Trends in Media Usage," *Public Opinion Quarterly* 57 (1993): 597, 610.

32. For example, Doris Graber, *Mass Media and American Politics* (Washington, DC: CQ Press, 1993), Ch. 7.

33. Russell Neuman, Marion Just, and Ann Crigler, *Common Knowledge: News and the Construction of Political Meaning* (Chicago: University of Chicago Press, 1992); and Jeffrey Mondak, "Newspapers and Political Awareness," *American Journal of Political Science* 39 (1995): 513–527.

34. William Kornhauser, *The Politics of Mass Society* (New York: Free Press, 1959).

35. An example is the study of the 1940 presidential campaign reported in Paul Lazarsfeld, Bernard Berelson, and Hazel Gaudet, *The People's Choice* (New York: Columbia University Press, 1948).

36. Joseph Klapper, *The Effects of Mass Communication* (New York: Free Press, 1960).

37. Bernard Cohen, *The Press and Foreign Policy* (Princeton, NJ: Princeton University Press, 1963), p. 13.

38. Presentation by Steven Livingston at the John F. Kennedy School of Government, Harvard University, March 1996.

39. Robert Rotberg and Thomas Weiss, eds., *From Massacres to Genocide* (Washington, DC: Brookings, 1996).

40. M. McCombs and D. Shaw, "The Evolution of Agenda-Setting: Twenty-Five Years in the Marketplace of Ideas," *Journal of Communications* 43 (1993): 58–67.

41. Steven Livingston and Todd Eachus, "Humanitarian Crises and U.S. Foreign Policy: Somalia and the CNN Effect Reconsidered," *Political Communication* 12 (1995): 413–429.

42. Shanto Iyengar and Donald Kinder, *News That Matters: Television and American Opinion* (Chicago: University of Chicago Press, 1987).

43. Jon Krosnick and Laura Brannon, "The Impact of the Gulf War on the Ingredients of Presidential Evaluations," *American Political Science Review* 87 (1993): 963–975.

44. Everett Carll Ladd, "As Much About Continuity as Change: As Much About Restoration as Rejection," *The American Enterprise* (January/February 1993): 49–50; and Marc Hetherington,

"The Media's Role in Forming Voters' National Economic Evaluations in 1992," *American Journal of Political Science* 40 (1996): 372–395.

45. The most extensive study of framing is by Shanto Iyengar, *Is Anyone Responsible?* (Chicago: University of Chicago Press, 1991).

46. Iyengar and Kinder, *News That Matters*, Chs. 6, 10.

47. Bernard Cohen, *The Press and Foreign Policy*. See also Lutz Erbring, Edie Goldenberg, and Arthur Miller, "Front-Page News and Real-World Clues: A New Look at Agenda-Setting by the Media," *American Journal of Political Science* 24 (1980): 16–49.

48. S. Robert Lichter and Stanley Rothman, "Media and Business Elites," *Public Opinion*, (October/November 1981): 43; and Freedom Forum survey cited in Jill Zuckman, "Dole Says Media Overplay GOP View on Abortion," *Boston Globe* (June 25, 1996): 10.

49. William Schneider and I. A. Lewis, "Views on the News," *Public Opinion* (August/September 1985): 6–11; and "Ordinary Americans More Cynical Than Journalists: News Media Differs with Public and Leaders on Watchdog Issues" (Washington, DC: Times Mirror Center on People and the Press, May 22, 1995).

50. Maura Clancy and Michael Robinson, "The Media in Campaign '84: General Election Coverage, Part I," *Public Opinion* (December/January 1985): 49–54, 59.

51. Daniel Amundson and S. Robert Lichter, "Heeeeeeree's Politics," *Public Opinion* (July/August 1988): 46.

52. Martha Moore, "Candidates Try to Reach Voters by Joking with Jay, Dueling with Dave," *USA Today* (March 1, 2000): 14A.

53. Schneider and Lewis note that in the Los Angeles Times study, "Views on the News," that they report on, one-quarter of the readership thought their papers were conservative, one-quarter thought they were liberal, one-quarter thought they were moderate, and one-quarter didn't know.

54. S. Robert Lichter, Stanley Rothman, and Linda S. Lichter, *The Media Elite: America's New Powerbrokers* (New York: Hastings House, 1990).

55. G. C. Stone and E. Grusin, "Network TV as Bad News Bearer," *Journalism Quarterly* 61 (1984), 517–523; R. H. Bohle, "Negativism as News Selection Predictor," *Journalism Quarterly* 63 (1986): 789–796; and D. E. Harrington, "Economic News on Television: The Determinants of Coverage," *Public Opinion Quarterly* 53 (1989): 17–40.

56. Larry Sabato, *Feeding Frenzy* (New York: Simon and Schuster, 1991).

57. Michael Robinson, "Public Affairs Television and the Growth of Political Malaise," *American Political Science Review* 70 (1976): 409–432. On TV making people more negative about human nature generally, see George Comstock, *The Evolution of American Television* (Newbury Park, CA: Sage, 1989), pp. 265–269.

58. A widely cited study of what constitutes news is provided by Herbert Gans, *Deciding What's News: A Case Study of CBS Evening News, NBC Nightly News, Newsweek and Time* (New York: Vintage, 1979).

59. The following account is based on Thomas Romer and Barry Weingast, "Political Foundations of the Thrift Debacle," in Alberto Alesina and Geoffrey Carliner, eds., *Politics and Economics in the 1980s* (Chicago: University of Chicago Press, 1981), pp. 175–214.

60. Ellen Hume, "Why the Press Blew the S&L Scandal," *New York Times* (May 24, 1990): A25.

61. Mark Rom, *Public Spirit in the Thrift Tragedy* (Pittsburgh, PA: University of Pittsburgh Press, 1996).

62. John David Rausch, Jr., "The Pathology of Politics: Government, Press, and Scandal," *Extensions: A Publication of the Carl Albert Congressional Research and Studies Center* (Norman, OK: Carl Albert Congressional Research and Studies Center, Fall 1990), pp. 11–12.

63. A Gallup survey of former Nieman Journalism Fellows found that more than three-quarters believe that traditional journalism is being replaced by tabloid journalism. See "The State of the Public Media Today" (Cambridge, MA: Nieman Foundation, April 1995).

64. Sabato, *Feeding Frenzy*.

65. James Fallows, *Breaking the News* (New York: Pantheon, 1966), p. 132.

66. Alison Carper, "Paint-by-Numbers Journalism: How Reader Surveys and Focus Groups Subvert a Democratic Press," discussion paper D–19, Barone Center on the Press, Politics and Public Policy, Harvard University Kennedy School of Government, April 1995.

67. John Kramer, vice president for Communication, Institute of Justice, personal communication, September 9, 1999.

68. Dave Barry, "Scandal Sheep," *The Boston Globe Magazine* (March 15, 1998): 12–13.

69. Peter Canellos, "Perot Ad Announcement Is Also-Ran Against Reruns," *Boston Globe* (September 13, 1996): A24.

70. Thomas Patterson, *Out of Order* (New York: Knopf, 1993), Ch. 2.

71. Kiku Adatto, *Picture Perfect* (New York: Basic, 1993), Ch. 25.

72. Ibid.

73. Elihu Katz and Jacob Feldman, "The Debates in the Light of Research: A Survey of Surveys," in Sidney Kraus, ed., *The Great Debates* (Bloomington, IN: University of Indiana Press, 1962), pp. 173–223.

74. Thomas Holbrook, "Campaigns, National Conditions, and U.S. Presidential Elections," *American Journal of Political Science* 38 (1994): 973–998.

75. David von Drehle and Ceci Connolly, "The Truth About Gore's Credibility: Republicans are Trying to Use the Tall Tales He Tells on the Stump to Trip Him Up," *Washington Post Weekly Edition*, (October 16, 2000): 11; Jim Hoagland, "The 'BS' Factor," *Washington Post Weekly Edition* (October 2, 2000): 5; Jonathan Alter, "Al Gore and the Fib Factor," *Newsweek* (October 16, 2000): 43; and "Face to Face Combat," *Newsweek* 94, 102–103.

76. Dan Balz, "Still Neck-and-Neck: With No Major Errors, The First Debate Nonetheless Exposed Weaknesses in Both Candidates," *Washington Post Weekly Edition* (October 9, 2000): 14; Dan Balz, "Tests Passed, But Questions Remain: Bush Showed a Mastery of Foreign Policy, and Gore Appeared Tentative in the Second Debate," *Washington Post Weekly Edition* (October 16, 2000): 14; David von Drehle, "The Candidates, Great and Small: Gore Looms Large in the 3rd Debate, But Is That Good?" *Washington Post Weekly Edition* (October 23, 2000): 11; Richard Morin, "For Better and for Worse: Post-Debate Polls Show No Clear-Cut Winner, with Good and Bad News for Both Candidates," *Washington Post Weekly Edition* (October 23, 2000): 34; and "Face to Face Combat," (November 20, 2000): 102.

77. Michael Robinson and Margaret Sheehan, *Over the Wire and on TV* (New York: Russell Sage, 1983).

78. S. Robert Lichter and Daniel Amundson, "Less News Is Worse News: Television News Coverage of Congress, 1972–92," in Thomas Mann and Norman Ornstein, eds., *Congress, the Press, and the Public* (Washington, DC: American Enterprise Institute, 1994), pp. 131–140.

79. Iyengar, *Is Anyone Responsible?*

80. David Broder, "The Heroism of Hard Work," *Boston Globe* (October 18, 1995): 23.

81. Lichter and Amundson, "Less News Is Worse News."

CHAPTER 13

1. Details for the McVeigh story came from the following sources: Lou Michel and Dan Herbeck,"Live from Death Row," *Newsweek* (April 9, 2001): 24–28; Michael Isikoff and Evan Thomas, "Waiting for Justice," *Newsweek* (May 21, 2001): 23–27; and Andrew Murr and Flynn McRoberts, "'It Just Goes On and On': For the Families and Survivors, the FBI Prolongs the Pain," *Newsweek* (May 21, 2001): 28.

2. Isikoff and Thomas, "Waiting for Justice," p. 27.

3. ABC News broadcast, June 11, 2001.

4. Michel and Herbeck, "Live from Death Row."

5. Peter Annin, "Inside the New Alcatraz: The ADX 'Supermax' Prison Redefines Hard Time," *Newsweek* (July 13, 1998): 35.

6. Michel and Herbeck, "Live from Death Row."

7. Jonathan Alter, "Why the Mess Really Matters," *Newsweek* (May 21, 2001): 29; Mike Tharp, Chitra Ragavan, and Angie Cannon, "A Notch in the Paranoia Belt," *U.S. News and World Report* (May 21, 2001): 20; and Jonah Goldberg, "Just Kill Him," *National Review Online* (May 14, 2001).

8. "The Executions Continue," *New York Times* (June 19, 2001): A22; and James Gill, "Europeans' Outrage Rings False," *New Orleans (LA) Times-Picayune* (June 20, 2001): 7.

9. Henry Steele Commager, ed., *Documents of American History*, Sixth Edition (New York: Appleton-Century-Crofts, 1958), pp. 125–126. Also see Willi Paul Adams, *The First American Constitutions: Republican Ideology and the Making of the State Constitutions in the Revolutionary Era* (Chapel Hill, NC: University of North Carolina Press, 1980).

10. Charles R. Ritcheson, "'Loyalist Influence' on British Policy Toward the United States After the American Revolution," *Eighteenth Century Studies* 7/1 (Autumn 1973): 1–17. See also Paul A. Smith, "The American Loyalists: Notes on Their Organization and Numerical Strength," *William and Mary Quarterly*, Third Series, 25/2 (April 1968): 259–277.

11. Arthur M. Schlesinger, *Prelude to Independence: The Newspaper War on Britain, 1764–1776* (New York: Alfred Knopf, 1958), p. 299.

12. *Barron* v. *Baltimore*, 1833, as quoted in C. Herman Pritchett, *Constitutional Civil Liberties* (Englewood Cliffs, NJ: Prentice-Hall, 1984), p. 6.

13. John Jay, Alexander Hamilton, and James Madison, writing under the pseudonym Publius, *The Federalist Papers* (New York: New American Library, 1961).

14. *Stromberg* v. *California* 283 US 359 (1931).

15. *Chaplinsky* v. *New Hampshire* 315 US 568 (1942).

16. *R. A. V.* v. *City of St. Paul, Minnesota* 112 S Ct. 2541 (1992).

17. *United States* v. *Carolene Products Co.* 304 US 144 (1938).

18. George Anastaplo, as quoted in Goldstein, *Political Repression*, p. 532.

19. *Papish* v. *the Board of Curators of the University of Missouri* 410 US 667 (1973).

20. *New York Times* v. *United States* 403 US 713 (1971)

21. Robert Goldstein, *Saving "Old Glory": The History of the Desecration Controversy* (Boulder, CO: Westview, 1995).

22. *Texas* v. *Johnson* 491 US 397 (1989).

23. *United States* v. *Eichman* 496 US 310, (1990).

24. *Jenkins* v. *Georgia* 418 US 153 (1974).

25. Linda Greenhouse, "Court, 9 0, Upholds State Laws Prohibiting Assisted Suicide, Protects Speech on Internet," *New York Times* (June 27, 1997): A1.

26. Michael W. McConnell, "Stuck with a Lemon: A New Test for Establishment Clause Cases Would Help Ease Current Confusion," *ABA Journal* (February 1997): 46–47.

27. Scalia concurrence, *City of Erie* v. *Pap's A. M.,* "Kandyland" 98-1161 (2000).

28. Kennedy partial concurrence, *County of Allegheny* v. *ACLU* 492 US 573 (1989).

29. Scalia dissent, *Lee* v. *Weisman* 505 US 577 (1992).

30. *Sante Fe* v. *Doe* 99-62 (2000).

31. As quoted in Charles L. Glenn, Jr., *The Myth of the Common School* (Amherst, MA: University of Massachusetts Press, 1987), p. 84.

32. *Sante Fe* v. *Doe* 99-62 (2000).

33. Benjamin I. Page and Robert Y. Shapiro, *The Rational Public: Fifty Years of Trends in Americans' Policy Preferences* (Chicago: University of Chicago Press, 1992), p. 113.

34. *Board of Education* v. *Mergens* 496 US 226 (1990).

35. *Mitchell* v. *Helms* 98-1648 (2000).

36. *Sherbert* v. *Verner* 374 US 398 (1963).

37. C. Herman Pritchett, *The American Constitution* (New York: McGraw-Hill, 1959), p. 477.

38. James F. Simon, *The Antagonists: Hugo Black, Felix Frankfurter and Civil Liberties in Modern America* (New York: Simon and Schuster, 1989), pp. 106–114.

39. Pritchett, *The American Constitution*, p. 478.

40. Paul E. Peterson, "The New Politics of Choice," in Diane Ravitch and Maris Vinovskis, eds., *Learning from the Past* (Baltimore, MD: Johns Hopkins University Press, 1995).

41. Joan Biskupic, "Vouchers for Religious Schools Allowed" *Washington Post* (November 10, 1998): A2.

42. *Griswold* v. *Connecticut* 381 US 479 (1965).

43. Ibid.

44. Michael J. Sandel, *Democracy's Discontent: American in Search of a Public Philosophy* (Cambridge, MA: Belknap Press of Harvard, 1996), pp. 93–94.

45. Bob Woodward and Scott Armstrong, *The Brethren: Inside the Supreme Court* (New York: Simon and Schuster, 1979), pp. 198–206.

46. *Harris* v. *McRae* 448 US 297 (1980).

47. *Webster* v. *Reproductive Health Services* 492 US 490 (1989).

48. *Planned Parenthood* v. *Casey* 112 SCt 291 (1992).

49. *Stenberg* v. *Carhart* 99-830 (3000).

50. Pamela Coyle, "Second State Court Overturns Sodomy Law," *New Orleans Times-Picayune* (March 18, 1999): A1; and Amy Argetsinger, "Maryland Judge's Ruling Protects Private, Consensual Sex Acts," *Washington Post* (January 20, 1999): B8.

51. "The Gallup Poll: Social and Economic Indicators–Homosexual Relations," accessed at www.gallup.com/poll/ indicators/indhomsexual.asp on March 22, 2000.

52. *New York Times* (November 12, 1993): 1.

53. Senator Joe Biden, as quoted in Chuck Henning, *The Wit and Wisdom of Politics: Expanded Edition* (Golden, CO: Fulcrum Publishing, 1992), p. 47.

54. *Mapp* v. *Ohio* 167 US 643 (1961).

55. *Washington* v. *Chrisman* 455 US 1 (1982), p. 182.

56. Joan Biskupic, "Police May Stop, Frisk Those Who Flee at Sight of Officer," *Washington Post* (January 13, 2000): A10.

57. Pritchett, *Constitutional Civil Liberties,* p. 78.

58. *Sheppard* v. *Maxwell* 384 US 333 (1966).

59. *Nebraska Press Association* v. *Stuart* 427 US 539 (1976).

60. Lisa J. McIntyre, *The Public Defender: The Practice of Law in the Shadows of Repute* (Chicago: University of Chicago Press, 1987), p. 162.

61. Jonathan D. Casper, *American Criminal Justice: The Defendant's Perspective* (Englewood Cliffs, NJ: Prentice-Hall, 1972), p. 101.

62. Toni Locy, "Okla. Trial for Nichols Rethought: New Prosecutor Reviewing Options," *USA Today* (June 19, 2001): 6A.

63. Casper, *American Criminal Justice;* and Jerome Skolnick, *Justice Without Trial* (New York: John Wiley, 1966).

CHAPTER 14

1. Amy Wallace and Diana Marcum, "Prop. 209 Foes Seize Building at UC Riverside," *Los Angeles Times* (November 12, 1996): A3.

2. Robert Pear, "The 1996 Elections: The Nation—The States; In California, Voters Bar Preferences Based on Race," *New York Times* (November 6, 1996): B7.

3. Wallace and Marcum, "Prop. 209 Foes Seize Building."

4. Bill Stall and Dan Morain, "Prop. 209 Wins, Bars Affirmative Action Initiatives," *Los Angeles Times* (November 6, 1996): A1.

5. Tanya Schevitz, "UC Berkeley Minority Applications on Rise," *San Francisco Chronicle* (January 27, 2000): A22; and "Affirmative Action in California: Passed," *The Economist* (April 8, 2000): 29.

6. Ruth Bader Ginsburg, "Employment of the Constitution to Advance the Equal Status of Men and Women," in Shlomo Slonim, ed., *The Constitutional Bases of Political and Social Change in the United States* (New York: Praeger, 1990), p. 188.

7. Robert F. Nagel, *Constitutional Cultures: The Mentality and Consequences of Judicial Review* (Berkeley, CA: University of California Press, 1989), Chs. 5–6.

8. Philip Converse, "The Nature of Belief Systems in Mass Publics," in David E. Apter, *Ideology and Discontent* (New York: Free Press, 1964), pp. 206–261.

9. John D. Hicks, *The American Nation* (Cambridge, MA: Riverside Press, 1949), p. 21.

10. Eric Foner, *A Short History of Reconstruction* (New York: Harper, 1990).

11. Richard M. Valelly, "National Parties and Racial Disfranchisement," in Paul E. Peterson, ed., *Classifying by Race* (Princeton, NJ: Princeton University Press, 1995), pp. 188–216.

12. U.S. Commission on Civil Rights, *Report of the Commission on Civil Rights* (Washington, DC: Government Printing Office, 1959), p. 32. Ellipses deleted.

13. V. O. Key, Jr., *Southern Politics* (New York: Random House, 1949).

14. J. Morgan Kousser, *The Shaping of Southern Politics: Suffrage Restriction and the Establishment of the One-Party South, 1880–1910* (New Haven, CT: Yale University Press, 1974), p. 61.

15. *Civil Rights Cases* 109 US 3 (1883).

16. *Plessy* v. *Ferguson* 163 US 537 (1896).

17. Edward Banfield and James Q. Wilson, *City Politics* (New York: Vintage Books, 1963); and

James Q. Wilson, *Negro Politics* (New York: Free Press, 1960). For caveats, see Steven P. Erie, *Rainbow's End: Irish-Americans and the Dilemmas of Urban Machine Politics, 1840–1985* (Berkeley, CA: University of California Press, 1990).

18. Gerald N. Rosenberg, *The Hollow Hope: Can Courts Bring About Social Change?* (Chicago: University of Chicago Press, 1991), p. 61.

19. *Smith* v. *Allwright* 321 US 649 (1944).

20. *Shelley* v. *Kraemer* 334 US 1 (1948).

21. Howard Ball and Phillip J. Cooper, *Of Power and Right: Hugo Black, William O. Douglas, and America's Constitutional Revolution* (New York: Oxford University Press, 1992), p. 172.

22. Simon, *The Antagonists*, p. 219–223; and Ball and Cooper, *Of Power and Right*, pp. 171–175.

23. Bob Woodward and Scott Armstrong, *The Brethren: Inside the Supreme Court* (New York: Simon and Schuster, 1979), Prologue.

24. *Brown* v. *Board of Education* 347 US 483 (1954), note 11. The citation of six psychological and sociological studies in this note led Herbert Garfinkel to charge that the Court was making decisions on the basis of sociology, not law. "Social Science Evidence and the School Segregation Cases," *Journal of Politics* 21 (Feb. 1959): 37–59. Kenneth B. Clark, "Effect of Prejudice and Discrimination on Personality Development" (Midcentury White House Conference on Children and Youth 1950, as cited in note 11 to *Brown*).

25. A. D. Morris, *Origins of the Civil Rights Movement: Black Communities Organizing for Change* (New York: Free Press, 1984).

26. Ibid., pp. 51–63.

27. Michael Lipsky, "Protest as a Political Resource," *American Political Science Review* LXII (December 1968): 1144–1158.

28. University of Georgia, Carl Vinson Institute of Government, "Historical Documents Related to Georgia," accessed at http://www.cviog.uga.edu/Projects/gainfo/gahisdoc.htm on April 6, 2000.

29. Rosenberg, *The Hollow Hope*, p. 50.

30. Gerald D. Jaynes and Robin M. Williams, Jr., eds., *A Common Destiny: Blacks and American Society* (Washington, DC: National Academy Press, 1989), p. 224.

31. Patricia Gurin, Shirley Hatchett, and James S. Jackson, *Hope and Independence: Blacks' Response to Electoral and Party Politics* (New York: Russell Sage, 1989), pp. 42–49.

32. Jaynes and Williams, *A Common Destiny*, p. 233.

33. Joint Center for Political and Economic Studies, *Focus* (Washington, DC: Joint Center for Political and Economic Studies 1993); and "Joint Center Releases 1998 National Count of Black Elected Officials," press release (Washington, DC: Joint Center for Political and Economic Studies, November 9, 1999).

34. William J. Grimshaw, *Bitter Fruit: Black Politics and the Chicago Machine, 1931–1991* (Chicago: University of Chicago Press, 1992).

35. Gary Orfield, *The Reconstruction of Southern Education: The Schools and the 1964 Civil Rights Act* (New York: Wiley, 1969); Gary Orfield, *Must We Bus?* (Washington, DC, Brookings, 1978); and Jennifer Hochschild, *The New American Dilemma* (New Haven, CT: Yale University Press, 1984).

36. Katherine Tate, *From Protest to Politics* (Cambridge, MA: Harvard University Press, 1993), Ch. 8.

37. *Milliken* v. *Bradley* I 418 US 717 (1974); 433 US 267 (1977).

38. *Regents of the University of California* v. *Bakke* 438 US 265 (1978).

39. U.S. Bureau of the Census, *Statistical Abstract of the United States, 1999*, Table 760.

40. U.S. Bureau of the Census, *Statistical Abstract of the United States, 1999*, Table 680; and Amitabh Chandra, "Is the Convergence in the Racial Wage Gap Illusory?" *American Economic Review* 90 (2000).

41. U.S. Bureau of the Census, *Statistical Abstract of the United States, 1999*, Tables 99 and 133.

42. Jaynes and Williams, *A Common Destiny*, p. 313.

43. U.S. Bureau of the Census, *Statistical Abstract of the United States, 1999*, Tables 298 and 302.

44. Lisa Handley and Bernard Grofman, "The Impact of the Voting Rights Act on Minority Representation: Black Officeholding in Southern State Legislatures," in Chandler Davidson and Bernard Grofman, eds., *Quiet Revolution in the South: The Impact of the Voting Rights Act, 1965–1990* (Princeton, NJ: Princeton University Press, 1994), pp. 335–350; Margaret Edds, *Claiming the Dream: The Victorious Campaign of Douglas Wilder of Virginia* (Chapel Hill, NC: Algonquin Books, 1990); and D. Stephen Voss and David Lublin, "Black Incumbents, White Districts: An Appraisal of the 1996 Congressional Elections," *American Politics Research* 29 (2001): 141–182.

45. Frederic Cople Jaher, *A Scapegoat in the Wilderness: The Origins and Rise of Anti-Semitism in America* (Cambridge, MA: Harvard University Press, 1994); Leonard Dinnerstein, *Anti-Semitism in America* (New York: Oxford, 1994); and Jack Nelson, *Terror in the Night: The Klan's Campaign Against the Jews* (New York: Simon & Schuster, 1993).

46. U.S. Census Bureau, *Statistical Abstract of the United States, 1999*, Table 13; and U.S. Census Bureau, *Profiles of General Demographic Characteristics* (Washington, DC: U.S. Department of Commerce, 2001).

47. Michael Jones-Correa, *Between Two Nations: The Political Predicament of Latinos in New York City* (Ithaca, NY: Cornell University Press, 1998).

48. National Election Studies; and *Newsweek* poll conducted by Princeton Survey Research Associates, June 25–30, 1999.

49. Geoffrey Fox, *Hispanic Nation: Culture, Politics, and the Constructing of Identity* (Secaucus, NJ: Birch Lane, 1996).

50. *Lau v. Nichols* 414 US 563 (1974).

51. Bernard Grofman, Lisa Handley, and Richard G. Niemi, *Minority Representation and the Quest for Voting Equality* (New York: Cambridge University Press, 1992), pp. 16–25. Also see Thomas Weyr, *Hispanic U.S.A.: Breaking the Melting Pot* (New York: Harper, 1959); and Peter Skerry, *Mexican Americans: The Ambivalent Minority* (New York: Free Press, 1993).

52. U.S. Bureau of the Census, *Statistical Abstract of the United States, 1999*, Tables 18 and 57.

53. Stanley Karnow and Nancy Yoshihara, *Asian Americans in Transition* (New York: Asia Society, 1992).

54. William Schneider, "Asian Americans Will Matter More," *National Journal* (August 14, 1999): 2398.

55. Asian Pacific American Institute for Congressional Studies, "Statement from APA Community Organizations," accessed at http://www.apaics.org/statement.html on April 10, 2000.

56. Vine Deloria, Jr., "The Distinctive Status of Indian Rights," in Peter Iverson, ed., *The Plains Indians of the Twentieth Century* (Norman, OK: University of Oklahoma Press, 1985), p. 241.

57. Deloria, ibid., pp. 237–248.

58. Deloria, ibid., p. 237.

59. John Agresto, *The Supreme Court and Constitutional Democracy* (Ithaca, NY: Cornell University

Press, 1984), pp. 148–149.

60. Theda Skocpol, *Protecting Soldiers and Mothers: The Political Origins of Social Policy in the United States* (Cambridge, MA: Harvard University Press, 1992); and Sara Evans, *Personal Politics: The Roots of Women's Liberation in the Civil Rights Movement and the New Left* (New York: Knopf, 1979).

61. Nancy McGlen and Karen O'Conner, *Women's Rights: The Struggle for Equality in the Nineteenth and Twentieth Centuries* (New York: Praeger, 1983), Ch. 9.

62. Jane J. Mansbridge, *Why We Lost the ERA* (Chicago: University of Chicago Press, 1986).

63. *Craig v. Boren* 429 US 190 (1976).

64. Ginsburg, *Employment of the Constitution,* p. 191.

65. *Rostker v. Goldberg* 453 US 65 (1981).

66. Mansbridge, *Why We Lost the ERA,* Ch. 7.

67. *Watson v. Fort Worth Bank & Trust* 487 US 997–999; *New York City Transit Authority v. Beazer* 440 US at 587, no 31; and *Griggs v. Duke Power,* 401 US at 432.

68. *Wards Cove v. Antonio* 490 US 642, (1989).

69. *Meritor Savings Bank v. Vinson* 477 US 57 (1986).

70. *Harris v. Forklift Systems* 510 US 77 (1993).

71. "Hillary's Class," *Frontline* (PBS television broadcast, No. 15, 1994), as cited in Karla Cooper-Boggs, "The Link Between Private and Public Single-Sex Colleges: Will Wellesley Stand or Fall with the Citadel?" *Indiana Law Review* 29 (1995), p. 137.

72. Cooper-Boggs, "The Link Between Private and Public Single-Sex Colleges," p. 135.

73. *United States v. Virginia* 116 SCt 2264 (1996).

74. Shawn Zeller, "Gay Rites: Giving to Democrats," *National Journal* (May 8, 1999): 1241.

75. Matthew Brelis, "From the Closet to the Campaign Trail; Being Gay Once Defined a Candidate. Now the Issues Do," *Boston Globe* (August 30, 1998): E1.

76. Deb Price, "Gays Need Democrats to Win 2000 Elections," *Detroit News* (November 1, 1999): A7; and Human Rights Campaign, accessed at http://www.hrc.org on April 11, 2000.

77. Stephen L. Percy, *Disability, Civil Rights, and Public Policy: The Politics of Implementation* (Tuscaloosa, AL: University of Alabama Press, 1989), p. 3.

78. Authors' 1995 estimate based on 1989 estimate provided by Percy, ibid., Ch 5.

79. Robert A. Katzman, *Institutional Disability: The Saga of Transportation Policy for the Disabled* (Washington, DC: Brookings, 1986).

80. Frederick J. Weintraub, ed., *Public Policy and the Education of Exceptional Children* (Washington, DC: Council for Exceptional Children, 1976).

81. Paul E. Peterson, "Background Paper," in Twentieth Century Fund, *Making the Grade: Report of the Twentieth Century Fund Task Force on Federal Elementary and Secondary Education Policy* (New York: Twentieth Century Fund, 1983), Ch. 5.

82. Rufus Browning, Dale Rogers Marshall, and David H. Tabb, *Protest Is Not Enough: The Struggle of Blacks and Hispanics for Equality in Urban Politics* (Berkeley, CA: University of California Press, 1984).

CHAPTER 15

1. Peter Bachrach and Morton S. Baratz, "Two Faces of Power," in Pietro S. Nivola and David H. Rosenbloom, eds., *Classic Readings in American Politics* (New York: Worth, 1999), pp. 113–125.

2. John Kingdon, *Agenda, Alternatives and Public Policies* (Boston: Little, Brown, 1984); and Paul

Light, *The President's Agenda* (Baltimore, MD: Johns Hopkins University Press, 1991).

3. Arthur Maass, *Congress and the Common Good* (New York: Basic Books, 1983).

4. Eugene Bardach, *The Implementation Game,* Fourth Edition. (Cambridge, MA: MIT Press, 1982); and Jeffrey L. Pressman and Aaron Wildavsky, *Implementation,* Third Edition. (Berkeley, CA: University of California Press, 1984).

5. Thomas R. Dye, *Politics, Economics and the Public: Policy Outcomes in the American States* (Chicago: Rand McNally, 1966).

6. Amy Goldstein, "Forgotten Issues; Welfare Reform's Progress Is Stalled," *Washington Post* (June 1, 2000): A1.

7. Timothy Smeeding, Michael O'Higgins, and Lee Rainwater, eds., *Poverty, Inequality and Income Distribution in Comparative Perspective* (New York: Harvester Wheatsheaf, 1990); and Lee Rainwater and Timothy M. Smeeding, "Doing Poorly: The Real Income of American Children in a Comparative Perspective," working paper no. 127, Maxwell School of Citizenship and Public Affairs, Syracuse University, Syracuse, NY, August 1995.

8. Neil Howe and Richard Jackson, *Entitlements and the Aging of America* (Washington, DC: National Taxpayers Union Foundation, 1994).

9. Martha Derthick, *Policymaking for Social Security* (Washington, DC: Brookings, 1979); and Theda Skocpol, *Protecting Soldiers and Mothers: The Politics of Social Provision in the United States* (Cambridge, MA: Harvard University Press, 1993).

10. R. Kent Weaver, *Automatic Government: The Politics of Indexation* (Washington, DC: Brookings, 1988).

11. Neil Howe and Richard Jackson, *1998 Chartbook: Entitlements and the Aging of America* (Washington, DC: National Taxpayers' Union Foundation, 1998), Chart 4-26.

12. Because these figures are in constant dollars, one should not compare Social Security benefits directly to other possible forms of investment.

13. *Boston Globe* (December 27, 1994): 70.

14. John F. Harris and Glenn Kessler, "Who Shrank the Surplus? Both Sides Place Blame as the Effects of a Slow Economy and a Tax Cut Set In," *Washington Post Weekly Edition* (July 16–22, 2001): 6.

15. *Budget of the United States Government, Fiscal Year 2001, Historical Tables* (Washington, DC: Office of Management and Budget, 2000), Table 16.1, p. 279.

16. Ibid.

17. Elizabeth Drew, *Showdown: The Struggle Between the Gingrich Congress and the Clinton White House* (New York: Simon & Schuster, 1996), pp. 238–242, 318–321.

18. U.S. Census Bureau, *Current Population Reports* (July 1998), pp. 20–504; and U.S. Census Bureau, *Current Populations Reports* (May 2000), pp. 20–523.

19. Susan A. MacManus, with Patricia A. Turner, *Young v. Old: Generational Combat in the 21st Century* (Boulder, CO: Westview, 1996), pp. 60, 141.

20. Employment information: Susan Levine, "AARP Hopes Boom Times Are Ahead," *Washington Post* (June 2, 1998): A1; membership and volunteer numbers, "What is AARP?" accessed at http://www.aarp.org/what_is.html on May 28, 2000; and budget figures, *AARP: 1999 Financial Statements* (Washington, DC: AARP, 2000).

21. Survey by the Luntz Research Companies/Mark A. Siegal and Associates, September 8–10, 1994; and *The Public Perspective: People, Opinions, & Polls* (February/March 1995).

22. *Publication 596: Earned Income Tax Credit* (Washington, DC: Internal Revenue Service, 1999); and John F. Harris and Dan Balz, "A Delicate Balance: The Steady Courtship of Senate Moderates Was Key to the Passage of the Tax Bill," Washington Post Weekly Edition (June 4–10,

2001): 8–10.

23. Percentage of monies going for services to the elderly in fiscal year 1993. Marilyn Werber Serafini, "Pinching Pennies," *National Journal* 27/37 (September 16, 1995): 2273. Also see Mark Rom, "Health and Welfare in the American States," *Politics in the American States,* Sixth Edition, Virginia Gray and Herbert Jacob, eds. (Washington, DC: CQPress, 1995).

24. Paul E. Peterson, "An Immodest Proposal," *Daedalus* 121 (Fall 1992): 151–174.

25. Calculated from Green Book, Table 1, 1579. Until 1995, the Green Book, issued annually since 1981, was one of the most comprehensive sources of information on U.S. social policy, U.S. House of Representatives, Committee on Ways and Means, Overview of Entitlement Programs: Background Material and Data on Programs within the Jurisdiction of the Committee on Ways and Means (otherwise known as the 1992 Green Book) (Washington, DC: U.S. Government Printing Office, 1992), Table 1, p. 1579. All subsequent references to this document in this chapter will be simply to the Green Book. They refer to the 1992 edition.

26. Green Book, Table 2, p. 1582.

27. U.S. Department of Health and Human Services, Administration for Children and Families, Office of Family Assistance, *TANF Selected Provisions of State Plans*, accessed at http://www.acf.dhhs.gov/ programs/ofa/provis.htm on July 24, 2000.

28. Paul E. Peterson and Mark Rom, *Welfare Magnets: A New Case for a National Standard* (Washington, DC: Brookings, 1990).

29. Green Book, Table 12, pp. 643–645.

30. Green Book, Table 12, p. 1212.

31. "Social Security Penalty on Earnings Is Repealed," *Los Angeles Times* (April 8, 2000): A14.

32. Skocpol, *Protecting Soldiers and Mothers.*

33. Charles Murray, *Losing Ground: American Social Policy, 1950–1980* (New York: Basic Books, 1984).

34. Christopher Jencks, "Is the American Underclass Growing?" in *The Urban Underclass,* Christopher Jencks and Paul E. Peterson, eds. (Washington, DC: Brookings, 1991), pp. 33, 88.

35. William J. Wilson, *The Truly Disadvantaged: The Inner City, the Underclass, and Public Policy* (Chicago: University of Chicago Press, 1987); and Christopher Jencks, "Is the American Underclass Growing?" in *The Urban Underclass,* Christopher Jencks and Paul E. Peterson, eds. (Washington, DC: Brookings, 1991), p. 56.

36. *Public Perspective* (February/March 1995): p. 39; and *The Gallup Poll,* accessed at www.gallup.com on July 24, 2000.

37. Jeff Shear, "The Credit Card," *National Journal* 27/32 (August 12, 1995): 2056–2058; and Marilyn W. Serafini, "Turning Up the Heat," *National Journal* 27/32 (August 12, 1995): 2051–2055.

38. Amy Pyle, "Bond Backers Weigh Second Try; Education: Bid to Cut Margin Needed to Pass School Measures Failed by So Little That Supporters Consider a Rush Job to Put Initiative on Fall Ballot," *Los Angeles Times* (March 24, 2000): A3; Randal C. Archibold, "School Budgets: Many Reasons Why Voters May Say No," *New York Times* (May 21, 2001): B1; Iver Peterson, "As Taxes Rise, Suburbs Work to Keep Elderly," *New York Times* (February 27, 2001): A1; Martha Groves and Duke Helfand, "Schools Prepare Fresh Set of Bond Issues," *Los Angeles Times* (November 9, 2000): A3; Martha Groves, "Voters Ready to Give Vouchers a Drubbing; Two-thirds of Those Likely to Turn Out Oppose Proposition 38. Proposition 39, Which Would Make It Easier to Pass; School Bond Measure Is in a Tighter Race," *Los Angeles Times* (October 26, 2000): A3; and Lisa Frazier, "In Bowie, 'White Angst' Bubbles Beneath Secession Movement,'" *Washington Post* (October 26,

2000): M2.

39. "Land Ordinance of 1785," in Henry S. Commager, ed., *Documents of American History,* Sixth Edition. (New York: Appleton-Century-Crofts, 1958), p. 124.

40. The Gallup Organization. Roper Center for Public Opinion Research Database, Question ID Numbers USGALLUP. 870.Q005A; USGALLUP. 99JNE25R11E

41. Eric A Hanushek, "School Resources and Student Performance," in *Does Money Matter? The Effect of School Resources on Student Achievement and Adult Success,* Gary Burtless, ed. (Washington, DC:Brookings, 1996), pp. 43–73.

42. Helen F. Ladd, "Introduction," in Helen F. Ladd, ed., *Holding Schools Accountable: Performance-Based Reform in Education* (Washington, DC: Brookings, 1996), pp. 1–22.

43. U.S. Department of Education, National Center for Education Statistics, *Digest of Education Statistics, 1999,* May 2000 (NCES 2000-031),Table 419, p. 471.

44. National Education Association Research Division, *Salaries Paid Classroom Teachers, Principals, and Certain Others, 1960–61, Urban Districts 100,000 and Over in Population;* ibid., 1970–71; Educational Research Service, *Salaries Paid Professional Personnel in Public Schools, 1974–75;* ibid., 1979–80; ibid., 1984–85; ibid., 1989–90; National Education Association, *Estimates of School Statistics,* 1960–61, p. 13; ibid., 1989–90, p. 19; and National Center for Education Statistics, *Digest of Education Statistics,* 1988,Table 57, p. 72.

45. *Statistical Abstract of the United States, 1999,* Table 163 and 1434.

46. David K. Kirkpatrick, *Choice in Schooling: A Case for Tuition Vouchers* (Chicago: Loyola University Press, 1990); and Terry Moe, ed., *Private Vouchers* (Stanford, CA: Hoover Institution Press, 1995).

47. William H. Clune and John F. Witte, eds., *Choice and Control in American Education,* Volumes I and II (New York: Falmer Press, 1990); and Henig, *Rethinking School Choice.*

48. Robert Manor, "Firms Linked in Plane Crash Ignored Rules, Oxygen Generators Improperly Loaded," *St. Louis Post-Dispatch* (June 2, 1996): 11A.

49. *Heart of Atlanta Motel* v. *United States* 322 US 533 (1964); and *United States* v. *South-Eastern Underwriters Association* 322 US 533 (1944).

50. Paul Attewell and Dean R. Gerstein, "Government Policy and Local Practice," *American Sociological Review* 44 (1979): 311–327. For a banking example, see John T. Woolley, "Conflict among Regulators and the Hypothesis of Congressional Dominance," *Journal of Politics* 55 (1993): 102–103.

51. Marc K. Landy, Marc J. Roberts, and Stephen R. Thomas, *The Environmental Protection Agency: Asking the Wrong Questions from Nixon to Clinton,* Expanded Edition. (New York: Oxford University Press, 1994).

52. Kenneth Meier, *Regulation: Politics, Bureaucracy, and Economics* (New York: St. Martin's, 1985).

53. Martha Derthick and Paul Quirk, *The Politics of Deregulation* (Washington, DC: Brookings, 1985); and Mark C. Rom, *Public Spirit in the Thrift Tragedy* (Pittsburgh, PA: University of Pittsburgh Press, 1996).

54. H. Craig Petersen, *Business and Government,* Second Edition. (New York: Harper & Row, 1985), p. 198.

55. A. W. Phillips, "The Relationship Between Unemployment and the Rate of Change of Money Wage Rates in the United Kingdom 1862–1957," *Economica* 25 (1958): 283–299.

56. Morris Fiorina, "Elections and Economics in the 1980s," in Alberto Alesina and Geoffrey Carliner, eds., *Politics and Economics in the 1980s* (Chicago: University of Chicago Press, 1991),

pp. 17–38.

57. For a summary of the relevant literature, see Fiorina, "Elections and Economics in the 1980s." Also see John Chubb, "Institutions, the Economy, and the Dynamics of State Elections," *American Political Science Review* 82 (1988): 133–154; and Dennis Simon, Charles Ostrom, and Robin Marra, "The President, Referendum Voting, and Subnational Elections in the United States," *American Political Science Review* 85 (1991): 1177–1192.

58. Paul Peretz, *The Political Economy of Inflation in the United States* (Chicago: University of Chicago, Press, 1983).

59. The following summary account is drawn from Allen Schick, *The Federal Budget* (Washington, DC: Brookings, 1995); and Steven Smith, *The American Congress* (Boston, MA: Houghton Mifflin, 1995), Ch. 11.

60. Tim Weiner, "Criticism Appears to Doom Republican Budget Tactic," *New York Times* (October 1, 1999,): A20.

61. Bruce Oppenheimer, "The Importance of Elections in a Strong Congressional Party Era: The Effect of Unified v. Divided Government," manuscript, 1995.

62. Donald Kettl, *Leadership at the Fed* (New Haven, CT: Yale University Press, 1986).

63. John M. Berry, "Where's the Rebound? The Fed, Increasingly Concerned That Its Rate Cuts Haven't Worked, Is Poised to Act Again," *Washington Post Weekly Edition* (June 25–July 1, 2001): 18.

64. Susan Milligan, "Greenspan Nominated to Fourth Term as Fed Chairman," *Boston Globe* (January 5, 2000): C1.

65. *Annual Report: Budget Review* (Washington, DC: Board of Governors of the Federal Reserve System, 1999).

66. James Livingston, *Origins of the Federal Reserve System* (Ithaca, NY: Cornell University Press, 1986).

67. John Woolley, *Monetary Politics: The Federal Reserve and the Politics of Monetary Policy* (New York: Cambridge University Press, 1984).

68. Douglas Hibbs, "The Partisan Model of Macroeconomic Cycles: More Theory and Evidence for the United States," *Economics and Politics* 6 (1994): 1–23.

69. Edward Tufte, *Political Control of the Economy* (Princeton, NJ: Princeton University Press, 1978), Ch. 2.

70. William Greider, *Secrets of the Temple: How the Federal Reserve Runs the Country* (New York: Simon & Schuster, 1987).

71. Michael Schrage, "It's Time to Put a Transaction Tax on Credit Card Purchases," *Washington Post* (October 17, 1990): F3.

72. "Steady Greenspan; Clinton Plays It Safe on Choice of Fed Chief," *San Diego Union-Tribune* (February 26, 1996): B4.

73. *Budget and Economic Outlook, Fiscal Years 2000–2009* (Washington, DC: Congressional Budget Office, January 1999).

74. David Bradford, *Untangling the Income Tax* (Cambridge, MA: Harvard University Press, 1986); plus surveys by the National Opinion Research Center.

75. Ballard C. Campbell, *The Growth of American Government: Governance from the Cleveland Era to the Present* (Bloomington, IN: Indiana University Press, 1995), p. 181

76. Calculated by authors from U.S. Bureau of the Census, *Statistical Abstract of the United States,*

1999, Tables 1434 and 1443.

77. Howard Schuman, *Politics and the Budget,* Third Edition. (Englewood Cliffs, NJ: Prentice Hall, 1992), p. 121.

78. The intellectual basis of such proposals is usually credited to Robert Hall and Alvin Rabushka, *The Flat Tax* (Stanford, CA: Hoover Institution Press, 1985).

79. "Why Tax Reform?" *The American Enterprise* (July/August 1995): 17; and Murray Weidenbaum, "The Nunn-Domenici 'USA Tax' Proposal," *The American Enterprise* (July/August 1995): 67.

80. For a critical survey, see Paul Krugman, *Peddling Prosperity* (New York: Norton, 1994), Ch. 5.

81. *U.S.* v. *Curtiss Wright Export Corporation* 299 US 304 (1936).

82. *Youngstown Sheet & Tube Co.* v. *Sawyer* 343 US 579 (1952).

83. Joint Resolution of Congress, H.J. RES 1145 August 7, 1964.

84. Louis Fisher and David Gray Adler, "The War Powers Resolution: Time to Say Goodbye," *Political Science Quarterly* 113/3: 1–20.

85. James L. Sundquist, *The Decline and Resurgence of Congress* (Washington, DC: Brookings, 1981), p. 93.

86. *United States* v. *Belmont* 301 US 324 (1937).

87. Ann Devroy, "Pact Reached to Dismantle Ukraine's Nuclear Force; Detailed Plan to Be Signed Friday, Clinton Announces," *Washington Post* (January 11, 1994): A1.

88. Aaron Wildavsky, "The Two Presidencies [1965]," in Steven A. Shull, *The Two Presidencies: A Quarter Century Assessment* (Chicago: Nelson Hall, 1991), pp. 11–25.

89. Wildavksy, "The Two Presidencies," p. 17.

90. Barry M. Blechman, *The Politics of National Security: Congress and U.S. Defense Policy* (New York: Oxford University Press, 1990); Duane M. Oldfield and Aaron Wildavsky, "Reconsidering the Two Presidencies," in Steve A. Shull, ed., *The Two Presidencies: A Quarter Century Assessment* (Chicago: Nelson Hall, 1991), pp. 181–90; Thomas Franck and Edward Weisband, *Foreign Policy by Congress* (New York: Oxford University Press, 1979); Thomas E. Mann, ed., *A Question of Balance: The President, the Congress and Foreign Policy* (Washington, DC: Brookings, 1990); and Stephen R. Weissman, *A Culture of Deference: Congress's Failure of Leadership in Foreign Policy* (New York: Basic Books, 1955).

91. James Baker, III, with Thomas M. DeFrank, *The Politics of Diplomacy: Revolution, War, and Peace, 1989–1992* (New York: Putnam, 1995), p. 116.

92. *Statistical Abstract,* 1996, p. 3.

93. Wildavksy, "The Two Presidencies," p. 16.

94. Wildavksy, "The Two Presidencies," p. 15.

95. John E. Mueller, *War, Presidents and Public Opinion* (New York: Wiley, 1973); and Gary King and Lyn Ragsdale, *The Elusive Executive: Discovering Statistical Patterns in the Presidency* (Washington, DC: CQ Press, 1988).

96. Mueller, *War, Presidents and Public Opinion.*

97. George F. Kennan, "Somalia, Through a Glass Darkly," *New York Times* (September 30, 1993): A25.

98. Jessica Mathews, "Policy vs. TV," *Washington Post* (March 8, 1994): A19.

99. Address at Westminster College, Fulton, Missouri, March 5, 1946, as reprinted in John Bartlett, *Familiar Quotations* (Boston: Little, Brown, 1980), p. 746.

100. George Marshall, secretary of state under Harry Truman, as quoted in Alexander De Conde, "George C. Marshall," in Norman A. Graebner, ed., *An Uncertain Tradition: American Secretaries of*

State in the Twentieth Century (New York: McGraw Hill, 1961), p. 252.

101. Henning, *Wit and Wisdom,* p. 69.

102. Barry Rubin, *Secrets of State: The State Department and the Struggle Over U.S. Foreign Policy* (New York: Oxford University Press, 1985), p. 64.

103. Stephen Holmes, "What Russia Teaches Us Now; How Weak States Threaten Freedom," *The American Prospect* (July–August 1997): 30.

104. Andrew Krepinevich, quoted in Justin Brown, "How Many Weapons Is Too Many?" *The Christian Science Monitor* (November 4, 1999): 1.

105. Bradley Graham, "Senators Scold Military Chiefs, Top Officers Accused of Failing to Warn Soon Enough of Readiness Decline," *Washington Post* (September 30, 1998): A2.

106. Loch K. Johnson, *America's Secret Power: The CIA in a Democratic Society* (New York: Oxford University Press, 1989), pp. 12, 43.

107. Ibid., Ch. 2.

108. Johnson, *America's Secret Power;* and Rhodri Jeffreys-Johnes, *The CIA and American Democracy* (New Haven, CT: Yale University Press, 1989).

109. *Director of Central Intelligence Annual Report for the United States Intelligence Community* (Washington, DC: Central Intelligence Agency, 2000).

110. Rubin, *Secrets of State,* p. 50.

111. As quoted in Robert Pastor, "Disagreeing on Latin America," in Paul E. Peterson, ed., *The President, the Congress, and the Making of Foreign Policy* (Norman, OK: Oklahoma University Press, 1994), p. 217.

112. Speech at the Constitutional Convention, as quoted in Hans J. Morgenthau, *Politics Among Nations,* Fourth Edition. (New York: Knopf, 1966), p. 12.

113. Speech in Philadelphia, February 22, 1861, as quoted in Morgenthau, *Politics Among Nations,* p. 35.

114. Annual Message to Congress, December 2, 1823, as quoted in Bartlett, *Familiar Quotations,* p. 408.

115. Address to Congress, asking for a declaration of war, April 2, 1917, as reprinted in Bartlett, *Familiar Quotations*, p. 682.

116. Carl B. Swisher, *American Constitutional Development,* Second Edition. (Boston: Houghton Mifflin, 1958), pp. 992–993.

117. George Washington, *Farewell Address*, September 17, 1796, as quoted in Bartlett, *Familiar Quotations,* p. 379.

118. Message to the Senate, August 19, 1914, as quoted in Bartlett, *Familiar Quotations,* p. 682.

119. Campaign speech in Boston, October 30, 1940, as reprinted in Bartlett, *Familiar Quotations,* p. 780.

120. "Fireside Chat to the Nation," December 29, 1940, as quoted in Bartlett, *Familiar Quotations,* p. 780.

121. Murphy Caryle, "The Roots of Hatred: Our Lack of Understanding Has Led Us to This Place," *Washington Post Weekly Edition* (September 24-30, 2001): 29; and Rachael Newman, "The Day the World Changed; I Did, Too," *Newsweek* (October 1, 2001): 9.

122. Benjamin Ginsberg, *The Fatal Embrace: Jews and the State, The Politics of Anti-Semitism in the United States* (Chicago: University of Chicago Press, 1993), Ch. 2.

123. Ben Wicks, *Dawn of the Promised Land: The Creation of Israel* (New York: Hyperion, 1997),

Chs. 3–5.

124. David S. Wyman, *The Abandonment of the Jews: America and the Holocaust, 1941–1945* (New York: Pantheon, 1984).

125. Lee Hockstader, "Allegations of Torture amid the Turmoil: Palestinian Civilians Report Abuse by Israeli Police," *Washington Post Weekly Edition* (August 27–September 2, 2001): 13; Muhanned Tull, "Do You Wonder Why We're Angry? Tales from the Road to Desperation," *Washington Post Weekly Edition* (September 3–9, 2001): 22; and Vincent Cannistraro, "Assassination is Wrong and Dumb," *Washington Post Weekly Edition* (September 3–9, 2001): 26.

126. Daniel Williams, "Arafat's Followers Ask: Does He Have a Vision for the Uprising?" *Washington Post Weekly Edition* (September 3-9, 2001): 15–16; Yezid Sayigh, "Not a Deadly Strategy, But an Absence of One," *Washington Post Weekly Edition* (September 3–9, 2001): 22–23; and Jackson Diehl, "Why Arafat is Winning?" *Washington Post Weekly Edition* (September 10–16, 2001): 27.

PHOTO CREDITS

CHAPTER 11

360 Reuters Newmedia Inc./Corbis. **370** Mark Reinstein/The Image Works. **373** PF Bently/PFPIX.COM. **378–379** Reuters/Bettmann/Corbis.

CHAPTER 12

393 Bettmann/Corbis. **409** Dilbert reprinted by permission of United Features Syndicate, Inc. **410** Calvin and Hobbes © Watterson, distributed by Universal Press Syndicate. Reprinted with permission. All rights reserved.

CHAPTER 13

426 HO/AP/Wide World Photos. **434** Robert Phillips/Black Star. **436** Bettmann/Corbis. **442** Corbis/Sygma. **446** AP/Wide World Photos. **448** Toby Talbot/AP/Wide World Photos. **454** AP/Wide World Photos.

CHAPTER 14

467 Hulton/Archive/Getty Images. **473** Hulton/Archive/Getty Images. **474** Hulton/Archive/Getty Images. **477** Reuters Newmedia Inc./Corbis. **484** Tina Fineberg/AP/Wide World Photos. **492** AP/Wide World Photos.

CHAPTER 15

523 Doug Mills/AP/Wide World Photos. **528** Dilbert reprinted by permission of United Features Syndicate, Inc. **533** Bettmann/Corbis.

NAME INDEX

SUBJECT INDEX

Page numbers in *italics* refer to charts, diagrams, or illustrations

ABC network
  in 2000 presidential election, 3
  television dominance by, 398
ABC News Political Nation, Web site for, 420
Abolitionism
  African American voting and, 466
  as social movement, 260
Abortion, 381, *493*
  American attitudes toward, 142–147, *145, 147*
  Catholic Church versus, 127
  Clarence Thomas on, 355
  as election issue, 190–191
  John Ashcroft and, 344
  moderate position on, 380
  original-intent theory and, 376
  privacy right and, 445–447
Abortion pill, 190–191
Abrams v. *United States*, 431
Absentee ballots, in 2000 presidential
    election, 5
Absentee voting, 166
Absolute power, government and, 6
Absolute rulers, 8. *See also* Tyrannies
Academic Information: Religion Gateway, Web
    site for, 122
Accuracy, of polling, 129
Accused, rights of, 450–453
Act frames, in polls, 146
Acting, being president as, 312
Active-negative presidents, 329, *330*
Active-positive presidents, 328, *330*
Activists
  in interest groups, 269–271
  among Supreme Court justices, 379
Activist voters, 13
  in 1968 presidential election, 218
  in nomination process, 221–224, *223*
Administrative caution, in bureaucracy, 350
Adolescents, killings by, 148
Advice and consent, presidential powers and, 44
Advisers, to president, 325–327. *See also*
    Cabinet
Advocacy advertising, by interest groups, 266
Affirmative action
  in civil rights movement, 476
  Clarence Thomas versus, 355
  constitutionality of, 479–480
  equality versus inequality and, 111
  Proposition 209 and, 462–463
  in redistricting, 481–482

Affluence
  of interest groups, 269
  party support and, *187*
  voter turnout and, 174–175
Africa, New World settled by, 95
African Americans
  in 1896 presidential election, 165
  in 1916 presidential election, 159
  in 1948 presidential election, 470, 471
  in 2000 presidential election, *245*
  affirmative action for, 111
  against Proposition 209, 462–463
  in American colonies, 95
  citizenship for, 99
  as Democrats, 186
  electoral power for, 469–470
  in fifth party system, 244–245
  homicide rate among, *451*
  human rights of, 105
  as immigrants, 99, 117
  individual responsibility and, 109–110, *110*
  party support by, *187*
  poverty among, 480
  progressive movement and, 254
  in Rodney King riots, 276
  on Supreme Court, 355–356
  unemployment among, 480
  voter turnout by, *171*, 172, 174–175
  voting rights lost by, 466–468
  voting rights of, 49, 50, 157, 283, 466–480
Age, voter turnout and, *171*, 172
Agencies, congressional oversight of, 343–350
Agency autonomy, 348–349
Agency reorganization, in bureaucracy, 344
Agenda setting
  mass media and, 404
  in policy making, 499, *499*, 500
Agostini v. *Felton*, 442
Agriculture
  federal regulation of, 70–71
  Mexican labor in, 100*n*
  protests by, 242
Agriculture department, *315*
  Food and Drug Administration versus, 346
Aid to Families with Dependent Children (AFDC),
    76, 505
Air force
  in Defense department, 541
  in Joint Chiefs, 542
Airline Deregulation Act, 515

ADDITIONAL TITLES
OF INTEREST

❯──────────·──────────❮

Note to Instructors: Any of these Penguin-Putnam, Inc., titles can be packaged with this book at a special discount. Contact your local Longman sales representative for details on how to create a Penguin-Putnam, Inc. Value Package.

Stephen E. Ambrose, *Rise to Globalism*

Alexis De Tocqueville (edited by
Richard D. Heffner), *Democracy in America*

The Federalist Papers
(edited by Clinton Rossiter and
new introduction by Charles R. Kesler)

Al Gore, *Earth in the Balance*

Peter Irons, *The Courage of Their Convictions*

Martin Luther King, Jr., *Why We Can't Wait*

Philip B. Kunhardt and Peter W. Kunhardt, *The American President*

Joe McGinniss, *Selling of the President*

David Osborne and Ted Gaebler, *Reinventing Government*

Thomas Paine, *Common Sense*

William L. Riordan, *Plunkitt of Tammany Hall*

Upton Sinclair, *The Jungle*

Harriet Beecher Stowe, *Uncle Tom's Cabin*

Stephen Waldman, *The Bill*

Juan Williams (introduction by Julian Bond), *Eyes on the Prize*